ORGANIZATIONAL PSYCHOLOGY

ORGANIZATIONAL PSYCHOLOGY

Critical concepts in psychology

Edited by Jo Silvester

**Volume IV
Looking to the Future: Work and
Organizational Psychology**

LONDON AND NEW YORK

First published 2008
by Routledge
2 Park Square, Milton Park, Abingdon, Oxon, OX14 4RN, UK

Simultaneously published in the USA and Canada
by Routledge
270 Madison Avenue, New York, NY 10016

*Routledge is an imprint of the Taylor & Francis Group,
an informa business*

Editorial material and selection © 2008 Jo Silvester;
individual owners retain copyright in their own material

Typeset in Times New Roman by Keyword Group Ltd.
Printed and bound in Great Britain by
TJI Digital, Padstow, Cornwall

All rights reserved. No part of this book may be reprinted or reproduced or utilised in any form or by any electronic, mechanical, or other means, now known or hereafter invented, including photocopying and recording, or in any information storage or retrieval system, without permission in writing from the publishers.

British Library Cataloguing in Publication Data
A catalogue record for this book is available
from the British Library

Library of Congress Cataloging in Publication Data
A catalog record for this book has been requested

ISBN 10: 0-415-40008-2 (Set)
ISBN 10: 0-415-40012-0 (Volume IV)

ISBN 13: 978-0-415-40008-4 (Set)
ISBN 13: 978-0-415-40012-1 (Volume IV)

Publisher's Note

References within each chapter are as they appear in the original complete work

CONTENTS

Acknowledgements ix

Introduction 1

PART 7
Globalization and new technology 5

51 Cross-cultural, social and organizational psychology 7
   MICHAEL HARRIS BOND AND PETER B. SMITH

52 Measuring organizational cultures: a qualitative and quantitative study across twenty cases 39
   GEERT HOFSTEDE, BRAM NEUIJEN, DENISE DAVAL OHAYV AND GEERT SANDERS

53 Managerial competency modelling and the development of organizational psychology: a Chinese approach 73
   ZHONG-MING WANG

54 Internet recruitment and selection: kissing frogs to find princes 92
   DAVE BARTRAM

55 Research on Internet recruiting and testing: current status and future directions 117
   FILIP LIEVENS AND MICHAEL M. HARRIS

CONTENTS

56 **Applicant and recruiter reactions to new technology in selection: a critical review and agenda for future research**   150
NEIL ANDERSON

57 **Call centres**   178
DAVID HOLMAN

58 **Managing a virtual workplace**   201
WAYNE F. CASCIO

PART 8
Next generation thinking   217

59 **Organizational behavior in the new organizational era**   219
DENISE M. ROUSSEAU

60 **Organizations of the future: changes and challenges**   252
LYNN R. OFFERMANN AND MARILYN K. GOWING

61 **The Internet and industrial/organizational psychology: practice and research perspectives**   281
MICHAEL M. HARRIS

62 **Selecting for change: how will personnel and selection psychology survive?**   294
PETER HERRIOT AND NEIL ANDERSON

63 **Personnel selection: looking toward the future—remembering the past**   329
LEAETTA M. HOUGH AND FREDERICK L. OSWALD

64 **Epistemology and work psychology: new agendas**   365
PHIL JOHNSON AND CATHERINE CASSELL

65 **The practitioner–researcher divide in Industrial, Work and Organizational (IWO) psychology: where are we now, and where do we go from here?**   386
NEIL ANDERSON, PETER HERRIOT AND GERARD P. HODGKINSON

CONTENTS

66 Any nearer a "better" approach? A critical view   **409**
KAREN LEGGE

67 Whither industrial and organizational psychology in a changing world of work?   **432**
WAYNE F. CASCIO

Index   457

ACKNOWLEDGEMENTS

The publishers would like to thank the following for permission to reprint their material:

The Annual Review of Psychology for permission to reprint Michael H. Bond and Peter B. Smith, 'Cross-cultural, social and organizational psychology', *Annual Review of Psychology*, volume 47, pp. 205–235, copyright © 1996 by Annual Reviews. www.annualreviews.org.

Administrative Science Quarterly for permission to reprint Geert Hofstede, Bram Neuijen, Denise D. Ohayv and Geert Sanders, 'Measuring organizational cultures: a qualitative and quantitative study across twenty cases', *Administrative Science Quarterly*, 35, 1990, pp. 286–316. Copyright 1990, all rights reserved.

Taylor & Francis for permission to reprint Zhong-Ming Wang, 'Managerial competency modelling and the development of organizational psychology: a Chinese approach', *International Journal of Psychology*, 38(5), 2003, pp. 323–334. www.tandf.co.uk/journals

Blackwell Publishing for permission to reprint David Bartram, 'Internet recruitment and selection: kissing frogs to find princes', *International Journal of Selection and Assessment*, 8(4), 2000, pp. 261–274.

John Wiley & Sons Ltd. for permission to reprint Filip Lievens and Michael M. Harris, 'Research on Internet recruiting and testing: current status and future directions', in C. L. Cooper and I. T. Robertson (eds), *International Review of Industrial and Organizational Psychology*, Vol. 18, 2003, pp. 131–165, copyright © 2003 John Wiley & Sons Ltd.

Blackwell Publishing for permission to reprint Neil Anderson, 'Applicant and recruiter reactions to new technology in selection: a critical review and agenda for future research', *International Journal of Selection and Assessment*, 11(2/3), 2003, pp. 121–136.

ACKNOWLEDGEMENTS

John Wiley & Sons Ltd. for permission to reprint David Holman, 'Call centres', in D. Holman, T. D. Wall, C. W. Clegg, P. Sparrow and A. Howard (eds), *The Essentials of the New Workplace: A Guide to the Human Impact of Modern Working Practices*, 2005, pp. 115–134, copyright © 2005 by John Wiley & Sons Ltd.

The Academy of Management (NY) in the format of Other Book via Copyright Clearance Center for permission to reprint Wayne F. Cascio, 'Managing a virtual workplace', *Academy of Management Executive*, 14(3), 2000, pp. 81–90. Copyright © 2000 Academy of Management (NY).

The Annual Review of Psychology for permission to reprint Denise M. Rousseau, 'Organizational behavior in the new organizational era', *Annual Review of Psychology*, volume 48, pp. 515–546, copyright © 1997 by Annual Reviews. www.annualreviews.org.

The American Psychological Association for permission to reprint Lynn R. Offermann and Marilyn K. Gowing, 'Organizations of the future: changes and challenges', *American Psychologist*, 45(2), 1990, pp. 95–108. Copyright © 1990 by the American Psychological Association.

The Journal of e-Commerce and Psychology for permission to reprint Michael M. Harris, 'The Internet and industrial/organizational psychology: practice and research perspectives', *Journal of e-Commerce and Psychology*, 1(1), 2000, pp. 8–24.

John Wiley & Sons Ltd. for permission to reprint Peter Herriot and Neil Anderson, 'Selecting for change: how will personnel and selection psychology survive?', in N. Anderson and P. Herriot (eds), *International Handbook of Selection and Assessment*, 1997, pp. 1–34, copyright © 1997 John Wiley & Sons Ltd.

The Annual Review of Psychology for permission to reprint Leaetta M. Hough and Frederick L. Oswald, 'Personnel selection: looking toward the future – remembering the past', *Annual Review of Psychology*, volume 51, pp. 631–664, copyright © 2000 by Annual Reviews. www.annualreviews.org.

The Journal of Occupational and Organizational Psychology for permission to reprint Phil Johnson and Catherine Cassell, 'Epistemology and work psychology: new agendas', *Journal of Occupational and Organizational Psychology*, 74, 2001, pp. 125–143. © The British Psychological Society.

The Journal of Occupational and Organizational Psychology for permission to reprint Neil Anderson, Peter Herriot and Gerard P. Hodgkinson, 'The practitioner–scientist divide in Industrial, Work and Organizational (IWO) psychology: where are we now, and where do we go from here?', *Journal of Occupational and Organizational Psychology*, 74, 2001, pp. 391–411. © The British Psychological Society.

John Wiley & Sons Ltd. for permission to reprint Karen Legge, 'Any nearer a "better" approach? A critical view', in D. Holman, T. D. Wall, C. W. Clegg, P. Sparrow and A. Howard (eds), *The New Workplace: A Guide to the Human Impact of Modern Working Practices*, 2005, pp. 393–412, copyright © 2005 by John Wiley & Sons Ltd.

The American Psychological Association for permission to reprint Wayne F. Cascio, 'Whither industrial and organizational psychology in a changing world of work?', *American Psychologist*, 50(11), 1995, pp. 928–939. Copyright © 1995 by the American Psychological Association.

Disclaimer

The publishers have made every effort to contact authors/copyright holders of works reprinted in *Organizational Psychology*. This has not been possible in every case, however, and we would welcome correspondence from those individuals/companies whom we have been unable to trace.

INTRODUCTION

In a speech at Harvard in 1943, Winston Churchill argued that 'the empires of the future are the empires of the mind': a statement that seems particularly apt in the case of organizational psychology. Whilst no academic discipline remains static, organizational psychology stands out as an area where research and practice have developed extremely quickly. It is also fair to say that given tremendous changes in the world of work, academic research has often been forced to follow rather than lead practical developments. Popular workplace activities such as 360-degree feedback, team working, assessment centres, quality circles and e-recruitment have all evolved from practical needs rather than theoretical innovations. As a consequence, research demonstrating validity or providing evidence to support (or refute) use has emerged several years later. Consequently, whilst most academics would like to see themselves as originators of innovative practice, more often than not research has been used to justify the implementation of activities designed to gain competitive advantage.

Organizational psychology has been dominated for many years by a management perspective and, despite important challenges (e.g., Hollway, 1991; Legge, 1984 and 2005 this volume), there have been comparatively few attempts to step back and take a more critical view with regard to what we do, the topics we research, and those that escape our attention. Perhaps academics and practitioners have been so occupied with the simple task of keeping up with a changing world of work that they have had little time to question basic and possibly unconscious assumptions. Yet, as Churchill quite rightly points out, what we build for the future depends on our vision of what that future might be. More importantly, it depends on us having a vision in the first place.

This fourth volume in the Critical concepts series is entitled 'Looking to the Future'. It includes papers that consider the opportunities and challenges for organizational psychology in changing work environments. Not only have these authors begun to vision the future, they provide us with an insight into possible empires of the future. 'Empire' is perhaps an unfortunate term, however, given that Churchill was speaking during the Second World War just before the decline of the British Empire. No doubt looking ahead to the future should go hand in hand with a healthy dose of self-reflection and critical challenge. Therefore, in order to ensure a robust, useful and defensible academic and practical discipline, it is important that organizational psychologists embrace rather than avoid critical reflection. The papers in this volume have been selected to illustrate the rich diversity of ideas and visions that organizational psychologists have for the future. Together they auger well for the future of organizational psychology as an innovative and strong discipline.

The first section in this volume considers how work and organizations are changing, with papers exploring the likely impact of globalization on employees. As managers and workers find themselves in different geographical locations or even different time zones, many work relationships are now virtual. The authors discuss what may be needed by managers in the future; they also consider how computer technology, 24/7 communication and feedback are influencing work design and performance management strategies. Whilst IT developments have provided incredible opportunities for workers and organizations, a darker side involves threat to autonomy, closer monitoring and control.

The first paper, by Smith and Bond (1996), argues that most organizational psychology research has been published by white, Western researchers, largely in relation to US organizations and working practices. Yet we know comparatively little about the impact of cultural differences on organizational functioning and employee behaviour: what happens when a South African business graduate applies to a Mexican-owned international mining organization for a job in Turkey? Wang's (2003) paper on developing competencies in China provides a practical illustration of the challenges posed when introducing traditional Western practices to organizations and employees with very different values and beliefs.

Another rapidly developing area is the use of the Internet to increase applicant pools and systematize recruitment processes. Human resource departments have been quick to understand how the Internet can provide a platform for profiling an organization to potential recruits. Company information can be provided online for a fraction of the cost of producing glossy graduate recruitment packs. Application forms can be standardized and individuals encouraged to apply online at any time of year. E-recruitment makes it possible to capture information about large numbers of individuals quickly and cheaply, something that is also an advantage for researchers keen to collect data quickly and efficiently. Yet the ethical implications of e-recruitment, and the darker side of mass recruitment, have yet to be explored. For example, e-recruitment has brought recruitment closer to marketing. Bartram (2000) discusses issues associated with using the Internet for computer-based assessment, including confidentiality, security and equality of access and skill. In their paper, Lievens and Harris (2003) explore the validity of Internet testing in more detail, and Anderson (2003) describes how the use of technology in recruitment can influence the perceptions and experience of applicants with potentially important implications for employers. The last two papers in this section consider how technology has changed the way in which people work. Holman (2005) looks at the newly prolific world of call centres and what research can tell us about this

INTRODUCTION

form of working. Cascio (2000) considers the skills that managers need in order to cope effectively and build employee trust, commitment and engagement in the virtual workplace.

Papers in the second section of this volume look ahead to future opportunities and challenges with authors considering how next generation thinking might help the discipline to evolve. Rousseau (1997) considers how behaviour is changing in the new organizational era. Written eighteen years ago, Offermann and Gowing's (1990) paper provides an interesting retrospective look at what we thought the future of organizations might be and an opportunity to compare how things have turned out. Harris (2000) continues the discussion about what the implications of the Internet will be for future researchers and practitioners. Herriot and Anderson (1997) critically discuss the limitations of traditional job analysis and selection methods in work environments where jobs and work roles are constantly changing. Hough and Oswald (2000) continue this discussion by considering the opportunities and challenges for personnel selection in the twenty-first century.

In the first of several more critical papers Johnson and Cassell (2001) challenge the prevailing scientific research epistemology within mainstream organizational psychology and argue for the importance of epistemological reflexivity. Anderson, Herriot and Hodgkinson (2001) also provide a challenging paper on the practitioner–researcher interface. They identify four types of research—pedantic, puerile, popularist and pragmatic—each driven by different stakeholder needs and set out a framework to help bridge the divide between researchers and practitioners. The final two papers include a critical view from Legge (2005) of organizational psychology as a discipline, and an upbeat paper from Cascio (1995) who returns to the question 'Whither industrial and organizational psychology in a changing world of work?'

Part 7

GLOBALIZATION AND NEW TECHNOLOGY

51

CROSS-CULTURAL SOCIAL AND ORGANIZATIONAL PSYCHOLOGY

Michael Harris Bond and Peter B. Smith

Source: *Annual Review of Psychology* 47 (1996): 205–235.

Abstract

This review considers recent theoretical and empirical developments in cross-cultural studies within social and organizational psychology. It begins with a description of the importance and the difficulties of universalizing psychological science. It then continues with an examination of theoretical work on both the internal-proximal and the external-distal constraints that mediate culture's influence on behavior. Influences on social cognition are documented by describing research on self-concept, self-esteem, emotions, attribution processes, person perception, interpersonal attraction, and justice. Group processes are addressed in the areas of leadership, decision-making, and negotiation, and research in organizational psychology is examined with respect to work motivation and work behavior. The review concludes that considerable improvement is evident in recent cross-cultural research. However, future research must include a broader range of cultures and attend more closely to the levels at which cultural effects should be analyzed, and cultural samples must be unpackaged in more psychologically useful ways.

[A] human race speaking many tongues, regarding many values, and holding different convictions about the meaning of life sooner or later will have to consult all that is human.

G Murphy (1969, p. 528)

Introduction

An American social psychologist, new to the cross-cultural area, attended the 1994 Congress of the International Association for Cross-Cultural Psychology. He later wrote:

> I have a sense that the field is suffering not just from an identity crisis, but from the overwhelming magnitude of that task we are undertaking and the enormous difficulty of doing valuable research in this area. I heard some fine talks, but it is clear that the field is really in its infancy, and to my way of thinking, it confronts the most difficult domain of knowledge in the social sciences. I found it stimulating and exciting, but also a bit daunting. I think we just have to plunge ahead and make the mistakes that will ultimately lead to progress (W Stephan, personal communication).

These astute observations capture the essence of our current challenge in cross-cultural psychology. Where have we cross-cultural psychologists come from? What have we found? Whither are we going? These are the issues we shall address in deciding if cross-cultural social and organizational psychology has indeed come of age.

The promise of the cross-cultural approach

Psychology is the scientific study of human behavior. Its presumptive goal is to achieve universal status by generalizing results found in particular ecological, social, legal, institutional, and political settings. Such generalization requires testing in maximally different cultures. "In no other way can we be certain that what we believe to be ... regularities are not merely peculiarities, the product of some limited set of historical or cultural or political circumstances" (Kohn 1987, p. 713).

Tests for generalizability often produce extensive discrepancies (Amir & Sharon 1987). Of course, these discrepancies can arise because of differences in testing methods. "To obviate the possibility that differences in findings are merely artifacts of differences in method, one tries to design studies to be comparable with one another in their methods, to establish both linguistic and conceptual equivalence in the wording of questions and in the coding of answers, and to establish truly equivalent indices of the underlying concepts" (Kohn 1987, p. 720).

This requirement is no mean challenge, and early, obvious failures have left cross-cultural psychology with a dubious legacy. Today, however, psychologists show greater vigilance and sophistication about the equivalence issue (van de Vijver & Leung 1996). Consequently, we may feel more confident about the validity of differences found across cultural settings.

With methodological concerns minimized, one can use discrepancies to comprehend the anomalous. As Kohn (1987) has noted, "what appear to be cross-national differences may really be instances of lawful regularities, if thought of in terms of some larger, more encompassing interpretation" (p. 716). This is mind-stretching work, but it is, however, essential if psychology is to claim universality. Carefully wrought cross-cultural psychology can serve as a midwife to this heady enterprise.

The current scene

The growth is illustrated by the recent appearance of textbooks in cross-cultural psychology as a whole (Berry et al 1992, Brislin 1993, Lonner & Malpass 1994, Segall et al 1990), cross-cultural social psychology (Matsumoto 1994, Moghaddam et al 1993, Smith & Bond 1994, Triandis 1994), and cross-cultural organizational psychology (Adler 1991, Erez & Earley 1993, Triandis et al 1993a), as well as by the appearance of volumes arising from the congresses of the International Association for Cross-Cultural Psychology (Bouvy et al 1994, Keats et al 1989, Iwawaki et al 1992, Pandey et al 1995) and of a completely new edition of the *Handbook of Cross-Cultural Psychology* (Berry et al 1996). The growth of cross-cultural research and the attention given to this area of study is encouraging. But how well positioned are we? How much progress are we able to report since the publication, in this series, of reviews of cross-cultural psychology by Kagitcibasi & Berry (1989) and Shweder & Sullivan (1993)?

Research in psychology is dominated by Americans. Prestigious psychology journals are largely monopolized by North Americans, who rarely cite the work of outsiders and who work on questions that are often themselves culturally distinctive (Hogan & Emler 1978). The state of affairs extends to cross-cultural psychology itself. Content analysis of the *Journal of Cross-Cultural Psychology* since its inception in 1970 reveals that, even there, North American theories and authors predominate (Ongel & Smith 1994). This ethnocentrism, as noted by Moghaddam et al (1993), is fueled by the general use of the English language in journals and at international conferences.

One small inroad into this North American domination of the field is the emergence of psychology both from and about Asian cultures (Bond 1986, 1995, Gudykunst 1993, Komin 1990, Misumi 1985). Sustained by the economic development of the Five Dragons, this work has stimulated and been responsive to the construct of cultural collectivism. Given researchers' predilection for two-culture comparisons, however, an East Asian variant of collectivism may be gaining a disproportionate scientific ascendancy (Singelis 1994). We need to decenter collectivism by undertaking studies in South America, Africa, and the former Communist Bloc (A Realo et al, submitted).

We note in fairness that many North American psychologists and journal editors are promoting the visibility of psychologists and psychology within other cultural groups (Rosenzweig 1992). There is some indication of growing reliance upon theories held by scholars indigenous to India (Adair et al 1993) and other countries (Kim & Berry 1993). Some textbooks are introducing more cross-cultural material, and the journal *Psychology and Developing Societies* has been established.

Greater attention is also being given to the development of procedures for ensuring the equivalence of measurements made at different locations. For instance, item response theory can be used to assess the equivalence of questionnaire responses (Bontempo 1993, Ellis et al 1993); careful thought can be given to item appropriateness (Lonner 1980); and cultural differences in response bias can be mapped (Hui & Triandis 1989, Marin & Marin 1991, Marin et al 1993) and controlled for by within-subject standardization of responses (Leung & Bond 1989), Methodological prerequisites are enumerated for valid cross-cultural experiments (Earley & Mosakowski 1995) and for studies of organizations (Lytle et al 1995, Shenkar & von Glinow 1994). All these developments contribute to a gradual cultural decentering of psychology, but the remaining obstacles are real and considerable (Ongel & Smith 1994, p. 50):

> High on the list of further impediments...must lie the difficulty of assembling diverse and truly collaborative research teams where members contribute equally toward research designs that will have validity in a number of different cultural settings. The development of such teams takes time, tact, and resources, and publication pressures militate against setting them up. Where some of the collaborating researchers are from high power distance cultures, [and hence are more likely to defer to project leaders from cultures low in power distance,] or are former graduate students of their present research partners, the encouragement to rely on established Western measures and theories is further intensified.

We hope this review will empower voices of science from other cultures to contribute to the universalizing of psychology.

Theoretical developments

Definitions of culture abound, and the sheer number displays the complexity of their referent (Krewer & Jahoda 1993, Misra & Gergen 1993, Soudjin et al 1990). We adopt Poortinga's (1992) broad position on culture as a set of "shared constraints that limit the behavior repertoire available to members of a certain...group" (p. 10). These "boundary conditions for behavior" (p. 12) include the internal constraints of genetic and cultural transmission and the external constraints of ecological, socioeconomical, historical, and situational contexts, with a range of distal to proximal effects within each type of constraint.

This definition of culture may be married to a position of universalism, in which "it is assumed that the same psychological processes are operating in all humans independent of culture" (Poortinga 1992, p. 13). Cultural constraints then limit and shape the behavioral expression of the universal process. Universals, as these psychological processes are called, are grist for the cross-cultural psychology mill. They may be identified conceptually by careful attention to the anthropological literature (Lonner 1980), by historical exegesis (Adamopoulos 1988), or through evolutionary analyses (Chasiotis & Keller 1994). Alternatively, they may also be identified empirically through careful cross-cultural replications, as seen in Kohn et al's (1990) work on class structure, job specialization, and the transmission of values in three cultures, or in Costa & McCrae's (1992) work on the Big Five factors of personality.

What typology of cultures and their behavioral constraints shall be used in the search for universals? We address this question on the basis of Poortinga's differentiation between internal and external constraints, each of which involves culturally transmitted values and beliefs in eco-socio-historical contexts.

Theories of internal-proximal constraints

Values

The dominant development of the past decade in theories of internal-proximal constraints has been Schwartz's (1992, 1994) work on values. A wide reading by Schwartz of previous theory, methodology, and cultural anthropology preceded the creation of a comprehensive values instrument that has been carefully administered to equivalent samples of teachers and students in almost 50 countries. The results of this work form the basis of a circumplex model of 10 universal value domains at the individual level (1992) and 7 at the cultural level with scores for 38 culture regions (1994). These culture-level scores have been related to Hofstede's (1980) four dimensions of cultural variation and to both Hofstede's and the Chinese Culture Connection's (1987) nation scores (Bond 1995). Schwartz's country-level scores have also been related to country-level indices of physical, economic, and social health (Chan & Bond 1995). In terms of both convergent and external validity, the Schwartz domains appear most promising.

Schwartz's initial work, however, was at the individual level, and his culture-level work was predicated on this foundation. Future cross-cultural work can proceed at the individual level through use of the Schwartz Value Survey (Feather 1994, Leung et al 1994). Such a "translation" of the Survey to the individual was not possible with Hofstede's (1980) classic results, eager as many psychologists were to leap from the study of culture to the study of the individual. We hope that Schwartz will soon publish the average scores of people from his culture samples on the 10 individual-level domains [as Bond (1988) did for the Chinese Culture Connection's nation scores (1987)], so researchers can work at their preferred level of study.

An additional development is Smith et al's (1995a) analysis of the Trompenaars (1993) data base. Data from 43 countries were derived from a questionnaire designed to show seven patterns of cultural variation. Smith et al identified two separate dimensions, i.e. conservatism–egalitarian commitment and loyal involvement–utilitarian involvement, which had been conflated in Hofstede's (1980) discussion of collectivism. This empirical refinement of the collectivism construct is important, given its current ascendancy in cross-cultural studies

(Kim et al 1994, Triandis 1995) and its further refinement at the individual level into horizontal as well as vertical components (Singelis et al 1995).

Beliefs

Values tap what is important, beliefs what is true. Scales measuring cultural constructs sometimes mix values and beliefs together. It is important, however, for theoretical (Feather 1988) and empirical (Leung et al 1994) reasons to keep these constructs separate. For example, Smith et al (1995b) have analyzed responses from 43 countries to Rotter's (1966) locus of control scale. This scale is used to tap beliefs, not values, about internal vs external control of reinforcement. Smith et al found three dimensions of belief about causality, only one of which paralleled Rotter's original formulation. These dimensions of beliefs along which countries may be arrayed overlap only moderately with country measures of value.

Locus-of-control beliefs are important in predicting individual behavior and are closely related to discussions of key cultural differences in individuals' experiences of control, harmony, and submission with respect to the environment. The experience of personal agency and people's needs to believe in their personal agency are probably universal; therefore, we would hope that locally valid measures of this belief will be developed and its role in explaining cross-cultural differences examined.

Other beliefs that vary cross-culturally, e.g. beliefs about a just world (Furnham 1993), global interdependencies (Der-Kerabetian 1992), and work behaviors (Furnham et al 1993), are promising areas for explaining cultural differences in behavior. A taxonomy of such beliefs would help to move the field beyond its excessive reliance on values (K Leung & MH Bond, unpublished observations).

Theories of external-distal constraints

Factor-analytic studies of ecological, social, economic, and political indicators may be exploited to provide a taxonomy of external-distal constraints on individual behavior. Studies in the 1970s yielded many factors, but economic development or so-called modernization was invariably the first obtained. The fact that this dimension is only one among many has been used to dismiss simplistic assertions about convergence (Smith & Bond 1994). We expect that variations along the remaining dimensions give considerable scope for nations and their constituent cultures to exert varying influences, once economic development has been partialled out (Bond 1991).

With the notable exceptions of Berry (1979) and Triandis (1984), recent researchers have been loath to grasp the nettle of external-distal constraints. The variables involved are perceived by many to lie outside the discipline. Their translation into the psychological realm is considered tenuous and uncharted or else probably isomorphic with cultural value dimensions. Although understandable, such avoidance is lamentable, especially in light of ubiquitous calls for cross-disciplinary integration (Easton & Shelling 1991, Gabrenya 1988). Much may be achieved in this area, however, as a recent study by Linssen & Hagendoorn (1994) on European nationality stereotypes can attest.

Almost all current models of cultural difference are thus proximal rather than distal. Fiske (1992), however, proposes a model of four domains of social relationship present in all cultures: communal sharing, authority ranking, equality matching, and market pricing. According to Fiske, cultural difference is defined in terms of the relative reliance on these four bases of relationship. Fiske (1993) replicated results of an earlier US study showing that when Koreans, Chinese, Bengalis, and Liberians made errors in naming a person, their errors referred to others within the same relationship type.

Social cognition

The self-concept

Triandis (1990), who has focused on the close relation of the self to the in-group and on the greater distance of the self from the out-group, hypothesizes that cultural collectivism leads its members to make more social responses on the "Who Are You?" test (Bochner 1994). Triandis (1993) defines culture-level collectivism as a cultural syndrome encompassing a broad range of behaviors. Triandis has also developed measures of the corresponding individual-level construct, allocentrism-idiocentrism, both within and across cultures (Triandis et al 1993b).

Markus & Kitayama (1991) have focused instead on the sense of interdependence that characterizes the experience of self in collective cultural systems. Such a socially shared, normative construction of the self has challenging implications for developmental (Kagitcibasi 1995), personality (Miller 1994), and social (Singelis et al 1995) areas of psychology. Surprisingly, attempts to measure the interdependent and independent components of the self-concept have shown them to be orthogonal, not bipolar constructs (Gudykunst et al 1994, Singelis 1994). Persons from collectivist cultures feel more interdependence, and interdependent peoples in all cultures endorse values such as restrictive conformity, prosociality, and security. Individuals from individualistic cultures feel more independence, and independent people in all cultures endorse self-direction (Gudykunst et al 1994). Scores on interdependence are positively related to emotional contagion (TM Singelis 1994, unpublished data) and embarrassability (Singelis & Sharkey 1995), both within and across cultures.

Self-concept clarity (SCC) is "the extent to which an individual's specific self-beliefs are clearly and confidently defined, internally consistent, and temporarily stable" (JD Campbell, PD Trapnell, SJ Heine, IM Katz, L Lavallee, DR Lehman, submitted). These authors argue that people with an interdependent self-concept should have less clarity. As a test of this prediction, they compared samples of Japanese and Canadians, who represent persons from a collectivist and individualist culture, respectively, and showed that Japanese are indeed lower on SCC than Canadians.

Gender self-concept

Williams & Best (1990) examined sex stereotypes in 30 countries and concluded that there is substantial agreement among cultures concerning the psychological characteristics differentially associated with men and women. The ratings were scored for activity, strength of affective meaning, and favorability. The content of the male stereotype turned out to be more active and stronger in affective meaning, but not any more favorable. Across cultures, stronger male stereotypes, i.e. greater attribution of affectively active, strong characteristics to males than to females, are associated with lower levels of literacy and socioeconomic development and with a lower proportion of women enrolled in college.

Best & Williams (1994) also showed that in all cultures, men and women differ in their self-reports of masculine and feminine characteristics, although the gender difference is typically less than that reflected in gender stereotypes. Best & Williams also reported that the gender difference in total affective meaning of self-reports was greater in countries in which power distance was high (i.e. more authoritarian social structure) and social-economic level, percentage of Christians, and proportion of female college graduates were low.

Ethnic identity

Weinreich (1986) defines ethnic identity as "that part of the totality of one's self-construal made up of those dimensions that express the continuity between one's construal of past ancestry and future aspirations in relation to ethnicity" (p. 308). This is a complex construct, and measures of one's ethnic identification can include assessments of one's ethnicity-related practices, the importance one attaches to those practices, one's subjective self-labeling, and the evaluation given to this self-labeling and to one's ascribed ethnicity (Rosenhhal & Feldman 1992). Weinreich has developed an idiographic technique called Identity Structure Analysis (ISA) that has been applied to cases of ethnic identification and conflicts arising from bicultural parenting, intergroup conflict, and superordinate group demands (Weinreich 1995).

Weinreich's thinking concerns how the individual negotiates the often treacherous cross-currents of ethnic identities ascribed to that individual by others. University students in Hong Kong, for example, perceive themselves as similar to but distinct from typical Hong Kong Chinese. They ascribe to themselves elements of a valued Western identity in equal measure to their Hong Kong identity (Weinreich et al 1994). This creative synthesizing of local identities provides an escape from the intergroup conflict that must arise when there is no alternative to ascribed ethnic identity. The identifications achieved by individuals rather than ascribed to them by others then become the basis for various forms of intergroup behavior, such as linguistic differentiation (Giles & Viladot 1994) and styles of conflict management (Ting-Toomey et al 1994).

Self-esteem

Because self-esteem is central to Western theories of psychopathology and social functioning (Taylor & Brown 1988), self-esteem measures have been much used in non-Western research (Leung & Leung 1992) and in cross-cultural comparisons (Bond & Cheung 1983).

Are self-esteem measures derived from cross-culturally equivalent ways of construing self-concept, from which self-esteem derives? The work of Watkins & Dong (1994) with Chinese, Nepalese, Nigerian, Filipino, and Australian children, using the Shavelson model (Shavelson & Bolus 1982) of the self-concept, confirms construct validity across cultures. Such models of the self-concept are, however, individualistic in conceptualization. When collective or group-based elements of the self-concept are included, construct similarity may break down.

Measures of self-esteem used in cross-cultural comparisons are often based on evaluations of one's individual attributes rather than on one's group attributes (Feather & McKee 1993). Cross-cultural comparisons may therefore miss differences in self-evaluation derived from one's collective identity (Luhtanen & Crocker 1992). Reported cultural differences in self-esteem may be misleading if the construct has not been fully assessed. Debates about whether people from certain cultural groups are more socially modest or internally depressed (DeGooyer & Williams 1992) may thus be premature.

The assessment question may also affect construct validity. Individually based levels of self-esteem seem to be derived from similar components of personality across cultural groups (Ho 1994) and to be meaningfully related to social responses in different cultures (Feather & McKee 1993). Collectively derived measures of self-esteem, however, predict important outcomes like psychological well-being for some ethnic groups but not for others (Crocker et al 1994). How one measures self-esteem across cultures will obviously affect what one discovers about the concept.

Emotion

The cross-cultural study of emotion (Mesquita & Frijda 1992) has been stimulated by Markus & Kitayama's (1991) seminal paper and a subsequent conference (Kitayama & Markus 1994). However, as Frijda & Mesquita (1994) have observed, cross-cultural researchers on emotion have been preoccupied with labels. Given the interpersonal focus of this chapter, we endorse Frijda & Mesquita's definition of emotions as "first and foremost, modes of relating to the environment: states of readiness for engaging, or not engaging, in interaction with that environment" (p. 51). Aspects of that engagement include "modifying inter-individual interactions ... at the moment; ... regulating the balance of power; ... determining general patterns of social interaction; ... and ... motivating social cohesion" (pp. 82–83).

This centrality of emotion in social life underscores its importance for understanding cross-cultural differences in behavior. Recent work has been concentrated on appraisal of the events that generate emotions (Ellsworth 1994). The dimensions of appraisal appear to be universal (Mauro et al 1992), as are appraisal patterns activated by many emotionally relevant situations (Mesquita 1993). The weight accorded to certain of these dimensions (e.g. controllability, causal agency) varies across cultures, as does the importance of certain emotions. These differences are explained by variations in cultural independence-interdependence, a construct that accounts for differences in the social embeddedness of the emotions (Frijda & Mesquita 1994).

In recent years fewer cross-cultural studies have examined how emotions are communicated to others (Russell 1994) and how emotional displays affect the responses of others to the actor, to the ongoing interaction, and to their social group (Frijda & Mesquita 1994). Such additional work would be most welcome to the field.

Attribution processes

Although a great deal of research on diverse aspects of attribution theory has been carried out, it has been criticized for committing the "fundamental attribution researcher's error" (Russell 1982), the assumption on the part of researchers that their conceptualization of what is under investigation corresponds to their subjects' ideas. The criticism particularly has force in cross-cultural research. Because researchers' conceptualizations and measures are almost always Western-based and subjects' attributional models are not, the dangers of "imposed-etic" research (Berry 1989) are present.

Watkins & Cheng (1995), for instance, showed that the perceived dimensions underlying the Revised Causal Dimension Scale, which was developed using American subjects, do not reflect the dimensions of causality used by Hong Kong students. The investigators argue that this difference arises because of the relative Chinese emphasis on the role of effort as an explanation for achievement (Leung 1995a). This difference in factor structure renders suspect cross-cultural comparisons on relative frequency of causal attribution categories. Part of a cross-culturalist's answer to this inconsistency is to work with more open-ended causal accounts (Kashima & Triandis 1986), which permit indigenous constructs such as the Chinese *yuan* (fatedness) (Yang & Ho 1988) to be included. Local instruments can then be developed that assess the dimensionality of causal categories in various cultures (Luk & Bond 1992). Equivalent categories may then be compared across cultures on issues such as salience, self-esteem maintenance, interpersonal modesty, and responsibility attribution. Crittenden (1995) explores these concerns within Chinese attribution research.

Nevertheless, a promising research theme has emerged in the study of attribution processes. Shweder & Bourne (1982) argued that many non-Western cultures inculcate a "holistic world view" that promotes "context-dependent, occasion-bound thinking." Accordingly, attributions made by members of non-Western cultures are more external/situational (Morris & Peng 1994). In research consistent with this assessment of non-Western attribution processes, Newman (1993) found US allocentrics less willing to make trait attributions, while Kashima et al (1992) found non-Westerners less likely to believe that others' behaviors are consistent with internal loci such as attitudes. This less-personal attributional logic can also aid our understanding of cultural variations in social processes such as morality judgments (Miller & Bersoff 1992).

Interpersonal behavior

Person perception

Dixon (1977) asserts that trait terms are used in every known language to distinguish persons. Studies of implicit personality theory in any language studied to date indicate that a five-factor model can describe the organization of perceived personality (Bond 1994; see Butcher & Rouse, this volume). The apparent universality of the broad categories of extroversion, agreeableness, conscientiousness, emotional stability, and openness to experience may arise from their importance in directing universal types of social behaviors such as association, subordination, and formality (Bond & Forgas 1984).

Within the general framework of this model, culture exercises its influence by accentuating certain of the Big Five dimensions over others. In free-response trait descriptions of themselves (Ip & Bond 1995) or of others (Chang et al 1994), Chinese, for example, use the category of conscientiousness more often and use the category of agreeableness less often than do Americans. Moreover, the rated importance of each of the five categories varies among cultural groups (Williams et al 1995), and these categories are differentially weighted in guiding social behavior (Bond & Forgas 1984).

Such differences may be explained by an ecological model emphasizing the adaptive significance of certain types of responding in different cultural environments (Zebrowitz-McArthur 1988). The universally adaptive significance of caring for immature members of the species is obvious. As a result, physical cues of immaturity, such as babyfacedness (McArthur & Berry 1987) and vocal softness (Peng et al 1993), have been related pan-culturally to personality perceptions of dependence and weakness. Similarly, mating with youthful members of the species is biologically adaptive, so people with youthful gaits are regarded as sexier across cultures (Montepare & Zebrowitz 1993). Likewise, the cues for physical attractiveness enjoy considerable universality (Perrett et al 1994) and connote reproductive fitness (Cunningham 1986). It may be for this latter, biological reason that the personalities of attractive persons are judged as more sociable across cultures (L Albright, Q Dong, TE Malloy, DA Kenney, D Yu, submitted). Through these examples, we can see how our common biological agenda accounts for universals of personality perceptions. The variable cultural impact of cues such as vocal speed (Peng et al 1993) or smiling (Matsumoto &Kudoh 1993) is harder to explain persuasively, because the linkage of these cues to dimensions of culture is less apparent.

Interpersonal attraction

People in individualistic cultures believe that internal dispositions drive behavior (Kashima et al 1992); therefore topics like interpersonal attraction and love engage Western psychologists almost exclusively (Hogan & Emler 1978). However, owing to modernization and the attendant increase in personal choice it offers people, scientific interest in interpersonal attraction is growing outside the West (Hatfield & Rapson 1993). This is a welcome development because only scattered evidence about the processes of interpersonal attraction exists from other cultures (Cheng et al 1995, Rai & Rathore 1988, Rodrigues & Iwawaki 1986). This evidence generally confirms Western models of similarity or balance.

Future work in other cultures must focus on the nature of attraction itself. For example, Shaver et al (1991) found that the mainland Chinese conceptualization of passionate love is dramatically different from Italian and American conceptualizations. Similarly, Ellis et al (1995) found that Mexicans assign a different subjective meaning to love than do Americans or Spaniards. Clearly, conceptual equivalence of key terms is an issue that must be carefully assessed in this area.

Cross-cultural work on behavioral benchmarks such as mate preferences (Liston & Salts 1988), friendship selection (Goodwin & Tang 1991), sexual activity (Hatfield & Rapson 1993), or attachment style (Wu & Shaver 1992) sidesteps this equivalence problem. The marriage relationship, for example, entails similar social requirements in all cultures, so it is perhaps not surprising that a high degree of cross-cultural agreement was found in Buss et al's (1990) multicultural study of desired spousal attributes. One complex of qualities, including chastity in women, domestic skills, and interest in home and children did, however, vary negatively as a function of cultural modernity. This latter variable and its associate, individualism, have been related to the importance of love itself in establishing and maintaining the marriage bond (KK Dion & KL Dion 1991, 1993, Levine et al 1995) and to the style of loving likely to be found in heterosexual relationships (KL Dion & KK Dion 1993). Research into how individualism and other cultural dimensions affect interpersonal attraction is still needed as modernization proceeds.

Justice

The topic of justice was first explored cross-culturally in the context of resource allocation. Bond et al (1982) argued and found that the concern of people in collectivist cultures for maintaining harmony should result in egalitarian resource divisions, and that the concern of people in individualistic cultures for performance should result in equitable resource divisions. Need-based allocations are also more likely in collectivist cultures because of concerns for group solidarity (Berman et al 1985).

Subsequent studies have revealed inconsistencies in research results based on the above reasoning (e.g. Chen 1995). Leung (1995b) has advanced a contextual model to integrate conflicting results. He argues that the nature of the social relationship between the allocator of the reward and the recipient (in-group or out-group member) and of the role relationship (supervisor allocating rewards to other performers, or coworkers allocating them to self and coworker) mediates the impact of culture on reward allocation. According to Leung, collectivists should only show an egalitarian division when allocating to an in-group member who is also a coworker. Otherwise, equity is observed. Leung (1995b) encourages cross-cultural researchers to test his model explicitly. He also challenges them to measure directly putative mediating variables such as performance enhancement that underlie reward distribution (Bond et al 1992). Only then can we build persuasive, pan-cultural theories of social behavior (Messick 1988).

Justice researchers have also focused on resource allocation procedures. Procedural concerns involve both the formal steps and the interpersonal style followed by allocators to reach their decisions (Tyler & Bies 1990). Judgments based on procedural justice are typically more convincing in cultures where authority and the decisions of people in power are widely accepted than are judgments based on outcome fairness. Tyler et al (submitted) extended this research across cultures. They argued that the preference for low power distance, which is evident in the United States, is associated with a relative emphasis on procedural rather than instrumental judgments in evaluating authorities. This conclusion was supported by Tyler et al both cross-culturally using Japanese respondents and within culture using an individual measure of preferred power distance.

Psychologists have recently examined human rights observance (Clemence et al 1995, Doise et al 1991, Humana 1992). Doise et al (1994) have linked individuals' positions on human rights to value structures. Future research might additionally consider the distinction between procedural and instrumental concerns.

Group processes

Many social scientists interested in group behavior assume that the phenomena identified in North America are universals. Whether these phenomena vary in strength by culture and whether indigenous approaches may identify wholly different additional phenomena is unclear. Studies of several known behavioral phenomena have found substantially different effects. Social loafing (Latané et al 1979) is not only absent but is significantly reversed in China (Earley 1989), Israel (Earley 1993), and Japan (Matsui et al 1987). In the China and Israel studies, subjects' endorsement of collectivist values predicted enhancement rather than curtailment of performance in group settings. Earley (1994) compared business employees in China and the United States and found Chinese performance was enhanced by a collectively focused training input, whereas US employees responded better to an individually focused input. Employees' collectivism scores predicted both culture-level and individual-level effects.

Bond & Smith (1995) report a meta-analysis of 133 replications of the Asch conformity study. After design variations are accounted for, Hofstede's collectivism scores predict higher levels of conformity. Replications of this type, however, can only detect the type of social influence processes captured by the Asch paradigm. Fernandez Dols (1992) proposes that in some cultures conformity processes may operate in a rather different manner. He finds a higher incidence of "perverse" norms in Spain than in Anglo countries. These are norms that are agreed to exist but that are only rarely enforced. Triandis (1995) identified cultures in which this type of norm is widespread as "loose" rather than "tight." Whereas the Asch paradigm shows conformity to depend upon majority size, Fernandez Dols argued that within a system of perverse norms, authority figures can maintain control by determining when norms will be enforced and when they will not.

Basic aspects of group performance, such as productivity and conformity, thus differ substantially by culture. These differences may well prove problematic in multicultural teams. Merritt & Helmreich (1995) found that US airline pilots and flight attendants endorsed lower power distance and collectivism than did pilots and attendants within the same airlines from seven East Asian countries. Anglo student groups were found to be less cooperative toward others than were non-Anglo groups (Cox et al 1991) and more in favor of risk-taking (Watson & Kumar 1992). However, although culturally diverse student teams experienced more difficulties in working together initially, Watson et al (1993) found their related performance three months later superior to that of culturally homogeneous teams.

Leadership

In his summary of an extensive program of leadership research in Japan, Misumi (1985) proposed that researchers distinguish between *general* or universal functions that effective leaders must carry out and the *specific* ways in which these functions are expressed. The P (Task Performance) and M (Group Maintenance) general leadership functions that, according to Misumi, predict leadership effectiveness resemble dimensions postulated by North American researchers. The more significant aspect of Misumi's Japanese results is that they consistently indicate that different *specific* behaviors contribute to each function in differing situations. Smith et al (1989) obtained similar results in their comparison of assembly-line workers' perceptions of supervisors in Japan, Hong Kong, the United States, and Great Britain. For instance, a *specific* behavior such as eating lunch with one's work team was associated with a high M score in some locations but not in others.

Misumi's work suggests a way in which one can better understand apparent contradictions between the results of different leadership studies. We may expect that studies that used relatively *general* characterizations of leader style will yield evidence of cross-cultural consistency in effectiveness, whereas studies of more *specific* leader attributes will detect cultural or organizational contingencies. In the remainder of this paragraph we consider studies that have used *general* style measures. Smith et al (1992) found that work teams within Japan, Hong Kong, the United States, and Great Britain led by leaders rated high for P and M all achieved higher work quality. Bass & Avolio's (1993) review of cross-cultural tests of their theory of transformational leadership indicates greater efficacy of the transformational style from 14 countries. Furthermore, Campbell et al (1993) found no difference in preference for participation in decision-making between US and Singaporean business students. Finally, Furnham & Stringfield (1994) found no difference in ratings on attributes such as innovation and commitment among Chinese and non-Chinese managers working for a Hong Kong airline. The results of these studies are as one may expect for studies using generalized measures of leader style.

Other cross-cultural studies of leadership (reviewed by Dorfman 1995) have been influenced by Western contingency theories and have consequently focused more upon *specific* attributes of effective leadership than the *general* functions that may underlie variations in leadership style. Okechuku (1994) found differences in the perceived traits associated with managers' ratings of effective subordinates in Canada, Hong Kong, and China, as did Black & Porter (1991), who compared managers' ratings in the United States and Hong Kong. Gerstner & Day (1994) asked students originally from eight different nations residing in the United States to rate how well 59 traits typified a business leader. The three country-level dimensions that were identified correlated highly with Hofstede dimensions of individualism, power distance, and uncertainty avoidance. Ayman & Chemers (1991) found some support for Fiedler & Chemers' (1984) contingency-based leader match theory among Mexican workers. Schmidt & Yeh (1992) compared leader influence in Japan, Taiwan, Australia, and Great Britain. Although a broadly similar range of influence strategies was found, they factored together distinctively within each national sample. Howell et al (1995), who contrasted business-leader effectiveness in Japan, Korea, Taiwan, Mexico, and the United States, found general effects for leader supportiveness and contingent reward, but cultural specificity for participation in decision-making and contingent punishment. Jago et al (1993) compared preferences to participate of managers in the United States and six European countries and found differences were correlated positively with power-distance scores for the seven countries. The Industrial Democracy in Europe International Research Group (IDE) (1993) carried out a longitudinal replication study of participation in 10 European countries and found differences reported in an earlier study were still apparent, though somewhat attenuated. These studies confirm that when more specific measures of leader style are employed, cultural differences are more apparent.

Decision-making

If the generality of some measures of leader style leaves unclear the relation of leader behavior to cultural constraints, then studies on the making of specific managerial decisions may provide greater clarity. Smith & Peterson (1988) proposed an analysis of leadership based around the concept of "event management," i.e. the exercise of choice in how events are managed. They suggest that managers handle events on the basis of their own experience, consultation with others, reliance upon rules, and so forth. Smith et al (1994a) surveyed managers in 16 countries and found that in individualist, low power distance nations, managers rely more heavily on their own experience and training than do those from collectivist, high power distance countries. Hofstede's country-level value measures thus predict reported managerial behaviors, despite a 25-year gap in data collection. Further studies of event management show differences in how Japanese, British, and American electronic assembly work teams handle events (Peterson et al 1990). Work teams judged most effective by their supervisors show, in Japan, more reliance on peers; in the United States, more reference to superiors; and, in Great Britain, greater self-reliance (Smith et al 1994b). Tse et al (1988) found Chinese managers more inclined than Hong Kong Chinese or Canadians to refer to their superiors. Wang & Heller (1993) compared decision-making of British and Chinese managers and found both nation and type of decision affected the degree of subordinate participation and supervisor consultation.

Yates & Lee (1995) found Chinese and several other East Asian groups (but not Japanese) more confident than Americans that their decisions were correct. They attribute this to a greater propensity to select the first adequate problem solution that is identified rather than to survey a range of alternatives before deciding. Radford et al (1991, 1993) found differences in decision-making style between Australian and Japanese students. Consistent with US counterparts from earlier research, Australians favored the "choice" style, which emphasizes careful individual thought. The Japanese, however, reported greater use of three other styles, which all involved greater reference to others. As Yates & Lee also found, the Japanese were less confident of their decisions. These differences may be explicable in terms of variations in individualism-collectivism among East Asian countries, Australia, and the United States.

Negotiation

Group processes within cross-cultural negotiation should provide particularly clear illustrations of the effects of divergence in values across cultures. Studies of intracultural simulated buyer-seller negotiations indicate that while cooperative problem-solving strategies are most effective in the United States, competitive behavior works better in Russia (Graham et al 1992), Taiwan (Graham et al 1988), Germany, Great Britain (Campbell et al 1988), Mexico, and Francophone

Canada (Adler et al 1987). Similarly, Gabrenya (1990) found that US students cooperated on a task better with strangers than did Taiwanese students. These results support the view that members of collectivist cultures are more competitive with out-groups than are members of individualist cultures. This proposition is tested more directly by DKS Chan, HC Triandis, PJ Carnevale, A Tam, MH Bond (submitted), who compared intracultural negotiation behavior of Hong Kong Chinese and US students and obtained measures of their individualist or collectivist values. Hong Kong students responded more to cooperation and yielded to an in-group negotiator more than to an out-group negotiator. Similar differences were obtained by Trubisky et al (1991), who compared intracultural conflict resolution preferences of US and Taiwanese students. The authors of both studies attributed their results to differences in individualism-collectivism. In a more detailed review of culture and negotiation, Leung (1995b) concludes that behavior is influenced both by variations in individualism-collectivism and by specific situational demands.

How closely the processes of intracultural and intercultural negotiation parallel one another remains unclear. Tse et al (1994) compared intracultural and intercultural negotiating behaviors of Chinese and Canadian executives. Neither party modified its approach when negotiating cross-culturally. Chinese negotiators sought to avoid conflict more than the Canadians, and when conflict did arise Chinese favored withdrawal or consultation with superiors more strongly. However, Adler & Graham (1989) did find some changes in negotiators' behavior when they engaged in intercultural negotiations. Japanese negotiators achieved lower payoffs negotiating with Americans than with other Japanese. Anglophone Canadians achieved lower payoffs in negotiations with Francophone Canadians, despite the fact that the Francophones became more cooperative when negotiating interculturally. Some caution is needed in equating payoff with success in this type of study because collectivists may regard maintenance of long-term links as a more important success criterion than short-term payoff.

Three studies show how social context and understanding of the other party's preferred communication styles are crucial to successful outcome. Qualitative analyses are provided by Goldman (1994) for US-Japanese negotiations and by Kimmel (1994) for US-Iraqi negotiations prior to the Gulf War. Marriott (1993) reports how seating arrangements affected Japanese-Australian business negotiations.

Organizational behavior

Work motivation

The role of work may be expected to reflect salient dimensions of a society's values. The Meaning of Working International Team (MOW) (1987) performed surveys in the United States, Japan, and six West European countries and found so-called "work centrality" highest in Japan, The MOW study has been replicated and extended to China and six East European countries (SA Ruiz Quintanilla & GW England, submitted). The MOW team conclude that work meanings can be represented along a single axis on which, at one end, are situated the costs to the individual and, at the other end, the collective benefits of work. The Work Socialization of Youth project (WOSY) (Touzard 1992) is a longitudinal study that compares work role socialization in seven West European countries and Israel and uses the same concepts developed by the MOW team. The WOSY researchers found that changes in patterns of work meaning over the first three years at work were predicted by both individual- and country-level variables, but the researchers did not analyze their results in terms of cross-cultural theory (Claes & Ruiz Quintanilla 1993).

Misra et al (1990) found greater linkage between work and family concerns in India than in Canada. Schwalb et al (1992) found that Japanese employees reported being motivated by the task itself, self-improvement, and financial reward, in contrast with a greater US emphasis upon affiliation, social concern, and recognition. Holt & Keats (1992) compared Anglo, Chinese, Lebanese, and Aboriginal Australians. While all valued achievement highly, the degree to which achievement related to work varied greatly. These results indicate the need for revision of the earlier view that achievement motivation is particularly strong in individualist cultures, and that individualistic entrepreneurialism is a prerequisite for economic development (McClelland 1961). Achievement motivation, at least in East Asian collectivist cultures, is more socially oriented (Yu 1995, Yu & Yang 1994), which may also foster entrepreneurial activity (Redding 1990). Whether achievement motivation centers upon work is dependent upon the values of a culture, and this variation can lead to unexpected findings. Xie & Jamal's (1993) study of Chinese managers, for example, illustrates that Type A managers reported more job stress than Type B managers, as in Western studies. However, the two groups showed no difference in psychosomatic problems, and Type A managers spent more time with their families. Thus the Western pattern of compulsive working with attendant health risks appears here to be attenuated by the centrality of family within Chinese culture.

Agarwal (1993) found positive effects of reliance on rules and normalization in handling role conflict and ambiguity among salespersons in India, but negative effects in the United States. Dubinsky et al (1992) compared role ambiguity and role conflict among salespersons in the United States, Japan, and Korea. Few effects due to culture were detected. Several researchers have examined the relation of work stress to Hofstede scores for particular countries. Shenkar & Zeira (1992) studied role ambiguity of chief executives within international joint ventures in Israel. Role ambiguity was greatest where the scores for power distance and masculinity among partners' countries were most divergent. Peterson et al (1995) surveyed managers in 21 countries and reported role overload was greatest in high power distance, collectivist nations whereas reported role ambiguity was greatest in low power distance, individualist nations.

Work behavior

Several studies discussed earlier that were designed to identify dimensions of cultural variation were based upon employees' reported values or behavior. This section considers more specific aspects of work behavior. Luthans et al (1993) made an observational study of Russian managers and compared the results to earlier studies of US managers. Although the pattern of their activities showed considerable similarities, the Russians spent less time on networking and more on planning, controlling, and coordinating. Boisot & Liang (1992) observed a small sample of Chinese managers. The managers spent more time with their superiors and received much more written material from them than was the case in earlier US studies.

Comparisons between Hong Kong and US managers have proved popular. Schermerhorn & Bond (1991) compared managers' preferred influence tactics and found Hong Kong respondents preferred assertiveness and the Americans preferred rationality, exchange, and ingratiation. Ralston et al (1992, 1993) found Hong Kong managers rated higher for Machiavellianism, external locus of control, dogmatism, and Confucian Work Dynamism. Most of these effects were found also among mainland Chinese managers. Black & Porter (1991) compared performance appraisals received by managers in the United States and Hong Kong with managers' self-rated traits derived from US leadership theory. High correlations between traits and performance appraisals were found in the United States but were not found for either Chinese or US managers working in Hong Kong. Similar conclusions were reached by Furnham & Stringfield (1993), who found that quite different traits were significantly linked to performance measures among Chinese and European managers working for the same Hong Kong airline.

Bochner & Hesketh (1994) studied Australian bank employees whose ethnic identity was with either high (e.g. Hong Kong) or low (e.g. Great Britain) power distance cultures. The high power distance group reported significantly more behaviors likely to be expected from high power distance, collectivist cultures and reported experiencing more discrimination than did respondents from the majority, low power distance group. Wong & Birnbaum-More (1994) found that among banks in Hong Kong the degree of centralization and hierarchy could be predicted by the Hofstede power distance score of the country owning the bank.

Organizational researchers have also sought to delineate the relationship between organizational culture and national culture. Morris et al (1994) compared the incidence of entrepreneurial corporate climate in US, South African, and Portuguese organizations. Within-country analyses revealed that within the United States and South Africa, respondents' endorsement of moderate levels of individualism-collectivism was associated with the highest endorsement of entrepreneurial values. Van Muijen & Koopman (1994) report results from the FOCUS 92 group, which surveyed perceptions of organizational climate in 10 European nations. Differences in mean country scores on preference for innovation paralleled Hofstede's individualism scores, but rules-orientation did not accord with any of the Hofstede scores. Janssens et al (1995) compared perceptions of safety policy within US, French, and Argentinian plants of the same US multinational corporation. Although a company-wide policy was in force, its implementation varied in ways that were interpreted in terms of individualism-collectivism. Hofstede et al (1990) identified six dimensions of organizational culture within organizations in Denmark and the Netherlands. Hofstede et al (1993) further illustrated the importance of employing the appropriate level of data analysis in characterizing individual values, organizational culture, or national culture.

Conclusions

Kagitcibasi & Berry (1989) concluded that three trends were apparent within the field of cross-cultural psychology in the late 1980s: a focus upon individualism-collectivism, increasing concern to develop indigenous psychologies, and the search for cultural universals. Our coverage indicates that since then the first of these issues has attracted the attention of more and more researchers. While this increased attention has served to focus cross-cultural psychology more clearly, it has led to the comparative neglect of other approaches deriving from Kagitcibasi & Berry's second and third areas. The search for universals and an emphasis upon indigenous culture-specifics are often cast as contradictory enterprises that exemplify contrasting etic and emic approaches. Yet these concepts are no more separable than nature and nurture. If the recently emerging dimensions of culture identified by Hofstede, Schwartz, Smith and others are to guide future research in fruitful directions, the methodological problems stemming from the etic-emic dilemma must be more clearly addressed.

Berry (1989) proposes a sequence in research whereby parallel indigenous studies within two or more societies may lead to a validly generalized universal or derived etic, in contrast to the currently much more widespread reliance on imposed-etic measures drawn from a small number of Western countries. Although many believe Berry's procedure is preferable, imposed-etic measures will likely continue to be much more widely used. In these circumstances, we need estimates of what types of cultural variance are missed by imposed-etic measures. Studies designed from a non-Western starting point such as the one by the Chinese Culture Connection (1987) are crucial. The increasing number of recent studies whose results compare well with already identified dimensions of cultural variation also enhance the argument for convergent validity (Bond 1995). The testing of hypotheses linking emergent dimensions of cultural values or beliefs to external-distal country-level data is another welcome trend (Best & Williams 1994, DKS Chan, submitted, Smith et al 1995a,b, Williams 1993).

However, numerous pitfalls along the path toward a well-validated framework for cross-cultural studies remain. First, this review demonstrates how the sampling of national cultures within recent studies is woefully biased. Current studies heavily overrepresent North America, East Asia, and Western Europe, with consequent neglect of Latin American, African, East European, Arab, South Asian, and other societies. Second, the strongly individualistic values of the cultures from which most researchers are drawn result in confusion regarding the appropriate levels of analysis of cross-cultural data. Most current culture-level analyses are based upon aggregation of individual-level data, and reviewers used by major North American journals rather often require that researchers engage in individual-level data analyses, which is inappropriate to a culture-level analysis. Appropriate-level variables must be used if we are to understand variation at a given level (Hofstede et al 1993). Equally invalid extrapolations are also widespread in the reverse direction: Researchers infer that because culture X has certain values, individuals within that culture will share those values. Separate individual-level variables are needed. Schwartz's (1994) recent large-scale surveys show how individual-level analyses yield results different from culture-level analyses and provide relatively comprehensive guidelines with respect to intracultural continuities in the structure of values.

Third, how do we define the boundaries of one's cultural samples? Most studies use national affiliation, but the existing and increasing cultural diversity of many nations makes this strategy unsatisfactory. However, if future researchers routinely include measures of the salient values and ethnic identities of the samples they study, comparisons with other studies with somewhat more established theoretical roots may be made. Furthermore, the growing cultural heterogeneity both of nations and of smaller social systems within them will require that researchers progress from documenting contrasts between different cultures toward examining the ways in which individuals and groups from different cultures relate to one another. In doing so, they may broaden the cultural range encompassed by existing literatures concerning intergroup relations, stereotyping, conflict, communication, and so forth.

Although the methodological problems facing cross-cultural researchers should not be minimized, we do not wish to conclude this review on a pessimistic note. Cross-cultural social and organizational psychology has for the first time a theoretical framework upon which studies may be designed and relevant samples may be selected. That framework must be scrutinized, of course, but a set of dimensions of cultural variation proven to predict social phenomena is now available to researchers. While the definition of individualism and collectivism as polar opposites will certainly prove unable to integrate the full range of global variations in social behavior, further progress can be expected in defining just how many dimensions are required for optimal parsimony.

Literature cited

Adair JG, Puhan BN, Vohra H. 1993. The indigenisation of psychology: empirical assessment of progress in Indian research. *Int. J. Psychol.* 28:761–73

Adamopoulos J. 1988. Interpersonal behavior: cross-cultural and historical perspectives. See Bond 1988, pp. 196–207

Adler NJ. 1991. *International Dimensions of Organizational Behavior*. Boston: PWS-Kent. 2nd ed

Adler NJ, Graham JL. 1989. Cross-cultural comparison: the international comparison fallacy. *J. Int. Bus. Stud.* 20:515–38

Adler NJ, Graham JL, Schwarz T. 1987. Business negotiations in Canada, Mexico and the United States. *J. Bus. Res.* 15:411–29

Agarwal S. 1993. Influence of formalisation on role stress, organizational commitment and work alienation of salespersons: a cross-national comparative study. *J. Int. Bus. Stud.* 24:715–39

Amir Y, Sharon I. 1987. Are social psychological laws cross-culturally valid? *J. Cross-Cult. Psychol.* 18:383–470

Ayman R, Chemers MM. 1991. The effect of leadership match on subordinate satisfaction in Mexican organisations: some moderating influences of self-monitoring. *Appl. Psychol.: Int. Rev.* 40:299–314

Bass BM, Avolio B. 1993. Transformational leadership: a response to critiques. In *Leadership Theory and Research*, ed. MM Chemers, R Ayman, pp. 49–80. San Diego: Academic

Berman JJ. Murphy-Berman V, Singh P. 1985. Cross-cultural similarities and differences in perceptions of fairness. *J. Cross-Cult. Psychol*, 16:55–67

Berry JW. 1979. A cultural ecology of social behavior. In *Advances in Experimental Social Psychology,* ed. L Berkowitz, 12:177–206. New York: Academic

Berry JW. 1989. Imposed etics-emics-derived etics: the operationalisation of a compelling idea. *Int. J. Psychol.* 24:721–35

Berry JW, Poortinga YH, Segall MH, Dasen PR. 1992. *Cross-Cultural Psychology: Research and Applications*. Cambridge: Cambridge Univ. Press

Berry JW, Segall MH. Kagitcibasi C, eds. 1996. *Handbook of Cross-Cultural Psychology*, Vol. 3, *Social Psychology, Personality and Psychopathology*. Needham, MA: Allyn & Bacon. In press

Best DL, Williams JE. 1994, Masculinity/femininity in the self and ideal self-descriptions of university students in fourteen countries. See Bouvy et al 1994, pp. 297–306

Black JS, Porter LW. 1991. Managerial behaviors and job performance: a successful manager in Los Angeles may not succeed in Hong Kong. *J. Int. Bus. Stud.* 22:99–113

Bochner S. 1994. Cross-cultural differences in the self concept: a test of Hofstede's individualism/collectivism distinction. *J. Cross-Cult. Psychol.* 25:273–83

Bochner S, Hesketh B. 1994. Power distance, individualism/collectivism and job-related attitudes in a culturally-diverse work group. *J. Cross-Cult. Psychol.* 25:233–57

Boisot M, Liang XG. 1992. The nature of managerial work in the Chinese enterprise reforms: a study of six directors. *Organ. Stud.* 13:161–84

Bond MH, ed. 1986. *The Psychology of the Chinese People*. Hong Kong: Oxford Univ. Press

Bond MH. 1988. *The Cross-Cultural Challenge to Social Psychology*. Newbury Park, CA: Sage

Bond MH. 1991. Chinese values and health: a cross-cultural examination. *Psychol. Health.* 5:137–52

Bond MH. 1994. Trait theory and cross-cultural studies of person perception. *Psychol. Inq.* 5:114–17

Bond MH, ed. 1995. *Handbook of Chinese Psychology*. Hong Kong: Oxford Univ. Press. In press

Bond MH, Cheung TS. 1983. The spontaneous self-concept of college students in Hong Kong, Japan, and the United States. *J. Cross-Cult. Psychol.* 14:153–71

Bond MH, Forgas JP. 1984. Linking person perception to behavioral intention across cultures: the role of cultural collectivism. *J. Cross-Cult. Psychol.* 15:337–52

Bond MH, Leung K, Schwartz S. 1992. Explaining choices in procedural and distributive justice across cultures. *Int. J. Psychol.* 27:211–25

Bond MH, Leung K, Wan KC. 1982. How does cultural collectivism operate? The impact of task and maintenance contributions on reward allocation. *J. Cross-Cult. Psychol.* 13:186–200

Bond R, Smith PB. 1995. Culture and conformity: a meta-anaiysis of the Asch line judgment task. *Psychol. Bull.* In press

Bontempo R. 1993. Translation fidelity of psychological scales: an item response theory analysis of an individualism-collectivism scale. *J. Cross-Cult. Psychol.* 24:149–66

Bouvy AM, van de Vijver FJR, Boski P, Schmitz P, eds. 1994. *Journeys into Cross-Cultural Psychology*, Amsterdam: Swets & Zeitlinger

Brislin R. 1993. *Understanding Culture's Influence on Behavior.* Fort Worth, TX: Harcourt, Brace, Jovanovich

Buss DM, Abbott M, Angelitner A, Asherian A, Biaggio A, et al. 1990, International preferences in selecting mates: a study of 37 cultures. *J. Cross-Cult. Psychol.* 21:5–47

Campbell D, Bommer W, Yeo E. 1993. Perceptions of appropriate leadership style: participation versus consultation across two cultures. *Asia Pac. J. Manage.* 10:1–19

Campbell N, Graham JL, Jolibert A, Meissner HG. 1988. Marketing negotiations in France, Germany, the United Kingdom and the United States. *J. Mark.* 52:49–62

Chan SCN, Bond MH. 1995. *Cultural values and social health.* Presented at Eur. Congr. Psychol., Athens

Chang YC, Lin W, Lohnstamm GA. 1994. *Parents' free descriptions of children's characteristics—a verified study of the Big Five in Chinese children.* Presented at Int. Soc. Stud. Behav. Dev., Beijing

Chasiotis A, Keller H. 1994. Evolutionary psychology and developmental cross-cultural psychology. See Bouvy et al 1994, pp. 6–82

Chen CC. 1995. New trends in rewards allocation preferences: a Sino-US comparison. *Acad. Manage. J.* 38:408–28

Cheng C, Bond MH, Chan SC. 1995. The perception of ideal best friends by Chinese adolescents. *Int. J. Psychol.* 30:91–108

Chinese Culture Connection. 1987. Chinese values and the search for culture-free dimensions of culture. *J. Cross-Cult. Psychol.* 18:143–64

Claes R, Ruiz Quintanilla SA. 1993. Work meaning patterns in early career. *Eur. Work Organ. Psychol.* 3:311–23

Clemence A, Doise W, Rosa AS, Gonzalez L. 1995. La representation sociale des droits de l'homme: une recherche internationale sur l'etendue et les limites de l'universalite. *Int. J. Psychol.* In press

Costa PT Jr. McCrae RR. 1992. Four ways five factors are basic. *Pers. Indiv. Diff.* 13:653–65

Cox T, Lobel S, McLeod PL. 1991. Effects of ethnic group cultural differences on cooperative and competitive behavior on a group task. *Acad. Manage. J.* 34:827–47

Crittenden KS. 1995. Causal attribution processes among the Chinese. See Bond 1995

Crocker J, Luhtanen R, Blaine B, Broadnax S. 1994. Collective self-esteem arid psychological well-being among White, Black, and Asian college students. *Pers. Soc. Psychol. Bull.* 20:503–13

Cunningham MR. 1986. Measuring the physical in physical attractiveness: quasi-experiments on the sociology of female facial beauty. *J. Pers. Soc. Psychol.* 50:925–35
DeGooyer MJ, Williams JE. 1992. A comparison of self-concepts in Japan and the United States. See Iwawaki et al 1992, pp. 279–88
Der-Kerabetian A. 1992. World-mindedness and the nuclear threat: a multinational study. *J. Soc. Behav. Pers.* 7:293–303
Dion KK, Dion KL. 1991. Psychological individualism and romantic love. *J. Soc. Behav. Pers.* 6:17–33
Dion KK, Dion KL. 1993. Individualistic and collectivistic perspectives on gender and the cultural context of love and intimacy. *J. Soc. Issues.* 49:53–69
Dion KL, Dion KK. 1993. Gender and ethnocultural comparisons in styles of love. *Psychol. Women Q.* 17:463–73
Dixon RMW. 1977. Where have all the adjectives gone? *Stud. Lang.* 1:19–80
Doise W, Dell' Ambrogio P, Spini D. 1991. Psychologic sociale et Droits del' Homme. *Rev. int. Psvchol. Soc.* 4:257–77
Doise W, Spini D, Jesuino JC, Ng SH, Emler N. 1994. Values and perceived conflicts in the social representations of human rights: feasibility of a cross-national study. *Swiss J. Psychol.* 53:240–51
Dorfman PW. 1995. International and cross-cultural leadership research. See Punnett & Shenkar 1995
Dubinsky A, Michaels RE, Kotabe M, Lim CU, Moon HC. 1992. Influence of role stress on industrial salespeople's work outcomes in the United States, Japan and Korea. *J. Int. Bus. Stud.* 23:77–99
Earley PC. 1989. Social loafing and collectivism: a comparison of the United States and the People's Republic of China. *Adm. Sci. Q.* 34:565–81
Earley PC. 1993. East meets West meets Mideast: further explorations of collectivistic and individualistic work groups. *Acad. Manage. J.* 36:319–48
Earley PC. 1994. Self or group: cultural effects of training on self-efficacy and performance. *Adm. Sci. Q.* 39:89–117
Earley PC, Erez M, eds. 1996. *New Perspectives on International Industrial/Organizational Psychology.* San Francisco: Jossey Bass. In press
Earley PC, Mosakowski E. 1995. A framework for understanding experimental research in an international and intercultural context. See Punnett & Shenkar 1995
Easton D, Shelling CS, eds. 1991. *Divided Knowledge: Across Disciplines, Across Cultures.* Newbury Park, CA: Sage
Ellis BB, Becker P, Kimmel HD. 1993. An item response theory evaluation of an English version of the Trier Personality Inventory (TPI). *J. Cross-Cult. Psychol.* 24:133–48
Ellis BB, Kimmel HD, Diaz Guerrero R, Canas J, Bajo MT. 1995. Love and power in Mexico, Spain and the United States. *J. Cross-Cult. Psychol.* 25:525–40
Ellsworth PC 1994. Sense, culture, sensibility. See Kitayama & Markus 1994, pp. 23–50
Erez M, Earley PC. 1993. *Culture, Self-Identity and Work.* New York: Oxford Univ. Press
Feather NT. 1988. From values to actions: recent applications of the expectancy-value model. *Aust. J. Psychol.* 40:105–24
Feather NT. 1994. Values, national identification and in-group favouritism. *Br. J. Soc. Psychol.* 33:467–76
Feather NT, McKee IR. 1993. Global self-esteem and attitudes toward the high achiever for Australian and Japanese students. *Soc. Psychol. Q.* 56:65–76

Fernandez Dols JP. 1992. Procesos escabrosos en psicologia social: el concepto de norma perversa. *Rev. Psicol. Soc.* 7:243–55

Fiedler FE, Chemers MM. 1984. *Improving Leadership Effectiveness: The Leader Match Concept.* New York: Wiley

Fiske AP. 1992. The four elementary forms of sociality: framework for a unified theory of social relations. *Psychol. Rev.* 99: 689–723

Fiske AP. 1993. Social errors in four cultures: evidence about universal forms of social relations. *J. Cross-Cult. Psychol.* 24: 463–94

Frijda NH, Mesquita B. 1994. The social roles and functions of emotions. See Kitayama & Markus 1994, pp. 51–87

Furnham A. 1993. Just world beliefs in twelve societies. *J. Soc. Psychol.* 133:317–29

Furnham A, Bond MH, Heaven P, Hilton D, Lobel T, et al. 1993. A comparison of Protestant work ethic beliefs in thirteen nations. *J. Soc. Psychol.* 133:185–97

Furnham A, Stringfield P. 1993. Personality and occupational behavior: Myers-Briggs Type indicator correlates of managerial practices in two cultures. *Hum. Relat.* 46:827–48

Furnham A, Stringfield P. 1994. Congruence of self and subordinate ratings of managerial practices as a correlate of supervisor evaluation. *J. Occup. Organ. Psychol.* 67:57–68

Gabrenya WK. 1988. Social science and social psychology: the cross-cultural link. See Bond 1988, pp. 48–66

Gabrenya WK. 1990. *Dyadic social interaction during task behavior in collectivist and individualist societies.* Presented at Workshop on individualism-Collectivism, Seoul, Korea

Gerstner CR, Day DV. 1994. Cross-cultural comparison of leadership prototypes. *Leadersh. Q.* 5:121–34

Gielen UP. 1994. American mainstream psychology and its relationship to international and cross-cultural psychology. In *Advancing Psychology and Its Applications: International Perspectives,* ed. AL Comunian, UP Gielen. pp. 26–40. Milan: Angel

Giles HA, Viladot A. 1994. Ethnolinguistic differentiation in Catalonia. *Multilingua: J. Cross-Cult. Interlang. Commun.* 13: 301–12

Goldman A. 1994. The centrality of 'ningensei' to Japanese negotiating and interpersonal relationships: implications for US-Japanese communication. *Int. J. Intercult. Relat.* 18:29–54

Goodwin R, Tang D. 1991. Preferences for friends and close relationship partners. *J. Soc. Psychol.* 131:579–81

Graham JL, Evenko LI, Rajan MN. 1992. An empirical comparison of Soviet and American business negotiations. *J. Int. Bus. Stud.* 23:387–418

Graham JL, Kim DK, Lin CY, Robinson R. 1988. Buyer-seller negotiations around the Pacific Rim: differences in fundamental exchange processes. *J. Consum. Res.* 15:48–54

Gudykunst WB, ed. 1993. *Communication in Japan and the United States.* Albany: S. Univ. NY

Gudykunst WB, Matsumoto Y, Ting-Toomey S, Nishida T, Karimi H. 1994. *Measuring self-construals across cultures: a derivedetic analysis.* Int. Commun. Assoc. Sydney

Hatfield E, Rapson RL. 1993. Historical and cross-cultural perspectives on passionate love and sexual desire. *Annu. Rev. Sex Res.* 4:67–97

Ho EKF. 1994. *Validating the five-factor model of personality.* BA thesis. Chinese Univ. Hong Kong

Hofstede G. 1980. *Culture's Consequences: International Differences in Work-Related Values.* Beverly Hills, CA: Sage

Hofstede G, Bond MH, Luk CL. 1993. Individual perceptions of organisational cultures: a methodological treatise on levels of analysis. *Organ. Stud.* 14:483–503

Hofstede G, Neuyen B, Ohayv DD, Sanders G. 1990. Measuring organizational cultures: a qualitative and quantitative study across twenty cases. *Adm. Sci. Q.* 35:286–316

Hogan RT, Emler NP. 1978. The biases in contemporary social psychology. *Soc. Res.* 45:478–534

Holt J, Keats DM. 1992. Work cognitions in multicultural interaction. *J. Cross-Cult. Psychol.* 23:421–43

Howell JP, Dorfman PW, Hibino S, Lee JK, Tate U. 1995. Leadership in Western and Asian countries: commonalities and differences in effective leadership processes and substitutes across cultures. Las Cruces: New Mex. State Univ.

Hui CH, Triandis HC. 1989. Effects of culture and response format on extreme response style. *J. Cross-Cult. Psychol.* 20:296–309

Humana C. 1992. *World Human Rights Guide.* New York: Oxford

Industrial Democracy in Europe international Research Group. 1993. *Industrial Democracy in Europe Revisited.* Oxford: Oxford Univ. Press

Ip GWM, Bond MH. 1995. Culture, values, and the spontaneous self-concept. *Asian J. Psychol.* 1:30–36

Iwawaki S, Kashima Y, Leung K, eds. 1992. *Innovations in Cross-Cultural Psychology.* Amsterdam: Swets & Zeitlinger

Jago AG, Reber G, Bohnisch W, Maczynski J, Zavrel J et al. 1993. *Culture's consequence? A seven nation study of participation.* Presented at Decis. Sci. inst., Washington, DC

Janssens M, Brett J, Smith FJ. 1995. Confirmatory cross-cultural research: testing the viability of a corporate-wide safety policy. *Acad. Manage. J.* 38:364–82

Kagitcibasi C, Berry JW. 1989. Cross-cultural psychology: current research and trends. *Annu. Rev. Psychol.* 40:493–531

Kagitcibasi C. 1995. *Family and Human Development Across Cultures: A View from the Other Side.* Hillsdale, NJ: Erlbaum

Kashima Y, Siegel M, Tanaka K, Kashima ES. 1992. Do people believe behaviors are consistent with attitudes? Towards a cultural psychology of attribution processes. *Br. J. Soc. Psychol.* 31:111–24

Kashima Y, Triandis HC. 1986. The self-serving bias in attributions as a coping strategy: a cross-cultural study. *J. Cross-Cult. Psychol.* 17:83–97

Keats DM, Munro D, Mann L. 1989. *Heterogeneity in Cross-Cultural Psychology.* Amsterdam: Swets & Zeitlinger

Kim U, Berry JW, eds. 1993. *Indigenous Psychologies: Research and Experience in Context.* Newbury Park, CA: Sage

Kim U, Triandis HC, Kagitcibasi C, Choi SC, Yoon G, eds. 1994. *Individualism and Collectivism: Theory, Method and Applications.* Newbury Park, CA: Sage

Kimmel PR. 1994. Cultural perspectives on international negotiations. *J. Soc. Issues* 50:179–96

Kitayama S, Markus HR, eds. 1994. *Emotion and Culture: Empirical Studies of Mutual Influence.* Washington, DC: Am. Psychol. Assoc.

Komin S. 1990. Culture and work-related values in Thai organisations. *Int. J. Psychol.* 25:681–704

Kohn ML. 1987. Cross-national research as an analytic strategy. *Am. Soc. Rev.* 52:713–31
Kohn ML, Schoonbach C, Schooler C, Slomczynski KM. 1990. Position in the class structure and psychological functioning in the United States, Japan and Poland. *Am. J. Soc.* 95:964–1008
Krewer B, Jahoda G. 1993. Psychologie et culture: vers une solution de Babel? *Int. J. Psychol.* 28:367–76
Latané B, Williams K, Harkins S, 1979. Many hands make light the work: causes and consequences of social loafing. *J. Pers. Soc. Psychol.* 37:822–32
Leung JP, Leung K. 1992. Life satisfaction, self-concept and relationship with parents in adolescence. *J. Youth Adolesc.* 21:653–65
Leung K. 1995a. Beliefs in Chinese culture. See Bond 1995
Leung K. 1995b. Negotiation and reward allocations across cultures. See Earley & Erez 1996
Leung K, Bond MH. 1989. On the empirical identification of dimensions for cross-cultural comparison. *J. Cross-Cult. Psychol.* 20:133–51
Leung K, Bond MH, Schwartz S. 1994. *How To Explain Cross-Cultural Differences: Values, Valences and Expectancies?* Hong Kong: Chinese Univ.
Levine R, Sato S, Hashimoto T, Verma J. 1995. Love and marriage in eleven cultures. *J. Cross-Cult. Psychol.* In press
Linssen H, Hagendoorn L. 1994. Social and geographic factors in the explanation of the content of European nationality stereotypes. *Br. J. Soc. Psychol.* 33:165–82
Liston A, Salts CJ. 1988. Mate selection values: a comparison of Malaysian and United States students. *J. Comp. Fam. Stud.* 19: 361–70
Lonner WJ. 1980. The search for psychological universals. See Triandis & Lambert 1980, pp. 143–204
Lonner WJ, Malpass R, eds. 1994. *Psychology and Culture.* Boston: Allyn & Bacon
Luhtanen R. Crocker J. 1992. A collective self-esteem scale: self-evaluation of one's social identity. *Pers. Soc. Psychol. Bull.* 18:302–18
Luk CL, Bond MH. 1992. Chinese lay beliefs about the causes and cures of psychological problems. *J. Clin. Soc. Psychol.* 11:140–57
Luthans F, Welsh DHB, Rosenkrantz SA. 1993. What do Russian managers really do? An observational study with comparisons to US managers. *J. Int. Bus. Stud.* 24:741–61
Lytle A, Brett JM, Barsness ZI, Tinsley CH, Janssens M. 1995. A paradigm for confirmatory cross-cultural research in organizational behavior. *Res. Organ. Behav.* 17:167–214
Marin G, Gamba RJ, Marin BV. 1993. Extreme response style and acquiescence among Hispanics: the role of acculturation and education. *J. Cross-Cult. Psychol.* 23: 498–509
Marin G, Marin BV. 1991. *Research with Hispanic Populations.* Newbury Park, CA: Sage
Markus HR, Kitayama S, 1991. Culture and the self: implications for cognition, emotion and motivation. *Psychol. Rev.* 98: 224–53
Marriott H. 1993. Spatial arrangements in Australian-Japanese business communication. *J. Asian Pac. Commun.* 4:107—26
Matsui T, Kakuyama T, Onglatco ML. 1987. Effects of goals and feedback on performance in groups. *J. Appl. Psychol.* 72: 407–15
Matsumoto D. 1994. *People: Psychology from a Cultural Perspective.* Pacific Grove, CA: Brooks/Cole
Matsumoto D, Kudoh T. 1993. American-Japanese cultural differences in attributions of personality based on smiles. *J. Nonverbal Behav.* 17:231–13

Mauro R, Sato K, Tucker J. 1992, The role of appraisal in human emotions: a cross-cultural study. *J. Pers. Soc. Psychol.* 62:301–17

McArthur LZ, Berry DS. 1987. Cross-cultural agreement in perceptions of babyfaced adults. *J. Cross-Cult. Psychol.* 18:165–92

McClelland DC. 1961. *The Achieving Society.* Princeton, NJ: Van Nostrand

Merritt AC, Helmreich RL. 1995. Human factors on the flightdeck: the influence of national culture. *J. Cross-Cult. Psychol.* In press

Mesquita B. 1993. *Cultural variations in emotions: a comparative study of Dutch, Surinamese and Turkish people in the Netherlands.* PhD thesis. Univ. Amsterdam

Mesquita B, Frijda NH. 1992. Cultural variations in emotions: a review. *Psychol. Bull.* 412:179–204

Messick DM. 1988. On the limitations of cross-cultural research in social psychology. See Bond 1988, pp. 41–47

Miller JG. 1994. Cultural diversity in the morality of caring: individually oriented versus duty-based interpersonal moral codes. *Cross-Cult. Res.* 28:3–39

Miller JG, Bersoff DM. 1992. Culture and moral judgment. How are conflicts between justice and interpersonal responsibilities resolved? *J. Pers. Soc. Psychol.* 62: 541–54

Misra S, Gergen K. 1993. On the place of culture in psychological science. *Int. J. Psychol.* 28:225–44

Misra S, Ghosh R, Kanungo RN. 1990. Measurement of family involvement a cross-national study of managers. *J. Cross-Cult. Psychol.* 21:232–48

Misumi J. 1985. *The Behavioral Science of Leadership.* Ann Arbor: Univ. Mich. Press

Moghaddam FM, Taylor DM, Wright SC. 1993. *Social Psychology in Cross-Cultural Perspective.* New York: Freeman

Montepare JM, Zebrowitz LA. 1993. A cross-cultural comparison of impressions created by age-related variations in gait. *J. Nonverbal Behav.* 17:55–68

Morris MH, Davis DL, Allen JW. 1994. Fostering corporate entrepreneurship: cross-cultural comparisons of the importance of individualism versus collectivism. *J. Int. Bus. Stud.* 25:65–89

Morris MW, Peng KP. 1994. Culture and cause: American and Chinese attributions for social and physical events. *J. Pers. Soc. Psychol.* 67:949–71

Murphy G. 1969. Psychology in the year 2000. *Am. Psychol.* 24:523–30

Newman LS. 1993. How individualists interpret behavior: idiocentrism and spontaneous trait inference. *Soc. Cogn.* 11:243–69

Okechuku C. 1994. The relationship of six managerial characteristics to the assessment of managerial effectiveness in Canada, Hong Kong and the People's Republic of China. *J. Occup. Organ. Psychol.* 67:79–86

Ongel U, Smith PB. 1994. Who are we and where are we going? JCCP approaches its 100th issue. *J. Cross-Cult. Psychol.* 25:25–53

Pandey J, Sinha D, Bhawuk DPS. eds. 1995. *Asian Contributions to Cross-Cultural Psychology.* New Delhi: Sage

Paranjpe AC, Ho DYF, Rieber RW, eds. 1988. *Asian Contributions to Psychology.* New York: Praeger

Peng Y, Zebrowitz LA, Lee HK. 1993. The impact of cultural background and cross-cultural experience on impressions of American and Korean speakers. *J. Cross-Cult. Psychol.* 34:203–20

Perrett DI, May KA, Yoshikawa S. 1994. Facial shape and judgments of female attractiveness. *Nature* 368:239–42

Peterson MF, Smith PB, Bond MH, Misumi J. 1990. Personal reliance on alternative event management processes in four countries. *Group Organ. Stud.* 15:75–91

Peterson MF, Smith PB, Akande D, Ayestaran S, Bochner S, et al. 1995. Role stress by national culture and organizational function: a 21 nation study. *Acad. Manage. J.* 38: 429–52

Poortinga Y. 1992. Towards a conceptualization of culture for psychology. See Iwawaki et al 1992, pp. 3–17

Punnett BJ, Shenkar O, eds. 1995. *Handbook of International Management Research.* Oxford: Blackwell. In press

Radford MH, Mann L. Ohta Y, Nakane Y. 1991. Differences between Australia and Japan in reported use of decision processes. *Int. J. Psychol.* 26:35–52

Radford MH, Mann L, Ohta Y, Nakane Y. 1993. Differences between Australian and Japanese students in decisional self-esteem, decisional stress and coping styles. *J. Cross-Cult. Psychol.* 24:284–97

Rai SN, Rathore J. 1988. Attraction as a function of cultural similarity and proportion of similar attitudes related to different areas of life. *Psychol. Ling.* 18:47–57

Ralston DA, Gustafson DJ, Elsacs PM, Cheung FM, Terpstra RH. 1992. Eastern values: a comparison of managers in the United States, Hong Kong and the People's Republic of China. *J. Appl. Psychol.* 77: 664–71

Ralston DA, Gustafson DJ, Terpstra RH, Holt DH, Cheung FM, et al. 1993. The impact of managerial values on decision-making behavior: a comparison of the United States and Hong Kong. *Asia. Pac. J. Manage.* 10:21–37

Redding SG. 1990. *The Spirit of Chinese Capitalism.* Berlin: de Gruyter

Rodrigues A, Iwawaki S, 1986. Testing the validity of different models of interpersonal balance in the Japanese culture. *Psychologia* 29:123–31

Rosenthal DA, Feldman SS. 1992. The naure and stability of ethnic identity in Chinese youth: effects of length of residence in two cultural contexts. *J. Cross-Cult. Psychol.* 23:214–27

Rosenzweig MR. 1992. *International Psychological Science: Progress, Problems and Prospects,* Washington, DC: Am. Psychol. Assoc.

Rotter JB. 1966. Generalised expectancies for internal versus external control of reinforcement. *Psychol. Monogr.* 80: (Whole No. 609)

Russell DW. 1982. The Causal Dimension Scale: a measure of how individuals perceive causes. *J. Pers. Soc. Psychol.* 42: 1137–45

Russell JA. 1994. Is there universal recognition of emotion from facial expression? A review of the cross-cultural studies. *Psychol. Bull.* 115:102–41

Schermerhorn JR, Bond MH. 1991. Upward and downward influence tactics in managerial networks: a comparative study of Hong Kong Chinese and Americans. *Asia Pac. J. Manage.* 8:147–58

Schmidt SM, Yeh RS. 1992. The structure of leader influence: a cross-national comparison. *J. Cross-Cult. Psychol.* 23:251–64

Schwalb DW, Schwalb BJ, Harnisch DL, Maehr ML, Akabane K. 1992, Personal investment in Japan and the USA: a study of worker motivation. *Int. J. Intercitlt. Relat.* 16:107–24

Schwartz SH. 1992. The universal content and structure of values: theoretical advances and empirical tests in 20 countries. In *Advanced Experimental Social Psychology,* ed. MP Zanna, 25:1–65. New York: Academic

Schwartz SH. 1994. Beyond individualism/collectivism: new cultural dimensions of values. See Kim et al 1994, pp. 85–119

Segall MH, Dasen PR, Berry JW, Poortinga YH. 1990. *Human Behavior in Global Perspective: An Introduction to Cross-Cultural Psychology*. New York: Pergamon

Shavelson RJ, Bolus R. 1982. Self-concept: the interplay of theory and methods. *J. Educ. Psychol.* 74:3–17

Shaver PR, Wu S, Schwartz JC. 1991. Cross-cultural similarities and differences in emotion and its representation: a prototype approach, In *Review of Personality and Social Psychology*, ed. MS Clark, 13: 175–212. Beverley Hills. CA: Sage

Shenkar O, von Glinow MA. 1994, Paradoxes in organizational theory and research: using the case of China to illustrate national contingency. *Manage. Sci.* 40:56–71

Shenkar O, Zeira Y. 1992. Role conflict and role ambiguity of chief executive officers in international joint ventures. *J. Int. Bus. Stud.* 23:55–75

Shweder RA, Bourne EJ. 1982. Does the concept of the person vary cross-culturally? In *Cultural Conceptions of Mental Health and Therapy*, ed. AJ Marsella. GM White, pp. 97–137. Dordrecht: Reidel

Shweder RA, Sullivan MA. 1993. Cultural psychology: Who needs it? *Annu. Rev. Psychol.* 44:497–523

Singelis TM. 1994. The measurement of independent and interdependent self-construals. *Pers. Soc. Psychol. Bull.* 20:580–91

Singelis TM, Sharkey WF. 1995. Culture, self-construal and embarassability. *J. Cross-Cult. Psychol.* In press

Singelis TM, Triandis HC, Bhawuk DW, Gelfand M. 1995. Horizontal and vertical dimensions of individualism and collectivism: a theoretical and measurement refinement *Cross-Cult. Res.* 29:240–75

Smith PB, Bond MH. 1994. *Social Psychology Across Cultures: Analysis and Perspectives*. Boston: Allyn & Bacon

Smith PB, Dugan S, Trompenaars F. 1995a. National culture and managerial values: a dimensional analysis across 43 nations. *J. Cross-Cult. Psychol.* In press

Smith PB, Misumi J, Tayeb MH, Peterson MF, Bond MH. 1989. On the generality of leadership styles across cultures. *J. Occup. Psychol.* 62:97–110

Smith PB, Peterson MF. 1988. *Leadership, Organizations and Culture: An Event Management Model*. London: Sage

Smith PB, Peterson MF, Akande D, Callan V, Cho NG, et al. 1994a. Organizational event management in 14 countries: a comparison with Hofstede's dimensions. See Bouvy et al 1994, pp. 364–73

Smith PB, Peterson MF, Misumi J. 1994b. Event management and work team effectiveness in Japan, Britain and the USA. *J. Occup. Organ. Psychol.* 67:33–44

Smith PB, Peterson MF, Misumi J, Bond MH. 1992. A cross–cultural test of Japanese PM leadership theory. *Appl. Psychol.: Int. Rev.* 41:5–19

Smith PB, Trompenaars F, Dugan S. 1995b, The Rotter locus of control scale in 43 countries: a test of cultural relativity. *Int. J. Psychol.* 30:377–400

Soudjin KA, Hutschmaekers GTM, Van de Vijver FJR. 1990. Culture conceptualizations. In *The Investigation of Culture: Current Issues in Cultural Psychology*, ed. FJR van de Vijver, GTM Hutschmaekers, pp. 19–39. Tilburg, Holland: Tilburg Univ. Press

Taylor SE, Brown JD. 1988. Illusion and well-being: a social psychological perspective on mental health. *Psychol. Bull.* 103: 193–210

Ting-Toomey S, Yee-Jung KK. Shapiro RB, Garcia W. 1994. *Ethnic identity salience and conflict styles in four ethnic groups: African Americans, Asian Americans, European*

Americans, and Latino Americans. Presented at Annu. Meet. Speech Commun. Assoc. New Orleans

Touzard H, ed. 1992. *Int. Rev. Soc. Psychol.* 5(1): whole issue

Triandis HC. 1984. Toward a psychological theory of economic growth. *Int. J. Psychol.* 19:79–95

Triandis HC. 1990. Cross-cultural studies of individualism and collectivism. In *Nebraska Symposium Motivation, 1989*, ed. JJ Berman, 37:41–134. Lincoln: Univ. Nebr. Press

Triandis HC. 1993. Collectivism and individualism as cultural syndromes. *Cross-Cult. Res.* 27:155–80

Triandis HC. 1994. *Culture and Social Behavior.* New York: McGraw-Hill

Triandis HC. 1995. *Individualism and Collectivism.* Boulder, CO: Westview

Triandis HC, Dunnette M, Hough LM, eds. 1993a. *Handbook of Industrial and Organizational Psychology,* Vol. 4, *Cross-Cultural Studies.* Palo Alto, CA: Consulting Psychologists. 2nd ed.

Triandis HC, McCusker C, Betancourt H, Iwao S, Leung K, et al. 1993b. An emic-etic analysis of individualism-collectivism. *J. Cross-Cult. Psychol.* 24:366–83

Triandis HC, Lambert WW, eds. 1980. *Handbook of Cross-Cultural Psychology,* Vol. 1, *Perspectives.* Boston: Allyn & Bacon

Trompenaars F. 1993. *Riding the Waves of Culture.* London: Brealey

Trubisky P, Ting-Toomey S, Lin SL. 1991. The influence of individualism-collectivism and self-monitoring on conflict styles. *Int. J. Intercult. Relat.* 15:65–84

Tse DK, Francis J, Walls J. 1994. Cultural differences in conducting intra- and inter-cultural negotiations: a Sino-Canadian comparison. *J. Int. Bus. Stud.* 25:537–55

Tse DK, Lee KH, Vertinsky I, Wehrung DA. 1988. Does culture matter? A cross-cultural study of executives' choice, decisiveness and risk adjustment in international marketing. *J. Mark.* 52:81–95

Tyler TR, Bies RJ. 1990. Beyond formal procedures: the interpersonal context of procedural justice. In *Applied Social Psychology and Organizational Settings,* ed. JS Carroll, pp. 77–98, Hillsdale, NJ: Erlbaum

Tyler TR, Lind EA, Huo YJ. 1995. Culture and reactions to authority: influence of situational and dispositional factors. *J. Pers. Soc. Psychol.* In press

van de Vijver FJR, Leung K, 1996. Methods and data analytic procedures in cross-cultural research. See Berry et al 1996

van Muijen J, Koopman P. 1994. The influence of national culture on organizational culture: a comparative study between ten countries. *Eur. Work Organ. Psychol.* In press

Wang ZM, Heller FA. 1993. Patterns of power distribution and managerial decision-making in Chinese and British industrial organizations. *Int. J. Hum. Res. Manage.* 4:113–28

Watkins D, Cheng C. 1995. The Revised Causal Attribution Scale: a confirmatory factor analysis with Hong Kong subjects. *Br. J. Educ. Psychol.* 65:249–52

Watkins D, Dong Q. 1994. Assessing the self-esteem of Chinese school children. *Educ. Psychol.* 14:129–37

Watson WE, Kumar K. 1992. Differences in decision-making regarding risk-taking: a comparison of culturally diverse and culturally homogeneous task groups. *Int. J. Intercult. Relat.* 16:53–65

Watson WE, Kumar K, Michaelsen LK. 1993. Cultural diversity's impact on interaction process and performance: comparing homogeneous and diverse task groups. *Acad. Manage. J.* 36:590–602

Weinreich P. 1986. The operationalization of identity theory in racial and ethnic relations. In *Theories of Race and Ethnic Relations*, ed. J Rex, D Mason, pp. 299–324. Cambridge: Cambridge Univ. Press

Weinreich P. 1995. Operationalization of ethnic identity: illustrative case studies of orientations to the European Community. In *National Identities in Europe: Problems and Controversies,* ed. E Sonsa. Lisbon: Portuguese Comm. to EC/ISPA. In press

Weinreich P, Luk C, Bond MH. 1994. *Ethnic identity: identification with other cultures, self-esteem and identity confusion.* Int. Conf. Immigr., Lang. Acquis, Patterns Soc. Integr., Jerusalem

Williams JE. 1993. *Young adults' views of aging: a 19 nation study.* Presented at Inter-Am. Soc. Psychol. Congr., Santiago, Chile

Williams JE, Best D. 1990. *Sex and Psyche: Gender and Self Viewed Cross-Culturally.* Newbury Park, CA: Sage

Williams JE, Saiz JL, FormyDuval DL, Munick ML, Fogle EE, et al. 1995. Cross-cultural variation in the importance of psychological characteristics: a seven country study. *Int. J. Psychol.* In press

Wong GYY, Brnbaum-More M. 1994. Culture, context and structure: a test on Hong Kong banks. *Organ. Stud.* 15:99–123

Wu S, Shaver PR. 1992. *Conceptions of love in the United States and the People's Republic of China.* Presented at Int. Soc. Study Pers. Relat., 6th, Orono, ME

Xie JL, Jamal M. 1993. The Type A experiences: stress, job-related attitudes and non-work behavior: a study of managers in China. *Int. J. Manage.* 10:351–60

Yang KS, Ho DYF. 1988. The role of *yuan* in Chinese social life: a conceptual and empirical analysis. See Paranjpe et al 1988, pp. 163–81

Yates JF, Lee JW. 1995. Chinese decision making. See Bond 1995

Yu AB. 1995. Ultimate Chinese concern, self, and achievement motivation. See Bond 1995

Yu AB, Yang KS. 1994. The nature of achievement motivation in collectivist societies. See Kim et al 1994, pp. 239–50

Zebrowitz-McArthur L. 1988. Person perception in cross-cultural perspective. See Bond 1988, pp. 245–65

52

MEASURING ORGANIZATIONAL CULTURES

A qualitative and quantitative study across twenty cases

Geert Hofstede, Bram Neuijen, Denise Daval Ohayv and Geert Sanders

Source: *Administrative Science Quarterly* 35 (1990): 286–316.

Abstract

This paper presents the results of a study on organizational cultures in twenty units from ten different organizations in Denmark and the Netherlands. Data came from in-depth interviews of selected informants and a questionnaire survey of a stratified random sample of organizational members. Data on task, structure, and control characteristics of each unit were collected separately. Quantitative measures of the cultures of the twenty units, aggregated at the unit level, showed that a large part of the differences among these twenty units could be explained by six factors, related to established concepts from organizational sociology, that measured the organizational cultures on six independent dimensions. The organizational culture differences found resided mainly at the level of practices as perceived by members. Scores of the units on the six dimensions were partly explainable from organizational idiosyncrasies but were also significantly correlated with a variety of task, structural, and control-system characteristics of the units.

Introduction

The "organizational culture" construct

The term "organizational cultures" entered the U.S. academic literature, as far as we know, with an article in *Administrative Science Quarterly* by Pettigrew in 1979 ("On Studying Organizational Cultures") and is thus a relatively recent addition.

In the U.S. management literature, the same term, in the singular, had been casually used by Blake and Mouton (1964) to denote what others then called "climate." More customary became "corporate culture," a term that had already figured in an article by Silverzweig and Allen in 1976 but which gained popularity after a book carrying this title, by Deal and Kennedy, appeared in 1982 and especially after the success of its companion volume, from the same McKinsey-Harvard Business School team, Peters and Waterman's *In Search of Excellence*, which appeared in the same year. Since then, an extensive literature has developed on the topic, which has also spread to the European language areas accessible to us.

"Culture" has become a fad, among managers, among consultants, and among academics, with somewhat different concerns. Fads pass, and this one is no exception. Nevertheless, we believe it has left its traces on organization theory. Organizational/corporate culture has acquired a status similar to structure, strategy, and control. Weick (1985) has even argued that "culture" and "strategy" are partly overlapping constructs. There is no consensus about its definition, but most authors will probably agree on the following characteristics of the organizational/corporate culture construct: it is (1) holistic, (2) historically determined, (3) related to anthropological concepts, (4) socially constructed, (5) soft, and (6) difficult to change. All of these characteristics of organizations have been separately recognized in the literature in the previous decades; what was new about organizational culture was their integration into one construct.

The literature on organizational cultures consists of a remarkable collection of pep talks, war stories, and some insightful in-depth case studies. There is, we believe, a dearth of ordinary research as taught by standard behavioral research methodology textbooks. Such textbooks (e.g., Selltiz et al., 1965; Blalock and Blalock, 1971) tell the student to start with a qualitative orientation and to follow up with a quantitative verification. The research project described below has attempted to do just that. We were guided by three main research questions:

First, can organizational cultures be "measured" quantitatively, on the basis of answers of organizational members to written questions, or can they only be described qualitatively? In operational terms, the issue is whether membership in one organization rather than another explains a significant share of the variance in members' answers to questions dealing with culture-related matters. Our hypothesis was that it would.

Second, if organizational cultures can be measured in this way, which operationalizable and independent dimensions can be used to measure them, and how do these dimensions relate to what is known about organizations from existing theory and research? Our hypothesis was that the analysis would produce a discrete number of independent dimensions and that these dimensions should correspond to issues covered in the organizational literature, since it was unlikely that we would find aspects of organizations that nobody had discovered before.

Third, to what extent can measurable differences among the cultures of different organizations be attributed to unique features of the organization in question, such as its history or the personality of its founder? To what extent do they reflect other characteristics of the organization, like its structure and control systems, which in themselves may have been affected by culture? To what extent are they predetermined by given factors like nationality, industry, and task? Our hypothesis was that organizational cultures are partly predetermined by nationality, industry, and task, which should be visible in significant effects of such factors on culture dimension scores. Partly, we expected them to relate to organization structure and control systems. However, we expected that correlations between culture measures and such nonculture data would leave sufficient variance unexplained to allow a considerable amount of uniqueness to each organization.

Previous research on national cultures

Our research project into organizational cultures was modelled after an earlier project by the first author that covered differences among national cultures (Hofstede, 1980, 1983a, 1983b, 1983c, 1983d). That study used an existing data bank from a large multinational business corporation (IBM), covering matched populations of employees in national subsidiaries in 64 countries. The data consisted of answers to questionnaires about employee values and perceptions of the work situation that were collected in the context of two worldwide rounds of employee attitude surveys. Their use for studying differences in national cultures was an unintended, serendipitous by-product, for which the corporation opened its files of 116,000 survey questionnaires collected between 1967 and 1973. Twenty different language versions were used. Initially, from the 72 different national subsidiaries for which data were available, only the 40 largest were selected for the analysis (Hofstede, 1980). Subsequent follow-up research showed data from another 24 subsidiaries to be usable, 10 as separate countries and 14 grouped into three historical/geographical regions (Arab-speaking countries, West Africa, and East Africa), thus raising the total number of units in the analysis to 53. In the remaining eight countries the number of native respondents was insufficient to allow statistical use of their data (Hofstede, 1983a).

The questions in the IBM surveys had been composed from initial in-depth interviews with employees in ten countries and from suggestions by frequent travellers in the international headquarters' staffs who reported on value differences they had noticed among subsidiaries. The surveys had been managed by an international team of social scientists (both from inside and outside the corporation) who were participant observers or observing participants in the daily life of one or more of the subsidiaries. During the years devoted to the analysis of the data, the first author and his family lived and worked in four different countries. This background provided a qualitative context to the cross-national study. The possibilities for quantitative analysis of the precoded answer scores were excellent. National idiosyncrasies and nuances of questionnaire translation weigh heavily in a two-, three-, or four-country study, but with the unusually large number of 40 or 53 countries and regions, national patterns start to show a global structure, which the "noise" of the idiosyncrasies of individual countries cannot suppress. The structure revealed by the IBM data consisted of four largely independent dimensions of differences among national value systems. These were labelled "power distance" (large vs. small), "uncertainty avoidance" (strong vs. weak), "individualism" vs. "collectivism," and "masculinity" vs. "femininity." All 53 countries and regions could be scored on all four dimensions; the four together accounted for 49 percent of the variance in country mean scores on 32 values and perceptions questions.

Differences in values among matched populations of employees of national subsidiaries of a multinational should be a conservative estimate of differences among the national populations at large, as respondents are supposed to share the same worldwide corporate culture. Differences found among IBM subsidiary personnel, as revealed by their scores on each of the four dimensions mentioned above, do correlate significantly with a multitude of comparative national data from other sources: results of surveys of other narrow but matched samples, results of representative samples of total national populations, and country-level indicators, such as indices of income inequality, government budget composition, or medical statistics (Hofstede, 1980: 326–331). The four-dimensional model of national culture differences certainly does not represent the ultimate truth about the subject, but it has so far served as a useful framework for teaching both practitioners (such as future expatriates) and students and for guiding research design in the previously fuzzy field of national cultures (e.g., Bourgoin, 1984; Triandis, 1984; Triandis et al., 1986; Kreacic and Marsh, 1986; Gudykunst and Ting-Toomey, 1988). Recently, another study on student populations from 23 countries using a survey questionnaire designed by Chinese scholars has revealed a fifth meaningful dimension independent of the four others (Hofstede and Bond, 1988; Bond and Mai, 1989). This fifth dimension, "Confucian dynamism," opposing a long-term to a short-term orientation in life and work, has the merit of providing a cultural explanation for the remarkable economic success within the past 25 years of the East-Asian countries.

A study of organizational cultures

Paradoxically, the cross-national research in IBM did not reveal anything about IBM's corporate culture, except that it engaged in a survey project of this size: all units studied shared the same corporate culture, and there were no outside points of comparison. However, the cross-national study was a model of how a cross-organizational study could be undertaken. Instead of one corporation in many countries, we would study many different organizations in one and the same country. The plan for this project had been formulated as early as 1980, at the time of the foundation of the Institute for Research on Intercultural Cooperation (IRIC), under the umbrella of which the research was carried out. At that time, the "organizational culture" construct was just gaining popularity. The logistics of such a cross-organizational study, however, proved quite formidable. Whereas in the cross-national IBM study existing data were used, the institute itself now had to acquire access to the participants and raise the necessary funds. We were finally able to go ahead with the research in 1985 and 1986. In order to find a sufficient number of participating organizations we had to include two national environments rather than one: besides in IRIC's home country, the Netherlands, we also operated in Denmark. On the national culture dimensions from the cross-national study, these two countries scored fairly similarly, and they belong to the same Nordic-Dutch cluster.[1]

Method

Sample

We attempted to cover a wide range of different work organizations, to get a feel for the size of culture differences that can be found in practice, which would then enable us to assess the relative weight of similarities and differences. A crucial question is what represents "an organization" from a cultural point of view. One organization may include several culturally different departments, and these departments may consist of culturally different work groups. Determining what units are sufficiently homogeneous to be used for comparing cultures is both a theoretical and an empirical problem. We took the pragmatic approach, to accept as units of study both entire organizations and parts of organizations and to follow management's judgment as to whether a unit was culturally homogeneous. In a few cases, the research results later gave us reason to doubt a unit's cultural homogeneity, but it is unlikely that the results have been substantially affected by this. In the end, we got access to 20 units from 10 different organizations, five in Denmark, five in the Netherlands. These 20 units were from three broad kinds of organizations: (1) private companies manufacturing electronics, chemicals, or consumer goods (six total divisions or production units, three head office or marketing units, and two research and development units); (2) five units from private service companies (banking, transport, trade); and (3) four units from public institutions (telecommunications, police). Unit sizes varied from 60 to 2,500 persons. Twenty units was a small enough number to allow studying each unit in depth, qualitatively, as a separate case study. At the same time, it was large enough to permit statistical analysis of comparative quantitative data across all cases.

Design

The project consisted of three phases. In the first phase, we conducted in-depth interviews of two to three hours' duration each with nine informants per unit, for a total of 180 interviews. These interviews allowed us to get a qualitative feel for the gestalt of the unit's culture and to collect issues to be included in the questionnaire for the subsequent survey. Informants were chosen nonrandomly in a discussion with our contact person(s) in the unit. They included, in all cases, the unit top manager and his (never her) secretary, and then a selection of men and women in different jobs from all levels, sometimes a gatekeeper or doorman, an oldtimer, a newcomer, an employee representative (equivalent to a shop steward). A criterion in their selection was that they were assumed to be sufficiently reflective and communicative to be valuable discussion partners. The interview team consisted of 18 members (Danish or Dutch), most of them with a social science training but deliberately naive about the type of activity going on in the unit studied. Each unit's interviews were divided among two interviewers, one woman and one man, so that the gender of the interviewer would not affect the observations obtained. All interviewers received the same project training beforehand, and all used the same broad checklist of open-ended questions. Interviews were taped and reports were written in a prescribed sequence, using respondents' actual words.

In the second phase, we administered a standardized survey questionnaire consisting of 135 precoded questions to a random sample from the unit, consisting of about 25 managers, 25 college-level nonmanagers ("professionals") and 25 non-college-level nonmanagers ("others"). Altogether, 1,295 usable questionnaires were collected, or an average of 65 per unit. About 60 of the questions in the survey were taken from the earlier cross-national study and its later extensions; the remaining questions, with a few exceptions, were developed on the basis of the interviews and were directed at the issues that the interviewers found to differ substantially between units. These included, in particular, many perceptions of daily practices, which had been almost entirely missing in the cross-national studies. The results of the interviews and of the surveys were discussed with the management of the units and were sometimes fed back to larger groups of unit members, if management chose to do so.

In the third phase, we used questionnaires, followed by personal interviews, to collect data at the level of the unit as a whole on such factors as its total employee strength, budget composition, key historical facts, or the demographics of its key managers. The first author collected all unit-level data personally, since finding out what comparable data *could* meaningfully be collected from such a varied set of organizations was a heuristic process difficult to share across researchers. The informants for the unit-level data were the top manager, the chief personnel officer, and the chief budget officer.

Interviews

The checklist used for the in-depth interviews was based on a survey of the literature on the ways in which organization cultures are supposed to manifest themselves and on our own ideas. We classified manifestations of culture into four categories: symbols, heroes, rituals, and values, as shown in Figure 1.

Symbols are words, gestures, pictures, or objects that carry a particular meaning within a culture. Heroes are persons, alive or dead, real or imaginary, who possess characteristics highly prized in the culture and who thus serve as models for behavior (Wilkins, 1984). Rituals are collective activities that are technically superfluous but are socially essential within a culture—they are therefore carried

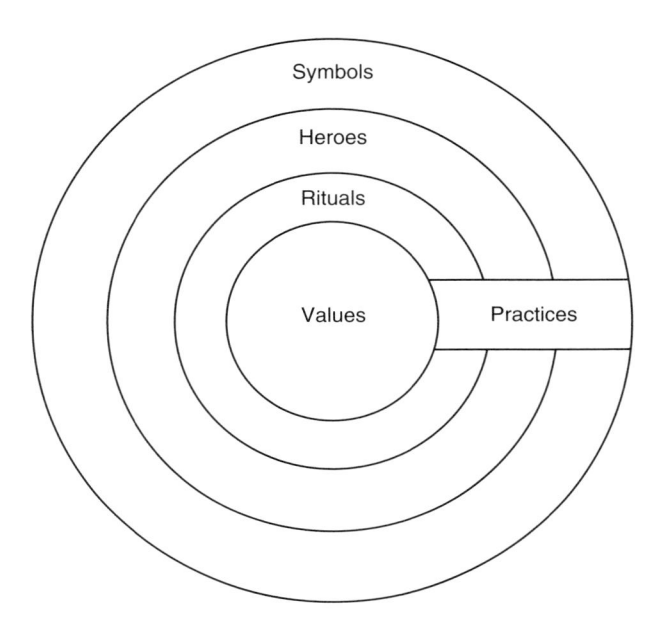

Figure 1 Manifestations of culture: From shallow to deep.

out for their own sake. In Figure 1, we have drawn these as the successive skins of an onion—from shallow, superficial symbols to deeper rituals. Symbols, heroes, and rituals can be subsumed under the term "practices," because they are visible to an observer although their cultural meaning lies in the way they are perceived by insiders. The core of culture, according to Figure 1, is formed by values, in the sense of broad, nonspecific feelings of good and evil, beautiful and ugly, normal and abnormal, rational and irrational—feelings that are often unconscious and rarely discussable, that cannot be observed as such but are manifested in alternatives of behavior. We selected these four terms from the terminology offered in the literature (e.g., Deal and Kennedy, 1982), because we believe them to be (1) mutually exclusive and (2) reasonably comprehensive, thus covering the field rather neatly.

The interview checklist contained questions like the following: "What are special terms here that only insiders understand?" (to identify organizational symbols); "What kind of people are most likely to make a fast career here?"; "Whom do you consider as particularly meaningful persons for this organization?" (to identify organizational heroes); "In what periodic meetings do you participate?"; "How do people behave during these meetings?"; "Which events are celebrated in this organization?" (to identify organizational rituals); and "What things do people very much like to see happening here?"; "What is the biggest mistake one can make?"; "Which work problems can keep you awake at night?" (to identify organizational values). Interviewers were free to probe for more and other information if they felt it was there.

The interviews were used to create a qualitative, empathic description of the culture of each of the twenty cases. The following are extracts from two of the twenty unit gestalt descriptions made on the basis of the interviews:

The TKB case

TKB is a 60-year-old production unit in the chemical industry. Many of its employees are oldtimers. Stories about the past abound. Workers tell about how heavy the jobs used to be, when loading and unloading was done by hand. They tell about heat and physical risk. TKB used to be seen as a rich employer. For several decades, the demand for its products exceeded the supply. Products were not sold, but distributed. Customers had to be nice and polite in order to be served. The money was made very easily. TKB's management style used to be paternalistic. The old general manager made his daily morning walk through the plant, shaking hands with everyone he met. This, people say, is the root of a tradition that still exists of shaking hands with one's colleagues in the morning. Rich and paternalistic, TKB has long been considered a benefactor, both to its employees in need and to the local community. Some of this has survived. Employees still feel TKB to be a desirable employer, with good pay, benefits, and job security. A job with TKB is still seen as a job for life. TKB is a company one would like one's children to join. Outside, TKB is a regular sponsor of local sports and humanitarian associations: "No appeal to TKB has ever been made in vain."

The working atmosphere is good-natured, with a lot of freedom left to employees. The plant has been pictured as a club, a village, a family. Twenty-fifth and fortieth anniversaries are given lots of attention; the plant's Christmas parties are famous. These celebrations are rituals with a long history, which people still value a lot. In TKB's culture, or, as people express it, in "the TKB way," unwritten rules for social behavior are very important. One doesn't live in order to work, one works in order to live. What one does counts less than how one does it. One has to fit into the informal network, and this holds for all hierarchical levels. "Fitting" means avoiding conflicts and direct confrontations, covering other people's mistakes, loyalty, friendliness, modesty, and good-natured cooperation. Nobody should be too conspicuous, in a positive or a negative sense. TKB-ers grumble, but never directly about other TKB-ers. Also, grumbling is reserved for one's own circle and is never done in front of superiors or outsiders. This concern for harmony and group solidarity fits well into the regional culture of the geographical area in which TKB is located. Newcomers are quickly accepted, as long as they adapt. The quality of their work counts less than their social adaptation, Whoever disrupts the harmony is rejected, however good a worker he or she is. Disturbed relationships may take years to heal: "We prefer to let a work problem continue for another month, even if it costs a lot of money, above resolving it in an unfriendly manner." Company rules are never absolute. The most important rule, one interviewee said, is that rules are flexible. One may break a rule if one does it gently. It is not the rule-breaker who is at risk, but the one who makes an issue of it.

Leadership in TKB, in order to be effective, should be in harmony with the social behavior patterns. Managers should be accessible, fair, and good listeners. The present general manager is such a leader. He doesn't give himself airs. He has an easy contact with people of all levels and is felt to be "one of us." Careers in TKB are made primarily on the basis of social skills. One should not behave too conspicuously; one needn't be brilliant, but one does need good contacts; one should know one's way in the informal network, being invited rather than volunteering. One should belong to the tennis club. All in all, one should respect what someone called "the strict rules for being a nice person."

This romantic picture, however, has recently been disturbed by outside influences. First, market conditions have changed, and TKB finds itself in an unfamiliar competitive situation with other European suppliers. Costs had to be cut and manpower reduced. In the TKB tradition, this problem was resolved, without collective layoffs, through early retirement. However, the oldtimers who had to leave prematurely were shocked that the company didn't need them anymore. Second, TKB has been severely attacked by environmentalists because of its pollution, a criticism that has received growing support in political circles. It is not impossible that the licenses necessary for TKB's operation will one day be withdrawn. TKB's management tries to counter this problem with an active lobby with the authorities, with a press campaign, and through organizing public visits to the company, but its success is by no means certain. Inside TKB, this threat is belittled. People are unable to imagine that one day there may be no more TKB. "Our management has always found a solution. There will be a solution now." In the meantime, attempts are made to increase TKB's competitiveness through quality improvement and product diversification. These also imply the introduction of new people from the outside. These new trends, however, clash with TKB's traditional culture.

The DLM case

DLM is a European airline company that in the early 1980s went through a spectacular turnaround. Under the leadership of a new president, the company switched from a product-and-technology to a market-and-service orientation. Before, planning and sales had been based on realizing a maximum number of flight hours with the most modern equipment available. Pilots, technicians, and disciplinarian managers were the company's heroes. Deteriorating results forced the reorganization. The president recognized that in the highly competitive air transport market, success depended on catering to the needs of current and potential customers. These needs should be best known by the employees with face-to-face customer contact. In the old situation, these people had never been asked for their opinions: they were a disciplined set of uniformed soldiers, trained to follow the rules. Now, they were considered to be on "the firing line," and the organization was restructured to support them rather than to order them around. Superiors became advisors; those on the firing line received a lot of discretion in dealing with customer problems on the spot, while only checking with superiors after the fact—which involves an acceptance of employees' judgment, with all risks that entails.

One of the units participating in the study is DLM's passenger terminal at its main station. The interviews were conducted three years after the turnaround. The employees and managers are uniformed, disciplined, formal, and punctual. They seem to be the kind of people who like to work in a disciplined structure. People work shift hours, and periods of tremendous work pressure alternate with periods of relative inactivity. They show considerable acceptance of their new role. Talking about the company's history, they tend not to go back to before the reorganization; only some managers do. They are proud of the company: their identity is to a large extent derived from it, and social relationships outside the work situation are frequently with other DLM-ers. The president is often mentioned as a company hero. In spite of the discipline, relationships between colleagues tend to be good-natured, and there is a lot of mutual help. A colleague who meets with a crisis in his or her private life is supported by others and by the company. Managers of various levels are visible and accessible, although more managers have trouble accepting the new role than nonmanagers. New employees enter via a formal introduction and training program, with simulated encounters with problem clients. This serves also as a screening device, to determine whether the newcomer has the values and the skills necessary for this profession. Those who pass feel quickly at home in the department. The employees demonstrate a problem-solving attitude toward clients: they show considerable excitement about original ways to resolve customers' problems, in which some rules can be twisted to achieve the desired result. Promotion is from the ranks and is felt to be on the basis of competence and collegiality.

It is not unlikely that this department, in particular, benefitted from a certain "Hawthorne effect" because of the key role it had played in a successful turnaround. At the time of the interviews, the euphoria of the successful turnaround was probably at its highest tide. Observers from inside the company commented that people's values had not really changed but that the turnaround had transformed a discipline of obedience toward superiors into a discipline of service toward customers.

Survey questionnaire and data analysis

The questionnaire was aimed at collecting information on the same four types of manifestations of culture as covered in the interview checklist: symbols, heroes, rituals, and values. The first three are subsumed under the common label "practices" (Figure 1). Values items describe what the respondent feels "should be," practices items what she or he feels "is."

The distinction between the two is present not only in the conception of the researchers but also in the minds of the respondents. In a factor analysis of all

135 survey items for all 1,295 respondents, values items and practices items loaded consistently on different factors, with very little overlap. The questionnaire contained the following items:

Values

Twenty-two questions assessed *work goals:* the characteristics of an ideal job, like "have an opportunity for high earnings" or "have security of employment," were each rated on a 5-point scale of importance. These were taken from the earlier cross-national research project and from later extensions of it. The interviews revealed no additional goals to add to the list.

Twenty-eight questions assessed *general beliefs*, like "competition between employees usually does more harm than good," each rated on a 5-point scale from "strongly agree" to "strongly disagree." Twenty-five of these stemmed from earlier cross-national research, mostly from the IBM studies and from Laurent (1983). Three were added based on the interviews.

Both work goals and general beliefs deal with values, but work goals represent "values as the desired" (what people claim to want for themselves) while general beliefs represent "values as the desirable" (what people include in their world view) (Hofstede, 1980: 20). Although items from the two categories tend to intercorrelate, answers are not necessarily logically consistent from the first category to the second (Hofstede, 1980: 21), and neither of the two is a perfect predictor of actual value-driven behavior in a choice situation. However, differences in verbal behavior (in questionnaire answers) between cultures do correlate with measures of collective actual behavior, at least in the national case (Hofstede, 1980: 328 ff).

Seven other questions were included, in a variety of formats, on other items statistically correlated with the previous values items, including questions on desired and actually perceived decision-making styles in one's boss. Five of these occupied a key role in the earlier cross-national research; the other two were added on the basis of the interviews.

Practices

Fifty-four questions assessed perceived practices in one's work situation. The first fifteen of these were inspired by Reynolds (1986), who did a thorough scan of the anecdotal U.S. literature on corporate cultures for suggested dimensions of differences. To Reynolds' questions, we added another 39 based on the interviews. We then cast all 54 questions into a bipolar format under the general heading "where I work..." and used 5-point scales on which, for example, 1 = "meeting times are kept very punctually" and 5 = "meeting times are only kept approximately." These 54 questions mostly cover symbols and rituals.

Seven questions asked about the "behavior of a typical member of the organization," using a 5-point "semantic differential" scale on which, for example, 1 = "slow" and 5 = "fast."

Thirteen questions asked about reasons for promotion and dismissal, rated on 5-point scales of importance or frequency. Both the typical-member and the promotion-and-dismissal questions cover the category of "heroes" and were inspired by the interviews.

Four demographic questions asked about the respondent's sex, age group, seniority with the employer, and education level. Finally, there was an open question, asking the respondent for any additions or remarks.

Results

Effects of organizational membership

For all 135 survey questions, without exception, unit mean scores differed significantly across the 20 organizational units. However, the 57 questions dealing with values tended to produce smaller differences between units than the 74 questions dealing with perceived practices. The range of mean scores for the group of values questions was from .32 to 2.09 (mean .87); the range for the group of perceived-practices questions was from .68 to 3.22 (mean 1.43). Because most questions were scored on 5-point scales, the mean scores from two units could maximally differ 4.0 points. A difference-of-means test showed that in view of the size of the samples and the standard deviations of the individual scores within these samples, a difference of means over .29 points was sufficient for significance at the .01-level in the most unfavorable case; in all other cases the limit was lower. Even the very lowest mean score range found, .32 for one of the values questions, still indicates a significant difference from the highest to the lowest scoring unit on this question. Most ranges were far over the significance limit (the .001-limit is at .41; all but one range are over this level).

The earlier cross-national study (Hofstede, 1980: 72) included analyses of variance (ANOVAs) for ten values questions across ten countries.[2] The same ten questions were also subjected to ANOVAs across the twenty organizational units in this study. Eighteen practices questions that we had identified as being key questions for determining the practices dimensions were subjected to similar ANOVAs.

The F-values shown in Table 1 are a measure of the variance explained by the criterion (country or organization). Again, all but one are significant at the .001-level. For the questions on values, country differences explain more variance than organization differences for any single question studied; for organizations, questions on practices have almost twice as much variance explained as questions on values.

Our first hypothesis was thus supported. Membership in an organization does explain a significant share of the variance in the answers by members for all 131 culture questions used in the survey. However, we found an unpredicted difference between questions dealing with values and questions dealing with perceived practices: the latter produced a much wider range of answers across organizations than

Table 1 F-values for analyses of variance for survey questions

	F-values for ANOVAs			
	Min.	Max.	Median	$p \leq .001$
10 questions on values across 10 countries*	3.2	46.7	8.0	3.1
10 questions on values across 20 organizations	1.6	6.4	4.0	2.5
18 questions on practices across 20 organizations	4.3	12.8	7.1	2.5

*From Hofstede, 1980:72.

the former. In the earlier research on national culture differences, the questions selected from the data bank because they discriminated among countries dealt almost exclusively with values. Where the same questions about values appeared in both studies, across countries and across organizations, the ANOVAs across countries explained a much larger share of the variance than the ANOVAs across organizations, although even across organizations the variances in answers on questions about values stayed above the significance level.

A possible explanation of the differences in explained variance between values and practices could be the process by which the questions were chosen: those about values were chosen for their potential to discriminate among countries, and those about practices for their supposed ability to discriminate among organizations. Our results could just be artifacts of this selection process. However, in selecting, we never deliberately associated "values" with "countries" only, or "practices" with "organizations." We only discovered this association after the fact. We did add five new questions about values on the basis of interviews in the organizations, but these discriminated only marginally better among organizations than those taken from the cross-national questionnaire, with mean scores ranging across the 20 units from .81 to 1.09, with a mean of .97. So we believe the "artifact" explanation does not hold.

Other criteria included in all the ANOVAs reported in Table 1 were occupation level, sex, and age. Their effects were not systematically different between the cross-national and the cross-organizational study, nor between values and practices questions in the cross-organizational study.

Dimensions of culture

The second research question, on the dimensions on which the cultures of the twenty organizational units could be measured, can be answered by multivariate analysis, reducing the data from the 131 survey items so as to explain the maximum share of their variance by the smallest possible number of meaningful factors.

As organizational cultures are supposed features of organizational units, not of individuals, the multivariate analysis here was not to be performed on the answers to the questions by individual respondents but on their mean scores for each of the twenty organizational units, so as to move from the individual level to the social system.

Multivariate analysis is based on correlations. If one wants to determine the correlation between two variables measured at the level of individual respondents, who are also members of particular organizational units, one has three choices: (1) an overall correlation across all individuals regardless of their organizational membership; (2) a series of within-unit correlations, one for each unit, across those individuals belonging to the unit, or (3) a between-unit correlation, based on the mean scores of the two variables for each unit. The three choices normally produce quite different correlation coefficients. First, the within-unit correlations may be significantly different from one unit to another and unlike the overall correlation. Second, whether or not the within-unit correlations are similar or different, the between-unit correlations are a different measure altogether. The latter are called "ecological correlations." It is easy to see why they differ from within-unit correlations if we consider two extreme cases. One is that for one of the two variables all units produce the same mean score. In this case, we find only within-unit correlations; the between-unit correlation is zero. The other extreme is that one of the variables is a constant for all members of a unit but that the value of this constant differs from one unit to the other. In this case, the within-unit correlations are all zero, but the between-unit correlation is not. Usually reality is somewhere between these extremes, so both types of correlations will be different from zero. However, they are not of equal magnitude; they may even have opposite signs. The mathematical relationship between individual and ecological correlations has been described by Langbein and Lichtman (1978).

There is a fairly extensive literature on the relative merits of analyzing correlations (or other covariance measures) at the individual versus the ecological level. The classic article is from Robinson (1950: 352) and deals with the "ecological fallacy": interpreting ecological correlations (in Robinson's example, between skin color and literacy in the U.S.A.) as if they applied to individuals. Various sociologists, political scientists, and cross-cultural psychologists have since shown that ecological correlations are not necessarily a source of fallacies but that they represent the proper focus for analysis when we are dealing with social systems (Menzel, 1950; Blau, 1960; Tannenbaum and Bachman, 1964; Scheuch, 1966; Przeworski and Teune, 1970: ch. 3; Leung and Bond, 1989). Meltzer (1963) produced a striking example: using data from a survey of 539 U.S. volunteers divided into 79 groups, he showed that on issues in which group processes played a role, individuals' attitudes could be better predicted from the group's mean scores on related questions than from the individuals' own scores on these questions.

Because organizational culture is a collective characteristic, the between-unit level is the correct level of analysis. The answers on each question by 1,295 individual respondents were aggregated into mean scores for 20 organizational units.[3] Each mean score was derived from a stratified sample of approximately equal shares of managers, professionals, and others.

Our purpose was to detect the structure in a 131 (variables, excluding the demographics) × 20 (cases) ecological matrix. We computed a 131 × 131 product-moment correlation matrix, correlating the 20 mean scores for each possible pair of questions. This showed that (1) values correlated with other values but rarely with practices (as we had already found in an earlier factor analysis of individual scores); (2) perceived practices and typical-member scores correlated among each other, and (3) reasons for promotion and dismissal correlated among each other but rarely with other items. We therefore decided to divide the questions, for analytic purposes, into three categories—57 values questions, 61 perceived practices and typical-member scores, and 13 reasons for promotion and dismissal—and to conduct separate factor analyses for these three categories.

Ecological factor analyses are of necessity characterized by flat matrices, that is, few cases in comparison to the number of variables, often fewer cases than variables. The textbooks on factor analysis generally require the number of cases to be much larger than the number of variables, although they remain vague on the allowable limit: "Unfortunately, nobody has yet worked out what a safe ratio of the number of subjects to variables is" (Gorsuch, 1983: 332). The reason for wanting a large number of subjects is that, otherwise, factors become unstable and unduly dependent on the whims of individual respondents. However, this constraint does not apply to factor analyses of ecological data, in which each case is basted on the mean of a large number of individual scores; such means are extremely stable. The stability of the factor structure for ecological matrices does not depend on the number of aggregate cases but on the number of independent individuals who contributed to each case. In our situation, it is based not on 20 (units) but on 1,295 (respondents), which is sufficient: both in the cross-national and in the cross-organizational study, factor scores derived through such analyses show many significant and theoretically meaningful correlations with outside data. However, if these factors were unstable, their factor scores would offer no more than random correlations with other phenomena. For the cross-national study, these outside validation data have been summarized in Hofstede (1980: 326–331); the validation data for the cross-organizational factors are shown in Table 4, below.

As ecological correlations tend to be stronger than individual correlations, we can expect to find high percentages of variance explained. To avoid paying attention to trivialities in factor analyzing ecological data it is therefore wise to keep the number of factors small, much smaller than the number of cases and smaller than what is technically possible based on the "eigenvalues" larger than 1.0. Also, one should only consider variables with high loadings on a factor, say over .50 or .60.

Value differences

For further treatment, the 22 questions on work goals had to be standardized. Items scored on "importance" tend to be subject to response-set bias (different categories of respondents choosing different parts of the 5-point scale across all items, regardless of content). Response-set bias in a factor analysis leads to all questions loading on one trivial response-set factor. Also, by definition, "importance" is a relative concept: something is more or less important than something else. The response-set bias can be eliminated by computing for each unit the grand mean across all 22 work-goal items and replacing the means per item by their distance from this grand mean, divided by the standard deviation of the 22 item means around this grand mean. For the other questions, which all used scales with a natural zero point (like agree-disagree), response-set bias does not normally play an important role, and the unit means can be used as they are.

For the 57 questions that we classified as dealing with values (22 standardized work goals, 28 general beliefs, and 7 other questions), an ecological principal component factor analysis was performed with orthogonal varimax rotation. A screen test indicated that we should limit the number of factors to three, which together explained 62 percent of the variance. We chose the following labels for these factors: V1 = need for security, V2 = work centrality, and V3 = need for authority. The results of the factor analysis are shown in Table 2.

V1 and V3 resemble two dimensions from the cross-national study: uncertainty avoidance and power distance, respectively. We may be dealing with basically the same value complexes, but only some questions with high loadings are the same in the cross-organizational and in the cross-national study. Uncertainty avoidance in the cross-national study deals with the extent to which a social system rejects unstructured and ambiguous situations. Power distance deals with the acceptance of inequality among ranks in the system. For the cross-organizational data in Table 2, uncertainty avoidance and power distance items from the cross-national study seem to have got somewhat mixed. V2, work centrality, does not appear among the cross-national dimensions: it expresses to what extent for most people in the system, work takes a central place in their total life pattern. It resembles the concepts of "job involvement" (Lodahl, 1964; Lodahl and Kejner, 1965) and "central life interest" (Dubin, Champoux, and Porter, 1975; Dubin and Champoux, 1977), but these were considered properties of individuals, not of the social system.

All three factors are strongly associated with the nationality of the unit: Danish or Dutch. In the cross-national study, the Danish and Dutch IBM subsidiaries, on scales from 0 to 100, differ 30 points in uncertainty avoidance (the Netherlands is more uncertainty avoiding), 20 points in power distance (Denmark shows smaller power distances), six points in individualism (both are quite individualist), and two points in masculinity (both are quite feminine). The relatively largest difference, therefore, is on the dimension of uncertainty avoidance, and this repeats itself as a difference on need for security in the cross-organizational study. However, in spite of the Danes' lower score on power distance in the cross-national study, the Danish units in the cross-organizational study scored higher than the Dutch on need for authority. Of course, the organizations in the two countries were not matched, so that the difference found may be an accidental effect of the particular sample of Danish and Dutch units studied. On work centrality, the Danish units all scored high, while the Dutch varied. All in all, having gone out to study organizational

Table 2 Results of factor analysis of unit mean scores on 57 values items across 20 units*

Factor V1: Need for Security
.92 Man dislikes work
.91 Variety and adventure in work unimportant
.89 Fringe benefits important
.87 Main reason for hierarchical structure is knowing who has authority
.87 When a man's career demands it, family should make sacrifices
.86 Having little tension and stress at work important
.83 Would not continue working if didn't need the money
.83 The successful in life should help the unsuccessful
.83 Pursuing own interest is not best contribution to society
.76 Working in well-defined job situation important
.75 Serving your country unimportant
.75 When people have failed in life it's not their fault
.74 Opportunity for advancement unimportant
.74 Opportunities for training unimportant
.73 Job you like is not more important than career
.69 Being consulted by boss unimportant
.66 Living in a desirable area unimportant
.63 Employees afraid to disagree with superiors
.63 Most people cannot be trusted
.63 Desirable that management authority can be questioned (second loading)

Factor V2: Work Centrality
.84 Work more important than leisure time
.78 Competition between employees not harmful
.65 Physical working conditions unimportant
.65 Opportunities for helping others unimportant
.64 No authority crisis in organizations
.63 Does not prefer a consultative manager
.62 Challenging tasks important
.62 Prestigious company or organization important
.61 Decisions by individuals better than group decisions
.60 Working relationship with boss important

Factor V3: Need for Authority
.81 Most organizations better off if conflicts eliminated forever
.70 Own manager autocratic or paternalistic
.70 Undesirable that management authority can be questioned
.65 Parents should stimulate children to be best in class
.64 Employee who quietly does duty is asset to organization
.62 Parents should not be satisfied when children become independent
.61 Staying with one employer is best way for making career
.61 Conflicts with opponents best resolved by compromise

*Loadings over .60 are shown; work-goal item scores were first standardized across 22 items; items with negative loadings have been reworded negatively. The three factors together explain 62% of the variance.

value differences and having done this in two countries for reasons of convenience, we seem to have mainly caught national value differences.

In an attempt to focus on the organizational differences, we reran the factor analysis after shifting the scores of the Dutch units so that, on average, they equalled the Danish. Thus we artificially eliminated the country effects. We again found three factors, which could be labelled (1) work orientation (intrinsic vs. extrinsic); (2) identification (with company vs. with noncompany interests); and (3) ambition (concern with money and career vs. family and cooperation, somewhat resembling the masculinity-femininity dimension in the cross-national study). The first factor was strongly related to the unit population's mean education level (the higher educated had a more intrinsic work orientation) and the second to their age, seniority, and hierarchical level. Thus, even if we eliminate the nationality effect, value differences between organizational units seem primarily dependent on demographics like age and education and only secondarily on membership in the organization as such. This is an important conclusion, to which we return in the Discussion section.

Practice differences

For fifty-four practice questions in the "where I work ..." format and seven "typical member" questions, another ecological principal component factor analysis was performed with orthogonal varimax rotation. A screen test showed that in this case the optimal number of factors was six, together explaining 73 percent of the variance. The labels we chose for these dimensions, partly based on their interpretation by members from the participating units during the feedback discussions, are as follows: P1 = process-oriented vs. results-oriented; P2 = employee-oriented vs. job-oriented; P3 = parochial vs. professional; P4 = open system vs. closed system; P5 = loose vs. tight control; and P6 = normative vs. pragmatic.

We computed scores for each unit on each of these dimensions, based on three "where I work ..." questions with high loadings (over .60) on the factor. We chose items that together represent the essence of the dimension, as we interpret it, and were suitable for conveying this essence to the members of the units in the feedback sessions. In Table 3, which presents the results, these key items are shown in boldface type. In an ecological factor analysis of only these 6 × 3 = 18 questions for the 20 units, they accounted for 86 percent of the variance in mean scores between units.

Dimension P1 opposes a concern with means (process-oriented) to a concern with goals (results-oriented). On a scale from 0 to 100, in which 0 represents the most process-oriented and 100 the most results-oriented unit among the 20, TKB scored 2 (very process-oriented, little concern for results), while DLM's passenger terminal scored 100—it is the most results-oriented unit we found. This dimension has often been identified in organization sociology. One of the best examples is Burns and Stalker's distinction between mechanistic and organic management systems. According to Burns and Stalker (1961: 120) mechanistic systems are

Table 3 Results of factor analysis of unit mean scores on 61 practices items across 20 units*

Factor P1: Process-Oriented vs. Results-Oriented
  .88 Employees are told when good job is done
  .88 Typical member fast
  .86 **Comfortable in unfamiliar situations**
  .85 **Each day brings new challenges**
  .78 Typical member initiating
  .75 Informal style of dealing with each other
  .73 Typical member warm
  .70 Try to be pioneers
  .70 Typical member direct
  .69 **People put in maximal effort**
  .67 Mistakes are tolerated
  .67 Typical member optimistic
  .63 Open to outsiders and newcomers (second loading)
  .60 Managers help good people to advance (second loading)

Factor P2: Employee-Oriented vs. Job-Oriented
  .84 **Important decisions made by individuals**
  .76 **Organization only interested in work people do**
  .69 Decisions centralized at top
  .68 Managers keep good people for own department
  .65 Changes imposed by management decree
  .64 Newcomers left to find own way
  .64 Management dislikes union members
  .62 No special ties with local community
  .60 **Little concern for personal problems of employees**

Factor P3: Parochial vs. Professional
  .87 **People's private life is their own business**
  .79 **Job competence is only criterion in hiring people**
  .73 **Think three years ahead or more**
  .63 Strongly aware of competition
  .62 Cooperation and trust between departments normal

Factor P4: Open System vs. Closed System
  .67 **Only very special people fit in organization**
  .67 Our department worst of organization
  .66 Management stingy with small things
  .64 Little attention to physical work environment
  .63 **Organization and people closed and secretive**
  .61 **New employees need more than a year to feel at home**

Factor P5: Loose Control vs. Tight Control
  .73 **Everybody cost-conscious**
  .73 **Meeting times kept punctually**
  .62 Typical member well-groomed
  .61 **Always speak seriously of organization and job**

Factor P6: Normative vs. Pragmatic
  .84 **Pragmatic, not dogmatic in matters of ethics**
  .68 Organization contributes little to society
  .63 **Major emphasis on meeting customer needs**
  .63 **Results more important than procedures**
  .63 Never talk about the history of the organization

*Loadings over .60 are shown; items with negative loadings have been reworded negatively; items in boldface have been chosen as key indicators for the dimension. The six factors together explain 73% of the variance.

among other things characterized by "the abstract nature of each individual task, which is pursued with techniques and purposes more or less distinct from those of the concern as a whole; i.e., the functionaries tend to pursue the technical improvement of means, rather than the accomplishment of the ends of the concern." Organic systems (Burns and Stalker, 1961: 121) are characterized by "the 'realistic' nature of the individual task, which is seen as set by the total situation of the concern." Results orientation also corresponds with Peters and Waterman's (1982) maxim number 1: "a bias for action."[4]

We found confirmation of Peters and Waterman's claim that "strong" cultures are more results-oriented. We have interpreted "strong" as "homogeneous" and operationalized it as the reverse of the mean standard deviation, across the individuals within a unit, of scores on the 18 key practices questions (three per dimension). A low standard deviation means that different respondents from the same unit perceived their environment in much the same way, regardless of the content of the perceptions. Actual mean standard deviations varied from .87 to 1.08, and the Spearman rank-order correlation between these mean standard deviations, as a measure of culture strength, and the unit's scores on "results orientation" was −.71, significant at the .001-level.

Dimension P2 opposes a concern for people (employee-oriented) to a concern for getting the job done (job-oriented). On a scale from 0 to 100, TKB scored 100 and DLM's passenger terminal 95—both of them extremely employee-oriented. This dimension corresponds to the two axes of Blake and Mouton's Managerial Grid (1964). The fact that Blake and Mouton claimed employee orientation and job orientation to be two independent dimensions seems to conflict with our placing them at opposite poles of a single dimension. However, Blake and Mouton's grid applies to individuals, while our analysis was made at the level of social systems. It simply means that the units in our analysis tend to vary along the line 9,1–1,9 in Blake and Mouton's grid.

Dimension P3 opposes units whose employees derive their identity largely from the organization, which we called "parochial," to units in which people identify with their type of job, which we called "professional." Sociology has long known this distinction as "local" versus "cosmopolitan," the contrast between an internal and an external frame of reference (Merton, 1968: 447 ff.). The parochial type of culture is often associated with Japanese companies. DLM passenger terminal employees scored as quite parochial (24); TKB employees scored about halfway (48).

Dimension P4 opposes open systems to closed systems. On this dimension, TKB again scored halfway (51) and DLM as extremely open (9). This dimension describes the communication climate (Poole, 1985), a focus of attention for both human resources and public relations experts.

Dimension P5 refers to the amount of internal structuring in the organization. It appears from the data that a tight formal control system is associated, at least statistically, with strict unwritten codes in terms of dress and dignified behavior. On a scale of 0 = loose and 100 = tight, DLM scored as extremely tight (96), and

TKB scored, once more, halfway (52); but halfway is loose for a production unit, as comparison with other production units shows. The tight-versus-loose distinction is well known from the literature on management control (e.g., Hofstede, 1967: 144 ff.).

Dimension P6 deals with the popular notion of "customer orientation." Pragmatic units are market-driven; normative units perceive their task toward the outside world as the implementation of inviolable rules. The DLM passenger terminal was the top scoring unit on the "pragmatic" side (100), which shows that the president's message came across. TKB scored 68, also on the pragmatic side; in the past, according to the interviews, it must have been more normative toward its customers, but the market changes already had their effect. This dimension receives enormous attention in the present-day business literature. The pragmatic pole corresponds with Peters and Waterman's maxim number 2: "staying close to the customer." It is interesting that our empirical data have identified "results orientation" and "customer orientation" as two separate and independent dimensions. We found examples of units being results-oriented but not customer-oriented (one of the two police corps). Examples of the opposite combination can be found in service businesses: trying to serve the customer does not automatically imply a results orientation.

Promotion and dismissal and relationships among values and practices

The questionnaire contained seven questions on reasons for promotion, and six on assumed reasons for dismissal. The reasons for promotion were, in order of average endorsement across all 20 units, as follows: personality, performance, commitment to the organization, creativity, collegiality, diplomas, and seniority. The reasons for dismissal were (in order of endorsement): stealing the equivalent of U.S. $500, same but $50, alcohol during working hours, poor performance, conflict with the boss, and sex with a subordinate. These items, as mentioned above, did not correlate strongly with any other parts of the questionnaire, but only among themselves. In a factor analysis of the 13 item means for the 20 units, there was a strong first factor (H1, H for heroes) opposing promotion for present merits (commitment, creativity, performance) to promotion for past merits (diplomas and seniority). A weaker second factor (H2) opposed dismissal for job-related misbehavior (stealing) to dismissal for off-the-job morals (sex).

In order to test the relationships between the three values factors (V1 through V3), the six practice factors (P1 through P6), and the two promotion and dismissal factors (H1 and H2), we did a second-order factor analysis of the scores on the eleven dimensions represented by these factors, plus five demographic indicators—sex, age, seniority, education and nationality—across the twenty units. We found the following three clusters: (1) V3 (larger need for authority), P1 (process-oriented), H2 (dismissal for off-the-job morals), and mean age, which we call a "bureaucracy" cluster; (2) V2 (strong work centrality), P3 (professional), and higher mean education level, clearly a "professionalism" cluster; and (3) V1 (stronger need for security), PA (closed system), H1 (promotion on past merits), and Dutch rather than Danish nationality, which we call a "conservation" cluster.

The three other practice factors, P2, P5, and P6 were not associated with other variables in the second-order analysis. The second-order analysis shows values and practices to be distinct but partly interrelated characteristics of culture. Apart from the "conservation" cluster, which reflects mainly national cultural differences among the two nations studied, the other two present major dichotomies among organizations known from organization sociology. The first, bureaucracy, opposes the mechanistic vs. organic systems described by Burns and Stalker (1961), and the second shows that the distinction between local and cosmopolitan also has a values component.

All in all, the results of the multivariate analysis of the survey data confirm our second hypothesis. We did find a discrete number of independent dimensions of organizational cultures, and these dimensions are well rooted in organizational theory and refer to quite classical distinctions among organizations. The six dimensions of perceived practices, P1 through P6, can be seen as a checklist for practical culture differences between organizations.

Relationships between organizational culture and other organizational characteristics

In our third hypothesis we assumed that organizational cultures are partly predetermined by nationality, industry, and task, partly related to organizational structure and control systems, and partly unique products of idiosyncratic features like the organization's history or the personality of its founder. Nationality, industry, and task of a unit are directly observable features. The results reported above show that nationality, as well as education, age, seniority, and hierarchical level, strongly affected the answers on questions dealing with values. For the answers on questions dealing with perceived practices no such dominant effect of demographic characteristics was evident.

For the organization's task, the scoring profiles of the twenty units on the six practice dimensions showed that dimensions P1 (process vs. results), P3 (parochial vs. professional), P5 (loose vs. tight), and P6 (normative vs. pragmatic) relate at least partly to the type of work the organization does and to the type of market in which it operates. In fact, these four dimensions form a major part of the industry culture, a frequently neglected component of the organizational culture (Pennings and Gresov, 1986). The two remaining dimensions, P2 (employee- vs. job-oriented) and P4 (open vs. closed) seem to be independent of the industry but more determined by the philosophy of founders and top leaders.

Of the quantitative data collected at the unit level, about forty out of a much larger number of quantifiable characteristics tried were really comparable across units. Unit scores on these forty characteristics were correlated with the unit scores on the six practices dimensions.

Table 4 lists those characteristics that yielded significant and meaningful correlations with practice dimension scores.[5] We checked for the possible effects of intercorrelations among the unit-level measures. There was a clear cluster of measures related to the unit's size, such as annual budget, total invested capital, and number of employees. From this cluster, number of employees appeared to be the indicator most strongly correlated with culture dimensions. Size strongly affected the correlations between culture and budget split (labor- vs. materials-intensive), so we controlled for it in the corresponding lines of Table 4. None of the other correlations in Table 4 were affected by controlling for size. Other intercorrelations among structural measures were of insufficient interest to be taken into account in the analyses presented in Table 4.

Table 4 contains 15 correlations significant at the .01-level and beyond and 28 at the .05-level. Crossing 40 characteristics with 6 dimensions we could expect two or three correlations at the .01-level by chance, and 12 at the .05-level. Chance, therefore, can only account for a minor part of the relationships found.

On practice dimension P1, process vs. results orientation, manufacturing and office units tended to score on the process-oriented side and research and development and service units on the results-oriented side.

Table 4 shows a strong correlation between dimension P1 and the balance of labor versus materials cost in the operating budget. Any operation can be characterized as labor-intensive, materials-intensive, or capital-intensive, depending on which of the three categories of cost takes the largest share of its operating budget. Labor-intensive units, holding number of employees constant, scored as more results-oriented, while materials-intensive units, again holding number of employees constant, scored as more process-oriented. If an operation is labor-intensive, people's efforts, by definition, play an important role in its results. This appears more likely to breed a results-oriented culture. The yield of materials-intensive units tends to depend on technical processes, which seems to stimulate a process-oriented culture.

The second highest correlation of results-orientation is with lower absenteeism. This is a nice validation of the fact that, as one of the key questions formulates it, "people put in a maximal effort."

There were three significant correlations between results orientation and structural characteristics. Flatter organizations (larger span of control for the unit top manager) scored as more results-oriented. This confirms Peters and Waterman's (1982) seventh maxim "simple form, lean staff." Three simplified scales were used, based on the Aston studies of organizational structure (Pugh and Hickson, 1976), to measure centralization, specialization, and formalization. Both specialization and formalization were negatively correlated with results orientation: more specialized and more formalized units tend to be more process-oriented. They correspond with the mechanistic systems of Burns and Stalker (1961).

The remaining correlations of results orientation are with having a top-management team with a lower education level and one that has been promoted

Table 4 Product-moment correlation coefficients between various unit-level characteristics and unit scores on six dimensions of practices across 20 units*

Structural characteristic	P1	P2	P3	P4	P5	P6
Measures of size						
Annual budget			.61			
Total invested capital		−.41	.53			
Number of employees			.60			
Private (−) vs. public (+)				−.39		−.39
Budget split in % (holding number of employees constant)						
Labor	.72					
Materials	−.46				.48	
Measures of structure						
Span of control, top manager	.41					
% Supervisory personnel				−.39		
Centralization score					.26[†]	
Specialization score	−.40		.41			.38
Formalization score	−.40			.43		
Control system						
Top manager's boss focuses on profits		.61				
Top manager's boss focuses on budgets		−.56				
Controversial issues in employee journal		−.55		−.39		
Time budget of top manager						
% Reading/writing memos					.66	
% Meetings/discussions			.51			
Profile of top 5 managers						
At least one woman				−.38		
Average education level	−.39	−.42	.58		−.46	
Average age			.46			
Promoted from ranks	−.40					
Profile of employees						
% Women				−.78	.45	
% Female managers				−.58	.54	
% Absenteeism	−.60				.39	
Average seniority			.53	−.39		
Average age			.38			
Average education men					−.47	
Average education women					−.41	
Recent growth in number					−.43	
Union membership	−.39		−.59			

*Only significant correlations are shown; limits: .05 at .38, .01 at .52. Positive correlations indicate associations with results orientation (P1), job orientation (P2), professional (P3), closed system (P4), tight control (P5), or pragmatic (P6).
[†]Highest correlation with centralization score, not significant.

from the ranks: doers rather than figureheads. Finally, in results-oriented units, union membership among employees tends to be lower.

Scores on dimension P2 (employee- vs. job-oriented) clearly reflected the philosophy of the unit or company's founder(s) and top leaders as we met them in the interviews. They also showed the possible scars left by past events: units that had recently been in economic trouble, especially if this was accompanied by collective layoffs, tended to score as job-oriented, even if, according to our informants, the past had been different. Opinions about the desirability of a strong employee orientation differed among the leaders of the units we studied; in the feedback discussions, we met top managers who wanted their unit to become more employee-oriented, as well as others who desired the opposite.

The strongest correlations with dimension P2 in Table 4 are with the way the unit is controlled by the organization to which it belongs. Where the top manager of the unit stated that his superiors evaluated him on profits and other financial performance measures, the members scored the unit culture to be more job-oriented. Where the top manager of the unit felt his superiors evaluated him on performance against a budget, the opposite was the case: members scored the unit culture to be more employee-oriented, it seems that operating against external standards (profits in a market) breeds a less benevolent culture than operating against internal standards (a budget). Where the top manager stated he allowed controversial news to be published in the employee journal, members felt the unit to be more employee-oriented, which validates the top manager's veracity.

The remaining correlations of employee orientation are with the average seniority and age of employees (more senior employees scored as being in a more job-oriented culture), with the education level of the top-management team (less educated teams corresponded with a more job-oriented culture), and with the total invested capital (not with the invested capital per employee). Large organizations with heavy investment tended to be more employee- than job-oriented.

On dimension P3 (parochial vs. professional), units with a traditional technology tended to score as parochial; high-tech units as professional. The strongest correlations of this dimension in Table 4 are with various measures of size: the larger organizations foster the more professional cultures. Professional cultures also have smaller labor union membership, their managers have a higher average education level and age, and they score higher on specialization. An interesting correlation is with the time budget of the unit top manager: in the units with a professional culture, the top managers claimed to spend a relatively large share of their time in meetings and person-to-person discussions. Finally, the privately owned units in our sample tended to score as more professional than the public ones.

In the same way as for employee versus job orientation, we believe the philosophy of the organization's founder(s) and top leaders plays a strong role in P4 (open vs. closed system). Communication climates in the units we studied seemed to have been formed historically without much outside rationale; some organizations had developed a tradition of being closed, others of remarkable openness.

In the national context, however, open vs. closed was the only one of the six practices dimensions that was significantly associated with nationality: an open organizational communication climate is more characteristic of Danish than of Dutch organizations. However, one Danish unit scored as extremely closed and had been perceived by its environment and by its own members as a very closed organization for over a century.

The open-closed dimension in Table 4 is responsible for the single strongest correlation in the matrix: .78 between the percentage of women among employees and the openness of the communication climate. The percentage of women among managers and the presence of at least one woman in the top-management team are also correlated with openness. However, this correlation is affected by the bi-national composition of the research population. Among developed European countries, Denmark has one of the highest participation rates of women in the workforce, and the Netherlands one of the lowest (although steeply increasing). Also, as reported above, Danish units as a group, with one exception, score as much more open than Dutch units. This does not necessarily exclude a causal relationship between the participation of women in the workforce and a more open communication climate. Among the Danish units taken separately, the correlation between the percentage of women employees and openness is also significant, but not among the Dutch units, which may be the effect of the restricted range of scores of the Dutch units on "openness." All in all, the relationship between female participation in the labor force and openness of the organization's communication climate is a finding that merits further research.

Other correlates of the open vs. closed dimension are an association of more formalization with a more closed culture (a suitable validation of both measures), of admitting controversial issues into the employee journal with a more open culture (another validation), of higher average seniority with a more open culture, and of a high percentage of supervisory personnel with a more open culture.

On dimension P5 (loose vs. tight control), units delivering precision or risky products or services (such as Pharmaceuticals or money transactions) tended to score as tight on control, those with innovative or unpredictable activities tended to score as loose. To our surprise, the two municipal police corps we studied scored on the loose control side (16 and 41): the work of a policeman, however, is highly unpredictable, and police personnel have considerable discretion in the way they want to carry out their task.

The strongest correlation of the loose vs. tight control dimension in Table 4 is with an item in the self-reported time budget of the unit top manager: where the top manager claims to spend a relatively large part of his time reading and writing reports and memos from inside the organization, we found tighter control. This makes perfect sense. We also found that materials-intensive units have more tightly controlled cultures. As the results of such units often depend on small margins of material yields, this makes sense, too.

Tight control in Table 4 is also correlated with the percentage of female managers and of female employees, in this order. This is most likely a consequence of the type of activities for which women tend to be hired. Tighter control is found in units with a lower education level among male and female employees and also among its top managers. In units in which the number of employees had recently increased, control was felt to be looser; where the number of employees had been reduced, control was perceived as tighter. Employee layoffs are obviously associated with budget squeezes. Finally, absenteeism among employees was lower where control was perceived to be not as tight. Absenteeism is evidently one way of escape from the pressure of a tightly controlled system.

On dimension P6 (normative vs. pragmatic), service units and those operating in competitive markets tended to score as pragmatic, while units involved in the implementation of laws and operating under a monopoly tended to score as normative. Table 4 shows only two correlations with this dimension: privately owned units in our sample were more pragmatic, public units more normative (like the police corps), and there was a positive correlation between pragmatism and specialization, which we would not have predicted.

Conspicuously missing from Table 4 are correlations with performance measures. It has been extremely difficult to identify measures of performance applicable to so varied a set of organizational units, and the ones we have tried did not yield significant correlations. Denison (1984), using employee survey data and financial performance figures for 34 U.S. business firms, found a positive relationship between participative decision-making practices (equivalent to our dimension P2, employee-oriented) and business success. However, we are unable either to confirm or refute such a relationship on the basis of our data.

While the task and market environment clearly affected the scores on at least four of the practice dimensions, some individual units showed surprising exceptions: a production plant with an unexpectedly strong results-orientation even on the shopfloor or a unit like TKB with a loose control system in relation to its task. These surprises confirm the possibility that a unit's culture may have distinctive elements. None of the correlations in Table 4 is so strong as to preclude deviations by individual units from general patterns, in our interviews and during the feedback discussions within the twenty participating units, we found idiosyncratic components of organization cultures within limits set by the task and the systems.

Our third hypothesis was thus confirmed as well: Organization cultures reflect nationality, demographics of employees and managers, industry and market; they are related to organization structure and control systems; but all of these leave room for unique and idiosyncratic elements.

Discussion

The popular literature on corporate cultures, following Peters and Waterman (1982), insists that shared values represent the core of a corporate culture. This study, however, empirically shows shared perceptions of daily practices to be the core of an organization's culture. Our measurements of employee values differed more according to the demographic criteria of nationality, age, and education than according to membership in the organization per se.

What we called "practices" can also be labelled "conventions," "customs," "habits," "mores," "traditions," or "usages." They have already been recognized as part of culture by Edward B. Tylor in the last century: "Culture is that complex whole which includes knowledge, beliefs, art, morals, law, customs and any other capabilities and habits acquired by man as a member of society" (Tylor, 1924: 1).

An explanation for the difference between the message of Peters and Waterman (and many other U.S. authors) and our findings about the nature of organizational cultures could be that the U.S. management literature rarely distinguishes between the values of founders and significant leaders and the values of the bulk of the organization's members. Descriptions of organizational cultures are often based only on statements by corporate heroes. In our case, we have assessed to what extent leaders' messages have come across to members. We conclude that the values of founders and key leaders undoubtedly shape organizational cultures but that the way these cultures affect ordinary members is through shared practices. Founders' and leaders' values become members' practices. Even in the case of the DLM passenger terminal, employees' values did not change, but because of the new president's orientation, the rules of the game were changed, so that new practices could be developed.

In organization theory, this process of a transfer of the founders' values into the members' practices has already been recognized by Weber (1948: 297): "... when the organization of authority becomes permanent, the staff supporting the charismatic ruler becomes routinized." In Weber's typology of social action, he distinguished (among other types) action toward a value (*wertrational*) from action dominated by habitual response ("traditional"; Burrell and Morgan, 1979: 83). Our findings suggest that actions by ordinary organization members are more often traditional than *wertrational*.

If members' values depend primarily on their demographics, the way values enter the organization is via the hiring process: a company hires people of a certain nationality, age, education, and sex and, therefore, with certain values. Their subsequent socialization in the organization is a matter of learning the practices: symbols, heroes, and rituals.

Organization culture differences are thus composed of other elements than those that make up national culture differences. We have pictured the distinction in Figure 2. Among national cultures—comparing otherwise similar people—we found considerable differences in values, in the sense of broad, nonspecific feelings, such as of good and evil, notwithstanding similarities in practices among IBM employees in similar jobs in different national subsidiaries. Among organizational cultures, the opposite was the case: we found considerable differences in practices for people who held about the same values. We believe this difference can be explained by the different places of socialization for values and for practices. Values are acquired in our early youth, mainly in the family and in the neighborhood, and later at school. By the time a child is ten, most of his or her basic

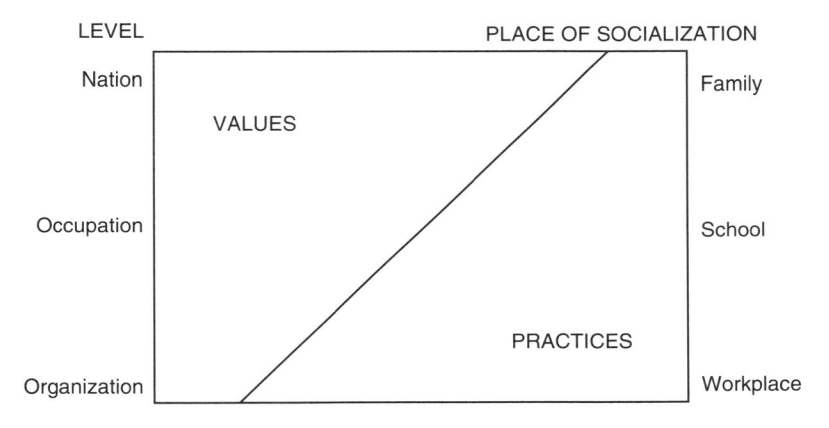

```
                LEVEL                              PLACE OF SOCIALIZATION
              Nation                                                    Family
                              VALUES


              Occupation                                                School


                                                    PRACTICES
              Organization                                              Workplace
```

Figure 2 Cultural differences: national, occupational, and organizational levels.

values are probably programmed into his or her mind. Organizational practices, on the other hand, are learned through socialization at the workplace (Pascale, 1985), which we usually enter as adults, with the bulk of our values firmly in place.

In Figure 2, we have placed an occupational culture level halfway between nation and organization, suggesting that entering an occupational field means the acquisition of both values and practices; the place of socialization is the school or university, and the time is between childhood and entering work. The place of occupational cultures in Figure 2 is supported by the results of the analyses of variance presented in Table 1: Occupation level was associated equally strongly with values as with practices. Occupational cultures have received considerably less attention in the literature than either national or organizational cultures, with a few exceptions (Van Maanen and Barley, 1984; Raelin, 1986).[6]

After having done both a large cross-national and a large cross-organizational culture study, we believe that national cultures and organizational cultures are phenomena of different orders: using the term "cultures" for both is, in fact, somewhat misleading, as has already been suggested by Wilkins and Ouchi (1983: 479).

The major outcome of our research project is a six-dimensional model of organizational cultures, defined as perceived common practices: symbols, heroes, and rituals that carry a specific meaning within the organizational unit. The source of our research data, twenty organizational units in two North-West-European countries, is obviously far too limited to claim any universality for the model. Certain types of organizations, like those in the health and welfare area, government offices, and military organizations, were missing from our set, and in other national environments, other practice dimensions could become relevant. Nevertheless, we predict that in other environments, too, differences among organizational cultures will be partly quantifiable and can be meaningfully described using perhaps five to seven practice dimensions, which should partly overlap with the six described in this paper. Information from some other sources seems to bear out this prediction. In Switzerland, Pümpin (Pümpin, 1984; Kobi, and Wüthrich, 1985) has described a seven-dimensional model, five dimensions of which are very similar to ours (results orientation, employee orientation, company orientation, cost orientation, and customer orientation); however, the source of his model, other than common sense, is not clear from the published materials. In India, Khandwalla (1985), in a study of managers across 75 organizations, using 5-point bipolar survey questions similar to our "where I work ..." questions, found a first factor closely resembling our process vs. results orientation.[7]

The usefulness of an approach that quantifies is that it makes a fuzzy field at least somewhat accessible. We do not want to deny that organizational cultures are gestalts, wholes whose flavor can only be completely experienced by insiders and which demand empathy in order to be appreciated by outsiders. However, in a world of hardware and bottom-line figures, a framework allowing one to describe the structure in these gestalts is an asset. Practitioners can use it to create awareness of cultural differences, for example, in cases of planned mergers of culturally different units. By allowing comparisons to be made with other organizations, it can suggest the cultural constraints that strategic planners will have to respect. It allows one to measure culture change over time. Finally, it can help both managers and researchers to decide whether an organization should be considered as one single culture or as a multitude of subcultures and to draw a cultural map of complex organizations.[8]

Our multidimensional model of organizational cultures does not support the notion that any position on one of the six dimensions is intrinsically "good" or "bad." Labelling positions on the dimension scales as more or less desirable is a matter of strategic choice, which will vary from one organization to another. For example, the popular stress on customer orientation (becoming more pragmatic on P6) is highly relevant for most organizations engaged in services and the manufacturing of custom-made, quality products. It may be unnecessary or even dysfunctional for, for example, the manufacturing side of organizations supplying standard products in a competitive price market or for units operating under government regulations. This conclusion stands in flagrant contradiction to the "one best way" assumptions found in Peters and Waterman's eight maxims. What is good or bad depends in each case on where one wants the organization to go, and a cultural feature that is an asset for one purpose is unavoidably a liability for another.

In this article we have reported on a piece of ordinary behavioral research in an area where, in relation to the amount of speculation offered in the literature, such research has been too rare. Our results, we believe, contribute to a demystification of the organizational culture construct, changing it from a passing fad into a regular element of the theory and practice of the management of organizations.

Notes

1 Earlier reports on this research project have appeared in Darish (Hofstede and Ohayv, 1987) and in Dutch (Sanders and Neuijen, 1987).
2 In that study, four work-goals questions were paired two by two, subtracting the score on one from the score on the other in order to eliminate acquiescence (Hofstede, 1980: 72). We repeated the same precaution for the ANOVAs across organizations.
3 Because some of the questions were scored on ordinal scales, we cannot guarantee that the answers are equidistant (which would make them into interval scales). In this case, the median would be the mathematically more correct measure of central tendency. However, for the type of 5-point scales used, mean and median have been shown to be almost identical (Hofstede, 1980: 70), and the mean is much easier to compute and to handle statistically.
4 Lammers (1986) has shown that Peters and Waterman's eight maxims for the "excellent corporation" correspond with the findings of a number of classics in organizational sociology on both sides of the Atlantic, among them Burns and Stalker.
5 The analysis of the relationships between the structural data and the culture dimension scores was partly done by Koop Boer and Bernd Mintjes of the University of Groningen in the context of a Master's thesis. For reasons of space, we have not listed all unit-level variables tried; interested readers are welcome to contact the first author about variables not mentioned.
6 In a methodological study, Hofstede and Spangenberg (1987) showed that the same work-goals questions form different clusters when factor analyzed at the individual, occupational, organizational, or national levels.
7 In Belgium, de Cock et al. (1984) developed a questionnaire aimed at assessing "organizational climate and culture." However, this one uses an imposed factor structure based on climate studies from the 1970s; its dimensions do not resemble ours. An article in a U.S. training journal, by Wallach (1963) describes an Organizational Culture Index with three dimensions: bureaucratic, innovative, and supportive. Some aspects of these overlap with our practice dimensions, but the source of Wallach's operationalization is not made clear.
8 Gibson, Ouchi, and Sung (1987) found considerable subsystem variable within a multinational "Type Z" firm. In a recent and as yet unpublished study of a large service company, we collected culture data from the full population of about < 2,500 employees, divided into 130 departments. A hierarchical cluster analysis revealed four clear subcultures, one of them with an almost "countercultural" profile (Martin and Siehl, 1983).

References

Blake, Robert R., and Jane S. Mouton (1964) *The Managerial Grid*. Houston, TX: Gulf.
Blalock, Hubert M., Jr., and Ann B. Blalock (1971) *Methodology in Social Research*. London: McGraw-Hill.
Blau, Peter M. (1960) "Structural effects." *American Sociological Review*, 25: 178–193.
Bond, Michael Harris, and Mai Ku Pang (1989) "Trusting to the Tao: Chinese values and the re-centering of psychology." Paper presented at the Conference on Moral Values and Moral Reasoning in Chinese Societies, Taipei, Taiwan.
Bourgoin, Henry (1984) *L'Afrique malade du management*. Paris: Jean Picollec.
Burns, Tom, and Stalker G. M. (1961) *The Management of Innovation*. London: Tavistock.
Burrell, Gibson, and Gareth Morgan (1979) *Sociological Paradigms and Organizational Analysis: Elements of the Sociology of Corporate Life*. London: Heinemann.

Deal, Terrence E., and Allan A. Kennedy (1982) *Corporate Cultures: The Rites and Rituals of Corporate Life*. Reading, MA: Addison-Wesley.

de Cock, Gaston, René Bouwen, K. de Witte, and J. de Visch 1984 *Organisatieklimaat en-Cultuur*. Leuven, Belgium: Acco.

Denison, Daniel R. (1984) "Bringing corporate culture to the bottom line." *Organizational Dynamics*, 13(2): 5–22.

Dubin, Robert, and Joseph E. Champoux (1977) "Central life interests and job satisfaction." *Organizational Behavior and Human Performance*, 18: 366–377.

Dubin, Robert, Joseph E. Champoux, and Lyman W. Porter (1975) "Central life interests and organizational commitment of blue-collar and clerical workers." *Administrative Science Quarterly*, 20: 411–421.

Gibson, David V., William G. Ouchi, and Byung H. Sung (1987) "Organizational culture, subsystem variation and environmental context." Unpublished manuscript. College of Business Administration, The University of Texas at Austin.

Gorsuch, Richard L. (1983) *Factor Analysis*, 2nd ed. Hillsdale, NJ: Lawrence Erlbaum.

Gudykunst, William B., and Stella Ting-Toomey (1988) *Culture and Interpersonal Communication*. Newbury Park. CA: Sage.

Hofstede, Geert (1967) *The Game of Budget Control*. Assen, Neth. and London: Van Gorcum/Tavistock.

——— (1980) *Culture's Consequences*. Beverly Hills, CA: Sage.

——— (1983a) "Dimensions of national cultures in fifty countries and three regions." In J. B. Deregowski, S. Dziurawiec, and R. C. Annis (eds.), *Expiscations in Cross-Cultural Psychology:* 335–355. Lisse, Neth.: Swets and Zeitlinger.

——— (1983b) "National cultures in four dimensions." *International Studies of Management and Organization*, 13: 46–74.

——— (1983c) "The cultural relativity of organizational practices and theories." *Journal of International Business Studies*, 14: 75–89.

——— (1983d) "National cultures revisited." *Behavior Science Research*, 18: 285–305.

Hofstede, Geert, and Michael Harris Bond (1988) "The Confucius connection: From cultural roots to economic growth." *Organizational Dynamics*, 16(4): 4–21.

Hofstede, Geert, and Denise D. Ohayv (1987) "Diagnosticering of Organisationskulturer." *Harvard Børsen*, 25: 60–69.

Hofstede, Geert, and John Spangenberg (1987) "Measuring individualism and collectivism at occupational and organizational levels." In Ç. Kagitçibasi (ed.), *Growth and Progress in Cross-Cultural Psychology:* 113–122. Lisse, Neth.: Swets and Zeitlinger.

Khandwalla, Pradip N. (1985) "Pioneering innovative management: An Indian excellence." *Organization Studies*, 6: 161–183.

Kreacic, Vladimir, and Philip Marsh (1986) "Organisation development and national culture in four countries." *Public Enterprise*, 6: 121–134.

Lammers, Cornelis J. (1986) "De excellente onderneming als organisatiemodel." *Harvard Holland Review*, 8: 18–25.

Langbein, Laura I., and Allan J. Lichtman (1978) *Ecological Inference*. Beverly Hills, CA: Sage.

Laurent, André (1983) "The cultural diversity of Western conceptions of management." *International Studies of Management and Organization*, 13: 75–96.

Leung, Kwok, and Michael Harris Bond (1989) "On the empirical identification of dimensions for cross-cultural comparisons." *Journal of Cross-Cultural Psychology*, 20(2): 133–151.

Lodahl, Thomas M. (1964) "Patterns of job attitudes in two assembly technologies." *Administrative Science Quarterly*, 8: 482–519.

Lodahl, Thomas M., and Mathilde Kejner (1965) "The definition and measurement of job involvement." *Journal of Applied Psychology*, 49: 24–33.

Martin, Joanne, and Caren Siehl (1983) "Organizational culture and counterculture: An uneasy symbiosis." *Organizational Dynamics*, 12(2): 52–64.

Meltzer, Leo (1963) "Comparing relationships of individual and average variables to individual responses." *American Sociological Review*, 28: 117–123.

Menzel, Herbert (1950) "Comment on Robinson's 'Ecological Correlations and the Behavior of Individuals'." *American Sociological Review*, 15: 674.

Merton, Robert K. (1968) *Social Theory and Social Structure*, rev. ed. New York: Free Press.

Pascale, Richard T. (1985) "The paradox of 'corporate culture': Reconciling ourselves to socialization." *California Management Review*, 27(2): 26–41.

Pennings, Johannes M., and Christopher G. Gresov (1986) "Technoeconomic and structural correlates of organizational culture." *Organization Studies*, 7: 317–334.

Peters, Thomas J., and Richard H. Waterman (1982) *In Search of Excellence: Lessons from America's Best-Run Companies*. New York: Harper & Row.

Pettigrew, Andrew M. (1979) "On studying organizational cultures." *Administrative Science Quarterly*, 24: 570–581.

Poole, Marshall S. (1985) "Communication and organizational climates: Review, critique, and a new perspective." In R. D. McPhee and P. K. Tompkins (eds.), *Organizational Communication*: 79–108. Beverly Hills, CA: Sage.

Przeworski, Adam, and Henry Teune (1970) *The Logic of Comparative Social Inquiry*. New York: Wiley-Interscience.

Pugh, Derek S., and David J. Hickson (1976) *Organizational Structure in its Context: The Aston Programme I*. Westmead, Farnborough: Saxon House.

Pümpin, Cuno (1984) "Unternehmenskultur, Unternehmensstrategie und Unternehmenserfolg." *GDI Impuls:* 2: 19–30. Bern, Switz.: Gottlieb Duttweiler Institut.

Pümpin, Cuno, J. M., Kobi, and H. A. Wüthrich (1985) *La culture de l'entreprise: le profil stratégique qui conduit au succès*. Bern, Switz.: Banque Populaire Suisse.

Raelin, Joseph A. (1986) *The Clash of Cultures: Managers and Professionals*. Boston: Harvard Business School Press.

Reynolds, Paul D. (1986) "Organizational culture as related to industry, position and performance." *Journal of Management Studies*, 23: 333–345.

Robinson, W. S. (1950) "Ecological correlations and the behavior of individuals." *American Sociological Review*, 15: 351–357.

Sanders, Geert, and Bram Neuijen (1987) *Bedrijfscultuur: diagnose en beïnvloeding*. Assen, Neth.: Van Gorcum.

Scheuch, E. K. (1966) "Aggregate data: Some problems." In R. L. Merritt and S. Rokkan (eds.), *Comparing Nations:* 148–157. New Haven, CT: Yale University Press.

Selltiz, Claire, Marie Jahoda, Morton Deutsch, and Stuart W. Cook (1965) *Research Methods in Social Relations*. London: Methuen.

Silverzweig, Stan, and Robert F. Allen (1976) "Changing the corporate culture." *Sloan Management Review*, Spring: 33–49.

Tannenbaum, Arnold S., and Jerald G. Bachman (1964) "Structural versus individual effects." *American Journal of Sociology*, 69: 585–595.

Triandis, Harry C. (1984) "Toward a psychological theory of economic growth." *International Journal of Psychology*, 19: 79–95.

Triandis, Harry C., Robert Bontempo, and Associates (1986) "The measurement of the etic aspects of individualism and collectivism across cultures." *Australian Journal of Psychology*, 38: 257–267.

Tylor, Edward B. (1924) *Primitive Culture*. (First published in 1871.) Gloucester, MA: Smith.

Van Maanen, John, and Stephen R. Barley (1984) "Occupational communities: Culture and control in organizations." In B. M. Staw and L. L. Cummings (eds.), *Research in Organizational Behavior*, 6: 287–365. Greenwich, CT: JAI Press.

Wallach, Ellen J. (1983) "Individuals and organizations: The cultural march." *Training and Development Journal*, February: 29–36.

Weber, Max (1948) From *Max Weber: Essays in Sociology*, H. H. Gerth and C. Wright Mills, trans. and eds. London: Routledge & Kegan Paul.

Weick, Karl E. (1985) "The significance of corporate culture." In P. J. Frost et al. (eds.), *Organizational Culture*: 381–389. Beverly Hills, CA: Sage.

Wilkins, Alan L. (1984) "The creation of company cultures: The role of stories and human resource systems." *Human Resource Management*, 23: 41–60.

Wilkins, Alan L, and William G. Ouchi (1983) "Efficient cultures: Exploring the relationship between culture and organizational performance." *Administrative Science Quarterly*, 28: 468–481.

53
MANAGERIAL COMPETENCY MODELLING AND THE DEVELOPMENT OF ORGANIZATIONAL PSYCHOLOGY
A Chinese approach

Zhong-Ming Wang

Source: *International Journal of Psychology* 38(5) (2003): 323–334.

Abstract

In recent years, China has undergone rapid economic reform and dynamic organizational changes. Several major developments have given special momentum to those changes: China entering the WTO, opening the western regions of China, building up an information network, transforming new management systems nationwide, and encouraging innovations and entrepreneurship. These developments call for more comprehensive and adaptive competencies and new approaches to organizational psychology in China. This provides a national and cultural context of personnel assessment, selection, and development of organizational psychology. Organizational psychology is one of the most active fields for research and application in psychology in China. Three aspects of recent trends are described under a framework of managerial competency modelling. (1) Leadership competence assessment for personnel selection and development has become one of the key aspects of human resources (HR) management in China. Based upon the results from the structured interview and strategic hierarchical job analysis, a model of leadership competency with four dimensions of leadership characteristics and the managerial performance was proposed. The four dimensions are: psychological traits; leadership predispositions; managerial skills; and professional knowledge (2) HR competency for person-job-organization fit. This includes competencies for compensation and motivational strategies, organizational commitment and career management competence, team competence, and group decision-making skills (3) Organizational competency for culture and change. This includes an integrative approach to link values with culture, and cross-cultural leadership skills. On the basis of the recent practice and research developments, a Chinese approach to organizational psychology with important characteristics is summarized: active theoretical development and conceptualization; continuous methodological improvement; close link with HR and management practices; and systematic cross-cultural socioeconomic perspective. This becomes a key framework for understanding organizational psychology. New directions for research and application in China are highlighted.

Introduction

In the last 20 years, industrial and organizational psychology has developed rapidly in China. This is mostly due to the significant development of economic reform and social changes and the great demand for organizational psychology and human resource management research and applications in Chinese organizations. As a result, the cross-cultural–socioeconomic perspective has been emphasized in relation to developments in various fields of psychology and human resource management in China (Drenth & Wang, 2000; Jing, 1994; Wang, 1993, 1995; Wang & Mobley, 1999). In recent years, China has undergone more dynamic organizational changes: entering the WTO, opening the western regions of China, building up an information network, and transferring management systems nationwide. These developments have given special momentum to changes and formed the national and cultural context for developing managerial competency and organizational psychology in China.

HR challenges for entering the WTO and strategic management for the western regions

Since China has entered the WTO, more international joint ventures have been established and more international business practices introduced. There are urgent needs to develop and formulate strategic HR competency models (Wang, 1997a, 1999; Wang & Mobley, 1999). Areas of international HR management have been active: (1) formulating expatriates' adaptation and training programmes; (2) developing the Third Culture management and cultural competencies; and (3) encouraging effective cross-cultural leadership teams (Wang, 1999, 2002). The motivational and regulative mechanism is becoming a key topic for executive development. New management development such as the implementation of various kinds of shareholding, the trial of stock options, and particularly the CEO compensation systems have called for more organizational psychology research.

In the late 1990s, China made a major decision to open the western regions of the country for rapid economic reform and international business. The organizations in the western area have mostly operated under traditional management values and practices, and are now in the process of transformation into a shareholding system or market-oriented management. More studies of organizational psychology are needed to explore values and leadership styles in order to develop effective strategic management schemes for the western regions of China.

Team networking for building up IT systems and transferring management systems

As technological innovation and E-commerce become active in China, more and more companies are preparing themselves for E-business development and virtual organization management. One of the key measures for rapid IT development is to formulate virtual team programmes and to restructure business models (Wang, 2001). Both teamwork skills and relevant HR support systems are recognized as important aspects of effective team networking approaches. Since the late 1990s, most of the state-owned enterprises have transformed into stockholding and/or shareholding systems. A multi-ownership system of enterprises has been recognized as an alternative model for Chinese firms. As a result, more attention has been paid to the quality of top management teams and their selection and development. A new leadership competence model is needed to provide a framework for recruitment, selection, placement, and development of leading cadres and key positions for managing new organization systems in China. Assessment and selection has become a part of the qualification process for management teams in China. The nature of employment has changed into a competitive practice rather than a practice of life-employment and iron-bowl welfare. Many Chinese companies have focused upon long-term person–job fit and succession planning, particularly among joint ventures, township companies, and private firms. More executive development programmes and overseas study tour programmes are conducted to enhance leadership competence among executives and managers. Attention has been paid to principles and methodology in the assessment and selection of both leaders and employees (Wang, 1997b; Wu & Zhang, 2001).

All of these recent changes have facilitated more systematic research and applications of organizational psychology in China. The focus of organizational psychology has shifted to managerial competency modelling for employees, teams, and organizational levels.

Leadership competence for assessment and selection

Developments in leadership assessment and selection

One important area of recent developments in organizational psychology in china has been leadership competence for assessment and selection. Although testing has been a traditional topic in Chinese society since ancient times, it was in the 1980s, when China adopted economic reform and open policy, that testing became widely studied. However, at the beginning research on testing mainly focused upon translation and adaptation of Western tests and formulated the Chinese norms of tests for children and students (H.C. Zhang, 1988). Up to the mid-1990s, more and more efforts were made to develop tests for selection of cadres for middle-management positions. A major example was the Personnel Assessment System for Middle Managers developed by the National Center for Personnel Examination with a group of psychologists from the main universities in China (Wang, 2001). By the late 1990s, the research focus of personnel assessment and selection had shifted to the top management group and executive levels. In the meantime, leadership competency modelling has become an important research task in this area in relation to some leadership studies.

Risk perception strategy and situational adaptability as leadership competence

A recent active research area is leadership competence under uncertainty and in real-life situations. Risk management competence and situational adjustment competence are shown to be correlated with managerial performance. X.F. Xie and Xu (2000) studied the risk perception strategies of 172 managerial staff from shareholding companies, private firms, and state-owned enterprises in China to explore how managerial staff perceived risks in their work situation. Large variations in risk perception strategies were found. Strategies of risk taking and progressive and stable perception were adopted by various groups of managerial staff in organizations. The study showed that not risk-taking strategy, but both progressive and stability strategies were highly correlated with leadership performance and productivity. Silverthorne and Wang (2001) conducted an empirical study among 79 managers and 234 subordinates from 20 Taiwanese high-tech business organizations to test the impact of Taiwanese leadership styles on productivity. They examined the effects of both adaptive and nonadaptive leaders on productivity measures such as absenteeism, turnover rate, quality of work, reject rates, profitability, and units produced. The results showed that the situational adaptability had positive effects on productivity indicators. The study provided evidence supporting the value of adaptive leadership styles in the high-tech industries in Taiwan region.

Tests of validation and assessment techniques developed in the Chinese context

As part of the recent development of organizational psychology, more attention has been paid to validation and quality management of various tests and other assessment techniques in the Chinese context. Most of these studies have been carried out in comparison with other cultures. Yu and Murphy (1993) conducted a study to test the cultural relativity hypothesis of modesty bias in the self-rating of performance using data from several organizations in China. They obtained self-, peer, and supervisory ratings of performance of industrial workers in three plants in and around Nanjing, China, and compared mean ratings on three specific and one summary dimension. The performance rating data were obtained for nonsupervisory workers in seven workshops, sampled randomly from three industrial plants (a machine manufacturing plant, an electrical meter plant, and a textile mill). Rating scales were distributed to 367 supervisor–subordinate dyads. They also obtained performance ratings for each worker from one peer, randomly sampled from the work group. It was found that Chinese workers didn't show leniency in self-ratings as was expected. In another study by L. F. Zhang (2001), individual differences were identified in academic achievement attributable to thinking styles over and above what can be explained by self-rated abilities. The study compared 209 university students from the Hong Kong region with 215 university students from mainland China. The Thinking Styles Inventory (Chinese version), based on Sternberg's theory of mental self-government, was adopted (Sternberg, 1988). Both academic achievement scores and self-ratings on their own analytical, creative, and practical abilities were obtained on a 10-point scale based on Sternberg's (1985) triarchic theory of intelligence. The prediction that thinking styles statistically predicted academic achievement was supported by data from both samples. Academic achievement and thinking styles are correlated differently in the two groups. In addition, cross-cultural differences were identified in the relationship between thinking styles and academic achievement.

Other studies focused more upon adaptation of Chinese scales and validation of assessment instruments. Based on self-monitoring to characterize individual differences in a person's ability and propensity to regulate self-presentation and some existing scales, Li and Zhang (1998) devised a 23-item two-dimensional Chinese Self-Monitoring Scale with subscales measuring the ability and propensity to regulate self-presentation according to situational cues. The results showed that two subscales displayed different correlational patterns with the Psychoticism, Extraversion, Neuroticism, and Lie subscales of the Eysenck Personality Questionnaire. The new scale may discriminate among self-presentational styles beyond the prototypes of his and low self-monitoring. Miao, Huang, Chia, and Ren (2000) conducted a validation study for the Chinese version of MBTI in terms of its content validity, criterion-related validity, and construct validity using relevant tests like EPQ, 16PF, MMP1-2, A-Type, and PM tests as criteria. Using a sample of 2123 college students, the Chinese MBTI proved to have high content validity, criterion-related validity, and construct validity. A more systematic validation study on Holland's Self-Directed Search by Long and Peng (2000) also used university students as subjects ($N = 1227$). Instead of just using test–retest reliability and correlational analysis, internal consistency and split-half reliability indicators as well as discriminant indicators were used in this study. A cluster analysis to test the structure and consistency across university programmes showed that the Holland Occupation Finder needed to be revised in order to adapt to the Chinese occupational and employment context. More recently, W. D. Zhang (2001) completed a comprehensive validation study on the dimensionality of the coping inventory (COPE). A LISREL model was built up showing that the dimensionality of the COPE was not all confirmed. Apparently, construct inequivalence in cross-cultural assessment of coping by the COPE inventory was shown.

Leadership competence structure for selection and development

It seems that there are culture-specific features of coping behaviour and occupational work patterns. Many recent studies and consulting projects in organizational psychology in China have focused upon specific features of leadership competencies (e.g., Leung, Wang, & Smith 2001; Wakabayashi & Chen 1999; Wang 2001). Wang and Schneider (2003) conducted a 3-year longitudinal research project examining the dynamics of multicultural leadership team development. With an emphasis on cross-cultural managerial competency–performance framework, four key competencies are found to be crucial for working in multicultural leadership teams in joint ventures: cultural competence, achievement competence, decision competence, and team competence. In a recent study on managerial competency modelling for assessment and selection in China, Wang and Chen (2002) used a strategic hierarchical job analysis technique to conduct critical leadership incident analysis, and a survey on leadership competence, in order to formulate a LISREL model of managerial competence structure. They interviewed 148 managers to generate critical leadership behavioural descriptions and designed a questionnaire distributed among a sample of 420 managers and their deputies from various companies in China. Both criticality and frequency of leadership competencies for manager and deputy manager positions were analysed. Based upon the results from the structured interview and the strategic hierarchical job analysis, a model of leadership competency with four dimensions of leadership characteristics and managerial performance was proposed. It was tested among 640 Chinese managers and proved to have good construct validity and predictive validity. The four dimensions of leadership competency are:

1. Psychological traits: Cognitive abilities of critical reasoning and problem-solving; personality traits of conscientiousness, emotional stability, group compatibility, extraversion, openness.
2. Leadership predispositions: Moral quality in leadership integrity, work values, job commitment, and enterprising, leadership motives of achievement, power, and relationship.
3. Managerial skills: strategic decision-making, relationship coordination, empowerment and facilitation, business monitoring, and innovation.

4. Professional knowledge: functional and financial knowledge and experience. Managerial performance: behavioural, functional, organizational performance.

The general results of this study showed an implicit and hierarchical leadership competency model behind the assessment indicators. In the Chinese context, relationship-based competencies showed a "diffusion effect" across other competence components and became the second-order competency factors, indicating the dominance of culture-specific competencies in the model.

In a study on developing the Chinese Personality at Work (CPW), Hui, Gan, and Cheng (2000) developed an indigenous instrument using Chinese-relevant personality constructs operationalized in situation-specific forms. The CPW items were chosen from an item pool developed by the Assessment and Development Center, which includes 15 dimensions: drive for personal achievement, deference to authority, planning and orderliness, attention-seeking, autonomy, need for affiliation, introspectiveness, support-seeking, dominance, nonabrasiveness and modesty, nursing and altruism, innovativeness and change-orientation, tenacity, client service orientation, and overall managerial readiness. These 15 dimensions presented three factors: ambition-altruism, order-independence, and management-subordination. The validation work showed that these personality and competence elements were crucial for managers. J.X. Zhang and Bond (1998) also carried out a study to examine the relationships between the endorsement of filial piety and both universal and indigenous personality trait factors among Chinese subjects. Two groups of college students from Hong Kong ($N = 125$) and Beijing ($N = 194$) participated in the study and completed a questionnaire composed of the Filial Piety Scale, the Five Factor Inventory (FFI), and five facets selected from the Chinese Tradition factor of the Chinese Personality Assessment Inventory (CPAI). The results showed (1) that the indigenous CPAI facets significantly contribute to predicting filial piety scores over and above the universal FFI factors; (2) that among the five factors of the FFI, Neuroticism and Openness significantly predicted filial piety; and (3) among the five facets of Chinese Tradition, Harmony and *Renqing* (relationship orientation) were the two significant predictors. Thus, improved prediction requires using indigenous measures in addition to the FFI.

In this review of recent studies on selection and decision in China, Wang (1997b) summarized four characteristics of an integrated approach to selection, appraisal, and decisions on leadership competence in China.

1. Multi-facet competency models of assessment and appraisal.
2. Mass assessment and organizational appraisal as criterion.
3. Procedural and nonprocedural control in process.
4. Multi-stage selection and decision-making.

HR competency for person–job–organization fit

Compensation and motivational strategies

Compensation and motivational strategy has recently been one of the most active areas of research in HR competence and organizational psychology in China. Traditionally, the patterns of compensation systems in China had very little variation across regions and industrial sectors. Since China started economic reform and an open policy, new forms of compensation programmes and motivational strategies have been developed and adopted in various types of organizations (Heneman, Charles, & Wang, 2001; Heneman, Tansky, Wang, & Wang, 2002; Wang, 2001a). Zhou and Martocchio (2001) used a policy-capturing approach to examine the extent to which four variables (work performance, relationship with co-workers, relationship with managers, and personal needs) affect the process through which Chinese and American managers make two types of compensation award decisions. Altogether, 71 Chinese executives and 218 American managers participated in the study, using scenarios of compensation award decision. Results showed that, compared with their American counterparts, Chinese managers put less emphasis on work performance when making bonus decisions, more emphasis on relationship with co-workers when making nonmonetary decisions, and more emphasis on personal needs when making bonus decisions. Relationship competence proved to be an important part of HR competency in China.

In a systematic research project of managerial motivation and its strategies, Du and Wang (2003) studied Chinese managers' achievement orientation, the structure of achievement motivation, the link with performance, situational assessment of achievement motivation, the functioning mechanism of achievement motivation, and reward decision-making. Altogether, 1616 managers and supervisors participated in the series of substudies. A two-dimensional model of motivation orientation was then established: self vs. social orientation, and process vs. result orientation. In an in-depth case analysis and then a questionnaire survey, four critical elements were found: hard-working behaviour, self-proceedings of goals, team cooperating, and interpersonal competing. Also, achievement motivation showed a close relationship with organizational culture. A critical leadership behaviour inventory was developed to assess achievement motivation. The structural equation modelling showed that Chinese managers had stronger self-achievement motivation than social-achievement motivation and that self-achievement motivation had a closer relationship with performance. Figure 1 presents the dimensions and assessment scores by the Chinese managers for achievement motivation. As is shown, Chinese managers are more process- and self-motive oriented although team cooperation is still an important motive.

Organizational commitment and career management

As the development of personnel and labour management reform, labour mobility, and career management have become active areas of research in organizational

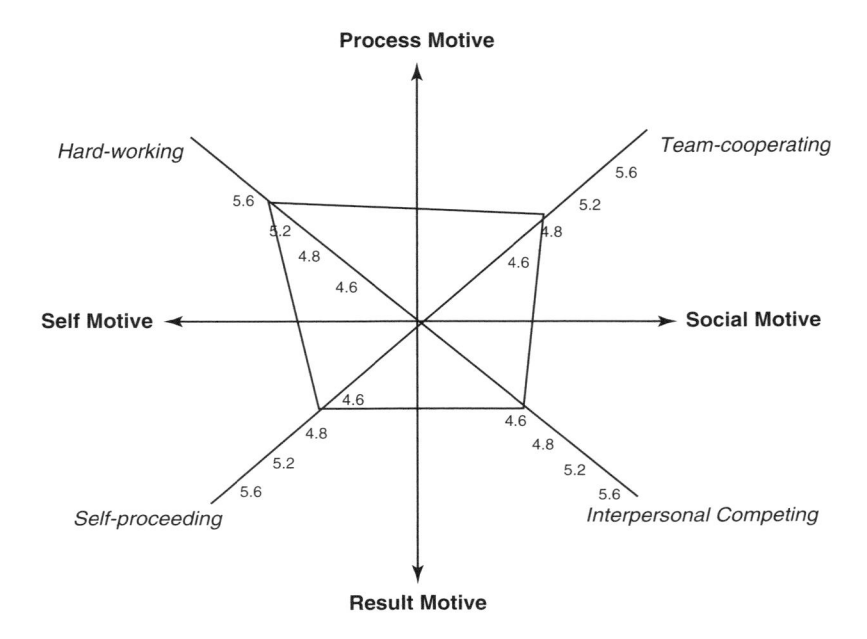

Figure 1 Dimensions and distribution of Chinese achievement motivation.

psychology in China, person–job–organization fit has become a main framework for HR competency research and practices. In a recent large-scale study on organizational commitment, Lin, Zhang, and Fang (2001) developed an instrument called the Chinese Employee Organizational Commitment Scale and tested it among 3236 employees. They looked at the main influencing factors such as organizational support, social exchange values, trust of supervisors, and work satisfaction and found them to affect organizational commitment. The results showed that trust of supervisors, organizational support, and socially fair exchange were among the most influential factors on organizational commitment, while affective, ideality, and opportunity commitment were among the most significant organizational commitment components. In another systematic research project carried out by Wang, Charles-Pauvers, and Liu (2001), the Chinese culture-based concept of organizational commitment was found to be closely related to a top-down social exchange between organization and employees, with the focus for employees on staying and developing in the organization. Figure 2 presents the cross-cultural differences in conceptualization of organizational commitment. As we can see, the solid circle represents the location of the Chinese culture-based concept of organizational commitment, emphasizing stay-development and social exchange, whereas the dashed circle indicates the location of the Western concept of organizational commitment, emphasizing leave-loss and economical exchange. Apparently, contextual boundaries in cultural characteristics could limit the applicability of some key concepts

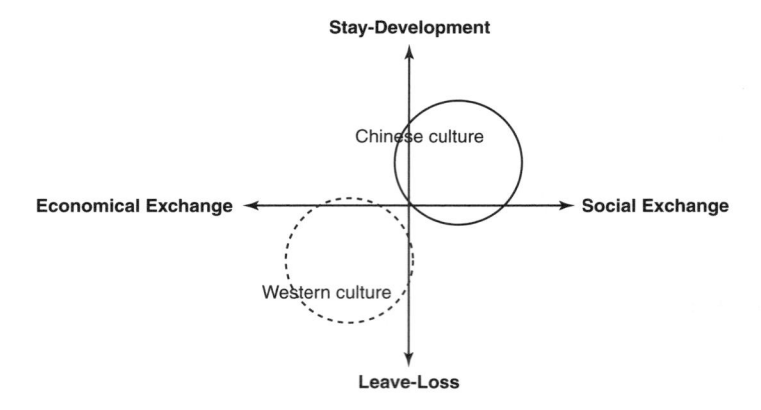

Figure 2 Cross-cultural differences concept of organizational commitment.

in non-Western countries such as China. Efforts have been made in recent organizational psychology research to identify these cultural and contextual boundaries and to formulate more culture-based concepts of HR and organizational behavior (Drenth & Wang, 2000; Wang, 2002).

Team competency and group decision making

Team competency is seen as key to leadership development and change (Earley, 1994; Wang, 1997a, 1999, 2002). In the recent 3-year longitudinal study on developing cross-cultural leadership teams in 40 Chinese companies and joint ventures. Wang and Schneider (2003) discovered six key dimensions of team readiness as a competency for leadership development and team effectiveness:

1. Career identity dimension: readiness for challenging jobs, career potential, and career task accomplishment.
2. Team responsibility dimension: readiness for team experimenting, risk-taking, and responsibility building in teamwork.
3. Relationship sharing dimension: readiness for peer discussion, joint problem-solving, and networking among team members.
4. Collective orientation dimension: readiness for team membership, group needs, and group actions.
5. Change initiative dimension: readiness for change, involvement, and opportunities in teamwork.
6. Interdependence dimension: readiness for team-member exchange, leader-member exchange, and unwritten rules.

The results of this research project showed that the first three dimensions of team readiness (career identity, team responsibility, and relationship sharing) significantly affected the effectiveness of cross-cultural leadership teams through team-member exchange, whereas the second three dimensions (collective orientation, change initiative, and interdependence) were functioning through leader-member exchange.

A related research topic is group cohesiveness and team climate as competence, X.L. Xie and Johnes (2000) examined the interactive effects of group cohesiveness and absence culture salience on absence and hypothesized that group cohesiveness and absence culture salience would be negatively related to work-group absence. The potential mediating effect of group absence norm was also tested. Eight hundred employees in a state-owned manufacturing enterprise in China took part in this study. The results showed that aggregate measures of salience and cohesiveness each had a negative relationship with work-group absenteeism respectively. Three levels of analysis revealed consistent support for the interactive effects: individual level, group level, and cross-level models. Yan and Wang's (2000) experimental study used social dilemmas and computer simulations to examine the effects of value orientation on group cooperative behaviour. Their results demonstrated that (1) value orientation significantly affected group cooperative behaviour and cooperation-oriented team members were more cooperative in working with their partners in the experiment; (2) partners' teamwork strategies facilitated group cooperation behaviour in solving social dilemma problems; and (3) value orientation and partner strategy interacted in determining group cooperative behaviour. Team value orientation and team strategies are proved to be among the key HR competencies.

Organizational competency through culture and change

Integrative approach to values and culture

One of the most active areas of research in organizational psychology in China is values and culture (Drenth & Wang, 2000; Higgins & Zheng, 2002; Wang, 1995, 1998, 2001). Morris, Leung, Ames, and Lickel (1999) examined different forms of synergy between emic and etic approaches to research on culture and cognition. The emic or inside perspective follows in the tradition of psychological studies of folk beliefs and in cultural anthropologists' striving to understand culture from "the native's point of view," whereas the etic or outside perspective follows in the tradition of behaviourist psychology and anthropological approaches that link cultural practices to external, antecedent factors, such as economic or ecological conditions, which may not be salient to cultural insiders. Both emic and etic approaches were traditional in studies of the Chinese culture. Drawing on the justice judgment literature, dynamics through which the two approaches proved to stimulate each other's progress, the integrative emic-etic frameworks overcome limitations of narrower frameworks in modelling culture and cognition. They therefore identified advantages of integrative frameworks in guiding responses to the diverse justice sensitivities in international organizations.

While trust and ethics for business practice have long been topics in psychological research in China (Wang, 1993, 1995), more attention has been paid to these areas in the highly competitive business and management environment. Recently, Atuahene-Gima and Li (2001) investigated the dual roles of sales controls and supervisor behaviours as antecedents of salespeople's belief in the benevolence of the supervisor. The study examined these antecedents as moderators of the relationship between supervisee trust and sales performance in the context of selling new products. The results of surveys among 215 field salespeople from high-tech firms in China and 190 from US firms suggested that factors such as supervisor accessibility engender supervisee trust but do not necessarily enhance sales performance. In the Chinese sample, supervisee trust enhanced sales performance when output control was adopted, when the supervisor had a high level of achievement orientation style, and when the salesperson had higher role ambiguity. The results also suggested that the supervisee trust–sales performance relationship was negative when supervisor accessibility was high. In examining business ethics, Ang and Leong (2000) studied Chinese business students in Hong Kong and Singapore. A model of corporate ethics and social responsibility (CESR) was developed and empirically tested. As predicted, it was found that CESR beliefs were negatively related to Machiavellianism and two Confucian concepts, *guanxi* (interpersonal connections) and *mianzi* (face). The authors pointed out several promising directions for future research: (1) to extend the research to the working population, possibly businessmen versus nonbusinessmen, and (2) to incorporate and assess the impact of the various environmental antecedents that drive differences in the levels of *guanxi*, *mianzi*, and Machiavellianism in the Chinese culture.

Cross-cultural competency as the key for leadership development

Several studies have recently focused upon cross-cultural competency models in relation to joint venture research in China (e.g., Leung et al., 2001). Kaye and Taylor (1997) interviewed and surveyed 89 joint-venture hotel expatriate managers about their cross-cultural training and work behaviour, inter-cultural sensitivity (collectivism, individualism, open-mindedness and flexibility), and reactions to the cultural shock. The results showed that cross-cultural orientation training was positively correlated with inter-cultural sensitivity and that, interestingly, expatriates of Asian origin showed greater cultural shock than the non-Asian origin expatriates for a given level of inter-cultural sensitivity. The study has implications for personnel policy in connection with selecting expatriate managers.

Smith, Wang, and Leung (1997) studied event management within 87 joint venture hotels in comparison with state-owned hotels in China. They found that in Chinese managers from the state-owned organizations, event management relied more on widespread beliefs in society, while event management by those managers working in the joint ventures relied more upon the line-management system and their own training and abilities, depending on their overseas partnerships. The cross-cultural competency of leadership teams was also investigated by Wang and Schneider (2003) in their 40-company longitudinal research project. The results of this project showed that four dimensions of leadership competencies were crucial for working in the multicultural leadership team in joint ventures in China. They are:

1. Cultural competence with two key components: the ability to adjust oneself to different cultures (national cultures, regional cultures, new cultures, etc.) and the skill of relationship management such as developing, adapting, and maintaining good relationships and networks with colleagues, superiors, and customers.
2. Achievement competence with two key components: the ability to organize, monitor, and control tasks and the skills of achievement management such as goal-setting and time, deadline, and performance management.
3. Decision competence with two components: the ability to take reasonable risks and responsibilities at work and the ability to make strategic decisions rapidly.
4. Team competence with two components: the high level of group compatibility and the skill of utilizing team resources, especially across cultures.

These four cross-cultural competency dimensions proved to have close relationships with organizational performance and could be used for assessment, selection, and development of multicultural joint venture leadership teams.

What are the key competency components specific to the Chinese culture? Kakabadese and Wang (2003) conducted leadership competence research with two objectives: (1) to change the traditional way of evaluating managers and supervisors, and (2) to identify a comprehensive structure of leadership competency for management selection and evaluation in China as well as in the UK. The results of the factorial structure of management competencies reflected Chinese characteristics in business leadership competency.

1. Holistic competency structure: the structure of Chinese management competencies was more holistic and showed larger competence factors than that of the British and Australian managers.
2. Culturally general competency factors: there appeared to be three culturally general factors—change uncertainty, independence, and work satisfaction. These are similar across several cultures.
3. Culturally specific competency factors: there were three more holistic competency factors—leadership skills, communication, feedback/people skills. These three factors followed the early findings of the three-dimensional organizational interface model from the Chinese enterprises (Wang, 1989), i.e., the personnel expertise (competence), the systems communication structure (networking) and the organizational participation (commitment).

In general, the research results indicated that managers in the Chinese state-owned enterprises had high levels of product-systems managerial competency, whereas joint venture managers showed high levels of business-action managerial competency. In addition, interpersonal relationship skill was the key competence for both types of ownership in China.

Bjorkman and Lu's recent study (2001) adopted a different approach. It demonstrated that institutionalization and bargaining power influenced HR and organizational competency in international joint ventures using a case analysis. They studied 63 Chinese-Western joint ventures and analysed how human resource management practices associated with local professionals and managerial-level employees in international joint ventures. The results showed that overall, the HRM practices resembled those of the foreign parent company more closely than those of local companies. Institutionalization and bargaining power perspective were instrumental in explaining the degree to which the HRM practices in the joint ventures were similar to their parent firms.

Other significant areas of research have focused on organization development and its approaches to organizational competency (Wang, 2000). Sun's work (2000) describes the major problems facing China's state-owned enterprises (SOEs) from the human resources perspective and the needs for organizational development (OD) and change. According to Sun's discussion, six abilities or competence components are needed for the Chinese organizational competencies.

1. Ability to adapt to the fast-changing environment and to resolve ineffectiveness and inefficiency problems.
2. Ability to deploy human resources rationally and resolve the overstaffed and understaffed sections.
3. Ability to improve social security systems and rechannel and laid-off or redundant workforce.
4. Ability to motivate employees and overcome the poor performance of organizations.
5. Ability to retain skilled innovative personnel and resolve labour disputes.
6. Ability to enhance management policies and develop human resource strategies.

In addition, the OD approach will have to overcome barriers from traditional culture values and behavioural patterns, motivation for top executives to change, training for management skills, and unavailability of experienced OD practitioners in China. In order to enhance organizational competency and adaptability, innovative executive training is undertaken, especially in the areas of strategic planning, interpersonal skills, leadership, problem solving, and communication skills. Efforts also need to be devoted to benchmarking the best practices and organizational learning, with an emphasis on OD tools such as survey feedback, organizational diagnosis, and basic change models. In general, building organizational competency becomes a key to future development.

Directions and conclusions

Characteristics of organizational psychology in China

As has been discussed in a number of previous review articles of psychology in China (e.g., Higgins & Zheng, 2002; Jing, 1994; Wang, 1993), the developments of psychology—especially organizational psychology—in China have been closely linked to rapid organizational changes. Recent HR-organizational behaviour practices and research developments also demonstrate the Chinese approach to build up managerial competency and enrich organizational psychology programmes. Recent developments revealed the following characteristics of organizational psychology in China:

1. Active theoretical development and conceptualization: Much research has adopted a competency-based theoretical approach in relation to the Chinese organizational and cultural context. A cross-cultural perspective has frequently been used to develop Chinese adaptive conceptual models.
2. Continuous methodological improvement: Recent studies in organizational psychology in China have significantly improved their methodology. The longitudinal paradigm is more commonly used as an important approach and we see more controlled experiments in relevant fields of organizational psychology research. In particular, more validation studies have been carried out in the areas of personnel assessment and selection, as well as research into HR topics.
3. Close links between research into HR and management practices: We see a closer link between theoretical studies and practical applications of organizational psychology in relation to the new developments in economic reform, high-tech, organization development, and social change.
4. Systematic cross-cultural socioeconomic perspective: This becomes a more frequently used framework for better understanding of the organizational psychology of Chinese employees and cadres under the context of changing corporate culture.

Directions for future research: a three-strategy model

In future research, we expect more systematic studies on organizational psychology. As a model for future research, a three-strategy managerial competency model is proposed and tested under the Chinese organizational setting. The model has three dimensions of strategy:

1. Leadership competence strategy: This strategy will be used to enhance leadership competence through recruitment, selection, training, and team building. A competency analysis method will be used to build up relevant competency models.

2. Leadership networking strategy: This strategy will be adopted to build up an adaptive organizational structure and formulate key networking requirements through strategic job modelling and organizational reengineering.
3. Leadership commitment strategy: This strategy will be implemented to create a participative and visionary leadership as well as a high organizational commitment through career development, participation, retention programmes, and succession planning.

Further research will be actively carried out in a number of new areas of managerial competency development. Executive competency structure will continue to be a key area of organizational research, particularly focusing upon new requirements under WTO and IT development. Entrepreneurship and intrapreneurship are among the active new areas of research in Chinese organizational psychology, HR, and organizational behaviour. While IT has been applied to many business areas, research on virtual teams and organizations will be more active in relation to development and E-commerce. Also, corporate culture and core values are recognized as the key for building up competitive advantages. A significant development will be the integration of organization development models with strategies in international management. The three-strategy managerial competency model will be more widely applied and further tested under various kinds of action research in organizational psychology in China.

References

Ang, S. H., & Leong, S. M. (2000). Out of the mouths of babes: Business ethics and youths in Asia. *Journal of Business Ethics, 28*, 129–144.

Atuahene-Gima, K., & Li, H. Y. (2001). When does trust matter? Antecedents and contingent effects of supervisee trust on performance in selling new products in China and the United States. *Journal of Marketing, 66*, 61–81.

Bjorkman, L., & Lu, Y. (2001). Institutionalization and bargaining power explanations of HRM practices in international joint ventures: The case of Chinese-Western joint ventures, *Organization Studies, 22*, 491–512.

Drenth, P. J. D., & Wang, Z. M. (2000). Work and organizational psychology. In K. Pawlik & M. R. Rosenzweig (Eds.), *International handbook of psychology* (pp. 479–496). London: Sage.

Du, H., & Wang, Z. M., (2003). A comprehensive study of managerial motivation in China. In Z. M. Wang (Ed.), *China HR and OB research review*. Shanghai: the Shanghai People's Press.

Earley, P. C. (1994). Self or group? Cultural effects of training on self-efficacy and performance. *Administrative Science Quarterly, 39*, 89–118.

Heneman, R. L., Charles, H. F. & Wang, Z. M. (2001). Compensation systems in the global context. In N. Anderson, D. S. Ones, H. K. Sinangil, & C. Viswesvaran (Eds.), *Handbook of Industrial, work and organizational psychology, Vol. 2* (pp. 77–92). London: Sage.

Heneman, R. L., Tansky, J. W., Wang, S., & Wang, Z. M. (2002). Compensation practices in small entrepreneurial and high-growth companies in the United States and China. *Compensation and Benefits Review, 34*, 13–22.

Higgins, L. T., & Zheng, M. (2002). An introduction to Chinese psychology: Its historical roots until the present day. *The Journal of Psychology, 136*, 225–240.

Hui, C. H., Gan, Y. Q., & Cheng, K. (2000). The conceptualization and validity of Chinese personality at work questionnaire (CPW). *Acta Psychologica Sinica, 32*, 443–452.

Jing, Q. C. (1994). Development of psychology in China. *International Journal of Psychology, 29*, 667–675.

Kakabadese, A., & Wang, Z. M. (2003). Leadership competency analysis and HR strategy in the Chinese state-owned enterprises and international joint ventures. In Z. M. Wang (Ed.), *China HR and OB research review*. Shanghai: The Shanghai People's Press.

Kaye, M. & Taylor, W. G. K. (1997). Expatriate culture shock in China: A study in the Beijing hotel industry. *Journal of Managerial Psychology, 12*, 496–508.

Leung, K., Wang, Z. M., & Smith, P. (2001). Job attitudes and organizational justice in joing venture hotels in China. *International Journal of Human Resource Management, 12*, 926–945.

Li, F., & Zhang, Y. L. (1998). Measuring self-monitoring ability and propensity: A two-dimensional Chinese scale, *The Journal of Social Psychology, 138*, 758–766.

Lin, W. Q., Zhang, Z. C., & Fang, L. L. (2001). The exploration of influential factors on organizational commitment. *Acta Psychologica Sinica, 33*, 259–263.

Long, L., & Peng, P. (2000). The development of college speciality finder for self-directed search in China. *Acta Psychologica Sinica, 32*, 453–457.

Miao, D. M., Huang, F. E., Chia, R. C., & Ren, J. J. (2000). The validity analysis of the Chinese version MBTI. *Acta Psychologica Sinica, 32*, 324–331.

Morris, M. W., Leung, K., Ames, D., & Lickel, B. (1999). View from inside and outside: Integrating emic and etic insights about culture and justice judgment. *The Academy of Management Review, 24*, 781–796.

Silverthorne, C., & Wang, T. H. (2001). Situational leadership style as a predictor of success and productivity among Taiwanese business organizations. *The Journal of Psychology, 135*, 399–412.

Smith, P. B., Wang, Z. M., & Leung, K. (1997). Leadership, decision-making and cultural context: Event management within Chinese joint ventures. *The Leadership Quarterly, 8*, 413–432.

Sternberg, R. J. (1985). *Beyond IQ: A triarchic theory of human intelligence*. New York: Cambridge University Press.

Sternberg, R. J. (1988). Mental self-government: A theory of intellectual styles and their development. *Human Development, 31*, 197–224.

Sun, J. M. (2000). Organization development and change in Chinese state-owned enterprises: A human resource perspective. *Leadership and Organization Development Journal, 21*, 379–389.

Wakabayashi, M., & Chen. Z. G. (1999). The practices of managerial skills for Asian managers: Comparisons based on managers in Japanese, Chinese and Taiwan corporations. *Forum of International Development Studies, 12*, Monograph, Nagoya University.

Wang, Z. M. (1989). Human-computer interface hierarchy model and strategies in systems development. *Ergonomics, 32*, 1391–1400.

Wang, Z. M. (1993). Psychology in China: A review dedicated to Li Chen. *Annual Review of Psychology, 44*, 87–117.

Wang, Z. M. (1995). Culture, economic reform and the role of industrial and organizational psychology in China. In M. D. Dunnette & L. M. Hough (Eds.), *Handbook of industrial and organizational psychology* (2nd ed.). Palo Alto, CA: Consulting Psychologists Press.

Wang, Z. M. (1997a). Effective team management and cooperative decisions in Chinese organizations. In C. Cooper (Ed.), *Trends in organizational behaviour*. New York: Wiley.

Wang, Z. M. (1997b). Integrated personnel selection, appraisal and decisions: A Chinese approach. In N. Anderson & P. Herriot (Eds.), *International handbook of selection and assessment*. New York: Wiley.

Wang, Z. M. (1998). Conflict management in China. In J. Selmer (Ed.), *International Management in China*. London: Routledge.

Wang, Z. M. (1999). Developing joint-venture leadership teams. In W.H. Mobley, M. J. Gessner, & V. Arnold (Eds.), *Advances in global leadership, Vol. 1*. New York: JAI Press.

Wang, Z. M. (2000). On organizational reform and sustainable business development. *Academy of Management Executives, 14*, 8–11.

Wang, Z. M. (2001). *Managerial psychology*. Beijing: People's Education Press.

Wang, Z. M. (2002). New perspectives and implicit managerial competency modeling in China. In C. L. Cooper & I. T. Robertson (Eds.), *International review of industrial and organizational psychology, Vol. 17*. New York: Wiley.

Wang, Z. M., Charles-Pauvers, B., & Liu, X. P. (2001). Organizational commitment and performance under the Chinese management setting. *Proceedings of the National Conference of Chinese Psychological Society*, 4–8 Nov., Guangzhou, China.

Wang, Z. M., & Chen, M. K. (2002). Managerial competency modeling: A structural equations analysis, *Psychological Science, 6*, 420–428.

Wang, Z. M., & Mobley, W. H. (1999). Strategic human resource management for twenty-first century China. In P. Wright, L. Dyer, J. Boudreau, & G. Milkovich (Eds.), *Research in personnel and human resources management*, Suppl 4 (pp. 353–366). New York: JAI Press.

Wang, Z. M., & Schneider, B. (2003). A longitudinal study on cross-cultural leadership team development in 40 Chinese local and joint venture companies. In Z. M. Wang (Ed.), *China HR and OB research review*. Shanghai: The Shanghai People's Press.

Wu, Z. M., & Zhang, H. C. (2001). The construct validity and structure modeling of assessment center. *Acta Psychologica Sinica, 33*, 372–378.

Xie, J. L., & Johnes, G. (2000). Interactive effects of absence culture salience and group cohesiveness: A multilevel and cross-level analysis of work absenteeism in the Chinese context. *Journal of Occupational and Organizational Psychology, 73*, 31–52.

Xie, X. F., & Xu, L. C. (2000). Risk perception of managerial staff under the working situation. *Acta Psychologica Sinica, 32*, 115–120.

Yan, J., & Wang, Z. M. (2000). The effects of calues orientation on group cooperation in social dilemmas. *Acta Psychologica Sinica, 32*, 332–336.

Yu, J. Y., & Murphy, K. R. (1993). Modesty bias in self-ratings of performance: A test of the cultural relativity hypothesis. *Peronnel Psychology, 46*, 357–363.

Zhang, H. C. (1988). Psychological measurement in China. *International Journal of Psychology, 23*, 101–177.

Zhang, J. X., & Bond, M. H. (1998). Personality and filial piety among college students in two Chinese societies: The added value of indigenous constructs. *Journal of Cross-Cultural Psychology, 29*, 402–418.

Zhang, L. F. (2001). Do thinking styles contribute to academic achievement beyond self-rated abilities? *The Journal of Psychology, 135*, 621–638.

Zhang, W. D. (2001). Study on the dimensionality of the coping inventory (COPE). *Acta Psychologica Sinica, 33*, 55–62.

Zhou, J., & Martocchio, J. J. (2001). Chinese and American managers' compensation award decisions: A comparative policy-capturing study. *Personnel Psychology, 54*, 115–145.

54
INTERNET RECRUITMENT AND SELECTION
Kissing frogs to find princes

Dave Bartram

Source: *International Journal of Selection and Assessment* 8(4) (2000): 261–274.

Abstract

The Internet has already had a dramatic impact on the way in which recruitment and selection are carried out in North America, and the impact is increasingly being felt in terms of changes in practice in Europe and Asia-Pacific. The paper presents a picture of the current development of the Internet as a medium in general and as a recruitment and selection medium in particular. The new medium has enabled the widespread adoption of computer-based assessment and it is predicted that it will replace paper as the default medium before very long. A range of issues are raised and discussed. These include security, confidentiality, authentication, control of assessment conditions, control over practice and equality of access. It is argued that as the second generation of users takes over from the first generation, so inequality of skill and access are becoming less and less of an issue. Finally, some potential areas of abuse of the system are noted and a call is made for the development of international standards to protect the rights and interests of test providers, test users and test takers.

Writing a paper on the topic of Internet Recruitment and Selection represents something of a challenge. The topic of study is relatively new. As a consequence there has been little time for research to have been carried out and found its way into the literature. A search of PsychLit for papers concerned with the Internet and selection or recruitment found nothing.

The field is not only a new one but also one that is changing so rapidly that much of what has been written is now out of date. This rate of change also makes it difficult to provide a clear 'position' paper, as even the current position is likely to have moved significantly by the time this paper appears in print.

One of the functions of this paper will, therefore, be to review the use of the Internet for Recruitment and Selection, how this has evolved in a brief life of four or five years and what the signs are for the future. Having done this, an attempt is made to identify those issues that are likely to be more than transient.

The attraction, recruitment, selection sequence

Before proceeding, it is worth considering the cycle of events involved in recruitment and selection. The process starts with job posting. This involves providing information about the vacancy in such a manner that relevant applicants come to know about it. Job posting is, therefore part of the 'attraction' stage, whereby potential applicants are made aware of the job and encouraged to apply for it. Recruitment can be seen as following on from this, and involves the initial gathering together of a pool of applicants, with the sifting out of those who fail to meet basic requirements. Having recruited a pool of potentially suitable applicants, we move into the selection process where various forms of assessment are used to select those applicants with the best potential for success in the job.

In effect, the first stage (Attraction) draws people into a large pool, the second stage (Recruitment) filters the numbers down by 'selecting out' those who fail to meet key criteria, and the third (Selection) 'selects in' from those who remain. Traditionally, the second-stage sifting has been required in order to reduce the numbers of applicants to a practical size for the more formal and more resource-intensive 'select-in' assessments (interviews, psychometric tests, assessment centre exercises, etc).

We will see that, to date, the Internet's impact has been mainly in the first two (Attraction and Recruitment) of these stages. However, it is increasingly impacting the third (Selection) as well.

Development in the use of computer-based assessment

Bartram (1997) commented on the fact that, despite the potential offered by technology for novel forms of assessment, the literature on computer-based assessment (CBA) within occupational assessment settings has been largely confined to a small number of issues. These have been dominated by the issues relating to the parallel use of computer-based and paper-based versions of the same tests and use of computers to generate descriptive and interpretative reports of test results (Bartram and Bayliss, 1984; Bartram, 1987b, 1989, 1993, 1994). Although computer technology has provided the possibility of implementing adaptive testing using, in particular, Item Response Theory models, the impact of this on general test practice has been slight in the occupational field. However, there are clear signs that attitudes to CBA are changing as people come to appreciate the real benefits of technology for assessment, and as the technological infrastructure needed to support these applications becomes increasingly ubiquitous.

Despite the increasing sophistication of computer-based assessment systems, the tests they contain are, typically, computer implementations of old paper-and-pencil tests. Outside of specialist applications (e.g. Bartram & Dale, 1983; Bartram, 1987a; Bartram, in press), there are very few examples of tests being published on computer that could not also be produced as paper-and-pencil versions. We are beginning to see this situation change.

The use of computer-based testing is increasing rapidly. It has been helped not only by the development of better interfaces, but by the dramatic increases in volume of and accessibility to hardware. The specification of the sort of system one can purchase in the UK for £1000 improves almost daily, with systems at that price being offered with Gigabytes of disc store, full multi-media including DVD and TV input, and masses of bundled software – including a range of Internet Service Providers packs. Internet connectivity is no longer an 'addon'. In addition we have seen the advent of email and restricted Internet services on digital TV systems. Within Europe, the new millennium heralded the appearance of the first generation of WAP mobile phones, with their ability to access the Internet in a wire-less environment. However, the pattern of development is not uniform around the world. Even where the technology is present, some users are more conservative than others in their adoption of that technology.

The impact of the Internet on computer-based assessment

A number of technological and cultural changes are likely to dramatically change the pattern of use over the next few years, making computer-based assessment the 'default' medium, with paper-and-pencil use being restricted to special applications or large scale group testing. However, even in these instances, while paper may remain as a preferred medium for some tests and some test situations, we are likely to see the response mechanism shift from pencil to an Internet-linked WAP device. Over the next five years we will witness a profound revolution in how occupational assessment and testing is carried out. This will have a major impact on the way assessment is carried out within recruitment and selection procedures.

In many ways we can look on 1995 as the real beginning of widespread use of the Internet, the time at which it started to become part of the fabric of many people's everyday lives. In the few years since then, the range of applications and volume of use have mushroomed. For all practical purposes, while the potential of the Internet has been known for many years, it has only just reached the stage of development at which that potential can begin to be realised. We are now at a significant watershed in its development for a number of reasons.

1   Within North America, Europe and Asia-Pacific, we now have widespread availability of inexpensive, high-powered computer systems.

2   As the hardware has become more widespread, so the range of service providers has increased. Now it is as easy to get onto the net as it is to have a phone installed. Indeed, wherever a phone or a cable TV connection has been installed, an Internet connection can be made. Once on the net, you have access to information and services that were previously restricted to expert users or specialists. You can be your own travel agent; you can buy books and other goods from anywhere in the world; you can consult experts, read government reports, or find a new job.
3   The convergence towards common standards has made it commercially viable for service providers to offer users more and more sophisticated applications.
4   The advances in technology have provided us with standard features we would hardly have dreamt of a few years ago: minimum screen resolutions of 1024 × 768 16bit colour; real-time animation, video and sound capabilities; multi-tasking and so on.
5   We have also witnessed an increase in reliability. This is key to the use of computers in testing. Though computer systems are still prone to crashes, hang-ups, and network failures, we are moving rapidly closer to the point where the user expectation is that computers should operate reliably.

Growth of the Internet

Computer networks have existed for a long time. The first use of a hyper-linked network by the US military occurred in 1957. Academic institutions in the UK joined in 1973 when University College London set up the first connection. The first commercial UK IP network was set up in 1989. At the start of this decade, Tim Berners Lee proposed the idea of using a standard graphical browser and a communication standard to provide access to data from any source, and so 'invented' the World-Wide Web (WWW). The Mosaic browser, the first of the WWW browsers, appeared in 1992. In 1994, Netscape was founded and a year later, Microsoft embraced the Internet, having previously dismissed it.

In order to evaluate the potential impact of the Internet on computer-based assessment in general and assessment for recruitment and selection in particular, it is important to get a realistic view of just how widespread the Internet is, and how rapidly accessibility is likely to increase. Like all demographic statistics, numbers of users of the Internet can only be estimated. However, the estimates can be quite robust: for example, the Internet is a system where it is possible to count the number of hosts and IP addresses.

By the year 2002, the Computer Industry Almanac has forecast that 490 million people around the world will have Internet access (CyberAtlas, 1999a). That represents 7.94% of the total world population. By 2005 this will be 11.8%. At the end of last year it was forecast that over 10% of the population of the top 25 user countries will be Internet users. Table 1 shows the numbers of users for the top 15 countries in 1997 and forecast for the end of 1999 (CyberAtlas, 1998, 2000a). Table 2 provides a summary by region (CyberAtlas, 1999a). The dominance of

Table 1 Top 15 nations for Internet usage (in 1,000s) at year-end 1997 and 1999

Country	1997	1999
United States	54,675	110,825
Japan	7,965	18,156
United Kingdom	5,828	13,975
Canada	4,325	13,277
Germany	4,064	12,285
Australia	3,347	6,837
Finland	1,250	
Norway	1,007	
Brazil	861	6,790
Switzerland	767	
China		6,308
France	1,175	5,696
S Korea		5,688
Taiwan		4,790
Italy	841	4,745
Sweden	1,311	3,950
Netherlands	1,386	2,933
Spain	920	2,905

Source: Computer Industry Almanac, cited in CyberAtlas, 1998, and 1999a. Rank order by 1999 figures.

Table 2 Actual and forecast Internet usage worldwide

Region	Users (millions)				Users (percent of population)			
	1995	1998	2000	2005	1995	1998	2000	2005
Worldwide	39.479	150.887	318.650	717.083	0.69	2.54	5.25	11.05
North America	26.217	82.989	148.730	229.790	8.9	27.57	47.91	71.54
Western Europe	8.528	34.741	86.577	202.201	2.17	8.75	21.75	50.14
Eastern Europe	0.369	2.983	9.487	43.767	0.13	1.02	3.27	15.18
Asia-Pacific	3.628	24.559	57.607	171.098	0.11	0.72	1.66	4.59
South & Central America	0.293	2.722	10.766	43.529	0.06	0.55	2.11	7.86
Middle East & Africa	0.444	2.893	7.482	26.708	0.05	0.29	0.72	2.36

Source: Computer Industry Almanac, cited in CyberAtlas, 1999a.

the US is expected to decline, relatively from its current position of having 43% of the total 259 million users to a projected 33% by 2002 and 27% by 2005. Usage within the Far East is growing rapidly and has overtaken Europe in a number of places since 1997.

The exact numbers tend to vary from survey to survey, partly through sampling effects and partly due to differences in the questions asked (e.g. how many people have access *versus* how many people are users). InternetTrak's survey in November 1998 found 7 million people online in the UK. NOP Research claimed that at least 10.6 million people accessed the Internet at least once during 1998. The Computer Industry Almanac estimated 8.1 million people on line at the end of 1998. (All three studies cited in CyberAtlas, 1999b). The Nielsen//Net Rating Inc. provide a more fine grain monthly analysis, distinguishing, for example, between those who have actually been online sometime during the month and those who could have been online. For home users, the Active Internet Universe (i.e. those who actually used the Internet) was 77 million in February 2000 while the Current Universe Estimate (i.e. those who have access from home) was 122.9 million (Nielsen Net Ratings Inc, 2000). What is clear, however, is that the numbers are substantial and that they are growing very rapidly.

The increasing numbers of users is not just a matter of increasing volume. The range of uses to which the Internet will be put will also increase dramatically. Almost certainly one big area for expansion is in business-to-business (B2B) commerce. This already dominates the e-commerce sector. In 1997, 92% of all e-commerce transactions in Europe were B2B. Even in UK retailing (business to customer, or B2C), it is predicted that Internet sales will constitute around 2.5% of all retail sales over the next few years, with more in the USA and other European countries.

The geographical divide

Estimates of volumes of trade vary considerably. However, there is agreement that there are clear geographical divides in access that are likely to remain for some time to come (see Table 2).

Erbschloe (quoted in CyberAtlas, 2000b) predicts that e-commerce activity in the regions of North America, Europe and Asia-Pacific will grow to $9.5 trillion by 2003, and account for 93% of the world total. For B2B transactions an expected $2.9 trillion in 2000 will grow to $9.2 trillion by 2003. For B2C, the rate of increase will be greater, but the value far less: a seven-fold increase on year 2000 expectations to a total of $0.3 trillion by 2003. B2C transactions are likely to be even more confined to the key geographical areas, with an expected 99.9% taking place in North America, Europe and Asia Pacific.

The number of businesses involved in e-commerce is increasing very rapidly in the areas where the infrastructure is now in place (US, Europe, Asia-Pacific). For example, (eBusiness Report cited in CyberAtlas, 2000b):

- In the US there are 590,000 firms conducting e-commerce. By the end of this year, the figure is expected to be 820,000.
- Small businesses will make the biggest advances in e-commerce revenues, growing from $14.3 billion (1999) to $177 billion by 2003.
- Medium and large businesses will continue to account for the majority of revenues, increasing from $57.1 billion (1999) to $477.3 billion by 2003.

Forrester Research predict that by 2002, 98% of large companies, 85% of medium sized ones (100-1000 employees) and 45% of small ones will be online.

Attraction and recruitment on the Internet

A major consequence of the rapid growth of the Internet and its increasing accessibility is that increasing numbers of organisations are recruiting and selecting applicants for jobs online. In addition, applicants for jobs and job-seekers are increasingly expecting to find work through the Internet rather than more traditional means.

The recent Electronic Recruiting Index (ERI, 2000) shows a substantial increase in spending on e-recruiting in 1999. For 1998 the total was about $4.5 billion, while in 1999 it jumped to over $15 billion. The ERI forecasts steady growth from around $18 billion in 2000 to nearly $40 billion by 2005. What is interesting is that spending on site development is expected to level off at $15 billion pa by this year, with the major source of growth being in job posting fees (rising from $1.425 billion last year to $15 billion by 2005).

It is interesting to note who visits job sites. The majority of visitors are employed people who are not actively thinking of changing jobs (71%). Of the remainder 15% are thinking about changing jobs, 10% are actively looking for a new job and 5% are unemployed (ERI, 1999). The 1999 ERI report (based on 1998 figures) estimated 150 million jobs posted on the Internet, served by more than 2,500 job boards (some more recent estimates suggest that the number of job boards is now around 5,000). The top two sites in April 1999 were AOL Workplace with over 3.2 million visitors and Monstor.com with 1.739 million (Media Matrix, 1999, cited in Lawrence, 1999), while the bottom of the top-10 sites recorded nearly 0.25 million visitors.

The following figures (Lawrence, 1999) provide some idea of the volume of traffic the top sites handle. In mid 1999, Monstor.com had 3 million registered users all of whom were getting customised email updates about jobs offered by 60,000 employers. There were 215,000 job vacancies listed and 1.5 million resumes/CVs on the site with about 4,000 new resumes/CVs coming in each day. Monstor.com's CEO claims that one in four users are offered a job, with those being offered getting an average of three offers each.

Lawrence (1999) notes that while, according to Forrester Research, only 14% of recruiting budgets were spent on online job boards in 1998, by now, the figure is likely to have risen to 32%, with newspaper classified advertising dropping from 70% to 52%. The recent Institute of Personnel and Development (IPD, 1999) survey on recruitment in the UK sampled 269 organisations and found that use of the Internet had risen from 14% of respondents in 1997, through 19% in 1998 to 32% in 1999.

Park HR and the Guardian carried out an interview survey of 100 senior HR executives and personnel directors in the UK in September 1998 (Park, 1999). Those interviewed represented organisations drawn mainly from the Times top 500, and were focused on graduate recruitment. In 1997 54% of them had access to the Internet. By the time of the survey this had increased to 73%, with a corresponding increase in the use of it for graduate recruitment. 88% of companies recruiting 50 or more graduates per year advertise on their own website. For those recruiting 20 or fewer, the figure was 29% (average 55%). Larger companies are also more likely to make use of other e-recruitment opportunities, while 40% of smaller companies did not make use of the Internet at all. Overall, in addition to 55% using their own website for job posting, 48% used specialist graduate recruitment websites, 44% accepted applications by email, and 22% used general recruitment websites.

More recently, the Association of Graduate Recruiters in the UK (AGR, 2000) reported the results of a survey that showed the number of recruiters recruiting online has doubled since 1999 from one third to two thirds of them all. Nearly 90% of graduates are now seeking their first jobs on the Internet and nearly 50% are applying online. What is more interesting is that employers report that the quality of applicants who apply online is higher than that of those who apply by traditional methods.

Interestingly, the major change envisaged by the respondents as a consequence of growing use of the Internet was the demise of the handwritten application form. This reflects the growing trend to move away from the posting of CVs and resumes, to the use of structured application forms systematically covering biographical data, experience, skills etc.

The downside

While job boards are able to handle very high volumes of both job seekers and recruiters, they do not, by themselves, solve the problem of quality. '… reaching a consistent set of quality candidates online is a goal yet to be realised for most corporate users. As one executive interviewed by Forrester so eloquently put it, "We have to sift through lots of résumés, like kissing frogs before you find the prince."' (Lawrence, 1999).

The key to sorting the frogs from the princes lies in using the new technology to apply valid objective assessment techniques to the initial sift process. At present most job search sifting is carried out using purely demographic criteria and checks on relevant experience. The future lies in developing structured assessments that can be completed online by job seekers and that can be shown to be job relevant. By doing this, it becomes possible to re-position online recruitment as a process of matching the competencies and capabilities of the applicant to the requirements of the job vacancy, and so produce a high quality shortlist that only contains princes.

These changes in technology need to be considered together with changes in recruitment practice. A major trend in personnel management has been the decentralisation of many operational responsibilities to staff at business unit, departmental or line-management level. The IPD (1999) survey referred to earlier showed that in the UK, line-managers are involved in determining recruitment criteria 97.4% of the time. The figures for central personnel staff (55.2%) and local personnel staff (36.6%) are much lower.

This trend to shift responsibility for recruitment and selection out to line management has implications for the design of selection systems. It is no longer safe to assume that a small number of highly trained personnel professionals will over-see the recruitment and selection procedures within their organisation. Thus, while needing to increase the sophistication of the recruitment and selection tools (to counter the increasing volumes of applicants available through online methods), we also need to 'de-skill' these tools from the point of view of the user. While it may be desirable, it is not practical to expect line managers in organisations to complete formal test training courses before they begin to recruit personnel. Given such realities, the challenge for occupational psychologists is to design tools that are objective and job-relevant but also easy and safe to use by relatively unskilled users.

Changing patterns in types of jobs advertised online

There is an assumption that the Internet is only really used to recruit people into technical positions (primarily IT). This is no longer the case. When HotJobs.com launched its site in 1996 it was almost entirely populated with listings for programmers. Now, less than half the listings on Hot Jobs represent traditional IS positions. Other main listings cover higher-salaried positions, marketing, and engineering. Sites that recruit for non-technical and management positions have become the major growth area (Hoffman, 1999). Futurestep (the net based arm of the executive search firm, Korn/Ferry) deals specifically with middle manager positions in the $75,000–$150,000 range (candidates' average salaries are $98,000).

Data from CareerMosaic (CyberAtlas, 1999c) supports the argument that the jobs people are searching for online are becoming less technical. Table 3 shows the figures for 25 job categories. The top two are management and sales – not IS. According to SBC Internet Services (cited in CyberAtlas, 1999d), 82% of college students in the US who are due to graduate this summer will use the Internet to search for job openings, and 66% of them will use e-mail to post their applications, with most posting them through an online job service. The same survey also found that 75% of 1999 graduates will use the Internet to research a specific job or career and 79% will use it to research prospective employers.

While Internet recruitment has moved into the middle management bands, it is deemed unlikely to replace traditional search methods for the top executive positions. However, it needs to be noted that the majority of people looking at job sites are people who have been defined as 'passive' job seekers (i.e. they are not currently actively seeking a new job). This is perhaps an unfortunate term, as such people may be in the process of actively managing their career and keeping up to date with what is available on the job market.

Table 3 Top job searches on CareerMosaic during January to June 1999 (CyberAtlas, 1999c).

Rank	Title/field	Searches
1	Manager/management	1,763,471
2	Sales	827,685
3	Engineer	642,723
4	Accounting	468,739
5	Marketing	430,465
6	Human Resource	396,366
7	Administrative/Clerical	373,601
8	Finance	351,165
9	Computer	310,066
10	Analyst	251,063
11	Programmer	230,732
12	Nurse	198,554
13	Technician	186,682
14	Network/Network Admin	175,715
15	Legal	174,578
16	Teacher	167,070
17	Customer Service	155,179
18	Consultant/Consulting	154,151
19	Secretary	152,957
20	Medical	148,630
21	Information Technology	146,594
22	Training/Trainer	133,096
23	Writer	122,022
24	Executive	115,952
25	Entry Level	102,983

Making the process more robust and user friendly

In larger organisations we are seeing the emergence of a new position in the HR department: that of Internet recruiter. A survey of over 1000 organisations found that half had hired up to 20% of their workforce as a direct result of Internet recruiting, more than 80% had career sites on their homepage and about 35% of the companies with more than 10,000 employees had at least one dedicated Internet recruiter (from poll carried out by Recruiter's Network, cited in CyberAtlas, 1999e).

It is being realised that the company's website is a key component in creating an image of the organisation. The most frequent use of the website is by job seekers who use it to move on to the organisation's career site. As the number of general job boards increase, so job seekers will increasingly need to target their searches effectively. Going direct to the careers site of preferred organisations is one way of doing this.

A recent report suggested that US corporations could be losing $30 million per day because their recruiting sites are too difficult for many job seekers to use (report from Creative Good, cited in CyberAtlas, 1999e). The survey looked at the problems job seekers encountered in applying for jobs on six corporate sites (including Cisco, Proctor & Gamble and Citibank). 74% of job seekers experienced some degree of failure in applying for the job online. More than 40% of tests ended in complete failure–a rate that would be quite unacceptable for any other medium.

On the more positive side, an SHL survey (Wroe, 2000) of over 45,000 candidates who completed an online selection process at two corporate web sites, showed that 92% were either positive or very positive about the process. 93% found it easy or very easy to complete, while only 1% found it difficult or very difficult. Even more interesting is that 48% of them viewed the company they were applying to more positively after completing the process, 51% reported no change, and only 1% viewed them less positively. Wroe concludes that 'the results may indicate that companies who provide an online application and true selection process on the Internet are viewed as more interactive, accessible and cutting-edge than companies who don't offer these services'.

Making the process faster

Futurestep claim they can fill vacancies in as little as 10 days (Hoffman, 1999). Our own research in the US indicates a typical time from job posting to hire of 16 days for Internet based recruitment as opposed to 32 days or more for traditional methods. Creative Good (CyberAtlas, 1999e), in the survey described above, found that a well-designed e-recruiting site can save a company $8000 per hire and reduce the hiring cycle time by 60 days.

Future job-seeking scenario

In the light of the above, consider how you will expect to look for a new job in the next few years. As a job seeker, you will access a job-seeker web-site, complete a general competency profile. Your personal Web Agent will then e-mail this to a number of job boards, with your multi-media structured CV attached. It will also search the net for you for information on companies that you might be interested in working for. You will be able to read the company reports, track back their performance on the stock market, and see who their key clients are. You may decide to view some realistic job previews and may try out some work sample exercises. If you like what you see, you can submit an initial application for a job.

Having declared an active interest in certain types of position, recruitment search processes will bring you to the attention of relevant companies, and you will receive invitations from some of these to make an application.

The companies you decide to apply to will sift your application and, if you're successful, contact you through your mobile WAP portal and ask you to provide additional information about yourself, complete some questionnaires and schedule an interview appointment. All this could be done within the space of a couple of hours, interactively through your digital mobile phone or TV Internet browser, all without you leaving your armchair. Even the initial interview could be carried out using a TV-based videophone.

Having passed the initial interview, you are invited to take some tests and complete some assessment exercises. As they have to be supervised, you are given the online booking form to book a convenient time at your local assessment centre, where your identity is checked, and the centre's administrator authenticates and supervises your assessments (which are, of course, all computer-administered).

Of course, you may not be sure what sort of job to apply for. The net will provide you with the opportunity to explore your profile of skills and competencies, work on personal development plans and help you consider your potential fit to various employers. As noted earlier, this is not only possible, but much of it is actually happening now. What we will see over the next few years is that this will become normal practice rather than exceptional.

Implications for selection procedures

To date, the main impact of the Internet has been on Attraction and Recruitment (the first two of the three stages identified earlier) rather than Selection. However, the future impact is likely to be increasingly seen on this final stage as well.

There are a number of selection assessment processes that will be affected:

- Interviews
- Reference checks
- Assessment Centre exercises
- Objective assessments (psychometric tests of personality, ability and so on).

Internet interviews

Some use is already made of the telephone for structured interviewing (Edenborough, 1994). However, the face-to-face interview serves a range of social functions other than the collection of information about the applicant (e.g. see Herriot, 1989). One of the defining elements of a job interview is that it is an interactive dialogue between at least two people. It provides the opportunity for the applicant to learn about their potential employers and acts as a forum in which negotiation can take place between the parties.

Through video-conferencing, the Internet provides the possibility of a halfway house between the telephone interview and the 'live' face-to-face interview. Video-conferencing provides the employer with the opportunity to conduct single, pair or panel interviews without having the cost of transporting applicants to a common interview site. Certainly for overseas applicants, video-conference interviewing provides a major saving in cost and (for the applicant) time. Most PCs can now have a low-cost video-camera attached to provide an Internet-based video-phone system. By the middle of this decade we will see domestic digital TV with built in cameras being used as video-phones as part of their role as general-purpose multi-media entertainment and information centres. This will enable high fidelity interviewing to take place without applicants having to leave their homes.

It is likely that for certain job there will remain a final stage at which the job applicant and the employer need to meet face-to-face before entering into a formal employment contract. However, the role of this final meeting could shift away from that of an assessment process (as the information can be collected more efficiently online) towards that of discussing and agreeing the psychological contract between applicant and employer. We could then see the interview become an event that occurs between the formal job offer being made and the applicant's acceptance or rejection of it.

Reference checks

It is already quite common to seek and transmit references by phone and by email. The use of the Internet to deliver structured and adaptive reference checks will add to the range of ways in which this information can be collected. It will also provide an effective means of providing a higher level of control over the administration of the reference-checking instrument. The same techniques can be used as are currently used in the systematic collection of information for 360 feedback.

Formal checking (subject to the necessary search and access permissions having been obtained) of medical, criminal and credit records could become very highly automated, as all the relevant data will be held on databases which have (secure) Internet access.

Key issues in relation to references and checks will be ones of permission and privacy. To avoid abuses, applicants should have to provide permission before data about themselves can be accessed and provided to a third party (i.e. the potential employer). Applicants should also have the right to see and comment on information provided by referees.

Assessment centres

It is in the area of both group and individual assessment exercises that some particularly exciting new possibilities emerge. One of the earliest applications of the Internet (well before the advent of the World Wide Web) was for multi-user games such as Dungeons and Dragons. It is now possible to create multi-user exercises (e.g. business simulations) that can be closely monitored and assessed. The users need not be brought together to a single location, but could form part of a virtual assessment or development centre. While such procedures may have a greater part to play in training and development, they could also be used in a selection context.

For single user exercises, web-based in-basket exercises are already being developed. These can be designed as relatively simple systems, for non-experienced users, or use software like MS Outlook. In either case, people can be provided with emails, phone messages, background information and have to work to obtain a set of objectives within some pre-defined constraints. The user can set tasks, make appointments, send emails and so on. All the actions and events can be logged, analysed and assessed. The great challenge is how to objectify the scoring of tasks such as this.

The potential advantage of making such tasks Internet based is that it removes the geographical constraints on having to bring people together to take part in an assessment.

Objective testing

Use of the Internet for the deliver of objective assessments is technically straightforward. Java applets, for example, can be written that provide high levels of control over the presentation of material and the timing of tests and responses. The use of downloaded applets also ensures that tests are not affected by denials of service from the user's ISP occurring during a test session.

As discussed earlier, there have been major developments in the science and technology of computer-based assessment (in the areas of IRT, item generation, task-based testing, simulations and so on). To date, these advances have not been translated into widespread commercial application. The Internet is likely to change that, as it provides the business infrastructure necessary for the commercial exploitation of these developments.

As the market for Internet-delivered computer-based testing develops, so the issue of ensuring those using such tests and assessment tools follow good practice will increase in importance. While issues of good practice apply generally to assessment over the Internet, they are of particular importance when we consider supervised testing.

Issues of good practice relating to the use of the Internet for assessment

The main issues are security, confidentiality, authentication, control over test conditions, control over practice and equality of access.

- Security: How does one protect the test publisher's and author's intellectual property rights and how does one ensure the security of people's confidential data?
- Confidentiality: How does one ensure that a test taker's results are held confidentially and only released to those with a right and a need to know?
- Authentication: How does one ensure that the person taking the test is the person they say they are?
- Control over test conditions: How does one ensure there is no breakdown of service in the middle of a test session? How does one ensure that they are taking the test unaided?

- Control over practice: How does one ensure that all test takers have had sufficient practice, without them having been over-exposed to specific test content?
- Equality of access: How does one ensure that relevant populations of job applicants have equivalent access to the Internet?

More generally, how does one provide the technological infrastructure to support and encourage good practice, and try to ensure that tests are not used inappropriately?

Security and control: the Internet, Intranets and Extranets

The controlled administration of computer-based tests to large groups of test takers has been possible for some time through the use of local-area networks on a single site – in one room – or on a more widely distributed basis. The former is currently used in many areas of centralised testing. For example, the MICROPAT pilot selection system (Bartram, 1995a) is currently being used on a 20-station network by the Republic of Singapore Air Force in Singapore and on a 10-station network by British Airways at Heathrow. In both cases, these are secure, closed networks over which it is possible to exercise direct administrator control.

Intranets and Extranets now provide the means of exercising this same level of control using web-based technology. An Intranet is, in effect, a closed-Internet that operates within an organisation. It can be designed so that it is not possible for people to enter it from outside, even though Intranet users can access the wider Internet. An Extranet operates, functionally, like an Intranet, but can be distributed throughout the Internet. Extranets could be used, for example, to provide a network of secure test administration stations, with only those stations on the Extranet being able to run tests.

The use of proxy servers, the embedding of transactions within SSL (Secure Socket Layer) and various forms of encryption all provide solutions to issues of ensuring adequate security over the transmission and storage of sensitive and confidential data. The concerns many people and businesses have relating to security of information on the Internet are often unrealistic or outdated. A well-designed Internet system can be far more secure than many local computer network systems or intranets, and certainly more secure than paper and filing cabinets.

In many cases, we are likely to see a mixture of Extra- and Intranet systems providing the vehicle for delivery of testing under controlled and secure conditions. By combining Intranet and secure Extranet technology we will see some of the biggest potential gains in terms of control over test materials and test data, data security and gains in assessment speed and efficiency in the short term. In the longer term, we will probably witness an increasing realisation that trying to keep your data secure at home rather than trusting it to a secure Internet provider is about as sensible as keeping your money under the mattress rather than in a bank.

Control over administration and authentication

It is quite possible not only to require a qualified test user or test administrator to log on, authenticate the test candidate, and log off confirming the session was properly completed, but also to prevent access to certain test materials outside particular physical locations. For example, MBA applicants are now tested on the GMAT via the Internet under supervision at authorised testing centres (see *http://www.gmat.org*). As part of their TOEFL 2000 program, Educational Testing Services (ETS) have developed Internet-based multi-media TOEFL assessments (*http://www.toefl.org*) that are managed by Sylvan Technology Centers at over 300 locations around the world.

It is difficult to envisage any alternative, at present, to the need for a 'responsible and accountable' other person to be present during any assessment where issues of authentication and control over 'cheating' matter. Thus, one still needs a test administrator for these situations. However, with well-designed tests, using interactive adaptive instructions and examples, the role of the test-administrator will become increasingly one of an invigilator. This is the most practical way of ensuring that the person taking the test does so unaided, and does not bring in to or remove from the testing situation materials that would constitute unfair aids to their performance. Just as stand-alone computer-based tests require the presence of a qualified test administrator, so will distance-assessment techniques (though TV video-surveillance technology could provide an alternative to the need for the physical presence of a test administrator).

In most areas, Internet-based assessment provides the potential for higher levels of control and security. The only material in the public domain will be the actual items that appear on the Web browser, and the reports generated by the software. All the sensitive materials remain secure on the host server: there are no scoring keys to pass on to unauthorised or unqualified users. Test scores are also potentially far more secure. Access to results can be controlled very precisely and made dependent on user qualification level and access rights. Detailed audit trails can be obtained of who did what, to whom and when.

Controlling test-taker experience

Current stand-alone testing technology provides no way for an employer to control or assess the number of times an applicant may have taken a particular test. The value of the information tests provide about differences between people depends on all those taking the test starting from a level playing field in terms of prior test experience and sophistication. It is well established that practice increases scores on ability tests (Kulik et al, 1984; Hunter et al, 1990; Feltham, 1991), and that cultural differences can interact with these effects (Jensen, 1980; Kurz, Lodh, & Bartram, 1993) through, for example, differential changes in speed/accuracy trade-off strategies. Recent evidence (Burke, 1997) suggests that practice effects are not only substantial for most types of ability test, but that they persist for periods of up to five years without any decrement.

It is widely acknowledged (e.g. Kellett, 1991; Callan & Geary, 1994) that we should provide people who are to be assessed, with the opportunity for practice, such that when the final assessment is taken, they are all performing at or close to their asymptotic level. In the past, this has not been possible. Until recently, the only practical mechanism for giving people experience of testing has been through the use of practice tests or dissemination of information leaflets that provide examples of test items.

The Internet provides an ideal mechanism for making practice test materials available to people. Indeed, where testing is being used in this 'formative assessment' mode, the complex issues of test user authentication and supervision are of lesser importance, so long as the test content is different from that used for selection testing. The SHL Direct for Students site[1] provides example items for verbal, numerical, and diagrammatic tests as well as personality inventory items in both rating and ipsative format. In addition, complete timed practice tests are available for potential test-takers. A range of other test publishers now provide Internet based practice (though these generally do not include timed test items).

Access and the 'digital divide'

There has been much concern expressed about the Internet creating a 'digital divide' between those with access to computer technology and those without (Keller, 1996). It has already ready been noted that this is currently true on a geographical basis, with nearly all of the infrastructure and development of business taking place in North America, Europe and Asia-Pacific. This will change over the coming decade, but for some time we will not be able to use the Internet as the sole source of recruitment and selection in countries outside these three main areas.

However, if we consider just those areas where the infrastructure is well developed, does everyone have equal access to it? In considering any selection and recruitment process we need to consider its potential for adversely impacting on one or more particular groups within the population. From the point of litigation, the main 'protected' groups are ethnic minorities, women, and people with disabilities. More generally we should be concerned about equality of access in terms of geographical dispersion (rural vs urban), age, educational background and any other factors that may not be directly job relevant, but have an effect on access to the recruitment process.

The Georgia Institute of Technology GVU surveys[2] have tracked changing demographic patterns in the use of the Web in a series of ten surveys carried out every 6 months, starting in January 1994. These show very interesting patterns of change in the demographics of web users as well as an increase in the total numbers.

Gender

The proportion of males in the web population has fallen steadily from nearly 95% in April 1994 to around 60% now (see Table 4). Similar figures are found from the Neilsen Media Research survey data. The latest GVU survey (Kehoe et al, 1999) shows some evidence of a reversal of this trend. However, it is argued that this may be an artifact of changes in sampling methodology rather than a general change in trend.

The growth in percentage of female users in Europe and other areas lags that in the USA, but is still showing a steady increase. Most interesting, is that regardless of geographic location, new users (those who have been online for less than a year) are quite gender-balanced with 48.5% being female and 51.5% being male. Furthermore, if one looks at the breakdown by level of user skill, then those who were novices were nearly equally divided between male and female.

Age

The Tenth GVU survey (Kehoe et al, 1999) shows an increase in average age from 35.1 years old in the Ninth survey (GVU, 1998) to 37.6 years old in the Tenth (see Table 5). The age profile for Europe is quite different from the US profile, showing again the 'lag' in development of the population. Males and females are identical in average age. The more experienced users tend to have been on the web longer and to be younger than the less experienced. This supports the view that the generation of new users is generally older than the generation of early Internet users: The average age for someone with less than one year on the Web increased by 4.5 years to 41.4 years old.

Table 4 Changing ratio of male to female web users from GVU Surveys 1 through 9 (GVU, 1998), Survey 10 (Kehoe et al, 1999), and CommerceNet, Nielsen Media Research surveys (cited in Tchong, 1999).

GVU Survey results		Nielsen results	
Date	Percent female	Date	Percent female
April 94	5.4		
Oct 94	9.7		
April 95	15.5		
Oct 95	29.3	Aug 95	33
April 96	31.5	Apr 96	34
Oct 96	31.4		
April 97	33.9	Jan 97	42
Oct 97	38.5	Sep 97	43
April 98	38.7	Jun 98	43
Oct 98	33.6	Apr 99	46

Table 5 Breakdown of average ages of users in the GVU 9 and GVU 10 surveys (Kehoe et al, 1999).

		GVU10	GVU9
Entire Sample	All	37.6	35.1
Location	USA	38.5	34.4
	Europe	30.9	35.5
	Other	34.4	36.0
Gender	Female	37.6	28.8
	Male	37.5	30.9
Years on the Web	< 1 Yr.	41.4	36.9
	1–3 Yrs	38.0	35.0
	> 3 Yrs	36.3	34.3
Skill Level	Novice	41.1	
	Intermediate	39.5	
	Experienced	36.3	
	Expert	34.1	

Race

As in all previous surveys, the respondents in the 10th GVU Survey are predominantly white (87.2% Tenth, 87.4% Ninth). Hoffman & Novak (1998) found that although income explained race differences in computer ownership and Web use, education did not (though education and income are related). Furthermore, they found no difference between white and African American students when students had a home computer. But when they did not have a home computer, white students were more likely to use the Web than African American students. The key concern within the US is that 'the Internet may provide for equal economic opportunity and democratic communication, but only for those with access' (Hoffman & Novak, 1999).

Hoffman & Novak (1999) report a detailed analysis of data from three surveys carried out by CommerceNet and Nielsen from Spring 1997 through to Spring 1998. Amongst the many complex findings, they note that 'although whites are still more likely to own a PC and to have PC access at work, these gaps are not increasing over time. Further, gaps in cable and satellite ownerships have disappeared.' As we see a move from PC-based to digital-TV based Internet provision, this shift could do much to equalise access. However, what remains unclear from the research is why there are differential rates of usage even when one controls for access. This suggests that some minority groups may regard the Internet as less relevant for them and be more pessimistic about the advantages it might offer. However, the data suggest that the picture is more complex than this. When one examines recent Web users (i.e. the Second Generation), a different pattern emerges. The gap between white and African American web use at home has decreased substantially and the latter group are now relatively more likely than whites to have used the Web from work, school or other locations.

Disability

People with disabilities that might hinder them in completing an application procedure, but which are not job relevant, must be provided with alternative means of application. Computer-based approaches to assessment provide a great deal of potential for accommodating a range of disabilities. On-screen content can be spoken, print size can be enhanced and so on. People with motor disabilities can also make use of alternative input devices (e.g. a mouth or foot operated mouse). The main concern is to ensure that the same good practice is applied to recruitment and selection using the Internet as would be applied when using other methods.

Second generation Internet users and the equalisation of access

We can define two generations of web users. The first generation users are those who were there in the early days, who transitioned from pre-WWW Internet to the WWW in the mid 90s and who are predominantly computer-skilled, young, white, male users. The second generation users are those who have come to use the WWW as it has become a part of the fabric of their work and home life (typically in the last two or three years in the USA and the last 12–18 months in Europe). The latter generation are pretty equally divided between males and females, reasonably balanced in terms of ethnic mix, are older than first generations users and do not aspire to the higher levels of technical user-skill of the earlier generation.

In relation to recruitment and selection, it will be important to ascertain that there is equality of access amongst the relevant applicant populations. The data suggest that inequality of access may be a greater issue for lower paid jobs than, say, for graduate level ones, and more of an issue when the only available means of application would be a home-based PC.

In taking such effects into account it will be important for recruiters to seek up-to-date information on relevant local demographics. As has been noted, patterns of access and use are changing very rapidly, and differ from country to country.

For positions where these considerations might create inequality of access, it is important that alternative routes of application are provided. However, this will create complications for recruiters, as traditional routes are slower than Internet ones. If one uses a mixed model, all the speed advantage of time to hire will be lost.

The impact of globalisation on assessment practice

A final set of issues to consider relates to the internationalisation of testing. There is now a wide range of possible geographical configurations for test-taker, test, test administrator and client organisation. Consider the following scenario:

> An Italian job applicant is assessed at a test centre in France using an English language test. The test was developed in Australia by an

international test developer and publisher, but is running from an ISP located in Germany. The testing is being carried out for a Dutch-based subsidiary of a US multinational. The position the person is applying for is as a manager in the Dutch company's Tokyo office. The report on the test results, which are held on the multi-national's Intranet server in the US, are sent to the applicant's potential line-manager in Japan having first been interpreted by the company's outsourced HR consultancy in Belgium.

Such a possibility raises a host of questions, including:

- Which country's test standards and codes of practice apply?
- Who is the test user?
- How does the test supplier decide on user qualification issues?
- In which country does the test user need to have their qualification?
- Where does the responsibility lie for ensuring that the test is suitably adapted to the culture and language of the test taker and that the report generated is appropriate for the client?
- Who chooses the language of assessment?
- What norms are used?
- What redress can the test taker have if they feel they have been treated unfairly, and to whom in which country?

While some of these are issues of standards and good practice, others have legal implications that have yet to be addressed internationally (e.g., the need for convergence on data protection legislation).

Future developments: opportunities and dangers

Before long, a high proportion of homes in North America, Europe and Asia-Pacific will have direct interactive access to the Web through the use of fibre-optic cable TV links. This is likely to dramatically increase levels of home-based traffic and will open up new possibilities for educational and occupational assessment in the home.

Technologies are converging to the point where it will be increasingly difficult to differentiate between PCs, TVs and telephones. As this happens, so interactive voice-response (IVR) technology will develop and merge with current Internet based and video-phone technologies to provide a future seamless interactive communication medium. Digital domestic phones have similar features to digital mobile phones. Last year the President and CEO of Nokia estimated that there would be 300 million mobile phone users by the end of 1998, rising to one billion by 2005, and that 'a substantial portion of the phones sold that year will have multimedia capabilities.' (These estimates are in line with those from a recent Dataquest survey). Key to this development is the Wireless Application

Protocol (WAP). This is the open global standard for providing wireless Internet access from handheld devices. WAP mobile phones are widely available in Europe. The total number of wireless portal users is expected to grow from 0.3 million users this year to 24.8 million by 2006 (Strategis Group report, cited in CyberAtlas, 2000c). Given the rapid growth in mobile telephony, especially in Europe, this may be an underestimate.

Access to the Web can now be obtained on a PC, TV or phone/palmtop, and the web can be used for making phone calls, both audio and video. Interactive digital TV will become increasingly portable and soon merge with the developments in mobile telephony. UMTS (universal mobile telephony services) will carry an average 144,000 bits/sec compared to the current 9,600 bits/sec of current mobile phones. It will be capable of performing multimedia functions, including Internet access and email.

All these developments will bring both advantages and disadvantages. The advantages will lie in the opening up of access to very sophisticated communications technology. Test producers and publishers will be able to assume the availability and accessibility of a ubiquitous infrastructure through which to deliver new products and services. Test users and test takers will have access to a wider range of services, better matched to their needs and better supported. Test designers will be able to consider new possibilities for assessment design: real-time interactive virtual group exercises using emails or videophone conferencing; realistic in-tray tasks; and so on.

The advantages of the internet are also its dangers. Anyone can now set up a home-page and 'publish' a test. Assessment authoring systems are already available for producing and delivering simple tests and questionnaires on the Web. Dozens of 'tests' can be found that provide interesting looking reports (a quick search of the web for measures of Emotional Intelligence, for example, found more than a dozen questionnaires). However, there is typically no indication of the quality of these and the unwary user can be forgiven for failing to distinguish between serious assessment and trivia.

Many authors of these 'tests' claim they are 'non-psychometric'. This is an odd claim, as a measurement instrument cannot be 'non-psychometric.' It may have good, bad or unknown psychometric properties, but that is a different matter. From the test user and test taker's points of view, it is becoming increasingly difficult to discriminate between good tests and bad. In testing, the medium is not the message, as the quality of the test is always hidden in the technical data. As a result, the emphasis placed by the major publishers on technical and ethical standards and good practice will become increasingly important.

We need to consider the implications of the new technology on standards and good practice in assessment (Bartram, 1995b, c). In particular, though, we need to do this at an international level. National professional associations and national publishers can no longer operate as closed systems. The presence of international networks, globalisation of industry and communications means that testing is now an international activity and individual nations need to be prepared to work as open systems within agreed international standards frameworks. The work of the International Test Commission on test adaptation and test user guidelines (Bartram, 1998) provides a valuable starting point for future developments at the international level. However, more needs to be done if standards are to keep pace with the changes in technology, and those involved in recruitment and selection procedures are to be protected from bad practice and poor assessment tools.

We are on the threshold of a very exciting revolution. We need radically to review our conception of assessment as a process and to reconsider the relationships between the various stakeholders in the assessment process: test developers, test publishers, test users, test takers, consumers of test results, professional bodies and lawmakers. Standards for assessment need to be reviewed and re-considered in terms of the relationships between virtual tests and roles in cyber space, rather than material tests and people in real geographical space.

Notes

1 See *http://www.shldirect.com/shldirect-homepage/SHLDirect-1.asp*
2 UEL: *http://www.gvu.gatech.edu/user_surveys*

References

AGR (2000) Going to work on the Web: Web-based graduate recruitment. AGR Briefing #11, June, 2000. Warwick, England: Association of Graduate Recruiters.

Bartram, D. (1987a) The development of an automated pilot testing system for pilot selection: the MICROPAT project. *Applied Psychology: an international review,* **36,** 279–298.

Bartram, D. (1987b) Future directions in Computer Based Assessment. *Bulletin of the British Psychological Society,* **40,** A27.

Bartram, D. (1989) Computer-based assessment. In Herriot, P (Ed.) *Handbook of Assessment in Organisations,* London: Wiley.

Bartram, D. (1993) 'Emerging trends in computer-assisted assessment'. In Schuler, H, Farr, JL and Smith M (eds) *Personnel Selection and Assessment: Individual and Organizational Perspectives,* Chapter 17, pp. 267–288. New Jersey: Lawrence Erlbaum Associates.

Bartram, D. (1994) Computer Based Assessment. In C.L. Cooper & I.T. Robertson (Eds.) *International Review of Industrial and Organizational Psychology,* **9,** 31–69.

Bartram, D. (1995a) Validation of the Micropat Battery. *International Journal of Selection and Assessment,* **3,** 84–95.

Bartram, D. (1995b) The development of standards for the use of psychological tests: The competence approach. *The Psychologist,* **8,** 219–223.

Bartram, D. (1995c) The role of computer-based test interpretation (CBTI) in occupational assessment. *International Journal of Selection and Assessment,* **3,** 178–185.

Bartram, D. (1997) Distance assessment: Psychological assessment through the Internet. *Selection Development Review,* **13,** 10–14.

Bartram, D. (1998) The need for international guidelines on standards for test use: A review of European and international initiatives. *European Psychologist,* **3,** 155–163.

Bartram, D. (in press) The MICROPAT Pilot Selection Battery: Applications of generative techniques for item-based and task-based tests. In Irvine, S., & Kyllonen, P. (Eds.) *Item Generation for Test Development*. NJ: Lawrence Erlbaum.

Bartram, D. & Dale, H.C.A. (1983) Micropat Version 3: A description of the fully automated personnel selection testing system being developed for the Army Air Corps. *Ministry of Defence Technical report, ERG/Y6536/83/7*, 14 pp.

Bartram, D. & Bayliss, R. (1984) Automated Testing: Past, Present and Future. *Journal of Occupational Psychology*, **57**, 221–237.

Burke, E. (1997) A short note on the persistence of retest effects on aptitude scores. *Journal of Occupational and Organizational Psychology*, **70**, 295–302.

Callan, A. & Geary, B. (1994) Best practice – putting practice testing to work. *Selection & Development Review*, 10, 2–4.

CyberAtlas (1998) Top 15 countries for net usage. *http://Cyberatlas.internet.com/ big_picture/demographics/article/0,1323,5911_151271,00.html.*

CyberAtlas (1999a) Worlwide Internet Users to Pass 500 Million Next Century. *http:// Cyberatlas.internet.com/big_picture/demographics/article/0,1323,5911_200001,00.html.*

CyberAtlas (1999b) UK numbers differ. *http://Cyberatlas.internet.com/big_picture/ demographics/article/0,1323,5911_151221,00.html.*

CyberAtlas (1999c) Internet job searches broaden. *http://Cyberatlas.internet.com/ big_picture/demographics/article/0,1323,5971_239621,00.html*

CyberAtlas (1999d) Net playing role in job searches. *http://Cyberatlas.internet.com/ big_picture/demographics/article/0,1323,5971_153281,00.html*

CyberAtlas (1999e) Corporate recruiting sites need help. *http://Cyberatlas.internet.com/ big_picture/demographics/article/0,1323,5971_197811,00.html*

CybsrAtlas (2000a) The World's online populations. *http://Cyberatlas.internet.com/ big_picture/demographics/article/0,1323,5911_151151,00.html.*

CyberAtlas (2000b) Web Commerce not yet Worldwide. *http://Cyberatlas.internet.com/ big_picture/demographics/article/0,1323.5911_309941,00.html*

CyberAtlas (2000c) Wireless portal users growing in number *http://Cyberatlas.internet. com/big_picture/demographics/article/0,1323,5931_309191,00.html*

Edenborough, R. (1994) *Using psychometrics*. London: Kogan Page.

ERI (1999) 1999 *Electronic Recruiting Index: The industry matures. Executive Summary. http://www.interbiznet.com*

ERI (2000) 2000 *Electronic Recruiting Index: Performance and the emergence of the middle market. Executive Summary. http://www.interbiznet.com/2000ERI*

Feltham, R. (1991) Practice effects in graduate testing – reply to Hunter, Keys, Wynne & Corcoran. *Guidance and Assessment Review*, **7**(1), 1–3.

GVU (1998) GVU's 9th WWW User Survey: General Demographics Summary. *http:// www.gvu.gatech.edu/user_surveys*

Herriot, P. (1989) Selection as a Social Process. In Smith, M., & Robertson, IT. (Eds). *Advances in Selection and Assessment*. London: John Wiley & Sons.

Hoffman, K.E. (1999) Recruitment sites changing their focus. Internet Careers, *http://www. iw.com/print/1999/03/15/intcareers/19990315-recruitment.html*

Hoffman, D.L., & Novak, T.P. (1999) The evolution of the digital divide: Examining the relationship of race to Interent access and usage over time. URL: *http://www2000. ogsm.vanderbilt.edu/*

Hunter, R.A., Keys, A., Wynne, K., & Corcoran, R. (1990) Graduate testing – the problem of practice effects. *Guidance and Assessment Review*, **6**(5), 1–4.

IPD (1999) *IPD Survey Report 5: Recruitment*. London: Institute of Personnel and Development.

Jensen, A. (1980) *Bias in mental testing*. London: Methuen.

Kehoe, C., Pitkow, J., Sutton, K., Aggarwal, G. & Rogers, J.D. (1999) *Results of GVU's Tenth World Wide Web User Survey. http://www.gvu.gatech.edu/user_surveys*

Keller, J. (1996) Public Access Issues: An Introduction. In Kahin, B., & Keller, J. (Eds.), *Public Access to the Internet*. The MIT Press.

Kellett, D. (1991) Practice tests in occupational selection – further steps. *Guidance and Assessment Review*, **7**(5), 1–3.

Kulik, J.A., Bangert-Drowns, R.L. & Kulik, C-L. (1984) Effectiveness of coaching for aptitude tests. *Psychological Bulletin*, **95**, 179–188.

Kurtz, R., Lodh, B., & Bartram, D. (1993) Practice and performance – the effects of systematic test preparation. Paper presented at the *BPS Occupational Psychology Conference*, Brighton, UK.

Lawrence, S. (1999) Employment Sites. *Iconocast*, 10 June 1999. URL: *<http://www.iconocast.com>*

Nielsen Net Ratings Inc (2000) Internet usage statistics for the month of February 2000, home. URL: *http://www.nielsen-netratings.com/hot_off.htm*

Park (1999) *Graduates in the eyes of employers*. London: Park HR and The Guardian.

Tchong, M. (1999) The Big Picture. *Iconocast*, 24 June 1999. URL: *http://www.iconocast.com*

Wroe, N. (2000) SHL survey suggests online selection process increases positive perception of companies. *SHL News Release*, Februray 1, 2000. Boulder, Colorado: SHL USA Inc.

55

RESEARCH ON INTERNET RECRUITING AND TESTING

Current status and future directions

Filip Lievens and Michael M. Harris

Source: C.L. Cooper and I.T. Robertson (eds), *International Review of Industrial and Organizational Psychology,* Vol. 18, Chichester: John Wiley, 2003, pp. 131–165.

Introduction

Over the last decade the Internet has had a terrific impact on modern life. One of the ways in which organizations are applying Internet technology and particularly World Wide Web (WWW) technology is as a platform for recruiting and testing applicants (Baron & Austin, 2000; Brooks, 2000; Greenberg, 1999; Harris, 1999, 2000). In fact, the use of the Internet for recruitment and testing has grown very rapidly in recent years (Cappelli, 2001). The increasing role of technology in general is also exemplified by the fact that in 2001 a technology showcase was organized for the first time during the Annual Conference of the Society for Industrial and Organizational Psychology. Recently, the American Psychological Association also endorsed a Task Force on Psychological Testing and the Internet.

It is clear that the use of Internet technology influences heavily how recruitment and testing are conducted in organizations. Hence, the emergence of Internet recruitment and Internet testing leads to a large number of research questions, many of which have key practical implications. For example, how do applicants perceive and use the Internet as a recruitment source or which Internet recruitment sources lead to more and better qualified applicants? Are Web-based tests equivalent to their paper-and-pencil counterparts? What are the effects of Internet-based testing in terms of criterion-related validity and adverse impact?

The rapid growth of Internet recruitment and testing illustrates that the answers to these questions have typically been taken for granted. Yet, in this chapter we aim to provide empirically based answers by reviewing the available research evidence. A second aim of our review consists of sparking future research on

Internet-based recruitment and testing. Despite the fact that there exist various excellent reviews on recruitment (e.g., Barber, 1998; Breaugh & Starke, 2000; Highhouse & Hoffman, 2001) and selection (e.g., Hough & Oswald, 2000; Salgado, 1999; Schmitt & Chan, 1998) in a traditional context, no review of research on Internet-based recruitment and testing has been conducted. An exception is Bartram (2001) who primarily focused on trends and practices in Internet recruitment and testing.

This chapter has two main sections. The first section covers Internet recruitment, whereas the second one deals with Internet testing. Although we recognize that one of the implications of using the Internet is that the distinction between these two personnel management functions may become increasingly intertwined, we discuss both of them separately for reasons of clarity. In both sections, we follow the same structure. We start by enumerating common assumptions associated with Internet recruitment (testing) and by discussing possible approaches to Internet recruitment (testing). Next, we review empirical research relevant to both these domains. On the basis of this research review, the final part within each of the sections discusses recommendations for future research.

Internet recruitment

Assumptions associated with Internet recruitment

Internet recruitment has, in certain ways at least, significantly changed the way in which the entire staffing process is conducted and understood. In general, there are five common assumptions associated with Internet recruitment that underlie the use of this approach as compared with traditional methods. A first assumption is that persuading candidates to apply and accept job offers is as important as choosing between candidates. Historically, the emphasis in the recruitment model has been on accurately and legally assessing candidates' qualifications. As such, psychometrics and legal orientations have dominated the recruitment field. The emphasis in Internet recruitment is on attracting candidates. As a result, a marketing orientation has characterized this field.

A second assumption is that the use of the Internet makes it far easier and quicker for candidates to apply for a job. In years past, job-searching was a more time-consuming activity. A candidate who wished to apply for a job would need to locate a suitable job opportunity, which often involved searching through a newspaper or contacting acquaintances. After locating potentially suitable openings, the candidate would typically have to prepare a cover letter, produce a copy of his or her resume, and mail the package with the appropriate postage. By way of comparison, the Internet permits a candidate to immediately seek out and search through thousands of job openings. Application may simply involve sending a resume via email. In that way, one can easily and quickly apply for many more jobs in a far shorter period of time than was possible before Internet recruitment was popularized. In fact, as discussed later, an individual perusing the Internet may be drawn quite accidentally to a job opening.

Third, one typically assumes that important information about an organization may be obtained through the Internet. The use of the Internet allows organizations to pass far more information in a much more dynamic and consistent fashion to candidates than was the case in the past. Candidates may therefore have much more information at their disposal before they even decide to apply for a job than in years past. In addition, candidates can easily and quickly search for independent information about an organization from diverse sources, such as chatrooms, libraries, and so forth. Thus, unlike years past where a candidate may have applied for a job based on practically no information, today's candidate may have reviewed a substantial amount of information about the organization before choosing to apply.

A fourth assumption is that applicants can be induced to return to a web site. A fundamental concept in the use of the Internet is that web sites can be designed to attract and retain user interest. Various procedures have been developed to retain customer interest in a web site, such as cookies that enable the web site to immediately recall a customer's preferences. Effective Internet recruitment programs will encourage applicants to apply and return to the web site each time they search for a new job. A final assumption refers to cost issues, namely that Internet recruitment is far less expensive than traditional approaches. Although the cost ratio is likely to differ from situation to situation, and Internet recruitment and traditional recruitment are not monolithic approaches, a reasonable estimate is that Internet recruitment is one-tenth of the cost of traditional methods and the amount of time between recruitment and selection may be reduced by as much as 25% (Cober, Brown, Blumental, Doverspike, & Levy, 2000).

Approaches to Internet recruitment

We may define Internet recruitment as any method of attracting applicants to apply for a job that relies heavily on the Internet. However, it should be clear that Internet recruitment is somewhat of a misnomer because there are a number of different approaches to Internet recruitment. The following describes five important Internet recruitment approaches. We start with some older approaches and gradually move to more recent ones. This list is neither meant to be exhaustive nor comprehensive as different approaches to Internet recruitment are evolving regularly.

Company web sites

Company web sites represent one of the first Internet-based approaches to recruiting. Many of these web sites also provide useful information about the organization, as well as a mechanism for applying for these jobs. A study in 2001 by iLogos showed that of the Global 500 companies, 88% had a company Internet recruitment site, reflecting a major surge from 1998, when only 29% of these companies had such a web site. Almost all North American Global 500 companies (93%) have a company Internet recruitment site. Most applicants would consider a medium- to large-size company without a recruitment web site to be somewhat strange; indeed, one report indicated that of 62,000 hires at nine large companies, 16% were initiated at the company Internet recruitment site (Maher & Silverman, 2002). Given these numbers, and the relatively low cost, it would seem foolish for an organization not to have a company Internet recruitment site.

Job boards

Another early approach to Internet-based recruiting was the job board. Monster Board (www.monster.com) was one of the most successful examples of this approach. Basically, the job board is much like a newspaper listing of job opportunities, along with resumes of job applicants. The job board's greatest strength is the sheer numbers of job applicants listing resumes; it has been estimated that they contain 5 million unique resumes (Gutmacher, 2000). In addition, they enable recruiters to operate 24 hours a day, examine candidates from around the world, and are generally quite inexpensive (Boehle, 2000). A major advantage of the job board approach for organizations is that many people post resumes and that most job boards provide a search mechanism so that recruiters can search for applicants with the relevant skills and experience. A second advantage is that an organization can provide extensive information, as well as a link to the company's web site for further information on the job and organization.

The extraordinary number of resumes to be found on the web, however, is also its greatest weaknesses; there are many recruiters and companies competing for the same candidates with the same access to the job boards. Thus, just as companies have the potential to view many more candidates in a short period of time, candidates have the opportunity to apply to many more companies. Another disadvantage is that having access to large numbers of candidates means that there are potentially many more applicants that have to be reviewed. Finally, many unqualified applicants may submit resumes, which increases the administrative time and expense. As an example, Maher and Silverman (2002) reported one headhunter who posted a job ad for an engineering vice president on five job boards near the end of the day. The next morning, he had over 300 emailed resumes, with applicants ranging from chief operating officers to help-desk experts. Despite the amount of attention and use of job boards, relatively few jobs may actually be initiated this way; combined together, the top four job boards produced only about 2% of actual jobs for job hunters (Maher & Silverman, 2002).

e-Recruiting

A completely different approach to Internet-based recruiting focuses on the recruiter searching on-line for job candidates (Gutmacher, 2000). Sometimes referred to as a 'meta-crawler' approach (Harris & DeWar, 2001), this approach emphasizes finding the 'passive' candidate. In addition to combing through various chat rooms, there are a number of different techniques that e-recruiters use to ferret out potential job candidates. For example, in a technique called 'flipping', recruiters use a search engine, like Altavista.com, to search the WWW for resumes with links to a particular company's web site. Doing so may reveal the resumes, email addresses, and background information for employees associated with that web site. Using a technique known as 'peeling', e-recruiters may enter a corporate web site and 'peel' it back, to locate lists of employees (Silverman, 2000).

The major advantage of this technique is the potential to find outstanding passive candidates. In addition, because the e-recruiter chooses whom to approach, there will be far fewer candidates and especially far fewer unqualified candidates generated. There are probably two disadvantages to this approach. First, because at least 50,000 people have been trained in these techniques, and companies have placed firewalls and various other strategies in place to prevent such tactics, the effectiveness of this technique is likely to decline over time (Harris & DeWar, 2001). Second, some of these techniques may constitute hacking, which at a minimum may be unethical and possibly could be a violation of the law.

Relationship recruiting

A potentially major innovation in Internet recruitment is called relationship recruiting (Harris & DeWar, 2001). A major goal of relationship recruiting is to develop a long-term relationship with 'passive' candidates, so that when they decide to enter the job market, they will turn to the companies and organizations with which they have developed a long-term relationship (Boehle, 2000). Relationship recruitment relies on Internet tools to learn more about web-visitors' interests and experience and then email regular updates about careers and their fields of interest. When suitable job opportunities arise, an email may be sent to them regarding the opportunity. For an interesting example, see http://www.futurestep.com. Probably the major advantage of this approach is that passive applicants may be attracted to jobs with a good fit. Over time, a relationship of trust may develop that will produce candidates who return to the web site whenever they are seeking jobs, thus creating a long-term relationship. At this point, it is unclear what disadvantages, if any, there are to relationship recruitment. One possibility may be that relationship recruitment may simply fail to generate enough applicants for certain positions.

Surreptitious approaches

Perhaps the most recent approach to Internet recruitment is the surreptitious or indirect approach. The best example is provided by www.salary.com, which provides free salary survey information. Because the web site enables one to request information by job title and geographic location, information about potential job opportunities can be automatically displayed. This site provides additional services (e.g., a business card, which can be sent with one's email address, to potential recruiters) that facilitate recruitment efforts. We imagine that if it is not happening yet, 'pop-up' ads for jobs may soon find their way to the Internet. Although it is too early to assess the strengths and weaknesses of surreptitious approaches to recruitment, they would appear to be a potentially useful way to attract passive job applicants. On the other hand, some of these techniques may be perceived as being rather offensive and overly direct.

Previous research

Despite the rapid emergence of Internet recruitment approaches, research studies on Internet recruitment are very sparse. To the best of our knowledge, the only topic that has received some empirical research attention is how people react to various Internet-based recruitment approaches.

Weiss and Barbeite (2001) focused on reactions to Internet-based job sites. To this end, they developed a web-based survey that addressed the importance of job site features, privacy issues, and demographics. They found that the Internet was clearly preferred as a source of finding jobs. In particular, respondents liked job sites that had few features and required little personal information. Yet, older workers and women felt less comfortable disclosing personal information at job sites. Men and women did not differ in terms of preference for web site features, but women were less comfortable providing information online. An experimental study by Zusman and Landis (2002), who compared potential applicants' preferences for web-based versus traditional job postings, did not confirm the preference for web-based job information. Undergraduate students preferred jobs on traditional paper-and-ink materials over web-based job postings. Zusman and Landis also examined the extent to which the quality of an organization's web site attracted applicants. In this study, poor-quality web sites were defined as those using few colors, no pictures, and simple fonts, whereas high-quality web sites were seen as the opposite. Logically, students preferred jobs on high quality web pages to those on lower quality pages. Scheu, Ryan, and Nona (1999) confirmed the role of web site aesthetics. In this study, impressions of a company's web site design were positively related to intentions to apply to that company. It was also found that applicant perceptions of a company changed after visiting that company's web site.

Rozelle and Landis (2002) gathered reactions of 223 undergraduate students to the Internet as a recruitment source and more traditional sources (i.e., personal referral, college visit, brochure about university, video about university, magazine advertisement). On the basis of the extant recruitment source literature (see Zottoli & Wanous, 2000, for a recent review), they classified the Internet as a more formal source. Therefore, they expected that the Internet would be perceived to be less realistic, leading to less positive post-selection outcomes (i.e., less satisfaction with the university). Yet, they found that the Internet was seen as more realistic than the other sources. In addition, use of the university web page as a source of recruitment information was not negatively correlated with satisfaction with the university. According to Rozelle and Landis, a possible explanation for these results is that Internet recruitment pages are seen as less formal recruitment sources than, for example, a brochure because of their interactivity and flexibility.

Whereas the previous studies focused on web-based job postings, it is also possible to use the Internet to go one step further and to provide potential applicants with realistic job previews (Travagline & Frei, 2001). This is because Internet-based, realistic job previews can present information in a written, video, or auditory format. Highhouse, Stanton, and Reeve (forthcoming) examined reactions to such Internet-based realistic job previews (e.g., the company was presented with audio and video excerpts). Interestingly, Highhouse et al. did also not examine retrospective reactions. Instead, they used a sophisticated micro-analytic approach to examine on-line (i.e., instantaneous) reactions to positive and negative company recruitment information. Results showed that positive and negative company information in a web-based job fair elicited asymmetrically extreme reactions such that the intensity of reactions to positive information were greater than the intensity of reactions to negative information on the same attribute.

Dineen, Ash, and Noe (2002) examined another aspect of web-based recruitment, namely the possibility to provide tailored on-line feedback to candidates. In this experimental study, students were asked to visit the career web page of a fictitious company that provided them with information about the values of the organization and with an interactive 'fit check' tool. In particular, participants were told whether they were a 'high' or a 'low' fit with the company upon completion of a web-based person–organization fit inventory. Participants receiving feedback that indicated high P–O fit were significantly more attracted to the company than participants receiving no feedback. Similarly, participants receiving low-fit feedback were significantly less attracted than those receiving no feedback.

Finally, Elgin and Clapham (2000) did not investigate applicant reactions to Internet-based recruitment but concentrated on the reactions of recruiters. The central research question was whether recruiters associated different attributes with job applicants with an electronic resume vs. job applicants with paper resumes. Results revealed that the electronic resume applicant was perceived as possessing better overall qualifications than the applicants using paper resumes. More detailed analyses further showed that the paper resume applicant was perceived as more friendly, whereas the electronic resume applicant was viewed as significantly more intelligent and technologically advanced.

Although it is difficult to draw firm conclusions due to the scarcity of research, studies generally yield positive results for the Internet as a recruitment mechanism. In fact, applicants seem to react favorably to Internet job sites and seem to prefer company web pages over more formal recruitment sources. There is also initial evidence supporting other aspects of Internet-based recruitment such as the possibility of offering realistic job previews and online feedback.

Recommendations for future research

Because of the apparent scarcity of research on Internet-based recruitment, this subsection discusses several promising routes for future research, namely applicant decision processes in Internet recruitment (i.e., decisions regarding which information to use and how to use that information), the role that the Internet plays in recruitment, and the effects of Internet recruitment on the turnover process.

How do applicants decide which sources to use?

Although there is a relatively large literature concerning applicant source (e.g., newspaper, employee referral) and applicant characteristics in the broader recruitment literature (Barber, 1998; Zottoli & Wanous, 2000), there is practically no research on how applicants perceive different Internet sources. In other words, do applicants perceive that some Internet sources of jobs are more useful than others? Several factors may play a role here. One factor, not surprisingly, would be the amount of available information and the quality of the jobs. A second factor may be the degree to which confidentiality and privacy is perceived to exist (for more information and discussion of this topic, see the section, 'Draw on psychological theories to examine Internet-based testing applications', about privacy in the section on Internet-based testing; see also the aforementioned study of Weiss & Barbeite, 2001). A third factor may be aesthetic qualities, such as the attractiveness of the graphics (see Scheu et al., 1999; Zusman & Landis, 2002). Technical considerations, such as the quality of the search engines, the speed with which the web site operates, and related issues (e.g., frequency of crashes), comprise the fourth factor.

Cober, Brown, Blumental, and Levy (2001) presented a three-stage model of the Internet recruitment process. The first stage in the model focuses on persuading Internet users to review job opportunities on the recruitment site. The model assumes that at this stage in the process, applicants are primarily influenced by the aesthetic and affective appeal of the web site. The second stage of the process focuses on engaging applicants and persuading them to examine information. This stage in turn comprises three substages: fostering interest, satisfying information requirements, and building a relationship. At this stage, applicants are primarily swayed by concrete information about the job and company. The final stage in this model is the application process, wherein people decide to apply on-line for a position. Cober et al. (2001) rated a select group of companies' recruitment web sites on characteristics such as graphics, layout, key information (e.g., compensation), and reading level. Using this coding scheme, they reported that most of these companies had at least some information on benefits and organizational culture. Relatively few of these companies provided information about such items as vision or future of the organization. The estimated reading level was at the 11th-grade level. Interestingly, reading level was negatively correlated with overall evaluation of the company's recruitment web site. The more aesthetically pleasing the web site, the more positively it was rated as well. Given the typology developed by Cober et al., the next logical step would be to study the effect on key measures such as number of applicants generated, how much time was spent viewing the web site, and the number of job offers accepted.

We believe that certain factors may moderate the importance of the things that we have already mentioned. One moderator may be the reputation of the organization; individuals may focus more on one set of factors when considering an application to a well-regarded organization than when viewing the site of an unknown organization. We also suspect that factors that initially attract job-seekers may be different than the factors that encourage candidates to return to a web site. Specifically, while aesthetic and technical factors may initially affect job-seekers, they are likely to play a less prominent role as job-seekers gain experience in applying for jobs. Cober et al.'s (2001) model and typology appears to be a good way to begin studying applicant decision processes.

Resource exchange theory (Brinberg & Ganesan, 1993; Foa, Converse, Tornblom, & Foa, 1993) is another model that may be helpful in understanding the appeal of different Internet-based recruitment sites. Yet, to our knowledge, this theory has not been extensively applied in the field of industrial and organizational (I/O) psychology. Briefly stated, resource exchange theory assumes that all resources (e.g., physical, psychological, etc.) can be sorted into six categories: information, money, goods, services, love, and status. Moreover, these six categories can be classified along two dimensions: particularism and concreteness. Particularism refers to the degree to which the source makes a difference—love is very high on particularism because it is closely tied to a specific source (i.e., person), while money is very low on particularism because it is the same, no matter what the source. Services, on the other hand, are higher on particularism than goods. The second dimension, concreteness, refers to the degree to which the resource is symbolic (e.g., status) or tangible (e.g., goods). Not surprisingly, status and information are the most symbolic, while goods and services are the most concrete (see Foa et al., 1993, for a good background to this theory).

Beyond the classification aspect of the theory, there are numerous implications. For present purposes, we will focus on some of the findings of Brinberg and Ganesan (1993), who applied this theory to product positioning, which we believe is potentially relevant to understanding job-seeker use of Internet recruitment. Specifically, Brinberg and Ganesan examined whether the category in which a consumer places a specific resource can be manipulated. For example, jewelry, described to a subject as a way to show someone that he or she cares, was more likely to be classified as being in the 'love' category than was jewelry, described to a subject as serving many practical purposes for an individual, which was more likely to be classified as being in the 'service' category. Based on the assumption that the perceived meaning of a particular product, in this case an Internet recruitment site, affects the likelihood of purchase (in this case, joining or participating), resource exchange theory may provide some interesting predictions. For example, by selling an Internet recruitment site as a service (which is more particularistic and more concrete) rather than information, job-seekers may be more likely to join. Thus, we would predict that the greater the match between what job-seekers are looking for in an Internet site (e.g., status and service) and the image that the Internet site offers, the more likely job-seekers will use the Internet site.

Finally, the elaboration likelihood model (Larsen & Phillips, 2001; Petty & Cacioppo, 1986) may be fruitfully used to understand how applicants choose Internet recruitment sites. Very briefly, the elaboration likelihood model separates variables into central cues (e.g., information about pay) and peripheral cues (e.g., aesthetics of the web site). Applicants must be both able and motivated to centrally process the relevant cues. When they are either not motivated or not able to process the information, they will rely on peripheral processing and utilize peripheral cues to a larger extent. Furthermore, decisions made using peripheral processing are more fleeting and likely to change than decisions made using central processing. We would expect that aesthetic characteristics are peripheral cues and that their effect is often fleeting. In addition, we would expect that first-time job-seekers use peripheral processing more frequently than do veteran job-seekers. Clever research designs using Internet sites should be able to test some of these assertions.

How is Internet-based information used by applicants?

As described above, one key assumption of Internet recruiting is that important information about an organization can be easily and quickly obtained through the use of search engines, as well as company-supplied information. A number of interesting research questions emanate from this assumption. First, there are many different types of web sites that may contain information about an organization. We divide these into three types: official company web sites, news media (e.g., www.lexisnexis.com), and electronic bulletin boards (e.g., www.vault.com). Paralleling earlier research in the recruitment area (Fisher, Ilgen, & Hoyer, 1979), it would be interesting to determine how credible each of these sources is perceived to be. For example, information from a chatroom regarding salaries at a particular organization may be considered more reliable than information about salaries offered in a company-sponsored web site. Likewise, does the source credibility depend upon the facet being considered? For example, is information regarding benefits considered more credible when it comes from official company sources, while information about the quality of supervision is perceived to be more reliable when coming from a chatroom?

A related question of interest is what sources of information candidates actually do use at different stages in the job search process. Perhaps certain sources are more likely to be tapped than others early in the recruitment process, whereas different sources are likely to be scrutinized later in the recruitment process. It seems likely, for example, that information found on the company web site may be weighted more heavily in the early part of the recruitment process (e.g., in the decision to apply) than in later stages of the process (e.g., in choosing between different job offers). In later stages of the recruitment process, particularly when a candidate is choosing between competing offers, perhaps electronic bulletin boards are more heavily weighted. Longitudinal research designs, which have already been used in the traditional recruitment domain (e.g., Barber, Daly, Giannantonio, & Phillips, 1994; Saks & Ashforth, 2000), should be used to address these questions.

Finally, researchers should explore the use of Internet-based information vs. other sources of information about the organization (see Rozelle & Landis, 2002). Besides the Internet, information may be obtained from a site visit of the organization, where candidates speak with their future supervisor, co-workers, and possibly with subordinates. As already noted above, there exists a voluminous literature on information sources in recruitment. How information from those traditional sources is integrated with information obtained from the Internet should be studied more carefully, particularly when contradictory information is obtained from multiple sources. Again, longitudinal research using realistic fields settings is needed here.

What role does the Internet play in recruitment?

Given the number of resumes on-line and use of Internet recruitment sites, one may conclude that the Internet plays a major role in recruitment. Yet, surveys indicate that networking is still by far the most common way to locate a job. There are several questions that should be investigated regarding the role of the Internet in recruitment. First, how are job-seekers using the Internet—is the Internet their first strategy in job search? Is it supplanting other methods, such as networking? Second, it seems likely that a host of demographic variables will affect applicant use of the Internet versus other recruitment methods. Sharf (2000) observed that there are significant differences in the percentage of households possessing Internet access, depending on race, presence of a disability, and income. Organizations may find that heavy dependence on Internet recruitment techniques hampers their efforts in promoting workforce diversity (Stanton, 1999). Finally, more research should be performed comparing the different methods of Internet recruitment. For instance, e-recruiting should be compared with traditional headhunting methods. We suspect that applicants may prefer e-recruiting over face-to-face or even telephone-based approaches. First, email is perceived to be more private and anonymous in many ways as compared with the telephone. Second, unlike the telephone, email allows for an exchange of information even when the sender and recipient are not available at the same time. Whether or not different Internet recruitment methods have different effects on applicants remains to be studied.

The effects of Internet recruitment on the turnover process

To date, there has been little discussion about the impact of Internet recruitment on the turnover process. However, we believe that there are various areas where the use of Internet recruitment may affect applicants' decision to leave their present organization, including the decision to quit, the relationships between withdrawal cognitions, job search, and quitting, and the costs of job search.

With regard to the decision to quit, there has been a plethora of research. The most sophisticated models of the turnover process include job search in the sequence of events (Hom & Griffeth, 1995). One of the most recent theories, known as the unfolding model (Lee & Mitchell, 1994), posits that the decision by an employee to leave his or her present organization is based on one of four 'decision paths'. Which of the four 'decision paths' is chosen depends on the precipitating event that occurs. In three of the decision paths, the question of turnover is raised when a shock occurs. A shock is defined as 'a specific event that jars the employee to make deliberate judgments about his or her job' (Hom and Griffeth, 1995, p. 83). When one's company is acquired by another firm, for example, this may create a shock to an employee, requiring the employee to think more deliberately about his or her job. According to Mitchell, Holtom, and Lee (2002), Path-3 leavers often initiate the turnover process when they receive an unsolicited job offer. It seems plausible, then, that with the frequency of individuals using Internet recruitment, there will be a significant increase in the number of individuals using the third decision path. As explained by Mitchell et al., individuals using the third path are leaving for a superior job. Thus, individuals who read Internet job postings may realize that there are better job alternatives, which to use Lee and Mitchell's terminology, prompts them to review the decision to remain with their current employer. Research is needed to further understand the use of Internet recruitment and turnover processes, using the unfolding model. Are there, for example, certain Internet recruitment approaches (e.g., e-recruiting) that are particularly likely to induce Path-3 processes? What type of information should these approaches use to facilitate turnover?

A second area relates to the relationships between withdrawal cognitions, job search, and quitting. As discussed by Hom and Griffeth (1995), one of the debates in the turnover literature concerns the causal paths among withdrawal cognitions, job search, and quitting. Specifically, there have been different opinions as to whether employees decide to quit and then go searching for alternative jobs, or whether employees first go searching for alternative jobs and then decide to quit their present company. Based on the existing evidence, Hom and Griffeth argue for the former causal ordering. However, using the assumption of Lee and Mitchell that different models of turnover may be relevant for different employees, it seems plausible that individuals using Internet recruitment might follow the latter causal order. In order words, individuals reviewing Internet job postings 'just for fun' may locate opportunities of interest, which compare more favorably than their current position. The existence of Internet recruitment may therefore affect the relationship between withdrawal cognitions, job search, and quitting.

The costs of job search constitute a third possible area where the use of Internet recruitment may affect applicants' decisions to leave their present organization.

As we noted above, the use of the Internet may greatly reduce the cost of job searching. Although there has been little research done on job search activity by I/O psychologists, it seems reasonable that the expectancy model, which includes an evaluation of the costs and benefits and the likelihood of success, will determine the likelihood of one engaging in job search behavior. Given that the use of Internet recruitment can greatly reduce the costs to a job-searcher, it seems reasonable to assume that individuals will be more likely to engage in a job search on a regular basis than in the past. Models of the turnover process in general, and the job search process in specific, should consider the perceived costs versus benefits of job hunting for the employee. In all likelihood, as the costs decline, employees would be more likely to engage in job hunting.

In sum, there are some interesting possible effects of Internet recruitment on turnover processes. In general, research linking recruitment theories and turnover theories appears to be lacking. It is time to integrate these two streams of research.

Internet testing

Common advantages associated with Internet testing

The use of the Internet is not only attractive for recruitment purposes. There are also a number of factors that lead organizations to invest in the web for testing purposes. On the one hand, testing candidates through the Internet builds further on the advantages inherent in computerized testing. Similar to computerized testing (McBride, 1998), Internet testing involves considerable test administration and scoring efficiencies because test content can be easily modified, paper copies are no longer needed, test answers can be captured in electronic form, errors can be routinely checked, tests can be automatically scored, and instant feedback can be provided to applicants. This administrative ease may result in potentially large savings in costs and turnaround time, which may be particularly important in light of tight labor markets. Akin to computerized testing, Internet-based testing also enables organizations to present items in different formats and to measure other aspects of applicant behavior. In particular, items might be presented in audio and video format, applicants' response latencies might be measured, and items might be tailored to the latent ability of the respondents.

On the other hand, web-based testing also has various additional advantages over computerized testing (Baron & Austin, 2000; Brooks, 2000). In fact, the use of the web for presenting test items and capturing test-takers' responses facilitates consistent test administration across many divisions/sites of a company. Further, because tests can be administered over the Internet, neither the employer nor the applicants have to be present in the same location, resulting in increased flexibility for both parties. Hence, given the widespread use of information technology and the globalization of the economy, Internet-based testing might expand organizations' access to other and more geographically diverse applicant pools.

Approaches to Internet testing

Because of the rapid growth of Internet testing and the wide variety of applications, there are many ways to define Internet-based testing. A possible straightforward definition is that it concerns the use of the Internet or an intranet (an organization's private network) for administering tests and inventories in the context of assessment and selection. Although this definition (and this chapter) focus only on Internet-based tests and Internet-based inventories, it is also possible to use the Internet (through videoconference) for conducting employment interviews (see Straus, Miles, & Levesque, 2001).

The wide variety in Internet-based testing applications is illustrated by looking at two divergent examples of current Internet-based testing applications. We chose these two examples for illustration purposes because they represent relative extremes. First, Baron and Austin (2000) developed a web-based cognitive ability test. This test was a timed, numerical reasoning test with business-related items and was used after an on-line application and before participation in an assessment center. Applicants could fill in the test whenever and wherever they wanted to. There was no test administrator present. The test was developed according to item response theory principles so that each applicant received different items tailored to his/her ability. In addition, there existed various formats (e.g., text, table, or graphic) for presenting the same item content so that it was highly improbable that candidates received the same items. Baron and Austin (2000) also built other characteristics into the numerical reasoning test to counter user identification problems and possible breaches to test security. For example, the second part of the test was administered later in the selection process in a supervised context so that the results of the two sessions could be compared. In addition, applicants were required to fill in an honesty contract, which certified that they and nobody else completed the Web-based test. The system also allowed candidates to take the test only once and encrypted candidate responses for scoring and reporting.

Second, Greenberg (1999) presented a radically different application of Internet testing. Probably, this application is more common in nowadays organizations. Here applicants were not allowed to log on where and when they wanted to. Instead, applicants were required to log on to a web site from a standardized and controlled setting (e.g., a company's test center). A test administrator supervised the applicants. Hence, applicants completed the tests in structured test administration conditions.

Closer inspection of these examples and other existing web-based testing applications illustrates (e.g., Coffee, Pearce, & Nishimura, 1999; Smith, Rogg, & Collins, 2001) that web-based testing can vary across several categories/dimensions. We believe that at least the following four dimensions should be distinguished: (1) the purpose of testing, (2) the selection stage, (3) the type of test, and (4) the test administration conditions. Although these four dimensions are certainly not orthogonal, we discuss each of them separately.

Regarding the first dimension of *test purpose*, Internet testing applications are typically divided into applications for career assessment purposes vs. applications for hiring purposes. At this moment, tests for career assessment purposes abound on the Internet (see Lent, 2001; Oliver & Whiston, 2000, for reviews). These tests are often provided for free to the general public, although little is known about their psychometric properties. The other side of the continuum consists of organizations that use tests for hiring purposes. Given this consequentiality, it is expected that these tests adhere to professional standards (Standards for Educational and Psychological Testing, 1999) so that they have adequate psychometric properties.

A second question deals with the *stage in the selection process* wherein organizations are using Internet testing. For example, some organizations might use Internet-based testing applications for screening ('selecting out') a large number of applicants and for reducing the applicant pool to more manageable proportions. Conversely, other organizations might use Internet-based testing applications at the final stage of the selection process to 'select in' already promising candidates.

A third dimension pertains to the *type of test* administered through the WWW. In line with the computerized testing literature, a relevant distinction opposes cognitive-oriented measures vs. noncognitive-oriented measures. Similarly, one can make a distinction between tests with a correct answer (e.g., cognitive ability tests, job knowledge tests, situational judgment tests) vs. tests without a correct answer (e.g., personality inventories, vocational interest inventories). At this moment, organizations most frequently seem to use noncognitive-oriented web-based measures. In fact, Stanton and Rogelberg (2001a) conducted a small survey of current web-based hiring practices and concluded that virtually no organizations are currently using the Internet for administering cognitive ability tests.

The fourth and last dimension refers to the *test administration conditions* and especially to the level of control and standardization by organizations over these conditions. Probably, this dimension is the most important because it is closely related to the reliability and validity of psychological testing (Standards for Educational and Psychological Testing, 1999). In Internet testing applications, test administration conditions refer to various aspects such as the time of test administration, the location, the presence of a test administrator, the interface used, and the technology used. Whereas in traditional testing, the control over these aspects is typically in the hands of the organizations, this is not necessarily the case in Internet testing applications. For example, regarding the *time* of test administration, some organizations enable applicants to log on whenever they want to complete the tests (see the example of Baron & Austin, 2000). Hence, they provide applicants with considerable latitude. Other organizations decide to exert a lot of control. In this case, organizations provide applicants access to the Internet test site only at fixed, predetermined times.

Besides test administration time, test administration *location* can also vary in web-based testing applications. There are organizations that allow applicants to log on where they want. For example, some applicants may log on to the web site from their home, others from their office, and still others from a computing room. Some people may submit information in a noisy computer lab, whereas others may be in a quiet room (Buchanan & Smith, 1999a; Davis, 1999). This flexibility and convenience sharply contrast to the standardized location (test room) in other web-based testing applications. Here, applicants either go to the company's centralized test center or to the company's multiple geographically dispersed test centers or supervised kiosks.

Another aspect of test administration conditions of Internet testing applications refers to the decision as to whether or not a *test-administrator* is used. This dimension of web-based testing is also known as proctored (supervised) vs. unproctored (unsupervised) web-based testing. In some cases, there is no test-administrator to supervise applicants. When no test-administrator is present, organizations lack control over who is conducting the test. In addition, there is no guarantee that people do not cheat by using help from others or reference material (Baron & Austin, 2000; Greenberg, 1999; Stanton, 1999). Therefore, in most Internet-based testing applications, a test-administrator is present to instruct testees and to ensure that they do not use dishonest means to improve their test performance (especially on cognitive-oriented measures).

In web-enabled testing, test administration conditions also comprise the type of *user interface* that organizations use (Newhagen & Rafaeli, 2000). Again, the type of interface used may vary to a great extent across Internet-based testing applications. At one side of the continuum, there are Internet-based testing applications that contain a very restrictive user interface. For example, some organizations decide to increase standardization and control by heavily restricting possible applicant responses such as copying or printing the items for test security reasons. Other restrictions consist of requirements asking applicants (a) to complete the test within a specific time limit, (b) to complete the test in one session, (c) to fill in all necessary information on a specific test form prior to continuing, and (d) neither to skip nor backtrack items. When applicants do one of these things, a warning message is usually displayed. At the other side of the continuum, some organizations decide to give applicants more latitude in completing Internet-based tests.

Finally, the *WWW technology* is also an aspect of test administration conditions that may vary substantially across Internet-based testing applications. In this context, we primarily focus on how technology is related to test administration conditions (see Mead, 2001, for a more general typology of WWW technological factors). Some organizations invest in technology to exert more control and standardization over test administration. For example, to guarantee to applicants that the data provided are 'secure' (are not intercepted by others), organizations may decide to use encryption technology. In addition, organizations may invest in computer and network resources to assure the speed and reliability of the Internet connection. To ensure that the person completing the test is the applicant, in the near future organizations may decide to use web cams, typing patterns, fingerprint scanning, or retinal scanning (Stanton & Rogelberg, 2001a). All these technological interventions are especially relevant when organizations have no control over other aspects of the web-based test-administration (e.g., absence of a test-administrator). Other organizations may decide not to invest in these new technologies. Instead, they may invest in a proctored test environment (e.g., use of a test administrator to supervise applicants).

Taken together, these examples and this categorization of Internet testing highlight that Internet-based testing applications may vary considerably. Unfortunately, no data have been gathered about the frequency of use of the various forms of Web-based testing in consultancy firms and companies. In any case, all of this clearly shows that there is no 'one' way of testing applicants through the Internet and that Web-based testing should not be regarded as a monolithic entity. Hence, echoing what we have said about Internet recruitment, we believe that the terms 'Internet testing' or 'Web-based testing' are misnomers and should be replaced by 'Internet testing applications' or 'Web-based testing applications'.

Previous research

Although research on Internet testing is lagging behind Internet testing practice, the gap is less striking than for Internet recruitment research. This is because empirical research on Internet testing has proliferated in recent years. Again, most of the studies that we retrieved were in the conference presentation format and had not been published yet. Note also that only a limited number of research topics have been addressed. The most striking examples are that, to the best of our knowledge, neither the criterion-related validity of Internet testing applications nor the possible adverse impact of Internet testing applications have been put to scrutiny. Moreover, most studies have treated Internet testing as a monolithic entity, ignoring the multiple dimensions of Internet testing discussed above. The remainder of this section summarizes the existing studies under the following two headings: measurement equivalence and applicant perceptions.

Measurement equivalence

In recent years, a sizable amount of studies have examined whether data collected through the WWW are similar to data collected via the traditional paper-and-pencil format. Three streams of research can be distinguished. A first group of studies investigated whether Internet data collection was different from 'traditional' data collection (see Stanton & Rogelberg, 2001b and Simsek & Veiga, 2001, for excellent reviews). Strictly speaking, this first group of studies dealt not really with Internet testing application because most of them were not conducted in a selection context. Instead, they focused on data collection of psychosocial data (Buchanan & Smith, 1999a, b; Davis, 1999; Joinson, 1999; Pasveer & Ellard, 1998; Pettit, 1999), survey data (Burnkrant & Taylor, 2001; Hezlett, 2000; Magnan, Lundby, & Fenlason, 2000; Spera & Moye, 2001; Stanton, 1998), or multisource feedback data (Fenlason, 2000). In general, no differences or minimal differences between

Internet-based data collection and traditional (paper-and-pencil) data collection were found.

A second group of studies did focus on selection instruments. Specifically, these studies examined the equivalence of selection instruments administered in either Web-based vs. traditional contexts. Mead and Coussons-Read (2002) used a within-subjects design to assess the equivalence of the Sixteen Personality Factor Questionnaire. Sixty-four students were recruited from classes and completed first the paper-and-pencil version and about two weeks later the Internet version. Cross-mode correlations ranged between 0.74 to 0.93 with a mean of 0.85, indicating relatively strong support for equivalence. Although this result is promising, a limitation is that the study was conducted with university students. Two other studies examined similar issues with actual applicants. Reynolds, Sinar, and McClough (2000) examined the equivalence of a biodata-type instrument among 10,000 actual candidates who applied for an entry-level sales position. Similar to Mead and Coussons-Read (2002), congruence coefficients among the various groups were very high. However, another study (Ployhart, Weekley, Holtz, & Kemp, 2002) reported somewhat less positive results with a large group of actual applicants for a teleservice job. Ployhart et al. used a more powerful procedure such as multiple group, confirmatory factor analysis to compare whether an Internet-based administration of a Big Five-type personality inventory made a difference. Results showed that the means on the Web-based personality inventory were lower than the means on the paper-and-pencil version. Although the factor structures took the same form in each administration condition, the factor structures were partially invariant, indicating that factor loadings were not equal across administration formats.

Finally, a third set of studies concentrated on the equivalence of different approaches to Internet testing. Oswald, Carr, and Schmidt (2001) manipulated not only test administration format but also test administration setting to determine their effects on measurement equivalence. In their study, 410 undergraduate students completed ability tests (verbal analogies and arithmetic reasoning) and a Big Five personality inventory (a) either in paper-and-pencil or Internet-based format and (b) either in supervised or unsupervised testing settings. Oswald et al. (2001) hypothesized that ability and personality tests would be less reliable and have a less clear factor structure under unsupervised and therefore less standardized conditions. Preliminary findings of multiple group confirmatory factor analyses showed that for the personality measures administered in supervised conditions, model fit tended to support measurement invariance. Conversely, unsupervised measures of personality tended not to show good fit, lending support to the original hypothesis. Remarkably, for cognitive ability measures, both supervised and unsupervised conditions had a good fit. In another study, Beaty, Fallon, and Shepherd (2002) used a within-subjects design to examine the equivalence of proctored (supervised) vs. unproctored (unsupervised) Internet testing conditions. So, interestingly, these authors did not also treat Internet-based testing as a monolithic entity. Another interesting aspect of the study was that real applicants were used. First, applicants completed the unproctored test at home or at work. Beaty et al. found that the average score of the applicants was 35.3 (SD = 6.5). Next, the best 76 candidates were invited to complete a parallel form of the test in a proctored test session. The average score for these candidates in the proctored testing session was 42.2 (SD = 2.0). In comparison, this same group had an average test score of 44.1 (SD = 4.9) in the unproctored test session ($t = 3.76, p < 0.05$). Although significant, the increase in test scores in unsupervised Web-based testing environments (due to cheating such as having other people fill in the test) seems to be less dramatic than could be anticipated.

In short, initial evidence seems to indicate that measurement equivalence between Web-based and paper-and-pencil tests is generally established. In addition, no large differences are found between supervised and unsupervised testing. Again, these results should be interpreted with caution because of the small number of research studies involved.

Applicant perceptions

Because test administration in an Internet-based environment differs from traditional testing, research has also begun to examine applicant reactions to Internet-based assessment systems. Mead (2001) reported that 81% of existing users were satisfied or quite satisfied with an on-line version of the 16PF Questionnaire. The most frequently cited advantage was the remote administration, followed by the quick reporting of results. The reported rate of technical difficulties was the only variable that separated satisfied from dissatisfied users. Another study by Reynolds et al. (2000) confirmed these results. They found more positive perceptions of actual applicants toward Internet-based testing than toward traditional testing. However, a confound was that all people receiving the Web-based testing format had opted for this format. Similar to Mead (2001), Reynolds et al. noted a heightened attention of applicants to technological and time-related factors (e.g., speed) when testing via the Internet as compared with traditional testing. No differences in applicant reactions across members of minority and non-minority groups were found.

Sinar and Reynolds (2001) conducted a multi-stage investigation of applicant reactions to supervised Internet-based selection procedures. Their sample consisted of applicants for real job opportunities. They first gathered open-ended comments from applicants to Internet-based testing systems. About 70% of the comments obtained were positive. Similar to Reynolds et al. (2000), the speed and the efficiency of the Internet testing tool was the most important consideration of applicants, especially if the speed was slow. Many applicants also commented on the novelty of Internet-based testing. User-friendliness (e.g., ease of navigation) was another theme receiving substantial attention. Sinar and Reynolds also discovered that comments about user-friendliness, personal contact provided, and speed/efficiency were linked to higher overall satisfaction with the process. Finally, Sinar and Reynolds explored whether different demographic groups had different reactions to these issues. Markedly, there were more positive reactions for racial minorities, but user-friendliness discrepancies for females and older applicants. It is clear that more research is needed here to confirm and explain these findings.

In light of the aforementioned dimensions of Internet-based testing, a noteworthy finding of Sinar and Reynolds (2001) was that, on average, actual applicants reported a preference for the proctored (supervised) Web-based setting instead of taking the Web-based assessment from a location of their choice (unsupervised). Perhaps applicants considered the administrator's role to be crucial in informing applicants and providing help when needed. It is also possible that candidates perceived higher test security problems in the unsupervised Web-based environment.

Other research focused on the effects of different formats of Internet-based testing on perceptions of anonymity. However, a drawback is that this issue has only been investigated with student samples. Joinson (1999) compared socially desirable responding among students, who either completed personality-related questionnaires via the Web (unsupervised) or during courses (supervised). Both student groups were required to identify themselves (non-anonymity situation), which makes this experiment somewhat generalizable to a personnel selection context. Joinson found that responses of the unsupervised Web group exhibited significantly lower social desirability than people completing the questionnaires during supervised courses. He related this to the lack of observer presence inherent in unsupervised Internet-based testing. In a similar vein, Oswald et al. (2001) reported greater feelings of anonymity for completing personality measures in the Web/unsupervised condition vs. in the Web/supervised condition. Oswald et al. suggested that students probably felt more anonymous in the unsupervised setting because this setting was similar to surfing the Internet in the privacy of one's home.

Taken together, applicant perceptions of Internet-based testing applications seem to be favorable. Yet, studies also illustrate that demographic variables, technological breakdowns, and an unproctored test environment impact negatively on these perceptions.

Recommendations for future research

Given the state-of-the art of research on Internet testing applications, this last section proposes several recommendations for future research. In particular, we posit that future research should (1) learn from the lessons of the computer-based testing literature, (2) draw on psychological theories for examining Internet-enabled testing applications, and (3) address questions of most interest to practitioners.

Be aware of the lessons from computer-based testing research

As already mentioned, some Internet testing applications have a lot of similarities to computerized testing. Therefore, it is important that future research builds on this body of literature (Bartram, 1994; Burke, 1993; McBride, 1998, for reviews). Several themes may provide inspiration to researchers.

Measurement equivalence is one of the themes that received considerable attention in the computerized testing literature. On the one hand, there is evidence in the computerized testing literature that the equivalence of computerized cognitive ability measures to traditional paper-and-pencil measures is high. Mead and Drasgow's (1993) meta-analysis of cognitive ability measures found average cross-mode correlations of 0.97 for power tests. On the other hand, there is considerable debate whether computerized noncognitive measures are equivalent to their paper-and-pencil versions (King & Miles, 1995; Richman, Kiesler, Weisband, & Drasgow, 1999). This debate about the equivalence of noncognitive measures centers on the issue of social desirability. A first interpretation is that people display more candor and less social desirability in their responses to a computerized instrument. This is because people perceive computers to be more anonymous and private. Hence, according to this interpretation, they are more willing to share personal information. A second interpretation posits that people are more worried when interacting with a computer because they fear that their responses are permanently stored and can be verified by other parties at all times. In turn, this leads to less self-disclosure and more socially desirable responding. Recently, Richman et al. (1999) meta-analyzed previous studies on the equivalence of noncognitive measures. They also tested under which conditions computerized noncognitive measures were equivalent to their paper-and pencil counterparts. They found that computerization had no overall effect on measures of social desirability. However, they reported that being alone and having the opportunity to backtrack and to skip items resulted in more self-disclosure and less socially desirable responding among respondents. In more general terms, Richman et al. (1999) concluded that computerized questionnaires produced less social desirability when participants were anonymous and when the questionnaire format mimicked that of a paper-and-pencil version.

Although researchers have begun examining the measurement equivalence issue in the context of Web-based testing, we believe that researchers may go even further because the computerized testing literature on measurement equivalence has important implications for future studies on Web-based testing. First of all, it does not suffice to examine measurement equivalence *per se*. The literature on computerized testing teaches us that it is crucial to examine under which conditions measurement equivalence is reduced or increased. Along these lines, several of the conditions identified by Richman et al. (1999) have direct implications for Web-enabled testing. For example, being alone relates to the Web-based test administration dimension 'no presence of test-administrator' that we discussed earlier. So, future research should examine the equivalence of Web-based testing under different test administration conditions. Especially lab research may be useful here. Second, the fact that Richman et al. (1999) found different equivalence results for noncognitive measures in the anonymous vs. the non-anonymous condition, calls for research in situations in which test results have consequences for the persons involved. Examples include field research with real applicants in actual selection situations or laboratory research in which participants receive an incentive to distort responses. Third, prior studies mainly examined the construct equivalence of Web-based tests. To date, no evidence is available as to how Internet-based administration affects the criterion-related validity of cognitive and noncognitive tests. Again, the answer here may depend on the type of Internet-based application.

Another theme from the computerized testing literature pertains to the impact of demographic variables on performance of computerized instruments (see Igbaria & Parasuraman, 1989, for a review). In fact, there is meta-analytic evidence that female college students have substantially more computer anxiety (Chua, Chen, & Wong, 1999) and less computer self-efficacy (Whitley, 1997) than males. Regarding age, computer confidence and control seems to be lower among persons above 55 years (Czaja & Sharit, 1998; Dyck & Smither, 1994). In terms of race, Badagliacco (1990) reported that whites had more years of computer experience than members of other races and Rosen, Sears, and Weil (1987) found that white students had significantly more positive attitudes toward computers. Research has begun to investigate the impact of these demographic variables in an Internet context. For example, Schumacher and Morahan-Martin (2001) found that males had higher levels of experience and skill using the Internet. In other words, as could be expected, the initial findings suggest that the trends found in the computerized testing literature (especially those with regard to gender and age) generalize to Internet-based applications. Although definitely more research is needed here, it is possible that Internet-enabled testing would suffer from the so-called digital divide because some groups (females and older people) are disadvantaged in Internet testing applications. For practitioners, the future challenge then consists of implementing Internet tests that produce administrative and cost efficiencies and at the same time ensure fairness (Stanton & Rogelberg, 2001a). Researchers should study differential item/scale/test functioning across Web-based testing and traditional paper-and-pencil administrations. In addition, they should investigate which forms of Web-based testing produce less adverse impact. For example, it is likely that there is an interaction between the Web-based testing conditions and the occurrence of adverse impact. In particular, when organizations do not restrict the time and location of Web-based testing so that people can complete tests in each Internet-enabled terminal (e.g., in libraries, shopping centers), we expect that adverse impact against minority groups will be less as compared with proctored Web-based testing applications.

Finally, we believe that research on Web-based testing can learn from the history of computer-based testing. As reviewed by McBride (1998), the first wave of computerized testing primarily examined whether using a computerized administration mode was cost-efficient, whereas the second wave focused on converting existing paper-and-pencil instruments to a computerized format and studying measurement equivalence. According to McBride (1998), only die third wave of studies investigated whether a computerized instrument can actually change and enhance existing tests (e.g., by adding video, audio). Our review of current research shows that history seems to repeat itself. Current studies have mainly concentrated on cost savings and measurement equivalence. So, future studies are needed that examine how use of the Internet can actually change the actual test and the test administration process.

Draw on psychological theories to examine Internet-based testing applications

Our review of current research on Internet-based testing illustrated that few studies were grounded on a solid theoretical framework. However, we believe that at least the following two theories may be fruitfully used in research on Internet-based testing, namely organizational privacy theory and organizational justice theory. Although both theories are related (see Bies, 1993; Eddy, Stone, & Stone, 1999; Gilliland, 1993), we discuss their potential benefits in future research on Internet-based testing separately.

Organizational privacy theory (Stone & Stone, 1990) might serve as a first theoretical framework to underpin research on Internet-based testing applications. Privacy is a relevant construct in Internet-based testing because of several reasons. First, Internet-based testing applications are typically non-anonymous. Second, applicants are often asked to provide personal and sensitive information. Third, applicants know that the information is captured in electronic format, facilitating multiple transmissions over the Internet and storage in various databases (Stanton & Rogelberg, 2001a). Fourth, privacy concerns might be heightened when applicants receive security messages (e.g., secure server probes, probes for accepting cookies, etc.). Although Bartram (2001) argued that these security problems are largely overstated, especially people who lack Internet experience, Internet self-efficacy, or the belief that the Internet is secure may worry about them.

So far, there has been no empirical research on the effects of Web-based testing on perceptions of invasion of privacy. Granted, there is some evidence that people are indeed more wary about privacy when technology comes into play, but these were purely descriptive studies. Specifically, Eddy et al. (1999) cited several surveys that found that public concern over invasion of privacy was on the rise. They linked this increased concern over privacy to the recent technological advances that have occurred. Additionally, Cho and LaRose (1999) cited a survey in which seven out of ten respondents to an online survey worried more about privacy on the WWW than through the mail or over the telephone (see also Hoffman, Novak, & Peralta, 1999; O'Neil, 2001).

In the privacy literature, there is general consensus that privacy is a multi-faceted construct. For example, Cho and LaRose (1999) made a useful distinction between physical privacy (i.e., solitude), informational privacy (i.e., the control over the conditions under which personal data are released), and psychological privacy (i.e., the control over the release of personal data). In a similar vein, Stone and Stone (1990) delineated three main themes in the definition of privacy. A first form of privacy is related to the notion of information control, which refers to the ability of individuals to control information about them. This meaning of privacy is related to the psychological privacy construct of Cho & LaRose (1999). Second, Stone and Stone (1990) discuss privacy as the regulation of interactions with others. This form of privacy refers to personal space and territoriality (cf. the physical privacy of Cho and LaRose, 1999). A third perspective on privacy views it in terms of freedom from the influence or control by others (Stone & Stone, 1990).

Several studies in the privacy literature documented that especially the perceived control over the use of disclosed information is of pivotal importance to the notion of invasion of privacy (Fusilier & Hoyer, 1980; Stone, Gueutal, Gardner, & McClure, 1983; Stone & Stone, 1990). This perceived control is typically broken down into two components, namely the ability to authorize disclosure of information and the target of disclosure. There is also growing support for these antecedents in the context of the use of information technology. For instance, Eddy et al. (1999) examined reactions to human resource information systems and found that individuals perceived a policy to be most invasive when they had no control over the release of personal information *and* when the information was provided to parties outside the organization.

How can privacy theory advance our understanding of applicants' view of Web-based testing? First, we need a clear understanding of which forms of privacy are affected by Web-based testing. Studies are needed to examine how the different forms of Web-based testing outlined above affect the various forms of privacy. Second, we need studies to shed light into the antecedents of applicants' privacy concerns. Studies are needed to confirm whether applicants' perceived decrease of control over the conditions under which personal information might be released and over the organizations that subsequently might use it are the main determinants to trigger privacy concerns in Web-based testing applications. Again, it would be interesting to examine this for the various dimensions of Web-enabled testing. Third, future studies should examine the consequences of applicants' privacy concerns in web-based testing. For example, when privacy concerns are heightened, do applicants engage in more socially desirable responding and less self-disclosure? What are the influences on their perceptions of the Web-based testing application? A final avenue for future research consists of investigating under which conditions these privacy concerns might be reduced or alleviated. To this end, research could manipulate the various dimensions of Web-based testing and examine their impact on different forms of privacy. For example, does a less restrictive interface reduce privacy concerns? Similarly, how do technology and disclaimers that guarantee security and confidentiality affect applicants' privacy concerns? What roles do the type of test and the kind of information provided play? What is the influence of the presence of a test-administrator? As mentioned above, there is some preliminary evidence that applicants feel more (physical) privacy and provide more candid answers when no test-administrator is present (see Joinson, 1999; Oswald et al., 2001). Such studies might contribute to our general understanding of privacy in technological environments but might also provide concrete recommendations for improving current Web-based testing practices.

A second theoretical framework that may be relevant is organizational justice theory (Gilliland, 1993; Greenberg, 1990). Organizational justice theory in general and a justice framework applied to selection in particular are relevant here because applicants are likely to compare the new Web-based medium with more traditional approaches. Hence, one of applicants' prime concerns will be whether this new mode of administration is more or less fair than the traditional ones. Gilliland (1993) presented a model that integrated both organizational justice theory and prior applicant reactions research. Two central constructs of the model were distributive justice and procedural justice, which both had their own set of distinct rules (e.g., job-relatedness, consistency, feedback, two-way communication). Gilliland (1993) also delineated the antecedents and consequences of possible violation of these rules.

Here we only discuss the variables that may warrant special research attention in the context of Web-based testing. First, Gilliland's (1993) model should be broadened to include technological factors as possible determinants of applicants' fairness reactions. As mentioned above, initial research on applicant reactions to Web-based testing suggests that these reactions are particularly influenced by technological factors such as slowdowns in the Internet connection or Internet connection crashes. Apparently, applicants expect these technological factors to be flawless. If the technology fails for some applicants and runs perfectly for others, fairness perceptions of Web-based testing are seriously affected. Gilliland's (1993) model should also be broadened to include specific determinants to computerized/Web-based forms of testing such as Internet/computer anxiety and Internet/computer self-efficacy. Second, Web-based testing provides excellent opportunities for testing an important antecedent of the procedural justice rules outlined in Gilliland's (1993) model, namely the role of 'human resource personnel' (e.g., test-administrators). As mentioned above, in some applications of Web-based testing, the role of test-administrators is reduced or even discarded. The question remains how this lack of early stage face-to-face contact (one of Gilliland's, 1993, procedural justice rules) affects applicants' reactions during and after hiring (Stanton & Rogelberg, 2001a). On the one hand, applicants might perceive the Web-based testing situation as more fair because the user interface of a computer is more neutral than a test administrator. On the other hand, applicants might regret that there is no 'live' two-way communication, although many user interfaces are increasingly interactive and personalized. An examination of the effects of mixed mode administration might also clarify the role of test-administrators in determining procedural justice reactions. Mixed mode administration occurs when some tests are administered via traditional means, whereas other tests are administered via the Internet. We believe that these different modalities of Web-based testing offer great possibilities for studying specific components of Gilliland's justice model and for contributing to the broader justice literature. Third, in current Web-based testing research, applicants' reactions to Web-based testing are hampered by the 'novelty' aspect of the new technology. This novelty aspect creates a halo effect so that it is difficult to get a clear insight into the other bases of applicants' reactions to Web-based testing applications. Therefore, future research should pay particular attention to one of the moderators of Gilliland's model, namely applicants' prior experience. In the context of Web-based testing, this moderator might be operationalized as previous work experience in technological jobs or prior experience with Internet-based recruitment/testing.

Address questions of interest to practitioners

The growth of Internet-based testing opens a window of opportunities for researchers as many organizations are asking for suggestions and advice. Besides answering questions that are consistent with previous paradigms (see our first two recommendations), it is equally important to examine the questions that are on the top of practitioners' minds.

When we browsed through the popular literature on Internet-based testing, cost benefits and concerns definitely emerged as a prime issue. To date, most practitioners are convinced of the possible benefits of Internet recruitment. Similarly, there seems to exist general consensus that Internet testing may have important advantages over paper-and-pencil testing. This is also evidenced by case studies. Baron and Austin (2000) reported results of a case study in which an organization (America Online) used the Internet for screening out applicants in early selection stages. They compared the testing process before and after the introduction of the Internet-based system on a number of ratios. Due to Internet-enabled screening the time per hire decreased from 4 hours and 35 minutes to 1 hour and 46 minutes so that the whole process was reduced by 20 days. Sinar and Reynolds (2001) also referred to case studies that demonstrated that companies can achieve hiring cycle time reductions of 60% through intensive emphasis on Internet staffing models. A limitation of these studies, however, is that they evaluated the combined impact of Internet-enabled recruitment and testing (i.e., screening), making it difficult to understand the unique impact of Internet testing.

More skepticism, though, surrounds the incremental value of supervised Internet-based testing over 'traditional' computerized testing within the organization. In other words, what is the added value of having applicants complete the tests at various test centers vs. having them complete tests in the organization? The obvious answer is that there is increased flexibility for both the employer and the applicant and that travel costs are reduced. Yet, not everybody seems to be convinced of this. A similar debate exists about the feasibility of having an unproctored Web-based test environment (in terms of user identification and test security). Therefore, future studies should determine the utility of various Web-based testing applications and formats. To this end, various indices can be used such as time and cost savings and applicant reactions (Jayne & Rauschenberger, 2000).

A second issue emerging from popular articles about Internet selection processes relates to practitioners' interest as to whether use of Web-based testing has positive effects on organizations' general image and their image as employers particularly. Although no studies have been conducted, prior studies in the broader selection domain support the idea that applicants' perceptions of organizational image are related to the selection instruments used by organizations (e.g., Macan, Avedon, Paese, & Smith, 1994; Smither, Reilly, Millsap, Pearlman, & Stoffey, 1993). Moreover, Richman-Hirsch, Olson-Buchanan, and Drasgow (2000) found that an organization's use of multimedia assessment for selection purposes might signal something about an organization's technological knowledge and savvy. Studies are needed to confirm these findings in the context of Web-based testing. Again, attention should be paid here to the various dimensions (especially technology and possible technological failures) of Web-based testing as potential moderators of the effects.

Conclusion

The aim of this chapter was to review existing research on Internet recruitment and testing and to formulate recommendations for future research. A first general conclusion is that research on Internet recruitment and testing is still in its early stages. This is logical because of the relatively recent emergence of the phenomenon. Because only a limited number of topics have been addressed, many issues are still open. As noted above, the available studies on Internet recruitment, for example, have mainly focused on applicant (student) reactions to the Internet as a recruitment source, with most studies yielding positive results for the Internet. However, key issues such as the decision-making processes of applicants and the effects of Internet recruitment on post-recruitment variables such as company image, satisfaction with the selection process, or withdrawal from the current organization have been ignored so far.

As compared with Internet-based recruitment, more research attention has been devoted to Internet testing. Particularly, measurement equivalence and applicant reactions have been studied, with most studies yielding satisfactory results for Internet testing. Unfortunately, some crucial issues remain either unresolved (i.e., the effects of Internet testing on adverse impact) or unexplored (i.e., the effects of Internet testing on criterion-related validity).

A second general conclusion is the lack of theory in existing research on Internet testing and recruitment. To this end, we formulated several suggestions. As noted above, we believe that the elaboration likelihood model and resource exchange theory may be fruitfully used to understand Internet job site choice better. We have also advocated that organizational privacy theory and organizational justice theory might advance existing research on Internet testing.

Finally, we acknowledge that it is never easy to write a review of an emerging field such as Internet-based recruitment and testing because at the time this chapter goes to print, new developments and practices will have found inroad in organizations and new research studies will have been conducted. Again, this shows that for practitioners and researchers the application of new technologies such as the Internet to recruitment and testing is both exciting and challenging.

Acknowledgements

This research was supported by a grant as Postdoctoral Fellow of the Fund for Scientific Research—Flanders (Belgium) (F.W.O.—Vlaanderen). We would like to thank Fred Oswald and Frederik Anseel for their comments on an earlier version of this chapter.

References

American Educational Research Association, American Psychological Association, and National Council on Measurement in Education (1999). *Standards for Educational and Psychological Testing*. Washington, DC: American Psychological Association.

Badagliacco, J. M. (1990). Gender and race differences in computing attitudes and experience. *Social Science Computer Review*, **8**, 42–63.

Barber, A. E. (1998). *Recruiting Employees: Individual and Organizational Perspectives*. Thousands Oaks, CA: Sage.

Barber, A. E., Daly, C. L., Giannantonio, C. M., & Phillips, J. M. (1994). Job search activities: An examination of changes over time. *Personnel Psychology*, **47**, 739–766.

Baron, H., & Austin, J. (2000). Measuring ability via the Internet: Opportunities and issues. Paper presented at the Annual Conference of the Society for Industrial and Organizational Psychology, New Orleans, LA.

Bartram, D. (1994). Computer-based assessment. In C. L. Cooper, & I. T. Robertson (eds), *International Review of Industrial and Organizational Psychology* (Vol. 9, pp. 31–69). New York: John Wiley & Sons.

Bartram, D. (2001). Internet recruitment and selection: Kissing frogs to find princes. *International Journal of Selection and Assessment*, **8**, 261–274.

Beaty, J. C. Jr, Fallon, J. D., & Shepherd, W. (2002, April). Proctored versus unproctored web-based administration of a cognitive ability test. In F. L. Oswald, & J. M. Stanton (chairs), Being virtually hired: Implications of web testing for personnel selection. Symposium presented at the 17th Annual Conference of the Society for Industrial and Organizational Psychology, Toronto, Canada.

Bies, R. J. (1993). Privacy and procedural justice in organizations. *Social Justice Research*, **6**, 69–86.

Boehle, S. (2000). Online recruiting gets sneaky. *Training*, **37** (May), 66–74.

Breaugh, J., & Starke, M. (2000). Research on employee recruitment: So many studies, so many remaining questions. *Journal of Management*, **26**, 405–434.

Brinberg, D., & Ganesan, S. (1993). An application of Foa's resource exchange theory to product positioning. In U. Foa, J. Converse, K. Y. Tornblom, & E. Foa (eds), *Resource Theory: Explorations and Applications* (pp. 219–231). San Diego, CA: Academic Press.

Brooks, P. W., Jr (2000, June). Internet assessment: Opportunities and challenges. Paper presented at the 24th Annual IPMAAC Conference on Professional Personnel Assessment, Washington, DC.

Buchanan, T., & Smith, J. L. (1999a). Using the Internet for psychological research: Personality testing on the World Wide Web. *British Journal of Psychology*, **90**, 125–144.

Buchanan, T., & Smith, J. L. (1999b). Research on the internet: Validation of a World-Wide Web mediated personality scale. *Behavior Research Methods, Instruments, & Computers*, **31**, 565–571.

Burke, M. J. (1993). Computerized psychological testing: Impacts on measuring predictor constructs and future job behavior. In N. Schmitt, & W. C. Borman (eds), *Personnel Selection in Organizations* (pp. 203–239). San Francisco: Jossey-Bass.

Burnkrant, S., & Taylor, C. D (2001, April). Equivalence of traditional and Internet-based data collection: Three multigroup analyses. Paper presented at the 16th Annual Conference of the Society for Industrial and Organizational Psychology, San Diego, CA.

Cappelli, P. (2001, March). Making the most of on-line recruiting. *Harvard Business Review*, **79**, 139–146.

Cho, H., & LaRose, R. (1999). Privacy issues in Internet surveys. *Social Science Computer Review*, **17**, 421–134.

Chua, S. L., Chen, D., & Wong, A. F. L. (1999). Computer anxiety and its correlates: A meta-analysis. *Computers in Human Behavior*, **15**, 609–623.

Cober, R. T., Brown, D. J., Blumental, A. J., Doverspike, D., & Levy, P. (2000). The quest for the qualified job surfer: It's time the public sector catches the wave. *Public Personnel Management*, **29**, 479–494.

Cober, R. T., Brown, D. J., Blumental, A. J., & Levy, P. E. (2001, April). What do the 'Best Companies' do? A qualitative analysis of internet recruiting practices. In S. Highhouse (chair), New approaches to research on job search and job choice. Symposium presented at the 16th Annual Conference of the Society for Industrial and Organizational Psychology, San Diego, CA.

Coffee, K., Pearce, J., & Nishimura, R. (1999). State of California: Civil service testing moves into cyberspace. *Public Personnel Management*, **28**, 283–300.

Czaja, S., & Sharit, J. (1998). Age differences in attitudes toward computers. *Journals of Gerontology: Series B: Psychological Sciences & Social Sciences*, **53**, 329–340.

Davis, R. N. (1999). Web-based administration of a personality questionnaire: Comparison with traditional methods. *Behavior Research Methods, Instruments, & Computers*, **31**, 572–577.

Dineen, B. R., Ash, S. R., & Noe, R. A. (2002). A web of applicant attraction: Person-organization fit in the context of web-based recruitment. *Journal of Applied Psychology*, **87**, 723–734.

Dyck, J. L., & Smither, J. A. (1994). Age differences in computer anxiety: The role of computer experience, gender and education. *Journal of Educational Computing Research*, **10**, 239–248.

Eddy, E. R., Stone, D. L., & Stone, E. F. (1999). The effects of information management policies on reactions to human resource information systems: An integration of privacy and procedural justice perspectives. *Personnel Psychology*, **52**, 335–358.

Elgin, P. D., & Clapham, M. M. (2000). Attributes associated with electronic versus paper resumes. Paper presented at the 15th Annual Conference of the Society for Industrial and Organizational Psychology, New Orleans, LA.

Fenlason, K. J. (2000, April). Multiple data collection methods in 360-feedback programs: Implication for use and interpretation. Paper presented at the 15th Annual Conference of the Society for Industrial and Organizational Psychology, New Orleans, LA.

Fisher, C. D., Ilgen, D. R., Hoyer, W. D. (1979). Source credibility, information favorability, and job offer acceptance. *Academy of Management Journal*, **22**, 94–103.

Foa, U., Converse, J., Tornblom, K. Y., & Foa, E. (1993). *Resource Theory; Explorations and Applications*. San Diego, CA: Academic Press.

Fusilier, M. R., & Hoyer, W. D. (1980). Variables affecting perceptions of invasion of privacy in a personnel selection situation. *Journal of Applied Psychology*, **65**, 623–626.

Gilliland, S. W. (1993). The perceived fairness of selection systems: An organizational justice perspective. *Academy of Management Review*, **18**, 694–734.

Greenberg, C. I. (1999). Technological innovations and advancements for psychologists working with organizations. *The Psychologist-Manager Journal*, **3**, 181–190.

Greenberg, J. (1990). Organizational justice: Yesterday, today, and tomorrow. *Journal of Management*, **16**, 399–342.

Gutmacher, G. (2000). Secrets of online recruiters exposed! *Workforce*, **79** (October), 44–50.

Harris, M. M. (1999, April). Practice network: I-O psychology.com-the internet and I-O psychology. *The Industrial-Organizational Psychologist*, **36**, 89–93.

Harris, M. M. (2000). The Internet and industrial/organizational psychology: Practice and research perspectives. *Journal of e-Commerce and Psychology*, **1**, 4–23.

Harris, M. M., & DeWar, K. (2001, April). Understanding and using Web-based recruiting and screening tools: Key criteria, current trends, and future directions. Workshop presented at the Annual Conference of the Society for Industrial and Organizational Psychology, San Diego, CA.

Hezlett, S. A. (2000, April). Employee attitude surveys in multi-national organizations: An investigation of measurement equivalence. Paper presented at the 15th Annual Conference of the Society for Industrial and Organizational Psychology, New Orleans, LA.

Highhouse, S., & Hoffman, J. R. (2001). Organizational attraction and job choice. In C. L. Cooper, & I. T. Robertson (eds), *International Review of Industrial and Organizational Psychology* (pp. 37–64). Chichester, UK: John Wiley & Sons.

Highhouse, S., Stanton, J. M., & Reeve, C. L. (Forthcoming). Asymmetries in reactions to positive and negative information in an organizational recruitment context. *Journal of Vocational Behavior*,

Hoffman, D. L., Novak, T. P., & Peralta, M. (1999). Building consumer trust online. *Communications of the ACM*, **42**, 80–85.

Hom, P. W., & Griffeth, R. W. (1995). *Employee Turnover*. Cincinnati, OH: South-Western.

Hough, L. M., & Oswald, F. L. (2000). Personnel selection: Looking toward the future—remembering the past. *Annual Review of Psychology*, **51**, 631–664.

Igbaria, M., & Parasuraman, S. (1989). A path analytic study of individual characteristics, computer anxiety and attitudes towards microcomputers. *Journal of Management*, **15**, 373–388.

Jayne, M. E. A., & Rauschenberger, J. M. (2000). Demonstrating the value of selection in organizations. In J. F. Kehoe (ed.), *Managing Selection in Changing Organizations* (pp. 123–157). San Francisco: Jossey-Bass.

Joinson, A. (1999). Social desirability, anonymity, and Internet-based questionnaires. *Behavior Research Methods, Instruments, & Computers*, **31**, 433–438.

King, W. C., & Miles, E. W. (1995). A quasi-experimental assessment of the effect of computerizing noncognitive paper-and-pencil measurements: A test of measurement equivalence. *Journal of Applied Psychology*, **80**, 643–651.

Larsen, D. A., & Phillips, J. I. (2001). Effect of recruiter on attraction to the firm: Implications of the elaboration likelihood model. *Journal of Business and Psychology*, **16**, 347–364.

Lee, T. W., & Mitchell, T. R. (1994). An alternative approach: The unfolding model of voluntary employee turnover. *Academy of Management Review*, **19**, 51–89.

Lent, R. W. (2001). Vocational psychology and career counseling: Inventing the future. *Journal of Vocational Behavior*, **59**, 213–225.

Macan, T. H., Avedon, M. J., Paese, M., & Smith, D. E. (1994). The effects of applicants' reactions to cognitive ability tests and an assessment center. *Personnel Psychology*, **47**, 715–738.

Magnan, S. M., Lundby, K. M., & Fenlason, K. J. (2000, April). Dual media: The art and science of paper and internet employee survey implementation. Paper presented at the 15th Annual Conference of the Society for Industrial and Organizational Psychology, New Orleans, LA.

Maher, K., & Silverman, R. E. (2002, January). Online job sites yield few jobs, users complain. *The Wall Street Journal*, January 2, A1, A13.

McBride, J. R. (1998). Innovations in computer-based ability testing: Promise, problems and perils. In M. D. Hakel (ed.), *Beyond Multiple Choice* (pp. 113–129). Mahwah, NJ: Lawrence Erlbaum.

Mead, A. D. (2001, April). How well does web-based testing work? Results of a survey of users of NetAssess. In F. L. Oswald (chair), Computers = good? How test-user and test-taker perceptions affect technology-based employment testing. Symposium presented at the 16th Annual Conference of the Society for Industrial and Organizational Psychology, San Diego, CA.

Mead, A. D., & Coussons-Read, M. (2002, April). The equivalence of paper- and web-based versions of the 16PF questionnaire. In F. L. Oswald, & J. M. Stanton (chairs), Being virtually hired: Implications of web testing for personnel selection. Symposium presented at the 17th Annual Conference of the Society for Industrial and Organizational Psychology, Toronto, Canada.

Mead, A. D., & Drasgow, F. (1993). Equivalence of computerized and paper-and-pencil cognitive ability tests: A meta-analysis. *Psychological Bulletin*, **114**, 449–458.

Mitchell, T. R., Holtom, B. C., & Lee, T. W. (2002). How to keep our best employees: Developing an effective retention policy. *Academy of Management Executive*, **15**, 96–108.

Newhagen, J. E., & Rafaeli, S. (2000). Why communication researches should study the Internet: A dialogue. *Journal of Communication*, **46**, 4–13.

Oliver, L. W., & Whiston, S. C. (2000). Internet career assessment for the new millennium. *Journal of Career Assessment*, **8**, 361–369.

O'Neil, D. (2001). Analysis of Internet users' level of online privacy concerns. *Social Science Computer Review*, **19**, 17–31.

Oswald, F. L., Carr, J. Z., & Schmidt, A. M. (2001, April). The medium and the message: Dual effects of supervision and web-based testing on measurement equivalence for ability and personality measures. In F. L. Oswald (chair), Computers = good? How test-user and test-taker perceptions affect technology-based employment testing. Symposium presented at the 16th Annual Conference of the Society for Industrial and Organizational Psychology, San Diego, CA.

Pasveer, K. A., & Ellard, J. H. (1998). The making of a personality inventory: Help from the WWW. *Behavior Research Methods, Instruments, & Computers*, **30**, 309–313.

Pettit, F. A. (1999). Exploring the use of the World Wide Web as a psychology data collection tool. *Computers in Human Behavior*, **15**, 67–71.

Petty, R. E., & Cacioppo, J. T. (1986). *Communication and Persuasion: Central and Peripheral Routes to Attitude Change*. New York: Springer-Verlag.

Ployhart, R. E., Weekley, J., Holtz, B., & Kemp, C. (2002, April). Web-based vs. paper and pencil testing: A comparison of factor structures across applicants and incumbents. In F. L. Oswald, & J. M. Stanton (chairs), Being virtually hired: Implications of web testing for personnel selection. Symposium presented at the 17th Annual Conference of the Society for Industrial and Organizational Psychology, Toronto, Canada.

Reynolds, D. H., Sinar, E. F., & McClough, A. C. (2000, April). Evaluation of an Internet-based selection procedure. In N. J. Mondragon (chair), Beyond the demo: The empirical nature of technology-based assessments. Symposium presented at the 15th Annual Conference of the Society for Industrial and Organizational Psychology, New Orleans, LA.

Richman, W. L., Kiesler, S., Weisband, S., & Drasgow, F. (1999). A meta-analytic study of social desirability distortion in computer-administered questionnaires, traditional questionnaires, and interviews. *Journal of Applied Psychology*, **84**, 754–775.

Richman-Hirsch, W. L., Olson-Buchanan, J. B., & Drasgow, F. (2000). Examining the impact of administration medium on examinee perceptions and attitudes. *Journal of Applied Psychology*, **85**, 880–887.

Rosen, L. D., Sears, D. C., & Weil, M. M. (1987). Computerphobia. *Behavior Research Methods, Instruments, & Computers*, **19**, 167–179.

Rozelle, A. L., & Landis, R. S. (2002). An examination of the relationship between use of the Internet as a recruitment source and student attitudes. *Computers in Human Behavior*, **18**, 593–609.

Saks, A. M., & Ashforth, B. E. (2000). Change in job search behaviors and employment outcomes. *Journal of Vocational Behavior*, **56**, 277–287.

Salgado, J. F. (1999). Personnel selection methods. In C. L. Cooper, & I. T. Robertson (eds), *International Review of Industrial and Organizational Psychology* (Vol. 14, pp. 1–54). Chichester, UK: John Wiley & Sons.

Scheu, C., Ryan, A. M., & Nona, F. (1999, April). Company web sites as a recruiting mechanism: What influences applicant impressions? Paper presented at the 14th Annual Conference of the Society for Industrial and Organizational Psychology, Atlanta, GA.

Schmitt, N., & Chan, D. (1998). *Personnel Selection; A Theoretical Approach*. Thousand Oaks, CA: Sage.

Schumacher, P., & Morahan-Martin, J. (2001). Gender, Internet and computer attitudes and experiences. *Computers in Human Behavior*, **17**, 95–110.

Sharf, J. (2000). As if 'g-loaded' adverse impact isn't bad enough, Internet recruiters can expect to be accused of 'e-loaded' impact. *The Industrial-Organizational Psychologist*, **38**, 156.

Silverman, R. E. (2000). Raiding talent via the Web. *The Wall Street Journal*, October 3, B1, B16.

Simsek, Z., & Veiga, J. F. (2001). A primer on Internet organizational surveys. *Organizational Research Methods*, **4**, 218–235.

Sinar, E. F., & Reynolds, D. H. (2001, April). Applicant reactions to Internet-based selection techniques. In F. L. Oswald (chair), Computers = good? How test-user and test-taker perceptions affect technology-based employment testing. Symposium presented at the

16th Annual Conference of the Society for Industrial and Organizational Psychology. San Diego. CA.

Smith, M. R., Rogg, K. L., & Collins, P. (2001, April). Applying Internet-based business simulations to individual assessment: Some results and implications. In M. L. Kelly, & M. T. Russell (chairs), *The use of assessment tools in leadership development*. Practitioner forum presented at the 16th Annual Conference of the Society for Industrial and Organizational Psychology, San Diego, CA.

Smither, J. W., Reilly, R. R., Millsap, R. E., Pearlman, K., & Stoffey, R. W. (1993). Applicant reactions to selection procedures. *Personnel Psychology*, **46**, 49–76.

Spera, S. D., & Moye, N. A. (2001, April). Measurement equivalence between paper and web survey methods in a multinational company. Paper presented at the 16th Annual Conference of the Society for Industrial and Organizational Psychology, San Diego, CA.

Stanton, J. M. (1998). An empirical assessment of data collection using the Internet. *Personnel Psychology*, **51**, 709–725.

Stanton, J. M. (1999). Validity and related issues in Web-based hiring. *The Industrial-Organizational Psychologist*, **36**(3), 69–77.

Stanton, J. M., & S. G. Rogelberg, S.G. (2001a, April). Challenges and obstacles in conducting employment testing via the Internet. In F. L. Oswald, (chair), Computers = good? How test-user and test-taker perceptions affect technology-based employment testing. Symposium presented at the 16th Annual Conference of the Society for Industrial and Organizational Psychology, San Diego, CA.

Stanton, J. M., & Rogelberg, S. G. (2001b). Using Internet/Intranet web pages to collect organizational research data. *Organizational Research Methods*, **4**, 199–216.

Stone, E. F., Gueutal, H. G., Gardner, D. G., & McClure, S. (1983). A field experiment comparing information-privacy values, beliefs, and attitudes across several types of organizations. *Journal of Applied Psychology*, **68**, 459–468.

Stone, D. L., & Stone, E. F. (1990). Privacy in organizations: Theoretical issues, research findings, and protection mechanisms. *Research in Personnel and Human Resources Management*, **8**, 349–411.

Straus, S. G., Miles, J. A., & Levesque, L. L. (2001). The effects of videoconference, telephone, and face-to-face media on interviewer and applicant judgments in employment interviews. *Journal of Management*, **27**, 363–381.

Travagline, A., & Frei, R. L. (2001, April). 21st century recruiting: A model for Internet-based realistic job previews. Paper presented at the 16th Annual Conference of the Society for Industrial and Organizational Psychology, San Diego, CA.

Weiss, E. M., & Barbeite, G. F. (2001). Internet as a job source and job site preference. Paper presented at the 16th Annual Conference of the Society for Industrial and Organizational Psychology, San Diego, CA.

Whitley, B. E. (1997). Gender differences in computer-related attitudes and behavior: A meta-analysis. *Computers in Human Behavior*, **13**, 1–22.

Zottoli, M. A., & Wanous, J. P. (2000). Recruitment source research: Current status and future directions. *Human Resource Management Review*, **10**, 353–382.

Zusman, R. R., & Landis, R. (2002). Applicant preferences for Web-based versus traditional job postings. *Computers in Human Behavior*, **18**, 285–296.

56
APPLICANT AND RECRUITER REACTIONS TO NEW TECHNOLOGY IN SELECTION
A critical review and agenda for future research

Neil Anderson

Source: *International Journal of Selection and Assessment* 11(2/3) (2003): 121–136.

Abstract

This paper presents a narrative review of recent research into applicant and recruiter reactions to new technology in employee selection. Different aspects of the use of new technology are noted including computer-based testing, Internet-based recruitment and candidate assessment, telephone-based and video-based interviews, video-based situational judgment tests, and virtual reality scenarios. It is argued that an appropriate way to conceptualize these advances is as 'technical innovations' as defined in the creativity and innovation research in Industrial, Work, and Organizational (IWO) psychology. Applicant reactions research is reviewed thematically, and studies into three main themes are discussed: *Applicant preferences and reactions, equivalence, and adverse impact*. Following Bartram (2001), an amphibian-monarchistic analogy is employed at several stages in the review. Four major criticisms of the extant applicant reactions research base are noted: *its atheoretical orientation, a short-termist concentration upon reactions level outcomes, an over-reliance on students as surrogates, and a patchiness of coverage of crucial research questions*. The second part of this paper explores neglected issues of recruiter adoption of new technology for employee selection. Again drawing from advances in the innovation and creativity literatures, this section explores likely antecedent factors at the individual and organizational levels of analysis. A general model of recruiter adoption of new technology is posited as a framework for future research in this area. For both applicant and recruiter reactions further research is called for and implications for practice are noted throughout.

Introduction

In recent years there has been a rapid growth in research into applicant reactions to new technology in employee selection procedures. Not surprisingly, given the increasing use of more advanced technology by organizations to deliver recruitment and assessment methods to applicant pools, this has spurred the interest of researchers and practitioners alike in the effects that new technology may be having upon applicant reactions, fairness, and equivalence, amongst other important considerations (e.g. Anderson, Born and Cunnigham-Snell, 2001; Harris, 1999, 2000; Highhouse and Hoffman, 2001; Hough and Oswald, 2000; Lievens and Harris, 2003). Although it has primarily been the growth in the use of computer-based testing procedures and Internet-based platforms for the delivery of company web sites for recruitment and prescreening tests which has driven these developments, other forms of new technology delivery of selection methods have also been evident including telephone-based interviews, video-based situational judgment tests, and virtual reality technology.

An appropriate way to conceptualize such advances, it is argued, is that they represent 'technical innovations' (Damanpour, 1990) as defined in the wider creativity and innovation literatures in IWO psychology (e.g. West and Farr, 1990). Regrettably the selection and innovation literatures have remained almost entirely separate, with each sub-field having developed in notable isolation from the other. This has been particularly unfortunate in the case of technological innovation in selection, it is argued, as advances in understanding of technical innovation processes in organizations could usefully have been applied to the introduction, adoption, and adaption of new technology in employee recruitment and selection. This paper therefore attempts to draw links and parallels between these two disparate sub-fields in IWO psychology. Particular emphasis is given to definitions of innovation, whether all forms of new technology in selection would meet the criteria for being described as 'innovations', and perhaps more innovatively in the final section of this paper, to developing and explicating a general model predicting recruiter adoption of new technology in selection.

Plethora and paucity

Overviewing developments in studies into applicant reactions to new technology in selection, the bulk of the research effort has actually been very recent, largely driven by the exponential growth in the use of the Internet and other computer-based testing batteries. Consequently, much of the research reviewed in this paper has been published only over the last decade or so. It is therefore timely to overview advances generally in research into new technology in staff recruitment and selection, to flag up important findings and themes of enquiry, and to highlight promising directions for future research. Compared with this plethora of recent research into applicant reactions to new technology, there has been a striking paucity of research into recruiter reactions to such advances. The second part of this paper therefore contrasts the rapid advances being made in our understanding of applicant reactions to new technology against the virtually unresearched range of questions which still remain over likely recruiter reactions to, and adoption of, new technological platforms. As an initial effort to structure the research agenda in this regard, again the field of innovation in organizations is argued to be a valuable and potentially synergistic topic area from which we can draw for future research into recruiter reactions (e.g. West, 2002). Indeed, the adoption of innovations by organizations has been a longstanding theme for research in the innovation literature and research in this area has uncovered a number of robust factors which influence willingness to adopt and adapt to new workplace practices (see for instance King and Anderson, 2002 for a comprehensive review). A recurrent theme in the innovation literature has been the adoption of new technology by organizations and so it is entirely appropriate to consider this issue with respect to the adoption of new technology by recruiters for staff selection and assessment procedures. For example, questions over the willingness of different recruiters to consider adopting newly emergent technological solutions for staff selection, their likely attitudes to different levels of technological complexity, their beliefs over the importance of the impact of company recruitment brochures and web site designs, adoption rates of new technology in selection by different sectors of organizations likely to be competing for staff with scarce skills or abilities, are all clearly important issues for pragmatic research. Yet, this 'side of the equation' in new technology research has been neglected by recent efforts among personnel psychologists, and as a result our understanding of these questions lags significantly behind our current state-of-knowledge into applicant reactions. The second part of this paper therefore highlights the importance of a balanced future research agenda which includes both applicant and recruiter reactions to new technology. Drawing from the now mature field of innovation and creativity in the workplace several key directions for future research are proposed as crucial outstanding issues for concern to which future research needs to be addressed.

Technological innovation in selection: definitions and trends

A cursory review of the journals, books, and other literature published over recent years reveals a range of examples of 'new technology' being used for employee recruitment and applicant assessment (e.g. Bartram, 2001; Lievens, Van Dam and Anderson, 2002). Of course, it is not immediately apparent how the term 'new technology' should be defined (see below), but for the present review a broad and encompassing interpretation of this term was used in order to include as many aspects of the proliferation of emergent technology in selection as possible. Our review covered all major journals (*Journal of Applied Psychology*, *Personnel Psychology*, *International Journal of Selection and Assessment*, *Academy of Management Journal*, *Human Performance*, etc.), several earlier special issues of journals (e.g. *International Journal of Selection and Assessment*, 1995, **3** (2)), numerous authored and edited books, unpublished technical and consultancy reports, and the published conference proceedings of international conferences where there has been a spate of recent symposia addressing particularly applicant reactions to Internet-based testing (e.g. Baron and Austin, 2000; Derous, 2003; Harris, Paajanen and Blunt, 2003). In addition, researchers active in this field were contacted with a request for offprints and in-press or in-progress papers. As mentioned previously, this area is relatively newly established in personnel psychology, a point vividly reflected in the recency of the publication dates of research cited in the present paper. Most developments have occurred since the early 1990s onwards, and in relation to applicant reactions there is a clear and encouraging pattern of exponential growth in the number and range of papers published.

Despite this proliferation of research interest, the moot point of how one is to define exactly what is, and what is not, 'new technology' in employee selection has received little attention in the literature. A valuable starting point is to refer to Damanpour's (1990) characterization of technical innovations which he states include new products, services or technological processes directly related to the primary work activity of the section or organization. In relation to the HRM function, this would clearly include the use of new technology in selection. However, there is undoubtedly considerable variation between organizations and HRM departments in their level of technical sophistication (Bartram, 2001, 2002). For some highly technologically-sophisticated organizations themselves involved in Internet solutions consultancy, possibly even the most advanced of our current platforms for delivery of assessment methods in staff selection would be perceived as outmoded, archaic software which by no means would qualify as 'new' technology. For other organizations where recruitment has been traditionally carried out via hard copy paper-based vitas and candidate assessment has involved only a series of unstructured face-to-face interviews, the prospect of conducting simple structured telephone-based interviews would be viewed as being radically innovative. From an applied perspective, therefore, it is likely that recruiters will vary considerably in what they would accept to fit the criteria of being 'new' and 'technological' in selection contexts.

Conversely, across the extant literature a common understanding and metric appears to have been adopted such that self-evidently new technology as the Internet, computer-based delivery of assessment instruments, and CD-ROM platforms for scenario presentations to applicants would undoubtedly fulfill the criteria. Indeed the present issue of this journal reports a number of studies into such applications. Before moving on to consider the existing research it is however important to clarify what precisely is meant by the term 'new technology'. West and Farr (1990) define innovation as follows:

> ... the intentional introduction and application within a role, group or organization of ideas, processes, products or procedures, new to the relevant unit of adoption, designed to significantly benefit the individual, the group, the organization or wider society (p. 9)

Their definition is constructive and valuable in several regards. First, West and Farr emphasize that innovation must confer an intended benefit at one or more levels of analysis – the job role, work group or wider organization. Most applications of new technology in selection will meet this criterion as they have typically been medium- to large-scale innovation projects intended to transfer existing or modified predictor methods onto a new platform for delivery to applicant pools. Second, but somewhat more problematic concerning new technology in selection, their definition argues that an innovation must be new to the 'relevant unit of adoption', what has been termed *relative* as opposed to *absolute novelty* in the innovation literature (Anderson and King, 1993; King and Anderson, 2002). In other words, that the *perception* of the innovation, in this context the use of new technology for selection, must be new only to the section which is now adopting it, usually HRM departments responsible for applicant screening. This is an important distinction since absolute novelty requires that the process or technology is not in usage anywhere else currently, that is, that it is unique. Hence, the adoption and use of computer-based testing by an HRM section which had in the past only used pen-and-paper tests would be deemed to be innovative in its use of new technology. Third, the innovation must necessarily demonstrate some benefits at the individual (recruiter job performance), group (HRM section), or organizational level of analysis. Thus, a failed attempt to introduce new technology into the screening process would clearly not meet this criterion as neither would the introduction of new technology which performed worse in comparison with existing, traditional methods. It is important to note, nonetheless, that the distinction between 'absolute' and 'relative' novelty implied in West and Farr's definition clearly has sensible limitations. It would not be reasonable to argue that the very last HRM department in an industrial sector to introduce Internet-based testing was being innovative, far from it. Merely following the trend long behind comparable departments or organizations would be at such a low point on a relative novelty scale as to make this conformity behavior rather than innovative behavior (see also, West, 2002). Additionally, innovation is most appropriately conceptualized as a cyclical, ongoing, and iterative set of events and processes of re-structuring (Anderson, De Dreu and Nijstad, in press). That is, it is not a single, outcome event, or in personnel psychology terminology, 'criterion measure'. Previous innovations spur changes in work role and work team functioning that are likely to be facilitative of a future propensity to innovate at either of these levels-of-analysis (Anderson *et al.*, *op. cit.*).

Although as Nicholson (1990) points out, these criteria and points of semantic debate simply push the definitional boundaries back a step so that one then has to define what is meant by 'intentional', 'beneficial', and even 'new', the West and Farr formulation is helpful. Moreover, as Amabile (1983) has argued, such definitions force researchers to attend to what study participants themselves perceive and rate to be innovative practice, rather than to impose upon them an isolated, irrelevant and amorphous terminology. Finally, these aspects of the innovation literature are valuable in that they highlight the dangers of adopting a so-called 'pro-innovation bias' (King and Anderson, 2002), that is the unverified assumption that new technology solutions are better than existing, traditional methods. Little research, if any, in the personnel selection field appears to have critically evaluated whether more highly advanced technological forms of delivering selection methods actually perform better than traditional modes of delivery, as discussed later in this paper.

If one accepts the West and Farr (1990) definition, which has indeed been widely the case in the innovation literature, an overview of the reported incidents and uses of new technology in selection over the last decade or so would most probably include all of the following: *Computer (PC)-based testing, Internet-based testing, telephone-based assessment procedures, computer-based realistic job previews and situational judgment tests, multimedia simulation tests, and virtual reality immersion testing*. In many of these applications, as noted earlier, it has been rapid advances in the power and cost-effectiveness of stand-alone personal computers and their use in connection with the Internet which has catapulted them into becoming viable tools for use in selection procedures (see Bartram, 2002; Harris and De War, 2001, for instance). Standing in relation to this list of new technology is the range of uses to which it has been put in selection, which includes the following: *Vacancy advertisements, company and job information provision, prescreening methods (recruitment short listing, biodata forms, candidate self-assessment, and so forth), candidate assessment methods (interviews, cognitive ability tests, personality tests, situational judgment tests, and so forth), feedback reports to applicants and to communicate outcome decisions, and finally, data collection for monitoring of adverse impact and test validation amongst other purposes*. Both lists are not intended to be exhaustive however, but they are representative of the apparently major forms and uses of new technology in selection reported in the literature.

In some areas, for instance the use of Internet-based recruitments and tests of general mental ability (GMA), developments have been particularly rapid and substantial research is already evident (for a comprehensive and up-to-date review see Lievens and Harris, 2003); in other areas the popularity of using the technology in practice appears to have outstripped the pace of developments in the validatory research base (e.g. concerns over use of the Internet for recruitment with regards potential adverse impact and inequalities of access); and in still other areas the new technology appears to be only being used by the most selection-sophisticated organizations who can afford the high start-up and maintenance costs (e.g. simulator training for pilot and police driver selection). Thus, there are considerable differences in both the *uptake* of new technology for delivery of different predictor methods, and simultaneously, in the *maturity* of the research-base to support and verify such use in practice. Whilst this is not surprising given the emerging nature of much of the hardware and software involved, this disparity in usage and validation remains a challenge for future research in this area.

Applicant reactions: three major research themes

Overview

This section presents a themed, targeted narrative review of the main research findings into applicant reactions to new technology in selection. It does not attempt to provide a complete, detailed review of all primary studies into every aspect of applicant reactions or every permutation of use of the new technology (see above) as this would be beyond the scope of a single paper. In addition, several comprehensive reviews of candidate reactions to selection procedures in general have been published elsewhere recently (e.g. Ryan and Ployhart, 2000; and Anderson, Born and Cunningham-Snell, 2001), as have several reviews of applicant reactions to specific aspects of new technology in selection (see Alkhadher, Anderson and Clarke, 1994; Bartram, 1994 for reviews of computer-based testing; Harris, 2002 on Internet-based GMA testing; and, Lievens and Harris, 2003 for a comprehensive review of Internet-based recruitment and testing). Three main themes are identified:

1 Applicant preferences and reactions
2 Equivalence
3 Adverse impact

Under each theme research findings are reviewed broadly in chronological order as the methods would occur in organizational selection practices – i.e. *recruitment, applicant prescreening methods (application forms, curriculum vitas, biodata forms), and candidate assessment methods (interviews, cognitive ability tests, personality inventories, other forms of testing, and assessment centers)*. The review focuses on key, replicated themes of findings rather than on an exhaustive review of all published studies across all areas of enquiry, therefore. Of necessity, some judgment calls had to be made by the present author over what these key themes of findings in the present research base were, but in all cases these were identified where (a) several independent studies had produced similar or identical findings, thus permitting some reliance upon the particular finding, and (b) where individual study methodologies were sufficiently robust as to warrant some weight being placed upon their findings, especially where multiple studies had used somewhat different but related and robust methodologies. In fact, applying these conditions, several of the emergent findings in applicant reactions to new technology in selection did not meet one or other of them and were thus omitted from the present review.

1. Applicant preferences and reactions

Research has only very recently begun to explore applicant reactions in *recruitment* phases particularly to Internet-based company information and application procedures. The popularity of company web sites certainly cannot be denied with one study in the USA reporting that 88 percent of Global 500 companies having recruitment sections to their company web sites (iLogos, 2001 cited in Lievens and Harris, 2003). Further, another US survey found that across nine larger American companies 16 percent of all subsequent hires originally applied through the company's Internet recruitment sites (Maher and Silverman, 2002). Thus, it would be premature to state that web-based recruitment has completely replaced traditional, paper-based application procedures, or even for that matter has become the majority route for attracting in applications. But certainly amongst larger, multinational organizations there has been a marked trend toward Internet-based recruitment over the last decade. Integral to this trend is undoubtedly the likelihood that applicants appreciate the possibility of being able to log-on from home to an organization's web site to download information directly. Thus, it is not clear at the present time whether this trend is largely being driven by organizational preferences, applicant preferences, or a combination of both. In contrast to this developing use in industry, research into applicant reactions to Internet-based recruitment has lagged behind. Only a couple of published and in-press studies can be located which examine in any detail the reactions of potential applicants to company web sites (see also, Salgado, this issue). However, these studies do show encouragingly positive findings, although both were conducted using university students as participants. Rozelle and Landis (in press) compared traditional forms of recruitment (college visits, company brochures, etc.) against Internet recruitment sites. They found that students perceived the latter as more realistic but also less formal compared against traditional methods for student selection. Similarly, Zusman and Landis (in press) reported that undergraduate students rated Internet-based postings for job placements more favorably than more traditional documentary sources. Whilst these are encouraging findings it is likely that students as younger applicants to the labor market will rate Internet-based recruitment media more favorably than older, more experienced, and possibly less computer-literate applicants. Note also that these studies concerned student recruitment (Rozelle and Landis) and job placement recruitment for students (Zusman and Landis) respectively so it would be unwise to generalize from these exploratory findings to other sectors of labor market recruitment. Care should even be taken in generalizing these findings to recruitment for permanent job vacancies in industry (e.g. Lievens, Van Dam and Anderson, 2002; Anderson, Lievens, Van Dam and Ryan, in press). Undoubtedly, future research is called for which extends these initial findings to investigate reactions of other types of applicants, to differing formats of web site design, follow-up procedures for applying online, and the longer-term impact of initial reactions of applicants upon later expectations of, and attitudes toward, organizational selection procedures.

Applicant reactions to *computer-based testing*, that is tests administered to applicants using personal computers or a networked internal computer system as opposed to Internet-based testing, have been a topic for research interest in the selection literature for a relatively longer period of time (e.g. Alkhadher *et al.*, 1994; Bartram, 1994). Overviewing the now quite voluminous number of studies conducted in this area, the findings can at best be described as varied and diffuse. On the one hand, a string of studies report positive applicant reactions to sitting computer-based tests as opposed to their pen-and-paper counterparts (e.g. Mathisen, Evans, Meyers and Kogan, 1985; Burke, Normand and Raju, 1987; Davis and Cowles, 1989; Arvey, Strickland, Drauden and Martin, 1990; Schmitt, Gilliland, Landis and Devine, 1993). On the other, several studies have either failed to find more positive reactions (Wiechmann and Ryan, 2003) or have reported negative reactions by applicants (e.g. Martin and Nagao, 1989; Meir and Lambert, 1991). Of all of these, the recent study by Wiechmann and Ryan (2003) reveals the importance of using carefully designed, experimental manipulations of test-taking conditions to participants. Simple, post-test only reactions designs may also fail to account for other important moderator variables such as applicant mood, exposure to computer-based tests in the past, computer anxiety, and so forth (Wiechmann and Ryan). Thus, the most probable explanation for these conflicting findings is that the design of the test itself together with moderator variables such as how it was administered, treatment of applicants during the selection process generally, and whether there existed an opportunity to receive feedback on test performance, influenced testee ratings of the computer-based testing session. Although some research into this mode of delivery of both cognitive ability and personality tests is on-going, much of the research attention has turned toward *Internet-based* delivery of such testing sessions (Bartram, 2002; Harris, 2002).

A flurry of studies has very recently appeared examining applicant reactions to *Internet-based testing procedures*. Indeed, the use of the Internet for both recruitment and testing functions appears to hold out considerable promise as a technology which may transform these aspects of selection in future (Buchanan and Smith, 1999; Bartram, 2001; Mead, 2001; Stanton and Rogelberg, 2001; Paronto *et al.*, 2003; Derous, 2003). But it has only been in the last four years or so that such developments have taken place and it appears at the moment that the research base is struggling to keep pace with the speed with which Internet-based testing is being adopted by organizations internationally (Lievens and Harris, 2003). So far, almost universally positive applicant reactions have been reported for Internet-based testing batteries. Mead (2001), and Reynolds, Sinar and McClough (2000) both found more positive candidate reactions to Internet-based personality tests than to traditional, pen-and-paper forms of administration. For cognitive ability testing via the Internet, Baron and Austin (2000) report positive reactions to GMA tests administered over the Internet. In a large-scale analysis Reynolds and Lin (submitted) also report favorable reactions by applicants to a range of tests being administered by Internet platforms, and so across this spate of recent studies, not one has yet reported negative reactions by applicants to web-based testing administration. Indeed, Internet-based test administration holds advantages for both the organization (e.g. cost savings, remote administration, data collection and monitoring) and the applicant alike (e.g. no need to physically attend the organization in the case of remote administration, freedom to choose when the test is taken, etc.), and so it is most likely that Internet-based testing will become substantially more popular in future years. Internet-based selection procedures can also have a positive impact on perceptions of the organization, that is company image, amongst potential applicants (Reynolds and Sinar, 2001). At present, it is the larger, multinational organizations recruiting larger numbers of employees that have adopted Internet-based recruitment and testing, especially organizations recruiting from a nationally or internationally mobile pool of applicants (Bartram, 2002; Lievens and Harris, 2003). In future, we are likely to see this technology proliferate downwards with Internet-based procedures being adopted by medium-sized and smaller organizations and with access to the World Wide Web becoming increasingly widespread internationally (Bartram, 2001; Harris, 2002; see also Van de Ven et al., 1989 for a review of innovation dispersion).

Applicant reactions to different modes of conducting *employment interviews* have been examined by a few studies (Straus, Miles and Levesque, 2001). Straus et al. (2001) evaluated student reactions to mock interviews conducted in face-to-face, videoconference, or telephone-based conditions. Although the sample size was small ($n = 59$) and these were simulated employment interviews with MBA students, applicants rated the videoconference condition significantly less favorably than face-to-face or telephone-based interviews. Other research into recruiter perceptions (Silvester, Anderson, Haddleton, Cunningham-Snell and Gibb, 2000; Silvester and Anderson, 2003) shows that interviewer reactions to information presented by interviewees may differ across modes of interview presentation, in this case face-to-face versus telephone-based interviews. This is considered below in the following part of this paper.

A handful of studies have been conducted into applicant reactions to *computerized job simulations and situational judgment tests* (SJTs) using new technology, in this case with more mixed findings. Shotland, Alliger and Sales (1998) report positive reactions to a computerized job simulation developed to select insurance claims personnel. Conversely, Paronto, Bauer and Truxillo (2003) compared reactions to a screening scenario test, similar in content to an SJT, across three conditions, interactive voice response by telephone, telephone-based interview screening, and face-to-face interview screening. Most positive responses were to the final condition, that is the face-to-face interview. Chan and Schmitt (1997) investigated whether differences in video-based versus paper-and-pencil SJTs were moderated by the ethnic origin of applicants. As hypothesized, they found overall that face validity was rated higher for the video-based condition, but also that face validity differences and test performance differences between whites and blacks were significantly smaller for the video-based SJT (see comments under Adverse Impact, below).

Finally, although not an empirical study into applicant reactions, Aguinis, Henle and Beaty (2001) usefully review potential applications for use of *virtual reality technology (or VRT)* in selection and assessment. They note that VRT incurs very high set-up costs compared with other modes of test or SJT delivery and so is probably only viable for use in high-demand, high-risk jobs such as pilot and other military personnel selection and training. Certain knowledge, skills, abilities, and other characteristics (KSAOs) are more suitable for assessment via VRT methods, it is argued, including manual dexterity, certain types of job knowledge, and cognitive and psychomotor functions.

2. Equivalence

With regard to *recruitment* there has been a notable shortage of research comparing the equivalence of traditional forms of sourcing applications against new technology sources. Perhaps this is to some extent due to methodological difficulties inherent in designing lab and field studies to examine equivalence with sufficient robustness. Whatever the reasons, existing studies appear to have limited their focus to that of applicant reactions to new technology rather than to encompass wider questions of whether outcome equivalence does indeed exist. The most central question is whether use of new technology produces the same quantity and quality of applicants for an organization, of course. Related to this is the question of whether new technology impacts upon applicants' decisions to self-select-out in any different manner to more traditional forms of recruitment (Breaugh and Starke, 2000; Dineen, Ash and Noe, 2002), in addition to the issue of potential adverse impact associated with this. Given the increasingly prevalent use of the Internet for staff recruitment this is a real shortcoming in our understanding.

In contrast a number of questions associated with the equivalence of pen-and-paper and both *computer-based tests* and *Internet-based tests* have been addressed by several primary studies. Indeed, for *computer-based tests* there has been a large number of studies that have examined the equivalence of particular pen-and-paper cognitive tests and personality inventories with computer based formats of the same measures (for major reviews and meta-analyses see Mead and Drasgow, 1993; Alkhadher *et al.*, 1994; Bartram, 1994; Finger and Ones, 1999; Harris and De War, 2001). Generally, the results have been positive and even the findings of the few studies which do report significant between-form differences may be attributable to sampling errors within individual studies (Finger and Ones, 1999), As Harris (2002) also points out, of greater import than simple questions of between-form measurement equivalence is whether predictive validities or adverse impact ratios differ (see below). For *Internet-based tests*, the present review failed to locate any papers published as yet into this question either for tests of cognitive ability or personality inventories. Internal, proprietary research may well be being conducted by commercial test publishers into this question, but as yet it does not seen to have appeared in the public domain. Given the growth in the use of the Internet as a platform for test delivery to applicants this is an area in which more research is sorely called for.

A few studies have been published into the equivalence of face-to-face, telephone-based, and video-based *interviews*. Silvester *et al.* (2000) and Silvester and Anderson (2003) compared face-to-face and telephone-based interviews.

In both studies they failed to find acceptable equivalence between each mode of delivery both in the response patterns of interviewees across conditions and the attributions made by interviewers from these responses. Recruiters rated applicants less leniently in the telephone-based condition and also attributed candidates' responses to structured questions less positively in this condition than in face-to-face interviews. Straus *et al.* (2001) found the opposite, however, that interviewers rated candidates more favorably in the telephone-based condition than face-to-face, but again equivalence was not demonstrated. It would seem that equivalence cannot be taken for granted in new technological administrations of selection methods even where this 'new' technology is more basic in nature, such as telephone-based interview procedures.

To summarize, the question of equivalence has received some research attention across different predictors with rather mixed findings. In terms of computer-based testing the findings are generally positive, for Internet-based tests there is a notable lack of published work, and for interviews the findings are contradictory but not in favor of equivalence. None of these studies has moved on to examine more demanding questions of differences between forms in the predictive validity of alternative modes of delivery in comparing traditional and innovative modes of presentation to applicants.

3. Adverse impact

The third, and in many ways most challenging issue to have received attention in research into applicant reactions to new technology is that of the potential for new modes of predictor method delivery to influence adverse impact in selection. Most interestingly, research suggests that this influence may be either beneficial or detrimental, or both, depending upon how the technology is used and at what stages in the recruitment and selection process. Indeed, the findings are actually *bimodal* in that on the one hand new technological approaches have been argued to exacerbate potential for adverse impact against minority groups, whereas on the other, several studies unequivocally reveal the potential for new technologies to ameliorate bias against minorities. In general this bimodal trend in the research findings splits conveniently between recruitment on one side and later stage selection methods on the other.

With regard to adverse impact in recruitment warning bells have been sounded by several authors of late (Sharf, 2000; Bartram, 2001; Harris, 2002; Lievens and Harris, 2003). This stems from differences between minority groups in being able to easily access the Internet via personal computers in the home, or so-called 'e-loaded' adverse impact (Sharf, 2000). Harris (2002) quotes most recent statistics in relation to household access to the Internet for homes in the USA. Internet usage percentages (as at September, 2001) were as follows: Whites, 60 percent; Asians, 60 percent; Blacks, 40 percent; and Hispanics, 32 percent. Thus, households of White or Asian ownership were almost twice as likely to have access to the Internet than for Hispanic occupants. In other countries it is likely that these socio-economic differences in Internet access will be similar in their effects, although of course the prevalence of Internet usage will be different as will the minority groups involved (see Bartram, 2001). Whatever these international differences, the implication is identical: minority groups that are concentrated in more socio-economically deprived areas will have substantially lower levels of access to the Internet via home computers. As Sharf (2000) and Bartram (2001) point out, this has important knock-on effects to the proportions of minority group members who will be able to access easily Internet-based recruitment sites. It also holds the potential for legal challenges against organizations using this technology but, in so doing, who may be unwittingly operating an anti-diversity policy through differential access to the Internet based upon socio-economic disadvantage. Harris (2002) in a landmark study based upon a huge sample of applicants for customer service jobs (total n = 1.3 million) did not, however, find percentage differences between traditional sources of recruitment referral and Internet sourced applications. Further, another study (Sinar and Reynolds, 2001) does suggest that once logged-on to Internet recruitment sites individuals from racial minorities tend in general to react more favorably. Combined, these two studies suggest that there may be few or no conversion-rate differences into actual applications between majority and minority group members once logged-on to organizational recruitment web sites. If so, the first imperative appears to be for organizations to ensure that sufficient proportions of minorities obtain access to their recruitment web sites in the first place.

However, this initial imperative opens-up a whole series of consequent issues and research questions. Some types of organization are likely to have better resources and knowledge in order to be able to cope with the potential of e-loaded adverse impact. For instance, organizations with a long experience of dealing with unfair discrimination professionally (e.g. state sector bodies), those with internal expertise on tap (e.g. military divisions with access to personnel psychologists), and those with sufficient slack resources to buy-in consultancy expertise (e.g. financial sector employers and multinational companies). Whether these organizations are the most attractive as potential employers to applicants from minority backgrounds is a question for empirical research. This leads onto another vexed issue: self-selection by minority group members themselves causing possible range restriction in the proportions of applicants received by an organization. Schmidt (2002) provides a seminal discussion of this very point in relation to general cognitive ability (GCA) or what has been termed elsewhere general mental ability (GMA), (see also, Kehoe, 2002). Currently, at least in the US, it has been argued that the lower proportions of minority group members who have *access* to the Internet is the cause for concern (cf. Sharf, 2000). I am indebted to the comments of one of the anonymous reviewers who noted that this may be ameliorated or exacerbated by self-selection effects by minority group members themselves. No published study appears so far to have investigated between-group preference differences for using Internet-based application procedures as opposed to traditional documentary methods. Additionally, *restriction of range* effects call for further research attention in this regard. For instance, if minority group applicants entering an organization's recruitment procedure are comparatively highly qualified and able, this introduces bias in favor of the minority applicant pool. This seems to be a likely scenario with regard to Internet-based recruitment and testing presently as applicants from minority groups are likely to be comparatively better educated, open to using new technology, possess a more informed network of contacts to be aware of organizational web sites, and be generally advantaged compared against even the majority group. These possible explanations may account for the following findings, that new technology can reduce minority-majority group differences in selection procedures.

Counter to the concerns over e-loaded adverse impact stand the results of several studies showing that selection methods being administered by new technology can reduce or even negate minority-majority group differences and recruiter discrimination. First, Silvester *et al.* (2000) suggest that telephone-based interviews may have reduced opportunities for recruiters to give less favorable ratings to ethnic minority applicants simply because the interviewer was not aware of the candidates ethnic origin. In this case, therefore, the lack of visual cues available to the interviewer conducting telephone-based interviews may have mediated against adverse impact, an unintentional but beneficial outcome from the use of technological innovations in interviewing (see also Silvester and Anderson, 2003). Visual cues were found to have a rather different effect by Chan and Schmitt (1997). They compared Black-White differences on a situational judgment test administered to subjects in both pen-and-paper and video-based conditions. It was found that ethnic differences in test performance were significantly smaller in the video-based condition than in the traditional pen-and-paper format. So, to summarize, the present position regarding adverse impact and new technology in selection can best be described as mixed; concerns over Internet access for ethnic minority groups have been voiced but against this there seem to be no conversion rate differences between Whites and ethnic minorities once logged-on to company recruitment sites. Finally, there is some initial evidence that the use of new technology for test and interview administration may reduce adverse impact, a highly beneficial potential effect that is surely worthy of further research attention.

Critique: kissing princes to find frogs

In critically reviewing this body of research into candidate reactions to new forms of technology in selection one is left with both a sense of excitement over an area which is newly emerging and vibrant, but also a sense of disappointment at the intellectual rigor and contribution to wider understanding that these studies combine to make. Should we be that surprised if applicants presented with better designed web sites react more positively to poorly designed ones? Or that reactions to computer-based and Internet-based tests are generally favorable if we limit our subject pool only to undergraduate students who have been brought up using computers as part of their everyday lives? Or that applicants prefer to sit

Internet-based tests in the comfort of their own homes as opposed to having to attend an organization's offices for group testing sessions? These comments are intentionally critical (and perhaps unfairly so), but overviewing this newly established research field one is forced to conclude that it now runs the risk of imploding into a quasi-science of empirically proving rather common sensical observations. We need to take steps at the present juncture to prevent this from happening as this would be to deny the wider field of selection research important on-going findings which have the potential to add significantly to our understanding of applicant and recruiter reactions. Ostensibly these refer to new technology, although it can be persuasively argued that such findings are likely to have wider generality to reactions to other impending changes in employee selection. How can the sub-field of reactions research make quantum leaps forward in the foreseeable future and in so doing avoid becoming encircled in a worthy but dull cul-de-sac of routine endeavor to quantify fairly obvious reactive outcomes? Research needs to move beyond immediate level reactions outcomes, to incorporate appropriate and competing theoretical rationales, and to move away from an excessive reliance upon students as surrogate samples to include other candidate groups applying for actual vacancies in the field.

First, much of the research has been rather *atheoretical* in its orientation, conceptualization, and design. Research has in general simply addressed rather descriptive level questions, such as applicant favorability reactions or between-forms equivalence, rather than being based upon articulated theoretical formulations or even postulated models of interactions between relevant variables (see also Lievens and Harris, 2003). This has led to dust-bowl empiricism. Indeed, it would at present be difficult to counter this criticism by pointing to a raft of studies in which a clearly articulated theory or model is postulated and empirically tested. This may again be due to the fact that this area is extremely recent in its emergence, but at times it does appear that studies are largely opportunistic efforts designed to address purely pragmatic and immediate questions. The *how much* of applicant reactions appears to have dominated any deeper empirical questions of the *why* of applicant reactions. This is regrettable as the field currently lacks any guiding theoretical frameworks or even specified models which attempt to explain why applicants react in the ways that they are found to do. A consequence of this largely atheoretical orientation has been a lack of inclusion of antecedent variables in applicant reactions studies, an important omission. Such variables as past exposure to computers, past experiences of new technology in selection, computerphobic reactions, and openness to new experience as a Five Factor Model personality variable are all likely to influence applicant reactions, yet have only been included in a couple of studies to date (see Wiechmann and Ryan (2003) for instance). Another useful theoretical framework which may be drawn from is noted by Lievens and Harris (2003). They also criticize this area for not basing research questions sufficiently on existing theory and point to organizational privacy theory and organizational justice theory as two related theoretical orientations. Given the relevance of both theoretical formulations to the impact of new technological forms in recruitment and selection, both of these frameworks do indeed appear prima facie to offer valuable psychological grounding for future research. To conclude, it is reasonable to challenge the field to become more theoretically sophisticated in its recourse to appropriate theoretical formulations and applied models. Ultimately our understanding of applicant reactions will benefit immeasurably from a more theoretical point of departure being taken by future studies, from alternative theoretical frameworks and models being tested empirically, and generally from more attention to underlying theoretical propositions and hypothesis formulation as to why applicants may react in the ways they are subsequently found to do.

Second, applicant reactions research can be criticized for its short-sightedness in terms of the type and longevity of outcomes it has chosen to address. The majority of studies have only considered immediate-level reactions outcomes and have largely ignored longer-term and potentially more permanent effects and outcomes. We can draw a parallel here with the training evaluation research and models of 'levels of outcomes' proposed as useful heuristics in this research (e.g. Goldstein, 1997). Why limit our research questions to the level of immediate, preferential and reactions outcomes by applicants to new technology in selection? Rather, important longer-term questions of how applicant reactions impact upon their intentions to remain in the selection procedure, organizational commitment, and most importantly, applicant decision making as a result of their exposure to different methods in selection need to be addressed by future studies (Anderson, 2001; Ryan and Ployhart, 2000). This necessarily implies the use of longitudinal research designs capable of tracking applicant reactions over time in selection procedures, and I would concur fully with Lievens and Harris (2003) who call strongly for the need to use such designs in future.

Third, research so far has fallen foul of the charge of becoming a 'science of the sophomore'. That is, the use of undergraduate student samples as surrogates for real-life applicant pools can be criticized as falling back on a convenience sample most readily accessible to researchers. One is forced to doubt the generalizability of the findings from undergraduate samples acting as surrogates, especially in relation to new technology in 'selection'. Subjects are highly educated, have been habitually exposed to computers on a daily basis, and in some of the extant studies are applying for mock vacancies not for actual job vacancies at a time when many may be only in their first or second years of undergraduate studies. Given the prolific growth in the use of some aspects of new technology by organizations for recruitment and selection, one is forced to question rather acerbically this recourse to laboratory-based experiments using student samples. This tactic would have been more defensible if researchers had been testing postulated theoretical models which demanded the control and manipulation of certain key variables. As noted above, however, this has not been the case. Would we likely expect older workers, manual workers, those having never used computers in either the work or home lives, or senior board directors whose subordinate staff typically use computers for them to react in identical ways to young, highly educated college students? Other research would suggest not. Czaja and Shark (1998) for instance found significantly less positive attitudes toward computer-based work tasks among older workers than amongst younger adults. The likelihood is then that our existing findings overestimate the favorability of reactions to new technology in selection, and as can be seen from this review, the majority of studies have indeed found positive results. Research in future should examine the reactions of different sectors of the labor market to different types of new technology in selection, and in the absence of needing to control key variables for imperative theoretical manipulations, to use field study designs of actual recruitment and selection scenarios for real-life job vacancies.

A fourth point of criticism and a direction for future research is the patchiness of coverage of research in this area alluded to earlier. For some issues there has been a spate of recent research (e.g. reactions to Internet-based recruitment and testing), whereas in others our research base lags woefully behind the rush to use new technology by practitioners in the field (e.g. adverse impact of GMA measures delivered to applicants via the Internet). Indeed, the use of new technology by recruiters, most notably those in large multinational organizations, has in some cases forged well ahead of the validatory research base generated to date by selection psychologists. This is most striking with regard to research into the implications of new technology for adverse impact. It appears that scholars are struggling to keep pace with the sheer rapidity of change in some aspects of the use of new technology by selection practitioners, and therefore, that research will need to catch-back some of this ground over the coming years. In addition to adverse impact, another pressing challenge for researchers in this area is the exponential growth in the use of Internet-based platforms for recruitment and assessment by major organizations. If, as cited by Dineen *et al.* (2002), 90 percent of large corporations in the USA use net-based recruitment (Cappelli, 2001; Martin, 1998) and 12 percent now use online screening methods (Cober *et al.*, 2000), the exposure of applicants at least in the US to Internet modes of delivery has already been pretty extensive. Questions of faking-good, impression management, and practice effects over the Internet therefore become prevalent, although again the huge growth in use by practitioners appears to have outstripped the ability of the research base to respond so speedily to such important issues. In some years time it will be most interesting to look back upon this review and to compare how the coverage of research on these key issues has developed and to review how the research base has progressed and expanded to redress some of these points of constructive criticism.

These four criticisms are therefore put forward as the reactions of one researcher, the author, to existing research in this area (which arrived on his desk in both paper-based and computer-based formats). Bartram (2001, p. 265) cites Lawrence (1999) who, when interviewing one recruiter forced to sift through many vitas before finding a strong one, likened it to 'kissing frogs before you find a prince'. The present author's expectations of this field of research were very high before beginning this review (*aka* Kissing princes), but in some respects this resulted in disappointments as one delved deeper into the studies (*aka* Finding frogs).

In offering this critique of the existing research, these comments are intended to be challenging but throughout to offer constructive points on which we may improve the robustness and coverage of this newly emerging field of research.

Recruiter reactions: toward a research agenda

Based upon surveys into Internet-based recruitment and testing use by organizations in the USA (e.g. Cober *et al.*, 2000; Cappelli, 2001), and anecdotal accounts by researchers in this area internationally (e.g. Bartram, 2002; Harris, 2002), there has been a headlong rush by larger organizations to use this technology as part of their recruitment procedures. For other technological innovations in selection method delivery, however, there is scant survey evidence to indicate just how popular and in widespread usage these methods are. Thus, for many of the other manifestations of new technology in selection we presently do not know precisely how popular these are amongst employer organizations and recruiters alike. It seems likely for many of these applications, including telephone- and video-based interviews, video-based SJTs, multimedia simulation tests, and virtual reality immersion testing, that only a handful of the most technologically sophisticated and well-resourced HRM departments are using them at present (including military applications, selection for commercial airline pilots, and so forth). In addition, light has not been shed upon cross-national differences in the use of these different technologies by organizations as most of the existing research has originated in the USA which may well be ahead of other countries in Europe and the rest of the world in terms of organizational take-up rates for new technology in selection. Regardless of the need for ongoing research to elucidate these questions, it seems reasonable at least in this narrative review to highlight an apparent split between the exponential growth in Internet-based recruitment usage which has occurred in recent years and the somewhat isolated examples of organizations using other technological innovations for candidate assessment and evaluation.

Why has this been the case? What factors may be influencing organizations and recruiters in their take-up of new technology in selection? What may be the trajectory of the innovation processes involved for organizations adopting such technological solutions to employee resourcing needs? And how best can future research in IWO psychology conceptualize, model, and empirically investigate these processes of innovation adoption by recruiters? These are the key questions that concern this section of this paper.

Past research into recruiter reactions to technological innovations in selection is somewhat scarce. Bartram (2001) usefully reviews a series of surveys carried out by professional and recruiter associations in the UK which also suggests a phenomenal growth in the use of Internet-based recruitment methods. However, the literature search carried out for the present paper could locate no published research by IWO psychologists which has examined recruiter attitudes to, expectations of, or adoption of new technology in selection. This is surprising for at least two main reasons. First, there has been a proliferation of very recent research into applicant reactions, as noted in the first section of this paper. Second, recruiters will usually be the client for consultancy organizations in IWO psychology keen to sell new technology in selection into HRM departments in industry and governmental sectors. It is therefore surprising that we have not witnessed more research that takes the recruiter's perspective to technological innovation in this area, especially since the dominant perspective in selection research in general over the years has been that of the organization and the recruiter (Ryan and Ployhart, 2000; Anderson *et al.*, 2001, in press).

Drawing from the findings of antecedent factors research in the innovation and creativity literatures, Figure 1 presents a general model of recruiter reactions to, and adoption of, new technology in selection. Two levels of variables are proposed as likely predictors of recruiter adoption: (1) Organizational level variables, which are postulated as 'necessary conditions' for adoption, and (2) individual level variables associated with the recruiter and their job role, which are proposed as 'sufficient conditions' over and above pre-existing necessary conditions.

Organizational level variables: necessary conditions

Several comprehensive reviews of primary studies and one quantitative meta-analytical summary into antecedent factors at the organizational level-of-analysis found to be predictive of innovation in organizations have been published (major reviews include, Zaltman, Duncan and Holbek, 1973; Van de Ven, Angle and Poole, 1989; West, 2001; and King and Anderson, 2002; see Damanpour, 1991 for a meta-analytic integration). The overwhelming volume of evidence now shows that organizations with organic strategic plans, flat organizational structures, democratic leadership styles, a culture and climate which is supportive of flexibility and change, less rule-governed working practices, and sufficient resources to fund research and development efforts, are unsurprisingly, more likely to be innovative in terms of both their product mix and their internal business processes (Damanpour, 1990). By extension, Figure 1 posits that HR departments possessing the same contextual antecedent factors will be more supportive of innovation adoption by recruiters working within the department. Without delving in detail into the innovation research, there is now accumulated a large body of studies to back these rather sensible (possibly even tautological) propositions (see West, 2002 for a recent discussion).

At this level-of-analysis these variables are hypothesized as 'necessary conditions' as opposed to 'sufficient conditions' underlying the adoption of technical innovations by recruiters (Damanpour, 1990). That is, that the presence of these antecedent factors is a *sine qua non* for even the potential for innovation adoption to occur in recruiter behavior. Put another way, if the organization habitually stifles new ideas, fails to support innovation attempts, and fails to provide basic funds and personnel resources to be able to even consider introducing technological innovation, then recruiters will continue to use traditional methods. However, the presence of these factors is not, in itself, sufficient for the adoption

Organizational Level Variables: 'Necessary Conditions'

Individual Level Variables: 'Sufficient Conditions'

Outcome

Organizational Strategy and Resources
- Mechanistic-organic strategic type
- Culture and climate for technological innovation
- Budget funds and resources
- Leadership style

HR Department Strategy and Resources
- Culture and climate for technological innovation
- Leadership style
- Budget funds and resources
- Exposure in new technology via external contacts and networks
- Climate for excellence in task performance

Job and Task Characteristics
- Autonomy, and job discretion ('slack innovation')
- Performance of existing systems ('distress innovation')
- Performance reward and management procedures
- Present and likely future workloads

Recruiter Characteristics and Educational Background
- Competence with new technology versus 'computerphobia'
- Personality
- Motivation and desire to succeed
- Propensity to innovate
- Rule-governed versus rule challenging behavior
- Educational background and past experiences with new technology

Moderator variables
- Labor market conditions
- Applicant characteristics, exposure to new technology, and likely reactions
- Selection ratios across different levels of organizational recruitment

- Recruiter adoption of new technology in selection

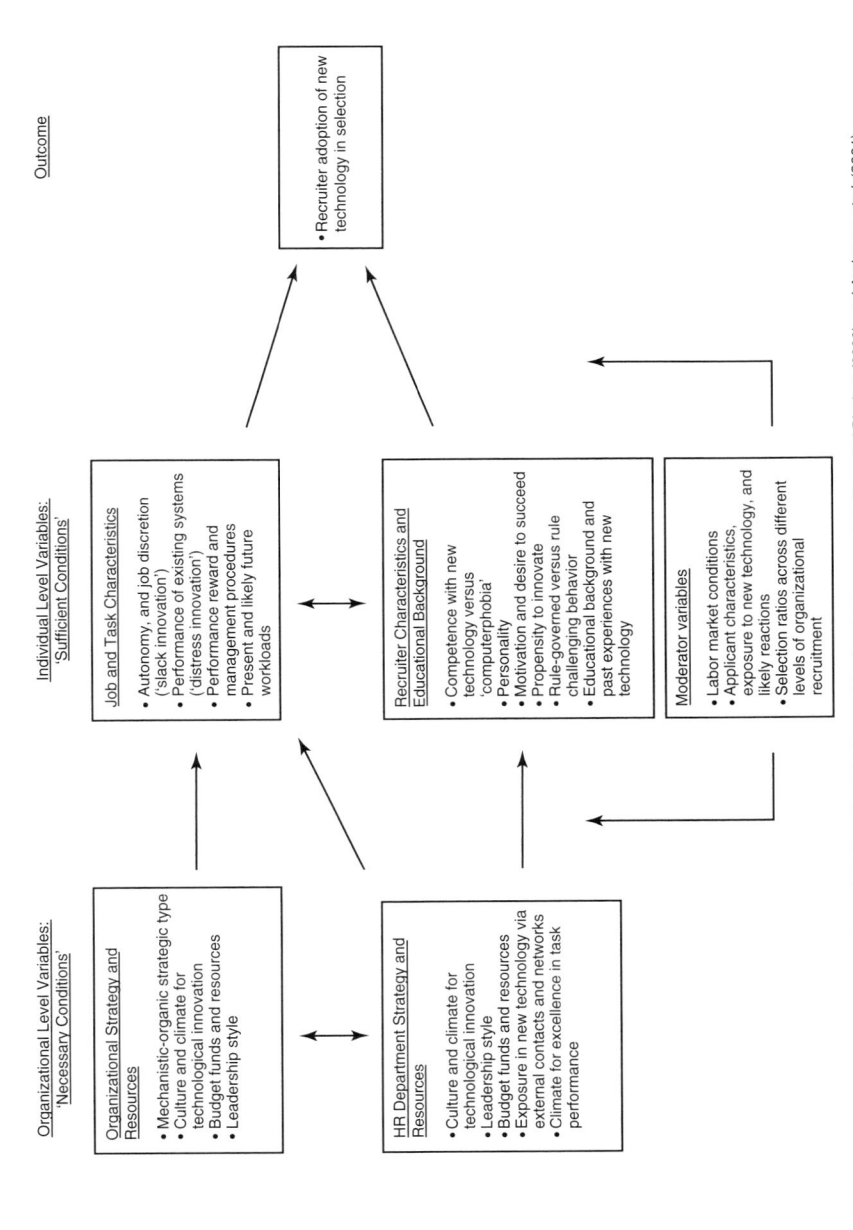

With acknowledgements to earlier models of applicant decision making in selection, especially Ryan and Ployhart (2000), and Anderson et al. (2001).

Figure 1 A general model of recruiter adoption of new technology in selection.

of technological innovation by recruiters. In addition to these organizational-level antecedent factors, Figure 1, again in common with validated models of individual innovation, posits that other individual-level variables will constitute 'sufficient conditions' for eventual innovation adoption.

Individual level variables: sufficient conditions

The model proposes that a further set of variables at the individual level-of-analysis will need to be present for technical innovation adoption by recruiters. These are specified as a series of sufficient conditions related to their job and task characteristics on one hand, and to recruiter personal characteristics on the other. Again in-keeping with major findings in the innovation research, this time regarding individual work role innovation and creativity, Figure 1 summarizes the range of variables which might affect the adoption process at this level.

First, several job characteristics found to be associated with propensity to work role innovation are specified. These include autonomy and job discretion (e.g. West, 1990), the perceived performance of existing recruitment and assessment procedures, reward structures for implementing improved ways of doing things in the job role (Amabile, 1983), and present and probable future workloads for the recruiter. A consistent finding in the innovation literatures is that individuals tend either to innovate in response to having time, energy and resources to be able to do so (so-called 'slack innovation': Kanter, 1983; Van de Ven, Polley, Garud and Venkataraman, 1999), or alternatively, in response to crisis situations and overload (so-called 'distress innovation': Kanter, 1983; Van de Ven et al., 1999; Anderson et al., in press). An example of the former in the context of recruitment is where an HR practitioner has relatively free time in between large-scale recruitment drives and has available sufficient resources to consider implementing a new company web site, for instance. Distress innovation may occur where the recruitment system manifestly fails to cope with the large numbers of applications received and the selector is confronted with the fall-out from this highly visible failure. In both cases, the model posits that suitable and sufficient job and task characteristics, which are in-keeping with the research findings into work role innovation, will need to be present as antecedents of technical innovation adoption.

Second, recruiter personal characteristics are also likely to substantively influence their propensity to innovate in their job role. Considerable research into work role innovation suggests that personal characteristics predictive of more innovative on-the-job behavior include openness to experience, task mastery, moderate levels of anxiety, high motivation to perform well, independence, above average cognitive ability, tolerance of ambiguity, self-confidence, and unconventionality (reviews include, Amabile, 1983; West, 2001; King and Anderson, 2002; Anderson, De Dreu and Nijstad, in press). Although these findings are as one might expect, the research in this area has generally found moderately strong effect sizes for these characteristics upon work role innovation. In addition,

Figure 1 proposes further variables as antecedent factors, namely recruiter mastery of new technology as opposed to 'computerphobia' (Torkzadeh and Angulo, 1992; Chua, Chen and Wong, 1999), their educational background, and previous experiences with new technology in selection, all posited to be positively related with innovation adoption.

Moderator variables

Finally, in common with recent models of applicant decision making in selection (Ryan and Ployhart, 2000; Anderson *et al.*, 2001), Figure 1 proposes that various moderator variables will influence final decisions as to whether to adopt new technology in the process. These include labor market conditions (difficult recruitment markets being likely to be positively associated with attempts to introduce technical innovations), applicant characteristics (applicants being well-versed in new technology, more highly educated, and having access to the Internet for instance, being positively associated with adopt decisions by recruiters), and selection ratios across the range of job roles being recruited for (high selection ratios being positively associated with technological adoption).

This model is therefore proposed as a general heuristic to explain and account for recruiter reactions to, and adoption of, technological innovation in staff selection. One contribution the model makes is to provide an initial structure for much-needed future research into recruiter adoption decisions, about which presently we know next to nothing. Further, the model attempts to draw some synergy from the volume of studies conducted in the innovation field in IWO psychology into organizational- and individual-level antecedents predictive of work role innovation and to apply these findings directly to recruiter adoption of new technology. Given the present author's earlier criticism that applicant reactions research has been too atheoretical in design, it is fitting that this model is put forward as one capable of being empirically tested by researchers active in this area. Perhaps it too will fail to live up to the 'frogs and princes' fable noted by Bartram (2001), but my intention is to provide an initial, general heuristic model which is capable of guiding future research studies into recruiter reactions.

Concluding comments

This paper has attempted to advance our understanding of the reactions research in selection in three ways: (1) to provide a critical, narrative overview of important and emergent themes of research into applicant reactions to new technology in selection, (2) to draw synergistically from disparate research into innovation and creativity in order to re-conceptualize the use of new technology in selection as technical innovation, and, (3) to propose directions for future research into both applicant and recruiter reactions in this field. As part of the third objective, a general model predicting recruiter adoption of new technology based upon organizational- and individual-level variables found to be important antecedents in the innovation literature is proposed as a framework to generate and guide future research in this area.

Research into applicant and recruiter reactions is in a highly anomalous state currently. Compared generally with research into selection and assessment, research in this area is commendably candidate-focused, embryonic in its state of maturity, strikingly patchy in both its band-width and fidelity of coverage of important issues, disappointingly atheoretical, short-termist in its myopic concentration upon only reactions level outcomes, restricted by an unwarranted reliance upon university students as surrogate samples, impressively cutting-edge in its rapid attention to growth in Internet-based recruitment and testing, and uniquely promising in its potential to address the inevitability of new technology being increasingly used for assessment purposes in the future. In ironic contrast to the historic concentration of research in selection upon recruiter and organizational decision making, research into the impact of new technology has been driven almost exclusively by concerns over applicant reactions and perceptions. We currently know next to nothing about recruiter reactions to, expectations of, and willingness to adopt different types of new technology for selection. Pragmatic concerns certainly appear to have underpinned many of the research questions into applicant reactions, including how applicant preferences and reactions impact upon their intention to apply, how favorably they rate different technological media, their impressions of the organization as a potential employer, and so on. But, as noted by Lievens and Harris (2003), lacking has been any coherent theoretical orientation across this newly established body of applicant reactions studies. Whilst it is undoubtedly useful to know something about reactions level outcomes, it would surely be far more useful to understand how these reactions impact longer-term upon applicant expectations of later stages in the selection process, their motivation to remain as a candidate, the previews they form of the job and the organization, and other aspects of more sustained, expectational and attitudinal outcomes. Research in this area would benefit from exposure to developments in studies into applicant decision making where such outcome variables are being included in both models and empirical investigations (Ryan and Ployhart, 2000; Anderson, 2001). Another issue which warrants attention by researchers active in this area is an overreliance upon undergraduate students as surrogate samples for actual applicants to organizational selection procedures. It may be that the reactions of students are generalizable to other populations active in the job market, but students are likely to be much more versed in their use of computers and the Internet than other types of applicants. In addition to concerns over ecological validity, one is forced to question whether surrogate samples have really been necessary given the prevalence of organizational use of some technological advances for actual selection procedures.

Research into recruiter reactions can at present best be described as being rather conspicuous solely by its absence. This stands not only as a critical weakness in our understanding of the effects of new technology in selection, but also as an aberration from the wider field of research in selection and assessment.

Historically selection research has emphasized the recruiter and the organization's perspective perhaps too heavily (see Ryan and Ployhart, 2000; Anderson et al., 2001 for instance) to the neglect of applicant perspectives, reactions, and decision-making processes. In stark contrast, the emerging body of research in new technology has focused almost exclusively upon applicant reactions to the detriment of addressing recruiter perceptions and reactions. The propensity of recruiters and their organizations to adopt new technology for staff selection has received little or no attention from researchers and yet this is without doubt an important, appropriate and viable topic for research within IWO psychology. Presently too little is known about the environmental drivers for adopting technical innovations by recruiters, their reactions to such technical change, and the performance of new systems in comparison to the old ones they replaced. Perhaps one explanation for this is that the whole field of reactions research is so new that the most immediate and pressing questions have been those relating to applicant reactions. So regrettably, questions into recruiter reactions have not yet made it onto the agenda in this fast-moving topic area. Even for applicant reactions it is true that published studies into some aspects of the new technology, such as Internet-based testing, have only begun to appear over the last three or four years. Despite the highly contemporaneous nature of these issues, it is important that research in future addresses a balanced agenda which includes both applicant and recruiter reactions and perspectives.

To conclude, new technology reactions research is at an early stage of development and in many areas somewhat lags behind the sheer pace of change in organization usage of increasingly widespread aspects of new technology. There is real evidence of some 'young princes' of themes of research here which hopefully will mature in the coming years, but also evidence of some bedeviling, methodological tadpoles which need to be screened out of future study designs in this area. Whilst research into applicant reactions has made a promising start toward investigating many pertinent issues and rapidly developing questions, psychologically-based research into recruiter reactions is almost non-existent. As organizations and applicants become increasingly accustomed to using such forms of new technology in selection it can only be hoped that the research base in IWO psychology will expand, diversify, and mature to keep pace with these inevitable advances.

Acknowledgment

I wish to thank Chockalingam Viswesvaran, Jesús Salgado, and the two anonymous reviewers for their helpful comments on earlier versions of this paper.

References

Aguinis, H., Henle, C.A. and Beaty, J.C. Jr (2001) Virtual reality technology: A new tool for personnel selection. *International Journal of Selection and Assessment*, **9**, 70–83.

Alkhadher, O., Anderson, N. and Clarke, D. (1994) Computer-based testing: A review of recent developments in research and practice. *European Work and Organizational Psychologist*, **4**, 169–187.

Amabile, T.M. (1983) *The Social Psychology of Creativity*. New York: Springer-Verlag.

Anderson, N. (2001) Towards a theory of socialization impact: Selection as pre-entry socialization. *International Journal of Selection and Assessment*, **9**, 84–91.

Anderson, N. and King, N. (1993) Innovation in organizations. In C.L. Cooper and I.T. Robertson (eds), *International Review of Industrial and Organizational Psychology* (pp. 1–34). Chichester: John Wiley & Sons.

Anderson, N., Born, M. and Cunningham-Snell, N. (2001) Recruitment and selection: Applicant perspectives and outcomes. In N. Anderson, D.S. Ones, H.K. Sinangil and C. Viswesvaran (eds), *Handbook of Industrial, Work & Organizational Psychology* **Vol. I,** (pp. 200–218). London: Sage.

Anderson, N., De Dreu, C.K.W. and Nijstad, B. (in press) The routinization of innovation research: A constructively critical review of the state-of-the-science. *Journal of Organizational Behavior*, in press.

Anderson, N., Lievens, F., Van Dam, K. and Ryan, A.M. (in press) Future perspectives on employee selection: Key directions for research and practice. *Applied Psychology: An International Review*, in press.

Arvey, R.D., Strickland, W., Drauden, G. and Martin, C. (1990) Motivational components of test taking. *Personnel Psychology*, **43**, 695–716.

Baron, H. and Austin, J. (2000) *Measuring Ability via the Internet: Opportunities and Issues*. Paper presented at the Annual Conference of the Society for Industrial and Organizational Psychology, New Orleans, LA.

Bartram, D. (1994) Computer-based assessment. In C.L. Cooper and I.T. Robertson (eds), *International Review of Industrial and Organizational Psychology* (pp. 31–69). Chichester: John Wiley & Sons Ltd.

Bartram, D. (2001) Internet recruitment and selection: Kissing frogs to find princes. *International Journal of Selection and Assessment*, **8**, 261–274.

Bartram, D. (2002) Testing on the Internet: Issues, Challenges and Opportunities. Paper presented at the International Conference on Computer-based Testing and the Internet, Winchester, England.

Breaugh, J. and Starke, M. (2000) Research on employee recruitment: So many studies, so many remaining questions. *Journal of Management*, **26**, 405–434.

Buchanan, T. and Smith, J.L. (1999a) Using the Internet for psychological research: Personality testing on the World Wide Web. *British Journal of Psychology*, **90**, 125–144.

Burke, M.J., Normand, J. and Raju, N.S. (1987) Examinee attitudes toward computer-administered ability testing. *Computers in Human Behavior*, **3**, 95–107.

Cappelli, P. (2001) Making the most of online recruiting. *Harvard Business Review*, March, 139–146.

Chua, D. and Schmitt, N. (1997) Video-based versus paper-and-pencil method of assessment in situational judgment tests: Subgroup differences in test performance and face validity perceptions. *Journal of Applied Psychology*, **82**, 143–159.

Chua, S.L., Chen, D. and Wong, A.F.L. (1999) Computer anxiety and its correlates: A meta-analysis. *Computers in Human Behavior*, **15**, 609–623.

Cober, R.T., Brown, D.J., Blumental, A.J., Doverspike, D. and Levy, P. (2000) The quest for the qualified job surfer: It's time the public sector catches the wave. *Public Personnel Management*, **29**, 479–494.

Czaja, S. and Sharit, J. (1998) Age differences in attitudes toward computers. *Journals of Gerontology: Series B: Psychological Sciences & Social Sciences*, **53**, 329–340.

Damanpour, F. (1990) Innovation effectiveness, adoption and organizational performance. In M.A. West and J.L. Farr (eds), *Innovation and Creativity at Work: Psychological and Organizational Strategies* (pp. 125–142). Chichester: John Wiley & Sons Ltd.

Damanpour, F. (1991) Organizational innovation: A meta-analysis of effects of determinants and maderators. *Academy of Management Journal*, **34**, 555–590.

Damanpour, F. and Gopalakrishnan, S. (2001) The dynamics of the adoption of product and process innovation in organizations. *Journal of Management Studies*, **381**, 45–65.

Davis, C. and Cowles, M. (1989) Automated psychological testing: Methods of administration, need for approval, and measures of anxiety. *Educational and Psychological Measurement*, **49**, 311–321.

Derous, E. (2003) *Applicant Reactions Toward Recruitment and Selection*. Symposium to the European Association of Work and Organizational Psychology Conference, Lisbon, 2003, May.

Dineen, B.R., Ash, S.R. and Noe, R.A. (2002) A web of applicant attraction: Person-organization fit in the context of web-based recruitment. *Journal of Applied Psychology*, **87**, 723–734.

Finger, M.S. and Ones, D.S. (1999) Psychometric equivalence of the computer and booklet forms of the MMPI: A meta-analysis. *Psychological Assessment*, **11**, 58–66.

Goldstein, I.L. (1997) Interrelationships between the foundations for selection and training systems. In N. Anderson and P. Herriot (eds), *International Handbook of Selection and Assessment* (pp. 529–542). Chichester: John Wiley and Sons Ltd.

Harris, M.M. (1999) Practice network: I-O psychology.com-the Internet and I-O psychology. *The Industrial-Organizational Psychologist*, **36**, 89–93.

Harris, M.M. (2000) The Internet and industrial/organizational psychology: Practice and research perspectives. *Journal of e-Commerce and Psychology*, **1**, 4–23.

Harris, M.M. (2002) *Patrolling the Information Highway: Creating and maintaining a safe, legal, and fair environment for test-takers*. Paper presented at the International Conference on Computer-based Testing and the Internet, Winchester, England.

Harris, M.M. and DeWar, K. (2001) *Understanding and using Web-based Recruiting and Screening Tools: Key Criteria, Current trends, and Future directions*. Workshop presented at the Annual Conference of the Society for Industrial and Organizational Psychology, San Diego, CA.

Harris, M.M., Paajanen, G. and Blunt, M. (2003) *Internet Recruitment: How does it Compare to other Sources?* Symposium to the Annual Conference of the Society for Industrial and Organizational Psychology, 2003, April.

Highhouse, S. and Hoffman, J.R. (2001) Organizational attraction and job choice. In C.L. Cooper and I.T. Robertson (eds), *International Review of Industrial and Organizational Psychology* (pp. 37–64). Chicester: John Wiley & Sons Ltd.

Hough, L.M. and Oswald, F.L. (2000) Personnel selection: Looking toward the future remembering the past. *Annual Review of Psychology*, **51**, 631–664.

International Journal of Selection and Assessment, (1995), Special Issue on computer-based testing, guest editor: D. Bartram, **3**, (2).

Kehoe, J.F. (2002) General mental ability and selection in private sector organizations: A commentary. *Human Performance*, **15**, 97–106.

King, N. and Anderson, N. (2002) *Managing Innovation and Change: A Critical Guide for Organizations*. London: Thompson.

Lievens, F. and Harris, M.M. (2003) Research on Internet recruitment and testing: Current status and future directions. In C.L. Cooper and I.T Robertson (eds), *International Review of Industrial and Organizational Psychology*. Chichester: John Wiley & Sons Ltd.

Lievens, F., van Dam, K. and Anderson, N. (2002) Recent trends and challenges in personnel selection. *Personnel Review*, **31**, 580–601.

Maher, K. and Silverman, R.E. (2002) Online job sites yield few jobs, users complain. *The Wall Street Journal*, January, **2**, A1–A13.

Martin, C.L. and Nagao, D.H. (1989) Some effects of computerized interviewing on applicant response. *Journal of Applied Psychology*, **74**, 72–80.

Martin, J. (1998) Changing jobs? Try the net. *Fortune*, **137**, 205–208.

Mathisen, K.S., Evans, F.J., Meyers, K. and Kogan, L. (1985) Human factors influencing patient-computer interaction. *Computers in Human Behavior*, **1**, 163–170.

Mead, A. D. (2001) How well does web-based testing work? Results of a survey of users of NetAssess. In F.L. Oswald (Chair), *Computers = Good? How Test-User and Test-Taker Perceptions Affect Technology-Based Employment Testing*. Symposium presented at the 16th Annual Conference of the Society for Industrial and Organizational Psychology, San Diego, CA.

Mead, A.D. and Drasgow, F. (1993) Equivalence of computerized and paper-and-pencil cognitive ability tests: A meta-analysis. *Psychological Bulletin*, **114**, 449–458.

Meier, S.T. and Lambert, M.E. (1991) Psychometric properties and correlates of three computer aversion scales. *Behavior Research, Methods, Instruments and Computers*, **231**, 9–15.

Nicholson, N. (1990) Organizational innovation in context: Culture, interpretation, and application. In M.A. West and J.L. Farr (eds), *Innovation and Creativity at Work: Psychological and Organizational Strategies*. Chichester: John Wiley & Sons Ltd.

Paronto, M.E., Bauer, T.N. and Truxillo, D.M. (2003). *Applicant Reactions to Three Screening Methods: What do Candidates Prefer*? Paper to the Annual Conference of the Society for Industrial and Organizational Psychology, 2003, April.

Reynolds, D.H. and Sinar, E. (2001) Applicant reactions to Internet-based selection techniques. In F. Oswald (Chair), *Computers = ''' Good?: How Test-User and Test-Taker Perceptions Affect Technology-Based Employment Testing*. Symposium conducted at the 16th Annual Conference of the Society for Industrial and Organizational Psychology, San Diego, CA.

Reynolds, D.H., Sinar, E.F. and McClough, A.C. (2000) Evaluation of a Internet-based selection procedure. In N.J. Mondragon (Chair), *Beyond the Demo: The Empirical Nature of Technology-Based Assessments*. Symposium presented at the 15th Annual Conference of the Society for Industrial and Organizational Psychology, New Orleans, LA.

Rozelle, A.L. and Landis, R.S. (in press) An examination of the relationship between use of the Internet as a recruitment source and student attitudes. *Computers in Human Behavior*.

Ryan, A.M. and Ployhart, R.E. (2000) Applicants' perceptions of selection procedures and decisions: A critical review and agenda for the future. *Journal of Management*, **26**, 565–606.

Schmidt, F.L. (2002) The role of general cognitive ability and job performance: Why there cannot be a debate. *Human Performance*, **15**, 187–210.

Schmitt, N., Gilliland, S.W., Landis, R.S. and Devine, D. (1993) Computer-based testing applied to selection of secretarial applicants. *Personnel Psychology*, **49**, 149–165.

Sharf, J. (2000) As if 'g-loaded' adverse impact isn't bad enough, Internet recruiters can expect to be accused of 'e-loaded' impact. *The Industrial-Organizational Psychologist*, **38**, 156.

Shotland, A., Alliger, G.M. and Sales, T. (1998) Face validity in the context of personnel selection: A multimedia approach. *International Journal of Selection and Assessment*, **6**, 124–130.

Silvester, J. and Anderson, N. (2003) Technology and discourse: A comparison of face-to-face and telephone employment interviews. *International Journal of Selection and Assessment*, **11**, 206–214.

Silvester, J., Anderson, N., Haddleton, E., Cunningham-Snell, N. and Gibb, A. (2000) A cross-modal comparison of telephone and face-to-face interviews in graduate recruitment. *International Journal of Selection and Assessment*, **8**, 16–21.

Sinar, E.F. and Reynolds, D.H. (2001) Applicant reactions to Internet-based selection techniques. In F.L. Oswald (Chair), *Computers = Good? How Test-User and Test-Taker Perceptions Affect Technology-Based Employment Testing*. Symposium presented at the 16th Annual Conference of the Society for Industrial and Organizational Psychology, San Diego, CA.

Stanton, J.M. and Rogelberg, S.G. (2001) Challenges and obstacles in conducting employment testing via the Internet. In F.L. Oswald (Chair), *Computers = Good? How Test-User and Test-Taker Perceptions Affect Technology-Based Employment Testing*. Symposium presented at the 16th Annual Conference of the Society for Industrial and Organizational Psychology, San Diego, CA.

Straus, S.G., Miles, J.A. and Levesque, L.L. (2001) The effects of videoconference, telephone, and face-to-face media on interviewer and applicant judgments in employment interviews. *Journal of Management*, **27**, 363–381.

Torkzadeh, G. and Angulo, I.E. (1992) The concept and correlates of computer anxiety. *Behaviour and Information Technology*, **11**, 99–108.

Van de Ven, A., Angle, H.L. and Poole, M. (eds) (1989) *Research on the Management of Innovation: The Minnesota Studies*. New York: Harper and Row.

Van de Ven, A., Andrew, H., Polley, D.E., Garud, R. and Venkataraman, S. (1999) *The Innovation Journey*. New York: Oxford University Press.

West, M.A. (2001) The human team: Basic motivations and innovations. In N. Anderson, D.S. Ones, H.K. Sinagil and C. Viswesvaran (eds). *Handbook of Industrial, Work and Organizational Psychology* **Vol. I and II**. London/New York: Sage.

West, M.A. (2002) Sparkling fountains or stagnant ponds: An integrative model of creativity and innovation implementation within groups. *Applied Psychology: An International Review*, **51**, 355–386.

West, M.A. and Farr, J.L. (1990) (eds.) *Innovation and Creativity at Work: Psychological and Organizational Strategies*. Chichester: Wiley.

Wiechmann, D. and Ryan, A.M. (2003) Reactions to computerized testing in selection contexts. *International Journal of Selection and Assessment*, **11**.

Zaltman, G., Duncan, R. and Holbeck, J. (1973) *Innovations and Organizations*. New York: Wiley.

Zusman, R.R. and Landis, R. (in press) Applicant preferences for Web-based versus traditional job postings. *Computers in Human Behavior*.

57

CALL CENTRES

David Holman

Source: D. Holman, T.D. Wall, C.W. Clegg, P. Sparrow, and A. Howard (eds), *The Essentials of the New Workplace: A Guide to the Human Impact of Modern Working Practices*, Chichester: John Wiley, 2005, pp. 115–134.

Call centres have long been part of the modern organisational landscape in one form or another. Emergency service telephone lines, operator services and customer help lines are just some of the types of call centre that have existed over the last 40–50 years, even if they have not been labelled as such. Yet, despite this historical presence, it is only recently that call centres have become of particular interest and significance. The most obvious reason for this is the recent, rapid increase in the number of call centres and those employed in them. For instance, in the UK, almost all call centre jobs have been created in the last 10 years (TUC, 2001) and a similar pattern of growth can be observed in the USA, Australia and the rest of Europe. Furthermore, it has been estimated that in 2002, 1.3% of the European working population will be employed in call centres, with the figure being 2.3% in the UK and 3% in the USA (Datamonitor, 1998). With call centres being found in almost all economic sectors, they have moved from occupying a relatively small niche to being a significant part of the global economy.

The growth in call centres is mainly attributable to technologies that combine call management systems (e.g. automatic call distribution systems) with networked information technologies (e.g. personal computers, display screen equipment, customer databases) (Waters, 1998). The use of these technologies enables the efficient distribution of incoming calls (or allocation of outgoing calls) to available staff, as well as enabling information such as customer details to be instantly accessed and/or easily inputted. Organisations have benefited because it has enabled them to rationalise and reduce the cost of existing functions (e.g. centralising back office functions in banks), to extend and improve customer service facilities (e.g. telephone banking) and to develop new avenues of revenue generation (e.g. exploiting customer databases for direct selling).

Although call centres offer organisations a number of clear benefits, the benefits for those employed in them, particularly front-line staff, are less clear. Thus, while some front-line staff enjoy call centre work, for many it is boring, demanding and stressful. It is these workplace experiences that have led some to label call centres as "electronic sweatshops" or "the dark satanic mills of the twenty-first century" (Garson, 1988; Incomes Data Services, 1997; Metcalf & Fernie, 1998).

One of the central issues, then, in the study of call centres has been how work organisation and human resource practices affect employee stress and well-being (e.g. anxiety, depression, job satisfaction). Other key concerns relate to how call centres are organised and managed, the nature of human resources (HR) practices in call centres and call centre performance. The aim of this chapter is to review research on these topics. To meet this aim, the chapter will be split into the following sections. First, I offer a brief and basic definition of a call centre. The second section outlines those features that differentiate call centres from other work environments and those features that are less unique to call centres but still important to an understanding of them. The third section focuses on how these features affect the experiences of front-line staff, particularly their well-being. Research on call centre performance is then examined, followed by some concluding comments.

Defining call centres

A call centre can be defined as a work environment in which the main business is mediated by computer and telephone-based technologies that enable the efficient distribution of incoming calls (or allocation of outgoing calls) to available staff, and permit customer–employee interaction to occur simultaneously with use of display screen equipment and the instant access to, and inputting of, information. It includes parts of companies dedicated to this activity, as well as the whole company (Health and Safety Executive, 1999).

This definition is useful, as it helps to distinguish a call centre environment from other working environments and it highlights two distinctive call centre features, the nature of call centre technology and the fact that customer–employee interaction is mediated by technology, particularly the telephone. However, the focus on technology tends to ignore other important but less unique call centre features, such as performance monitoring, work and job design, and human resource management practices. The following section is therefore devoted to a full exploration of these in order to delineate the distinctive and significant features of call centres.

Features of call centres

Call centre technologies

Information and computer technologies are central to call centres and much of the debate among practitioners is on the technological possibilities afforded by, for example, automatic call distribution systems, interactive voice recognition, web enablement/joint browsing, E-mail and WAP mobile phone technology. Discussion often focuses on issues such as the effectiveness of call management systems, the integration of different technologies and software systems, and how customer service or revenue generation can be best promoted by technology. However, to argue that call centres are defined simply by the technologies used would be mistaken, because call centre technologies can be used in different ways, and it ignores the equally important social systems of call centres, e.g. work organisation and human resource practices. Thus, the interest here is not on the details of call centre technology *per se*, but on the relationship between the technological and social practices in call centres. In other words, our interest is in call centres as socio-technical systems (Cherns, 1987).

A good starting point when examining this socio-technical relationship is to consider how one aspect of the social system, the stakeholders who are involved in the design and implementation of call centre technology, can affect the final form of that technology (Clark *et al.*, 1998; Orlinowski, 1992). For example, Boddy (2000) described how, during the development of a call centre, management utilised the possibilities of the IT system by opting to introduce an individualised electronic monitoring and reporting system. They chose to do this in order to further their aim of achieving greater control over the work process. The interests of management, together with the capability of the technology, shaped its final form. Other case studies have revealed how a cost minimisation strategy can shape call centre technology. One way of cutting costs is to employ cheaper, less skilled staff, a particularly attractive option in service industries where labour costs can account for up to 60% of total costs (Batt, 2000). However, to employ less skilled staff, work must be broken down into small, simple tasks (Callaghan & Thompson, 2001; Knights & McCabe, 1998; Taylor & Bain, 1999). These simple tasks then become embedded and relatively fixed within technology in the form of scripts or fixed procedures. In this way, technology has an enduring effect on other aspects of the social system, such as job design, performance appraisal and customer–employee interaction.

Call centre technology can vary according to technical factors (e.g. processing speed, call capacity, usability) and organisational and social factors (e.g. work design, monitoring). As many of these factors affect employee well-being (see later), attention to this during the design process would seem imperative. Yet, although it is increasingly recognised that the design of display screen equipment ergonomics can affect physical and psychological well-being (Vandevelde, 2001), there is little evidence that organisational and social factors are considered in relation to employee well-being during the design process. Indeed, the technologically-driven concerns of management, and a singular focus on cost minimisation, can shape technology in ways which produce deleterious effects on its users. Furthermore, the opportunity for customer service representatives (CSRs) to shape a technology according to their needs often arises only during its implementation, when, of course, the scope for change is much restricted (Boddy, 2000).

Customer–employee interaction

Another distinctive feature of a call centre is that customer–employee interaction is mainly mediated by the telephone (but can also be supplemented by face-to-face, letter or E-mail contact). Yet, this does not necessarily imply that customer–employee interaction in call centres is radically different to that occurring in other organisations. Indeed, customer–employee interaction in call centres differs little from customer–employee interaction in other service organisations, as defined by Gutek (1995, 1997). Gutek classified customer–employee interactions as "relationships", "encounters" or a hybrid of these, "pseudo-relationships" (see Table 7.1 for the main properties of relationships and encounters). In a relationship the participants have a shared history and attempt to know each other as individuals and as role occupants. This shared history and mutual understanding can be drawn on to make the service efficient, effective and customised. In time, this can lead to the development of trust and to increased satisfaction and loyalty for both parties (Chaudhuri & Holbrook, 2001; Singh & Sirdeshmukh, 2000).

Encounters are almost the reverse of relationships and typically involve a single, short interaction between strangers. The standardised nature of encounters makes them efficient, and it is easy to change the provider without affecting the service. In encounters, there is less room for authentic emotional expression, particularly for the service provider, and less opportunity to understand the reasons for a person's behaviour. This can lead to the customer making errors of attribution, such as attributing good service to organisational rules and bad service to individual traits.

Although relationships can be found in call centres (e.g. counselling, stock brokering or sex chat-lines!), encounters are more common (Batt, 2000). Given this,

Table 7.1 Characteristics of relationships and encounters (based on Gutek, 1997)

Relationships	Encounters
Provider and customer are known to each other	Provider and customer are strangers: can be anonymous
All providers not equivalent	Providers interchangeable, functionally equivalent
Based on trust	Based on rules
Elitist: customers treated differently	Egalitarian: all customers treated alike
Customized service	Standardized service
Difficult to start	Easy to enter
Difficult to end, loyalty is a factor	No obligation to repeat interaction
Does not need infrastructure	Is embedded in infrastructure
Fosters emotional involvement	Often requires emotional expressions not felt
Become more effective over time, e.g. therapist, lawyer, doctor, financial advisor	Designed to be operationally efficient, e.g. fast-food worker, bank teller, shop worker
Call centre example: counsellor (e.g. Samaritans, sex-lines, stockbroker)	Call centre examples: telephone banking, ticket sales, operator services

does telephone-mediated interaction prevent the development of relationships? There is some evidence that it does, because telephone-mediated interaction can reduce gestural cues, make interaction more formal, make complex problems more difficult to solve and slow down the development of trust (Grundy, 1998; Muscovici, 1967; Nohria & Eccles, 1992; Morely & Stephenson, 1970; Rutter, 1987; Rutter & Stephenson, 1979). However, people also seem to adapt readily to the medium and to regulate telephone interaction with some ease. The telephone can also make certain forms of communication easier, e.g. discussing personal issues (Short, Williams & Christie, 1976; Rosenfield, 1997). The telephone may not, therefore, significantly impede the development of relationships, which suggests that other factors are likely to account for the dominance of encounters over relationships in call centres. One reason is that, for simple services such as getting a ticket, a relationship may not be needed, possible or desired. However, it must be remembered that the simplified service on offer may be a result of choices about how a call centre is organised.

Although certain factors may prevent relationships developing, relationships "serve as a model for encounters because relationships have many positive features" for the organisation, for employees and for customers (Gutek, 1997, p. 149). Gutek (1997) suggests that, in order to emulate some of the qualities of relationships in service interactions, organisations try to develop pseudo-relationships with customers. One way is to encourage employees to develop an "instant rapport" with the customer. This might be achieved by customer-relationship management systems that track customers' interactions with the organisation and enable the employee to know a customer's service history and anticipate his/her needs. An alternative to promoting individualised relationships is to try to get the customer to feel that he/she has a trusting relationship with the organisation. The development of individual–organisational trust is supported by economic and social structures (e.g. contracts, rules expressing standards of service) rather than the quality of personal relationships (Hosmer, 1995).

Performance monitoring

Although performance monitoring is not unique to call centres, the overt, pervasive nature of performance monitoring within many call centres is fairly distinctive. Indeed, it is the pervasiveness of performance monitoring in call centres that has provoked much debate, due to its perceived negative impact on CSRs' wellbeing. This impact will be discussed later, but first performance monitoring will be described.

Performance monitoring involves the observation, examination, recording and feedback of employee work behaviours and exists in both "traditional" and "electronic" forms[1] (Stanton, 2000). Traditional forms of performance monitoring encompass methods such as direct observation, listening to calls, work sampling and customer surveys. Electronic performance monitoring involves the automatic and remote collection of quantitative data (e.g. call times). The characteristics of both forms can be clustered into content or purpose (Carayon, 1993; Stanton, 2000).

The "content" of performance monitoring covers the more "objective" qualities of the monitoring process, such as its frequency, the feedback process and the type and range of performance criteria. The content of traditional monitoring in call centres is typified by a supervisor assessing call quality by listening to a call while at the side of a CSR or by listening to a call remotely (with or without the CSR's knowledge). As this is resource-rich, the monitoring of call quality is episodic, and the number of calls being assessed can vary from five times per week in some call centres to once a month in others (Frenkel *et al.*, 1998; Holman, Chissick & Totterdell, 2001). Some call centre technologies permit every call to be recorded, meaning that every call can potentially be assessed. A call's quality is normally evaluated against a mixture of technical, social and attitudinal criteria that includes: adherence to a script; call opening and closing; accuracy of information; product knowledge; helpfulness; empathy; enthusiasm; and professional tone (Bain *et al.*, 2001; Holman *et al.*, 2002). Assessments are normally fed back in one-to-one discussions and summated results fed back in team meetings. In addition to call quality, CSRs are assessed against a range of non-call-related criteria, such as teamwork, helpfulness and attendance.

Electronic performance monitoring in call centres is generally conducted in a continuous manner, with the results often being fed back daily (Bain & Taylor, 2000; Frenkel *et al.*, 1998; Holman *et al.*, 2002). The types of performance criteria used include call length, wrap-up time (i.e. time spent in administrative duties), time spent logged-off the system and number of sales.

The purpose of performance monitoring relates to the uses to which performance data is put. For example, performance monitoring can be deployed punitively to inform disciplinary proceedings. It can also be used to improve employee performance, particularly through the identification of training needs and goal setting; to reduce costs; to ensure customer satisfaction; and, to enable the correct allocation of resources by matching employee numbers to call levels (Aiello & Kolb, 1995; Alder, 1998; Chalykoff & Kochan, 1989).

Somewhat surprisingly, there is little evidence for the assumed performance benefits of monitoring in a call centre context. Indeed, most research on monitoring and performance is laboratory-based, conducted on tasks that are quite different to those employed in call centres (e.g. non-telephone-based data-entry tasks) and has revealed no conclusive benefit to individual performance. In contrast, filed research has revealed that performance monitoring can be used to improve resource allocation, i.e. balancing employee numbers to call volumes (Betts, Meadows & Walley, 2000). If the evidence linking performance monitoring to performance is so poor, why is it so pervasive in call centres? One explanation is that organizations do it because they simple *believe* that monitoring improves individual performance, and because they have some knowledge that it improves resource allocation. According to this scenario, performance monitoring has become, to management at least, an undisputed good. Another explanation is that, while performance monitoring is "dressed up" as a developmental tool for employees, this actually hides its "real" purpose, i.e. a method to enforce adherence to organizational norms. Whatever the reason, due to the effects of performance monitoring on stress levels (see later), questions should be raised about the extent to which high levels of performance monitoring are really necessary or desirable (Holman *et al.*, 2002).

Job and work design

The design of a CRS's job is another salient feature of call centres that, like performance monitoring, has attracted much attention. A reason for this is that some CSR jobs do seem to be an expression of an advanced form of Taylorism (Knights & McCabe, 1998; Taylor & Bain, 1999) and, as such, have been criticised for being a primary cause of job-related stress. However, not all CSR jobs are designed in this manner, with most falling on a continuum running from "Tayloristic" to "empowered" (Batt, 2000; Frenkel *et al.*, 1998, 1999; Holman, 2002).

At the "Taylorist" end of the continuum, jobs are unskilled, repetitive and monotonous. Calls are of a short duration, are required to be completed within a specified time and there is no choice as to whether a call can be answered or not. Calls are often conducted in accordance to a script that specifies the opening and closing of the call and, in some cases, the entire call. These factors mean that the CSRs have little control over the timing of their work, the methods they use and what they can say. CSRs also spend most of their time answering calls, a consequence being that little time is spent doing other tasks, such as administration. Variety comes from answering different call types, although actual differences may be small. The level of problem-solving demand is not high and when problems do arise there is a general expectation that these should be handed on to a supervisor. Tayloristic jobs also tend to have lower degrees of task interdependence. As a result, works is more individualised and fewer interactions with other CSRs are needed to ensure service delivery, although coworkers do interact to offer social support and help each other to learn the job (Frenkel *et al.*, 1999).

In the "empowered" job, a semi-professional CSR has more control over how he/she works and is required to combine an extensive product or service knowledge (often of a complex product or service, such as mortgages or computer repair) with IT and customer service skills to provide a customized service (Winslow & Bramer, 1994; Frenkel *et al.*, 1998). CSRs are engaged in a variety of calls and tasks in which problems are handled at source. Calls are longer and generally unscripted apart from the call's opening and closing. Empowered jobs tend to have higher degrees of task interdependence, as CSRs often need to draw upon others' knowledge.

It might be expected that empowered jobs would be associated with the use of self-managed teams and off-line teams, such as quality circles. Work by Batt (2000) suggests that there is little evidence of this in call centres[2]. This indicates that self-managed teams and off-line teams may be used to increase variety and participation in Tayloristic jobs when it is perceived that there is little room for achieving these aims through the redesign of the core job task.

Human resource management

HR practices vary considerably in call centres. To explore this variation and the reasons for it, three issues will be addressed. The first concerns whether particular HR and work organisation practices are found bundled together or whether the relationship between practices is more idiosyncratic, i.e. there is an *internal fit or alignment between* practices. The second issue focuses on whether there is an *organisational fit or alignment* between bundles of practice and a particular feature of the organisation and whether this results in performance benefits. For example, Batt (2000, p. 542) argues that "the customer–worker interface is a significant factor in defining the organisation of work and HR practices in services" and that both should be aligned to ensure maximum productivity. The third issue focuses on whether there is an alignment between the organisation's strategy and bundles of practices and whether such a *strategic fit or alignment* is beneficial.

Before these issues are explored, it is useful to note that previous work has suggested that two models of service management exist, the "mass service" model and the "high-commitment service" (HCS) model (Bowen & Schneider, 1988; Frenkel *et al.*, 1999; Levitt, 1972; Schlesinger & Heskett, 1991)[3]. In addition, a number of writers argue that, in high-performing organisations, bundles of particular work organisation and HR practices will align with other features of the organisation and with its strategic aims (Batt, 2000; Schuler & Jackson, 1995; Wright & McMahon, 1992). Applied to the call centre context, and by drawing on the work of Batt (2000), Frenkel *et al.* (1998, 1999), Holman (2002) and Kinnie, Purcell & Hutchinson (2000), two ideal models of call centre practice referred to above can be envisaged (see Table 7.2). In each model, the bundles of practice (internal alignment), the organisational alignment and strategic alignment will be as follows.

In the ideal mass service call centre, there is a strategic alignment between a mass market customer segment, a cost-minimisation strategy and a bundle of work organisation and HR practices that includes Tayloristic job designs, low rates of pay and discretionary pay, low levels of training, temporary contract in core workers and minimum recruitment criteria. An alignment of this sort is advantageous, as the small profit margins of the market served mean that costs, particularly labour costs, must be minimised. This is achieved by using Tayloristic job designs, which leads to less skilled, cheaper labour being employed and fewer resources being devoted to recruiting and retaining a skilled workforce. The use of standardised products also means that it makes economic sense to ensure an organisational alignment between the customer–employee encounter, Tayloristic job designs and low-cost HR practices.

With the high-commitment service (HCS) model, the strategy is to generate high profit margins and sales revenues by providing a customised service to a specialised

Table 7.2 Call centre models: "mass service" and "high commitment service"

Mass service	High commitment service
Customer segment Mass Market	*Customer Segment* Specialist, high-earning private customers, businesses
Market High-volume, low added value	*Market* Low-volume, high added value
Strategy Cost-minimisation	*Strategy* Customisation of service, cross-selling, bundling of services
Product/service Simple, one or few product or services on offers Standardised service	*Product/service* Complex and/or multiple products and services on offer Customised service
Customer–worker interaction Encounter	*Customer–worker interaction* Relationship or pseudo-relationship
Job design Taylorist, e.g. low control and variety, low skill, high use of scripts, short call times	*Job design* Empowered, e.g. high control and variety, little scripting, long calls
Work design Low interdependence Work groups Off-line work groups	*Work design* High interdependence High use of semi-autonomous work groups Off-line work groups
Performance monitoring High levels of monitoring Emphasis on quality and quantity Higher tendency to use monitoring to discipline and control	*Performance monitoring* Low levels of monitoring Emphasis on quality Use of monitoring for developmental purposes
Human resource practices Low cost Recruitment—minimal criteria Pay—relatively low rates of pay, low percentage of total pay that is commission-based Training—mainly induction training Career—little career structure, poor promotion prospects Job security—low, high use of temporary contracts in core workers	*Human resource practices* High cost Use of selection tests and competency models Relatively high rates of pay, higher percentage of total pay that is commission-based, good additional benefits Induction training and continuing training Better promotion prospects High job security, lower use of temporary contracts in core workers
Management/supervisor relations with CSRs Hierarchical Low trust	*Management/supervisor relations with CSRs* Supportive, facilitative High trust

customer segment. To do this, the organisation needs to devote resources to recruiting, training and keeping a skilled workforce (e.g. through effective recruitment and continuous training). HR practices also reward discretionary behaviour (e.g. by the use of performance-related pay) and cultivate employee commitment to the organisation through job security and good terms and conditions. Empowered work designs permit a customised service to be provided, a relationship or pseudo-relationship between employee and customer to be developed (thus there is an organisational as well as a strategic alignment) and discretionary behaviour to be exhibited. Greater employee commitment means that less monitoring is needed to gain adherence to organisational goals and norms.

Research indicates that work organisation and HR practices in call centres do vary in a manner similar to that predicted by the models outlined above. The strongest evidence comes from Batt's (2000) study of telecommunications call centres that were serving four different customer segments and which were pursuing different strategic aims. The four customer segments were operator services (mass market), residential consumers, small businesses, and middle market (customised/specialised market). She found that empowered jobs (high control, low scripting, high skill requirements) were associated with HR practices such as low performance monitoring and high levels of discretionary pay. Moreover, this bundle was associated with relationship-type interactions and with the residential, small business and middle market customer segment. In other words, there was both an internal, organisational and strategic alignment akin to that posited in the ideal HCS call centre model. In contrast, the internal, organisational and strategic alignments akin to the mass service call centre were found in the operator services call centres. However, the match to theory was not complete, as she found little difference with regard to the use of teams, training, promotion and job security, although operator service call centres did stand out as having lower training and job security.

The respondents in the Batt (2000) survey were managers. Evidence from CSR-level data comes from Holman & Fernie (2000), who compared CSRs working in a banking call centre serving mass market customers with those in a call centre giving mortgage advice to residential and small business customers. CSRs in the banking call centre reported more-encounter-type interactions, lower job control and variety, lower skill use, higher monitoring and poorer relations with managers. Thus, there were different bundles of practice and the organisational alignments were as suggested by the models. A similar pattern was reported by Frenkel *et al.* (1999) who, using case study and CSR-level survey data, found that work roles, job designs and HR practices consistent with the ideal mass service call centre were aligned with customer–employee encounters and a mass market customer segment. A case study by Hutchinson, Purcell & Kinnie (2000) also demonstrated that "the driving force for the adoption of HCM (high-commitment management) was the need to realign business strategy and organisational structure" (p. 74). In the call centre in question, HR practices were changed in response to a new strategic aim of adding value, particularly for customers, and the provision of a more complex service that combined previously distinct sales and service tasks. The HR changes included greater use of induction and continuing training, more sophisticated recruitment and selection techniques, a wider use of performance-related pay and greater involvement in quality improvement teams.

Work on HR in call centres, while limited in extent, does indicate that bundles of work organisation and HR practice do exist (i.e., there is an internal fit), that there is a degree of organisational alignment between these bundles and customer–employee interaction, and that call centres do exhibit a degree of strategic alignment to the customer segment pursued. However, the following caveats are required. First, there are many "anomalies" in the data. Some mass service call centres adopt some high commitment work practices (e.g. self-managed work teams in mass service call centres; Batt, 2000, Houlihan, 2001) and some HCS call centres adopt some mass service work practices (e.g. high levels of performance monitoring in HCS call centres; Kinnie *et al.*, 2000). Indeed, it is probable that most call centres are a hybrid of mass service call centres and HCS call centres, which Frenkel *et al.* (1998) have labelled "mass customized bureaucracies". The "anomalies" in the data also imply that managers consider other factors when choosing which practices to adopt. For example, when local labour markets are very competitive, it may not be possible to use practices such as low pay or Tayloristic job designs that exacerbate recruitment and turnover problems. Indeed, Houlihan (2001) reports that some mass service call centres use empowered job designs in response to concerns about the effects of Tayloristic jobs on employee well-being. Other factors affecting the adoption of work practices include costs, alternative organisational goals, legal requirements and problems of implementation. This implies that a true alignment or "best fit" may not be possible.

Second, a best fit may not be desirable. Internal, organisational and strategic alignments of the kind described may be easily mimicked by other organisations and may therefore fail to provide the unique organisational practices, services or products that enable the organisation to secure a niche position in the market place and to compete successfully (Boxall, 1996).

Third, any organisational or strategic alignment may not be the result of top-down strategic choice. Rather, alignment may emerge from the pragmatic choices made by managers when trying to make sense of the dynamic call centre environment (Hutchinson *et al.*, 2000; Kinnie *et al.*, 2000). Korczynski *et al.* (2000) suggest that these choices are informed by the sometimes competing rationales of "bureaucratic efficiency" and "customer orientation", which can be equated respectively with the rationale underlying the mass service call centre and that which underlies the HCS call centre. These rationales and the dynamic between them can be expressed in different ways, but include:

- Service quality vs. service quantity (Knights & McCabe, 1998; Bain *et al.*, 2001).

- Ensuring employee empathy with the customer whilst also ensuring employee instrumentality, i.e. doing just enough to satisfy the customer and not waste time (Sturdy, 2000).
- Providing a customised service and having standardised procedures (Korczyniski et al., 2000).
- Gaining the commitment of employees whilst ensuring adherence to organisational norms (i.e. the control of employees).

In summary, research on HR in call centres demonstrates how work organisation and HR practices vary, that they do form "messy" bundles, and that the type of bundle found is contingent upon the particular conglomeration of factors that includes customer–worker interaction, the customer segment, the local labour market, the actions and views of employees, and internal organisational resources. However, it is open to question whether any organisational or strategic alignment is the result of a top-down strategy, or whether it emerges from the pragmatic choices that managers make when trying to make sense of a dynamic call centre environment.

The experience of call centre work

Call centre work, particularly that of CSRs, has attracted much attention due to its perceived impact on job-related stress. In response, there is a growing literature on the causes of stress in call centres. Another body of work has focused on how CSRs actively resist managerial control and deleterious working practices. It is heavily influenced by labour process theory but not entirely disconnected from the literature on well-being.

The experience and causes of stress, stress-related outcomes and affect

Those factors outlined in the previous sections (e.g. job design, performance monitoring, HR practices) have a significant impact on employee stress and stress-related outcomes in call centres (Frenkel et al., 1998; Holman, 2002; Incomes Data Services, 1997; Knights & McCabe, 1998; Taylor & Bain, 1999), as they do in other work settings[4].

Job design research has demonstrated that low control, lack of variety and high demands are important predictors of stress (i.e. anxiety, depression, emotional exhaustion) and stress-related outcomes (e.g. absence) (Karasek & Theorell, 1990; Spector, 1987; Terry & Jimmieson, 1999). Studies of job design in call centres report similar findings (Batt & Appelbaum, 1995; Batt & Moynihan, 2001; Zapf et al., 1999), but highlight how little control CSRs have (Holman, 2001) and the impact of scripts on stress (Deery, Iverson & Walsh, 2001).

Performance monitoring is another practice that has attracted attention, due to its assumed effect on stress. Arguments in favour of monitoring are that employees benefit because they can improve their performance and develop new skills (Grant & Higgins, 1989), which in turn helps the CSR to cope better with demands (Aiello & Shao, 1993; Bandura, 1997; Stanton, 2000). Arguments against performance monitoring are that it is threatening to employees because the information gained may affect employees' remuneration or co-worker relationships (Alder, 1998). Monitoring is also considered to be a demand in itself (Smith et al., 1992). The threat of monitoring and the consequent feeling of increased demand are thought to negatively affect employee well-being.

Both arguments have found support. On the one hand, laboratory and field studies have reported that monitored employees (or participants) are generally found to have higher levels of stress and dissatisfaction than non-monitored employees (Aiello & Kolb; 1995; Irving, Higgins & Safeyeni, 1986; Smith et al., 1992). On the other hand, in one of the few studies conducted in a call centre, Chalykoff & Kochan (1989) discovered that the performance-related content of the monitoring system (i.e. immediacy of feedback, the use of constructive feedback and the clarity of the rating criteria) was positively related to satisfaction with the monitoring system, which in turn was related to job satisfaction.

The positive and negative associations between performance monitoring and well-being suggests that various performance monitoring characteristics may be differentially related to employee well-being. This proposition found support in a study by Holman et al. (2002) that examined the relationship between well-being and three performance monitoring characteristics in a call centre, viz. its performance-related content (i.e. immediacy of feedback, clarity of performance criteria); its beneficial purpose (i.e. does it have developmental rather than punitive aims?) and its perceived intensity (i.e. was it felt to be pervasive?). The results revealed that the performance-related content of performance monitoring reduced depression, that the beneficial purpose of monitoring reduced depression, anxiety and emotional exhaustion, whilst perceived intensity increased anxiety, depression and emotional exhaustion. Furthermore, the perceived intensity of monitoring had much stronger effects on the other two characteristics of performance monitoring. These findings support arguments both for and against performance monitoring. They show that, while performance monitoring can reduce stress if it is conducted in a developmental manner and is based on regular feedback and clear criteria, these positive effects can be wiped out if monitoring is perceived by CSRs to be too intense. Indeed, excessive monitoring may, over the long term, make employees more depressed, less enthusiastic and have the opposite effect of that intended.

Customer–employee interaction can also affect well-being. The strongest evidence comes from work on emotional labour, the regulation and expression of emotion in exchange for a wage (Grandey, 2000; Hochschild, 1983). Central to theories of emotional labour is the idea that organisations implicitly or explicitly specify what and how emotions should be expressed. Dissonance can occur when emotions felt do not match the emotional expression required. In response, the employee can either display his/her "true" emotions or he/she can try to display the required emotions. If he/she chooses the latter option, two modes of emotional regulation may be deployed, surface acting or deep acting (Hochschild, 1983). Surface acting involves displaying the required emotions, but there is little attempt to feel those emotions, e.g. an employee may "smile down the phone" (Belt, Richardson & Webster, 1999). Deep acting involves trying to feel and display the required emotions, e.g. by reappraising the situation so that its emotional impact is lessened (Grandey, 2000). Research findings in call centres are in line with these propositions (Holman et al., 2002; Zapf et al., 1999) and have also revealed that emotional labour only has negative effects (i.e. anxiety, depression, emotional exhaustion) when the emotions expressed are negative and when surface acting is engaged in (Zapf et al., 1999). This is because the expression of positive emotions can be pleasant in itself and lead to a sense of personal accomplishment, and because the suppression of feelings is more demanding on personal resources than other forms of regulation, such as deep acting (Holman et al., 2002; Totterdell & Holman, 2002; Zapf et al., 1999). These studies have also illuminated the extent to which CSRs engage in emotional regulation throughout their working day. A diary study revealed that CSRs hid negative feelings from customers for one-half of their time at work and suppressed positive feelings for one-fifth of the time (Totterdell & Holman, 2001). This suggests that surface acting may be fairly common in call centres and that customer–employee interaction may be an important cause of stress in them.

Other aspects of customer–employee interaction that can affect well-being are the provision of good customer service (Frenkel et al., 1999), the expression of positive emotions, and pleasant customers (Totterdell & Holman, 2001). These can have a positive effect on well-being. In contrast, short unemotional calls may be associated with stress, although what may be more important is whether the person can control the call and whether a CSR receives a variety of calls.

Research on other causes of stress in call centres is less comprehensive. For instance, with regard to HR practices and team leader support, the perceived fairness of the payment system, the usefulness of performance appraisal and the adequacy of training, all have been linked to low anxiety, low depression and job satisfaction (Batt & Appelbaum, 1995; Frenkel et al., 1998; Holman, 2002). Technology has also been cited as a determinant of physical and psychological well-being and, although I have yet to find a study that has examined the ergonomic impact of call centre work-station design and the usability of the human–computer interface, their effect is probably little different to that elsewhere (Grieco et al., 1995, Health and Safety Executive, 1992).

While many factors have been shown to be associated with stress, those practices with the strongest associations to anxiety, depression and job satisfaction are job control, the intensity of monitoring, the adequacy of the coaching and training and team leader support (Holman, 2002). In addition to the differential effects of practices on stress, differences in levels of stress between different types of call centre have been identified. Holman & Fernie (2000) compared levels of well-being between a mass service-type call centre, an HCS-type call centre, and a hybrid type falling somewhere in between. Depression and job dissatisfaction were generally lower at the HCS and hybrid call centres. Against expectations, however, anxiety was lower at the mass service call centre. It was argued that CSRs were managing their anxiety by leaving the mass service call centre. CSRs at the other call centres, which had better terms and conditions, were more likely to stay and "sweat it out". Other studies have revealed quit rates to be lower in HCS call centres (Batt & Moynihan, 2001). Call centre work has been highlighted as particularly stressful and, by implication, more stressful than comparable forms of work. But studies show no clear pattern of findings[5]. In one study, call centre workers were found to be less satisfied than sales workers and knowledge workers (e.g. IT systems designers) (Frenkel *et al.*, 1999). In another, call centre work compared favourably with shop floor manufacturing work and clerical work with regard to anxiety, depression and job satisfaction (Holman, 2001).

Control and resistance in call centre work: the active agent

Research on stress in call centres tends to paint the CSR as a rather passive figure, i.e. as someone always responding to work conditions. In contrast, studies inspired by labour process theory (Braverman, 1974; Sturdy, Knights & Willmott, 1992) have been concerned with how CSRs actively consent to, comply with and resist managers' efforts to exert control over their work. Management control practices in call centres are fairly overt and wide-ranging and include:

- The measurement of output through IT systems.
- The measurement of behaviour through call monitoring and observation.
- The inculcation of norms through training, customer awareness programmes, socialisation, coaching, performance appraisal and feedback.
- The structuring of work tasks through scripts and IT systems.

As noted, CSRs may not consent to the above control practices. CSRs may have different ideas from management on the management of the call centre or how customers should be served. CSRs are also likely to disagree with practices they view as having deleterious personal consequences. Labour process theory has illuminated the individual and collective ways in which CSRs resist those control practices they disagree with or find deleterious. For example, at an individual level, a CSR may resist managerial exhortations to deal with calls more rapidly as a means of improving customer service. This may occur because a CSR's sense of customer service is different. The CSR may have an embodied sense of customer service, i.e. to the customer she is serving, and this makes her attend to the needs of the individual without regard to those other customers waiting in the queue (Korczynski *et al.*, 2000; Sturdy, 2000). At a collective level, resistance may take the form of trade union activity that aims to alter job designs or performance monitoring practices (Keefe & Batt, 2001; Taylor & Bain, 2001; Trades Union Congress, 2001) (see Table 7.3 for more examples of individual and collective

Table 7.3 Individual and collective forms of CSR resistance to management control

Individual resistance	Collective resistance
Cutting customers off	Trades union activity
Not following the script	Humour
Not selling	Sharing knowledge of how to beat the system
Deliberately cheating the IT system	
Pretending to be speaking to a customer	
Challenging targets set	
Not filling in information properly	

forms of resistance). From these different forms of resistance it can be concluded that CSRs do not passively accept their work conditions, particularly those that may decrease their well-being, and that CSRs are actively engaged in attempting to change their working conditions to ones which, in their eyes, are preferable. CSR resistance also demonstrates that, even in the most regimented call centres, total control cannot be achieved and that comparisons with panopticans are grossly overdrawn (Bain & Taylor, 2000; Metcalf & Fernie, 1998; Frenkel *et al.*, 1999).

Finally, the labour process literature has highlighted how CSRs often use similar rationales to those used by management and that they too are faced by similar demands (e.g. quality vs. quantity, service vs. selling, etc.). What is more, whereas managers have to contend with these issues at a system level, the CSR has to balance the tensions that these demands create in every call.

Call centre performance

Only a small number of studies have examined performance in call centres, and they have focused on the contribution that call management, employee behaviour and work practices make to two outcomes, viz, perceptions of service quality (which includes customer satisfaction) and sales. With regard to perceptions of service quality, management's ability to regulate call volumes, and in particular their ability to reduce waiting times, is a key determinant of customer satisfaction (Evenson, Harker & Frei, 1999; Feinberg *et al.*, 2000). Yet, managing call volumes so that demand is matched by resources has proved to be problematic with current technologies and procedures, particularly when calls are long (Betts *et al.*, 2000). This would indicate that management's control over a key determinant of customer satisfaction is limited. Customer satisfaction has also been linked to employee behaviours, such as empathy, assurance, the authority to deal with requests, adaptiveness and displays of negative emotion (Burgers *et al.*, 2000; Doucett, 1998). Clearly the CSR needs to have the opportunity and ability to engage in such behaviours if customer satisfaction is to be achieved. Batt's (1999) work would appear to support this. She found that groups with greater self-regulation (akin to the processes involved in self-managed teams), coaching support, level of education, training and better work group relations had higher scores on an employee-reported measure of service quality. This study also showed that group–self-regulation, coaching support and level of education were also positively related to sales volume. Another study, by Batt & Moynihan (2001), showed that those call centres adopting appropriate HR practices (i.e. high-commitment practices when serving high-value customers) achieved higher sales growth.

Conclusion

Viewing all call centres as "electronic sweatshops" is misguided and such a simplistic view should be given short shrift. Call centres are diverse entities. This diversity is a result of the pragmatic and strategic choices made by the stakeholders involved in them. Permeating these choices are various rationales that suggest what is plausible and justifiable. From this chapter it is possible to suggest that the two most dominant rationales are the economically-based rationales of bureaucratic efficiency (which includes a focus on cost minimisation) and customer orientation (Korczynski et al., 2000). Respectively, these can be seen to inform the design and running of the mass service call centre and the HCS call centre. For example, the use of a bureaucratic efficiency rationale by IT consultants and managers during the design of a call centre will often lead to standardised services and simplified job designs. Further evidence of these rationales being at work comes from those studies showing an organisational and strategic alignment of practices, although whether call centres are *explicitly* designed in accordance with these rationales is open to debate.

Yet, while these rationales enable action by suggesting what is justifiable and workable, they also constrain action by ignoring or de-legitimating other issues, such as employee well-being. The choices stakeholders make will be further constrained by the conditions in which they are made. As shown earlier, the use of Taylorist jobs can cause difficulties in labour market conditions that make high levels of labour turnover problematic. As such, the dominance or role of these two economic logics must not be overplayed. Practices may be introduced for a number of reasons and be based on alternative rationales (e.g. legal, moral), as is evidenced by mass service call centres adopting self-managed work teams to alleviate the harmful effects of Tayloristic jobs (Houlihan, 2001).

Work in the labour process tradition also shows that all stakeholders are able to use the same rationales to justify and inform their practice, although it must be said that the effect of each rationale may differ according to who uses it and when. For example, the use of a customer orientation logic by IT consultants and call centre managers may have more global effects during the design of call centre practices than the use of the same rationale by a CSR when talking to a customer. Managers also have a greater opportunity to determine the work conditions of CSRs. Ultimately, the choices of managers affect CSR well-being. This means that call centre managers can take a proactive approach to employee well-being and try to reduce stress through the design of call centre work. Furthermore, as the causes of well-being in call centres are similar to the causes in other organisations, the "old rules" still apply in a "new" setting. Call centres are not radically new forms of work organisation. As a result, many of the job redesign or system redesign methods, including socio-technical methods and the like, may be usefully applied in a call centre setting (see Chapter 17, this volume; for review, see Parker & Wall, 1998). These tools may be used most effectively on technologies, on job design and on performance monitoring systems, particularly during their design and implementation. With regard to performance monitoring, it seems imperative that it should be part of a system that aims to develop employees' skills and performance and that it should be closely linked to coaching (see Chapter 12, this volume, by Pritchard and Payne). It would also seem sensible to minimise the number of performance criteria used when monitoring to reduce the perception that it is intense.

However, in a mass service call centre, do stress-alleviating work designs and HR practices prevent the optimal alignment of work organisation, HR practices, customer–employee interaction and strategy? According to theory, the answer is yes; that in mass service call centres there must be a trade-off between effectiveness and employee well-being. Yet, although there is evidence that loose alignments occur, there is little evidence to date that aligned call centres have higher organisational or employee performance than non-aligned call centres. Furthermore, it might also be the case that employee performance, as measured by customer satisfaction, could be worse in mass service call centres, despite the best attempts of employees to engage in emotional labour, because "what employees experience, gets transmitted to customers" (Schlesinger and Heskett, 1991, p. 71). In addition, the direct and indirect costs of poor job design and extensive monitoring may prove excessive in some circumstances. This shows that there are economic as well as moral reasons which have led some "mass service" call centres to introduce empowered job designs and HR practices. These call centres have been called "compensatory", suggesting that the simple distinction between mass service and HCS call centres may be too crude (Houlihan, 2001). Therefore, not only is research needed that examines the relationship between call centre design, employee well-being, organisational performance and employee performance, but it should also examine the possibility that several types of call centre design may exist.

Research in the future should also focus on how new technologies will affect call centre employees. One current argument is that technologies will remove the more boring aspects of call centre work and make it more pleasant. This is reminiscent of previous claims about computer technologies, which subsequently turned out to have a range of impacts, positive, negative and neutral, on employee work experiences (Wood, 1982). Researchers, consultants and managers should therefore concentrate on the reasons for this variation, focus on how centre technology and its associated work practices are shaped, and take a more proactive role in shaping call centre technologies so that they do not negatively effect employee well-being.

It is evident that the causes of stress in call centres are similar to those in other organisations. Therefore, researchers in the future would do best to focus on factors particularly pertinent to a call centre environment. Such factors would include a more detailed look at performance monitoring, an examination of the effects of technology (e.g. usability, work station design) relative to other factors, and quasi-experimental redesign studies comparing the performance and well-being effects of different job designs and different performance monitoring designs.

In conclusion, this chapter has sought to demonstrate that the design and diversity of call centres emerges from the pragmatic and strategic choices made by stakeholders who, informed by various rationales, attempt to achieve their goals in the context of the unique set of contingencies with which they are faced. This dynamic understanding of call centres means that managers do have a choice in how they run and organise call centres, and that well-being can be designed into call centres. It has also demonstrated that CSRs contend with many of the same issues in their daily interactions with customers (i.e. quality vs. quantity) as those faced by managers. However, CSRs generally have little influence on how the organisation deals with these issues at a more systemic level. But the lessons from other types of organisation are that worker knowledge, when it is called upon, often improves the design of customer service, technology and HR practices (Clegg et al., 1996, 2000; Clark et al., 1998). Perhaps it is time that CSRs are given greater opportunity to engage in the design of call centre technologies and practices.

Notes

1 While not ideal labels, we keep them as they are used by others in this field (cf. Stanton, 2000).
2 Batt (2000) found that although 38% of organisations with empowered jobs used self-managed teams a lot, and that 18% of organisations with Tayloristic jobs used self-managed teams a lot, this difference was not significant. Batt also found that, with 90% usage of off-line teams in each, there were no differences between organisations with Tayloristic or empowered jobs.
3 These are the functional equivalent of the mass production and high commitment/involvement models present in the manufacturing literature (Ichniowski et al., 1996; Wood, 1995).
4 Nearly all research or stress in call centres has been in relation to CSRs. The following relates to this group unless otherwise stated.
5 Zapf et al. (1999) and Batt & Appelbaum (1995) reported differences but did not examine whether the differences were significant.

References

Aiello, J. R. & Kolb, K. J. (1995). Electronic performance monitoring and social context: impact on productivity and stress. *Journal of Applied Psychology*, **80**, 339–353.

Aiello, J. R. & Shao, Y. (1993). Electronic performance monitoring and stress: the role of feedback and goal setting. In M. J. Smith & G. Salavendy (Eds), *Human–Computer Interaction: Applications and Case Studies* (pp. 1011–1016). Amsterdam: Elsevier Science.

Alder, G. S. (1998). Ethical issues in electronic performance monitoring: a consideration of deontological and teleological perspectives. *Journal of Business Ethics*, **17**, 729–743.
Bandura, A. (1997). *Self-efficacy: the Exercise of Control*. New York: W. H. Freeman.
Bain, P. & Taylor, P. (2000). Entrapped by the "electronic panoptican"? Worker resistance in the call centre. *New Technology, Work and Employment*, **15**, 2–18.
Bain, P., Watson, A., Mulvey, G., Taylor. P. & Gall, G. (2001). Taylorism, targets and quantity–quality dichotomy in call centres. 19th International Labour Process Conference, Royal Holloway College, University of London, March.
Batt, R. (1999). Work organization, technology and performance in customer service and sales. *Industrial and Labor Relations Review*, **52**, 539–564.
Batt, R. (2000). Strategic segmentation in front line services: matching customers, employees and human resource systems. *International Journal of Human Resource Management*, **11**, 540–561.
Batt, R. & Appelbaum, E. (1995). Worker participation in diverse settings: does the form affect the outcome, and if so, who benefits? *British Journal of Industrial Relations*, **33**, 353–378.
Batt, R. & Moynihan, L. (2001). The viability of alternative call centre production models. Paper presented at Call Centres and Beyond: the Human Resource Management Implications, Kings College, London, November.
Belt, V., Richardson, R. & Webster, J. (1999). Smiling down the phone: women's work in telephone call centres. Paper presented at RGS–IBG Annual Conference, University of Leicester, January.
Betts, A., Meadows, M. & Walley, P. (2000). Call centre capacity management. *International Journal of Service Industry Management*, **11**, 185–196.
Boddy, D. (2000). Implementing interorganizational IT systems: lessons from a call centre project. *Journal of Information Technology*, **15**, 29–37.
Bowen, D. E. & Schneider, B. (1988). Services marketing and management: implications for organizational behaviour. In B. M. Staw & L. L. Cummings (Eds) *Research in Organisational Behavior*, Vol 10 (pp. 43–80). Greenwich: JAI Press.
Boxall, P. (1996). The strategic HRM debate and the resource based view of the firm. *Human Resource Management Journal*, **6**, 59–75.
Braverman, H. (1974). *Labour and Monopoly Capital*. New York: Monthly Review Press.
Burgers, A., de Ruyter, K., Keen., C. & Streukens, S. (2000). Customer expectation dimensions of voice to voice service encounters: a scale development study. *International Journal of Service Industry Management*, **11**, 142–161.
Callaghan, G. & Thompson, P. (2001). Edwards revisited: technical control and call centres. *Economic and Industrial Democracy*, **22**, 13–37.
Carayon, P. (1993). Effects of electronic performance monitoring on job design and worker stress: review of the literature and conceptual model. *Human Factors*, **35**, 385–395.
Chalykoff, J. & Kochan, T. (1989). Computer-aided monitoring: its influence on employee job satisfaction and turnover. *Personnel Psychology*, **42**, 807–834.
Chaudhuri, A. & Holbrook, M. B. (2001). The chain effects from brand trust and brand affect to brand performance: the role of brand loyalty. *Journal of Marketing*, **65**, 81–93.
Cherns, A. (1987). Principles of socio-technical design revisited, *Human Relations*, **40**, 153–162.
Clark, J., McLoughlin, I., Rose, H. & King, J. (1998). *The Process of Technological Change: New Technology and Social Change in the Workplace*. Cambridge: Cambridge University Press.

Clegg, C. W., Axtell, C., Damodaran, L., Farby, B., Hull, R., Lloyd-Jones, R., Nicholl, J., Sell, R., Tomlinson, C., Ainger A. & Stewart, T. (1996). Failing to Deliver: the IT Performance Gap. Report to Economic and Social Research Council, Institute of Work Psychology, Memo No. 64, University of Sheffield.

Clegg, C. W. (2000). Sociotechnical principles for system design. *Applied Ergonomics*, **31**, 463–477.

Datamonitor (1998). *Call Centres in Europe: Sizing by Call Centres and Agent Positions in 13 European Countries*. London: Datamonitor.

Deery, S. J., Iverson, R. D. & Walsh, J. T. (2001). Work relationships in telephone call centres: understanding emotional exhaustion and employee withdrawal. *Journal of Management Studies* (in press).

Doucett, L. (1998). Responsiveness: emotion and information dynamics in service interactions. Working Paper 98–15, Financial Institutions Center, The Wharton School, University of Pennsylvania.

Evenson, A., Harker, P. T. & Frei, F. X. (1999). Effective call center management: evidence from financial services. Working Paper 99–110, Financial Institutions Center, The Wharton School, University of Pennsylvania.

Feinberg, R. A., Kim, I-K., Hokama, L., de Ruyter, K. & Keen, C. (2000). Operational determinants of caller satisfaction in the call center. *International Journal of Service Industry Management*, **11**, 131–141.

Frenkel, S., Korczyniski, M., Shire, K. & Tam, M. (1999). *On the Front-line: Organization of Work in the Information Economy*. Ithaca, NY: Cornell University Press.

Frenkel, S., Tam, M., Korczynski, M. & Shire, K. (1998). Beyond Bureaucracy? Work organisation in call centres. *International Journal of Human Resource Management*, **9**, 957–979.

Garson, B. (1988). *The Electronic Sweatshop: How Computers are Transforming the Office of the Future into the Factory of the Past*. New York: Simon & Schuster.

Grant, R. A. & Higgins, C. A. (1989). Computerised performance monitors: factors affecting acceptance. *IEEE Transactions on Engineering Management*, **38**, 306–314.

Grieco, A., Moltini, G., Piccolo, B. & Occhipiati, E. (1995). *Work with Display Units*. Amsterdam: Elsevier Science.

Grandey, A. A. (2000). Emotion regulation in the workplace: a new way to conceptualise emotional labour. *Journal of Occupational Health*, **5**, 95–110.

Grundy, J. (1998). Trust in Organizational Teams. *Harvard Business Review*, **73**, 40–50.

Gutek, B. (1995). *The Dynamics of Service: Reflections on the Changing Nature of Customer/Provider Interactions*. San Fransisco, CA: Jossey-Bass.

Gutek, B. (1997). Dyadic interactions in organisations. In C. L. Cooper & S. E. Jackson (Eds), *Creating Tomorrows Organizations Today*. Chichester: Wiley.

Health and Safety Executive (1992). *Display Screen Equipment Regulations*. London: HMSO.

Health and Safety Executive (1999). *Initial Advice Regarding Call Centre Working Practices*. Local Authority Circular 94/1, Health and Safety Executive, Sheffield.

Hochschild, A. (1983). *The Managed Heart: the Commercialization of Human Feeling*. Los Angeles, CA: University of California Press.

Holman, D., (2001). Employee Stress in call centres. *Human Resource Management Journal* (at press).

Holman, D. Chissick, C. & Totterdell, P. (2002). The effects of performance monitoring on emotional labour on well-being in call centres. *Motivation and Emotion*, **26**(1), 57–81.

Holman, D. & Fernie, S. (2000). Employee Well-being in Call Centres. Institute of Work Psychology, Memo No. 260, University of Sheffield.

Hosmer, L. T. (1995). Trust: the connecting link between organisational theory and philosophical ethics. *Academy of Management Review*, **20**, 379–403.

Houlihan, M. (2001). Control and commitment in the call centre? More evidence from the field. Paper presented at Conference on Call Centres and Beyond: the Human Resource Management Implications, Kings College, London, November.

Hutchinson, S., Purcell, J. & Kinnie, N. (2000). Evolving high commitment management and the experience of the RAC call centre. *Human Resource Management Journal*, **10**, 63–78.

Ichniowski, C., Kochan, T., Levine, D., Olson, C. & Strauss, G. (1996). What works at work: overview and assessment. *Industrial Relations*, **35**, 299–334.

Incomes Data Services (1997). *Pay and Conditions in Call Centres*. London: Incomes Data Services.

Irving, R. H., Higgins, C. A. & Safeyeni, F. R. (1986). Computerised performance monitoring systems: use and abuse. *Communications of the ACM*, August **29**, 794–801.

Karaseck, R. A. & Theorell, T. G. (1990). *Healthy Work: Stress, Productivity and the Reconstruction of Working Life*. New York: Basic Books.

Keefe, J. & Batt, R. (2001). Telecommunications services: union–management relations in an era of industry re-consolidation. In P. Clark, J. Delaney & A. Frost (Eds), *Collective Bargaining: Current Developments and Future Challenges*. IRRA Research Volume. Madison, WI: IRRA.

Kinnie, N., Purcell, J. & Hutchinson, S. (2000). Managing the employment relationship in call centres. In K. Purcell (Ed.), *Changing Boundaries in Employment* (pp. 133–159). Bristol: Bristol Academic Press.

Knights, D. & McCabe, D. (1998). What happens when the phone goes wild? Staff, stress and spaces for escape in a BPR telephone banking call regime. *Journal of Management Studies*, **35**, 163–194.

Korczynski, M., Shire, K., Frenkel, S. & Tam, M. (2000). Service work in consumer capitalism: customers, control and contradictions. *Work, Employment and Society*, **14**, 669–687.

Levitt, T. (1972). Production line approach to services. *Harvard Business Review*, **50**, 41–50.

Metcalf, D. & Fernie, S. (1998). (Not) hanging on the telephone: payment systems in the new sweatshops. *Centrepiece*, **3**, 7–11.

Morley, I. E. & Stephenson, G. M. (1970). Formality in experimental negotiations: a validation study. *British Journal of Psychology*, **61**, 383–384.

Muscovici, S. (1967). Communication processes and properties of language. In L. Berkovitz (Ed.) *Advances in Experimental Social Psychology*, Vol. 3 (pp. 225–270), Academic Press, New York.

Nohria, N. & Eccles, R. G. (Eds) (1992). *Networks and Organizations*. Boston, MA: Harvard Business School Press.

Orlinowski, W. J. (1992). The duality of technology: rethinking the concept of technology in organisations. *Organization Science*, **3**, 398–427.

Parker, S. K. & Wall, T. D. (1998). *Job and Work Design*. London: Sage.

Rosenfield, M. (1997). *Counselling by Telephone*. Sage: London.

Rutter, D. R. (1987). *Communicating by Telephone*. Oxford: Pergamon.

Rutter, D. R. & Stephenson, G. M. (1979). The role of visual communication in social interaction. *Current Anthropology*, **20**, 124–125.

Schlesinger, L. & Heskett, J. (1991). Breaking the cycle of failure in services. *Sloan Management Review*, **32**, 17–28.

Schuler, R. S. & Jackson, S. E. (1995). Linking competitive strategies with human resource management strategies. *Academy of Management Executive*, **1**, 207–219.

Short, J., Williams, E. & Christie, A. (1976). *The Social Psychology of Telecommunications*. Chichester: Wiley.

Singh, J. & Sirdeshmukh, D. (2000). Agency and trust in consumer satisfaction and loyalty judgements. *Journal of the Academy of Marketing Science*, **28**, 150–167.

Smith, M. J., Carayon, P., Sanders, K. J., Lim, S. Y. & LeGrande, D. (1992). Employee stress and health complaints in jobs with and without monitoring. *Applied Ergonomics*, **23**, 17–27.

Spector, P. E. (1987). Interactive effects of perceived control and job stressors on affective reactions and health outcomes for clerical workers. *Work and Stress*, **1**, 155–162.

Stanton, J. M. (2000). Reactions to employee performance monitoring: framework, review and research directions. *Human Performance*, **13**, 85–113.

Sturdy, A. (2000). Training in service—importing and imparting customer service culture as an interactive process. *International Journal of Human Resource Management*, **11**, 1082–1103.

Sturdy, A., Knights, D. & Willmott, H. (Eds) (1992). *Skill and Consent*. London: Routledge.

Taylor, P. & Bain, P. (1999). An assembly line in the head: the call centre labour process. *Industrial Relations Journal*, **30**, 101–117.

Taylor, P. & Bain, P. (2001). Trades unions, workers' rights and the frontier of control in UK call centres. *Economic and Industrial Democracy*, **22**, 39–66.

Terry, D. & Jimmieson, N. (1999). Work control and well-being: a decade review. In C. Cooper & I. Robertson (Eds), *International Review of Industrial and Organizational Psychology*, Vol. 14 (pp. 95–148). Chichester: Wiley.

Totterdell, P. & Holman, D. (2001). Just trying to keep my customers satisfied: a diary study of emotional dissonance in a call centre. Paper presented at European Congress of Psychology Conference, London, 3 July.

Totterdell, P. & Holman, D. (2002). Emotional regulation in customer service roles: testing a model of emotional labour. *Journal of Occupational Health Psychology* (in press).

Trades Union Congress (2001). *It's Your Call: TUC Call Centre Workers' Campaign*. London: TUC.

Vandevelde, H. (2001). Call centres don't have to be hellish. *Sunday Times*, 25 November, Public Appointments (p. 9).

Waters, R. (1998). *Computer Telephony Integration*. London: Artech House.

Winslow, C. D. & Bramer, W. L. (1994). *Futurework*. New York: Free Press.

Wood, S. (Ed.) (1982). *The Degradation of Work?* London: Hutchninson.

Wood, S. (1995). Can we speak of high commitment management on the shop floor? *Journal of Management Studies*, **32**, 215–247.

Wright, P. & McMahon, G. (1992). Theoretical perspectives for strategic human resource management. *Journal of Management*, **18**, 295–320.

Zapf, D., Vogt, C., Seifert, C., Mertini, H. & Isic, A. (1999). Emotion work as a source of stress: the concept and development of an instrument. *European Journal of Work and Organisational Psychology*, **8**, 371–400.

58

MANAGING A VIRTUAL WORKPLACE

Wayne F. Cascio

Source: *Academy of Management Executive* 14(3) (2000): 81–90.

Executive overview

Virtual workplaces, in which employees operate remotely from each other and from managers, are a reality, and will become even more common in the future. There are sound business reasons for establishing virtual workplaces, but their advantages may be offset by such factors as setup and maintenance costs, loss of cost efficiencies, cultural clashes, isolation, and lack of trust. Virtual teams and telework are examples of such arrangements, but they are not appropriate for all jobs, all employees, or all managers. To be most effective in these environments, managers need to do two things well: Shift from a focus on time to a focus on results; and recognize that virtual workplaces, instead of needing fewer managers, require better supervisory skills among existing managers. Taking these steps can lead to stunning improvements in productivity, profits, and customer service.

The virtual workplace, in which employees operate remotely from each other and from managers, is a reality for many employers now, and all indications are that it will become even more prevalent in the future. Virtual organizations are multisite, multiorganizational, and dynamic.[1] At a macro level, a virtual organization consists of a grouping of businesses, consultants, and contractors that have joined in an alliance to exploit complementary skills in pursuing common strategic objectives.[2] The objectives often focus on a specific project.[3] In and of itself, this grouping represents a dramatic change in how we work, and it presents two new challenges for managers. The challenges stem from the physical separation of workers and managers wrought by such information-age arrangements wrought by such information-age arrangements as telework and virtual teams. "How can I manage them if I can't see them?" is a question that many managers are now asking. It defines the first managerial challenge of the virtual workplace: making the transition from managing time (activity-based) to managing projects (results-based).

The second managerial challenge of the virtual workplace is to overcome uncertainty about whether managers will still be valued by their companies if they are managing employees who are not physically present. In one case, a first-level manager recalled his boss coming out of his office, looking at the empty cubicles around him, and saying, "What do I need you for?"[4] As we shall see in this article, the need is not for fewer managers, but for better supervisory skills among existing managers.

This article identifies the business reasons for, as well as some potential arguments against, virtual workplaces; examines alternative forms of virtual workplaces, along with the advantages and disadvantages of each; and provides tools and information to managers of virtual workplaces, based on advances in research on this topic.

Business reasons for virtual workplaces

Many companies have instituted virtual workplaces, and have reaped the following benefits:

- *Reduced real estate expenses*. IBM saves 40 to 60 percent per site annually by eliminating offices for all employees except those who truly need them.[5] Northern Telecom estimates the savings gained from not having to house an employee in a typical 64-square-foot space, considering only rent and annual operating costs, at $2,000 per person per year.[6] Others estimate the savings at $2 for every $1 invested.[7]
- *Increased productivity*. Internal IBM studies shows gains of 15 to 40 percent. USWest reported that the productivity of its teleworking employees increased, some by as much as 40 percent.[8]
- *Higher profits*. Hewlett-Packard doubled revenue per salesperson after moving its sales people to virtual workplace arrangements.[9]
- *Improved customer service*. Andersen Consulting found that its consultants spent 25 percent more time face-to-face with customers when they did not have permanent offices.[10]
- *Access to global markets*. John Brown Engineers & Constructors Ltd., a member of the engineering division of Trafalgar House, the world's third largest engineering and construction organization, with 21,000 employees around the globe, was able to access local pharmaceutical engineering talent at a project site in India. Using virtual work arrangements, the firm was able to traverse national boundaries, enabling it to work with and present a local face to its global clients. This enhanced its global competitiveness.[11]
- *Environmental benefits*. At Georgia Power, 150 people, or 13 percent of the workers at headquarters, are teleworkers. This has reduced annual commuting mileage by 993,000 miles, and automobile emissions by almost

35,000 pounds.[12] A U.S. government study showed that if 20,000 federal workers could telecommute just one day a week, they would save over two million commuting miles, 102,000 gallons of gasoline, and 81,600 pounds of carbon dioxide emissions each week. The emissions savings for one week under this arrangement are equivalent to the amount of carbon dioxide produced by the average car over 9.3 years.[13]

Potential disadvantages of virtual workplaces

Offsetting these advantages, however, are some potentially serious disadvantages that managers should consider carefully before institutionalizing virtual-work arrangements:

- *Setup and maintenance costs.* For individual employees, the additional cost required to equip a mobile or home office varies from roughly $3,000 to $5,000, plus about $1,000 in upgrades and supplies every year thereafter.[14] In addition, to be viable, virtual offices require online materials that can be downloaded and printed; databases on products and customers that are accessible from remote locations; well-indexed, automated, central files that are accessible from remote locations; and a way to track the location of mobile workers. Technology is the remote worker's lifeline. In the absence of the administrative and technical support that one might find at the home office, the technology must work flawlessly, and technical support should be available 24 hours a day, seven days a week. (Or at least a help desk should be staffed from 8 a.m. to midnight.) Decision makers need to consider the incremental costs associated with setting up and maintaining virtual workplaces.
- *Loss of cost efficiencies.* When expensive equipment or services are concentrated in one location, multiple users can access them. When the same equipment or services are distributed across locations, cost efficiencies may be lost. For example, in the securities industry, certain real-time information sources are necessary. Most stock quotes are available on the Internet on a 15-minute delay, which is adequate for most people's needs. However, for brokers and traders quoting prices to customers, it is imperative that quotes be up-to-the-second. Companies such as Bloomberg, Bridge Financial System, Reuters Quotron, and ILX Systems provide this real-time service. Each is willing to install its system at the customer's place of choice. Typical costs are about $1,200 per month for the first installation of such a system, and about $200 per month to install each additional system in the same location. When a securities firm needs this information for 50 brokers, along with related services (e.g., CDA Spectrum, Multex.com's Market Guide, and First Call/Thomson Financial), it is more cost-effective to have all employees at one location, rather than working at many different locations.[15]
- *Cultural issues.* Virtual organizations operating in the global arena often have to transfer their business policies and cultures to work with dispersed business

teams across collaborating organizations, geography, and cultures. This can lead to potential clashes of business and national cultures, which, in turn, can undermine the entire alliance.[16] If the members of a virtual organization or a virtual team are not empowered to make decisions, the technology that enables their collaboration will add little value, and the competitive advantage associated with rapid responses to demands in the market place will be lost.

- *Feelings of isolation.* Some level of social interaction with supervisors and coworkers is essential in almost all jobs. Without it, workers feel isolated and out of the loop with respect to crucial communications and contact with decision makers who can make or break their careers.
- *Lack of trust.* A key ingredient to the success of virtual work arrangements is trust that one's coworkers will fulfill their obligations and behave predictably. Lack of trust can undermine every other precaution taken to ensure successful virtual work arrangements, such as careful selection of employees to work in the virtual environment, thorough training of managers and employees, and ongoing performance management.

When virtual work arrangements are appropriate

Virtual workplaces are not appropriate for all jobs. In fact, an organization must first understand the parameters of each job it considers for a virtual work environment. To do so, it must determine what function the job serves; if the work is performed over the phone, in person, via computer, or in some combination; how much time the employee spends in direct contact with other employees, customers, and business contacts; if the location of the office is critical to performance; whether the hours have to be 9 to 5; and whether the employee must be reachable immediately.[17]

Jobs in sales, marketing, project engineering, and consulting seem to be best suited for virtual workplaces because individuals in these jobs already work with their clients by phone or at the client's premises. Such jobs are service- and knowledge-oriented, dynamic, and evolve according to customer requirements.[18] Even in these jobs, however, virtual work arrangements are not recommended for new employees or those who are new to a position. Newcomers require a period of socialization during which they learn to adapt to their new company, new environment, and new managers and coworkers. They need time to learn business skills, how and why things are done in the new company or new position, and the dos and taboos of the company's culture.

For employees whose jobs are appropriate for virtual work arrangements, and who are internally motivated self-starters who know their jobs well and are technically self-sufficient, the key is to work with them well ahead of planned transitions. Firms such as Lotus, IBM, and Hewlett-Packard have written guidelines, training, and networks of peers to facilitate the transition. For example, Hewlett-Packard's guidelines for virtual workplaces address topics such as who can participate, family and household issues, remote office setup, and administrative processes.

Just as not all employees are suited to work away from their primary business locations during scheduled work hours, not all managers are suited to manage employees with virtual-work arrangement. Those who are seem to have the following characteristics:

- An open, positive attitude that focuses on solutions to issues rather than on reasons to discontinue virtual-work arrangements.
- A results-oriented management style. Those who need structure and control are unlikely to be effective managers in virtual-work environments.
- Effective communications skills, both formal and informal, with employees working remotely and at the primary business location.
- An ability to delegate effectively, and to follow up to ensure that work is accomplished.

While these characteristics apply to progressive managers in conventional as well as virtual-work environments, the need is greater in virtual environments that lack the attributes of traditional social contexts, such as physical proximity, verbal and nonverbal cues, norms of behavior, and, in the case of teams, a sense of cohort.

Virtual teams

In a virtual team, members are dispersed geographically or organizationally. Their primary interaction is through some combination of electronic communication systems. They may never meet in the traditional sense. Further, team membership is often fluid, evolving according to changing task requirements.[19] Such an arrangement provides several advantages:

- It saves time, travel expenses, and provides access to experts.
- Teams can be organized whether or not members are in proximity to one another.
- Firms can use outside consultants without incurring expenses for travel, lodging, and downtime.
- Virtual teams allow firms to expand their potential labor markets, enabling them to hire and retain the best people regardless of their physical location, or, in the case of workers with disabilities, whether or not they are able to commute to work.
- Employees can more easily accommodate both personal and professional lives.
- Dynamic team membership allows people to move from one project to another.
- Employees can be assigned to multiple, concurrent teams.
- Team communications and work reports are available online to facilitate swift responses to the demands of a global market. For example, Veriphone uses

a so-called relay race to develop software products faster than its competitors. Software engineers at the firm's Dallas headquarters work a full day on a project, then put their work product online on the company's intranet. Veriphone engineers in Honolulu take up the project, then post it for their counterparts in Bombay. As the Bombay software engineers leave work, they transmit their work product electronically back to headquarters in Dallas, where the originators are arriving for the next day's work. Electronic communications media make the relay race possible. Clients benefit from the firm's speedy response to their needs.

Disadvantages of virtual teams

The major disadvantages of virtual teams are the lack of physical interaction—with its associated verbal and nonverbal cues—and the synergies that often accompany face-to-face communication. These deficiencies raise issues of trust. Trust is critical in a virtual team because traditional social control based on authority gives way to self-direction and self-control. Members of virtual teams need to be sure that all others will fulfill their obligations and behave in a consistent, predictable manner.

An empirical analysis of the development of trust in 29 global virtual teams that communicated strictly by e-mail over a six-week period found that teams with the highest levels of trust tended to share three traits. First, they began their interactions with a series of social messages—introducing themselves and providing some personal background—before focusing on the work at hand. Second, they set clear roles for each team member, thus enabling all team members to identify with one another. Third, all team members demonstrated positive attitudes. Team members consistently displayed eagerness, enthusiasm, and an intense action orientation in all of their messages.[20] The lessons from this research are that first impressions are critical, and that especially in virtual-work environments, initial messages need to be handled well. Keep the tone of all messages upbeat and action-oriented. One pessimist in the group has the potential to undermine trust in the entire virtual team, and lack of trust affects overall group productivity. Not surprisingly, low-trust teams were less productive than high-trust ones.

Training members and managers of virtual teams

Because virtual teams are growing in popularity, it is important to address the issue of how best to train members and managers of virtual teams. A majority of U.S. corporations use some form of team structure in their organizations.[21] Virtual teams add another layer of complexity to any teamwork situation. They have created a rich training agenda, for example:

- How to use the software to enhance team performance.
- How to manage the anonymous environment, and when to use it.

- How to provide anonymous participation and feedback when ideas or criticism need to be brought out. This is particularly important since the traditional cues of social interaction—body language and hand gestures—may not be available.
- Social protocol for virtual teams.
- Since changes in team membership must occur with seamless continuity, it is important to teach common cultural values.

These issues imply that managers should think carefully about the kinds of behaviors that are most likely to enhance a virtual team's ability to function effectively. Empirical findings with global virtual teams suggest that these behaviors fall into three key areas: virtual-collaborative skills, virtual-socialization skills, and virtual-communication skills.[22]

Key virtual-collaboration behaviors include the ability to exchange ideas without criticism, develop a working document in which team members' ideas are summarized, exchange it among team members for editing, track member comments in a working document with initials, agree on activities, and meet deadlines.

Key virtual-socialization behaviors include the ability to communicate with other team members immediately, solicit team members' feedback on the process the team is using to accomplish its tasks, disclose appropriate personal information, express appreciation for ideas and completed tasks, apologize for mistakes, volunteer for roles, and acknowledge role assignments.

Key virtual-communication behaviors include the ability to obtain local translator help when language skills are insufficient to be understood, rephrase unclear sentences so that all team members understand what is being said, use e-mail typography to communicate emotion, acknowledge the receipt of messages, and respond within one business day.

There is also much to learn from other research on teams in general, especially with respect to self-limiting behaviors by team members.[23] Team members may limit their involvement for any one of the following reasons: the presence of someone with expertise, the presentation of a compelling argument, lack of confidence in one's ability to contribute, an unimportant or meaningless decision, pressures from others to conform to the team's decision, or a dysfunctional decision-making climate in which members become frustrated, indifferent, unorganized, or unwilling to commit to making an effective decision.

To avoid these problems, managers should choose team members carefully and give each member a good reason for being on the team. They should also frame the team's decision task appropriately, emphasizing clear, well-defined goals and the consequences of the team's decision. The first team meeting is crucial and will establish lasting precedents for the team. Managers should set productive team norms, for example, and clarify whether decisions will be made by consensus and whether all team members will share responsibility for implementing the final decision. Managers should also monitor the team's process. If this proves difficult, they should include a team-development specialist to serve as a resource to the team, assisting it with technical problems, and facilitating their interaction when necessary.[24] Finally, they should provide honest feedback to group members about their individual behaviors and the final outcome of the team's work. Doing so may uncover unproductive behaviours that will enable group members to work better the next time around.

Teleworking

Telework is work carried out in a location remote from central offices or production facilities, where the worker has no personal contact with coworkers, but is able to communicate with them electronically.[25] Teleworking is a popular and rapidly growing alternative to the traditional, office-bound work style. Two of every three *Fortune* 500 companies employ teleworkers. Forty million employees telework on a global basis, and by 2003 more than 137 million workers world-wide are expected to telework at least on a part-time basis.[26] Survey results indicate that employees want more opportunities for telework, and that their top priority is to gain the flexibility to control their own time.[27] Some companies are actively encouraging the trend. In February, 2000, both Ford Motor Company and Delta Air Lines announced that they are giving employees personal computers for home use.[28]

Telework may also assume other forms:

- *Hoteling*: Ernst & Young workers in Washington, D.C., use workstations and meeting rooms in nearby hotels. The firm has hoteled eight offices and is converting seven more, and has found that workers focus less on the office and more on the customer.[29]
- *Hot desking*: About 20,000 IBM employees, primarily those in sales and service, share offices with four other people, on average. Cisco Systems, a technology firm in San Jose, California, has several thousand people sharing a variety of spaces around the world. As noted earlier, however, hoteling and hot desking are not for everyone.[30]
- *Telework centers*: Corporate office environments in miniature, offering more technology than an employee has at home, may be located in residential neighborhoods. Small groups of employees who live nearby work in these centers, rather than commute. For example, the Ontario Telebusiness Work Center near Los Angeles offers electronically equipped suites to companies.[31] The suburban location minimizes commuting time, while maximizing productive time.

Telework and the balance between work and family

Although there is little empirical research on the effect of telework on work-family relations, a recent study in three Canadian organizations revealed that teleworkers had significantly lower levels of interference from work to family, significantly lower levels of interference from family to work, and significantly fewer problems managing their family time than they did before teleworking.[32] These data support the positive view of telework and suggest that working from home helps employed parents balance work and family demands.[33]

Implications of telework research for decision makers

Decision makers should be skeptical of claims about the effects of telework that are not grounded in rigorous empirical research. For example, several studies have suggested that the level of teleworking participation will have a negative impact on visibility, and, therefore on career advancement.[34] But empirical research has not addressed this out-of-sight, out-of-mind argument. Before drawing conclusions about telework and framing organizational policy on this issue, decision makers should also consider the extent to which research findings might apply to their own industries and organizational cultures, and to employees at different stages of their careers.

Traning managers and employees for telework

In a telework relationship, time is not important. This is one of the harder lessons for managers of teleworkers to learn, and many have to rethink completely how they view supervision. They need to understand that managing employees they can't see differs considerably from walking around offices to see that employees are at their desks. Learning to make the transition from managing time to managing projects is critical and will determine the success of an organization's telework program.[35]

Before a telework arrangement is finalized at Merrill Lynch, process consultants study how employees in a given area communicate and do business, and identify what the barriers to teleworking will be. This alleviates managers' concerns and focuses attention on areas that need to be addressed. Formalized training for telework is divided into teleworker training, supervisor and manager training, and team training, in which teleworkers and their managers come together to discuss issues that affect their relationship. Some organizations also set aside time to train and educate the entire staff, from the mail room to the board room.[36]

In teleworking arrangements, cultural, managerial, and interpersonal implications also need to be addressed. Training for workers and managers should begin together so they hear the same message, and understand the business case for implementing telework arrangements. Both groups address such issues as the lack of face-to-face time (which may create resentment among workers who remain in the office), potential losses in creativity from lack of personal interaction with coworkers and managers, and potential losses in productivity from absence from the office. Employees and managers who already have experience with telework arrangements should make presentations. Both groups should be encouraged to begin measuring productivity through assignments and projects, rather than hours spent in the office.[37]

Project management is especially important in instances where teleworkers or virtual members are not part of the same organization. Each person is hired to accomplish a specific task, and that person often has no vested interest in monitoring the end result. If a manager does not actively monitor the progress of the overall project and the usefulness of the final product, the team's productivity will never result in improved profitability.

The time frame for completion can cause problems for some managers who are new at managing teleworkers or virtual teams. Most managers establish completion dates, which are necessary. However, completion of a project may be delayed if managers do not establish milestone activities, critical completion points within the overall duration of a project. Through the use of milestones, a manager can see early in a project's life cycle whether or not the necessary pieces are progressing satisfactorily. This allows corrections and changes during the project that ensure timely completion, or at least forewarn of problems.[38] The principles of effective project management are not new, and they do not change in virtual work environments. They simply become more important.

Managers and workers should be wary of naive expectations about what working away from the office is really like. To provide a realistic preview for prospective teleworkers. Merrill Lynch uses a simulation lab, a large room with work stations where employees work for two weeks without face-to-face contact with their managers. After the two-week trial, some employees decide that telework is not for them.[39] While some firms use short, self-scored surveys to help workers identify how likely they are to succeed as teleworkers, there is really no substitute for a job tryout, such as a simulation lab provides.

A final component of telework training is to bring managers into the evaluation process about six months after the implementation of the telework program, using productivity measurements as the basis for a business case analysis. Examining the impact of telework on productivity, cost, and customer satisfaction allows for adjustments or enhancements to the program, or to its cancellation.

Virtual office challenges for managers

It is important at the outset to ensure that all departments that will interact with members of virtual teams or teleworkers accept and support the concept of the virtual-work arrangement. If they do not, it will fail.[40] As the vice chairman of American Express noted: "It's important to have a multifunction team of senior managers promoting and supporting a virtual-office initiative from the start. We had three departments involved in our effort: HR, technology, and real estate. The individuals must be enthusiastic and not unnecessarily fettered by traditional approaches. And they must be made knowledgeable about all the key issues.[41]

Broad support alone is not enough to guarantee the success of virtual workplaces. Managers also must set and enforce ground rules for communication, and institute a comprehensive process of performance management.

Communication

Communication is a major challenge for managers implementing a virtual-work environment. Many managers have to learn new communication skills to prevent team members from feeling isolated and not part of a larger group. It is important not to rely solely on e-mail, which is one-way communication. Managers should learn how to conduct effective audio meetings, and to balance e-mail, voice mail, video conferencing, and face-to-face communications.

Begin with some ground rules so that all team members understand the method of communication and what is expected during those communication sessions. For example, use e-mail for reports, and the computer-based chat room to discuss project issues. In addition, all team members should be available by phone between certain hours.[42]

Scheduled virtual meetings are essential and attendance must be enforced strictly to ensure that all team members participate. Face-to-face meetings on a regular basis, if at all possible, allow team members to put faces to e-mail. Forging personal relationships among team members contributes to successful implementation. Since facial expressions and body language cues are not available in the virtual work environment, teleworkers must compensate with other forms of communication in order to understand each other fully. This generally means asking more questions and conversing more frequently. The manager or team leader should communicate with all team members, not just a few, and include all team members on distribution lists. This ensures that all members are accounted for and are equal contributors to the team. Regular updates and status reports are necessary to replace hallway conversations, networking, and the daily stimulation of a traditional office environment.

When team members do not work at the same time, or in the same location, members themselves must make exceptional efforts to ensure accurate, timely communications. Some virtual teams must contend with different time zones. Others must disseminate detailed information, perhaps on spreadsheets or by using computer-aided design (CAD) software. Managers can provide guidance and coaching on how to improve communications, but team members themselves have to shoulder responsibility for providing accurate, timely information.

Performance management

By far the biggest challenge is performance management, which requires that managers do three things well: define, facilitate, and encourage performance.[43] While these principles are important to follow in conventional working environments, they are even more imperative in virtual working environments.

Define performance

On a virtual team, a fundamental requirement is that all team members understand their responsibilities.[44] A manager trying to define performance might ask the following questions to help clarify these responsibilities:

- What is the team's overall objective?
- Do you expect each team member to fulfill more than one role on the team?
- Which responsibilities will team members share (e.g., selecting new members, rating one another's performance)?
- Will the team elect a leader? What responsibilities will this person have?
- Who is responsible for disciplinary action if the need arises?
- How will the team make decisions (e.g., by consensus, or by majority-rule)?
- Which decisions does the team have the authority to make?

The next step is to develop specific, challenging goals, measures of the extent to which goals have been accomplished, and assessment mechanisms so that workers and managers can stay focused on what really counts. To be useful, the measures should be linked to the strategic direction, business objectives, and customer requirements for the company.[45] For a cable-television company, a major strategic thrust might be to increase the number of new subscribers, or the number of current subscribes who pay for premium channels. For a firm that provides outsourcing services in information technology, major customer requirements might be timeliness of response to inquiries, and cost savings relative to in-house capability.

In defining performance, regular assessment of progress toward goals focuses the attention and efforts of an employee or team. A manager who identifies measurable goals, but then fails to assess progress towards them, is asking for trouble.

The overall objective of goals, measures, and assessment is to leave no doubt in the minds of remote workers what is expected of them, how it will be measured, and where they stand at any given point in time. The need for such ground rules is even more pressing in a virtual work environment. There should be no surprises in the performance management process, and regular feedback to remote employees helps ensure that there won't be.

Facilitate performance

Managers who are committed to managing remote workers effectively recognize that two of their major responsibilities are to eliminate roadblocks to successful performance and to provide adequate resources to get a job done right and on time.

Obstacles that can inhibit maximum performance include outdated equipment or technology, delays in receiving critical information, and inefficient design of work processes. Employees are well aware of these, and are usually willing to identify them when managers ask for their input. Then it is the manager's job a eliminate these obstacles.

Adequate capital resources, material resources, and human resources are necessary if remote workers or members of virtual teams are to reach the challenging goals they have set. In the words of one observer. "It's immoral not to give people tools to meet tough goals."[46] Conversely, employees really appreciate their employer's providing everything they need to perform will. Not surprisingly, they usually do perform well under those circumstances.

Encourage performance

To encourage performance, especially repeated good performance, it is important to provide sufficient rewards that employees really value, in a timely and fair manner.

Begin by asking remote workers what's most important to them. For example, is it pay, benefits, free time, technology upgrades, or opportunities for professional development? Then consider tailoring your awards program so that remote workers or teams can choose from a menu of similarly valued options.

Next, provide rewards in a timely manner, soon after major accomplishments. For example, North American Tool & Die, a metal-stamping plant in San Leandro, California, provides monthly cash awards for creativity. This is important, for an excessive delay between effective performance and receipt of the reward may mean the reward loses its potential to motivate subsequent high performance.

Finally, provide rewards in a manner that employees consider fair. Procedures are fair to the extent that they are consistent across persons and over time, free from bias, based on accurate information, correctable, and based on prevailing moral and ethical standards.[47] Not surprisingly, employees often behave very responsibly when they are asked in advance for their opinions about what is fair. Indeed, it seems only fair to ask them.

Implications for managers

New business realities, coupled with demands by workers for more flexibility and empowerment, suggest that virtual workplaces are here to stay. The challenges of managing a virtual workplace will escalate in scope. The use of new technology and tools only enables competitive advantage. Realizing competitive advantage requires effective management coupled with new ways of doing business. Organizations in which virtual-work arrangements thrive will be flatter than they are today. Knowledge workers within these environments will have more autonomy and responsibility than in traditional organizations, yet lines of authority, roles, and responsibilities will still need to be defined clearly. New ways of communicating and interacting among workers in virtual environments will need to be developed and implemented, yet face-to-face communications will remain essential ingredients of successful workplaces. Heavy emphasis will be placed on establishing and maintaining the technical tools that are the lifeblood of workers in virtual environments. Workers as well as managers will need continual training in both new tools and new processes to operate effectively in these environments.

Managers who are committed to virtual-work environments will understand that basic principles of management are not different in virtual-work environments, but that the principles need to be followed more closely than ever. They understand that better, not fewer, management skills and managers will be needed.

To be a beneficiary, rather than a victim, of emerging virtual-workplace trends, institute the performance-management systems, information-access capabilities, and training systems to develop skills that will be important in the future. Always look ahead; learn from the past, but don't live in it. By embracing these emerging changes in the world of work, proactive managers can lead change, not just react to it.

Endnotes

1 Snow, C. C., Lipnack, J., & Stamps, J. 1999. The virtual organization: Promises and pay-offs, large and small. In C. L. Copper & D. M. Rousseau (Eds.), *The virtual organization*: 15–30, New York: Wiley.
2 Dess, G. G., Rasheed, A. M. A., McLaughlin, K. J., & Priem, R. L. 1995. The new corporate architecture. *The Academy of Management Executive*, 9(3):7–18.
3 Igbaria, M., & Tan, M. (Eds.). 1998. *The virtual workplace*. Hershey, PA: Idea Group Publishing.
4 Grensing-Pophal, L. 1999. Training supervisors to manage teleworkers. *HRMagazine*, January, 67:72.
5 O'Connell, S. E. 1996. The virtual workplace moves at warp speed. *HRMagazine*, March 51:77. See also: *Business Week*. 1996. The new workplace. April 29:105–113.
6 Cooper, R. C. 1997. Telecommuting: The good, the bad, and the particulars. *Supervision*, 57(2):10–12.
7 McCune, J. C. 1998. Telecommuting revisited. *Management Review*, 87:10–16.
8 Matthes, K. 1992. Telecommuting: Balancing business and employee needs. *HR Focus*, 69(3)December: 3.
9 O'Connell, op. cit.
10 Ibid.
11 Grimshaw, D.J., & Kwok, P.T.S. 1998. The business benefits of the virtual organization. In Igbaria & Tan (Eds.), op. cit. 45–70.
12 McCune, op. cit.
13 The Green Commuter. *http://libertynet.org/cleanair/green/summer98/greentext8-98.html.*
14 Clark, K. 1997. Home is where the work is. *Fortune*. November 24:219–221.
15 Arko, D. et al. 1999. Virtual teams. Unpublished manuscript. University of Colorado Executive MBA Program, Denver.
16 Serapio, M. G., Jr., & Cascio, W. F. 1996. End-games in international alliances. *The Academy of Management Executive*, 10(1):62–73. See also Cascio, W. F., & Serapio, M. G. Jr. 1991, Human resource systems in an international alliance: The undoing of a done deal? *Organizational Dynamics*, Winter:63–74.
17 Apgar, M., IV. 1998. The alternative workplace: Changing where and how people work. *Harvard Business Review*, May–June:121–136.

18 Townsead, A. M., DeMarie, S. M., & Hendrickson, A. R. 1998. Virtual teams: Technology and the workplace of the future. *The Academy of Management Executive*, 12(3):17–29.
19 Ibid.
20 Coutu, D. 1998. Trust in virtual teams. *Harvard Business Review*, May–June:20–21. See also Jarvenpaa, S. L., Knoll, K., & Leidner, D. E. 1998. Is anybody out there? Antecedents of trust in global virtual teams. *Journal of Management Information Systems*, 14(4):29–64.
21 Townsend et al., op. cit.
22 Knoll, K., & Jarvenpaa, S. L. 1998. Working together in global virtual teams. In Igbaria & Tan (Eds.), op. cit.:2–23.
23 Mulvey, P. W., Veiga, J. F., & Elsass, P. M. 1996. When teammates raise a white flag. *The Academy of Management Executive*, 10(1):40–49.
24 Townsend et al., op. cit.
25 Gupta, Y., Karimi, J., & Somers, T. M. 1995. Telecommuting: Problems associated with communications technologies and their capabilities. *IEEE Transactions on Engineering Management*, 42(4):305–318.
26 Anderson, C., Girard, J., Payne, S., Pultz, J., Zboray, M., & Smith, C. 1998. *Implementing a successful remote access project: From technology to management*. New York: Gartner Group, Report R-06-6639, Nov. 18.
27 The new world of work: Flexibility is the watchword. 2000. *Business Week*. January 10:36. See also Conlin, M. 1999. 9 to 5 isn't working anymore. *Business Week*, September 20:94–98.
28 Rivenbark, L. 2000. Employees want more opportunities to telecommute, report reveals. *HRNews*. April:14–16.
29 *Business Week*, 1996, op. cit.
30 "Office Hoteling" isn't as inn as futurists once thought. 1997. *The Wall Street Journal*, September 2:A1.
31 O'Connell, S. E., op. cit.
32 Duxbury, L., Higgins, C., & Neufeld, D. 1998. *Telework and the balance between work and family: Is telework part of the problem or part of the solution?* In Igbaria & Tan (Eds.) op. cit.: 218–255.
33 Ibid.
34 Austin, J. 1993. Telecommuting success depends on reengineering the work processes. *Computing Canada*, 19:37–38. See also DuBrin, A. J., & Barnard, J. C. 1993. What telecommuters like and dislike about their jobs. *Business Forum*, 18:13–17. See also Dutton, G. 1994. Can California change its corporate culture? *Management Review*, 83:49–54.
35 Grensing-Pophal, op. cit.
36 Ibid.
37 Grensing-Pophal, L. 1998. Training employees to telecommute: A recipe for success. *HRMagazine*, Dec:76–82.
38 Arko et al., op. cit.
39 Grensing-Pophal, op. cit.
40 Anderson, C. 1998, *The top 10 non-technical reasons telecommuting programs fail*. New York: Gartner Group, Report COM-04-0431, March 25.
41 Apgar, op. cit.:125.
42 Telecommuting: Practical option or management nightmare? http://www.eeicom/eye/telecomm.html.
43 Cascio, W. F. 1998. *Managing human resources: Productivity, quality of work life, profits* (5th ed.). Burr Ridge, IL: Irwin/McGraw-Hill. See also Cascio, W. F. 1996. Managing for maximum performance. *HRMonthly* (Australia), September:10–13.

44 Townsend et al., op. cit.
45 Moravec, M. 1996. Bringing performance management out of the stone age. *Management Review*, February:38–42.
46 Kerr, S. in Sherman, S. 1995. Stretch goals: The dark side of asking for miracles. *Fortune*. November 13:31.
47 Greenberg, J. 1987, Reactions to procedural justice in payment distributions: Do the means justify the ends? *Journal of Applied Psychology*, 72:55–61.

Part 8

NEXT GENERATION THINKING

59

ORGANIZATIONAL BEHAVIOR IN THE NEW ORGANIZATIONAL ERA

Denise M. Rousseau

Source: *Annual Review of Psychology* 48 (1997): 515–546.

Abstract

Changes in contemporary firms and their competitive environments translate into a new focus in organizational research. This chapter reviews organizational behavior research reflecting the shift from corporatist organizations to organizing. Key research themes include emerging employment relations, managing the performance paradox, goal setting and self-management, discontinuous information processing, organization learning, organizational change and individual transitions, and the implications of change for work-nonwork relations. Research into organizing is building upon and extending many of the field's traditional concepts. This chapter suggests that some assumptions of organizational behavior research are being superseded by those more responsive to the new organizational era.

Introduction

Contemporary organizations are changing, and the field of organizational behavior is changing with them. This chapter describes the shifts organizational research manifests as firms transition to a new era of flexible, lateral forms of organizing (Davis 1987, Miles & Creed 1995). It seeks answers to two questions. First, how are core features of organizational research influenced by the changes contemporary organizations are undergoing? Second, what new dynamics and features are emerging as important organizational research issues?

The central problems in organizational behavior are influenced by changes in organizations themselves (Barley & Kunda 1992, Goodman & Whetten 1995). Although *Annual Review of Psychology* (*ARP*) authors often have reported the durability of such traditional categories as work motivation and performance, absenteeism and turnover, climate and culture, and groups and leadership (e.g. O'Reilly 1991), other recent commentaries report more substantial shifts. The time frame used to review a body of research is probably the greatest determinant of whether we observe change or stability. For example, Barley & Kunda's (1992) investigation of trends in managerial thought ranged from the 1870s to the present and reported alternating cycles of rational (e.g. scientific management) and normative (e.g. human relations) thinking among managers and scholars predicated on the degree of expansion or contraction in the economy of the time. From their starting point in the 1950s, Goodman & Whetten (1995) noted an adaptive quality in the field's work that shifts attention toward particular applied problems firms face within a given decade: Organizational development was a theme in the 1950s and 1960s, and organizational decline and interorganizational relations were themes in the 1980s and 1990s. In the *ARP*, the historic reach of chapters typically centers around the intervening years since a subject's last review, a practice that can highlight stability and mask trends.

Several previous *ARP* reviewers have characterized the field as "moribund" (O'Reilly 1991) or "fallow" (Mowday & Sutton 1993), concluding pessimistically that neither innovation nor progress was evident. However, both the time frame of a review and the categories reviewers focus on shape how dynamic or stable the field appears. I conducted a content analysis of *ARP* chapters (described in the Appendix of this chapter) to determine the field's key content areas and their stability over time. That analysis provides evidence of both change and stability in the field's major topics. It suggests that though a stable core of topics reappear—focusing on organizational and individual performance, motivation, and worker responses—the correlation of categories over time is moderate, with issues emerging and receding with the field's advances and shifts in the problems organizations face. A trend toward increased specialization is evident, which may make overall progress in the field difficult to gauge. With this in mind, the present chapter focuses on research particularly responsive to contemporary organizational changes. In contrast with the conclusions of earlier reviewers, I show that there is cause for optimism about the progress being made in organizational research.

A new era in organizational research

This review is predicated on the premise that the meaning of organization is changing. The term organization has two principal definitions. "The act or process of organizing" is the longest established meaning. The second refers to "a body of persons organized for some end or work," or alternatively "the administrative personnel or apparatus of a business" (Merriam-Webster Inc. 1989). As Drucker (1994) noted, the second definition—"the" organization as an entity—has been widely used only since the 1950s, which is concurrent with the era of the industrial state. This second definition has been operative in organizational research. Now, however, there is evidence that organizational behavior researchers are reconnecting with the more traditional meaning of organization as process, given the increasing attention to group-level—particularly team-level—phenomena, social networks, managerial cognition and information processing, and entrepreneurship (e.g. Arthur & Rousseau 1996, Drazin & Sandelands 1992, Snow et al 1992, Weick 1996). In his *ARP* chapter, Wilpert (1995) described the related "social construction of organizations" perspective as a respected tradition in European research. However, more is going on here than just a shift in epistemological assumptions.

Increasing interest in social construction occurs at a time when firms and work roles themselves have an emergent quality in response to an era of upheaval and transition. Changes in several institutional sectors are influencing firms (Davis 1987, Handy 1989): The Reagan Era's conservative approach to antitrust laws opened up a set of previously illegal interorganizational relationships; global competition has heightened; information technology has exploded in the manufacturing and service sectors; distressed educational institutions are struggling to meet new skill demands; and escalating pressures coupled with lagging resources stress families and other social institutions caught in the transition. These institutional forces often operate quite differently across societies and can yield distinct local variations in firms (Rousseau & Tinsley 1996). In most industrialized societies, institutional forces are manifesting themselves in several related organizational changes: the movement to small-firm employment in the United States (Small Business Association 1992), the United Kingdom (Storey 1994), and elsewhere (Castells 1992); reliance on interfirm networks to substitute for corporate expansion, one product of which is outsourcing work among firms (Bettis et al 1992): new and more differentiated employment relations [e.g. core and peripheral part-time workers and independent contractors, guest workers such as technical-support people employed by a vendor but working inside a client firm (Handy 1989)]; and new forms of interdependence among workers and work groups, which in turn link rising performance standards with the concurrent assertion of the interests of many stakeholders, such as customers, workers, and stockholders (Davis 1987). Inevitably, transition costs occur, for people, firms, and society (Mirvis & Hall 1994, Perrow 1996).

The shift from organization to organizing translates into activities that were once predominately repetitive becoming predominately novel, networks formerly based on roles now forming around knowledge, careers once firm-based now depending more on personal resources, and work structures once rule-centered now constructed by the people doing the work (cf Drazin & Sandelands 1992, Manz 1992). The disappearance of old work structures along with expansion of small-firm employment and the demise of hierarchical advancement—particularly the decline in middle-management posts and the concomitant rise of professional and technical jobs—removes cues provided to people from traditional internal labor markets and career paths. The shift from managerial prerogatives to self-management removes a good deal of formal control over work. With the erosion of traditional external guides for behavior, internally generated guides are needed to operate within and around the more fluid boundaries of firms, interfirm networks, and work groups. With fewer external guides for work, greater value is placed on improvisation and learning (Weick 1996).

Research themes regarding organizing

Shifting to more flexible ways of organizing work and employment introduces new elements to established organizational research topics and, more significantly, gives new meanings to existing concepts. We can observe the most significant changes in those areas where the effects of organizing are greatest.[1]

New employment relations

Since 1987, 7 million Americans have lost their jobs (Cascio 1995), and several industrial sectors have expanded their hiring concomitantly. This evident mobility is tied to the formation of new and more varied employment relationships across industries as well as within specific firms. Worldwide shifts in personnel management practices are evident, including decline of seniority-based wages in Japan (Mroczkowski & Hanaoka 1989), decline in job security coupled with higher performance demands in England (Herriot & Pemberton 1995), and higher unemployment prolonging postsecondary school education and apprenticeships in Germany (Roberts et al 1994). In addition, Eastern Europe has undergone a strategic reorientation from placement via centralized workforce planning to recruitment through labor markets (Roe 1995).

Research on the employment relationship reflects both new employment arrangements and the by-products of transition. The shift to organizing is evident in the weaker role of hierarchy and greater decentralization of personnel practices, the role of strategic and environmental factors in shaping incentives for workers and work groups, and generally increased turbulence and uncertainty in employment. Central themes include rewards available from labor force participation and performance, how workers understand new psychological contracts, and the impact of these contracts on equity, worker attachment, and other responses.

Accessing rewards

The rewards that motivate workforce participation and performance—such as compensation and benefits, career opportunities, and fulfilling work—are central to research on motivation. Accessing rewards entails issues of who distributes rewards, how they are allocated, and what the parties understand the exchange to mean. Reward distribution is a major theme in organizational research, particularly regarding the locus of decision making about incentives and personnel actions. Control over hiring, firing, and pay levels appears to be increasingly decentralized to permit responsiveness to local market conditions (Cappelli 1996). Wages are now more sensitive to the influence of local labor markets (Katz & Kruger 1991), while rewards based on seniority have declined (Chauvin 1992). Decentralizing personnel decisions means relations with immediate superiors and coworkers are important in the accessing of rewards. Impression management—particularly with superiors—has been found to impact performance ratings and the ability to access rewards beyond an individual or group's actual level of performance (Ancona 1990, Tsui et al 1995). Most reward distribution remains mediated by managers, even as their roles shift under self-management (Manz & Sims 1987).

Delayering coupled with broader spans of control complicates the role leaders play in distributing rewards and motivating employees. High-quality leader-member exchanges (LMX) have been found to increase the opportunities both parties have to perform well and access rewards (Graen & Scandura 1987). However, LMX has historically depended upon two conditions—a long-term supervisor-subordinate relationship and demographic similarity (Graen & Scandura 1987)—that are increasingly unlikely in a mobile, heterogeneous workforce. The meaning of quality LMX under conditions of organizing is unclear. Nonetheless, trust-based relations between workers and managers appear to be increasingly critical as workers are held accountable for their performance across more dimensions (e.g. internal and external customers) (Miles & Creed 1995). The problem of how to distribute rewards appropriately with fewer managers increases the relevance of "substitutes for leadership" (Kerr & Jermier 1978, Podsakoff et al 1993) such as member socialization, computer-based performance monitoring, and client/customer feedback (Podsakoff et al 1993). Gainsharing has been found to increase peer monitoring of coworker behavior (Welbourne et al 1995), which suggests that social comparisons and peer pressure increase when an individual's rewards are tied to peer performance. Rearranged jobs and a rising proportion of pay that is performance-contingent combine to make individual and team performance more observable, as occurs in organizing around projects. Contingent pay and peer pressure generated by teams are emerging as substitutes for both managerial influence and internalized member commitment, in effect creating short-term contracts that are heavily leveraged on individual or team performance.

The rewards themselves are changing. Promotions and formal status gains are being reduced and replaced by lateral moves presented as "career-building" assignments (Arthur 1994, Kanter 1989). In particular, autonomous work groups and job rotation tend to break down narrow job descriptions and reduce the number of job titles, a process referred to as "broad banding" (Katz 1985). Employability, the ability to access alternative work on the external labor market (Kanter 1989), is replacing job security in some segments. High-involvement work systems have been found to offer job security to valued, highly skilled workers in whom the firm has considerable investments (Handy 1989). These shifts are evidence that external labor-market factors drive employee experiences within the firm.

Workers often perceive training as a reward, providing self-actualization and the motivation to learn; career development with increased responsibility, autonomy, and likelihood of advancement; and personal psychosocial benefits, including increased confidence, new friendships, and better functioning in nonwork life (Noe & Wilk 1993, Nordhaug 1989). However, employer-provided training varies widely with market forces. Bartel & Sicherman (1994) reported that training is more frequent where unemployment rates are low, which suggests that employers provide skills through training where labor markets are tight but that they are less likely to do so when they can buy skills on the outside market. Hicks & Klimoski (1987) provided evidence that reactions to development opportunities can be enhanced when employees receive realistic information about the benefits of training; yet environmental uncertainty can make it difficult to forecast accurately the benefits of training. In any case, as the context of training is altered, the meaning workers attach to it is likely to change as well.

Traditional organizational research has viewed rewards as discrete exchanges (e.g. pay for performance). Increasingly, rewards and other conditions of employment are viewed as compensation "bundles" (Gerhart & Milkovich 1992). Koys (1991) found that employees' attitudes toward the firm are influenced by their perceptions of the motives that underlie reward systems and other human resource practices. Though increasingly threatened by cost cutting and shifts to peripheral employment (contractors, temporaries), the availability of benefits and employee perceptions of their importance contribute jointly to employee commitment and their perception of organizational support (Eisenberger et al 1986, Greenberger et al 1989, Sinclair et al 1995).

Although rewards are traditionally thought of as static and discrete, with workers having similar understandings of the firm's, management's, or supervisor's intentions in reward distribution, the concept of a psychological contract suggests otherwise. Psychological contracts are beliefs individuals hold about the exchange relationship between themselves and an employer, in essence, what people understand the employment relationship to mean [e.g. a high-involvement relationship or limited transactional employment (Rousseau 1995)]. Introducing the concept of a psychological contract distinguishes traditional notions of discrete rewards from the meaning ascribed to the whole exchange relationship. They have been characterized as schemas or mental models that capture how employees interpret bundles of rewards. The same reward (e.g. training or development) can signal distinct kinds of relationships (e.g. short-term incentive or long-term benefit) depending on the employment context in which it occurs. Contracts are dynamic, with time playing two important roles: First, employment duration can alter the rewards accrued. Second, psychological contracts can undergo unannounced changes in terms and meaning giving rise to idiosyncratic work roles (Miner 1990) and employment relationships (Rousseau 1995). Trusted senior workers who have more flexibility in responsibilities and work hours than do their junior colleagues are likely to perceive themselves party to a more relationally oriented contract with their employer. As mental models of the employment relationship, psychological contracts are formed typically at certain points in time (e.g. at hiring or when undergoing socialization for new assignments) and resist revision except when circumstances signal the need to revise an old schema or create a new one (Rousseau 1995). Those who had the strongest attachment to their employers have been found to react more adversely to contract violations (Robinson & Rousseau 1994), and these violations of promised contractual commitments engender more adverse reactions than do unmet expectations (Robinson 1995). When psychological contracts are congruent with changes in work practices, workers have been found to more fully implement change (Rousseau & Tijoriwala 1996).

Inequality and shifting reward allocations

Polls of public opinion in the United States observe that the optimistic attitudes of the 1960s toward one's economic success have given way in the 1990s to fear of losing affluence (Yankelovich 1993). Workplace justice, a long-standing topic in organizational research, is an increasing concern with the often uneven consequences of transitions. Critics of organizational restructurings have raised concern that short-term shareholder value is being increased by appropriating valued employment conditions, such as job security, for which workers have contracted (Smolowe 1996). Compensation research has focused on specific distributive issues, including the disparity between "haves and have nots" across organizational hierarchies (Cowherd & Levine 1992), particularly the high salaries and bonuses of corporate executives in comparison to those of rank-and-file employees. Cowherd & Levine reported higher product quality in firms with less disparity in compensation between executives and the rank and file. Redistributing rewards among workers with different employment relations raises issues of employee equity and of appropriate management practices for firms not used to dealing simultaneously with distinct types of workers. Firms most likely to have internal labor markets, that is, firms with more than 1000 employees, demonstrate the greatest expansion in use of temporary help (Magnum et al 1985). This means that firms with the most extensive commitments to some employees are also using workers to whom they make few commitments, and that these firms are still learning how to manage each type of employee simultaneously. Full-time employees often benefit from the presence of temporaries. Although firms requiring greater amounts of technical skills were less likely to use temporaries (Davis-Blake & Uzzi 1993), even a limited presence of temporary workers can enhance the quality of work life for full-time core employees because promotion opportunities are typically limited to core workers. Pearce (1993) found that managers are more likely to assign temporary workers tasks that require little knowledge and to shift complex assignments involving teamwork to full-timers. Although wages are about the same for part-time and temporary workers as for full-time employees (from a 1988 Bureau of National Affairs survey cited by Cappelli 1996, p. 19), benefits were perhaps half as likely. This rise in dual (or even multiple) labor markets within the same organization raises issues of social comparison and equity, as well as broader issues of employment relations (e.g. social questions such as whether temporary or noncore workers should be invited to holiday parties or participate in company orientations). Legal issues surrounding the contingent workforce are still being sorted out (Feldman & Klaas 1996).

New employment relations bring new meanings to old dependent variables

New distinctions among core, peripheral, temporary, and contingent workers raise issues for microorganizational behavior's typical measures of individual-level responses. Traditionally, commitment has been viewed as an individual outcome, largely motivated by individual differences (Mathieu & Zajac 1990). Commitment—particularly its behavioral component, the intention to remain—has recently been examined as a two-way street (Eisenberger et al 1986, Shore & Wayne 1993), the product of an interaction between individual and employer. Measures of employee-firm attachment, such as commitment, are problematic for new employment relations. Quite commonly, employees of temporary-help agencies work for more than one agency (National Association of Temporary Staffing Services 1994). Where the employment relationship takes on the form of an organized open market, a hiring hall, people may stay within the same occupation but not necessarily with the same employer for any length of time. Thus, occupational commitment may be a better indicator of attachment than organizational commitment. Increasingly, workers are "participants," if not necessarily "employees," in several firms (e.g. the technician paid by Xerox to work out of an office at Motorola headquarters exclusively servicing the Xerox equipment Motorola uses). However, it is also possible that outsourcing has merely shifted loyalties such that outsourced information systems staff who once were committed to a multifunctional corporation (e.g. AT&T) are now similarly committed to the specialty firm for which they work (e.g. EDS).

Research on dual commitments has focused on union and organizational commitment (e.g. Gordon & Ladd 1990), but we know very little about multiple commitment to several employers or multiple clients or customers. Hunt & Morgan (1994) tested competing models contrasting organizational commitment as one of many distinct commitments (e.g. commitments to work group, supervisor) with organizational commitment as a mediating construct in the relations between constituency-specific commitments and outcomes, such as citizenship and intention to quit. Their analysis supported the role of organizational commitment as a mediator between attachment to different constituencies and outcomes. Finding no evidence of conflict among different commitments, they concluded that employee commitments to different parties within the organization either promote global organizational commitment or are not significantly related to it. More research can be expected regarding multiple commitments, that is, commitments to occupation, employer, client, internal customers, team, union, and others.

Trust, particularly between labor and management, has long been considered important to organizational success (for an extensive historical review, see Miles & Creed 1995). Its base rate may have declined in recent years even while its value has risen (Barney & Hansen 1994). Trust for the general manager in a chain of restaurants has been found to be significantly related to sales, profits, and employee turnover (Davis et al 1995). Davis et al (1995) argued that trust fulfills Barney's (1986) requirements for competitive advantage: Trust adds value by reducing transaction costs, it is rare between employees and management, and it is not easily copied. Mayer et al (1995) offer an integrative framework defining organizational trust as "the willingness to be vulnerable" to another. Under conditions of organizing, the parties associated with organizational trust include but are not limited to coworkers, immediate superiors, senior managers and executives, and the organization in general. Organizing can, however, signal a shift in the dynamics of trust. Traditionally, trust derived from long-term experiences of reciprocity (Creed & Miles 1996); however, the rise of temporary work systems such as product design teams, film crews, and campaign organizations requires what has been termed "swift trust" (Meyerson et al 1996) supported by social networks and vulnerability to social reputation. In organizing, trust plays a fluid role as both cause and result.

Organizational citizenship is a correlate and possible outcome of trust (Organ 1990). It has been found to be influenced by perceptions of procedural though not distributive fairness (Ball et al 1994, Moorman 1991). As competitive pressure increases performance demands, the meaning of citizenship may shift as "performance beyond expectations" becomes expected. Perhaps due to organizational transitions, there has been a shift in the types of citizenship behaviors investigated, with increasing focus on more negative citizenship, or retributive behaviors (such as sabotage or theft) that directly work against the interests of the organization. Using multidimensional scaling, Robinson & Bennett (1995) developed a typology of deviant workplace behavior that varies along two dimensions: minor vs serious, and interpersonal vs organizational. Consistent with distinctions made by Hollinger & Clark (1982), organizationally relevant behaviors fall into two types: production deviance (e.g. leaving early, taking excessive breaks), assessed as relatively minor; and property deviance (e.g. sabotaging equipment, stealing from the company), assessed as serious. In their framework for research on organizationally motivated aggression, O'Leary-Kelly et al (1996) proposed that organizational insiders (e.g. members) are primarily responsible for violence in the workplace (as opposed to outsiders), but that poor treatment by the organization and hierarchical or control-oriented organizational norms influence both the incidence and targets of violence. Surveying human resource management executives in public corporations, Griffin (R Griffin, unpublished manuscript) respondents reported that violence in the form of threats, verbal attacks, and racial and sexual harassment is increasing in their organizations. Human resource (HR) managers attributed these changes to the effects of downsizing, reengineering, and increased employee workload.

In conclusion, research on the employment relationship in the new organizational era has two overarching themes: the greater complexity of the worker-firm relationship than appreciated previously and the often-negative consequences that have resulted in the shift from organization to organizing. Awareness has increased regarding the importance of trust in the employment relationship as well as how misleading it can be to atomistically study that relationship's terms in isolation.

Performance: measurement and management

Performance issues have long been a central theme in organizational research. Escalating competition and expanded performance-measurement capabilities have made greater scrutiny of organizational performance evident in all sectors of the economy. This attention has led to the recognition of a phenomenon referred to as the "performance paradox" (Meyer & Gupta 1994, National Research Council 1994). This paradox has two features: First, measures of performance often are observed to be only loosely interrelated. Second, performance improvements in subunits do not necessarily translate into productivity gains for the firm. An example of the first feature is that organizational success in obtaining market share often bears little relationship to other performance indicators: Those organizations good in some areas may be poor in others. Although this pattern was observed in early studies of organizational performance (e.g. Seashore et al 1960), it largely went unnoted. An example of the second would be a division whose successful innovations do not lead to firm-wide innovation (e.g. the Saturn division of General Motors). As competitive pressures and performance expectations have increased, both researchers and managers are becoming more aware of the two features of this paradox, calling attention to the need for enhanced coordination within firms (Goodman et al 1994) as well as performance monitoring, reconciling diverse sources of performance information (client, peer, subordinate, task/technical), customer responsiveness, organizational learning, and more systematic performance management (Pritchard 1994, Sink & Smith 1994).[2]

So what does organizational research say for firms seeking to be good at several things at once? More mature firms have been found to be most successful in their efforts to perform well on several indicators concurrently, which suggests that it takes time to learn how to do several things well at once (Meyer & Gupta 1994). A meta-analysis of management by objectives (an amalgam of participative management, goal setting, and performance feedback) and its impact on organizational productivity indicate the critical role of top management commitment [56% average gain under high commitment vs 6% under low commitment (Rodgers & Hunter 1991)]. Absence of top management commitment was reported also to give rise to local innovations that go unused by the larger firm and to coordination problems for units seeking to obtain a high-priority objective that conflicts with the goals of another unit with which it is interdependent. It is a truism that top management commitment promotes productivity improvement. As firms become smaller and less hierarchical, the critical processes for productivity improvement may change. Research is needed on the effects of concurrent feedback from a multiplicity of performance indicators for groups, individuals, and organizations, in decentralized as well as hierarchical settings. Effects might range anywhere from responsiveness and high performance to vigilance and overload.

The goal of high-performance work teams is to perform well on multiple dimensions (financial, customer satisfaction, employee well-being). Huselid's (1995) study of 968 firms in major industries indicates that human resource management practices associated with high-performance work systems (bundling training, participative decision making, incentive systems, and open communications) impact both employee outcomes (turnover and productivity) and corporate financial results. Findings suggest that firms that have top managers focused on a set of clearly defined goals supported by integrated HR practices are less likely to manifest the suboptimal performance paradox.

ProMES (Productivity Measurement and Enhancement System), a methodology for measuring and managing organizational performance developed by Robert Pritchard (1990), is designed to address some of the difficulties related to the performance paradox. Using consensus-building among stakeholders, ProMES combines the integration of multiple conflicting goals and performance feedback that can be readily understood and acted upon, with incentives and other managerial support for performance improvement. As the demand for high performance escalates, successful new performance-management methodologies are likely to find ways of increasing the firm's capacity to focus its attention broadly enough to reflect major constituents and interests, while being sufficiently selective to provide feedback useful in directing and coordinating efforts to improve performance.

Goal setting becomes self-management

Goal setting has been essential to organizational research on motivation and performance at many levels: individual, group, and organization. Its centrality makes it a bellwether for issues in the new organizational era. Goal setting's stylized fact has been that moderately difficult goals motivate high performance (Locke & Latham 1990). However, researchers in this area acknowledge that it largely has focused on repetitive tasks (see Locke et al 1981), often in the context of assignment of performance objectives by a hierarchical superior. There is a striking shift toward studying goal setting as it relates to more complex tasks and social arrangements (e.g. Smith et al 1990). In field settings, research investigates the role of goal setting to a firm's (as well as an individual's or group's) planning processes, strategy, and performance (Rodgers & Hunter 1991) and has shown significant effects of goal setting on firm productivity.

Perhaps the most significant shift is a new (or perhaps renewed) focus on self-management in goal setting (Gist et al 1990, Latham & Locke 1991). Self-regulation has long been implicit in goal-setting theory, because setting goals and translating them into action is a volitional process (Latham & Locke 1991), where acceptance of goals, when they are not self-set, is critical to their achievement. Frederick Kanfer (1975) focused attention on self-control mechanisms as a basis in clinical practice to modify addictive behavior, training people to stop smoking or overeating. Self-management teaches people to assess their problems, set specific hard goals to address these problems, self-monitor the effects of the environment on goal attainment, and appropriately administer rewards or penalties while working toward the goals. Although goal setting and self-management have been linked theoretically for many years, "classic" goal-setting research emphasized goal setting alone, while self-management focused attention on the learning and orchestration of cognitive processes for acquiring skills, self-monitoring progress, and providing self-reinforcement (Gist et al 1990). Gist et al found that goal setting per se is less effective in novel, complex tasks than is self-management, a process in which more skills are learned and actively displayed, even when the effects of goal level are controlled. Goal setting and the cognitive and behavioral processes surrounding goal achievement remain at the core of self-management practices, but the latter focus attention on learning, adaptation, knowledge transfer, and the flexibility to adapt to changing circumstances.

Organizational delayering and the rise of smaller, often entrepreneur-based, firms give self-management new meaning [including self-leading teams, (Manz 1992)]. This new meaning gives rise to debates over the distinction between the personal autonomy of self-management and the interdependent forms of shared governance, where the self in "self-managed" can mean person (Gist et al 1991), work group (Manz 1992), or broader institution (Welch 1994). At the heart of this shift in meanings is a debate over who sets the strategic goals for the firm, coupled with questions about the legitimacy and competence of stakeholders involved in these strategic choices (Manz 1992). Case analysis of W.L. Gore and Associates, the firm that developed the product Gore-tex, provides evidence that self-management practices where learning is emphasized can yield a fluid ad hoc work system, reflecting organizing processes rather than formal structure and resulting in innovation, high performance, and collaborative shaping of the firm's goals (Shipper & Manz 1992). In Brazil, similar self-management practices—based on a combination of profit sharing, collaborative decision making, and shared financial information—are reported to be successful (Semler 1989).

Self-management in the achievement of personal and organizational goals introduces a new twist to research on organizational leadership, both stretching and challenging how leadership is conceptualized. Podsakoff et al (1993) conducted an empirical investigation of Kerr & Jermier's (1978) model of Substitutes for Leadership. Originally developed to account for the often-limited effect of managers and supervisors on subordinate performance, this model identified factors that might neutralize the effects of (or minimize the need for) leaders. Podsakoff et al reported that contingent rewards, professional orientation, nonroutine work, organizational formalization, and spatial distance from others contribute to employee criterion variables while reducing the impact of leader behaviors. However, leader support appears to aid employees experiencing role ambiguity. Under conditions of organizing, self-management practices coupled with appropriate rewards and developments appear to enhance performance in the absence of formal leaders. In a highly turbulent business environment, Howell & Avolio (1993) found that transformational leadership positively predicted business-unit performance over a one-year interval, while transactional leadership, including contingent rewards, was negatively related to business-unit performance. They suggest it may be counterproductive for leaders to spend too much time focusing on meeting goals as opposed to promoting freedom of action in dynamic environments.

The concept of stretch goals (Sherman 1996) is predicated on the idea that seemingly impossible goals can motivate high performance by mandating creativity and assumption-breaking thinking that takes the performer "out of the box." On the surface, stretch goals appear to violate an essential premise of goal theory, that workers cannot accept a goal that does not seem feasible. Related to the concepts of transformational leadership, where performance expectations are elevated well beyond the limits of past experience (Bass 1985), and double-loop learning (Argyris & Schoen 1996), where previously successful frameworks are questioned, revised, or discarded, the fact that prior experience is often a poor guide for stretch-goal achievement shifts the performers' attention away from old routines and assumptions toward novel and creative approaches. Wood et al (1987) reported that "do-your-best" goals worked better than difficult, specific goals when the task was novel and highly complex. Plausibly, both worker self-efficacy and the credibility of the people setting the stretch goal contribute to the resulting performance. Kelly & McGrath (1985) have suggested dysfunctional consequences for groups working on especially difficult tasks, such as stringent time deadlines, where they spend less time discussing task ideas (e.g. agreements or modifications) that might affect product quality or interpersonal issues (e.g. conflicts, needs) that can affect member support and well-being. Further, they reported that these negative interaction processes carry over even to later trials for which time limits have changed.

Employers that reward only extreme performance have been found to foster some unexpected consequences. In a study of high-technology firms, Zenger (1992) reported that performance-based compensation that aggressively rewards extreme performance while largely ignoring performance distinctions at moderate levels yields retention of extremely high and moderately low performers. In contrast, moderately high and extremely low performers were likely to depart. New issues arise as organizations and goal-setting researchers turn their attention to more complex circumstances and ever more challenging levels of performance.

Information processing: discontinuous and multiphased

Turbulent competitive environments, technological sophistication, and flexible organizing give rise to greater novelty and complexity in work, which contributes to an expanding interest in individual and managerial cognition (Kiesler & Sproull 1992) and the broader domain of information processing by firms and individuals (Fiol 1994, Louis & Sutton 1991). Evidence that people process information differently in novel vs routine situations has led to the development of the concept of "discontinuous information processing" (Sims & Gioia 1986). Organizing promotes use of controlled information processing, where information is actively sought and carefully processed to make a quality decision when there is little experience on which to rely. This phenomenon has been used to characterize the vigilance and flexibility required to operate American aircraft carriers as "high-reliability organizations" (Weick & Roberts 1993), where even hierarchy must be adaptable. Models of rational decision making such as expectancy theory (Vroom 1964) tend to work well in accounting for behavior in nonroutine decisions such as choosing a career (Wanous et al 1983) but do less well in explaining routine behaviors. In routine situations such as sustained performance in a stable situation over time, controlled processes give way to reliance on automatic processes using established mental models and routines (Bartunek & Moch 1987, Fiol 1994, Sims & Gioia 1986).

An individual's capacity to switch back and forth between routine and nonroutine information processing ["shifting the gears" (Louis & Sutton 1991)] is postulated to be influenced by personality characteristics (e.g. locus of control) as is an individual's capacity to enact the "weak situations" characteristic of work settings where organizing is required (Weick 1996). Research is needed on the impact of personality and cognitive styles on both discontinuous information processing and enactment of weak situations. Cascio (1995) has suggested that personality tests offer important predictive power for successful performance in new forms of work.

"Shifting the gears" in cognitive processes is evident in research on training (Hesketh et al 1989), socialization (Louis & Sutton 1991), and organizational learning (Argyris 1991, Nicolini & Meznar 1995). In training, unpredictability and variation tend to cause difficulties for the learner. Yet these factors also enhance the ability to apply training in the future, when diverse circumstances arise that are not necessarily anticipated at the time of training (Neal et al 1995). In socialization, individuals may be open to learning about the organization only at certain points in time (Guzzo & Noonan 1994, Louis & Sutton 1991). Organizational learning based on active thinking has been advocated (Fiol & Lyles 1985), while strategic failings have been traced to overreliance upon automatic processing (Starbuck & Milliken 1988).

Organizational learning

Although organizational learning has played a role in the organizational literature for decades (e.g. Congelosi & Dill 1965), until recently there was little empirical research on the subject. Rising competitive pressures have fueled interest in organizational learning as a major determinant of sustainable organizational performance, which suggests that to survive and thrive firms will need to learn at an increasingly rapid rate. Competition has been observed to promote organizational learning in single-unit firms, typically small, frequently entrepreneurial enterprises, while larger multiunit firms tend to manifest less learning in response to competition, instead levering their market position to obtain competitive advantage (Barnett et al 1994). Learning necessitates a facility for discontinuous information processing on the part of both firms and individuals, the capability to deploy knowledge and demonstrable skills in novel ways and flexible combinations (Argyris & Schoen 1996). Organizational learning can occur within a firm when it involves diffusion of knowledge between members and across units (e.g. Epple et al 1996) or between firms, with dissemination and implementation of new knowledge obtained through external monitoring or benchmarking and interpersonal contact (Miner & Robinson 1994).

Within-firm: memory and shared understanding

To a point, organizational learning displays several features of individual learning, particularly in its need for memory and the transfer of learning to new settings and problems. The major distinction is organizational learning's requirement that members convey their learning to one another, develop shared understandings or common cognitive structures regarding application of shared knowledge, and otherwise externalize what they learn (Lyles & Schwenk 1992; Goodman & Darr 1996). The prevalence of the second feature of the performance paradox (above), where innovations in a subunit do not necessarily translate into innovations for the firm as a whole, suggests that within-firm learning is difficult. Nonetheless, it does occur. In an empirical study of a large financial firm, Fiol (1994) observed that gradual consensus building with interactions among different subgroups played a critical role in overcoming resistance to change and led to a collective understanding that acknowledged both differences and agreement regarding a new venture. In pizza franchises, unit cost declined significantly as stores gained experience in production (Darr et al 1994). Knowledge transferred across stores owned by the same franchisee but not across stores owned by different franchisees. Employee turnover contributed to "forgetting," or knowledge depreciation, in this high-turnover industry.

The repeated finding that turnover leads to organizational "forgetting" raises questions about whether organizational learning has really occurred when performance gains are manifest. It can be difficult to distinguish between gains due to individual learning among many members as opposed to organizational learning embedded in new processes and procedures. In a laboratory simulation, paired subjects developed interlocked task-performance patterns that displayed characteristics of organizational routines (Cohen & Bacdayan 1994). Procedural memory explains how such routines arise, stabilize, and change. Procedures can become enduring properties of organizations. But unless they are externalized (e.g. written down or incorporated into training programs), they may not be effectively retained when knowledgeable individuals leave.

Internal organizational barriers often inhibit within-firm learning. Goodman & Darr (1996) report that even a multiunit firm ostensibly committed to learning may find it difficult to disseminate information and create shared understandings about new processes and capabilities. If shared cognitive structures are critical for organizational learning, these may be easier to achieve in smaller, single-unit firms. Embedding knowledge in technology has been found to facilitate transfer across shifts (Epple et al 1996). This research suggests useful directions for research into transfer mechanisms (e.g. representations, flow diagrams, and procedures) that inhibit forgetting induced by employee turnover. These transfer mechanisms themselves may distinguish organizational learning from that of individuals.

Learning between firms: careers and social networks

New organizational forms such as joint ventures, outsourcing among organizational networks, research consortia, and other forms of organizing (Aldrich & Sasaki 1995) provide evidence that organizational learning will occur across increasingly blurry boundaries. While outsourcing has been linked to declines in organizational learning in outsourced functions (Bettis et al 1992), networked organizations with flexible memberships can promote it (Snow et al 1992). These "boundaryless" organizations, defined here as organizations whose membership, departmental identity, and job responsibilities are flexible (Kanter 1989, Miner & Robinson 1994), yield a pattern of more flexibly structured careers. Career patterns are found to contribute to organizational learning by generating diverse frames of reference for problem solving, redirecting old routines in new ways, and harvesting organizational memory (Miner & Robinson 1994). Job transitions (loss, rehire, rotation, transfers, international assignments, horizontal moves, demotions) become commonplace and can promote organizational and individual learning (Miner & Robinson 1994). Transitions out of firms complicate retention but create opportunities for learning in new firms, particularly given the movement of employees from large to smaller firms where routinization is often lower. Nonhierarchical careers recombine personal and organizational learning in novel ways and themselves can become repositories of knowledge (Bird 1994).

Social networks outside corporations and other firms have become sources of career advantage (DeFilippi & Arthur 1994) and expertise (Miner & Robinson 1994), functioning in ways similar to occupational communities that influence career decisions and transitions of members (Van Maannen & Barley 1984). Firms that cultivate relationships with educational institutions such as high schools improve their access to appropriately skilled workers (Rosenbaum et al 1990). The impact social networks outside the firm have on career advancement may be particularly important to the career development of women and minorities. Evidence suggests that within-firm social networks can work to the advantage of white men over women (Ibarra 1992) and over African-Americans (Thomas & Higgins 1996).

In sum, organizing—with its flexible work arrangements, personnel movements, reliance upon personal expertise, and systematic information processing—places a premium on experimentation and collective learning. As boundaries between firms blur, we can expect more rapid organizational learning and possibly a similar rate of forgetting, along with greater attention to mechanisms for retaining knowledge with or without a stable membership. The shift toward network organizations (Snow et al 1992) suggests that knowing who is becoming as important as knowing how (DeFillippi & Arthur 1994).

Managing organizational change and individual transitions

Transitions abound in the new organizational era both for firms and for the workforce. Managing organizational change and individual transitions is an overarching research theme.

Organizational change

Change management focuses on the implementation and ultimately the successful institutionalization of new technology, culture, strategy, and related employment arrangements. Organizational Development (OD), the traditional practice side of organizational research, has long had a shaky reputation among organizational scientists for its lack of rigor and "pop" style. However, the boundary between OD and organizational science has become blurred as more researchers tackle the problems of implementing change (e.g. Kiesler & Sproull 1992, Novelli et al 1995).

Organizing is typically a radical departure from the traditional ways people think and act in firms. Stable and enduring mental models or schemas have been found to contribute to reactions to change (e.g. Bartunek & Moch 1987). Lau & Woodman (1995) identify three features of schemas pertinent for change: causality (attributions used to understand causes of change), valence (meaning and significance), and inferences (predictions of future outcomes). They reported that organizational commitment is related to these features of change schemas, consistent with the argument that a fundamental realignment in how people understand the firm is needed to foster organizational change.

Organizational change also has become a justice issue (Novelli et al 1995). Distributive justice, the perceived fairness of the outcomes, is a particular focus because the departures from the status quo that constitute change are commonly experienced as losses, and gains from change may take time to realize, particularly when mastery of a radical new organizational form is required. Offsetting losses from work system changes has been found to improve distributive fairness by helping people gain the skills needed to be successful and gain rewards under the new system (Kirkman et al 1994).

Interactional justice pertains to the communication process in managing change. Presenting bad news with politeness and respect (Folger 1985) and providing credible explanations or social accounts foster more positive reactions (Bies & Moag 1986). In labor disputes, the general public was found to react with stronger perceptions of unfairness, more sympathy, and more support for grievances based on interactional justice rather than procedural justice, which in turn generated more intense reactions than grievances based on distributive injustice (Leung et al 1993). For victims of change, when outcomes are particularly severe, explanations high on specificity were judged to be more adequate and led to more positive reactions than did explanations emphasizing interpersonal sensitivity. Effects are enhanced when the explanation is delivered orally rather than via memo or letter (Shapiro et al 1994).

Procedural justice in change refers to the processes whereby implementation decisions were made. Voice mechanisms that allow affected people to participate in deciding upon the change or planning its implementation enhance procedural justice, as do procedures to correct for biases or inaccuracy of information used in the process (Sheppard et al 1992). In a study of new technology implementation, employee strain increased during the implementation phase and was highest among those individuals who were not included in the implementation process (Korunka et al 1993). However, voice had no effect in reactions to seven facility relocations (Daly & Geyer 1994), although the researchers speculate that employees may not have expected to have a voice in relocation decisions. The timing and phases of change may also play a role in effective implementation (Jick 1993), but these have received less systematic attention.

Individual transitions

Employment displacements are occurring at faster rates than in the past and are predicted to continue (Handy 1989). Job loss has been associated with lower self-esteem (Cohn 1978), increased anxiety, and psychological distress (Winefield et al 1991). Moreover, workers who are pressured to leave but opt to stay report unusually high levels of psychological distress (Price & Hooijberg 1992). Reemployment can mean settling for unsatisfactory new jobs (Liem 1992), which can engender long-term adverse consequences. In a longitudinal study of laid-off industrial workers, Leana & Feldman (1996) found that financial pressures, levels of optimism and self-blame, and the amount of problem-focused and symptom-focused coping individuals engage in were significant predictors of reemployment, which supports previous research on the importance of individual differences in successful searches (Kanfer & Hulin 1985). Jobs programs coupled with interpersonal support have been found to play a role in successful reemployment (Vinocur et al 1991).

Forecasting repeated cycles of employment and unemployment for skilled as well as unskilled workers, several organizational researchers predict that transitions will become less disruptive as people develop skills for adapting to change (Weick 1995) and as personal expectations and definitions of psychological success recast "unemployment" as an opportunity for personal development or family benefit (Mirvis & Hall 1994). A major factor in worker adaptation is likely to be the broader societal supports—educational, cultural, and economic—for workers and nonworkers alike.

Leisure, nonwork, and community: personal and institutional supports

Escalating pressures on the workforce due to restructuring manifest in the attention paid to work-nonwork relations (Mirvis & Hall 1994). Decline of corporatist firms and their traditional benefits raises concerns about the infrastructure needed to support both new forms of employment and organizing and individual workers and their families—evident in an emerging area of scholarship on social capital (Etzioni 1993, Perrow 1996).

Social capital refers to civic life and public trust, the societal infrastructure from which workers and organizations receive support. Social institutions such as family and schools are reported to have difficulty responding to the prevailing economic pressures (Etzioni 1993), a fact suggesting that more active individual involvement in community life may be required to sustain these institutions. Greater involvement in off-the-job activities has been associated with reduced role interference and psychological strain (Gutek et al 1991, O'Driscoll et al 1992). Kirchmeyer (1995) found that employee commitment is enhanced when organizations provide resources to help employees fulfill family and other nonwork responsibilities. She further reported that workers prefer benefits that let them manage their responsibilities themselves (e.g. flexible scheduling) rather than have the firm do it for them (e.g. on-site child care).

Kanter (1977) suggested that early in the twentieth century, corporations tried to "swallow the family and take over its functions." Subsequently, firms moved to separate work and family in order to exclude competing loyalties. Demographic changes, particularly working mothers and dual income-career families, have increased the interdependence of work and family and intensified conflicts, particularly regarding time allocation. Recent studies support the significance of institutional factors, including societal beliefs about the role of women and work-family relations, in expanded organizational emphasis on work-nonwork relations (Goodstein 1994, Ingram & Simons 1995). Consistent with institutional arguments, larger (i.e. more publicly visible) firms seek legitimacy by adopting child-care benefits and work flexibility (Goodstein 1994). However, Ingram & Simons (1995) reported that institutional pressures explain late adoption of "family friendly" HR practices, while early adopters are likely to do so instead to gain strategic advantage (e.g. professional firms coping with labor shortages by filling positions with qualified women and dual-career spouses). Early adoption is linked to significant numbers of women in a firm's workforce, while late adoptions are less affected by firm-specific demographics (Galinsky & Stein 1990, Goodstein 1994).

Traditional corporate firms have been implicated in an erosion of community and civic life (Etzioni 1993, Perrow 1996). If corporations did in fact erode social capital, the shift to organizing does not reverse such effects. Organizing may require more social capital than did organizations with huge internal infrastructures, particularly in respect to education (Handy 1989), portable retirement and health-care benefits (Lucero & Allen 1994), and family support (Mirvis & Hall 1994). As a result, organizational researchers are likely to expand their consideration of work-nonwork relations to include a broader array of support systems and community institutions.

Conclusion

The evolution from organization to organizing changes both the phenomena traditionally studied by organizational research and the meaning of some traditional concepts. The answer to the opening questions of this review are apparent. Core features of organizational research, including its focus on performance and worker-firm relations, endure, but they do so with new dimensions. Performance now involves a multiplicity of results pursued concurrently and with an expanded focus on adaptive and sustained learning. Goal setting and leadership may converge into self-management. However, new dynamics are evident in the shift toward an interactive view of the employment relationship, reoriented from a focus on what managers offer workers to how workers across all ranks access rewards contingent upon the firm's strategic concerns. We see an increasingly complex view of information processing, reflecting a more rapid cycling from novel to routine and back again, characteristic of a more dynamic environment. There is also a broader concern for the personal and societal impact of the way work is organized.

This chapter has focused on topics particularly sensitive to the dynamics of organizing. Assuming the shift from organization to organizing will not be quickly undone, what are its implications for organizational research as a whole? Barley & Kunda (1992) maintain that periods of economic contraction lead to more emphasis on relationship building, organizational support, and strengthening of employee-firm commitment (witness Elton Mayo's Human Relations movement during the depression of the 1930s). Formerly, firms displaced workers only when the economy was shrinking. The recent coupling of massive terminations with economic expansion fragments the managerial ideologies that both justify and guide organizational actions. They may do the same for research ideologies. As a result, we might expect to find more researchers investigating competing hypotheses from more distinct and often divergent frameworks. A central theme may be the drive to increase shareholder value coupled with concern about the costs of displacement and transition for the workforce which creates that value. Clearly, organizational research needs to dig into the messy problems of serving multiple constituencies.

This chapter is not an attempt to create a "short" list of research topics; no prescriptions are intended for future researchers about topics to "buy" or to "sell." Several key research themes, including customer service (Schneider & Bowen 1995), quality (Dean & Bowen 1994), and the adoption of new technology (Leonard-Barton & Sinha 1993) were omitted because of space limitations.

Rather, this chapter highlights broad areas where the effects of organizing are more visible, where our learning progresses even as further research needs appear. If the past is a prologue, we can expect that relevant organizational changes will manifest themselves in other areas, too. However, while new topics such as the performance paradox appear, established ones keep their labels but shift their focus. Perhaps it is for this reason that in the many years of *ARP*s reviewed in preparation for this chapter, certain core themes have endured. Yet, at some point, we might need to acknowledge that changes in firms are profound enough to alter further basic assumptions on which the field is based. In any case, a new era in organizational behavior appears to be in the making.

Appendix

In preparing this chapter, a content analysis was conducted on the 23 *ARP* chapters since 1979 dealing with organizational research (organizational behavior, industrial/organizational psychology, personnel and human resource management, training and development, and organizational development and change). Substantive topics covered were categorized by having two raters read each chapter and identify their central concepts. Raters generated a set of categories and then coded chapters according to their content (rate of agreement was 85%). In the case of the 1979 *ARP*, for example, Mitchell's (1979) chapter on organizational behavior was coded as including personality, job attitudes, commitment, motivation, and leadership. That volume contained a second organizationally relevant chapter, Dunnette & Borman's (1979) "Personnel Selection and Classification Systems," which was coded as including categories of validity, job analysis, performance ratings, equal opportunity, and selection practices. Content coding identified 94 discrete categories altogether.

Correlations computed between category matrices for each time period assess the degree of stability in category patterns over time. Using the QAP correlation technique (Krackhart 1987), correlations were computed between entries in two matrices, and the observed correlations were compared to the frequency of random correlations to provide a test of statistical significance (based on 500 permutations). This analysis, using normalized data (Table 1), indicates moderate stability in *ARP* categories with slightly greater convergence in categories in *ARP* chapters across periods 1 and 3. It also suggests a fair degree of variety over time in the issues addressed.

Examination of frequently cited categories across the three periods (Table 2) suggests that categories related to the general topics of performance (e.g. predictors of individual performance, measurement, organizational performance, ineffectiveness, and failure), motivation (e.g. effort resulting from goal setting or rewards offered), and employee responses (e.g. stress, satisfaction, and commitment) form a stable core. These categories comprise what apparently are the central dependent variables or outcomes operationalized in organizational behavior research.

Table 1 Annual Review of Psychology: summary information

Time period	ARP # of articles	ARP # of categories	Times	ARP[a]
Time 1: 1979–1984	9	47	1 × 2	0.23
Time 2: 1985–1990	8	57	2 × 3	0.24
Time 3: 1991–1995	6	44	1 × 3	0.34
Total[b]	23	94		

[a] Correlations are significantly different from 0.00, the average correlation across all cells in matrix.
[b] Represents total number of total distinct categories where many categories may appear in several time periods.

Table 2 Frequent categories

	ARP
TIME 1	Performance predictors = 5 Stress = 5 Job analysis = 4 EEO = 4 Motivation = 4 Personnel selection = 3 Satisfaction = 3 Equity = 3 Performance appraisal = 3 Job design = 2 Methodology = 2 Fairness = 2 Organizational performance = 2 Personality = 2 Individual difference = 2 Personnel training = 2
TIME 2	Job analysis = 6 Leadership = 6 Motivation = 5 Performance predictors = 3 Affect = 2 Organizational culture = 2 Organizational change = 2 Performance appraisal = 2 Personnel selection = 2 Personnel layoffs = 2

Table 2 cont'd

	ARP
TIME 3	Organization context/cross level effects = 3 Motivation = 2 Stress = 2 Performance predictors = 2 Organizational technology = 2 Organizational performance = 2 Performance appraisal = 2 Personality = 2 Job analysis = 2 Legal issues = 2 Organizational demography = 2

Other durable categories with basically consistent levels of research/citation throughout this extended period include the personnel-related areas of job analysis and performance appraisal. Topics where reports of research activities are increasing over time include individual cognition, organizational change, and organizational performance. A multidimensional scaling (MDS) of the *ARP* categories within each time period (Krackhardt et al 1994) suggests that the field has moved from three core areas (Change, Personnel, and Micro OB) of earlier years to a more highly differentiated set of category clusters (Personnel, Micro OB, Context Power and Influence, Organization environment). Figures 1 and 2 display MDS for the first and third periods. Categories in ellipses bridge two or more areas, thus Pers (Personality) bridges Personnel and Micro-OB in both periods while Operf (Organizational Performance) emerges as a bridge among Micro OB, Personnel, and Context in period 3. Bridging categories provide an opportunity for integration across disciplines and paradigms. Nonetheless, from 1979 to 1995, a trend toward specialization is evident. Further information about this analysis is available from the author.

Acknowledgments

I wish to thank Colin Housing for his help with the literature review, Tiziana Casciaro for her work with the quantitative review, and both Tiziana and Kristina Dahlin for their assistance in coding the data. David Krackhardt merits special thanks for help with the multidimensional scaling analysis and the figures. Michael Arthur, Kathleen Carley, Paul Goodman, and Laurie Weingart provided useful input at various points in this chapter's preparation. Thanks also to Catherine Senderling for her editorial work and to Carole McCoy for wordprocessing.

This chapter is dedicated to Herbert Simon on the occasion of his eightieth birthday.

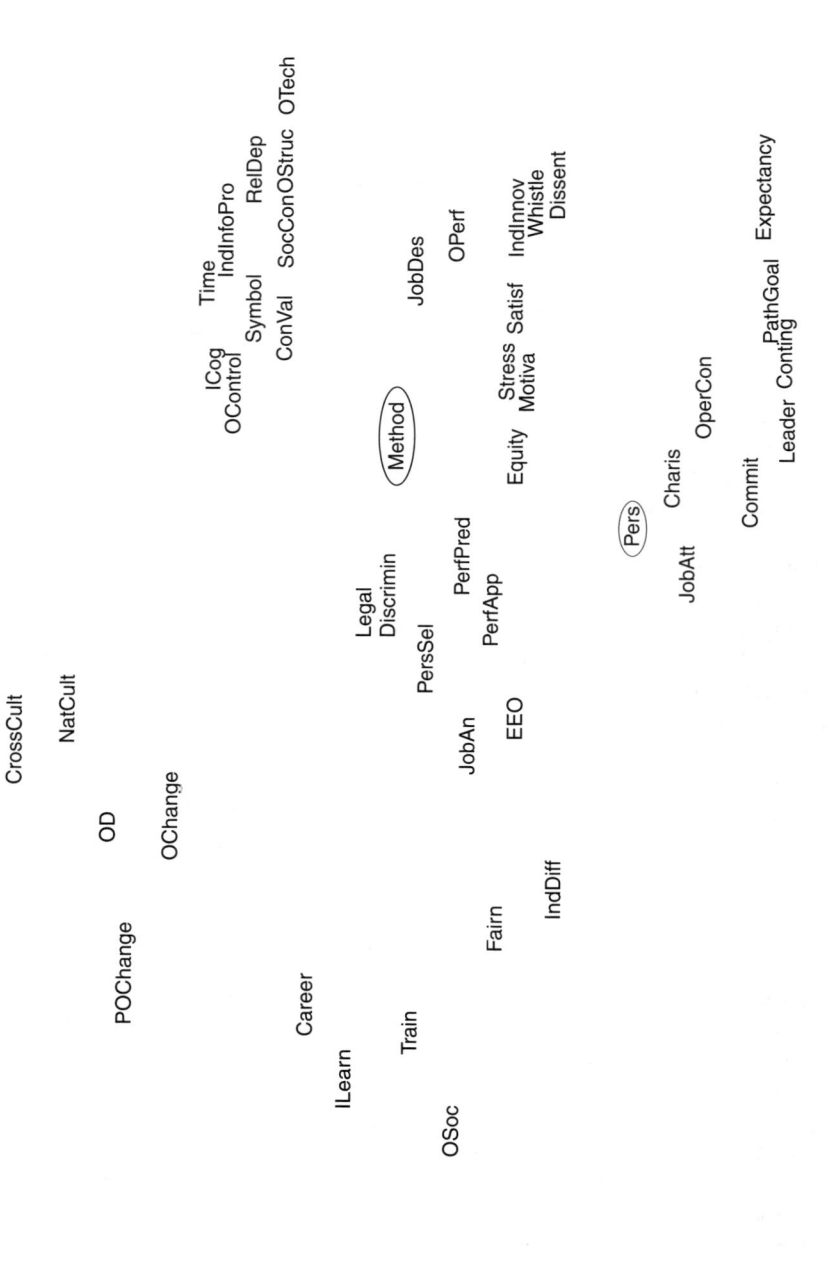

Figure 1 MDS on *ARP* for Period 1.

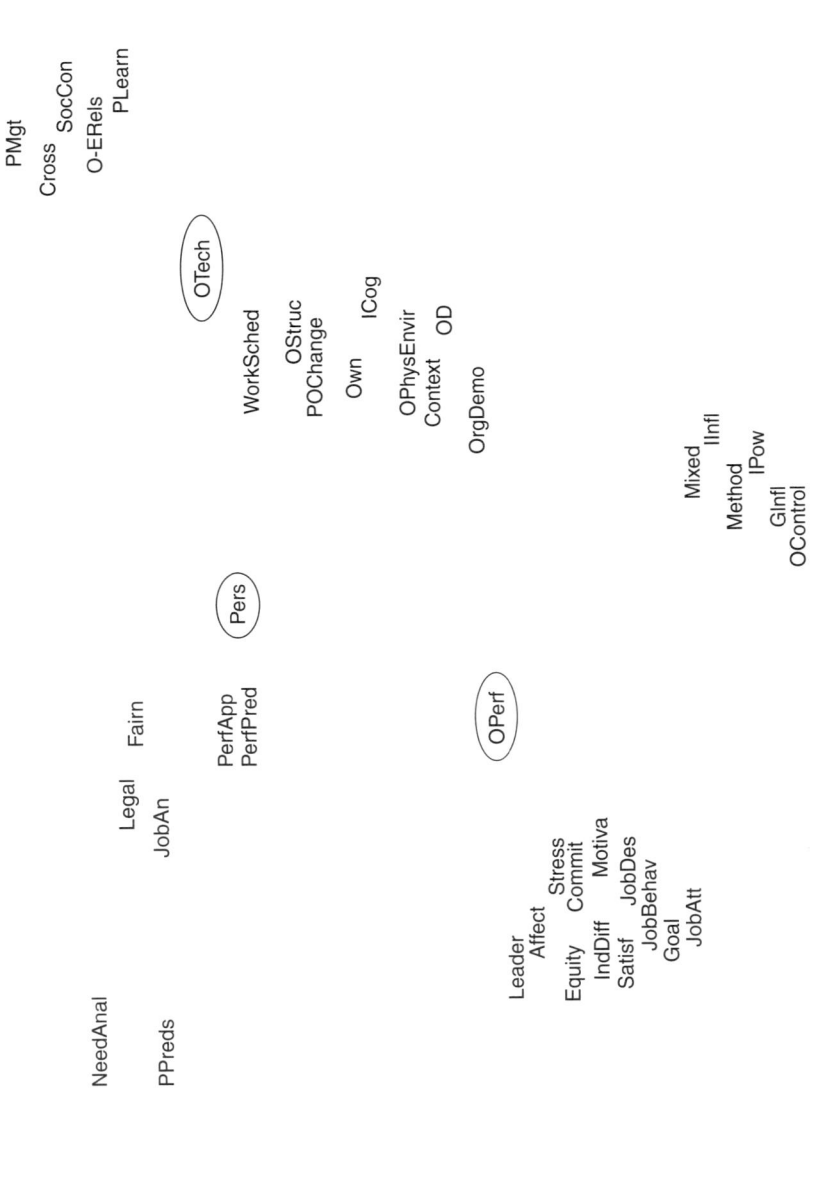

Figure 2 MDS of *ARP* for Period 3.

Notes

1. The present chapter omits areas relevant to organizing that are already treated in contemporary reviews: teams (Guzzo & Dickson 1996), personnel selection, and other human resource practices (Borman et al 1997, Cascio 1995).
2. In this section, we focus primarily upon research pertinent to the first feature of the paradox. The second is addressed in the later section on within-firm organizational learning. Research into high-reliability organizations indicates that major—and sometimes catastrophic—errors can occur, while other performance indicators are positive (Perrow 1984, Sagan 1993). Organizational factors contributing to high performance in indicators such as customer satisfaction are likely to be different from those contributing to safety or cost containment. Firms may also have limited focus of attention, which can constrain their ability to gather information and provide support for performance in more than a few areas.

Literature cited

Aldrich HE, Sasaki T. 1995. R&D consortia in the United States and Japan. *Res. Policy* 24:301–16

Ancona DG. 1990. Outward bound: strategies for team survival in an organisation. *Acad. Manage. J.* 33:334–65

Argyris C. 1991. Teaching smart people how to learn. *Harvard Bus. Rev.* 69:99–109

Argyris C, Schoen DA. 1996. *Organizational Learning II*. Reading, MA: Addison-Wesley

Arthur MB. 1994. The boundaryless career: a new perspective for organizational inquiry. *J. Organ. Behav.* 15:295–306

Arthur M, Rousseau DM, eds. 1996. *The Boundaryless Career: A New Employment Principle for a New Organizational Era*. New York: Oxford Univ. Press

Ball GA, Trevino LK, Sims HP Jr. 1994. Just and unjust punishment: influences on subordinate performance and citizenship. *Acad. Manage. J.* 37:299–322

Barley S, Kunda G. 1992. Design and devotion: surges of rational and normative ideologies of control in managerial discourse. *Adm. Sci. Q.* 37:463–99

Barnett WP, Greve HR, Park DY. 1994. An evolutionary model of organizational performance. *Strateg. Manage. J.* 15:11–28

Barney JB. 1986. Organizational culture: Can it be a source of sustained competitive advantage? *Acad. Manage. Rev.* 11:656–65

Barney JB, Hansen MH. 1994. Trustworthiness as a source of competitive advantage. *Strateg. Manage. J.* 15:175–90

Bartunek JM, Moch MK. 1987. First-order, second-order, and third-order change and organizational development interventions: a cognitive approach. *J. Appl. Behav. Sci.* 23:483–500

Bass BM. 1985. *Leadership and Performance Beyond Expectations*. New York: Free Press

Bettis RA, Bradley SP, Hamel G. J992. Outsourcing and industrial decline. *Acad. Manage. Exec.* 6:7–22

Bies RJ, Moag JS. 1986. Interactional justice: communication criteria of fairness. In *Research on Negotiations in Organizations*, ed. MH Bazerman, R Lewicki, B Sheppard, pp. 1:43–55. Greenwich, CT: JAI

Bird A. 1994. Careers as repositories of knowledge: a new perspective on boundaryless careers, *J. Organ. Behav.* 15:325–44

Borman W, Hanson M, Hedge J. 1997. Personnel selection. *Annu. Rev. Psychol.* 48:299–337

Cappelli P. 1996. Rethinking employment *Br. J. hid. Relat.* In press
Cascio WF. 1995. Whither industrial and organizational psychology in a changing world of work? *Am. Psychol.* 50:928–39
Castells M. 1992. Four Asian tigers with a dragon head: a comparative analysis of the state, economy and society in the Asian Pacific Rim. In *States and Development in the Asian Pacific Rim*, ed. RP Applebaum, J Henderson, pp. 33–70. Newbury Park, CA: Sage
Chauvin K. 1992. Declining returns to tenure for managerial jobs. *Manage. Econ.*
Cohen MD, Bacdayan P. 1994. Organizational routines are stored as procedural memory: evidence from a laboratory study. *Organ. Sci.* 5:554–68
Cohn R. 1978. The effects of employment status change on self-attitudes. *Soc. Psychol.* 41:81–93
Congelosi VE, Dill WR. 1965. Organizational learning: observations toward a theory. *Adm. Sci. Q.* 10:175–203
Cowherd DM, Levine DI. 1992. Product quality and pay equity between lower-level employees and top management: an investigation of distributive justice theory. *Adm. Sci. Q.* 37:302–20
Creed WED, Miles RE. 1996. Trust in organizations: a conceptual framework linking organizational forms, managerial philosophies, and the opportunity costs of controls. See Kramer & Tyler 1996, pp. 16–38
Daly JP, Geyer PD. 1994. The role of fairness in implementing large-scale change: employee evaluations of process and outcome in seven facility relocations. *J. Organ. Behav.* 15:623–38
Darr E, Argote L, Epple D. 1994. The acquisition transfer, and depreciation of knowledge in service organizations. *Manage. Sci.* 41:1750–62
Davis JH, Mayer RC, Schoorman FD. 1995. *The trusted general manager and firm performance: empirical evidence of a strategic advantage*. Presented at Strateg. Manage. Soc. Meet., Oct., Mexico City
Davis S. 1987. *Future Perfect*. Reading, MA: Addison-Wesley
Davis-Blake A, Uzzi B. 1993. Determinants of employment externationalization: the case of temporary workers and independent contractors. *Adm. Sci. Q.* 29:195–223
Dean JW Jr, Bowen DE. 1994. Management theory and total quality: improving research and practice through theory development. *Acad. Manage. Rev.* 19:392–418
DeFillippi RJ, Arthur MB. 1994. The boundaryless career: a competency-based perspective. *J. Organ. Behav.* 15:307–24
Drazin R, Sandelands L. 1992. Autogenesis: a perspective on the process of organizing. *Organ. Sci.* 3:230–49
Dracker PF. 1994. The age of social transformation. *Atl. Mon.* 275:53–80
Dunnette MD, Borman WC. 1979. Personnel selection and classifcation systems. *Annu. Rev. Psychol.* 30:477–526
Eisenberger R, Huntington R, Hutchinson S, Sowa D. 1986. Perceived organizational support. *J. Appl. Psychol*, 71:500–7
Epple D, Argote L, Murphy K. 1996. An empirical investigation of the micro structure of knowledge acquisition and transfer through learning by doing. *Manage. Sci.* In press
Etzioni A. 1993. *The Spirit of Community: Rights, Responsibilities, and the Communitarian Agenda*. New York: Crown
Feldman DC, Klaas BS. 1996. Temporary workers: employee rights and employer responsibilities. *Empl. Responsib. Rights J.* 9:1–21
Fiol M. 1994. Consensus, diversity, and learning in organizations. *Organ. Sci.* 5:403–20

Fiol MC, Lyles MA. 1985. Organizational learning. *Acad. Manage. Rev.* 10:803–13

Folger R. 1985. *The Churchill Effect*. A. B. Freeman Sch. Bus., Tulane Univ., New Orleans

Galinsky E, Stein PJ, 1990. The impact of human resource policies: balancing work and family issues. *J. Fam. Issues* 11:368–83

Gerhart B, Milkovich GT. 1992. Employee compensation: research and practice. In *Handbook of Industrial and Organizational Psychology*, ed. MD Dunnette, LM Hough, pp. 481–569. Palo Alto, CA: Consult. Psychol. Press. 2nd ed.

Gist ME, Bavetta AG, Stevens CK. 1990. Transfer training method: its influence on skill generalization, skill repetition, and performance level, *Pers. Psychol.* 43:501–23

Gist ME, Stevens CK, Bavetta AG. 1991. Effects of self-efficacy and post-training intervention on the acquisition and maintenance of complex interpersonal skills. *Pers. Psychol.* 44:837–61

Goodman PS, Darr E. 1996. Exchanging best practices through computer-aided systems. *Acad. Manage. Exec.* 10(2):7–19

Goodman PS, Lerch J, Mukhopadhyay T. 1994. Linkages and performance improvements. See National Research Council 1994, pp. 54–80

Goodman PS, Whetten DA. 1997. Fifty years of organizational behavior from multiple perspectives. In *A Half Century of Challenge and Change in Employment Relations*, ed. M Neufeld, J McKelvey. Ithaca, NY: ILR Press, In press

Goodstein JD. 1994. Institutional pressures and strategic responsiveness: employer involvement in work-family issues. *Acad. Manage. J.* 37:350–82

Gordon ME, Ladd RT. 1990. Dual allegiance: renewal, reconsideration, and recantation. *Pers. Psychol.* 43:37–69

Graen GB, Scandura TA. 1987. Toward a psychology of dynamic organizing. In *Research in Organizational Behavior*, ed. LL Cummings, BM Staw, 9:175–208. Greenwich, CT: JAI

Greenberger E, Goldberg WA, Hamill S, O'Neill R, Payne CK. 1989. Contributions of a supportive work environment to parents' well-being and orientation to work. *Am. J. Commun. Psychol.* 17:755–83

Griffin R. 1995. *Stress, aggression, and violence in the new workplace*. Cent. Hum. Resour. Manage., Tex. A&M Univ., College Station

Gutek B, Searle S, Klepa L. 1991. Rational versus gender role explanations for work-family conflict. *J. Appl. Psychol.* 76:560–68

Guzzo RA, Dickson MW. 1996. Teams in organizations: recent research on performance and effectiveness. *Annu. Rev. Psychol.* 47:307–38

Guzzo RA, Noonan KA. 1994. Human resource practices as communications and the psychological contract. *Hum. Res. Manage.* 33:447–62

Handy C. 1989. *The Age of Unreason*. Cambridge: Harvard Bus. Sch. Press

Herriot P, Pemberton C. 1995. *New Deals: The Revolution in Managerial Careers*. Chichester: Wiley

Hesketh B, Andrews S, Chandler P. 1989. Training for transferable skills: the role of examples and schema. *Educ. Train. Technol. Int.* 26:156–65

Hicks WD, Klimoski RJ. 1987. Entry into training programs and its effects on training outcomes. *Acad. Manage. J.* 30:542–52

Hollinger RC, Clark JP. 1982. Formal and informal social controls of employee deviance. *Sociol. Q.* 23:333–43

Howell JM, Avolio B. 1993. Transformational leadership, transactional leadership, locus of control, and support for innovation. *J. Appl. Psychol.* 78:891–902

Hunt SD, Morgan RM. 1994. Organizational commitment: one of many commitments or key mediating construct? *Acad. Manage. J.* 37:1568–87

Huselid MA, 1995. The impact of human resource management practices on turnover, productivity, and corporate financial performance. *Acad. Manage. Rev.* 3:635–72

Ibarra H. 1992. Homophily and differential returns: sex differences in network structure and access in an advertising firm. *Adm. Sci. Q.* 37:422–47

Ingram P, Simons T. 1995. Institutional and resource dependence determinants of responses to work-family issues. *Acad. Manage. J.* 38:1466–82

Jick TD, 1993, *Managing Change: Cases and Concepts.* Burr Ridge, IL: Irwin

Kanfer FH. 1975. Self-management methods. In *Helping People Change*, ed. FH Kanfer. pp. 309–55. New York: Wiley

Kanfer R, Hulin CL. 1985. Individual differences in successful job searches following layoff. *Pers. Psychol.* 38:835–47

Kanter RM. 1977. *Work and Family in the United States: A Critical Review and Agenda for Research and Policy.* New York: Russell Sage Found.

Kanter RM. 1989. *When Giants Learn to Dance.* New York: Simon & Schuster

Katz HC. 1985. *Shifting Gears: Changing Labor Relations in the U.S. Automobile Industry.* Cambridge, MA: MIT Press

Katz LF, Kruger AB. 1991. Changes in the structure of wages in the public and private sectors. In *Research in Labor Economics*, ed. RG Ehrenberg. 12. Greenwich, CT: JAI

Kelly JR, McGrath J. 1985. Effects of time limits and task types on task performance and interaction of four-person groups. *J. Pers. Soc. Psychol.* 49:395–107

Kerr S, Jermier JM. 1978. Substitutes for leadership: their meaning and measurement. *Organ. Behav. Hum. Perform.* 22:375–403

Kiesler S, Sproull L. 1992. Managerial response to changing environments: perspectives on problem sensing from social cognition. *Adm. Sci. Q.* 27:548–70

Kirchmeyer C. 1995. Managing the work-non-work boundary: an assessment of organizational responses. *Hum. Relat.* 48:515–36

Kirkman BL, Shapiro DL, Novelli L Jr. 1994. *Employee resistance to work teams: a justice perspective.* Presented at Acad. Manage. Meet., Aug., Dallas

Korunka C, Weiss A, Karetta B. 1993. Effects of new technologies with special regard for the implementation process per se. *J. Organ. Behav.* 14:331–48

Koys DJ. 1991. Fairness, legal compliance, and organizational commitment. *Empl. Responsib. Rights* 4:283–91

Krackhardt D. 1987. QAP partialling as a test of spuriousness. *Soc. Netw.* 9:171–86

Krackhardt D, Blythe J, McGrath C. 1994. KrackPlot 3.0: an improved network drawing program. *Connections.* 17:53–55

Kramer RM, Tyler TR, eds. 1996. *Trust in Organizations: Frontiers of Theory and Research.* Thousand Oaks, CA: Sage

Latham GP, Locke EA. 1991. Self-regulation through goal setting. *Organ. Behav. Hum. Decis. Process.* 50:212–47

Lau C, Woodman R. 1995. Understanding organizational change: a schematic perspective. *Acad. Manage. J.* 38:537–54

Leana CR, Feldman DC. 1996. Finding new jobs after a plant closing: antecedents and outcomes of the occurrence and quality of reemployment. *Hum. Relat.* In press

Leonard-Barton D, Sinha DK. 1993. Developer-user interaction and user satisfaction in internal technology transfer. *Acad Manage. J.* 36:1125–39

Leung K, Chiu W, Au Y. 1993. Sympathy and support for industrial actions. *J. Appl. Psychol.* 78:781–87

Liem R. 1992. Unemployed workers and their families: social victims or social critics? In *Families and Economic Distress*, ed. P Voydanoff, LC Majka, pp. 135–51. Beverly Hills, CA: Sage

Locke EA, Latham GP. 1990. *A Theory of Goal Setting and Task Performance*. Englewood Cliffs, NJ: Prentice-Hall

Locke EA, Shaw KN, Saari LM, Latham GP. 1981. Goal setting and task performance: 1969–1980. *Psychol. Bull.* 90:125–52

Louis MR, Sutton RI. 1991. Switching cognitive gears: from habits of mind to active thinking. *Hum. Relat.* 44:55–76

Lucero MA, Allen RE. 1994. Employee benefits: a growing source of psychological contract violations. *Hum. Res. Manage.* 33:425–46

Lyles MA, Schwenk CR. 1992. Top management strategy, and organizational knowledge structures. *J. Manage. Stud.* 29:155–74

Magnum G, Mayhall D, Nelson K. 1985. The temporary help industry: a response to the dual internal labor market. *Ind. Labor Relat. Rev.* 38:599–611

Manz CC. 1992. Self-leading work teams: moving beyond self-management myths. *Hum. Relat.* 45:1119–40

Manz CC, Sims HP Jr. 1987. Leading workers to lead themselves: the external leadership of self-managing work teams. *Adm. Sci. Q.* 32:106–28

Mathieu JE, Zajac DM. 1990. A review and meta-analysis of the antecedents, correlates, and consequences of organizational commitment. *Psychol. Bull.* 98:224–53

Mayer RC, Davis JH, Schoorman FD. 1995. An integrative model of organizational trust. *Acad. Manage. Rev.* 20:709–34

Merriam-Webster Inc. 1985. *Webster's Third International Dictionary*. Springfield, MA: Merriam-Webster

Meyer M, Gupta V. 1994. The performance paradox. In *Research in Organizational Behavior*, ed. B Staw, LL Cummings, 16: 309–69. Greenwich, CT: JAI

Meyerson D, Weick KE, Kramer RM. 1996. Swift trust and temporary groups. See Kramer & Tyler 1996, pp. 166–95

Miles RE, Creed WED. 1995. Organizational forms and managerial philosophies. In *Research in Organizational Behavior*, ed. LL Cummings, BM Staw, 17:333–72. Greenwich, CT: JAI

Miner AS. 1990. Structural evolution through idiosyncratic jobs: the potential for unplanned learning. *Organ. Sci.* 1:195–210

Miner AS, Robinson DF. 1994. Organization and population level learning as engines for career transitions. *J. Organ. Behav*: 15:345–64

Mirvis PH, Hall DT. 1994. Psychological success and the boundaryless career. *J. Organ. Behav.* 15:365–80

Mitchell TR. 1979. Organizational behavior. *Annu. Rev. Psychol.* 30:243–82

Moorman RH. 1991. Relationship between organizational justice and organizational citizenship behaviors: do fairness perceptions influence employee citizenship. *J. Appl. Psychol.* 76:845–55

Mowday R, Sutton RI. 1993. Organizational behavior: linking individuals and groups to organization contexts. *Annu. Rev. Psychol.* 44:195–229

Mroczkowski T, Hanaoka M. 1989. Continuity and change in Japanese management. *Calif. Manage. Rev.* 31:39–53

National Association of Temporary and Staffing Services. 1994. *Temporary Help/Staffing Services Industry Continues to Create Employment Opportunities.* Alexandria, VA:Natl. Assoc. Temp. Staff. Serv.

National Research Council, ed. 1994. *Organizational Linkages: Understanding the Productivity Paradox.* Washinaton, DC: Natl. Acad. Press

Neal A, Hesketh B, Andrews S. 1995. Instance-based categorization: intentional versus automatic forms of retrieval. *Mem. Cogn.* 23:227–42

Nicolini D, Meznar MB. 1995. The social construction of organizational learning: conceptual and practical issues in the field. *Hum. Relat.* 48:727–46

Noe RA, Wilk SL. 1993. Investigation of the factors that influence employees' participation in development activities. *J. Appl. Psychol* 78:291–302

Nordhaug O. 1989. Reward functions of personnel training. *Hum. Relat.* 42:373–88

Novelli L, Kirkman BL, Shapiro DL. 1995. Effective implementation of organizational change: an organizational justice perspective. In *Trends in Organizational Behavior*, ed. CL Cooper, DM Rousseau, pp. 2:15—36. Chichester: Wiley

O'Driscoll MP, Ilgen DR, Hildreth K. 1992. Time devoted to job and off-job activities, interrole conflict, and affective experiences. *J. Appl. Psychol.* 77:272–79

O'Leary-Kelly AM, Griffin RW, Glew DJ. 1996. Organization-motivated aggression: a research framework. *Acad. Manage. Rev.* 21:225–53

O'Reilly CA. 1991. Organizational behavior: where we've been, where we're going. *Annu. Rev. Psychol.* 42:427–58

Organ DW. 1990. The motivational basis of citizenship behavior. In *Research in Organizational Behavior*, ed. LL Cummings, BM Staw, 12:43–72. Greenwich. CT: JAI

Pearce JL. 1993. Toward an organizational behavior of contract laborers: their psychological involvement and effects on employee co-workers. *Acad Manage. J.* 36: 1082–96

Perrow C. 1984. *Normal Accidents: Living with High-risk Technologies.* New York: Basic Books

Perrow C. 1996. The bounded career and the demise of civil society. See Arthur & Rousseau 1996, pp. 297–313

Podsakoff PM, Niehoff BP, MacKenzie SB, Williams ML. 1993. Do substitutes for leadership really substitute for leadership? An empirical examination of Kerr and Jermier's situational leadership model. *Organ. Behav. Hum. Decis. Process.* 54:1–44

Price RH, Hooijberg R. 1992. Organizational exit pressures and role stress: impact on mental health. *J. Organ. Behav.* 13:641–52

Pritchard RD. 1990. *Measuring and Improving Organizational Productivity.* New York: Praeger

Pritchard RD. 1994. Decomposing the productivity linkages paradox. See National Research Council 1994, pp. 161–92

Roberts K, Clark SC, Wallace C. 1994. Flexibility and individualisation: a comparison of transitions into employment in England and Germany. *Soc.* 28:31–54

Robinson SL. 1995. Violation of psychological contracts: impact on employee attitudes. See Tetrick & Barling 1995, pp. 91–108

Robinson SL, Bennett RJ. 1995. A typology of deviant workplace behaviors: a multidimensional scaling study. *Acad. Manage. J.* 38:555–72

Robinson SL, Rousseau DM. 1994. Violating the psychological contract: not the exception but the norm. *J. Organ. Behav.* 15:245–59

Rodgers R, Hunter JE. 1991. Impact of management by objectives on organizational productivity. *J. Appl. Psychol.* 76:322–36

Roe RA. 1995. Developments in Eastern Europe and work and organizational psychology. In *International Review of Industrial and Organizational Psychology*, ed. CL Cooper, IT Robertson. Chichester: Wiley

Rosenbaum JE, Kariya T, Settersten R, Maier T. 1990. Market and network theories of the transition from high school to work. *Annu. Rev. Soc.* 16:263–99

Rousseau DM. 1995. *Psychological Contracts in Organizations: Understanding Written and Unwritten Agreements*. Newbury Park, CA: Sage

Rousseau DM, Tijoriwala S. 1996. It takes a good reason to change a psychological contract. Presented at Soc. Ind./Organ. Psychol., April, San Diego

Rousseau DM, Tinsley K. 1996. Human resources are local: society and social contracts in a global economy. In *Handbook of Selection and Appraisal*, ed. N Anderson, P Herriot. London: Wiley. In press

Sagan S. 1993. *The Limits of Safety: Organizations, Accidents, and Nuclear Weapons*. Princeton, NJ: Princeton Univ. Press

Schneider B, Bowen DE. 1995. *Winning the Service Game*. Boston: Harvard Bus. Sch. Press

Seashore SE, Indik BP, Georgopolons BS. 1960. Relationships among criteria of job performance. *J. Appl. Psychol.* 44:195–202

Semler R. 1989. Managing without managers. *Harv. Bus. Rev.* 67(5):76–84

Shapiro DL, Buttner EH, Barry B. 1994. Explanations: What factors enhance their perceived adequacy? *Organ. Hum. Decis. Process.* 58:346–68

Sheppard BH, Lewicki RJ, Minton JW. 1992. *Organizational Justice: The Search for Fairness in the Workplace*. New York: Lexington Books

Sherman S. 1995. Stretch goals: the dark side of asking for miracles. *Fortune*, Nov. 13. pp. 231–32

Shipper F, Manz CC. 1992. Employee self-management without formally designated teams: an alternative road to empowerment. *Organ. Dyn.* 20:48–61

Shore LM, Wayne SJ. 1993. Commitment and employee behavior: comparison of affective commitment and continuance commitment with perceived organizational support. *J. Appl. Psychol.* 78:774–80

Sims HP, Gioia DA, eds. 1986. *The Thinking Organization: The Dynamics of Organizational Social Cognition*. San Francisco: Jossey-Bass

Sinclair RR, Hannigan MA, Tetrick LE. 1995. Benefit coverage and employee attitudes: a social exchange perspective. See Tetrick & Barling 1995, pp. 163–85

Sink DS, Smith GL. 1994. The influence of organizational linkages and measurement practices on productivity and management. See National Research Council 1994, pp. 131–60

Small Business Administration 1992. *The State of Small Business*. Washington, DC: US Gov. Print. Off.

Smith KG, Locke EA, Barry D. 1990. Goal setting, planning, and organizational performance: an experimental simulation. *Organ. Behav. Hum. Decis. Process.* 46:118–34

Smolowe J. 1996. *Reap as ye shall sow: pay-for-performance standards are a jackpot this year for executives but not for workers. Time*, Feb. 5. p. 45

Snow CC, Miles RE, Coleman HJ. 1992. Managing 21st century network organizations. *Organ. Dvn.* 20:5–20

Starbuck WH, Milliken FJ. 1988. Executives' perceptual filters: what they notice and how they make sense. In *The Executive Effect: Concepts and Methods for Studying Top Managers*, ed. D Hambrick. Greenwich, CT: JAI

Storey DJ. 1994. *Understanding the Small Business Sector*. London: Routledge

Tetrick LE, Barling J, eds. 1995. *Changing Employment Relations: Behavior and Social Perspectives*. Washington, DC: Am. Psychol. Assoc.

Thomas D, Higgins M. 1996. Mentoring and the boundaryless career: lessons from the minority experience. See Arthur & Rousseau 1996. In press

Tsui AS, Ashford SJ, St. Clair L, Xin KR. 1995. Dealing with discrepant expectations: response strategies and managerial effectiveness. *Acad. Manage. J.* 38:1515–43

Van Maannen J, Barley SR. 1984. Occupational communities: culture and control in organizations. In *Research in Organizational Behavior*, ed. BM Staw, 8:287–364. Greenwich, CT: JAI

Vinocur AD, van Ryn M, Gramlich EM, Price RH. 1991. Long-term follow-up and benefit-cost analysis of the jobs program: a preventive intervention for the unemployed. *J. Appl. Psychol.* 76:213–19

Vroom V. 1964. *Work and Motivation*. New York: Wiley

Wanous JP, Keon TL, Latack JC. 1983. Expectancy theory and occupational organizational choices: a review and test. *Organ. Behav. Hum. Perform.* 32:66–85

Weick KE. 1995. *Sensemaking in Organizations*. Thousand Oaks, CA: Sage

Weick KE. 1996. Enactment and the boundaryless career: organizing as we work. See Arthur & Rousseau 1996, pp. 40–57

Weick KE, Roberts KH. 1993. Collective mind in organizations. *Adm. Sci. Q.* 38:357–81

Welbourne TM, Balkin DB, Gomez-Mejia LR. 1995. Gainsharing and mutual monitoring: a combined agency–organizational justice interpretation. *Acad. Manage. J.* 38:881–99

Welch R. 1994. European works councils and their implications: the potential impact on employer practices and trade unions. *Empl. Relat.* 16:48–61

Wilpert B. 1995. Organizational behavior. *Annu. Rev. Psychol.* 46:59–90

Winefield A, Winefield H, Tiggeman M, Goldney R, 1991. A longitudinal study of the psychological effects of unemployment and unsatisfactory employment on young adults. *J. Appl. Psychol.* 76:424–31

Wood R, Mento A, Locke E. 1987. Task complexity as a moderator of goal effects: a meta-analysis. *J. Appl. Psychol.* 72:416–25

Yankelovich D. 1993. How changes in the economy are reshaping American values. In *Values and Public Policy*, ed. HJ Aaron, TE Mann, T Taylor. Washington, DC: Brookings Inst.

Zenger TR. 1992. Why do employers only reward extreme performance? Examining the relationships among performance, pay, and turnover. *Adm. Sci. Q.* 37:198–220

60

ORGANIZATIONS OF THE FUTURE

Changes and challenges

Lynn R. Offermann and Marilyn K. Gowing

Source: *American Psychologist* 45(2) (1990): 95–108.

Abstract

Widespread societal change is radically altering the traditional face and place of work in the United States. In this article, we examine some of the existing and projected work force changes and the ways in which organizations themselves are evolving. Issues that will demand the attention of psychologists and others interested in human behavior at work are highlighted, and implications for the education and training of industrial/organizational psychologists are presented. It is suggested that we view these changes as challenges that allow psychologists to gain greater understanding of human behavior at work, while at the same time contributing to the creation of healthier, safer, and more productive work environments.

As we approach the year 2000, there is steadily increasing interest among individuals in all sectors of society in attempting to project what the 21st century holds in store for us. Once the purview of science fiction, the incredible pace of change over the last several decades has given new importance to forecasting future trends that will present new challenges. The nature of work, the work force, and the workplace have undergone and will continue to undergo enormous change, bringing both upheaval and opportunity for those involved in organizations. Psychologists interested in organizational behavior are no exception.

Psychologists have had a long history of involvement in studying human behavior in organizations, an endeavor that has evolved along with changes in organizations. From the early efforts of American Psychological Association (APA) president Hugo Münsterberg to study industrial accidents and human safety, to the efforts of APA president Robert Yerkes in involving psychologists in the development and validation of sound psychometric instruments for personnel selection in World War I, to recent efforts to understand the dynamics of individual and systemic responses to the wave of "merger mania" characterizing the 1980s, we psychologists have been involved. For us, the changes taking place in the workplace of today and tomorrow offer opportunities both to gain insight into basic processes of human behavior in the important domain of work and to contribute to making organizations both more productive and humane. In doing so, we have the opportunity to advance the field of psychology, the welfare of the work force (in which most of us are also participants), and the larger goals of our nation to meet the demands of a competitive, global environment.

This special issue was designed to (a) document and highlight some of the recent theoretical developments and significant practical applications made by psychologists and others in organizational settings and (b) present avenues of opportunity for future contributions based on our understanding of trends affecting organizational environments today and in the future. Many of the contributions discussed herein were made by industrial/organizational (I/O) psychologists, and many, though not all, of the implications of these works have their most direct impact on the field of I/O psychology. Yet this issue is by no means a summary of I/O psychology or one whose topics are of concern only to I/O psychologists. A single journal issue cannot cover *all* organizational matters to which psychologists can contribute or have contributed. Consequently, we chose a sample of topics from the organizational side of "I/O" inquiry whose results and ramifications bear directly on psychologists as researchers, practitioners, workers, or concerned citizens.

On this basis, we focus on four major categories that are critical to the establishment of progressive and dynamic organizations and that are clearly amenable to the activities and competencies of psychologists. Each of these four categories is reflected in a section of this issue: (a) The Changing Face and Place of Work, (b) Developing and Maintaining Organizational Competitiveness, (c) Developing Leaders for Tomorrow, and (d) Workplace Wellness. In each section, authors have been requested to discuss what is known about their topic theoretically, empirically, and practically, with a special focus on what needs to be done in the future. Some articles highlight programs currently in place, their results, and what has been learned from them. Other articles focus on expanding opportunities for the involvement of psychologists that have resulted from theoretical developments. All articles summarize what is, and is yet to be known, in each selected area.

In the present article, we examine some of the larger societal and organizational issues that impact most of the specific areas of research and practice which follow in subsequent articles. We describe existing and projected work force changes, and the ways in which organizational systems are changing. We then outline the subsequent articles of this special issue, and conclude with implications for the education and training of psychologists seeking to understand organizational behavior.

The changing work force

Projections about who will be employed in the year 2000 are less conjectural than might be imagined. The entire work force of the year 2000 has already been born, and over two thirds of those in this group are working today. Each of these groups—the new workers of the year 2000 and those presently employed and continuing to work in 2000—present different concerns and issues for organizations.

New workers

Numbers

Concern is generally greatest about the cohort of workers who will enter the labor market in the year 2000. The first issue is mere size: Relative to previous age cohorts, there will be fewer young people entering the job market than in the past. The "baby boom" generation (those born between 1946 and 1961) produced a plentiful group of workers from whom organizations could selectively choose. In the late 1970s, there were about 3 million people entering the work force each year at around age 18. By 1990, there will be 1.3 million new workers per year, and by 1995, there will be about 1.3 million *fewer* workers in the 18- 24-year-old group (Odiorne, 1986). The labor force will be increasing at a slower rate than at any time since the 1930s (Rauch, 1989).

This slow growth in the size of the labor force can impact our national productivity. When the labor force is steadily increasing in size, lower individual productivity can be countered by the sheer numbers of individuals working to still allow for overall increases in national economic growth. Slower increases in work force size mean that either the national rate of economic growth will fall well below the rates that could be expected if the size increases of the 1960s and 1970s were continued or that organizations must foster increased productivity in each worker, making maximal use of each employee.

Skills

The skill level of the entry-level worker of the year 2000 is of prime concern to organizations. Here, many organizations feel that they are on a collision course with demographics. When the labor supply seemed endless, organizations could easily be selective, retaining the skilled, and discarding the undereducated. Already many organizations are having difficulty in recruiting new entry-level workers and have had to invest in training those selected on basic skills such as simple mathematics and writing (Hamilton, 1988). This is not surprising given that the National Assessment of Educational Progress (NAEP) survey conducted by the Educational Testing Service found that only 34% of Whites, 20% of Hispanics, and 8% of Blacks of the 3,600 21- 25-year-olds surveyed could figure out the tip and change for a two-item restaurant meal (Hamilton, 1988). The present concern with the level of literacy and basic skills of today's entry-level workers is compounded by the realization that virtually all prognostications of the nature of work in the years ahead project an increase in the level of skill needed to perform well. Computer software can check the spelling of words in an article but cannot proofread for meaning and context. As robots take over routine assembly work from people, jobs will open requiring the monitoring and troubleshooting of computerized equipment. Yet the NAEP finds that among their 21- 25-year-old sample, only 25% of Whites, 7% of Hispanics, and 3% of Blacks can interpret a complex bus schedule. It should not be surprising, then, to find that U.S. businesses are spending a record 210 billion dollars for on-the-job training and education, an effort about equal in size to public elementary, secondary, and higher education institutions combined (Hamilton, 1988).

Sex

Just as women accounted for about 60% of the total growth of the U.S. work force between 1970 and 1985 (Committee for Economic Development, 1987), women are expected to make up a similar percentage of new entry-level workers between 1985 and 2000 (Johnston & Packer, 1987). Sometimes called the "feminization" of the work force, much of the increase has come from the increased participation of women with children. The current rate of maternal employment in two-parent families with school-aged children is 71%, rising a little each year (Hoffman, 1989). In particular, one of the fastest growing parts of the labor market are mothers of infants (U.S. Bureau of the Census, 1986). In 1987, 53% of married mothers with children aged one or under were in the labor market, more than double the rate in 1970 (U.S. Bureau of Labor Statistics, 1987).

The influx of women, particularly women with children, into the workplace is having tremendous impact. With the increase of dual-earner and single-parent families, concern is growing with balancing the demands of work and family settings (e.g., Zedeck & Mosier, this issue, pp. 240–251). The United States is unusual among industrialized nations in our lack of a clear, coherent family policy. More than 60 countries, including most of the industrial ones, have family or children's allowances, typically paying families the equivalent of 5% to 10% of the average wage per child, and over 100 countries give one or both parents cash and time off (typically about four months of paid leave) when they have a new baby (Rauch, 1989). Although only 10% of U.S. companies currently provide employees with childcare assistance, a recent survey by the Society for Human Resources Management (1988) indicated that nearly half of U.S. employers are actively considering some form of childcare assistance for their employees. Private and public sector organizations alike are experimenting with innovative solutions to re-solving work-family problems (Ropp, 1987), often without much research to guide them. Like their elected representatives, however, there is considerable debate on how best to provide this assistance.

In addition to child-care assistance, the presence of large proportions of dual-career couples in the work force creates other demands on organizations. No longer able to relocate employees with the assumption of one spouse who is free to "trail" the other, organizations are now forced to engage in what Schein (1981) referred to as "joint career management" (p. 90). Consideration for spousal employment opportunities must be given in relocation planning.

Race/ethnicity

It is projected that a third of the new entrants into the work force between now and the year 2000 will be minority group members (Johnson & Packer, 1987). Those future workers are today's minority children, more than half of whom are being raised in poverty (Horowitz & O'Brien, 1989). As a result, the ranks of new workers in the future will be dominated by those who have traditionally been ill-served by the nation's school system—the poor, minorities, and immigrants (Hamilton, 1988). One societal effect of this trend has been to increase the focus of corporate executives, legislators, and educators on poverty as an economic issue affecting national productivity rather than exclusively as a social issue (Rauch, 1989). It is hoped that this broader view will widen support for poverty reduction and early educational intervention programs.

Blacks and Hispanics are also 35% more likely to be employed in occupations projected by the Bureau of Labor Statistics to lose the most employees between 1978 and 1990 (Johnston & Packer, 1987). New jobs will generally require higher education and skill levels than those that were made obsolete (Miller, 1989). Such findings make issues of retraining for new occupations of critical importance to the economic status of minority groups. Recent indications of a decline in labor force participation among Black men is an additional concern. By 2000, Black women will outnumber Black men in the work force, in contrast to the 3 to 2 ratio of men to women in the White population in the work force (Johnston & Packer, 1987).

Continuing workers

The middle-aged "spread"

The American work force is aging along with the baby boomers. Although the Age Discrimination in Employment Acts of 1967, 1978, and 1986 defined "older" workers as those over 40, the age group showing the largest expansion in the work force and the one that will have the most impact on it, is made up of those in the younger part of this older worker classification. These baby boom workers comprise one of the fastest growing groups in the work force (Bureau of National Affairs, 1987). Between 1986 and 2000, the number of persons aged 35 to 47 will increase by 38%, the number between age 48 and 53 will jump 67%, while the overall population growth will be only 15% (Johnston & Packer, 1987).

This tremendous expansion in the number of middle-aged individuals will mean increased competition for scarce high-level organizational positions. In 1987, one person in 20 was promoted into top management; in 2001, that ratio is expected to be one in 50 (Arnett, 1989). The traditional lure of promotion as an incentive to motivation and commitment may be threatened by such staggering odds, creating a need to consider alternate ways to keep workers invested and productive. However, the lowered odds of promotion within an organization may also lead talented individuals to become more entrepreneurial and to seek more actively to create new business ventures for themselves. Those choosing to deal with the scarcity of top positions in this way could be a boon to economic growth, particularly considering projections that 85% of the work force in the year 2000 will work for firms employing fewer than 200 people (Arnett, 1989).

For organizations, the increasing age of the work force may carry with it increasingly high payrolls, as organizations employ greater numbers of people with more seniority. In the past, these workers have been shown to be less likely to relocate or retrain for new occupations than younger workers (Johnston & Packer, 1987).

Attitudes toward older workers

Despite attempts to improve attitudes toward older workers, there is still evidence of bias. A study comparing attitudes toward older workers, defined as those over age 50, in 1953 and 1983 found less positive attitudes reported toward the older worker at both times, with no overall improvement (Bird & Fisher, 1986). These attitudes are in contrast to consistent meta-analytic evidence that age is typically unrelated to job performance for most jobs (e.g., McEvoy & Cascio, 1989; Waldman & Avolio, 1986). The few exceptions to this finding may be jobs with heavy physical requirements or where the small but significant slowing in reaction time with advanced age would be problematic (Rhodes, 1983). Despite similarity in performance across age groups, there is widespread belief that biases against older workers in performance appraisals continue to exist (e.g., Sterns & Alexander, 1988).

Such appraisal biases may stem less from current performance levels and more from fears about the future prospects of older workers. The lower willingness of older workers to retrain or relocate has already been noted. Although research suggests that older workers are evaluated positively in terms of loyalty, productivity, and work habits, there are also negative perceptions revolving around flexibility, adaptability to technology, and aggressiveness—all imperatives of the current focus on competitiveness in American business (Dennis, 1988). Issues surrounding the management of an aging work force should be included in management training programs in order to dispel myths, prevent discrimination, and maximize the participation of an important and growing segment of society.

Retirement issues

Although age-based mandatory retirement was prohibited beginning in 1986, and the physical health of individuals in the 55- 65-year-old group has increased, the percentage of men of this age in the work force has fallen from above 90% in the 1960s to about 75% today (Colburn, 1989). A recent study indicates that mental health considerations, particularly job stress, may be one reason older men are choosing early retirement (Mitchell & Anderson, 1989). Although some opinion surveys show employee interest in retiring later, the trend toward early retirement continues unabated.

However, the percentage of workers over 55 in the years after 2000 will be affected by a group whose future retirement plans are less predictable now—women. Lacking past experience on which to base forecasts, the retirement rates of baby-boom women who have spent most of their lives at work are difficult to forsee (Riche, 1988). Many experts feel that in order to maintain staffing levels in the face of demographic shifts, there will be a need for the increasingly older population of workers, men and women, to stay on the job longer (Faley, Kleiman, & Lengnick-Hall, 1984).

Job attitudes

The changing demographics discussed earlier are being accompanied by modifications in employee attitudes, motivations, and values (Odiorne, 1986). Increased desire for autonomy, self-development, and balance between work and family life is surfacing among many workers (Hall, 1986). People are seeking more meaningful work experiences, as well as more involvement in the decisions pertaining to themselves (London & Strumpf, 1986). Furthermore, there is evidence that compared with past generations of workers, today's workers have a growing perception of entitlement to such meaning and involvement in their work.

As the labor market tightens in coming years, employers will need to pay greater attention to attitudes such as these as they compete to attract and keep talent within their organizations. Increased attention has been given to career planning and management, with individual abilities and interests being balanced with organizational needs (Gilley, 1988; Quaintance, 1989) in an effort to increase organizational productivity. Many organizations have developed Quality of Work life (QWL) programs to deal with changes in work values and attitudes. Although they are used in numerous ways by different organizations, most programs adopt a common philosophy advocating increased worker autonomy and opportunities for personal self-development on the job, fostering a sense of belonging to the organization, and providing both material rewards and recognition to successful employees (Stein, 1983). QWL programs such as quality circles (small groups of employees who meet to discuss and suggest product and process improvements) are becoming popular. There is some evidence that quality circles result in initial improvements in job attitudes and effective performance, with those improvements diminishing over time (Griffin, 1988).

Summary

In terms of new workers, the message for the year 2000 is clear: We must find a way to educate and train *all* individuals. The disturbing figures presented earlier mask a glimmering hope for groups of individuals who were previously disenfranchised. Their talents are needed, and their needs can no longer be ignored. The causes and solutions to these problems go beyond any single organization. Joint cooperation between educators, legislators, and the business community is required if the work force needs of the year 2000 are to be met.

For both new and continuing workers, issues of motivation and attitudes toward work will become ever more critical. As the work force continues to diversify, organizations will need to be especially attuned to the potentially different expectations of different groups. The notion of America as a melting pot is giving way to a view of America as a rich assortment of different talents to be preserved rather than homogenized. The traditional organizational focus on conformity through assimilation needs to be replaced by a true understanding of integration.

The changing organization

The evolving nature of organizations

Just as the nature of the work force is changing, so, too, are organizations. A number of trends are currently converging to alter the nature of organizations themselves.

Failures and downsizing

Companies are failing at a very substantial rate. There were more than 57,000 corporate failures in 1986; others are avoiding bankruptcy through successful downsizing efforts (Ropp, 1987). Whereas downsizing once was undertaken only in the presence of dire financial or competitive pressures, it is now viewed as a management prerogative that may be used repeatedly, both in good times and in bad (Skrzycki, 1989). A survey by the American Management Association showed that in 1988, 39% of the 1,084 companies and nonprofit organizations surveyed reduced their work forces, cutting an average of 162 employees as compared to 35% a year earlier (Skrzycki, 1989). Corporate mergers and acquisitions frequently were the driving force behind these downsizing efforts.

With the perceived need to downsize comes the decision about how to best accomplish the work force reduction. Options include natural attrition, layoffs, early retirements, shortened work weeks, and job transfers, with different options generating different costs for organizations and their employees (Greenhalgh, Lawrence, & Sutton, 1988). Organizations must be sensitive to the fact that there are concerns among the employee "survivors" as well as among those forced to leave. For example, five major employee concerns have been identified among employees in an acquired firm: loss of identity, lack of information and anxiety, an often obsessive concern about their own continued survival, lost talent, and family repercussions (Schweiger, Ivancevich, & Power, 1987).

Mergers and acquisitions

In 1986, $122.7 billion was spent for mergers, acquisitions, leveraged buy-outs, and divestitures—up 21% from 1985 (Ropp, 1987). From 1985 to 1988, approximately 15 million workers were affected by mergers (Fulmer & Gilkey, 1988). A recent study of 150 large mergers and acquisitions conducted by an executive recruiting firm suggested that nearly half the senior executives in an acquired company will leave within one year of the merger and almost three quarters will leave within three years (Fulmer & Gilkey, 1988). Such significant changes in top management often portend significant alterations in management practices, as well as organizational culture. Many acquisitions fail to live up to expectations, at least partly as a result of a failure to understand and manage the process itself (Jemison & Sitkin, 1986).

The expanding service sector

The focus of today's organizations has shifted from manufacturing to service. Services are defined as all those economic activities in which the primary output is neither a product nor a construction. The service sector now accounts for more than 68% of the nation's gross national product (GNP) and 71% of its employment (Quinn & Gagnon, 1986). Value is added to this output by means "like convenience, security, comfort, and flexibility ... the output is consumed when produced" (Quinn & Gagnon, 1986, p. 95). Service organizations have grown so rapidly in number and size that they accounted for nearly 90% of all new, nonfarm jobs created in the United States between 1953 and 1984 (Grover, 1987).

Unfortunately, the growth of service organizations has not been accompanied by comparable gains in productivity. According to the Committee for Economic Development (1987), nonmanufacturing, nonfarm productivity showed zero growth between 1973 and 1985, while manufacturing productivity grew 2.2%. Future concerns about national productivity will inevitably emphasize improving performance in the service sector, and psychologists will undoubtedly be focusing increased attention on this sector as well.

The international challenge

The United States is part of an increasingly global economy. According to Cascio (1986), about 100,000 U.S. companies do business overseas, including 25,000 firms with foreign office affiliates and 3,500 major multinational companies. He further calculated that one third of the profits of U.S. companies are derived from international business, along with one sixth of the nation's jobs.

Charged with increasing productivity in this international environment, American business is hampered by the inability to formulate U.S. trade policy. Advances in organizational productivity will increasingly require an understanding of a complex external environment involving policymakers at home and abroad. It is important to recognize and consider a variety of available trade policy options, beyond the extremes of either free trade or protectionism (Lenway, 1985).

Changes in organizational culture and climate

Diverse organizational cultures have been formed through restructuring activities that largely stem from management's desire for access to new U.S. and worldwide markets, products, technology, resources, or management talent (Jemison & Sitkin, 1986). Similarly, multinational organizations with cross-cultural work forces represent new types of organizational culture that must be directed in a rapidly changing world economy (Drucker, 1987). The challenge for management is to institute a new organizational culture that reflects shared values, regardless of previous organizational affiliation or geographic location.

Managing change

Levinson (1988) predicted that top managers will have to adjust their styles considerably to be effective in these new organizational environments. Specifically, Levinson stated,

> When costs have been cut to the bone and controls tightened into rigidity, the resulting insensitivity and lack of flexibility will inhibit competitive adaptation. ...Managers and executives will necessarily have to be more closely involved with their subordinates over the longer period of time required to establish and maintain commitment. ...They will have to become more psychologically minded; that is they will have to understand the personalities of their subordinates better, particularly the unconscious factors in motivation. (pp. 119–121)

In addition to changing managerial style, the human resource problems created specifically by mergers and acquisitions may be addressed through the application of organizational development interventions, with some suggesting that strategies found to be effective with blended families be applied to the "blended corporate family" (Fulmer & Gilkey, 1988). Both blended families and corporations must deal with new structure and systems, territorial battles and start-up problems, among others. In both sets of circumstances, conscious attempts can be made to alleviate problems by clarifying roles and relationships, maintaining prompt and open communication, developing a common historical perspective, and building a new culture (Fulmer & Gilkey, 1988).

Others view managerial rewards as powerful means of developing corporate culture. Kerr and Slocum (1987) found that a hierarchy-based reward system in which performance was defined in qualitative terms and evaluated subjectively, with subordinates being dependent on their superiors for evaluations and rewards, supported a "clan culture." Clan cultures were characterized by long socialization, high commitment, peer pressure to conform and the importance of superiors as mentors. Kerr and Slocum concluded that this type of system is useful for firms that pursue a product-driven strategy, supporting the development and marketing of a product with specified quality. In contrast, a performance-based reward system based on quantitative definitions of performance, objective evaluations, and rewards based on formulas such as return on investment connected to results, with subordinates less dependent on superiors for guidance or evaluation, supported a "market culture." Market cultures were characterized by short-term commitment, independence from peers, little socialization, and superiors as resource allocators. Kerr and Slocum (1987) maintained that this type of culture is useful in firms pursuing acquisitive, high diversification strategies that must be responsive to the desires of the marketplace.

Communications and training

When instituting a new organizational culture, the communications of management become critical. One of the concerns of recently acquired employees is a lack of timely and accurate information, specifically information regarding the future of the employees and the company (Schweiger et al., 1987). The selection of appropriate media facilitates effective communication of the values and performance expectations of the new organizational culture. Lengel and Daft (1988) have labeled the selection of communication media an executive skill.

Formal training programs can play a crucial role in the communication of organizational culture. One such program for top-level executives was held by Allied-Signal after they acquired Bendix, where managers from different parts of the merged organization were brought together in order to facilitate acquaintanceship, the exchange of information, and to bring about cultural change that emphasized common objectives and shared values (Fulmer & Gilkey, 1988).

The challenge of maintaining organizational productivity

In the presence of their changing internal work environments, corporations must strive to become and to remain competitive with their external counterparts in the business world. Some argue that the United States has lost its competitive edge and cite statistics to support the erosion of U.S. ability to compete in the world economy (e.g., Mitroff & Mohrman, 1987). Indicators of such erosion include a substantial reduction in America's share of the world GNP and exports, and a trade balance that has declined both in absolute terms and as a percentage of

GNP (Lodge & Crum, 1985). Recent estimates set the trade deficit at $166 billion (Steers & Miller, 1988).

Some suggest that the solution to organizational competitiveness lies in theories of quality control, that is, defining the standards of quality for the company's products or services and holding employees accountable for reaching those standards (e.g., Dumas, Cushing, & Laughlin, 1987; Garvin, 1987). However, Hitt and Ireland (1987) argued that organizations cannot be evaluated as to their progress until there is agreement on what constitutes "excellence" in organizational performance. These authors challenged the criteria proposed by Peters and Waterman (1982) in their well-known book *In Search of Excellence.*[1]

The growth and poor performance of the service sector fosters the realization that management techniques may need to be altered to ensure ongoing organizational effectiveness. A new concept called *service management*, which encompasses a structured, systemic approach for planning, organizing, and controlling the design, development, and delivery of a product and/or service that promotes superior consumer satisfaction and results, has received increasing attention (e.g., Albrecht, 1988; Albrecht & Zemke, 1985; Bowen & Schneider, 1988).

Optimizing organizational structure

As a result of these shifting emphases, organizations are restructuring along flatter, leaner lines, with fewer layers of management and fewer people at upper levels (Galagan, 1987). Hill, Hitt, and Hoskisson (1988) noted that the trend toward diversification in products and services in organizations has also had an effect on the organizational structure of U.S. firms. This trend led to the development of a decentralized, multidivisional or "M-form" structure with the following characteristics: Each distinct business is in its own operating division; the divisions are responsible for day-to-day operating decisions; and the corporate office is responsible for overall financial control of the divisions and the overall strategic development of the firm. Hill et al. (1988) suggested that the M-form organizational structure establishes a number of quasi-autonomous operating divisions allowing for a separation between short-run operating and long-run strategic decisions. It has been argued for many years that these strategic divisions are essential for U.S. organizations to regain the competitive advantage (Hayes & Abernathy, 1980). Others point out that the traditional hierarchical model of organizations, frequently represented by the M-form structure with centralized control of finances and strategy by the corporate office, may no longer be the most appropriate model. Rather they envision an "organizational map" including customers, suppliers, distributors, and franchisees, with the organizational layers in a circular rather than hierarchical format (Peters, 1988). Still others believe that globalization will increasingly require joint ventures and cooperative managements, with a resulting organizational structure that is a network of contracted relationships and strategic alliances (Galbraith & Kazanjian, 1988).

Restructuring work

Organizations are emphasizing the formation of self-contained, close-to-the-customer work groups that learn customer preferences and cater to them and that require integrated team performance from the employees (Galagan, 1987). Numerous companies, including IBM and Digital, are describing their strategies for making teams work (Galagan, 1986; Hardaker & Ward, 1987). Specifically, Hardaker and Ward (1987) recommended that as a first step, the team members develop a clear understanding of the team's mission, what its members collectively are paid to do, and what they need to do in the future as well as what they are currently doing, and then attempt to reach consensus on the factors critical to success. This process of goal formulation and consensus building may be the first step in an integrated team development effort (e.g., Sundstrom, DeMeuse, & Futrell, this issue, pp. 120–133).

Maximizing the use of technology

Managers have also turned their attention to ergonomics and human factors considerations in an effort to address their productivity problems (Dainoff & Dainoff, 1987). These considerations attempt to maximize performance through the optimal combination of human and automated capabilities. Ergonomic training programs are being examined for their potential contributions to reducing visual display terminal operator complaints and to increasing productivity (Gross & Chapnik, 1987).

Corporations now have numerous sources of information on how to design the "electronic office" (Lueder, 1986). Automation is being introduced to boost sales and marketing (Moriarty & Swartz, 1989) and to provide managers with essential information on their human resources (Davey & Jacobson, 1987) and on their financial control systems (Bruns & McFarlan, 1987). Well-conceived and implemented changes to automation may certainly boost productivity. For example, a division of Vanity Fair reduced the time for order processing from two weeks to three days, increased order accuracy and customer satisfaction, and realized a 10% increase in sales following the introduction of computers capable of giving salespeople up-to-date inventory and order status information (Moriarty & Swartz, 1989).

We must also consider the social aspects of technology. The effects of new technology may be far broader than first imagined, and not always positive. Only by making careful decisions about the introduction and management of technology, and by monitoring the forseen and unforseen effects of changes associated with it, can we exercise conscious choice about how to best use and control technology without being controlled by it (Kraut, 1987).

Creating an effective work environment

Companies are experimenting with alternative formats to the traditional office (Collins, 1936) and in some cases, with placing the office wherever the employee is located (Stone & Luchetti, 1985). It has been estimated that about 15.8 million corporate employees now work out of offices in their homes at least part of the time, with about one third of those people having formal arrangements with their employers (Martin, 1989). The prospect of so-called "virtual organizations" whose members do not meet face-to-face but are linked together through computer technology clearly presents new challenges to traditional theories of management and organization.

Companies are also beginning to take a new look at the physical and social environments in which their employees are working, looking to the principles of environmental psychology to link those environments to effective work behaviors (Proshansky, Ittelson, & Rivlin, 1976; Sundstrom, 1986). Rather than single all-purpose workstations, some companies are establishing activity settings where workers move around various settings such as conference rooms, quiet spaces, and equipment areas as tasks change (Stone & Luchetti, 1985). Empirical work on this topic to date has been limited, and with work environments changing so rapidly many vital questions remain unanswered (see Sundstrom, 1986, for a comprehensive review).

Improving products and services

Although improvements in organizational competitiveness and productivity can be made through such strategies as optimizing the organizational structure, restructuring work, maximizing the use of technology, and creating an effective work environment, most corporate managers recognize that the improvement of product and service quality may have the greatest payoff to their organizations. Smith (1987) described some basic commonsense approaches that were taken by Quasar that resulted in the reduction of the average defect rate for every 100 sets built to a defect rate of 15, which is 10 times better than the U.S. average. These approaches included thorough life-cycle testing of product components, use of a pilot line to plan production and work out some of the flaws, and the predesign of workstations to minimize changes of operation error. In this case, quality assurance principles and the application of some of the earlier strategies including a redesign of the work environment resulted in an enhanced quality product.

Summary

Strategic planning efforts have frequently led the organizations of today to adopt either dramatic downsizing or acquisition policies. Undoubtedly these trends will exist in the future, along with the global expansion of markets and the delivery of services. Such strategies place renewed emphasis on the need to manage change within the organization and to strive to establish and/or influence the corporate culture through communication and training.

The challenge to future management is to maintain organizational competitiveness and productivity through new models of structural design and creative approaches to work assignments that maximize human and machine resources. Simultaneously, future managers must deal with a new, diversified work force characterized by changing attitudes and values. We hope that their efforts to make their organizations more efficient will be balanced by a sensitivity to human resource management issues. This combination ultimately will enhance the quality of the products and services offered by the organization, as well as the quality of work life for employees.

Overview of the contents of this issue

The changing face and place of work

The demographic and organizational forces outlined in the preceding section have led to a changing face and place of work, with a new diversity in the work force and new conditions under which work is accomplished. Companies that grow rapidly through acquisitions and mergers gain new managerial talent, who bring with them their own, sometimes conflicting, definitions of organizational culture. Psychologists and other interventionists frequently must assist these newly formed corporations in defining their new company culture (including mission identification, vision building, and the identification of top management values), as well as the consequences of that culture for company performance (Plant & Ryan, 1988). Training mid-management personnel in the new culture becomes particularly challenging when international facilities are involved.

In his article on organizational culture, Schein (this issue, pp. 109–119) suggests that culture is a complex phenomenon that manifests itself in observable artifacts, values, and basic underlying assumptions. He describes how culture is developed as well as how it evolves over time and is maintained, and he recommends that those interested in assisting organizations to define their cultures adopt more ethnographic approaches.

Organizational culture has been identified as one contextual factor that influences the work of individuals performing as teams within an organization. There is considerable agreement that team structures will play an increasingly key role in the organization of the future (e.g., Tuttle, 1988). Sundstrom et al. (this issue, pp. 120–133) suggest that work team effectiveness is a function of team type, organizational context (including such things as culture, technology/task design, mission clarity, and training), team boundaries, and team development of processes, norms, cohesion, and roles. They present a model of team functioning, summarize existing studies of team development, and suggest avenues for future explorations into work group performance.

Developing and maintaining competitiveness

Many solutions have been proposed for the problem of developing and maintaining organizational competitiveness. The articles in this section focus on developing competitiveness through organizational training, organizational development, motivating employees, negotiating and resolving conflicts, and maximizing the contributions of human factors and technology in the workplace.

Nowhere will the impact of the changing demographics of the workplace be felt more than in the area of organizational training. Goldstein and Gilliam (this issue, pp. 134–143) relate these demographic changes to the challenges facing training to ensure that each individual is working to his or her full potential, regardless of that individual's level in the organization. Additionally, they suggest that organizations need research on basic skill and support programs to permit greater numbers of unskilled youth to enter the world of work. Simultaneously, organizations need to stress top quality managerial development programs to help future managers and leaders work with a more diverse work force.

Although some companies rely heavily on training programs as an intervention for quality improvement (Cocheu, 1989), others have extolled organization development interventions for assisting managers to increase both organizational effectiveness and member well-being. Beer and Walton (this issue, pp. 154–161) summarize a variety of current interventions and describe a process for transforming organizations, noting the critical role of change leaders in that process. They conclude by discussing the role of consultants in assisting organizations with their transformations.

Another option for improving competitiveness deals with the enhancement of individual worker motivation. Changes in workers and organizations are changing our view of appropriate motivational techniques. Katzell and Thompson (this issue, pp. 144–153) provide a comprehensive description of the major theories of work motivation and present key practical strategies for improving work motivation in organizational settings.

Intra-organizational conflict is recognized as a potential factor in the destruction of an organization (Phillips, 1988). Certainly, at a minimum level, such conflict can require resources and energies that would be better placed on programs designed to maintain organizational competitiveness. Brett, Goldberg, and Ury (this issue, pp. 162–170) describe the strategies of dispute system designers, specialists attempting to intervene in organizational conflict, intended to reduce the costs of conflict to the organization and to the individual while simultaneously resulting in conflict resolution.

With increasing office automation and the introduction of advanced technology to employee and managerial workstations, corporations have renewed interest in the potential contributions of ergonomics to the design of effective person–machine systems. Turnage (this issue, pp. 171–178) discusses the impact of the new technologies on the individual employee, on management methods, and on organizational structure and design. She stresses the need for a balance between technological development and human resource management needs.

Developing leaders for tomorrow

Psychologists have long been interested in the study of leadership processes; organizations have long been interested in the problems of selecting and developing managerial and executive talent. This section of the special issue presents what psychologists know about leadership in organizations and about how that knowledge can be applied to the problems of management and executive development.

An important place to begin is with an understanding of the concepts of power and leadership. Power is a major factor of organizational life, one that cannot be ignored if we hope to understand and improve the functioning of organizations from within (Mintzberg, 1983). It is also clearly intertwined with an understanding of leadership processes (Hollander, 1985). Hollander and Offermann (this issue, pp. 179–189) review the extensive literature on power and leadership, arguing for the increasing importance of considering the dynamics of followership in the study of leadership. They document growing organizational concern for the sharing of leadership functions through participation and teamwork and discuss the challenges and issues ahead for organizations as they attempt to integrate increasing numbers of individuals into roles and functions previously reserved for "leaders." These developments are consistent with the changing job attitudes and concerns of workers for more autonomy and self-development discussed earlier.

One of the key applications of psychological research on leadership in organizations is in the area of leadership development. Simulations have been used extensively for this purpose, and Thornton and Cleveland (this issue, pp. 190–199) carefully detail their forms, successes, and problems. They also propose a sequential model of management development activities based on the arrangement of training activities in terms of increasing cognitive complexity requirements.

The demand for innovative and creative leaders who can form successful new companies has led to studying entrepreneurship (Stevenson & Gumpert, 1985), the process of new business ventures being created by individuals with a vision of how to do things better by establishing their own firms. Likewise, traditional organizations have been concerned with trying to duplicate the kind of spirit and enthusiasm of entrepreneurial activity within their own corporate structures through a process now called "intrapreneurship." Hisrich's article (this issue, pp. 209–222) outlines the current research on entrepreneurship and intrapreneurship, much of which to date has focused on characteristics of entrepreneurs themselves. Opportunities for psychological research on new venture creation are discussed, and appear ripe for study.

The demographic destiny discussed earlier highlights the importance of integrating persons of different sexes and races into the organizational mainstream. Although progress has been made in getting women and minorities into organizations, there is a growing concern with their advancement prospects. Women and minorities in top management positions are still exceedingly rare. In 1986, only 1.7% of Fortune 500 corporate officers were women, and the existence of a "glass ceiling" for women where the top can be seen, but not reached, has been proposed (Morrison, White, & Van Velsor, 1987). The situation for minorities is no better. The Bureau of Labor Statistics found that the percentage of minority managers rose from 3.6% in 1977 to 5.2% in 1982 (Jones, 1986). Yet even with this increase, minorities are underrepresented in middle management and almost absent from boardrooms and positions of corporate leadership (London & Strumpf, 1986). Morrison and Von Glinow (this issue, pp. 200–208) address the issues of integrating women and minorities into management positions, discussing the progress and promise of organizations that truly use the strengths of a diverse work force.

Many leadership concerns are unfortunately not well integrated into the strategic planning process of organizations. There is now an increasing awareness that the characteristics of the organization's human resources—its people—must be matched with the nature and strategies of the business (Schuler & Jackson, 1987). No longer can organizations blithely assume that needed personnel—particularly top managers—will be there on demand with the requisite skills and experience to move the company forward or to manage a new acquisition. Again, the demographics of a shrinking work force with fewer individuals possessing the high level of required skills have forced organizations to reconsider practices. Human resource planning programs can integrate job requirements and human resource capabilities to allow for optimal staffing practices, as well as smooth transitions in management succession. Jackson and Schuler (this issue, pp. 223–239) discuss the state of human resource planning and suggest ways in which the needed integration of human resource plans with organizational strategy can be accomplished. They highlight the example of how future leadership needs can be anticipated and met through a comprehensive management succession plan.

Workplace wellness

The workplace, as a prime center for much of the life activity for millions of workers, is also surfacing as a prime center of interest for those concerned about promoting individual health and welfare. This final section of the issue deals with the relationship between work environments and individual health and well-being, including issues of work and family, and the promotion of health through the management of work stress and through establishing employee fitness programs. The section concludes by describing the role of industrial/organizational psychologists in contributing to the creation of healthier workplaces.

There is a growing national concern about the relationship between work and family. Increases in the mean number of hours people work, the growing number of women in the work force, and the increased participation of women with preschool children in the work force discussed earlier have led to concern about balancing the demands of work and family settings. Zedeck and Mosier (this issue, pp. 240–251) review proposed theoretical links between work and family and suggest needed areas for psychological research. They further examine current corporate responses to work and family issues, including child care, parental leave policies, and flexible work arrangements.

Job-related stress is another growing corporate concern (Matteson & Ivancevich, 1987). Pressure and consequent strains on the job may help induce stress-related illnesses (Hall & Savery, 1986). Workers are now suing organizations—sometimes successfully—for worker's compensation in cases of claimed job-induced stress (Ivancevich, Matteson, & Richards, 1985). Between 1982 and 1986, employee damage suits for stress-related illnesses in California increased five-fold (Roberts & Harris, 1989). Ivancevich, Matteson, Freedman, and Phillips (this issue, pp. 252–261) discuss the state of the art of stress management interventions in the workplace, including the targets of change, levels of activity, and desired outcomes. They review published studies of implemented organizational programs and suggest areas for future study.

One option being implemented in many organizations is a physical fitness program. Although some employers are investing large sums of money on such programs, their value in reducing stress and increasing productivity have yet to be firmly established (Falkenberg, 1987). Gebhart and Crump (this issue, pp. 262–272) describe some of the major corporate attempts at fostering physical fitness and evaluate the claims made for their impact on the individual and corporate "bottom line."

Finally, Ilgen (this issue, pp. 273–283) overviews research on health at work, with a particular focus on how industrial/organizational psychologists can contribute to its understanding and improvement. Although programs directed toward individual coping and health are important, Ilgen argues that the unique training of industrial/ organizational psychologists fosters a broader, problem-solving approach toward health at work. Options such as job redesign, which can be directed at changing the organization to reduce the stresses placed on workers, should be extremely useful. Thus, a combined individual and organizational approach to health at work may be optimal.

Implications for education and training of industrial/organizational psychologists

Just as the myriad changes in organizations are putting demands on the American school system to better prepare today's students to become tomorrow's workers, these changes need to be considered by programs training psychologists to work in tomorrow's organizations. The roles of I/O psychologists are broadening and may include being an analyst, technical expert, educator, consultant, change agent, facilitator, manager, team builder, or human resource strategist (London & Moses, 1989). Organizations of the future will place numerous demands on psychologists hoping to work with them, study them, and improve them.

I/O psychologists must communicate with nonpsychologists

The framework for understanding human behavior at work that psychology offers can be of enormous assistance to organizations. The articles in this issue give ample testament to the kind of contributions psychologists can make. These contributions stem from the strong training I/O psychologists receive in the scientific method. We are able to design studies that help management make better decisions based on empirical data. However, our contributions can be made only if our studies are understood and valued and our recommendations given close consideration. Ultimately, we, as psychologists, have limited abilities to make any real change in organizations ourselves without the support and backing of top corporate management. In the final analysis, we often must "sell" our research and its resulting implications to organizations, making them aware of its potential and limitations. We can help make organizations more productive and allow management to make data-driven decisions rather than purely judgmental ones if we can communicate the importance of our methods and techniques to decision makers. Because they are trained in different areas, many of these individuals will not immediately grasp some of the values that we accept without hesitation. The need for costly control groups must be explained, and the state-of-the-art statistics taught with pride in graduate courses may be less believed than simple percentages. We must maintain high professional standards ourselves while translating our results effectively to those who do not know—or do not want to know—all the impressive evidence on which we have based our conclusions.

Our function as practitioners in organizations is to take our psychological training and integrate it with the demands of business. We may be the experts on research design and methodology, but without justifying the costs in lay terms, our designs may acquire more threats to validity than we would hope for. Our ability to translate existing research into workable organizational solutions requires strong communication skills. One successful I/O psychologist who is also a corporate manager claims an acid test for deciding whether to hire a new I/O PhD for his organization. The candidate is asked to summarize his or her dissertation in five minutes or less in lay terms. Failure on this task does not bode well for later communication with decision makers who lack psychological training.

I/O psychologists must speak the language of business

In garnering support for our activities, I/O psychologists need to be able to speak the language of business. Many I/O PhD recipients graduate without any exposure to key areas of business and economics. Basic competencies in these areas would facilitate communication enormously. So would the ability to cost out our research, testing programs, and training and development programs in terms of the ultimate "bottom line" of dollars. Recent work by Cascio (1987) and others on costing human resource activities is vitally important to convincing those in power that dollars spent on human resource activities can be dollars saved in the long run. Given the current focus on competitiveness, appeals to altruism, scientific advancement, or societal gain are less likely to meet with success.

For example, the recent widespread burst of interest in child care and family issues by organizations is undoubtedly due to the need to attract and retain well-trained, talented workers who are also young parents. Companies with good childcare arrangements and flexible working hours are those routinely rated as the best companies for which to work. As talent becomes scarce, it makes good economic sense for companies to use such progressive policies as tools for recruitment. Similar arguments could be made for worksite health promotion. We must be prepared to make and support those economic arguments.

I/O psychologists must understand individual and organizational diversity

The changes documented earlier show that both workers and organizations are becoming increasingly diverse. Psychologists have traditionally been well-trained in understanding individual differences, a strength that should be retained. Social psychological perspectives on group differences and methods for understanding and fostering cooperation in and between groups also provide important insights. Yet in order to be maximally effective in organizations, psychologists also need to comprehend the myriad differences between organizations. Different corporate strategies, goals, and cultures produce radically different organizations. In addition to formal study of organizational culture, exposure to multiple organizations during graduate training through multiple internships or practicums should be encouraged to broaden perspectives on organizational environments and their impact.

I/O psychologists must be open to interdisciplinary solutions

Many of the areas of concern highlighted in this issue cross over speciality areas within psychology and over academic disciplines as well. For example, work in team development should integrate basic research in group processes from social psychology and sociology into the applied concerns of organizational psychologists. Workplace wellness issues clearly concern individuals with backgrounds in medicine and physiology as well as those in the areas of I/O and clinical psychology. Integration of human and machine resources requires an overlap between psychology, computer science, cognitive science, and engineering.

Broader training in psychology will be important for I/O psychologists, who will increasingly need to be familiar with the developmental issues inherent in the study of careers, gerontological research on older workers, clinical issues in the mental health of workers, and learning theory perspectives on training and retraining (N. W. Schmitt, personal communication, October 5, 1989). A broad grounding in psychology may be our best hope in assuring our ability to bring a unique psychological perspective to organizations. As our individual subspecialities take shape in the course of graduate training, exposure to nonpsychological fields of study should be encouraged as well. Exposure to different perspectives during graduate training may help I/O psychologists to develop an appreciation of, and ability to work with, individuals from differing academic backgrounds as psychologists collectively strive to deal with problems requiring an interdisciplinary perspective. We I/O psychologists need to know not only the unique contributions of our own approaches but also how those contributions can be meshed with others for maximal benefit.

I/O psychologists must find ways to manage their own obsolescence

Psychologists are not immune from the need to refresh and update their own areas of expertise. As indicated by Goldstein and Gilliam in this issue, the "half-life" of engineers is approximately five years—that is, five years after graduation an engineer will be functionally obsolete. What is the "half-life" of an I/O psychologist? How can we best provide for the continuing education needs of I/O psychologists?

Workshops offered twice a year through the Society for Industrial and Organizational Psychology (SIOP, APA's Division 14) are one solution. SIOP's Frontiers of Industrial Organizational Psychology Series (Campbell, Campbell, & Associates, 1988; Goldstein, 1989; Hall & Associates, 1986) is another. A series of books on professional practice issues is also in preparation, with the first volume under the editorship of Douglas Bray. Perhaps there should be other formal methods for psychologists to keep abreast of recent trends and findings. Keeping abreast of the published literature and contributing to its advancement through the conduct and sponsorship of quality research is vitally important. Judging by the preponderance of authors with academic affiliations in our journals, much of the knowledge being amassed by those in full-time practice in organizations is receiving limited exposure. Mechanisms for further broadening this exposure warrant exploration. One purpose of the current special issue is to present relevant, up-to-date information to a broad audience of psychologists working in organizations.

Conclusions

Research and practice in the psychology of work behavior have always responded to the needs of workers and organizations. From the turn of the century to the present, psychologists have been making contributions to understanding workplace behavior and intervening to create safer, healthier working environments. At the same time, needs for increased productivity and competitiveness must also be met if our organizations are to thrive. "The foundation of national wealth is really people—the human capital represented by their knowledge, skills, organizations, and motivations ... the primary assets of a modern corporation leave the workplace each night to go home to dinner" (Johnston & Packer, 1987, p. 116). The challenge of managing and maintaining these precious resources pose unique opportunities for those interested in applying psychological knowledge to the workplace.

Although researchers can, and undoubtedly will, be responsive to the challenges and problems endemic in tomorrow's organizations, they are likely to be always a step behind the changes themselves. When a merger occurs, we can seize the opportunity to study the formation of a new organizational culture and the responses of survivors. Yet what thoughtful consideration about change and transition gives us most is the opportunity to study proactively the one underlying constant of today and tomorrow—change itself.

We need to more fully understand how people react to organizational change and help promote positive, healthy responses to change. For example, why do many people refuse retraining opportunities when offered? How can we change individual coping to more effectively deal with new work environments? There are ample opportunities to study the implementation of change as well. For example, before widespread introduction of a new technology, limited introduction in a carefully studied area might prevent large-scale problems for the organization and generate valuable insight into human responses to a changing work environment.

The changes coming in the next decade will be enormous. The trends described in this article outline a reasonable scenario for what lies ahead. Yet the data we present are *projections,* not reality. The reality of the year 2000 will be affected by decisions being made in organizations today. Policies that encourage or discourage retirement, or facilitate or inhibit the participation of parents in the work force, will undoubtedly influence work decisions made by those groups. Equal opportunity at all organizational levels will also affect employment patterns. Changes in organizations themselves must be brought into line with changes in the nature of the work force. Our best hope for the future is reasoned action in the present.

Acknowledgments

The opinions expressed in this article are those of the authors and do not necessarily reflect the official policy of the U.S. Office of Personnel Management or of the Society for Industrial and Organizational Psychology (Division 14, APA). We thank Robert D. Caplan, Manuel London, George Rebok, and Neal Schmitt for their helpful comments on an earlier draft of this article.

Special thanks are extended to Leonard Goodstein for championing this special issue, to Matthew Zalichin for his editorial expertise, and to the many authors and reviewers whose professionalism and patience throughout a long process made coordinating this project much easier.

Note

1 The criteria for excellence proposed by Peters and Waterman (1982) include a bias for action; staying close to the customer; autonomy and entrepreneurship; productivity through people; hands-on, value driven (executives stay in touch with the firm's essential business); stick to the knitting (remain with the business the company knows best); simple

form, less staff, fewer layers of administration, fewer people at the top; and simultaneous loose-tight properties (i.e., a climate where there is dedication to the central values of the company with tolerance for all employees accepting those values).

References

Age Discrimination in Employment Act of 1967, Pub. L. 90–202, 81 Stat. 602 (Title 29, Sect 621–634).

Age Discrimination in Employment Act Amendments of 1978, Pub. L. 95–256, 92 Stat. 189 (Title 5, Sect 8335, 8339; Title 29, Sect 621 note, 623, 624, 626, 631, 633a, 634).

Age Discrimination in Employment Act Amendments of 1986, Pub. L. 99–592, 100 Stat. 3342 (Title 29, Sect 621 note, 622 note, 623, 623 note, 624 note, 630, 631).

Albrecht, K. (1988). *At America's service: How corporations can revolutionize the way they treat their customers.* Homewood, IL: Dow Jooes-Invin.

Albrecht, D., & Zemke, R. (1985). *Service America.* Homewood, IL: Dow Jones-Invin.

Arnett, E. C. (1989, July 20). Futurists gaze into business's crystal ball. *Washington Post*, pp. F1–F2.

Beer, M., & Walton, E. (1990). Developing the competitive organization: Interventions and strategies. *American Psychologist, 45*, 154–161.

Bird, C. P., & Fisher, T. D. (1986). Thirty years later: Attitudes toward the employment of older workers. *Journal of Applied Psychology, 71*, 515–517.

Bowen, D. E., & Schneider, B. (1988). Services marketing and management: Implications for organizational behavior. In B. M. Staw & L. L. Cummings (Eds.), *Research in organizational behavior* (Vol. 10, pp. 43–80). Greenwich, CT: JAI Press.

Brett, J. M., Goldberg, S. B., & Ury, W. L. (1990). Designing systems for resolving disputes in organizations. *American Psychologist, 45*, 162–170.

Bruns, W. J., Jr., & McFarlan, E. W. (1987, September–October). Information technology puts power in control systems. *Harvard Business Review*, pp. 89–94.

Bureau of National Affairs. (1987). *Older Americans in the workforce: Challenges and solutions.* Washington, DC: Author.

Campbell, J. P., Campbell, R. J. & Associates. (1988). *Productivity in organizations.* San Francisco: Jossey-Bass.

Cascio, W. (1987). *Costing human resources: The financial impact of behavior in organizations* (2nd ed.). Boston: Kent.

Cascio, W. F. (1986). *Managing human resources.* New York: McGraw-Hill.

Cocheu, R. (1989). Training for quality improvement. *Training and Development Journal. 43*, 56–62.

Colburn, D. (1989, August 29). Early retirement by men linked to job stress. *Washington Post* (Health Supplement), p. 5.

Collins, E. G. C. (1986). A company without offices. *Harvard Business Review, 1*, 127–136.

Committee for Economic Development. (1987). *Work and change: Labor market adjustment policies in a competitive world.* New York: Author.

Dainoff, M. J., & Dainoff M. H. (1987). *A managers guide to ergonomics in the electronic office.* New York: Wiley.

Davey, B. W., & Jacobson, L. S. (Eds.). (1987). *Computerizing human resource management.* Alexandria, VA: International Personnel Management Association.

Dennis, H. (1988). Management training. In H. Dennis (Ed.), *Fourteen steps to managing an aging workforce* (pp. 141–154). Lexington, MA: Lexington Books.

Drucker, P. F. (1987). Management: The problems of success. *Academy of Management Executive, 1*, 13–19.

Dumas, R. A., Cushing, N., & Laughlin, C. (1987, February). Making quality control theories workable. *Training and Development Journal*, pp. 30–33.

Faley, R. H., Kleiman, L. S., & Lengnick-Hall, M. L. (1984). Age discrimination and personnel psychology: A review of the legal literature with implications for future research. *Personnel Psychology, 37*, 327–349.

Falkenberg, L. E. (1987). Employee fitness programs: Their impact on the employee and the organization. *Academy of Management Review, 12*, 511–522.

Fulmer, R. M., & Gilkey, R. (1988). Blending corporate families: Management and organizational development in a postmerger environment. *Academy of Management Executive, 2*, 275–283.

Galagan, P. (1986, November). Work teams that work. *Training and Development Journal*, pp. 33–35.

Galagan, P. (1987, July). Here's the situation: A quick scan of the trends that experts think will affect you most. *Training and Development Journal*, pp. 20–22.

Galbraith, J. R., & Kazanjian, R. K. (1988). Strategy, technology, and emerging organisations. In J. Hage (Ed.), *Futures of organizations* (pp. 29–41). Lexington, MA: Lexington Books.

Garvin, D. A. (1987, November–December). Competing on the eight dimensions of quality. *Harvard Business Review*, pp. 101–109.

Gebhardt, D. L., & Crump, C. E. (1990). Employee fitness and wellness programs in the workplace. *American Psychologist, 45*, 262–272.

Gilley, J. (1988). Career development as a partnership. *Personnel Administrator, 33*, 62–68.

Goldstein, I., & Associates. (1989). (Ed.). *Training and development in organizations*. San Francisco: Jossey-Bass.

Goldstein, I. L., & Gilliam, P. (1990). Training system issues in the year 2000. *American Psychologist, 45*, 134–143.

Greenhalgh, L., Lawrence, A. T., & Sutton, R. L. (1988). Determinants of work force reduction strategies in declining organizations. *Academy of Management Review, 13*, 241–254.

Griffin, R. W. (1988). Consequences of quality circles in an industrial setting: A longitudinal assessment. *Academy of Management Journal, 31*, 338–358.

Gross, C. M., & Chapnik, E. (1987, November). Ergonomic training for tomorrow's office. *Training and Development Journal*, pp. 56–61.

Grover, R. A. (1987). The management of service organizations. *Academy of Management Review, 12*, 558.

Hall, D. T. (1986). An overview of current career development theory, research, and practice. In D. Hall and Associates (Eds.), *Career development in organizations* (pp. 1–20). San Francisco: Jossey-Bass.

Hall, D. T., & Associates (Eds.). (1986). *Career development in organizations*. San Francisco: Jossey-Bass.

Hall, K., & Savery, L. K. (1986, January–February). Tight rein, more stress. *Harvard Business Review*, pp. 160–164.

Hamilton, M. H. (1988, July 10). Employing new tools to recruit workers, *Washington Post*, pp. H1, H3.
Hardaker, M., & Ward, B. K. (1987, November–December). Getting things done: How to make a team work. *Harvard Business Review*, pp. 112–119.
Hayes, R. H., & Abernathy, W. J. (1980, July–August). Managing our way to economic decline. *Harvard Business Review*, pp. 67–77.
Hill, C. W. L., Hitt, M. A., & Hoskisson, R. E. (1988). Declining U.S. competitiveness: Reflections on a crisis. *Academy of Management Executive, 2*, 51–60.
Hisrich, R. D. (1990). Entrepreneurship/intrapreneurship. *American Psychologist, 45*, 209–222.
Hitt, M. A., & Ireland, R. D. (1987). Peters and Waterman revisited: The unended quest for excellence. *Academy of Management Executive, 1*, 91–97.
Hoffman, L. W. (1989). Effects of maternal employment in the two-parent family. *American Psychologist, 44*, 283–292.
Hollander E. P. (1985). Leadership and power. In G. Lindzey & E, Aronson (Eds.), *Handbook of social psychology* (3rd ed., pp. 485–537). New York: Random House.
Hollander, E. P., & Offermann, L. R. (1990). Power and leadership in organizations: Relationships in transition. *American Psychologist, 45*, 179–189.
Horowitz, F. D., & O'Brien, M. (1989). In the interest of the nation: A reflective essay on the state of our knowledge and the challenges before us. *American Psychologist, 44*, 441–445.
Ilgen, D. R. (1990). Health issues at work: Opportunities for industrial/organizational psychology. *American Psychologist, 45*, 273–283.
Ivancevich, J. M., Matteson, M. T., Freedman, S. M., & Phillips, J. S. (1990). Worksite stress management interventions. *American Psychologist, 45*, 252–261.
Ivancevich, J. M., Matteson, M. T., & Richards, E.P.III (1985, March–April). Who's liable for stress on the job? *Harvard Business Review*, pp. 60–72.
Jackson, S. E., & Schuler, R. S. (1990). Human resource planning: Challenges for industrial/organizational psychologists. *American Psychologist, 45*, 223–239.
Jemison, K. B., & Sitkin, S. B. (1986, March–April). Acquisitions: The process can be a problem. *Harvard Business Review*, pp. 107–116.
Johnston, W. B., & Packer, A. H. (1987). *Workforce 2000: Work and workers for the twenty-first century.* Indianapolis, IN: Hudson Institute.
Jones, E.W., Jr. (1986, May–June). Black managers: The dream deferred. *Harvard Business Review*, pp. 84–93.
Katzell, R. A., & Thompson, D. E. (1990). Work motivation: Theory and practice. *American Psychologist, 45*, 144–153.
Kerr, J., & Slocum, J. W., Jr. (1987). Managing corporate culture through reward systems. *Academy of Management Executive, 1*, 99–108.
Kraut, R. E. (1987). Social issues and white-collar technology: An overview. In R. E. Kraut (Ed.), *Technology and the transformation of white-collar work* (pp. 1–21). Hillsdale, NJ: Erlbaum.
Lengel, R. H., & Daft, R. L. (1988). The selection of communication media as an executive skill. *Academy of Management Executive, 2*, 225–232.
Lenway, S. A. (1985). *The politics of U.S. international trade: Protection, expansion, and escape.* Boston: Pitman.

Levinson, H. (1988). You won't recognize me: Predictions about changes in top-management characteristics. *Academy of Management Executive, 2*, 119–125.

Lodge, G. C., & Crum, W. C. (1985, January–February). U.S. competitiveness: The policy tangle. *Harvard Business Review*, pp. 34–42, 46–52.

London, M., & Moses, J. L. (1989, August). *The changing roles of the industrial/organizational psychologist: From analyst/technician to change agent/strategist.* Paper presented at the meeting of the American Psychological Association, New Orleans.

London, M., & Strumpf, S. A. (1986). Individual and organizational career development in changing times. In D. T. Hall and Associates (Eds.), *Career development in organizations* (pp. 21–49). San Francisco: Jossey-Bass.

Lueder, R. K. (1986) *The ergonomics payoff: Designing the electronic office.* Lawrence, KS: Ergosyst Associates.

Martin, A. (1989, July). There's no place like home ... to work. *Human Resource Executive*, pp. 50–51.

Matteson, M. T., & Ivancevich, J. M. (1987). *Controlling work stress.* San Francisco: Jossey-Bass.

McEvoy, G. M., & Cascio, W. F. (1989). Cumulative evidence of the relationship between employee age and job performance. *Journal of Applied Psychology, 74,* 11–17.

Miller, K. (1989). *Retraining the American workforce.* Reading, MA: Addison-Wesley.

Mintzberg, H. (1983). *Power in and around organizations.* Englewood Cliffs, NJ: Prentice-Hall.

Mitchell, J. M., & Anderson, K. H. (1989, Summer). Mental health and the labor force participation of older workers. *Inquiry*, pp. 262–271.

Mitroff, I. I., & Mohrman, S. A. (1987). The slack is gone: How the United States lost its competitive edge in the world economy. *Academy of Management Executive, 1,* 65–70.

Moriarty, R. T., & Swartz, G. S. (1989, January–February). Automation to boost sales and marketing. *Harvard Business Review*, pp. 100–109.

Morrison, A. M., & Von Glinow, M. A. (1990). Women and minorities in management. *American Psychologist, 45,* 200–208.

Morrison, A. M., White, R. P., & Van Velsor, E. (1987). *Breaking the glass ceiling: Can women reach the top of America's largest corporations?* Reading, MA: Addison-Wesley.

Odiorne, G. S. (1986). The crystal ball of HR strategy. *Personnel Administrator, 31,* 103–106.

Peters, T. J., & Waterman, R. (1982). *In search of excellence.* New York: Harper & Row.

Peters, T. J. (1988). Restoring American competitiveness: Looking for new models of organizations. *Academy of Management Executive, 2,* 103–109.

Phillips, R. C. (1988, September). Manage differences before they destroy your business. *Training and Development Journal*, pp. 66–71.

Plant, R., & Ryan, M. (1988, September). Managing your corporate culture. *Training and Development Journal*, pp. 61–65.

Proshansky, H. M., Ittelson, W. H., & Rivlin, L. G. (Eds.). (1976). *Environmental Psychology: People and their physical settings.* New York: Holt, Rinehart & Winston.

Quaintance, M. K. (1989). Internal placement and career management. In W. Cascio (Ed.), *Human resources planning, employment, and placement* (pp. 200–235). Washington, DC: Bureau of National Affairs.

Quinn, J. B., & Gagnon, C. E. (1986, November–December). Will services follow manufacturing into decline? *Harvard Business Review*, pp. 95–103.
Rauch, J. (1989). Kids as capital. *The Atlantic*, August, 56–61.
Rhodes, S. R. (1983). Age-related differences in work attitudes and behavior: A review and conceptual analysis. *Psychological Bulletin, 93*, 328–367.
Riche, M. (1988). America's new workers. *American Demographics, 10*, 34–41.
Roberts, M., & Harris, G. T. (1989, May). Wellness at work, *Psychology Today*, pp. 54–56, 58.
Ropp, K. (1987, February). Restructuring: Survival of the fittest. *Personnel Administrator*, 45–47.
Schein, E. H. (1981). Increasing organizational effectiveness through better human resource planning and development. In D. E. Klinger (Ed.), *Public personnel management: Readings in contexts and strategies* (pp. 87–104). Palo Alto, CA: Mayfield).
Schein, E. H. (1990). Organizational culture. *American Psychologist, 45*, 109–119.
Schuler, R. S., & Jackson, S. E. (1987). Linking competitive strategies with human resource management practices. *Academy cf Management Executive, 1*. 207–219.
Schweiger, D. M., Ivancevich, J. M., &.Power, F. R. (1987). Executive actions for managing human resources before and after acquisition. *Academy of Management Executive, 1*, 127–138.
Skrzycki, C. (1989, August 20). The drive to downsize. *Washington Post*, pp. B1.
Smith, M. R. (1987). Improving product quality in American industry. *Academy of Management Executive, I*, 243–245.
Society for Human Resource Management. (1988). *Survey of childcare practices.* Alexandria, VA: Author.
Steers, R. M., & Miller, E. L. (1988). Management in the 1990s: The international challenge. *Academy of Management Executives, 2*, 21–22.
Stein, B. A. (1983). *Quality of work life in action: Managing effectiveness.* New York: American Management Association.
Sterns, H. L., & Alexander, R. A. (1988). Performance appraisal of the older worker. In H. Dennis (Ed,), *Fourteen steps to managing an aging workforce.* (pp. 85–93). Lexington, MA: Lexington Books.
Stevenson, H. H., & Gumpert, D. E. (1985, March–April). The heart of entrepreneurship. *Harvard Business Review*, pp. 85–94.
Stone, P. J., & Luchetti, R. (1985, March–April). Your office is where you are. *Harvard Business Review*, pp. 102–117.
Sundstrom, E. (1986). *Work places: The psychology of the physical environment in offices and factories.* New York: Cambridge University Press.
Sundstrom, E., De Meuse, K. P., & Futrell D. (1990). Work teams: Applications and effectiveness. *American Psychologist, 45*, 120–133.
Thornton, G. C., & Cleveland, J. N. (1990). Developing managerial talent through simulation. *American Psychologist, 45*, 190–199.
Turnage, J. J. (1990). The challenge of new workplace technology for psychology. *American Psychologist, 45*, 171–178.
Tuttle, T. C. (1988). Technology, organizations of the future, and non-management roles. In J. Hage (Ed.), *Futures of organizations*, (pp. 163–180). Lexington, MA: Lexington Books.

U.S Bureau of Labor Statistics. (1987, August). *Press release* (No. 87-345). Washington, DC: U.S. Department of Labor.

U.S. Bureau of the Census. (1986). *Estimates of the population of the U.S. by age, sex, and race. 1980–1985* (Current Population Reports, Series P-25, No. 985). Washington, DC: U.S. Government Printing Office.

Waldman, D. A., & Avolio, B. J. (1986). A meta-analysis of age differences in job performance. *Journal of Applied Psychology, 71*, 33–38.

Zedeck, S., & Mosier, K. L. (1990). Work in the family and employing organization. *American Psychologist, 45*, 240–251.

61

THE INTERNET AND INDUSTRIAL/ORGANIZATIONAL PSYCHOLOGY

Practice and research perspectives

Michael M. Harris

Source: *Journal of e-Commerce and Psychology* 1(1) (2000): 8–24.

Abstract

This paper addresses practice and research perspectives regarding the Internet and Industrial/Organizational (I/O) Psychology. First, I discuss some current and near future uses of, as well as issues regarding, the Internet in I/O psychology. Although current use of the Internet by I/O psychologists is primarily for collection of data and dissemination of information, potential challenges such as privacy concerns, demand for very fast decisions, and competition from non-I/O psychologists (e.g., technologically-oriented companies) exist. At the same time, the Internet provides new opportunities for I/O psychologists. Second, I propose suggestions for research in various areas, such as recruiting, selection, performance management, and training. This new technology offers some fascinating possibilities for scholarly research.

Introduction

Without doubt, the Internet ranks with television, radio, and probably even the printing press in its importance and effect on the world. As an indication of the widespread influence of the Internet, some now refer to the youngest generation as the "Net Generation." The term "outernet" has come to refer to non-Internet media, such as newspapers and magazines (Silverman, 2000). Despite the ubiquity of the Internet, there has been very little written about the Internet and Industrial/Organizational (I/O) psychology. What has been written by I/O psychologists has focused on professional practice issues (e.g., Harris, 1999; Most & Avolio, 1997). Nonetheless, the technology is rapidly changing and therefore an updated examination of this topic is in order. Just as importantly, there has been practically no writing on the *research* implications of the Internet for I/O psychology. The purpose of the present article is twofold. One purpose is to discuss the implications of the Internet for the practice of I/O psychology. A second purpose is to provide suggestions for research on the Internet within the field of I/O psychology. I begin first with some general thoughts about the Internet, and provide a broad example of an area where the Internet has been heavily used, with implications for I/O psychology.

General thoughts about and one use of the Internet

The Internet, as everyone knows, is widely used for many different purposes. While U.S. retail sales over the Internet were about $20 billion in 1999, they are estimated to reach almost $200 billion by 2004 (Waclawski, 2000). Some experts predict that entire occupations, such as floor traders on the stock exchanges, will become obsolete (Cohen & Silverman, 2000). Others predict that industries that operate in traditional ways, such as banks, will become obsolete as a result of the Internet and other new technologies (Wysocki, 2000). Regardless of the specific outcomes, the Internet will have many profound influences on business, society, and human interaction.

What effect will the Internet have on I/O psychology? I would like to begin by describing in some detail the effect the Internet has had on one area of I/O psychology, namely, recruitment. Although recruitment is not an area that I/O psychologists usually have much direct involvement with in their practice (there is much research, however, on this topic), I believe it is instructive to consider because of the many implications. As is widely known, the Internet has rapidly become a key recruitment source for many companies and job seekers. Its appeal for organizations is that it allows for rapid responses from anywhere in the world that the Internet can be accessed, offers an easy mechanism for applicants to submit resumes, and provides for the efficient sharing of information between organizations and applicants. Applicants have the advantage of being able to very quickly search for jobs of interest and they can sort through those jobs by geographic preference. Some companies have used the Internet for self-screening purposes. For example, Texas Instruments has a web site that contains personality and interest questions and provides a score as to the degree of "fit" with the company (see www.ti.com/recruit/docs/fitcheck.shtml). But the advent of the Internet has generated different forms of recruitment as well. Consider Brett Prager, who recently hired a part-time database programmer for his brother. Rather than going the traditional newspaper or trade newsletter route, Brett contacted FreeAgent.com, a web site where contract professionals list their availability and employers post their job positions. Brett searched through the list of professionals and located resumes of five individuals. His email to them produced three responses in less than one hour. A short time later, he telephoned the top person and settled on an agreeable wage (Ip, 2000).

I find this story fascinating for a number of different reasons. First, and most obviously, I believe that it provides a good illustration of how recruiting has changed. Secondly, I find the speed with which this recruiting assignment was completed to be astonishing. Third, this story appeared in the Wall Street Journal, under the heading "Buying and Selling," and was used to illustrate how the Internet has changed the buying and selling of goods and services, including workers. What I glean from this story, and from other sections of the article, is that I/O psychology's paradigm which implicitly assumes, among other things, a population of full-time, permanent employees, may have to change (see Harris & Greising, 1998). Instead, I/O psychology may need to adopt a different paradigm, at least in some areas. For example, some economists believe that organizations exist only to minimize transaction costs. With a tool like the Internet, which minimizes transaction costs, far more people may be independent contractors (Ip, 2000). Alternatively, perhaps I/O psychologists might argue that the existence of a cadre of permanent, full-time employees can create a sense of commitment, which has additional payoffs to the organization. In short, if a large segment of the workforce becomes contingent workers, and if more organizations use a "virtual" design, what role will I/O psychologists play? I would argue that we could still have a significant role, but our basic theories and models of the workplace *may* need to change.

More to the point, the Internet has the potential to affect many areas of I/O psychology. Just what the effects will be may be more complex than one might initially think. Next, I describe how the Internet is being used in I/O psychology, as well as some trends for the future of the Internet in I/O psychology.

Practice: the Internet and I/O psychology

To learn about how the Internet is being used in I/O psychology and relevant issues, I contacted eight practicing I/O psychologists (their names and affiliations are provided in the Appendix) towards the end of 1999. I aimed for a mix of respondents from both consulting firms and industry. The basic questions I asked each of my respondents revolved around current use of the Internet, how the Internet had changed their work, and their thoughts about the future effects on I/O psychology. I have organized their reactions, and added some of my own ideas, into a section on current uses and a section on challenges and opportunities resulting from the Internet.

Current and near future uses of the Internet

Despite all of the hype in the popular media about the Internet, I/O psychologists are currently using this technology in a less dramatic way than I expected. Specifically, the respondents I talked with indicated that they were using the Internet primarily for two purposes: information collection and information dissemination. In terms of information or data collection, employee surveys and psychological tests appear to becoming increasingly Internet-based. The Internet also appears to becoming the method of choice for disseminating a variety of kinds of information. For example, the Internet is being used to provide updates on change initiatives and to send candidate reports to clients. Neither of these uses is particularly surprising, given that computer-administered testing via CD-ROM has been available for a number of years now, and sending e-mails with attachments has rapidly become a very popular substitute for traditional ways of sending documents (e.g., snail mail or FAX). In short, then, the Internet has become yet another "platform" for a number of I/O psychology products.

Only two respondents indicated a current or near future use that I would count as a major change. One respondent indicated that his/her consulting business had changed as a result of the Internet. This was attributed to the fact that whereas prior to the Internet the firm served only a regional market, this technology enabled the business to have a global market. Aside from the obvious point that products and services can now be used by anyone with a connection to the Internet, the company attributed its expanded market to two features of the Internet. First, the Internet has provided the ability for search engines to identify the company, which has led to more business. Second, the fact that the company is now able to build alliances over the Internet has provided the opportunity for additional business. Thus, for consulting firms at least, the Internet has the potential to make for some big changes. Of course, the disadvantage is the potential for more competition from other quarters, an issue that I will address below in more detail.

Another respondent described how the nature of the jobs his firm works with has changed, which in turn has implications for some of the I/O products provided. Specifically, the firm has changed from supporting "telephone" centers to "contact" centers, as the communication medium is changing from telephone to the Internet. As a result of this job change, the firm is changing its selection systems to assess applicant ability to communicate using email and chat rooms, rather than ability to communicate over the telephone. By implication, then, communication skills differ, depending on the medium used.

To summarize, at present the Internet is having some effect on I/O psychology, but the change it is producing is hardly radical. Some emerging trends, however, suggest that over time the Internet may lead to greater change in I/O psychology. I present those possibilities in the next section in terms of how each issue may present a challenge, as well as an opportunity, for I/O psychology.

The Internet and I/O psychology: challenges and opportunities

My respondents offered a number of different issues that will affect I/O psychology now and in the future. Practically all of the issues they raised may be viewed as challenges or opportunities, depending on how one perceives them and how I/O psychologists will address them.

I/O psychologists with some Internet skills versus Webmasters with some I/O skills

Using the Internet will require I/O psychologists to understand how to capitalize on the strengths of the Internet. Although I/O psychologists will *not* have to know how to create Web pages and implement hardware, I/O psychologists will need to understand how the Internet may best be used. I/O psychologists will increasingly be expected to be able to use the various modalities offered by the Internet to communicate with managers and other users of I/O psychology information. I view this as an opportunity for I/O psychologists to becoming increasingly valuable to their customers. At the same time, I believe that the Internet poses a threat because businesses with technical expertise, but little I/O psychology background, may begin to encroach on the practice of I/O psychology. As an example, I conducted a Web search on hotbot.lycos.com using the key words "employment testing." I was surprised by how many "hits" I received (over 50,000). I examined one such testing site in more detail. The information about the president and developer of this web site indicated that he had a Master's degree in psychology. No information was provided about his experience, research background, or expertise. In short, the Internet can facilitate business opportunities for individuals without the necessary expertise to offer I/O products and services. On the other hand, like many other products offered over the Internet, I believe that "brand names" along with "bricks and mortar" will become increasingly important and merely having a Web page will not be enough for a business to survive.

More information versus privacy concerns

Several respondents mentioned that a major advantage of the Internet is that it will facilitate the creation of large, longitudinal databases. For example, selection testing data, training outcome data, and performance data of various kinds could be input in the same database for each applicant who is hired, facilitating data analysis. An additional advantage of the Internet is that an email message could automatically be sent as a reminder to the responsible party if data is not input for a particular applicant or employee by a predetermined date. One respondent suggested that information might even be stored across companies, if, for example, they are using the same developmental program. The ease with which such information could be stored and manipulated would seem to provide opportunities to develop very large and detailed databases, producing a wealth of scientific information.

At the same time, the challenge for I/O psychologists will be to address possible concerns about the privacy of information. Legislation governing privacy of information provided over the Internet has been discussed in several states (Simpson, 2000), which has the potential to affect I/O psychologists. For example, pending legislation in California would create a state office to investigate the unlawful release of personal information by a government or private enterprise. This pending legislation would also allow for a civil lawsuit if information was released without permission (Simpson, 2000). One of my respondents astutely pointed out that employee concerns about the privacy of information collected over the Internet may be largely a function of the culture of the organization. This is yet another good reason for organizations to develop and maintain a positive culture.

The promise of the Internet versus the acceptance of the Internet

Most respondents described the efficiency of the Internet in collecting, delivering, and disseminating information. For example, one respondent stressed the vast amount of information that users of I/O products and services will be able to access. Personally, I believe that "just in time" training, where trainees will be able to "attend" a training program when they need the information, rather than when the program is offered, is one of the greatest strengths of Internet-based training. Despite the many advantages of the Internet, concern was raised as to whether people will accept the Internet as a means of collecting and disseminating data or whether people will resist this new technology. I am not aware of any studies on this topic, but given the amount of commerce, particularly "business-to-business" commerce on the Internet, it would appear that within the next five years a large number of workers in the U.S will be required to use the Internet in order to perform their jobs effectively. (It would be interesting to determine what percentage of jobs in the U.S. currently involve some use of the Internet.) If this is correct, it would suggest that many employees will be using the Internet, so that it is likely to become as acceptable as the telephone or a paper-and-pencil questionnaire. Of course, it is possible that workers will use the Internet for certain purposes (e.g., purchasing materials), but resist using it for other purposes (e.g., 360-feedback), but I suspect that this will not be the case.

More importantly, however, is the message that the organization may be sending by using the Internet rather than a different vehicle. Take, for example, the case of training. It has been suggested that the way in which training is conducted sends a strong message to employees. The use of classroom training for instance may send a quite different message than Internet-based training. Last year I had the opportunity to present a "live" training program on human resources to a medium-sized non-profit organization. I was informed that the executive director, who attended both four-hour sessions, had just returned from a trip to Asia. When we reached the section on harassment, the executive director communicated briefly, but very clearly, his position of zero tolerance for such behavior to the group. I believe that the message communicated both by his presence and verbal statement sent a far stronger signal than could have been the case in an Internet session. In sum, the challenge will be for I/O psychologists to create and relate the same information and message, both implicit and explicit, using the Internet as compared to other media (e.g., "live" training). I do not think this will be a simple task.

While I believe that certain training may be more efficiently provided over the Internet (e.g., computer skills), I also feel that other training (e.g., employee orientation) may be better provided in a "live" setting.

Data-based decisions versus fast decisions

A theme I heard echoing throughout my discussions was that I/O psychologists, as well as the consumers of I/O psychology, will have more data to work with and will be better able to work with that data than ever before. Take for instance human resource planning. The ability to gather performance data from multiple sources (e.g., 360 feedback) and quickly analyze changes and trends by time and department, can greatly facilitate decision making about future needs and problems. This should mean that data-based decisions become more popular, which I/O psychologists have always championed. But the challenge, as one of my respondents asserted, is to address the speed with which companies perceive they need to make decisions. This respondent felt that our research process has simply become too slow in a world where speed is becoming increasingly important. Will our research become increasingly irrelevant and delayed to be of much use for businesses? I believe that the counter argument is that good research must sometimes proceed slowly. But, as this respondent noted, is that because we have a slow process (e.g., most of the research is done by small teams of researchers, submitting their research to journals that use an extensive, thorough, but slow review and publication process) or is it because our research takes a long time? As this respondent argued, there are faster ways to do research (e.g., use consortia of research groups; enter data to an "on-line" database; gather data from multiple sites) that could produce faster answers to pressing questions. Of course, this leads to questions regarding the rewards for doing research and the value that businesses place on I/O psychology research. I do *not* believe however that this is a new question. It is just that the speed with which businesses want answers is faster than ever.

In sum, I believe that the Internet provides some interesting challenges and opportunities for I/O psychologists. I would submit that how we collectively and individually address these issues will affect the demand for our products and services. Next, I turn to a discussion of research questions regarding the Internet and I/O psychology. Areas to be discussed include recruiting, selection, performance management, and training.

Research: the Internet and I/O psychology

Recruiting

Given the widespread use of the Internet as a recruitment source, it seems reasonable to compare the Internet to other, more traditional forms of recruitment. Aside from the obvious, practical research questions, such as whether the Internet is really quicker and cheaper than other forms, the standard research questions regarding quality and quantity of the applicants are of interest. Assuming that the Internet produces more qualified applicants compared to other sources, the question would be "why?" Is it because more qualified applicants are more likely to use the Internet, because applicants can do a better job of self-screening with the vast amount of information available on the Internet, or are there other reasons? I strongly suspect that the nature of the job (e.g., production worker versus professional employee) will be a moderating variable here. Another important issue that has been raised is whether Internet recruiting will lead to more disparate impact and less diversity in the workforce, due to the demographic characteristics of Internet users (Stanton, 1999). However, this potential issue seems likely to change, as saturation of the Internet continues throughout North America. In short, many questions that have been addressed with regard to traditional recruiting sources need to be explored for the Internet.

The use of the Internet for recruiting opens the door to some additional issues that may be of interest. For example, from a marketing perspective, what are the features of Web pages that most attract potential job applicants? Features may include both graphics, as well as content (for example, the EDS web site provides quotes from and pictures of employees). Some web sites provide extensive information about the nature of the work, pay, benefits, and other topics of concern for job applicants. Web sites might even include the opportunity to exchange email and have chat room discussions, so that recruiters can easily communicate with job applicants. Questions that have been asked with regard to the relative importance of recruiter characteristics compared to job attributes might be reexamined in the context of the Internet. How influential is the Internet web site in attracting applicants? What type of information does the Internet best provide? To what degree does a Web page replace or augment a live recruiter? These and related questions would seem to provide the basis for some interesting, yet highly practical, research for I/O psychologists.

Selection processes

For the I/O psychologist, especially one who focuses on the "I" side of the house, the most obvious application of the Internet is to conduct psychological assessments. Many researchable issues arise in this regard. One need, which was examined years ago in the context of computer-administered testing, involves comparing Internet-based assessments to other delivery methods, such as CD-ROM administrated versions and the classical "paper-and-pencil" approach. The challenge for researchers investigating this question is to offer theory as to why the psychometric properties of an internet-administered test differ from other delivery methods (Lautenschlager & Flaherty, 1990; Richman et al., 1999). Assuming differences emerge, I believe that one cause may be perceptions of the privacy of alternative technologies. Concerns regarding who will see the information provided through the Internet and who may subsequently gain access to such information may compel applicants or even employees to be more careful about sharing socially undesirable information. Beyond psychometric differences, it would be interesting to examine other perceptions, such as test-taker ease completing an Internet-based assessment as compared to paper-and-pencil versions. The growing literature on procedural justice also may be a useful starting point here (e.g., Gilliland, 1993).

The employment interview represents another interesting area for research with regard to the Internet. Surprisingly, in my discussions with I/O psychologists both in a previous paper (Harris, 1999) and for the present paper, there was not a single mention of the effect of the Internet on the interviewing process. I would submit that there are a number of interesting research ideas that derive from the application of the Internet to the interviewing process. First, using the Internet, whether through a chat room or email system, one can completely eliminate the face-to-face component of the employment interview. At first blush, this form of communication would seem to be an improvement for the interview, as it is typically assumed that sources of bias (e.g., race and sex), as well as distracting nonverbal cues, would be eliminated. Research by Motowidlo and his associates, however, has suggested that nonverbal cues may provide incremental validity over the content of interview answers (DeGroot & Motowidlo, 1999; Motowidlo & Burnett, 1995). Comparison of "chat room" interviews, "email" interviews, and live interviews might provide both practically and theoretically rich findings. In addition, much has been written about interviewer-applicant dynamics in the context of the traditional, "face-to-face" interview (e.g., Jablin, Miller, & Sias, 1999). Whether the same set of dynamics apply or whether a different set of dynamics apply in an Internet-based interview needs to be addressed. Because e-mail and chat room discussions can be easily recorded, saved, and retrieved, I believe there is much opportunity for researchers to do interesting research on communication and interaction in the context of Internet-based interviews.

Performance management

I/O psychologists have conducted a vast amount of research regarding certain aspects of performance management, such as the effect of the rating scale, the rater (e.g., self versus supervisor), and the cognitive processes that are involved in making performance judgments. At the same time, there has been relatively less research on such questions as the communication processes and rater/ratee motivation. I believe that the use of the Internet for performance management activities leads to a number of interesting questions to be researched.

In terms of the communication processes, there is some research indicating that people provide the least accurate ratings in a face-to-face meeting with a subordinate (Klimoski & Inks, 1990). Although the exact reason for this is not clear, it seems as though managers are reluctant to provide bad news when they are meeting with subordinates in a face-to-face setting. I believe that using email or a chat room is a more comfortable way for managers to give bad news and therefore they would be more willing to give low ratings and negative feedback to someone over e-mail or even in a chat room as compared to a face-to-face meeting. Thus, I would hypothesize that using these Internet-based communication devices would lead to more accurate ratings. As a corollary, if they are more critical in their ratings, managers will be forced to be more specific and precise in explaining why the ratings are low. Thus, I would expect some interesting ramifications of using an Internet-based performance management system. Of course, in many cases, an Internet-based feedback mechanism might simply be a prelude to a "face-to-face" meeting with one's subordinate, which could change the dynamic of using the Internet, as well as the dynamics of the "live" meeting.

The effect of the Internet on rater and ratee motivation is another interesting topic to examine. As described above, the Internet may help managers feel more comfortable giving low ratings because they do not have to provide the information in a face-to-face manner. Use of the Internet as a way to facilitate the performance management process, by helping develop the rating scale, creating the desired narrative, and providing an easy way to recall previous ratings, may work to make the manager more motivated to engage in performance management activities. For the same reasons, I expect that employees may find the performance management process less intimidating and more useful. Internet-based documents that explain the process, the meaning of the terms, and offer suggestions for improvement may make the performance management process more useful to those being evaluated.

Training

Besides recruiting, employee training is probably the next area of I/O psychology where the Internet's influence has been most profound. As indicated above, I believe that we will find that Internet-training works best for certain areas (e.g., computer skills) and less well for other areas (e.g., employee orientation programs). I believe there is a large number of research questions that might be asked here. I present two of these issues in greater detail.

First, are there certain learning styles that are more conducive to Internet-based training than others? Researchers have investigated individual learning styles and found that they may influence the effectiveness of different training methods. It seems as though in the future, employees might be directed to the method that will be most effective for them, depending on their learning style. This might even be built into an Internet site, where depending on the trainee's score, he or she would be encouraged to go to another Web page or to seek out a "live" training session.

Second, more research on the motivational effects of training, including transfer of training, is needed here. One question to investigate is the motivational impact of the Internet versus "live" training on trainees. As someone who regularly conducts diversity training, I believe that there are trainees who come to such training only because they are required to, but once they begin to listen to the discussions and participate in the exercises, they gain a great deal. I seriously question whether the Internet can really substitute for those "live" experiences. Are there other types of skills, attitudes, and knowledges that are better suited for the Internet setting? This question needs to be examined. In discussions with my graduate and undergraduate students, I have discovered less support for Internet-based classes than I would have expected. Among the major objections, two stand out. First, students seem to indicate that they enjoy the "live" interaction between the instructor and each other, something they seem to feel they cannot reproduce in a chat room or using an electronic bulletin board. Second, students seem to feel that there is more structure in a "live" class, which forces them to keep up with the work. Alternatively, the Internet might be used to augment, rather than supplant, the traditional, "face-to-face" class. At the University of Missouri-St. Louis, for example, we have introduced the On-Line MBA program, which utilizes a combination of "live" meetings with Internet-based sessions. I believe, then, that successful trainers of the future will know how to take advantage of both "face-to-face" as well as Internet options for maximal effectiveness.

Conclusions

I have reviewed practice and research issues regarding the role of the Internet in I/O psychology. My belief is that the Internet provides yet another medium for collecting and exchanging relevant information between organizations, managers, I/O psychologists, employees, and job applicants. I also believe that the Internet opens the door to new tactics and fresh ways of thinking about I/O issues. I do *not* believe, however, that the Internet will immediately produce radical changes in the field of I/O psychology. I believe this latter statement to be true for two reasons.

First, I/O psychology is much different from "commodity" services and products. The most important effect of the Internet is eliminating the "middleman," who helped link the seller with the buyer. As some have indicated, the new opportunity for the traditional "middleman" lies with providing expert advice. This is precisely what the I/O psychologist has always done best. I/O psychologists have never "mass marketed" their products in the sense that books, music, or other commodities are sold.

Second, there are other evolving technologies that may overshadow the Internet in terms of its importance for I/O psychology. Take, for example, virtual reality, which has been available for a couple of decades now. Cox (2000) notes that improving technology, as well as ever faster computers, are leading the way to a variety of new uses of virtual technology. Boeing, for instance, uses virtual technology to allow engineers to work together in a virtual airplane, even though they are working in two different cities. In terms of I/O psychology, in seems quite likely that virtual reality would permit highly life-like, interactive assessment exercises, especially for jobs where complex skills (e.g., law enforcement officers) are important. Training programs could become much more life-like and sophisticated. Telecommuting might become even more popular.

At the same time, over the long-term, I believe that some of our most important paradigms may change as a result of the Internet (Jones, 2000). I strongly encourage

I/O psychologists to stay current with new developments in and applications of the Internet and e-business and to continue to talk with their customers about ways to take advantage of the Internet to provide better services and products.

References

Cohen, A., & Silverman, R. (2000). Expert forecast: Floor traders, manufacturing and money. *Wall Street Journal*, January 1, R25.

Cox, P. (2000). (Un)real world. *Wall Street Journal*, January 1, R40.

DeGroot, T., & Motowidlo, S. (1999). Why visual and vocal interview cues can affect interviewers' judgments and predict job performance. *Journal of Applied Psychology, 84*, 986–993.

Gilliland, S. (1993). The perceived fairness of selection systems: An organizational justice perspective. *Academy of Management Review, 18*, 694–734.

Harris, M.M. (1999, April). Practice network: I-O psychology.com—the internet and I-O psychology. *The Industrial-Organizational Psychologist, 36*, 89–93.

Harris, M.M., & Greising, L. (1998). Contract employment as a full-time career: Implications for HRM/OB constructs. In M.A. Rahim, R. Golembiewski, & L. Pate (Eds.), *Current topics in management* (Vol. 3), Stanford, CT: JAI Press.

Ip, G. (2000). Buying and selling. *Wall Street Journal*, January 1, R23.

Jablin, F., Miller, V., & Sias, P. (1999). Communication and interaction processes. In R. Eder & M. Harris (Eds.), *The employment interview handbook*. Thousand Oaks, CA: Sage.

Jones, J.W. (2000, May). Catching the "virtual HR" wave without wiping out. Invited address, e-HR World.com Conference and Exposition, Anaheim, CA.

Klimoski, R., & Inks, L. (1990). Accountability forces in performance appraisal. *Organizational Behavior & Human Decision Processes, 45*, 194–208.

Lautenschlager, G., & Flaherty, V. (1990). Computer administration of questions: More desirable or more social desirability? *Journal of Applied Psychology, 75*, 310–314.

Most, R., & Avolio, B. (1997, April). On the horizon: Industrial/Organizational psychology in the Web age. *The Industrial-Organizational Psychologist, 34*, 21–30.

Motowidlo, S., & Burnett, J.R. (1995). Aural and visual sources of validity in structured employment interviews. *Organizational Behavior and Human Decision Processes, 61*, 239–249.

Richman, W., Kiesler, S., Weisband, S., & Drasgow, F. (1999). A meta-analytic study of desirability distortion in computer-administered questionnaires, traditional questionnaires, and interviews. *Journal of Applied Psychology, 84*, 754–775.

Silverman, R. (2000). The words of tomorrow. *Wall Street Journal*, January 1, R10.

Simpson, G. (2000). E-Commerce firms start to rethink opposition to privacy regulation as abuses, anger rise. *Wall Street Journal*, January 6, R24.

Stanton, J. (1999, January). Validity and related issues in Web-based hiring. *The Industrial-Organizational Psychologist, 36*, 69–77.

Waclawski, J. (2000, January). The real world: The E-Business revolution—faster than a speeding bullet. *The Industrial-Organizational Psychologist, 37*, 70–80.

Wysocki, B. (2000). The big bang. *Wall Street Journal*, January 1, R34.

Appendix

Respondents
Seymour Adler, Assessment Solutions, Inc.
Andrew Cella, Olsten Corporation
Wade Gibson, Psychological Services, Inc.
Sherry Hoy, Square D Company-Schneider Electric
Jo Ann Johnson McMillan, Bigby, Havis & Associates
Dennis Joy, Reid Psychological Systems
Mark Schmit, Personnel Decisions Inc.
T. Joe Thomas, Nike, Inc.

62

SELECTING FOR CHANGE

How will personnel and selection psychology survive?

Peter Herriot and Neil Anderson

Source: N. Anderson and P. Herriot (eds.), *International Handbook of Selection and Assessment*, Chichester: John Wiley, 1997, pp. 1–34.

Introduction

Traditional personnel and selection psychology is in danger of terminal decline. What an opening assertion in an editorial for the *International Handbook of Selection and Assessment!* Overwhelming changes in the international business environment have fundamentally shifted the nature of work, and therefore the aetiology of organization structures and work design in most industrialized countries over recent years. Personnel and selection psychologists have operated within a period of disjuncture and threat virtually unparalleled in our history. As many practitioners would willingly testify, the demand characteristics on their role in the recruitment process have been transformed from fitting individuals into discrete and stable jobs into selecting for newly created jobs, flexible and transient work roles, innovation potential, organizational fit, teamworking skills, and de-selection, amongst many other newly emergent pressures. This shift is the result of global changes in the business environment, changes that strike at the heart of the dominant criterion-related validity paradigm in personnel and selection psychology and which are rendering it increasingly outmoded and impotent in the world of work.

But surely the evidence fails to support our prophecy of gloom and doom? Membership numbers of both the American Psychological Association Division 14 (SIOP) and the British Psychological Society Occupational Division continue to rise, as do the figures for organizational psychology professional bodies in many other countries. Attendances at organizational psychology conferences are growing in both Europe and the United States; new journals have been launched in several countries; and there has been an increasing number of university programmes in organizational psychology, particularly outside the United States. All of these 'health of the profession' indicators are surely positive? But all are input and demand indicators, driven by an international recognition of the potential role that personnel and selection psychology could play in the modern, post-bureaucratic business environment. None points up the growing concerns, voiced in several quarters over recent years, that elements of traditional selection theory and practice are becoming noticeably obsolete and archaic.

The tenets of traditional selection theory and practice remain rooted in an era of bureaucratic work organization, where stable, specialized jobs in large numbers were prevalent and which largely supported assumptions key to the paradigm. Post-bureaucratic forms of work organization have shifted the ground under the feet of personnel psychologists, resulting in the dominant paradigm becoming increasingly maladaptive. Cascio (1995) aptly quotes Albert Einstein's comment following the first atomic reaction in 1942: 'Everything has changed, except our way of thinking' (*Workplace of the Future*, 1993, p. 2). We hope that this editorial chapter will serve as a paradigmatic 'wake-up call' for personnel and selection psychology, since continuing to ignore the sweeping changes in the environment upon which we theorize and in which we practice will undoubtedly lead to marginalization and eventually to terminal decline. No institution or organization survives unless its culture adapts to the changing demands of its environment (Schein, 1985). We will demonstrate in this chapter that the culture of personnel psychology is changing painfully slowly in response to the immense global challenges of today. And the task is indeed immense. As Howard (1995, p. 548) observes: '... the practice of I/O psychology in the twenty-first century will need to be more like the work environment—fluid, varied, and complex, but customer oriented and just in time'.

We put forward four main arguments. First, that there exist a number of hugely powerful 'environmental drivers' in modern day international business. Secondly, that these drivers have resulted in deep rooted changes in the nature of work within organizations. Thirdly, that the dominant predictivist paradigm is curtailing selection psychologists' responses to these changes, and is becoming increasingly maladaptive to its environment. Fourthly, and by inescapable implication, that these changes in the context of personnel psychology give rise to several far-reaching challenges for selection research and practice, among them the following four:

(i) selecting for change,
(ii) multiple and interactive levels of analysis,
(iii) cross-cultural applicability of meta-analytical findings, and
(iv) generating wider theoretical frameworks.

Figure 1.1 illustrates these themes and therefore overviews the structure of this chapter.

```
Environmental drivers → Changing nature of work roles → Emergent themes in selection and assessment

1. Globalism              1. Restructuring                                    1. Selecting for change
2. Information technology 2. Alternative forms of employment                  2. Multiple and interactive levels of analysis
                                                    Dominant paradigm
3. Knowledge and learning 3. Modified psychological   in personnel and        3. Cross-cultural applicability of meta-analytic findings
                             contracts                selection psychology
4. Markets                4. Requirements for flexibility and innovation      4. Generating wider theoretical frameworks
5. Pace of change         5. Teamworking
```

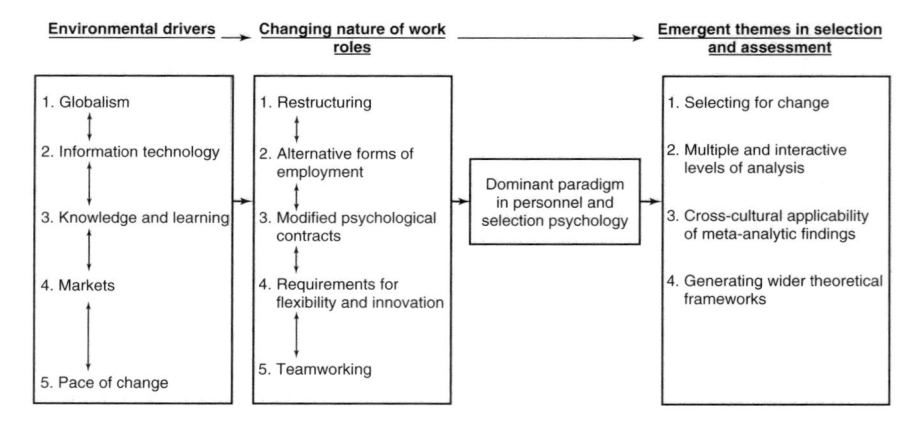

Figure 1.1 The changing nature of personnel and selection psychology

The drivers of change

The changes currently assailing us all are each huge in their own right. In sum they are formidable; in interaction, feeding off each other as they do, they represent a revolutionary shock, a discontinuity in the development of human society (Davis, 1995). Perhaps the most fundamental of them all is 'globalism'. The barriers of space and time are overturned, and finance capital can be transferred at a moment's notice. Tiny changes in interest or exchange rates can have global consequences. Organizations can transfer their functions to wherever offers the most cost-competitive business environment. Some are so at home anywhere in the world that they are no longer identified with a particular country; they are truly transnational (Bartlett and Ghoshal, 1989). Huge corporations can form alliances with each other to open up new markets on the other side of the globe. We are all interdependent now—in terms of our environment, finance, health, safety, mobility and careers.

The main engine for change is information technology (IT). The instantaneous transfer of capital, for example, depends upon the communicative power of IT. Research and development (R&D) teams on the opposite sides of the world can interactively formulate and reformulate scientific models (Sproull and Kiesler, 1986). IT also offers the possibility of adding to our knowledge by enabling us to perceive patterns in data—of 'informating' (Zuboff, 1988). It helps us to learn by providing instant symbolic feedback from our actions. And it can control processes or aid decisions.

The growth of knowledge is exponential, and according to Prahalad and Hamel (1990), knowledge in the form of the core competence of the corporation is now the major source of competitive advantage. Such knowledge is hard to imitate and adds unique value to the customer. Knowledge is three sided—*knowing that, knowing how*, and *knowing beyond* (Herriot and Pemberton, 1994). Gaining information, using it in practice, and learning from that use to envisage a different future are now the key processes in knowledge-based organizations.

With the erosion of many trade barriers and the deregulation of various industry sectors, new markets are constantly opening up, and competition for them is ever keener. Organizations both annexe and create new niche markets for themselves, and prospector companies (Sonnenfeld and Peiperl, 1988) move into and out of markets with speed and effect. The need to satisfy the short-term requirements of the shareholders for dividends, especially in the United States and the United Kingdom (Hutton, 1994), adds to the attractiveness of such a strategy.

The diversity of the new markets results in strongly differentiated demand and the need to customize goods and services to suit different markets and even individual customers or clients. 'Think global but act local' is the new motto. And speed to market of goods and services is a source of competitive advantage, with compressed design cycles being critical in the time spent in development, production and transportation. Moreover, obsolescence of these same goods and services is even faster, so the product cycle is under constant pressure from both ends.

The pace of change is thus increasing exponentially, with its speed and unpredictability making long-term planning next to impossible (Hosking and Anderson, 1992). Furthermore, the adaptations required of organizations and individuals are now so frequent that the pressure of new learning and new relationships, and feelings of never returning to a steady, routinized state, are highly prevalent amongst individuals at work. As we mentioned above, the impact of each of these environmental drivers is multiplicative and is a function of their interaction with one another. For example, globalism continuously opens up new markets, which further differentiate demand. Information technology adds to knowledge, which increases the rate of change.

The changing nature of work roles

Organizational responses

Faced with an environment that is transforming itself, how are organizations to survive? The evolutionary analogy has proved irresistible to commentators. To quote Howard again (1995, p. 522):

> An organism's survival doesn't depend on overall 'fitness', which is impossible to define, but on the niche it is filling, what other organisms are around, what resources it can gather, and to some extent its past history. Organizations likewise must engage in this dance of co-evolution with their wafting webs of economic and political dependencies. They must keep open as many options as possible and strive for what is not necessarily optimal, but advantageous and workable.

But this is a prescriptive rather than a descriptive account. There are three strategic responses which organizations have favoured over the last decade: cost-cutting, customer-facing and innovation (Williams and Dobson, Chapter 11 in this volume). Of these, cost-cutting has been favoured in the Anglo-Saxon countries (e.g. North American and Northwest European countries), and has consequently received most attention. Moreover, when we consider the drivers of change to which cost-cutting is a strategic response, it is clear that it is only the increase in competition that this strategy is fundamentally designed to address.

Cost-cutting has been addressed in two basic ways. First, by various forms of restructuring, and secondly by attempts to increase productivity so that the same amount of work can be done by fewer and fewer employees. Restructuring has had the fundamental purpose of reducing headcount and hence employment costs. The reduction of cost is immediate, and is instantly recognizable to shareholders and financial analysts as a response to the impact of competition. Downsizing, often by means of compulsory redundancies, is the favoured option. Delayering (the elimination of levels in the hierarchy) and devolution of the corporation to profit centres are also frequent, and these latter restructurings also have the purpose of empowering those who deal with customers to meet their needs faster and more flexibly.

Mergers, acquisitions and bankruptcies are ever more frequent; the first two have the purposes of adding to the organization's core capability and at the same time ridding it of a competitor. They often have the additional longer-term consequence of reducing overall headcount. Finally, much of what is not core to the organization's purpose is now being contracted out to external suppliers, on the grounds that this decreases costs by removing the expense of permanent employment. A wide variety of temporary and part-time employment contracts are also now in vogue (Feldman, 1995). Such contracts enable organizations both to reduce costs and also to have employees available for periods of peak demand. There are even so-called zero hour contracts, whereby 'employees' are guaranteed no work at all, but required to work whenever they are needed. It is important to note that while operatives and others at the lower levels of the organizational hierarchy have historically been liable to suffer from these uncertainties, they are now universal throughout organizations (Heckscher, 1995). There are, of course, unavoidable and far-reaching implications from these contractual developments for the theory and practice of personnel selection.

The second major element of the strategy to survive by means of cost competitiveness has been the attempt to increase productivity. This has taken many forms, and has been dominated by a series of management fads (Huczynski, 1993). These have been marketed as packaged solutions by management consultants, and include individual performance-related pay as a means of performance management, and business process re-engineering to reduce and simplify the work-flow. While many organizations have quietly filleted these fads for those elements that are appropriate to their own needs and culture, others have believed that they are the solution to their problems. In general, such fads have been sold to top management, who then passed down the responsibility for implementation to middle managers already doing the work of two. Fads have a shelf life of about two years, and few become deeply embedded in organizations. The consequence is a sequence of fads to which employees have to pretend to adapt.

The results of evaluations of corporate restructuring and management fads are now beginning to come through. It seems that financial performance assessed in a variety of ways has not reliably improved as a consequence of downsizing (DeMeuse, Vanderheiden and Bergmann, 1994). Moreover, a variety of other often deleterious consequences has ensued (Cascio, 1995). These include a variety of hidden costs, such as the need to manage external contractors, and loss of reputation as a good employer. The same applies to the fads, where the psychological consequences of the various interventions were unforeseen, in particular the concerns for equity. Indeed, it is important to explore the impact of restructuring and management fads on individuals and groups in the workplace in more detail, since it is the arena in which we would have expected personnel psychologists to have had an influence. Again, these changes are not without impact upon the field of selection psychology, whether one sits on the practitioner or the academic side of the fence.

Moreover, what we know of the process of innovation in organizations suggests that the psychological consequences of restructuring are actively hostile towards innovation. Yet innovation and creativity at work have become the norm in employers' expectations of the day-to-day behaviour of their staff, not merely a desirable supplementary quality displayed periodically by just a few. Innovation requires: a degree of security so that risks may be taken; autonomy from over-zealous control; a sense of agency such that individuals believe that they can have an impact upon outcomes: and working in teams so as to benefit from diverse perspectives (West and Altink, 1996). Yet restructuring has resulted in job and personal insecurity; tighter control through budget targets; helplessness engendered by a series of organizational and environmental events over which one has had no control; and the reward of individual performance rather than teamwork. It will consequently be extremely difficult to move from a strategy of cost cutting to one of innovation, since the consequences of the former are actively hostile to the latter. Conversely, it is arguable that in the longer term this is the only alternative for post-industrial societies; cost competitiveness will be a necessary but not a sufficient condition for survival. And certainly, many organizations are already selecting for innovation potential amongst prospective employees (King and Anderson, 1995).

The decline of jobs and the emergence of work roles

One way to understand the consequences of restructuring on jobs and individuals is to use the concept of the psychological contract, i.e. the perception of what each party to the employment relationship owes the other (Rousseau, 1995; Herriot and Pemberton, 1996). Downsizing and delayering may be construed by employees as reneging on an existing contract by the organization in which individuals had historically traded their loyalty, expertise and conformity for security and regular promotion and pay increases. As a consequence, both those made redundant and those who survive are likely to experience a range of emotional responses. Insecurity, inequity, powerlessness and loss of organizational commitment are amongst them (Stroh, Brett and Reilly, 1994), especially if the manner of the redundancy pays no attention to the relational nature of the psychological contract (Brockner, Tyler and Cooper-Schneider, 1992; Jackson, Chapter 31 in this volume). Long-serving employees are likely to have gone the extra mile for the organization and been good organizational citizens over and above their job descriptions. Is this the way they are to be repaid from now on, think the survivors? Rousseau (1990) distinguishes such relational from strictly explicit and transactional contracts, and believes (Rousseau, 1995) that the trend will be towards the latter. The employment relationship is becoming shorter; it is moving from insiders to outsiders; and it is changing from being implicit to being explicit in its terms and conditions. And the ideology of human resource management, which construes employees as human capital to be used to achieve business objectives, has taken fast hold upon Anglo-Saxon business culture.

The consequences of such pressures toward business restructuring are already being acutely felt in most sectors of business, whether public service or private sector. The traditional Taylorian-derived, specialized job consisting of discrete tasks and activities is dying, and is being replaced by ever-more flexible forms of work organization (Bridges, 1994; Cascio, 1995; Howard, 1995). Larger organizations which for years had been structured around classical principles of bureaucratic control, authority structures and job specialization (e.g. the armed forces, public sector utilities, monopolistic and oligopolistic companies) are being decentralized, privatized and downsized, and many of their job tasks out-sourced to sub-contractors. And these organizations, we need to acknowledge, are inextricably tied into the historical roots of personnel and selection psychology, particularly in Anglo-Saxon countries. In these organizations stable jobs in large numbers permitted the application of various assumptions, validation techniques, methods and practices. But this context is disappearing, with an increasing emergence of small to medium sized companies, the downsizing of military personnel numbers, sub-contracted labour, homeworking and teleworking, and the inexorable trend toward more flexible, changeable work roles as the latter-day replacements for stable, specialized jobs (see also Sackett and Arvey, 1993; Schmidt, 1993; and Howard, 1995). Of course, we acknowledge that probably there will always be job roles in organizations structured around the design principles of classical bureaucracy, but these are rapidly declining in numbers as internal markets, outsourcing and sub-contracting all take their toll.

Six specific responses

These pressures have resulted in six main responses:

- flexible work roles
- newly created jobs (NCJs)

- teamworking
- concerns over organizational fit
- moves towards a segmented labour market
- proactive career management by the individual

Work roles

Work roles less and less consist of predictable and regular tasks, but of high involvement in solving problems and adding value in new ways (Lawler, 1992). Role-senders are many and varied—colleagues, bosses, customers, clients, suppliers and allies. To meet their changing expectations requires flexibility and adaptability. Employees need a whole range of skills and knowledge over and above their functional or technical competence (which, of course, is itself subject to ever faster obsolescence). Yet the dominant paradigm presupposes a set of tasks that can be defined and which will remain the same for the predictable future (Lawler, 1994).

Newly created jobs

An increasing proportion of job roles being recruited for have not previously existed. Organizational restructuring, downsizing programmes, entry into new markets and the impact of new technology are all drivers toward newly created jobs (NCJs). In a survey of British managers conducted by Nicholson and West in the 1980s (Nicholson and West, 1988), between one-third and one-half of respondents reported that their last move was into an NCJ. It is impossible to use traditional methods of job analysis for jobs that do not yet exist, and so the classical opening gambit of selection psychologists—job analysis—is not relevant.

Teamworking

Innovation and speed to market require teamworking of a high order (Mohrman and Cohen, 1995). Individuals are increasingly interdependent, and work is coming to be seen more and more as the completion of projects. Hence analysis by the organization at the level of individual performance is becoming increasingly questionable and obsolete. The team itself can manage its own members' contributions. Moreover, if selection is for team role rather than for job, then it will have to be for the short term and just-in-time. So will the selection of those on temporary contracts. People will be selected on the basis of reputation, recent performance and team fit. Yet the dominant paradigm implies that selection is always of individuals for long-term jobs, and its artefacts are designed to that end.

Organization fit

For the organizational core, however, selection will be for the longer term. But it is more for organization fit than for job fit that they will be assessed (Schneider, 1987, and Schneider *et al.*, Chapter 19 in this volume). This does not necessarily imply homogeneity, however. To meet its needs for innovation, the organization may require a variety of perspectives (Amabile, 1983; West and Farr, 1990). To understand and deal with its customers better, it may need a comparable demographic mix of employees. In both cases the criterion is fit to the organization rather than to a job. Again, the dominant psychological culture makes the wrong assumption that it is person-job fit which is the sole concern in selection decision-making.

Segmented labour market

As organizations become more knowledge based, the labour market will become more segmented and differentiated; for many of their core experts and managers, the labour market will become a seller's rather than a buyer's one (Mirvis, 1993). Where labour market power is more evenly divided than recently has been the case, the selection procedure becomes more of a negotiation. Each party is trying to decide whether it wishes to select the other as employee or employer, and on what terms. The procedure is a subjective dynamic social process rather than a one-way objective assessment (Herriot, 1989). This is perhaps one of the reasons why the interview is so popular, together with the belief that organization fit is best assessed face-to-face (Anderson, 1992). As Murphy (1986) pointed out, utility estimates are of little use when your first choice turns you down. Of course, these changes in labour market power will not be true of all sectors of the labour market. For unskilled and semi-skilled or workers whose activities can be outsourced or sub-contracted to developing countries to reduce labour costs, the picture looks increasingly bleak. Without reskilling, the labour market (for these workers) looks set to reduce or even disappear. We are therefore facing an increasingly segmented and divided labour market; not by sex or race, as has been the concern for affirmative action over recent decades, but by skills and knowledge. Moreover, selection practices will need to cope with new contractual and geographically distant forms of employment—fixed-term contracts, zero hours contracts, international secondments and placements, and homeworking and tele-working, to name but a few. Once again, we need to critically review the capability of the dominant paradigm to embrace such a diversity of selection scenarios.

Career management

The rapidity of change and the need for everyone in the organization to adapt implies a requirement for career-resilient employees who can take charge of their own development and manage their own careers (Waterman, Waterman and Collard, 1994). Yet at the same time organizations will seek to ensure that their supply of top management talent is developed by job moves designed to remove the gaps in their experience (Hall and Associates, 1986). Self-management implies ownership of assessment information by the individual, and the use of instruments that have other purposes than to predict job performance (see Kidd, Chapter 30 in this volume). And developmental job postings imply selecting people who may not be the best performers. The implication is that selection will change from being a one-off barrier to entry into the organization, so long a taken-for-granted assumption in the predictivist paradigm. It will become a continuous and repeated internal process where appraisal increasingly begins to take on facets of re-assessment and attempted behaviour modification. We return to this final implication later in this chapter.

The compound effect of these six major drivers is to raise pertinent questions over the paradigm-environment fit of personnel psychology, and whether such a fit as presently exists is less than compelling and becoming ever less so. More seriously, we may argue that the dominant paradigm fails to address the present and future needs of organizations. If customer-facing and innovation strategies are going to become more necessary in an era of demanding markets, sharp competition and increasing knowledge, then various changes in personnel strategies and practice become inevitable.

The dominant paradigm

Cultural assumptions

If these environmental drivers and the organizational responses to them are the environment in which personnel and selection psychology itself has to survive, how well adapted is its culture? The dominant paradigm in personnel psychology derives from North America, and may be described in terms of a set of fundamental assumptions, general beliefs, specific values and artefacts. While the following account is doubtless sufficient of an over-simplification as to invite the charge of caricature, it is a useful starting-point.

The culture of the dominant paradigm may be described briefly as follows (Herriot, 1992). Its *fundamental assumptions* are:

- Work is done by individuals
- Work consists of tasks
- Groups of tasks form jobs
- Jobs do not change very much
- Individuals' job performance can be measured and attributed to the individual
- Job tasks require specific attributes
- Individuals' attributes predict job performance
- Individual differences in attributes are the biggest source of performance variability
- Attributes can each be measured independently of each other

- Attributes change relatively little over time
- Selection is by the organization of the applicant, not the reverse
- The main purpose of selection is to predict job performance
- The best job performers are the most suitable employees
- The better the selection, the better the job, team and organizational performance.

In addition to these assumptions about work, people and selection, there are certain more *general beliefs* about the nature of personnel psychology itself, as follows:

- Personnel psychology is a branch of academic psychology
- Psychology is a science
- The theories and findings of science are universal
- Personnel psychology is therefore universal.

Among the *specific values* of the dominant culture in the academic wing of the discipline are the following:

- Approval of one's academic peers and seniors
- Publication in prestigious scientific journals
- Analysis rather than intervention
- Methodological rigour
- Quantitative and statistical sophistication
- Continued membership of invitation-only researcher discussion groups and workshops
- Conferment of honorary awards and titles by academic peers.

The *artefacts* of the dominant culture include:

- Selection procedures designed in terms of the classic criterion-related validity paradigm
- Meta-analysis, validity generalization and utility analysis
- Job analysis and job descriptions
- Theories of individual differences
- Performance ratings of individuals

The consequence of these latter assumptions is a stance towards the environment whereby personnel and selection psychologists perceive themselves as detached scientists and expert practitioners, standing outside both the environmental drivers and the efforts of organizations to adapt to those drivers. They have formulated a body of esoteric knowledge of which, if they are wise, organizations will take account in their personnel policies and practices. This is the classic self-definition of scientists as objective external investigators of the phenomena that they seek to explain and control. Unfortunately, the ground has moved under the feet of academic personnel psychologists: selection research is now *following slowly* after changing events in the workplace in a reactive manner, *not* generating novel perspectives to drive innovative practice.

Problems with the culture

Let us begin by debunking some of these rather grandiose assumptions. Foremost amongst them is the myth that personnel psychology could ever attain the status of a 'pure science'. We would strongly endorse the recent stance of Landy, Shankster-Cawley and Moran (1995, pp. 253–254):

> Adopting a systems perspective requires that we discard the traditional view of selection and placement activities as neutral technologies to be inserted into a system in a rational manner. Personnel activities are part of a system, and as they change or are developed, they influence and are influenced by social, economic, and organizational contexts.

Likewise, the role of the personnel psychologist can never be that of a completely detached expert-scientist, and it is folly to believe that surrounding ourselves with the 'trappings of scientism' will ever raise the status of the discipline. It will not; it will merely marginalize the profession and reduce its influence upon its environment.

The dominant paradigm in personnel psychology values quantified empirical studies, formulaic reconfigurations of established methods and the production of generalized knowledge, the jewels in the crown of the profession over the last two decades being meta-analysis and validity generalization. But the maturation of personnel psychology as a scientific discipline, whilst reaping the benefits of increasingly robust and sophisticated empirical research, has led to a predominant cultural code of mass epistemological conformity. No other sub-discipline in the organizational sciences has exhibited such a paucity of theoretical perspectives, such a lack of debate over guiding paradigmatic assumptions and such unquestioned conformity to naive, managerialist positivism. And if the discipline fails to stimulate a diversity of theoretical perspectives and epistemological approaches, then it runs the risk of becoming an overheated enginehouse of remote, blind empiricism.

Already, the opportunities for an academic personnel psychologist to hole-up in her or his office have become seductive. One can quite feasibly nowadays handle most communications by electronic media, request offprints by remote electronic means, send graduate students out to do all necessary fieldwork, run analyses of secondary data sets, and thus never have to leave the office. Indeed, for academic personnel psychologists there are strong pressures toward isolationism: analysis and writing-up work is less interrupted, a degree of detachment from the day-to-day hubbub of the commercial world helps independent reflection; and one can avoid those troublesome queries from people who should know better (organizational clients, human resource practitioners, students, colleagues, etc.). And if one specializes in meta-analytic procedures, then one need only ever collect-in reports of other people's data sets, thereby avoiding entirely the tiresome need for fieldwork which, after all, is the demeaning workaday world of 'second division' academics.

This leads on to the second concern we have over prevalent beliefs, values and assumptions, namely that the dominant predictivist paradigm can only *ever* furnish an incomplete understanding of the myriad of phenomena and issues that go to make up the dynamic, social psychological milieu of current selection processes. Again, the list that follows is not exhaustive but illustrative of phenomena in the selection process that the dominant paradigm either cannot account for, or would dismiss as inappropriate or inconsequential research questions:

- The processes of selection as opposed to the validity of individual methods
- Psychological and developmental processes that occur in applicants between the times a predictor measure and the criterion measure are taken
- The impact of selection procedures upon applicants
- Applicant rights
- Recruiter abuse of applicants and power-based mistreatment of candidates
- Irrational beliefs and practices amongst recruiters and applicants
- Processual variance between recruiters in their idiosyncratic styles of conducting even highly structured methods
- Erosion of standardization over time (e.g. following the organization-wide introduction of structured interviewing)
- Candidate decision-making—whether to apply, to remain in the selection process, or to accept a job offer
- Impression management by recruiters and candidates
- How the psychological contract is formed and developed by both parties throughout the selection process
- The 'socialization impact' of selection methods as a moderator of predictive validity
- Changes in the job role that alter the criterion domain
- Selecting for organizational and team-level fit
- Cultural, national, historical and societal impacts upon recruitment and selection processes
- The reasons *why* discrimination occurs in practice.

Scientific paradigm or psychic prison?

The above list is clearly a lengthy one, and no amount of organization-specific validity studies or large-scale meta-analyses will begin to address these phenomena. All these practical issues are, in our view, worthy of research attention, and ironically, many will directly impact upon predictive validity but have received little or no attention within the dominant paradigm. Nonetheless, the dominant paradigm is extremely coherent; the values and artefacts that underpin its culture follow logically from its assumptions. We venture that these assumptions have now taken on the characteristics of an ideology, in the sense of an explicit set of beliefs that are embraced as a whole; to question a part is tantamount to rejecting the whole (see also Dachler, 1994). It is likely to be extremely difficult to adapt the culture to its environment if its assumptions are not capable of being evaluated in terms of their appropriateness to the current and future environment. So potent and pervasive is this culture that it almost feels sacrilegious to dare to raise questions over its value.

A comparison with other sub-disciplines in the organization sciences reveals, in stark contrast, just how restrictive the predominant paradigm in personnel psychology has become. In management science and organizational behaviour, for instance, a vociferous dialectic has raged for years between managerial-positivists, post-bureaucratic organization theorists and advocates of labour process theory (Legge, 1995). So vigorous has this debate been that, in comparison, the field of personnel psychology appears bland beyond belief, at least in terms of published outputs and the near absence of theoretical debate. In personnel psychology we have allowed a creeping asphyxiation of published disagreement to occur in which a conservative and conventional epistemological stance has become ingrained into the deepest layers of our culture. It may be that differences of opinion are now only expressed under the cover of the anonymous review process, but certainly the situation has not been helped by our main journals publishing almost exclusively quantitative, empirical studies. Why does selection psychology have no equivalent journal to the *Academy of Management Review* which specializes in theory-building articles? Of course, the *Journal of Applied Psychology* includes theoretical papers in its terms of reference, but how many have appeared over the years? And this is not, we believe, a function of over-restrictive editorial policy so much as a manifestation of the cultural artefacts we listed earlier in this chapter.

The paucity of theoretical frameworks has serious implications, for it limits the range of topic areas that are considered appropriate subjects for study. Yet the environment is forcing governments, organizations and individuals to address other and quite different issues. If the dominant paradigm prevents these issues being addressed, then other professions will annex our territory (Abbott, 1988). It is no accident that, certainly in the Anglo-Saxon countries, HR practitioners and academics have gained prominence in recent years. It is a salutary lesson for personnel psychologists that this increase in the influence of human resource management (HRM) has occurred despite its prescriptive nature and the relative paucity of the evidence it quotes. Whilst personnel practitioners have moved with the times to embrace many of the issues in selecting for change, academic personnel psychologists appear to have fortified themselves into a paradigm that has begun to take on the appearance of a psychic prison. Researchers at times have appeared to obstinately cling to taken-for-granted assumptions that have been by-passed in the real world of post-bureaucratic work organizations. The psychic prison may indeed be built upon the impressive foundations of pure science, its facade monolithic and imposing to the uninitiated, and its interior culture safe and predictable to the privileged longer-term guests, but it is a prison nevertheless. And its institutionalizing effects undoubtedly need to be challenged periodically.

Academic conformity

We raised the spectre earlier that the structure of rewards in the academic wing of our discipline has become dysfunctional. Excessive conformity pressures have starved the discipline of paradigmatic innovation, radical theoretical perspectives, alternative model-building, and attempts toward and the acceptance of novel methodological approaches to applied studies. Many readers will have heard similar arguments in the past, but usually confined to hushed conversations between small cliques of trusted friends in darkened corners of conference anterooms. What exactly are the conformity pressures, how are they enacted, and what effects are they ultimately having upon the well-being of our discipline?

The competition for tenure-track posts amongst early-career faculty is intense, and is followed up by a three-, five- or seven-year period (dependent upon the country in question) of what is effectively probation and socialization. Allying oneself with a powerful senior professor as mentor, together with ingratiating oneself to senior colleagues in the department and in the wider scientific community, are further determinants of survival. Altruistic contributions to the professional society and upholding journal standards by furnishing timely reviews of manuscripts both help. But above all, avoiding controversy, radicalness or ostracism by one's peers is crucial in the repertoire of impression management tactics learned by early-career faculty. The advancement of scientific understanding in personnel psychology would be immensely better served if younger researchers perceived themselves as radical academicians rather than as fledgling apparatchics of their respective professional societies; and if this was reflected by the reward structure. Regrettably, many countries with developed selection research communities have allowed the opposite to become the case.

But such pressures are not confined solely to pre-tenured academics. Far from it. The pressures to 'play the game' by sticking to safe empirical studies, to locate oneself within the confines of the predominant managerialist-positivist paradigm, and not to alienate oneself from an academic elite who wield considerable power have become excessive. Taken in combination, these pressures have resulted in theoretical stagnation, methodological homogeneity, piecemeal deductivism, and the hegemony of 'dust-bowl' empiricism. The evidence of constructive controversy and challenge to the predominant paradigm is sparse, let alone any signs of radical theoretical advance. What controversy there is appears to be almost entirely within-paradigm: disagreements over the calculation of SDy estimates, banding procedures for test cut-off scores, parameters for including studies in meta-analyses, the number of generic personality dimensions, and so forth.

Academic endeavour in personnel psychology seems to have been reduced to a cosy quasi-bureaucratic industry, where multiple empirical factories compete with one another, playing out a game for which the rules are well known, the norms for output type and frequency well established, and an accommodation reached between academics that managerialist-positivist paradigmatic assumptions are better left unchallenged.

How maladaptive is the dominant culture?

What are the indicators that an applied scientific discipline is becoming isolated from its environment? They include:

- An increasing gulf between the interests of academics, consultants and practitioners
- Segregation of practitioners from academics and early-career exclusive specialization into either branch
- Growth of academic numbers sufficient to permit the evaluation of colleagues on all occasions by fellow academics
- Increasing competition for funding from government grants reviewed by academic peers and a decline in direct industrial funding of research
- Acceptance of the need to publish a quantity of outputs above the desire to contribute to an understanding of, or impact upon, phenomena in the field
- Concerns expressed by practitioners that tenure is no longer needed to protect academics engaged in radical or politically sensitive research
- Concerns expressed by academics that practitioners are more at the cutting edge of developing innovative responses in the field
- Practitioners regarding the premier journals in the field as 'irrelevant'
- Academics regarding the premier journals in the field as 'boring'.

Of course, the presence of just one or two of these indicators in isolation does not imply maladaption or marginalization. It is their combined effects over time that is likely to lead to this. There are two lines of argument which suggest that the dominant culture in personnel and selection psychology is on the verge of becoming maladaptive. The first consists of evidence that those who should be acting upon the understandings and recommendations of its exponents are failing to do so. The second delineates the inappropriateness of its assumptions, values and artefacts to either its present and likely future environment or to developing scientific understanding of phenomena in the selection process.

Organizations are part of the environment to which personnel psychology has to adapt, although whether organizations rather than other academics are the more powerful role-senders in the research environment is open to debate. What is clear from the evidence is that although the use of psychometric instruments is widespread, actual practice in organizations does not follow the recommendations that are implied by the dominant culture. If it did, then those instruments most used would be those that had high validity; and selection decisions would be made on an actuarial rather than a clinical judgemental basis.

Smith and Abrahamsen (1992) brought together survey results from six countries: France, Germany, Israel, the Netherlands, Norway, and the United Kingdom. Interviews and application forms were the most frequently used selection techniques in all of them, with cognitive, personality and trainability tests used for between 10% and 20% of vacancies, and assessment centres and biodata used very rarely. The correlation between the frequency of usage of instruments and their validity was negative: $r = -0.25$. The same infrequency of usage of the most valid instruments is also true in the United States (Muchinsky, 1994), where it is rare for information derived from psychometric instruments to be used actuarially (Ryan and Sackett, 1987). Whatever the reasons for these findings, it is clear that the findings from validation studies and meta-analyses as key artefacts of the dominant academic culture have had only a limited impact upon their supposed constituency.

Other evidence suggests that researchers have committed substantial effort toward questions which are regarded by practitioners as being banal, esoteric and self-indulgent. In no other area has this been more blatantly obvious than in utility analysis. Countless minor modifications in the calculation of SDy estimates, excruciatingly slight twists in the configuration of formulae, and tweaks to include hitherto overlooked variables, have spawned literally hundreds of published papers. Many are impressively sophisticated and intricately detail-conscious in their endeavour, but all are grounded upon the fundamental premiss that financial payback is a critical factor in practitioner choice between selection methods. In other words, that the rational-quantitative assumptions and cultural artefacts prevalent amongst the personnel psychology research community will naturally be applicable to practising HR specialists and line managers. They simply are not. In a paper provocatively titled *'The futility of utility analysts'*, Latham and Whyte (1994) found that experienced managers were indeed influenced by the provision of utility analysis findings in addition to general validity information and expectancy tables—but in a negative direction! Managers were *less* likely to implement more valid selection methods when given the financial payback results of utility analysis. Yet, the power to persuade practitioners to adopt more valid methods supposedly conferred upon personnel psychologists by utility analysis has been the justification offered for the monumental research effort in this area.

The thorny question of whether researchers have wasted their time, undoubted talents and technical expertise is subservient in our view to the concern we have of why it has taken so long for a paper challenging the guiding premise that financial payback is paramount to be published. Our point then is not to criticize utility analysis *per se*. Indeed, Boudreau, Sturman and Judge (Chapter 15 in this volume) present a cogently argued case for on-going and important work in this area. Rather, this is just one of several possible exemplars of taken-for-granted assumptions in personnel psychology being unchallenged and left uncriticized. In such a climate there is always a danger that false consensus may lead to the myopia of technical–statistical sophistication over-stepping its rational and epistemological bounds. It may remain unchecked by a telling lack of constructive controversy over underlying assumptions within the research community, or by any concern about whether practitioners find it in the least useful. We argue that researchers need to critically examine more often the veracity of taken-for-granted assumptions in personnel psychology; in short, to ask of ourselves the ultimatums *why* and *for what purpose* much more frequently than seems to be the case at the moment.

A multi-cultural framework

Questions of reason and purpose are critical. We argue that the fundamental beliefs of the dominant paradigm about the nature of personnel psychology itself are now outmoded. If we are to adapt successfully, then we will have to engage in double-loop learning (Argyris and Schon, 1978), which forces us to reflect upon our beliefs and activities. We need to question why particular research questions are being pursued, who is likely to benefit from such knowledge, and make self-regulatory judgements over the appropriate level of resourcing and time dedicated to each, competing research question. Personnel psychology, particularly in North America, has developed notable strengths in single-loop learning—questioning and improving how we do what we do (Argyris and Schon, 1978). Indeed, it can be argued that this is one factor that accounts for the methodological sophistication and quantitative–empirical excellence so evident in North American journals. Our point is that, in a period of environmental disjuncture and upheaval such as we are presently witnessing, single-loop learning alone is not enough. We need to critically appraise our underlying beliefs and values.

To recapitulate, these beliefs suggest that personnel and selection psychology is an objective body of knowledge that has universal application; it is an applied science. Such assumptions reflect a narrow, largely Anglo-Saxon view of the way in which psychological knowledge is acquired and applied. We would argue that national cultures are pivotal. It is true that they are being affected by the environmental drivers, but cultural differences are deep and will ever remain so. Such differences will profoundly influence the ways in which organizations and individuals in those nations or regions respond to the environmental drivers. They will also influence the culture of personnel psychology within them in two ways. First, the assumptions, values and artefacts of the national culture will affect those of its psychologists, just as they influence the organizations based in that country. Secondly, different stakeholders in personnel psychology have different degrees of influence in different countries; such differences in role-senders affect the culture's response to them. Hence the impact of personnel psychology upon organizations is mediated through national cultures. It follows that to ignore such differences and to attempt to apply globally the assumptions, values and artefacts of the dominant Anglo-Saxon personnel culture is doomed to failure (see Figure 1.2).

Recently, the effects of national cultural differences upon business and organization have been suggested (Hofstede, 1980; Trompenaars, 1993). Underlying

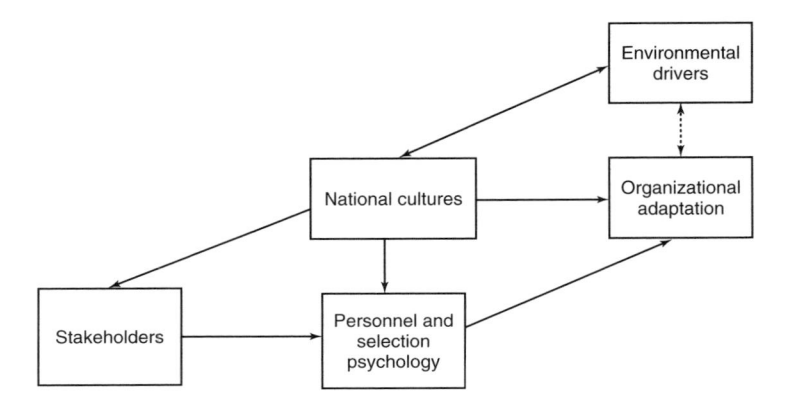

Figure 1.2 The role of personnel and selection psychology: a cross-cultural perspective

dimensions of the different assumptions embodied in various national cultures are now clear. They are (with some differences in terminology and emphasis): *universalism* versus *particularity*; *individualism* versus *collectivism*; *affectively neutral* versus *affectivity*; *specific* versus *diffuse*; *achievement* versus *ascription*; and *internal* versus *external locus of control*. The Anglo-Saxon cultures tend towards the first-mentioned polarity of each of these dimensions.

So, universalist Anglo-Saxons are more likely to believe the abstract generalizations and moral laws apply everywhere, whereas other cultures (e.g. Japan) are more likely to think differently about particular situations or relationships. Individualist Anglo-Saxons focus on their own individuality and their personal objectives rather than on their group or community membership and common objectives. The French, Italians, Irish and Japanese are more collective. Objectivity, detachment and instrumentality are recommended in American and Northwest European business activity, allowing people to remain affectively neutral, or at least to separate the emotional from the reasoning processes. Others such as the Italians mix them together. Specific Anglo-Saxons split up relationships at work into areas, e.g. collaboration on a task, whereas others generalize across from the particular to the diffuse, or require general personal relations to be established before specific business can be done (China, Japan and South America). Accomplishments and recent performance are what counts in an achievement-oriented country such as the United States, where you are only as good as your last success. In Germany and Japan, individual status is ascribed as a result of your position and in France of your education. Particularly in Germany and Japan, however, there is a strong emphasis on corporate rather than individual achievement. A strong tendency towards an internal locus of control enables Americans to attribute outcomes to individual effort and ability almost regardless of context; hence individual performance-related pay is a natural artefact. Reference outwards to the situation or to other people as determinants of outcomes (Japan and Singapore) may actually lead to better adaptation to customers and better response to feedback. As Trompenaars (1993) observes, feedback can be used to help us change our objectives in response to external realities, or it can simply inform as to how well we are achieving our internally set targets.

National cultures and personnel and selection psychology

Clearly, the above account of differences in national cultures is grossly oversimplified. However, it can be argued that national cultures affect the personnel psychology culture in two ways: directly, inasmuch as psychologists themselves embody their national culture and operate within it, and indirectly, different stakeholders have more influence in some cultures than in others. We characterized the American and British cultures as typical Anglo-Saxon cultures operating towards one end of each of the six cultural dimensions above. It is only too clear how closely these national assumptions and values are related to the dominant personnel psychology culture. It, too, is individualist, concentrating on the individual level of analysis; it is universalist, assuming its scientific theories can be applied everywhere; it is specific, concerning itself with analysis down into job tasks and personal attributes; it is achievement oriented, concentrating as it does on performance; it largely ignores emotions, assuming rationality and measuring aptitudes; and it assumes that individuals are responsible for outcomes, an internal locus of control. The dominant personnel psychology culture admirably reflects the culture of its nation of origin. This is why it has been so successful in its idiosyncratic context.

Other countries, however, have different psychology cultures which accord with their national culture and situation. In Spain, for example, academics and practitioners are closely aligned in the development of theory and practice (Prieto and Avila, 1994). In China, group structure and processes have long been major areas of applied research (Xu and Wang, 1991). In Latin America, the major emphasis of applied psychology is on community psychology (Wiesenfeld and Sanchez, 1991), and personnel psychology needs to treat organizations as impacting upon local communities.

Moreover, different stakeholders dominate in different countries. In the United States, for example, academics are well supported by their universities (although some might not think so!) which provide them with research facilities and support staff. Their academic peers are consequently their main reference group and stakeholders since they are not forced to go externally for their resources, and the origin of issues and problems is mainly the academic literature. It is reviewers and editors of the academic journals who determine what are the issues worth addressing, since the most valued product is the refereed journal article. In Britain and the Netherlands, the same stakeholders are gaining power, but indirectly: their national governments award resources partly on the basis of research performance, which is assessed by publications in prestigious European and American journals. In Western Europe, large organizations have close connections with university-based consultancies, and individual tenure is partially determined by the value of external funding won by faculty members. In Eastern Europe, national government is often the most prominent stakeholder, demanding help from psychologists in addressing pressing economic and social issues. Clearly, stakeholders have a profound effect on which issues are addressed and how, and on what behaviour is valued—methodological purity or practical intervention, for instance.

There are therefore many cultural influences upon the role of personnel psychologists in different countries. What are the implications of this realization? The most important is surely the need to stand outside one's own cultural perspective and view it in comparison with the perspectives of others. Attempts to transpose the dominant North American culture and paradigm in personnel psychology to other countries and cultures are thus again doomed to failure. The second is the ability to work through the consequences of each of these different perspectives for organizations and work in different countries. And the third is the willingness and ability to engage in these latter two activities in collaboration with people from other countries, since without such collaboration the enterprise is doomed to failure. These activities are obviously necessary for those engaged in work in an international context. They are also increasingly vital for people working in their own national culture, since it may well be crucial to the successful local adaptation of personnel psychology to incorporate a few assumptions, values and artefacts from elsewhere. Those who happen to work in one of the countries where personnel psychology is more developed would benefit from expanding their field of vision and experience beyond the source of the next refereed article to collaborating with international colleagues. Assumptions of scientific superiority need to be kept carefully in check since personnel psychologists in different countries can learn much from each other, and the profession stands to gain immeasurably from an internationalization of its perspectives and *modus operandi*.

Emergent themes in personnel selection and assessment

The preceding sections of this chapter offer little comfort to personnel psychologists who would prefer a universally applicable system in a steady state where routinized responses are the order of the day. We have suggested that overwhelming forces in globalized business markets have, and will continue, to transform work organizations. If this is not enough, then we have argued, perhaps more controversially, that the dominant paradigm in personnel psychology is outmoded and retrogressive; maladaptive to its changing environment; and incapable of sustaining an eclectic culture of research able to generate a wider understanding of recruitment selection processes across the world. We expect that some will disagree with our broad-brush analysis and applied cross-cultural stance—fine. Whatever the reader's impressions so far, the conclusion that issues and challenges in personnel selection running into the next millennium will dictate core rather than superficial, artefactual revisions to the scientific paradigm and organizational practice is inescapable. We now identify four main issues that will have to be addressed, each subsuming a number of specific themes. In this way we seek to make more specific some of the ways in which the dominant paradigm will have to change. These issues and themes are as follows:

1. Selecting for change
   - bimodal prediction
   - compressed validation cycles
   - selecting for emergent knowledge, skills, abilities and other factors (KSAOs)
   - the need for on-going, internal re-assessment.

2. Multiple and interactive levels of analysis
   - Person–team (P–T) fit
   - Person–organization (P–O) fit
   - Complementary, neutral and contradictory interactive terms.

3. Cross-cultural applicability of meta-analytic findings
   - International generalizability
   - Generalizability to expatriate selection.

4. Generating wider theoretical frameworks
   - Examples of innovative perspectives
   - Facilitating theoretical eclecticism.

Selecting for change

Our first theme—selecting for change—subsumes four interdependent issues: *bimodal prediction, compressed validation cycles, selecting for emergent knowledge, skills, abilities and other factors (KSAOs)* and *the need for on-going internal re-assessment.*

Bimodal prediction

The traditional paradigm in selection has, as we have already argued, assumed the existence of on-going, stable, analysable jobs comprised of discrete sets of tasks. Person–job fit was therefore the primary concern, with the job being conceptualized as a given 'target' to be hit through the application of valid and reliable methods of candidate assessment. The responsibility of the personnel psychologist was one of *unimodal prediction*—predicting the degree of fit to a given job. Increasingly we will be responsible for what can best be termed *bimodal prediction*—predicting the likely composition of the work role *as well as* person–work role fit. And we use the term 'work role' intentionally: as we have seen, clusters of activities and tasks performed by employees are likely to be much more fluid and transient in the future (Howard, 1995).

Predicting person–job fit alone was difficult enough, but bimodal prediction constitutes a daunting challenge, and one which demands a reconceptualization of the predictivist paradigm. In the past, as long as a job analysis had been performed, personnel psychologists could safely concentrate their efforts on the development of methods to evaluate applicant qualities. In the future, we will need to have available valid and reliable methods to predict the short- and medium-term composition of work roles (see also Visser *et al.*, Chapter 21 in this volume). This challenge, we believe, is one of crucial import to the survival of the discipline. There is thus a demonstrable need for personnel psychologists to turn their attention to the development of projective methods and techniques to predict future work roles. There is also the need for a major paradigmatic shift to incorporate this expansion of the prediction equation, and to refocus theory and practice around the strictures of bimodal prediction.

Some evidence of activity in bimodal prediction is already apparent by both American and British personnel psychologists. In the United States, Arvey, Salas and Gialluca (1992) used a task–ability intercorrelation matrix for present jobs to forecast the requirements for future possible job scenarios. In Britain, Henderson, Anderson and Rick (1995) report the development of a future-oriented competency framework for use as assessment centre dimensions. Structured interviews and repertory grids were conducted with groups of organizational staff to elicit expected competency dimensions for the job–family (graduate entrant jobs) for three to five years in the future. The assessment centre was subsequently reorganized around these future-oriented competencies. Sparrow (Chapter 17 in this volume) describes competency-based approaches to selection which depend upon the organization identifying and recruiting for a 'stock' of behavioural competencies. He argues persuasively that some clusters of competencies will be maturing (declining in importance), some emerging (increasing in importance) and some core (of on-going importance). The organization thus selects to develop or re-stock the behavioural repertoire present in its labour pool.

Compressed validation cycles

Production engineers talk of 'compressed design cycles' to indicate that the time needed to move from a product prototype to the finished and saleable item is now considerably shorter than in the past. In personnel psychology, the shorter-term stability of work roles presents a series of challenges to the classical paradigm, which historically has rightly emphasized the value of predictive validity studies. Why bother to validate a selection method or procedure against a criterion which is already out of date by the time the study has been completed? Validation cycles, which in the past could quite conceivably have held true over a period of several years, are becoming of increasingly dubious value. This, we believe, will lead to the need for *compressed validation cycles*. By this we mean that validation studies will need to be conceived of and completed in a period of weeks/months rather than months/years. The 'shelf-life' of validation study findings will be determined by how quickly the work role changes; the quicker the change, the shorter the shelf-life.

Of course, the wider availability of personal computers loaded with powerful database management and statistical analysis programs should help. But the challenge to our way of thinking is that in future the criterion problem, as we have already implied, will be of a magnitude and transience hitherto not conceived of. Personnel psychologists will need to adapt their approach from being that of a 'one-off' definitive validation study, maybe spanning years, toward an ethos of continuous improvement through a series of shorter-cycle validation studies followed by selection system re-adjustment (see also Roe, 1989). Moreover, as Fletcher (1996) argues, it is likely that concurrent validation studies will become more prevalent than predictive designs, since they are quick to complete because they do not rely on longitudinal data collection. Whatever the strengths of the traditional purist stance that predictive validity studies will always be needed, the imperative is for personnel psychologists to develop methodological approaches which are rapid enough to function within compressed validation cycles. Shorter delays after selection and before taking initial performance measures; using ratings of potential given in appraisal as predictors of performance over subsequent months; and regularly updating the criterion space for alpha, beta and gamma changes in dimension composition are just some of the possible ways of responding to the challenge of compressed validation cycles.

Selecting for emergent KSAOs

The changes in work organization described earlier in this chapter have given rise to several applicant KSAOs becoming more attractive to employers. Sparrow (Chapter 17 in this volume) would describe these as 'emergent competencies'. Amongst other factors, it is clear that organizations are placing greater emphasis on employee *flexibility*, *personality*, and *potential to innovate.*

First, *flexibility* and adaptability, in technical and social competencies, attitudes to work, and task- and non-task-related behaviour will be called for. As work roles will themselves be transient, assessment criteria for selection will widen from being the evaluation of specific technical competencies, to the assessment of flexibility as a psychological–behavioural construct. To our knowledge, little research exists into how to evaluate flexibility or its psychological antecedents. Indeed, personnel researchers will need initially to establish whether it makes sense to talk of 'flexibility' as a single construct—it may conceivably break down into several antecedent attitudinal dimensions (e.g. openness to change, rule independence, openness to experience, etc.) and observable, behavioural dimensions (e.g. ease of transition between task domains, ability to learn new skills, adaptability to work role changes, etc.). Each set of dimensions might be best assessed by different methods (e.g. attitudinal domains by personality instruments, behavioural domains by assessment centre exercises), so it is clear that much further research and applied technical development is called for.

Secondly, as several recent reviews have concluded, *personality* assessment is currently enjoying something of a renaissance in interest (Robertson, 1993; Robertson and Kinder, 1993; Landy, Shankster-Cawley and Moran, 1995; Ostroff and Rothausen, 1996; Hogan, Hogan and Roberts, 1996; Borman, Hanson and Hedge, in press). Landy, Shankster-Cawley and Moran quote Goldberg (1993): *'Once upon a time, we had no personalities. Fortunately, times change.'* Times do indeed change, but it still seems rather peculiar for *psychologists* to admit to a resurgence of interest in personality. Indeed, this appears largely specific to the context of the United States where the popularity of personality testing was adversely affected by earlier sceptical reviews and the strict legislative framework (e.g. Guion, 1991; Landy, Shankster-Cawley and Moran, 1995; Hough and Schneider, 1996). In many European countries, particularly Britain and the Netherlands, personality testing has long been popular (Shackleton and Newell, 1994; and Chapter 4 in this volume). In Britain, for instance, personality inventories are used by up to 80% of all organizations in recruitment for graduate and managerial vacancies (Keenan, 1995). Debate continues over the 'Big Five' structure of personality (e.g. Barrick and Mount, 1991; Schneider and Hough, 1995), as does discussion over the bandwidth-fidelity dilemma (e.g. Barrett *et al.*, 1996; Hough and Schneider, 1996; Ones and Viswesvaran, 1996). However, from the perspective of this chapter the critical point is that the need to assess personality is inextricably linked to the emergence of flexible job roles which permit greater behavioural freedom and expression at work.

Thirdly, selecting for *innovation potential* is becoming more prevalent amongst organizations. We have confined our comments so far in this chapter to situations where changes in the work-role are imposed from above as a result of environmental, technological or business pressures. Somewhat different implications arise for selection where organizations are actively recruiting for individuals with the motivation, skills and knowledge to change their work-role from within—that is, to innovate. Two challenges arise in relation to selection decision making. First, there is a dearth of methods specifically designed and validated to measure applicants' propensity to innovate (King and Anderson, 1995). Several personality instruments contain innovation or creativity-type dimensions, but little dimension-specific evidence exists to support their construct or criterion-related validity (King and Anderson, 1995). This leads on to the second major challenge in selecting for innovation potential. By definition, innovation implies changing the work role for the better in some *unforeseen* way, and therefore shifting the criterion domain in a manner which is unknown at the time of prediction. Of course, this is not such a new phenomenon; innovation research has long shown that job-holders in even non-discretionary and extensively regulated roles attempt to modify their position through innovation (Amabile, 1983; Van de Ven, Angle and Poole, 1989; West and Altink, 1996). The challenge for selection psychologists is thus to adapt to new recruits' *wilful disruption*, as it were, of the criterion domain.

The need for on-going, internal re-assessment

The fourth and final issue subsumed within our 'selecting for change' theme is the need for assessment to be viewed as an on-going activity rather than as a one-off barrier to entry into an organization. Why is this so, especially as some would hold that it is sufficient to measure general intellect (g) and possibly conscientiousness (c) as stable 'panacea predictors' of any foreseeable criterion? The reasons stem from our assertion that work-role change is endemic, exponential in its effects, and the only likely stable characteristic of future work organization. Again, selection psychologists need literally to 'select for change', whether the causes of such instability are environmental pressures, the changing of roles from below by innovative employees or, most likely, a mixture of the two.

Here the implication is that we will need to extend our traditional restricted focus on organizational entry up until the first or second performance appraisal (although, of course, longer-term validity and validity decrement studies have been conducted). Selection needs to shift from being a one-off barrier to entry to being an on-going, periodic re-appraisal of the fit between individual competencies and organizational, team and work-role demands. The timing and duration of this cycle will be determined by how quickly the work-role changes, how fundamental the changes are, and how 'fine-tuned' an organization wishes to maintain the degree of fit between employee competencies and work-role demands. Of course, in these circumstances, the staff appraisal procedure of an organization is likely to take on this function of the periodic re-assessment of individual competency. This raises the question: Are many organizational appraisal processes up to the task? The valid and reliable measurement of cognitive and behavioural dimensions has always been treated as critical in selection procedures, but less so in appraisal where the fidelity of measurement has taken second place behind concerns over facilitating performance feedback. Appraisal schemes may therefore need considerable upgrading if they are to meet this challenge.

Multiple and interactive levels of analysis

Organizations of the future will need to select not only for person–work role fit but also for person–team (P–T) fit and for person–organization (P–O) fit. This trend has certainly been acknowledged elsewhere (e.g. Chatman, 1991; Guion, 1991; Ostroff and Rothausen, 1996; Borman, Hanson and Hedge, in press) where excellent reviews of studies into P–T fit and P–O fit are presented. Again, we confine our comments to the implications for the dominant scientific paradigm and for practice implied by the need to select for P–T fit and P–O fit. The critical challenge is to expand our conceptual horizon beyond the level of person–job fit and to incorporate multiple and interactive levels of analysis into selection decision-making. Fortunately, progress has already been made in theorizing issues for multiple levels of analysis in I/O psychology (e.g. Ostroff, 1993; George and James, 1994). At the team level of analysis, the work of Campion and Stevens shows considerable promise in elucidating the range of individual KSAOs needed to be an effective team member (Campion, 1994; Stevens and Campion, 1994a; see also West and Allen, Chapter 24 in this volume). These authors have also developed a useful psychometric test (Stevens and Campion, 1994b) which shows promise as a diagnostic tool to evaluate P–T fit. In a similar vein, Cannon-Bowers *et al.* (1995) propose an alternative typology of individual-level KSAOs for teamworking. Other recent research by Borman and Motowildo (1993) into *contextual performance*—performance on non-task-related elements of a job—also shows real promise in advancing our understanding of, and methods to predict, P–T fit.

However, all these approaches are again grounded firmly in the dominant paradigm since they focus exclusively at an individual level of analysis. Assessing P–T fit and P–O fit comprehensively demands that personnel psychologists extend their foci of analysis beyond solely the individual level. The selection of entire *ad hoc* project teams, selecting a cohort of newcomers into an organization, and selecting for longer-term fit into the organization culture are all instances where P–T and P–O fit are crucial and cannot be accounted for by individual-level measurement alone. We therefore coin the term *multiple and interactive levels of analysis* to highlight this challenge.

In terms of *multiple* levels of analysis, we refer to P–T fit and P–O fit in addition to the traditional concern for person–job fit. Of course, these three levels of analysis are interdependent and, to some extent, overlapping. Contextual performance, as operationalized by Borman and Motowildo (1993), clearly encroaches upon many micro-analytical issues of team level fit, for example. So the dividing lines between the three levels of analysis will inevitably be somewhat arbitrary.

Furthermore, we propose that there is an *interaction* between the levels of analysis. Interaction terms will be either *complementary*, *neutral*, or *contradictory*. A *complementary* interaction occurs where a high scale score at one level of analysis is desirable in combination with a high scale score at another level of analysis. For example, in a work-role involving substantial interpersonal contact the criterion of a high scale score on sociability is likely at the individual level of analysis, and if this work-role also requires team-working skills, then this criterion is appropriate also at the team level of analysis. *Neutral* interactions, if not a contradiction in terms, occur where a high scale score desired at one level combines with a middling scale score or where this dimension is simply not applicable at another level of analysis. More problematic, naturally, are *contradictory* interactions. Here an organization simultaneously desires a high scale score at one level of analysis, but a low scale score at another. For instance, high sociability at the individual level, but a low scale score on this dimension in order for the person to fit into an organization culture which values modesty, introspection and self-effacing behaviour by its employees. Given three levels of analysis (individual, team and organization) in combination with three interaction terms (complementary, neutral and contradictory) being applied to multiple measurement dimensions, the opportunities for research and improving current practice are immense.

Cross-cultural applicability of meta-analytic findings

Meta-analysis and validity generalization techniques have contributed much to the development of knowledge in selection psychology. The combination of multiple validity studies involving up to several thousand subjects in procedures that allow the analyst to partial-out measurement errors omnipresent in individual studies have permitted definitive conclusions over the mean validity of selection methods (e.g. Schmidt *et al.*, 1995; Schmitt *et al.*, 1984). Of course, the vast majority of meta-analyses have been conducted in the United States, inputting the findings of validity studies almost all of which were also conducted there. This is understandable since it has been eminent American I/O psychologists who have championed developments in meta-analysis and their computation procedures. However, the findings from meta-analyses have been unreservedly cited by personnel psychologists in other countries and appear to have been unquestioningly accepted as being generalizable to different national contexts. Social, cultural, legislative, and recruitment and appraisal differences have been overlooked, and certainly in many European countries the results of meta-analyses conducted in the United States have been cited as applying without caveat. These findings may indeed be transferable to other countries, but then again they may not be, given the pervasive cultural differences we outlined earlier in this chapter.

Schmidt (1993) quotes the intriguing statistic that the United States has around 5% of the world's population but 70% of the world's lawyers. This inequality of distribution is probably quite comparable to the numbers of personnel psychologists, and even more so in terms of the citation impact of published papers, especially in the area of meta-analysis. At a rough guess, possibly up to seven-tenths of the world's personnel psychologists reside in the United States, whereas at least nine-tenths of the citation impact of published articles is probably attributable to American academic personnel psychologists. The distribution is changing rapidly, however, with considerable growth in the numbers of personnel psychologists in other countries. Although some meta-analysts have not been shy or reticent in their claims over the generality of their findings (see Guion, 1991; and Murphy, Chapter 16 in this volume), claims of *international generalizabiliy* are notably absent. In fact, proponents of meta-analysis have often supported their efforts by citing the possible utility payback to the American economy of using more valid methods of staff selection (e.g. Schmidt, 1993; Schmidt, Ones and Hunter, 1992). It is therefore down to personnel psychologists in other countries who have been remiss in not establishing the international generalizability of meta-analytic findings.

We would argue that international generalizability will inevitably be influenced by the selection method in question. For example, interviews will be subject to national, social and cultural differences in their format and conduct. Thus, the findings from US meta-analyses may be generalizable to those Northwest European countries which share an Anglo-Saxon culture, but not to countries in Southern Europe, Asia or Africa. For other methods, for instance ability and personality tests, the tests comprising the original meta-analytic samples need to be established. Popular tests in America (e.g. the Wonderlic, DAT, GATB, HPI, and MMPI) and others upon which several meta-analyses have been based, are virtually unused for selection in other countries. Consequently, the generalizability of meta-analytic findings may be questionable, especially as some countries (e.g. Britain) have moved toward the use of tests of specific cognitive ability and tests of work-related or occupational personality.

Two issues warrant further comment. First, the generalizability of findings to expatriate selection, and secondly, the situation-specific reactions of personnel practitioners regardless of the country in question. In relation to the former, Schmidt, Ones and Hunter (1992) claim:

> We would add that ability and some personality-based predictors used in *expatriate selection* (selection of overseas assignees) may prove to be valid and generalizable across cultures as well (p. 661).

The authors clearly stop short of claiming the international generalizability of American meta-analytic findings *per se*, but suggest they may be so for recruitment decisions for foreign assignments. This is not an uncontroversial claim. Are we really to believe that validity findings will generalize to expatriate assignments in *all* other countries In the world from Afghanistan to Zambia? This is a claim of incredible scope which cries out for empirical research given the trends toward globalization outlined earlier in this chapter. It is, perhaps, based upon the assumption that 'scientific' findings must in principle be universally applicable.

Finally, we must acknowledge the reality of the position of personnel practitioners in any country. Being employed by a single organization and perceiving this employer as the focus of their loyalties inevitably moderates their reactions to meta-analytic and validity generalization findings. Why should HR practitioners pay any attention to average validity findings, especially if these findings emanate from another country? Certainly, the variations in every organization-specific validity study so clinically (and quite correctly) dispatched to measurement error by meta-analysts are more likely to be perceived by that organization's personnel practitioners as verification of Its uniqueness, individuality and their own *raison d'être*. However irrational it may appear to academic selection psychologists, practitioners are likely to value above all the situational specificity of their employing organization and, paradoxically, to dismiss the claim that validity findings will be generalizable to their own context as being equally irrational.

Generating wider theoretical frameworks

As noted earlier in this chapter, the dominant concern in much selection research has been the prediction of person–job fit. As a consequence, the organizational perspective has tended to be emphasized above all other considerations. This, in itself, is of course an entirely legitimate concern. It is the circumscription of this focus within the predominant predictivist–quantitative paradigm that has falsely restricted the range of issues and phenomena addressed by personnel researchers. One cannot deny the methodological and statistical sophistication with which researchers are nowadays examining relationships between predictors and criterion, and undoubtedly Anglo-Saxon cultures lead the world in the statistical–analytical complexity of their research in selection psychology. Whether such a degree of statistical complexity is warranted given the unreliability of measures of many variables in applied-organizational settings is a moot point. Nevertheless, in our attempts to mimic the physical sciences personnel psychology has been successful in constructing a body of research that exhibits all the hallmarks of 'proper' scientific enquiry: hypotheses specified a priori, state-of-the-art statistical analyses, empirical incrementalism, quantitative studies grounded upon existing theory and previous findings, acknowledged limitations of the study design, sanitized study reports which obscure the messy realities of conducting organizational research and, above all, responsibly conducted and written-up deductivism.

Having stated that the dominant vantage point has been that of the organization, there have been several themes of research which have expounded quite different views. These include:

- Applicant rights in the selection process (e.g. de Wolff and Van den Bosch, 1984)
- The psychological impact of selection procedures upon candidates (e.g. Iles and Robertson, Chapter 27 in this volume; Fletcher, 1991; Rynes, 1993).
- Procedural and distributive justice in the selection process (e.g. Gilliland, 1993).
- Selection as a social negotiation of the psychological contract (e.g. Herriot, 1989).
- Selection as a developmental model of mutual accommodation (e.g. Hesketh and Robertson, 1993).
- Selection as mutual attraction and bi-directional decision-making (e.g. Schneider *et al.*, Chapter 19 in this volume; Wanous *et al.*, 1992).
- Selection as the co-construction of mutual realities (e.g. Dachler, 1994).
- Selection as the domination of one group over another (e.g. Hollway, 1991).
- Radical feminist perspectives of the selection process (e.g. Hollway, 1991).

The themes of concern underlying all of these innovative perspectives are worlds away from those that preoccupy those at the heart of the predictivist paradigm. But these are the few exceptions to the overwhelming volume of work which sits neatly within the dominant and convergent paradigm. Our call, then, is for greater divergence and diversity of theoretical perspectives, but also for such radical approaches to embrace an appropriate level of methodological rigour. Only through this combination of theoretical innovation coupled with methodological rigour will the discipline flourish in response to environmental changes.

Conclusion

We are presently witnessing a watershed in personnel and selection psychology. To attempt to stand above this in aloof splendour, relying upon the regalia and the trappings of scientism built up over the years, is a temptation especially for the academic wing of our discipline. Personnel psychologists, we argue, need to put down their calculators and pick up their thought processes. The time has come for a moratorium on any further meta-analyses of popular selection methods in the United States, slight modifications to the configuration of utility formulae, and replication studies in areas that have been intensively researched. The opportunity costs are simply too great. Instead, it is time to take stock of the theoretical health and dynamism of the discipline; to rejuvenate its early roots as an applied science, but one which is becoming increasingly influenced by the globalization of business and therefore needs to become a truly global applied science that reflects important national and cultural differences.

We return to our opening aim that this chapter should be a 'paradigmatic wake-up call' and our original statement that *traditional* personnel and selection psychology is in danger of terminal decline. Unless we can stimulate a quantum leap in our paradigmatic assumptions, beliefs, values and artefacts, the prospect of marginalization will loom ever larger. We need to break free of the restrictive and narrow paradigm that has dominated our thinking and practice hitherto. For only by engaging in critical, self-imposed constructive controversy, healthy epistemological debate and dialectic, are we likely to be able to stimulate the double-loop learning in personnel psychology needed to cope with an environment that is changing at an exponential rate. Only then will we begin adequately to understand and address the issues facing our key clients: individuals, work groups, organizations and governments. Applied personnel psychology is not primarily an academic discipline with academic peers as clients; it is psychology applied to the world of work.

References

Abbott, A. (1988). *The System of Professions*. Chicago: University of Chicago Press.

Amabile, T.M. (1983). *The Social Psychology of Creativity*. New York: Springer-Verlag.

Anderson, N.R. (1992). Eight decades of employment interview research: A retrospective meta-review and prospective commentary. *European Work and Organizational Psychologist*, **2**, 1 32.

Argyris, C. and Schon, D.A. (1978). *Organisational Learning*. Reading, MA: Addison-Wesley.

Arvey, R.D., Salas, E. and Gialluca, K.A. (1992). Using task inventories to forecast skills and abilities. *Human Performance*, **5**, (3), 171–190.

Barrett, P., Kline, P., Paltiel, L. and Eysenck, H.J. (1996). An evaluation of the psychometric properties of the concept 5.2 Occupational Personality Questionnaire, *Journal of Occupational and Organizational Psychology*, **69**, 1–20.

Barrick, M.R. and Mount, M.K. (1991). The big five personality dimensions and job performance: A meta-analysis. *Personnel Psychology*, **44**, 1–26.

Bartlett, C.A. and Ghoshal, S. (1989). *Managing Across Borders.* London: Hutchinson.
Borman, W.C. and Motowildo, J.J. (1993). Expanding the criterion domain to include elements of contextual performance. In N. Schmitt, W.C. Borman & Associates, *Personnel Selection in Organizations.* San Francisco: Jossey-Bass.
Borman, W., Hanson, M. and Hedge, J. (in press). Personnel selection, *Annual Review of Psychology.*
Bridges, W. (1994). *Jobshift.* Reading, MA: Addison-Wesley.
Brockner, J., Tyler, T.R. and Cooper-Schneider, R. (1992). The effects of prior commitment to an institution on reactions to perceived unfairness: The higher they are, the harder they fall. *Administrative Science Quarterly,* **37**, 241–261.
Campion, M.A. (1994). Job analysis for the future. In M.G. Runsey, C.B. Walker and J.H. Harris (eds.) *Personnel Selection and Classification.* Hillsdale: NJL Erlbaurn.
Cannon-Bowers, J.A., Tannenbaum, S.I., Salas, E. and Volpe, C.E. (1995). Defining competencies and establishing team training requirements. In R.A. Guzzo and E. Salas (eds.), *Team Effectiveness and Decision Making in Organizations.* San Francisco: Jossey-Bass.
Cascio, W.F. (1994). Downsizing: What do we know? What have we learned? *Academy of Management Executive,* **7** (1), 95–104.
Cascio, W.F. (1995). Whither industrial and organizational psychology in a changing world of work? *American Psychologist,* **50** (11), 928–939.
Chatman, J.A. (1991). Matching people and organisations: Selection and socialisation in public accounting firms. *Administrative Science Quarterly,* **36**, 459–484.
Dachler, M.P. (1994). A social-relational perspective of selection. Paper presented at the 23rd International Congress of Applied Psychology, Madrid, Spain, July 1994.
Davis, D.D. (1995). Form, function and strategy in boundaryless organisations. In A. Howard (ed.), *The Changing Nature of Work.* San Francisco: Jossey-Bass.
DeMeuse, K.P., Vanderheiden, P.A. and Bergmann, T.J. (1994). Announced lay-offs: Their effect on corporate financial performance. *Human Resource Management,* **33** (4), 509–530.
Feldman, D.C. (1995). Managing part-time and temporary employment. In M. London (ed.), *Employees, Careers, and Job Creation.* San Francisco: Jossey-Bass.
Fletcher, C. (1991). Candidates' reactions to assessment centres and their outcomes: A longitudinal study. *Journal of Occupational and Organizational Psychology,* **64**, 117–127.
Fletcher, C. (1996). Challenge and change for psychometrics: The need for a new approach. Paper presented at the Conference on Ethics and Good Practice in Assessment and Psychological Testing, Cheltenham, UK, July 1996.
George, J.M. and James, L.R. (1994). Levels issues in theory development. *Academy of Management Review,* **19**, 636–640.
Gilliland, S.W. (1993). The perceived fairness of selection systems: An organizational justice perspective. *Academy of Management Review,* **18**, 694–734.
Goldberg, L.R. (1993). The structure of phenotypic personality traits. *American Psychologist,* **48**, 26–34.
Guion, R.M. (1991). Personnel assessment, selection, and placement. In M.D. Dunnette and L.M. Hough (eds.), *Handbook of Industrial and Organizational Psychology,* Vol. 2, Palo Alto, CA: Consulting Psychologists Press, Inc.
Hall, D.T. and Associates (1986). *Career Development in Organisations.* San Francisco: Jossey-Bass.

Heckscher, C. (1995). *White Collar Blues*. New York: Basic Books.
Henderson, F., Anderson, N.R. and Rick, S. (1995). Future competency profiling. *Personnel Review*, **24**, 19–31.
Herriot, P. (1989). Selection as a social process. In M. Smith and I.T. Robertson (eds.), *Advances in Staff Selection*. Chichester: John Wiley.
Herriot, P. (1992). Selection: The two subcultures. *European Work and Organizational Psychologist*, **2**, 129–140.
Herriot, P. and Pemberton, C. (1994). *Competitive Advantage through Diversity*. London: Sage.
Herriot, P. and Pemberton, C. (1996). Contracting careers. *Human Relations*, **49**, 757–790.
Hesketh, B. and Robertson, I.T. (1993). Validating personnel selection: A process model for research and practice. *International Journal of Selection and Assessment*, **1**, 3–17.
Hofstede, G. (1980). *Culture's Consequences*. London: Sage.
Hogan, R., Hogan, J. and Roberts, B.W. (1996). Personality measure and employment decisions. *American Psychologist*, May, 469–477.
Hollway, W. (1991). *Work Psychology and Organizational Behaviour*. London: Sage.
Hosking, D.M. and Anderson, N.R. (eds.) (1992). *Organizational Change and Innovation: Psychological Perspectives and Practices in Europe*. London: Routledge.
Hough, L.M. and Schneider, R.J. (1996). Personality traits, taxonomies, and applications in organizations. In K.R. Murphy (ed.), *Individual Differences and Behaviour in Organizations*. San Francisco: Jossey-Bass.
Howard, A. (1995). Rethinking the psychology of work. In A. Howard (ed.), *The Changing Nature of Work*. San Francisco: Jossey-Bass.
Huczynski, A.A. (1993). Explaining the succession of management fads. *International Journal of Human Resource Management*, **4** (2), 443–464.
Hutton, W. (1994). *The State We're In*. London: Heinemann.
Keenan, A. (1995). Graduate recruitment in Britain: A survey of selection methods used by organizations. *Journal of Organizational Behavior*, **16**, 303–317.
King, N. and Anderson, N.R. (1995). *Innovation and Change in Organizations*. London: Routledge.
Landy, F.J., Shankster-Cawley, L. and Moran, S.K. (1995). Advancing personnel selection and placement methods. In A. Howard (ed.), *The Changing Nature of Work*. San Francisco: Jossey-Bass.
Latham, G.P. and Whyte, G. (1994). The futility of utility analysis. *Personnel Psychology*, **47**, 31–46.
Lawler, E.E. (1992). *The Ultimate Advantage: Creating the High-involvement Organisation*. San Francisco: Jossey-Bass.
Lawler, E.E. (1994). From job-based to competency-based organizations. *Journal of Organizational Behavior*, **15**, 3–15.
Legge, K. (1995). *Human Resource Management: Rhetorics and Realities*. London: Macmillan.
Mirvis, P.H. (ed.) (1993). *Building a Competitive Workforce*. New York: John Wiley.
Mohrman, S.A. and Cohen, S.G. (1995). When people get out of the box: New relationships, new systems. In A. Howard (ed.), *The Changing Nature of Work*. San Francisco: Jossey-Bass.
Muchinsky, P.M. (1994). A review of individual assessment methods used for personnel selection in North America. *International Journal of Selection and Assessment*, **2**, 118–124.

Murphy, K.R. (1986). When your top choice turns you down: Effects of rejected offers on the utility of selection tests. *Psychological Bulletin*, **99**, 133–138.

Nicholson, N. and West, M.A. (1988). *Managerial Job Change: Men and Women in Transition*. Cambridge: Cambridge University Press.

Ones, D.S. and Viswesvaran, C. (1996). Bandwidth-fidelity dilemma in personality measurement for personnel selection. *Journal of Organizational Behavior*, **17**, 609–626.

Ostroff, C. (1993). Comparing correlations based on individual-level and aggregated data. *Journal of Applied Psychology*, **78**, 569–582.

Ostroff, C. and Rothausen, T.J. (1996). Selection and job matching. In D. Lewin, D.J.B. Mitchell and M.A. Zaidi (eds.), *Human Resource Management Handbook*. Greenwich, CT: JAI Press.

Prahalad, C.K. and Hamel, G. (1990). The core competence of the corporation. *Harvard Business Review*, **90** (3), 79–91.

Prieto, J.M. and Avila, A. (1994). Linking certified knowledge to labour markets. *Applied Psychology*, **43** (2), 113–130.

Robertson, I.T. (1993). Personality assessment and personnel selection. *European Review of Applied Psychology*, **43**, 187–194.

Robertson, I.T. and Kinder, A. (1993). Personality and job competencies: The criterion-related validity of some personality variables. *Journal of Occupational and Organizational Psychology*, **66**, 225–244.

Roe, R.A. (1989). Designing selection procedures. In P. Herriot (ed.), *Assessment and Selection in Organizations*. Chichester: John Wiley.

Rousseau, D.M. (1990). New hire perceptions of their own and their employer's obligations: A study of psychological contracts. *Journal of Organizational Behavior*, **11**, 389–400.

Rousseau, D.M. (1995). *Psychological Contracts in Organisations*. California: Sage.

Ryan, A.M. and Sackett, P.R. (1987). A survey of individual assessment practices by I/O psychologists. *Personnel Psychology*, **40**, 455–488.

Rynes, S.L. (1993). Who's selecting whom? Effects of selection practices on applicant attitudes and behavior. In N. Schmitt, W.C. Borman and Associates, *Personnel Selection in Organizations*. San Francisco: Jossey-Bass.

Sackett, P.R. and Arvey, R.D. (1993). Selection in small N settings. In N. Schmitt, W.C. Borman and Associates, *Personnel Selection in Organizations*. San Francisco: Jossey-Bass.

Schein, E. (1985). *Organizational Culture and Leadership*. San Francisco: Jossey-Bass.

Schmidt, F.L. (1993). Personnel psychology at the cutting edge. In N. Schmitt, W.C. Borman and Associates, *Personnel Selection in Organizations*. San Francisco: Jossey-Bass.

Schmidt, F.L., Ones, D.S. and Hunter, J.E. (1992). Personnel selection. *Annual Review of Psychology*, **43**, 627–670.

Schmidt, F.L., Pearlman, K., Hunter, J.E. and Hirsch, H.R. (1985). Forty questions about validity generalization and meta-analysis. *Personnel Psychology*, **38**, 697–798.

Schmitt, N., Gooding, R.Z., Noe, R.A. and Kirsch, M. (1984). Meta-analyses of validity studies published between 1964 and 1982 and the investigation of study characteristics. *Personnel Psychology*, **37**, 407–422.

Schneider, B.W. (1987). The people make the place. *Personnel Psychology*, **40**, 437–453.

Schneider, R.J. and Hough, L.M. (1995). Personality and industrial-organisational psychology. In C. Cooper and I.T. Robertson (eds.), *International Review of Industrial and Organisational Psychology*. Chichester: John Wiley.

Shackleton, V.J. and Newell, S. (1994). European management selection methods: A comparison of five countries. *International Journal of Selection and Assessment*, **2**, 91–102.

Smith, M. and Abrahamsen, M. (1992). Patterns of selection in six countries. *The Psychologist*, **5**, 205–207.

Sonnenfeld, J.A. and Peiperl, M.A. (1988). Staffing policy as a strategic response: A typology of career systems. *Academy of Management Review*, **13**, 588–600.

Sproull, L. and Kiesler, S. (1986). Reducing social context cues: Electronic mail in organisational communication. *Management Science*, **32** (11), 1492–1512.

Stevens, M.J. and Campion, M.A. (1994a). The knowledge, skill and ability requirements for teamwork: Implications for human resource management. *Journal of Management*, **20**, 503–530.

Stevens, M.J. and Campion, M.A. (1994b). Staffing work teams: Development and validation of a selection test for teamwork settings. Unpublished manuscript.

Stroh, L.K., Brett, J.M. and Reilly, A.H. (1994). A decade of change: Managers' attachment to their organisations and their jobs. *Human Resource Management*, **33** (4), 531–548.

Trompenaars, F. (1993). *Riding the Waves of Culture*. London: Nicholas Brealey.

Van de Ven, A., Angle, H.L. and Poole, M.S. (eds.) (1989): *Research on the Management of Innovation: The Minnesota Studies*. New York: Harper & Row.

Wanous, J.P., Poland, T.D., Premack, S.L. and Davis, K.S. (1992). The effects of met expectations on newcomer attitudes and behaviours: A review and meta-analysis. *Journal of Applied Psychology*, **77**, 168–176.

Waterman, R.H., Waterman, J.A. and Collard, B.A. (1994). Toward a career-resilient workforce. *Harvard Business Review*, **12** (4), 87–95.

West, M.A. and Altink, W. (1996). Innovation at work: Individual, group, organizational and socio-historical perspectives. *European Journal of Work and Organizational Psychology*, **5**, 3–11.

West, M.A. and Farr, J.L. (eds.) (1990) *Innovation and Creativity at Work*. Chichester: John Wiley.

Wiesenfeld, E. and Sanchez, E. (1991). Introduction: The why, what, and how of community social psychology in Latin America. *Applied Psychology*, **40** (2), 113–118.

de Wolff, C.J. and van den Bosch, G. (1984). Personnel selection. In P.J. Drenth, H. Thierry, P.J. Willems and C.J. de Wolff (eds.), *Handbook of Work and Organizational Psychology*, Vol. 1. Chichester: John Wiley.

Workplace of the Future: A report of the Conference on the Future of the American Workplace (1993). New York: US Departments of Commerce and Labor.

Xu, L-C. and Wang, Z.-M. (1991). New developments in organisational psychology in China. *Applied Psychology*, **40** (1), 3–14.

Zuboff, S. (1988). *In the Age of the Smart Machine*. Oxford: Heinemann.

63

PERSONNEL SELECTION

Looking toward the future—remembering the past

Leaetta M. Hough and Frederick L. Oswald

Source: *Annual Review of Psychology* 51 (2000): 631–664.

Abstract

This chapter reviews personnel selection research from 1995 through 1999. Areas covered are job analysis; performance criteria; cognitive ability and personality predictors; interview, assessment center, and biodata assessment methods; measurement issues; meta-analysis and validity generalization; evaluation of selection systems in terms of differential prediction, adverse impact, utility, and applicant reactions; emerging topics on team selection and cross-cultural issues; and finally professional, legal, and ethical standards. Three major themes are revealed: (a) Better taxonomies produce better selection decisions; (b) The nature and analyses of work behavior are changing, influencing personnel selection practices; (c) The field of personality research is healthy, as new measurement methods, personality constructs, and compound constructs of well-known traits are being researched and applied to personnel selection.

Introduction

Global, widespread, and diverse forces impact today's economies and marketplaces, with important implications for personnel selection (Dunnette 1997, Howard 1995, Ilgen & Pulakos 1999, Kraut & Korman 1999a, Pearlman & Barney 1999, Schmitt & Chan 1998). Indeed, Herriot & Anderson (1997) call for new selection methods. Our personnel selection review identifies emerging topics, covers traditional ones, and suggests new avenues for research and practice.

Job and work analysis

Recognizing the changing nature of work, many researchers and practitioners conduct "work" analysis, focusing on tasks and cross-functional skills of workers, rather than "job" analysis with its focus on static jobs (Cascio 1995, Nelson 1997, Pearlman 1997, Sanchez & Levine 1999). Perhaps the O*NET, the computerized delivery system for the *Dictionary of Occupational Titles* (*DOT*), has made the greatest operational strides in addressing this shift (Peterson et al 1999). The O*NET is a flexible database containing occupational information structured around a "content model" linking work behaviors to worker attributes, much in line with Dunnette's call to bridge these "two worlds of behavioral taxonomies" (1976, p. 477), As information on work (e.g. jobs, organizational contexts, and work characteristics) and the worker (e.g. knowledge, skills, interests, and motivation) changes, the computerized nature of the O*NET allows an equally responsive change in its database. Collecting and using such information to select individuals for jobs, tasks, or roles is becoming more critical than ever (Campbell 1999).

Work/job analysis now includes personality variables alongside traditional cognitive, behavioral, and situational variables. The National Skill Standards Board (K Pearlman, unpublished manuscript) and O*NET (Peterson et al 1999) both incorporate personality-based work requirements. One personality-based job analysis instrument generates job profiles along seven personality scales (Hogan & Rybicki 1998). Another personality-based job analysis evaluated 260 jobs, meaningfully distinguishing 12 *DOT*-based job clusters (Raymark et al 1997).

Sixteen potential cognitive and social sources of rating inaccuracy in job analysis may influence different dimensions and psychometric properties of job analysis (Morgeson & Campion 1997). Type of job data and method for clustering jobs affect similarities and distinctions between jobs (Colihan & Burger 1995), and Q-factor analysis of rated task importance for two job titles shows meaningful within-title variation (Sanchez et al 1998). Future job analysis studies might identify substantive sources of variance attributable to types of raters, workers, or both.

Criteria

Taxonomic issues

Job performance constitutes all measurable work behaviors relevant to organizational goals and within the individual's control (Campbell et al 1996). Job performance is complex, dynamic, and multidimensional, and consequently personnel selection systems might predict individual differences for several types of job performance (e.g. task proficiency and leadership behaviors). Models incorporating multiple predictors and multiple criteria first apply rational weights to performance criteria and then derive least-squares optimal weights for the predictors. Meta-analytic correlations between ability, conscientiousness (predictors), individual task performance, and organizational citizenship (criteria) illustrate how validity can vary greatly depending on criterion weights (Murphy & Shiarella 1997). Absent criterion data for establishing regression weights, rational weighting of a selection battery increases appropriateness and legal defensibility. Weights could multiply job analysis ratings of importance, time spent, consequences of errors, and time-to-proficiency (Arthur et al 1996).

Contextual performance, or organizational citizenship behavior, is a relatively new and multifaceted job performance construct (Borman & Motowidlo 1997). Coleman & Borman (1999) classified organizational citizenship behaviors into three broad categories: interpersonal citizenship behavior (benefiting employees), organizational citizenship performance (benefiting organizations), and job/task conscientiousness (benefiting work itself). Hierarchical regression analyses suggest that interpersonal facilitation is a part of contextual performance, but job dedication (similar to job/task conscientiousness within the organizational citizenship framework) is a part of task performance (Van Scotter & Motowidlo 1996). Organizations clearly require both task and contextual performance (Kiker & Motowidlo 1999).

Measurement issues

Regarding criterion reliability, interrater reliability coefficients are more appropriate to use than intrarater (coefficient alpha) or test-retest reliabilities, and interrater reliabilities of supervisory ratings of overall and dimensional job performance are higher than peer ratings (Viswesvaran et al 1996). A greater understanding of "unreliable" criterion variance is needed to address biases in measures of constructs (Schmitt et al 1995). Similarly, criterion range restriction (or enhancement) may be a legitimate organizational phenomenon affecting criterion-related validities and not merely a statistical artifact (James et al 1992). Organizational climate, for instance, does not always attenuate correlations between procedural fairness and customer-perceived performance relationships (Burke et al 1996). Further research should investigate how individual differences, job types, and their interactions influence the mean and variance of criterion measures (see Hattrup & Jackson 1996).

Dynamic criteria

Job performance and the relative contributions of its determinants (job knowledge, skill, and motivation) change, calling for longitudinal models of reliability and validity (Tisak & Tisak 1996). The nature of performance change (e.g. systematic vs random change or reversible vs irreversible change) and how constructs relate between individual and group levels are critical theoretical and methodological issues (Chan 1998a,b). Nonlinear mixed-effects models simultaneously estimate individual and group levels of change (Cudeck 1996), accommodating missing data, prespecified error structures (see DeShon et al 1998a), and individuals not measured at the same time points. For a review and tutorial of quadratic and linear models of longitudinal change, see Chan (1998a).

Personality items predicted change in eight consecutive quarters of securities sales performance, with a curvilinear group mean increase over time (i.e. greater increase initially) and different rates of increase for each individual (Ployhart & Hakel 1998). Psychomotor ability predicted initial piece-rate performance of sewing machine operators, and cognitive ability predicted performance change. Individuals with less experience and lower levels of initial performance changed more (Deadrick et al 1997).

Predictors

Cognitive abilities and job knowledge

Self-selection on cognitive ability may precede personnel selection. Job seekers may select into or "gravitate" toward jobs with ability requirements commensurate with the seekers' own general cognitive ability (Wilk & Sackett 1996). Ability self-evaluations might lead to seeking coaching and practice on ability tests. Firefighter applicants with lower cognitive ability scores are likely to attend a free test preparation program, although the program's effects on raising ability test scores (reading, listening, and spelling) are minimal (Ryan et al 1998b).

General cognitive ability

Various cognitive ability tests (e.g. verbal, numerical, and spatial tests) intercorrelate positively, and the common variance often operationalizes g, a single general cognitive ability factor. For many jobs and practical work outcomes (job knowledge acquisition, training performance, and job performance), g predicts well (e.g. Levine et al 1996). For prediction in less complex jobs or in later stages of complex learning, g is less useful but rarely useless (Gottfredson 1997). Greater understanding of g is needed (Campbell 1996), as its determinants and theoretical meaning are debated (see Lubinski 2000). Individuals higher in g show lower intercorrelations between specific abilities (Legree et al 1996). Matching individuals' specific abilities (or ability profiles) to particular jobs may therefore be especially important for individuals with higher g (Lubinski & Benbow 1999). Item response theory and computerized adaptive testing have clarified relationships between g and specific abilities contributing to it (Sands et al 1997, Segall 1999). Developers of good cognitive ability selection tests cannot rely on knowledge of g alone.

Ability and job knowledge

Multiple-ability test battery data from 3000 Air Force enlistees supported a hierarchical ability structure (Carretta & Ree 1996) that fit the data well, considerably better than two nonhierarchical models or a *g*-only model (see also Carretta et al 1998). Men and women show similar hierarchical ability structures (Carretta & Ree 1997).

Carretta & Doub (1998) tested the mediating effect of prior mechanical and electrical knowledge on the relationship between *g* and subsequent job knowledge of Air Force trainees. Comparing racial groups (White, Black, and Hispanic) resulted in little moderating effect. Comparing gender groups prior job knowledge mediated subsequent job knowledge for males but not for females. The effect of *g* was weaker in individuals with more prior job knowledge; conversely, *g* was stronger in individuals with less prior job knowledge. It seems that *g* predicts the rate of job knowledge acquisition, which in turn has a larger direct influence on performance ratings than the indirect effect of *g* (Ree et al 1995).

Academic achievement and language proficiency

Meta-analysis found that undergraduate college grade point average (GPA) predicted job performance across many types of organizations, especially for job performance measured closer in time to the GPA (Roth et al 1996). Another meta-analysis reported substantial criterion-related validities for aptitude tests predicting GPA in graduate school. Subject-specific tests (possibly a job knowledge analog) had higher validities than verbal and mathematical tests, but both were of useful magnitude (Kuncel et al 1999).

Increasing immigration and concomitant workforce diversity suggest measuring English language proficiency when selecting for certain jobs. For entry-level meat trimmers ($N = 87$) whose native language was not English, a written and spoken English proficiency test was internally consistent and clearly linked to job analysis information. The test predicted supervisory ratings of overall job performance (Chan et al 1999). Spoken English proficiency assessment is now possible via real-time computer processing and analysis of human speech (Bernstein 1999).

Adverse impact

Cognitive ability measures tend to show nontrivial racial-group mean differences. Helms' (1992) hypothesis states that White-Black mean differences might be reduced by couching ability test content within a social context. An expert panel modified abstract ability items to reflect everyday organizational, social, and life situations. Contrary to the hypothesis, marked White-Black differences remained under the new test format, even under large-sample replication and parallel test forms (DeShon et al 1998b). Research needs to expand the number and types of items, explore different administration formats, and examine other specific abilities.

Short-term memory tests (digit span and digit-symbol substitution) show promise as an alternative or supplement to traditional ability tests, with lower adverse impact and good validities with job performance. Meta-analysis estimated White-Black mean differences on short-term memory tests at 0.48 SD, about half the 1.0 SD difference typically found in general cognitive ability tests. Short-term memory tests are reliable and correlate with training performance and job performance [$r \approx 0.45$ (Verive & McDaniel 1996)]. Lower adverse impact combined with respectable overall criterion-related validity encourages future research in this area.

The Armed Services Vocational Aptitude Battery (ASVAB) and an experimental ability test battery predicted training performance criteria in 17 military jobs (Sager et al 1997), showing some necessary tradeoffs. One cannot completely (a) minimize adverse impact for all subgroups compared (see Hoffman & Thornton 1997 for this issue in utility context), (b) maximize both criterion-related validity within jobs and classification efficiency across jobs, or (c) satisfy both (a) and (b). A selection strategy aimed at minimizing adverse impact may differ somewhat from a selection strategy aimed at maximizing mean predicted performance (Sackett & Roth 1996).

Personality

Personality taxonomies and constructs

The Five Factor Model (FFM), consisting of Extraversion, Agreeableness, Conscientiousness, Neuroticism (Adjustment), and Openness to Experience (see Wiggins & Trapnell 1997), enjoys considerable support. Factor analysis supports the robustness and generalizability of the FFM across different theoretical frameworks, assessments, rating sources, and cultures (see Hogan & Ones 1997b, Saucier & Goldberg 1998, Wiggins & Trapnell 1997). The model is useful for summarizing information and guiding theory and research (e.g. Mount & Barrick 1995, Tokar et al 1998).

The FFM yields information about the higher-order factor structure of personality; however, it ignores, confounds, or otherwise obscures understanding of variables combined into five broad factors (Hough 1997,1998b; Hough & Schneider 1996). FFM factors contain facets with high and low criterion-related validities, diluting the criterion-related validity of the factors. A review of meta-analyses concluded the FFM factors do not correlate highly with job performance (Matthews 1997). As alternatives, researchers are turning to nonhierarchical models such as the circumplex (Plutchik & Conte 1997) and other hierarchies. Hough (1997, 1998b) argues for a more refined taxonomy, distinguishing achievement from conscientiousness and extraversion and affiliation from extraversion. Meta-analyses demonstrate the importance of these distinctions for predicting managerial performance (Hough et al 1998) and sales performance (Vinchur et al 1998). Ghiselli's (1966) personality framework was compared with the FFM framework in the Barrick & Mount (1991) meta-analysis: the median uncorrected validity in the Ghiselli meta-analysis was 0.24; the highest mean uncorrected validity for an FFM variable in the Barrick & Mount (1991) study was 0.15 (Hough 1997). Several important personality constructs not within the FFM have been used for predicting work behavior:

EMOTIONALITY

Emotionality, or affectivity, consists of two bipolar dimensions at the most general level: negative-positive and aroused-unaroused (Averill 1997, Russell & Carroll 1999). A state measure of emotionality did not correlate with job performance, but a dispositional measure did (Wright & Staw 1999). In social welfare workers, negative affectivity correlated positively with emotional exhaustion or "burnout," and emotional exhaustion correlated negatively with job performance (Wright & Cropanzano 1998).

SOCIAL COMPETENCE

Social competence is a compound variable consisting of social insight, social maladjustment, social appropriateness, social openness, social influence, warmth, and extraversion (Schneider et al 1996). Reliable self-report measures of social insight (e.g. Gough 1968) and empathy (e.g. Hogan 1968) have a long history, as do situational judgment measures of social intelligence (e.g. Moss et al 1955). Variables subsumed under social competence might increment predictive validity for criteria emphasizing interpersonal effectiveness.

Conscientiousness

Many claim that conscientiousness, a FFM factor, is a valid predictor across organizations, jobs, and situations (Hogan & Ones 1997b, Mount & Barrick 1995, Salgado 1997a, 1998). Others question this wholesale conclusion (Hough 1997, 1998b; Robertson & Callinan 1998). Whether or in what direction conscientiousness predicts performance obviously depends on the criterion construct and how conscientiousness is defined and operationalized. Based on the Hogan & Ones' (1997) definition of conscientiousness as conformity and socially prescribed impulse control, conscientiousness would likely not predict performance across organizations, jobs, or situations in which creativity or innovation is important (Hough 1997, 1998b; Hough et al 1998).

Integrity tests

Meta-analyses of relations between integrity tests and FFM variables indicate that integrity tests are compound variables consisting primarily of conscientiousness, agreeableness, and adjustment (Ones & Viswesvaran 1998b). Four themes account for most of the variance in overt and personality-based integrity tests: punitive attitudes, admissions of illegal drug use, reliability, and admissions of theft (Hogan & Brinkmeyer 1997). Importantly, integrity tests differ from tests of deception (Murphy & Luther 1997). Sackett & Wanek (1996) provided an insightful and thorough review of integrity testing that dealt with construct- and criterion-related validity evidence; moderator variables; social desirability and applicant reactions; and legal, professional, and governmental evaluations. Meta-analysis indicates that integrity and conscientiousness tests usefully supplement general cognitive ability tests when predicting overall job performance (Schmidt & Hunter 1998). Converging evidence exists for the construct, criterion-related, and incremental validity of integrity tests (Miner & Capps 1996, Ones & Viswesvaran 1998b), but considerable variability may accompany the overall findings.

For example, criteria often used in integrity-testing research are problematic. Self-report or admission of counterproductive behavior confounds reliability with validity for overt integrity tests and underestimates the extent of counterproductive work behaviors, as do more direct measures (e.g. detected theft). Moreover, counterproductivity is not a unitary construct (Ashton 1998, Sackett & Wanek 1996). Two recent meta-analyses summarized correlations between integrity test scores and two facets of counterproductivity: reported drug abuse [$r = 0.21$ (Schmidt et al 1997)] and number of job-related accidents [$r = 0.52$ (Ones & Viswesvaran 1998b)]. Workplace violence, a facet of counterproductivity, tends to be better predicted by narrow measures such as aggression and violence scales than by broad honesty tests. Meta-analysis indicates that the validity for predicting workplace violence is higher for violence scales than for integrity tests [$r = 0.48$ vs 0.26 (Ones et al 1994)]. A physical-aggression measure predicted aggressive penalty minutes ($r = 0.33$) in high school hockey games, but not nonaggressive penalty minutes ($r = 0.04$) (Bushman & Wells 1998).

Customer service orientation

Meta-analysis finds that customer service orientation is a compound variable consisting of agreeableness ($r = 0.70$), adjustment ($r = 0.58$), and conscientiousness ($r = 0.43$) (Ones & Viswesvaran 1996), and customer service scales correlate with performance in customer service jobs ($r = 0.31$) (Frei & McDaniel 1998).

Core self-evaluation

Core self-evaluation is a compound variable consisting of self-esteem, generalized self-efficacy, locus of control, and emotional stability (Judge et al 1998). Meta-analysis estimated the validity of core self-evaluation for predicting job performance at 0.30 (TA Judge & JE Bono, submitted for publication). A much larger meta-analysis suggests that self-efficacy, a facet of core self-evaluation, correlates higher with job performance than does core self-evaluation as a whole [$r = 0.38$ (Stajkovic & Luthans 1998)].

Other meta-analyses

Meta-analysis of the Five Factor Model validities in U.S. studies from 1992 through 1997 produced results similar to past U.S. meta-analyses (Anderson & Viswesvaran 1998), but meta-analyses involving only European samples produced somewhat different results (Salgado 1997a, 1998). Both conscientiousness and emotional stability correlated positively with job performance across occupational groups, and both contributed incremental variance beyond general mental ability in predicting overall job performance. Other meta-analyses of validities of FFM factors indicate that agreeableness, as well as conscientiousness and emotional stability, predicts performance in jobs involving interpersonal interaction (Mount et al 1998). Managerial potential scales predict overall managerial job performance [$r \approx 0.40$ (Ones et al 1998)], although meta-analytic validities tend to be low for FFM factors predicting overall managerial performance (Hough et al 1998). Some FFM facets had much higher validities, shedding light on how facet-level variables might combine to form managerial potential scales with high criterion-related validity. Many of these meta-analytic researchers corrected study correlations for predictor range restriction by using national norm SDs from personality test manuals. This practice of using norm SDs appears warranted, because SDs of job applicants on personality measures are about 2%–9% less than those based on national norms (Ones & Viswesvaran 1999).

Conditional reasoning

Pioneered by James (1998, 1999), conditional reasoning assumes that individuals' personalities are differentiated by the type of logical reasoning used to justify their actions. For example, people who score high on achievement motivation tend to attribute success to internal rather than external sources and consider demanding tasks challenging rather than frustrating. An achievement conditional reasoning scale correlated positively with scholastic criteria, in-basket performance, and other achievement scales (James 1998, Migetz et al 1999a, Smith et al 1995). An aggression conditional reasoning scale correlated negatively with overall job performance (Hornick et al 1999, James 1998) and positively with counterproductive work behavior (Burroughs et al 1999, Migetz et al 1999b, Patton et al 1999). This approach appears to overcome many problems related to intentional distortion.

Intentional distortion

Not surprisingly, meta-analysis shows large mean-score differences between honest and directed-faking conditions (Viswesvaran & Ones 1999). The amount of distortion in naturally occurring applicant settings is uncertain however. Rosse et al (1998) found that applicants ($N = 197$) scored on average 0.69 SD higher than incumbents ($N = 73$) on FFM facet-level scales. In contrast, three separate samples involving over 40,500 applicants and over 1700 incumbents found significantly less distortion on similar scales (Hough 1998a). Ability and motivation to fake may be key determinants in the amount of distortion found in applicant settings (Snell et al 1999). Meta-analysis indicates that explicit warnings not to distort do reduce distortion [0.23 SD (Dwight & Donovan 1998)].

A slew of recent studies has investigated intentional distortion effects on criterion-related validities. Many assert that distortion does not tend to moderate, mediate, suppress, or attenuate the criterion-related validities of personality scales (Barrick & Mount 1996; Hogan 1998; Hough 1997, 1998a,b; Ones & Viswesvaran 1998b,c; Ones et al 1996). Others, such as Douglas et al (1996), Snell & McDaniel (1998), and Zickar & Drasgow (1996), contend that distortion seriously reduces criterion-related validity. Hough (1998a) resolved the apparent conflict by stratifying results by employment setting. In directed-faking settings, self-report scale scores have dramatically lower criterion-related validities than those obtained in applicant or incumbent settings; in applicant settings, self-report scale scores have the same or slightly lower criterion-related validities than those obtained from job incumbents in research-only settings. Similarly, construct validity may be negatively affected in directed-faking studies (Ellingson et al 1999a), but the effect does not seem to be as serious in applicant settings (Collins & Gleaves 1998, Ellingson et al 1999b, Ones & Viswesvaran 1998c).

Coaching individuals on personality tests potentially threatens the effectiveness of traditional social desirability scales. Subtle items can be more resistant to coaching and distortion than obvious items (Alliger et al 1996). Theory-driven approaches to scale development and validity data to refine items produce subtle items resistant to distortion and with excellent validity (Gough 1994).

Race and ethnic background

Similar personality factor structures for Blacks and Whites are found (Collins & Gleaves 1998). Meta-analyses of White, Black, Hispanic, and Native American groups indicate minimal group mean differences for three overt integrity tests (Ones & Viswesvaran 1998a) and for FFM factors, although Hispanics scored 0.60 SD higher than Whites on social desirability scales (Hough 1998b). Personality variables have little adverse impact against minorities, if any. Score correction strategies using social desirability scales to correct distortion in content scale scores might affect Hispanics more than others.

Multiple predictor domains

Applied psychology has long postulated that ability and motivation interact in predicting job performance: High performers must have the requisite ability and effort to do the job; neither ability nor effort alone suffices. However, regression analyses of data across job samples, performance criteria, and different ability and motivation measures have yielded nonexistent or very slight incremental ability-motivation interaction effects (Sackett et al 1998). A combined meta-analysis of ability-personality correlations and review of the empirical findings on ability-interest and personality-interest relationships have produced an integrated model identifying four categories or "trait complexes": science/math, clerical/conventional, social, and intellectual/cultural (Ackerman & Heggestad 1997). A vocational interest structure was empirically linked to Gottfredson's (1986) ability-based job classification framework, yielding four similar categories (Oswald & Ferstl 1999). Linking different predictor domains to a common job classification framework may clarify the constellations of predictors that are useful for selection into various types of jobs (see Arthur & Bennett 1995, Hattrup et al 1998, Johnson et al 1997, Mael et al 1996b, Vinchur et al 1998) and may improve synthetic validity efforts.

Assessment methods

Interview

Interview structure

Compared with unstructured interviews, structured employment interviews define content more explicitly. Their successes are therefore more likely to replicate, and they are better analyzed and meta-analyzed to determine their transportability to other jobs and work settings. Nonetheless, organizations still prefer unstructured interviews by a wide margin (Graves & Karren 1996). A comprehensive review indicates that various components of structured interviews influence the interview's psychometric properties, legal defensibility, and applicant/interviewer reactions (Campion et al 1997). Recent research offers at least three other compelling reasons for structuring the core of the interview (see also the Dipboye 1997 review).

RELIABILITY

Structured interviews tend to have higher interrater reliability than unstructured interviews. Meta-analysis reports average interrater reliabilities of 0.67 for high structure vs 0.34 for low structure (Conway et al 1995).

STANDARDIZATION

Standardized interviews place more burden on the instrument than any particular interviewer's interviewing and assessment skills. A highly standardized situational interview, in which applicants respond to hypothetical critical work incidents, can be less susceptible to rating biases (Kataoka et al 1997). Computerized phone interviews have efficiently obtained standardized applicant information, with validity coefficients similar to those for traditional interviews (Schmidt & Rader 1999). Interviewer experience and training further standardize the interview

(Conway et al 1995, Campion et al 1997, Huffcutt & Woehr 1999). Training in note taking improves attention, encoding, recall, and evaluation of interview information focusing on work behaviors (Burnett et al 1998).

FAIRNESS

Structured interviews treat applicants in a consistent manner. Mean differences by race are more likely reduced in highly structured interviews containing content related to noncognitive constructs, especially for high-complexity jobs (Huffcutt & Roth 1998). Court outcomes on disparate impact and disparate treatment have favored organizations high on three interview characteristics: standardized administration, high job relatedness, and multiple raters (Williamson et al 1997).

Interpersonal and nonverbal behavior

Interviewee characteristics (e.g. gaze, hand movement, and physical attractiveness) can predict several dimensions of managerial effectiveness (leadership, teamwork, and planning/organization), even when characteristics are coded independently of the content (Burnett & Motowidlo 1998; see also Motowidlo & Burnett 1995). The convergent and discriminant validities between interpersonal behavior in the interview and different job performance criteria should be considered.

Assessment centers

Assessment centers (ACs) have long been haunted by evidence of content- and criterion-valid ratings lacking construct validity (Arthur et al 1999, Spychalski et al 1997, Woehr & Arthur 1999). Confusion about the constructs being measured, rating errors, type and form of rating procedures, and participant inconsistencies in behavior across exercises are possible explanations (Arthur & Tubre 1999, Guion 1998). Features improving AC ratings include having (a) only a few conceptually distinct constructs, (b) concrete, job-related construct definitions, (c) frame-of-reference assessor training with evaluative standards, (d) cross-exercise assessment, and (e) several psychology-trained assessors (Lievens 1998, Woehr & Arthur 1999). An AC designed and implemented on the basis of research and professional-practice guidelines (see Task Force on Assessment Center Guidelines 1989) produced construct-valid AC ratings. Generalizability theory facets associated with individuals and constructs accounted for 60% of the total variance, and facets associated with assessors and exercises accounted for 11% of the total variance (Arthur et al 1999).

ACs are expensive and prone to cost-benefit comparisons with other predictors. AC ratings have significant incremental validity over personality variables, and vice versa, when predicting managerial performance (Goffin et al 1996, with $N = 68$). AC ratings also have incremental validity over cognitive ability, although some AC exercise validities are founded primarily on their cognitive component

(Goldstein et al 1998). By using policy capturing and meta-analysis, overall AC ratings have been predicted from both cognitive ability and personality variables [$R = 0.77$ (Collins et al 1999)]. The key question is whether policy-captured predictors predict job performance better than AC ratings (Howard 1999). Black-White mean exercise score differences have ranged from 0.03 to 0.40 SDs, with Blacks scoring lower (Goldstein et al 1999). Exercises emphasizing interpersonal skills more than cognitive ability have resulted in less or no adverse impact for Blacks (Goldstein et al 1999, Bobrow & Leonards 1997).

Biodata

Several researchers have focused on much-needed construct-oriented approaches to biodata (biographical information). CN MacLane (submitted for publication) refined the federal government's Individual Achievement Record biodata scales, which measure social and cognitive abilities (see Gandy et al 1994). Personality-based biodata scales predict leadership (Stricker & Rock 1998) and life insurance sales (McManus & Kelly 1999). A review of eleven studies examined the validity of biodata scales based on Mumford & Stokes' (1992) rigorous construct-oriented item-generation procedures. Scales were content and construct valid, with criterion-related validities similar to those for traditional empirical keying (Mumford et al 1996).

Biodata theory relies heavily on the principle that past behavior is the best predictor of future job performance (i.e. die "consistency" principle). Failure or negative life experiences also explain why biodata predict performance (Russell 1999). Moxie (i.e. courage or "ego-resiliency") may moderate how negative life experiences influence development and subsequent job performance (Dean et al 1999, Muchinsky 1999). "Negative" is often in the eye of the beholder, however. Both positive and negative responses to elements of a broader life-events taxonomy may be needed.

Conclusions about the effectiveness of rational, empirical-keying, and factor-analytic biodata scale development strategies are inconsistent. Rational scales have predicted sales performance at least as well as empirically keyed and factor-analytic scales (Stokes & Searcy 1999). Factor-analytic and rational scales have predicted several customer service criteria much better than empirical keying (Schoenfeldt 1999). A meta-analysis found similar levels of criterion-related cross-validities across all three scale construction strategies (Hough & Paullin 1994). Rational, empirical-keying, and factor-analytic scale strategies need not be executed and compared separately; the strategies may iteratively inform one another.

Regarding the generalizability of biodata, the reliability, factor structure, and validity of biodata keys appear stable across two English-speaking countries (Dalessio et al 1996). Validity for a biodata inventory predicting managerial progress generalized across organizations and educational levels (Carlson et al 1999). "Contemporary" items tend to be more valid than "future/hypothetical" or "historical" items, and items that ask respondents about others' opinions of them are more valid than direct self-report items (Lefkowitz et al 1999). Meta-analysis found that the amount and task-level specificity of work experience correlated most highly with job performance (Quiñones et al 1995). Rational biodata scales may produce inadequate levels of validity for separate racial/ethnic groups, but empirical item analysis can be used to produce a scale valid across groups (Schmitt & Pulakos 1998, Schmitt et al 1999). Whitney & Schmitt (1997) discovered differential item functioning between racial subgroups in about one quarter of the biodata items they examined.

Measurement issues and validation strategies

Measurement issues

Many published studies in personnel selection continue to suffer from low statistical power due to small sample sizes (Mone et al 1996, Salgado 1998). Confidence intervals directly convey the impact of sample size on the accuracy of statistics (Hunter 1997). A computer program calculates confidence intervals on correlation coefficients corrected for measurement unreliability and range restriction (Salgado 1997b). Formulas are accurate in the large-sample case; for the small-sample case, the bootstrap method (i.e. calculating a distribution of correlations by resampling data with replacement) has generated accurate confidence intervals for ability-training performance validities (Russell et al 1998). Instead of confidence intervals, Murphy & Myors (1999) provide noncentral F tables and real-world examples that test minimum-effect null hypotheses for t-tests, correlations, and ANOVAs.

Measurement error variance can distort patterns of research results and mislead conclusions. Circumstances in 26 applied-research situations show when to correct validities for such error by using the appropriate reliability coefficient (Schmidt & Hunter 1996). Structural equation modeling can test the statistical significance of corrected correlation coefficients and the difference between two such correlations (Hancock 1997). Recent studies considered maximizing the reliability of a linear composite by weighting the constituent variables as a function of their reliabilities (Cliff & Caruso 1998, Li et al 1996, Raykov 1997, Wang 1998).

Estimation formulas for the population validity (expected prediction in the entire population) and cross-validity (expected prediction in other independent samples) were thoroughly reviewed (Raju et al 1997), and formulas were compared in a Monte Carlo study with data from a large sample of Air Force enlistees (Raju et al 1999). Generally, the Ezekiel, Smith, and Wherry procedures all provided good squared population validity estimates, and Burket's formula best estimated the squared population cross-validity. In stepwise regression, results showed that the sample size-to-predictor ratio had to be relatively large (10:1 at least) to yield good cross-validity estimates. All cross-validity estimation formulas performed similarly well; none was clearly superior (Schmitt & Ployhart 1999). Instead of stepwise regression, researchers often judge the relative size of regression weights to decide on the important variables within a particular model. A new type of relative importance weights enhances the interpretability of regression results when predictors are highly intercorrelated (Johnson 1999).

Finally, personnel selection research must often deal with missing data. Generally, pairwise deletion is better than listwise deletion, and estimating missing scores via regression is better than substituting missing scores with their unconditional mean (Roth et al 1996). Personnel selection would profit from understanding substantive processes underlying "missingness." Job promotions or transfers, emotional exhaustion from work, and organizational redesign all may reflect different types of longitudinal and cross-sectional attrition processes.

Meta-analysis and validity generalization

Meta-analysis has had a far-reaching impact on policymaking, real-world application, and academic research (Hunter & Schmidt 1996) and is a useful quantitative tool for summarizing large bodies of personnel selection research (Murphy 1997). The meta-analytic mean effect size across studies (e.g. mean correlation coefficient) tends to be fairly accurate. In contrast, estimates of the variance of effect sizes (after correcting for statistical artifacts) can deviate from their actual population values by practically significant amounts (Oswald & Johnson 1998), which may affect meta-analytic conclusions about selection research. Variance estimates can be downwardly biased if one ignores the fact that individuals were selected on a variable correlated with the variables in the meta-analysis [i.e. incidental range restriction (Aguinis & Whitehead 1997)]. Statistical homogeneity tests of the variance have low statistical power and tend to discourage the search for moderator effects (Sánchez-Meca & Marín-Martínez 1997).

Meta-analysis is one of many lines of evidence supporting the use of a selection test. In addition to meta-analytically averaging correlations, researchers might consider what predicts group or organizational mean differences on predictors and criteria (Ostroff & Harrison 1999). Hierarchical linear modeling (HLM) has been advocated for this purpose; Hofmann (1997) presented some practical organizational examples. Synthetic validity evidence may provide additional validity information (Hoffman & McPhail 1998).

Evaluation of selection systems

Differential prediction

A selection test with equal regression slopes across subgroups (e.g. race, gender, and age groups) does not necessarily measure a latent construct the same way across subgroups. Only data conforming to a special set of mathematical constraints will show a lack of differential prediction and latent construct equivalence simultaneously (Millsap 1995, 1997). To the extent that these constraints are violated, this finding may challenge previous selection research suggesting a lack of differential prediction (e.g. cognitive ability research).

Aguinis & Stone-Romero (1997) examined range restriction effects on the statistical power of moderated multiple regression for detecting differential prediction. Range restriction often mistakenly led to concluding no differential prediction when validity differences were moderate (0.4 correlation units). Larger validity differences were detected, and smaller differences were not, regardless of range restriction. Computer software for estimating the statistical power of differential prediction in moderated multiple regression is available (Aguinis & Pierce 1998b). Future software could incorporate violations of the assumption of equal error variances between subgroup regression models. Assumption violations occur when larger subgroup sample sizes are paired with the smaller subgroup validity coefficient (e.g. Aguinis & Pierce 1998a, DeShon & Alexander 1996), but for some organizational data, violations are not severe enough to affect statistical inferences from moderated multiple regression (Oswald et al 1999). Error variance in the independent variables affects differential prediction (Terris 1997), and errors-in-variables regression addresses this problem. Errors-in-variables regression detected differential prediction more accurately than moderated multiple regression when reliability coefficients were >0.65 and sample sizes were >250 (Anderson et al 1996).

Adverse impact

Common sense might assert that combining low-adverse-impact predictors with a high-adverse-impact predictor improves adverse impact over using the high-adverse-impact predictor alone. However, Sackett & Ellingson (1997) presented tables illustrating reduced subgroup differences for some composites but increased differences for others. Composite measures invariably reduce subgroup differences less than expected. In particular, the "four-fifths rule" set out in the Uniform Guidelines (U.S. Equal Employment Opportunity Commission et al, 1978) is usually met only under very high selection ratios (≥ 0.90) or very slight composite group-mean differences ($d \leq 0.20$).

Similar conclusions came from in meta-analytic estimates of criterion-related validities for a cognitive ability measure, a noncognitive composite (interview, biodata, and conscientiousness), and a composite of both, all independently predicting overall job performance. Selection batteries excluding cognitive ability almost always satisfied the four-fifths rule; batteries that included cognitive ability alone or in a composite almost never satisfied the rule (Schmitt et al 1997). Findings are echoed in two large-sample studies of firefighter and police officer job applicants selected on cognitive ability and personality measures (Ryan et al 1998a). Bobko et al (1999) updated the Schmitt et al (1997) meta-analytic matrix, discovering that even a noncognitive composite could violate the four-fifths rule when selection ratios were $\leq 50\%$. Group-mean differences on noncognitive composites should be determined before assuming they reduce adverse impact.

Also, adverse impact is partly a function of the criteria chosen and how they are weighted (Hattrup et al 1997).

Alternative forms of administration potentially reduce adverse impact and increase overall validity. Videotaped versions of situational judgment test material can reduce adverse impact and have greater face validity than paper-and-pencil versions. Presumably, validity improves because the content in the video format is preserved, and irrelevant variance related to reading comprehension is removed (Chan & Schmitt 1997). Similar conclusions come from comparing a video-based ability test to a traditional ability test (Pulakos & Schmitt 1996).

Banding

Given subgroup differences on selection tests (most notably cognitive ability tests), statistical banding can fulfill important goals such as maintaining workforce diversity and improving perceptions of process and outcome fairness in a selection procedure (Truxillo & Bauer 1999). Linearly transforming bands on predicted criterion scores into bands on predictor scores (Aguinis et al 1998) may improve banding because criterion differences tend to matter more to organizations than predictor differences (see Campbell 1996, Gottfredson 1999). Further advances in banding might consider that reliable predictors tend to produce smaller statistical bandwidths, in which differences larger than the band may still not be practical differences or translate into practical criterion differences.

Utility

A few recent studies focus on how utility information communicates the effectiveness of a selection system to organizational stakeholders. Whyte & Latham (1997) replicated the counterintuitive results of Latham & Whyte (1994), discovering that communicating positive utility information can actually decrease managers' intentions to use a selection system. Utility information may prove beneficial as supplementary information, not delivered face-to-face as a "hard sell" (Cronshaw 1997). Communicating utility in terms of multiple outcomes (e.g. dollars, job performance, and organizational effectiveness) may lead to greater acceptance of the utility message by different stakeholders (Roth & Bobko 1997). Considering and balancing all particular stakeholder positions is difficult but beneficial to organizations (Austin et al 1996).

Applicant reactions

Positive applicant reactions increase the chances of hiring the best applicants, facilitate the ability to recruit effectively, avoid the possibility of costly litigation, and contribute to the organization's reputation (Gilliland & Steiner 1999, Ryan & Greguras 1998, Schmitt & Chan 1999). Selection systems can be viewed as socialization mechanisms imparting job information to applicants and affecting their work-related thoughts, attitudes, and behaviors (Anderson & Ostroff 1997). Managing applicant reactions does not imply making the organization attractive to all individuals; accurate perceptions can lead to applicant withdrawal. Black-White test-taking attitude differences may not affect group differences in applicant withdrawal (Schmit & Ryan 1997), but they might, which would add to adverse-impact concerns (Chan 1997).

Chan et al (1998) discovered that (a) pretest reactions affected cognitive ability test performance, and test performance affected posttest reactions, and (b) personality test performance was unrelated to either pretest or posttest reactions. Integrity test results paralleled the personality test conclusions, and the overt integrity test had greater perceived job relatedness than the personality-based test (Whitney et al 1999).

Test outcome (passing or failing) contributes strongly to subsequent applicant reactions. Applicants passing a test for a clerical position rated organizational attractiveness, intentions to work for the organization, and test fairness higher than their initial reactions (Bauer et al 1998). Test outcome affects the perceived fairness of the hiring decision much more than the selection ratio (Thorsteinson & Ryan 1997). Ployhart et al (1999) determined that fairness perceptions of cognitive and job knowledge tests increased with a positive selection outcome and with sensitively conveyed personal and procedural information regardless of outcome. Selected applicants' self-perception improved with personal or procedural information; rejected applicants' self-perception declined. Sensitive explanations amplified this result, implying that providing information about the selection procedure would increase fairness and organizational perceptions but be counterbalanced by lower self-perceptions for rejected applicants.

Invasiveness of personnel selection measures has been investigated. Verifiable, impersonal, and face-valid biodata items tend to be perceived as less invasive, especially for individuals who understand the general purpose of biodata (Mael et al 1996a). Ways to obtain potentially invasive information without violating applicants' needs for privacy have been offered [e.g. explaining the job relevance of the item (Mael 1998)].

Emerging topics

Team member selection

Organizations increasingly use team-based structures for organizing, motivating, and performing work (see Guzzo & Salas 1995, Howard 1995, Kehoe 1999, Klimoski & Zukin 1999, Kraut & Korman 1999b, O'Neil 1997, Sundstrom 1999). Much has been learned about factors affecting team performance and effectiveness (see reviews by Cohen & Bailey 1997, and West & Allen 1997), but more work remains for personnel selection. Selection systems need to consider differences between team selection and traditional selection methods, particular work team circumstances (task type, role differentiation, and resources), and selection into new versus preexisting work teams.

Individual characteristics and types of tasks interact within a team to influence team performance and effectiveness. On a creative problem-solving task, a midrange of extraverts appears best; too many or too few depress performance ratings slightly. Conscientiousness did not predict team performance on the creative task (Barry & Stewart 1997), as Hough (1992) found at the individual level of analysis. In other team studies (LePine et al 1997, Barrick et al 1998), conscientiousness did predict task performance. Given a designated leader and group members each with unique expertise, team decision-making accuracy over time tends to be best when all members are high in conscientiousness and general cognitive ability (LePine et al 1997). Barrick et al (1998) found that conscientiousness, general cognitive ability, and extraversion all predicted overall team performance ratings in manufacturing work teams, where team members contributed independently to the outcome. Team agreeableness predicted teamwork for those tasks in which intergroup conflict was possible. One disagreeable team member was often enough to disrupt team performance, indicating the importance of interpersonal skills when selecting for some teams. Negotiation, an interpersonal skill, was validly measured with a simulation exercise (O'Neil et al 1997a,b). Significant advances in team selection research await good taxonomies of "team difference" variables (the analog of individual-difference variables for individuals) and situational variables relevant to teams.

Cross-cultural selection issues

With their expanding global markets, culturally diverse work teams, and expatriate work assignments, international and multinational organizations place new demands on selection processes and measurement tools. Validities of domestic selection instruments may not generalize to international sites, because different predictor and criterion constructs may be relevant, or, if the constructs are the same, the behavioral indicators may differ. Interpersonal skill, open-mindedness, and adaptability are important factors for expatriate success, and family situation is the most commonly cited reason for failure (Arthur & Bennett 1995, Nyfield & Baron 1999). The vast majority of companies base their expatriate selection decisions on technical competence alone (Aryee 1997), so finding a very high failure rate among expatriates is unsurprising [between 15% and 40% (Shackleton & Newell 1997)]. A clear need for improving expatriate selection exists.

Several personality inventories originally developed in English have demonstrated similar psychometric properties across languages and cultures (see Katigbak et al 1996, McCrae & Costa 1997, Nyfield & Baron 1999). The International Committee on Test Standards produced a set of stringent standards for translating tests into another language (see Hambleton 1999). Psychologists from many different cultures might be involved in all phases of inventory development and validation, a strategy used to develop the Global Personality Inventory

(Schmit et al 1999). Cultural variables likely moderate the validity of selection procedures. The House et al (1997) review concluded that Hofstede's (1980) four constructs (power distance, uncertainty avoidance, individualism vs collectivism, and masculinity vs femininity) described and differentiated cultures most usefully.

Professional, legal, and ethical standards

Professional

Three initiatives sponsored by the American Psychological Association provide guidelines and policies regarding test-taker rights and responsibilities, test standards, and test-user qualifications. First, the American Psychological Association is in the final stages of approving 10 test-taker rights and corresponding responsibilities (Joint Committee on Testing Practices 1999). Second, the "Standards for Educational and Psychological Testing" (unpublished manuscript) revises and updates standards for psychological tests and for psychological measurement in general. All parties involved in employment decisions involving psychological assessment should become familiar with these new standards. Third, the "Test User Qualifications" document is currently under review (Fox 1999). These three documents will impact personnel selection practices and have significant legal and ethical implications.

Legal

Over the past 20 years or so, more employment litigation has been brought under common-law torts than under federal or state equal employment opportunity statutes (Highberger 1996). Nevertheless, legal challenges to personnel selection decisions are often based on the Civil Rights Acts, Americans with Disabilities Act (ADA), and Age Discrimination in Employment Act. In the vast majority of these cases, the Equal Employment Opportunity Commission is typically not involved (Sharf & Jones 1999), although commission guidelines provide important compliance information for the public and the courts. Unstructured interviews account for the majority of federal court cases involving selection tools, followed by cognitive ability tests, and physical ability tests; together, they were judged to be discriminatory in about 40% of the cases, with cognitive tests faring somewhat better (Terpstra et al 1999). For important practical guidance and discussions of the many issues, risks, and myths regarding fair employment as well as trends in employment litigation, see Barrett (1996, 1998), Jeanneret (1998), and Sharf & Jones (1999).

The U.S. Supreme Court significantly limited the scope of ADA, ruling that impairments should be evaluated in their corrected or "mitigated" state (*Sutton vs United Airlines* 1999, *Murphy vs United Parcel Service* 1999). The U.S. Equal Employment Opportunity Commission (1999) answered 46 frequently asked questions pertaining to employers' legal obligations and the rights of the disabled in both the application and employment settings. Tippins (1999) provided practical ADA guidance for several testing scenarios, and Bruyére (1999) outlined the psychologist's role in upholding ADA provisions in all phases of the employment process.

Affirmative action and reverse discrimination

Although individuals differ greatly in their perceptions of affirmative action programs (Kravitz et al 1997), negative consequences consistently occur when employees or applicants believe hiring is based on group membership rather than merit (Heilman 1996, Heilman et al 1998, Kravitz et al 1997, Stanush et al 1998). Affirmative action programs are associated with slight improvement in employment conditions for women and racial minorities and appear to have virtually no effect on organizational effectiveness (Kravitz et al 1997).

No general agreement exists on how to prevent discrimination or remedy past discrimination (Campbell 1996). Reverse-discrimination court cases have clarified that race or other job-irrelevant class membership can not be used when making employment-related decisions. Therein lies a conflict: The Uniform Guidelines indicate that organizations should seek out valid non- or less-discriminating predictors, yet developing a selection system with such measures requires attention to class membership. In *Hoyden vs County of Nassau* (1999), the claim that an entrance exam designed to minimize discriminatory impact on minority job candidates necessarily discriminated against nonminority job candidates was ruled to be without merit. This case sets a precedent in affirming the reasonableness of designing selection systems to minimize adverse impact against protected groups.

Ethical

Ethical issues in personnel selection are complex, context-specific, and relative to each concerned party. We refer the reader to two important new sources in the field. Lowman (1998) authored an updated ethics casebook for human resource professionals practicing within organizations, and Jeanneret (1998) discussed ethical issues involved in individual assessment, detailing the responsibilities for both assessors and organizations.

Parting remarks

New areas in personnel selection are unfolding, and traditional areas continue to improve. (*a*) Greater conceptual and methodological attention has been devoted to understanding and predicting how organizationally relevant criteria might change over time. Given the present and future state of rapid change in the world of work, this line of research is critically important for improving personnel selection and overall organizational effectiveness. (*b*) Personality theory and measurement within a personnel selection context have burgeoned. New personality constructs and compound constructs of well-known traits are being brought into the fold. (c) Applicant reactions to personnel selection procedures have been energetically studied. (d) Team member and cross-cultural selection issues have drawn greater research attention. (e) Refined taxonomic structures are being developed across many different domains in personnel selection, both from the worker and work perspectives. We predict that selection systems will become more complex as a consequence of all this work; selection systems will mirror today's realities and prove to be more effective and rewarding for individuals and organizations alike. We also predict that Guion's (1998) book on personnel selection will fast become a classic. It is readable, practical, thoughtful, and thorough, and it assures its readers that much has been learned in personnel selection. Although the turn of the millennium marks a distinct ending and beginning, personnel selection theory and practice remain in constant process, looking toward the future while remembering the past.

Literature cited

Ackerman PL, Heggestad ED. 1997. Intelligence, personality, and interests: evidence for overlapping traits. *Psychol. Bull.* 121:219–45

Aguinis H, Cortina J, Goldberg E. 1998. A new procedure for computing equivalence bands in personnel selection. *Hum. Perform.* 11:351–65

Aguinis H, Pierce CA. 1998a. Heterogeneity of error variance and the assessment of moderating effects of categorical variables: a conceptual review. *Organ. Res. Methods* 1:296–314

Aguinis H, Pierce CA. 1998b. Statistical power computations for detecting dichotomous moderator variables with moderated multiple regression. *Educ. Psychol. Meas.* 58:668–76

Aguinis H, Stone-Romero EF. 1997. Methodological artifacts in moderated multiple regression and their effects on statistical power. *J. Appl. Psychol.* 82:192–206

Aguinis H, Whitehead R. 1997. Sampling variance in the correlation coefficient under indirect range restriction: implications for validity generalization. *J. Appl. Psychol.* 82:528–38

Alliger GM, Lilienfeld SO, Mitchell KE. 1996. The susceptibility of overt and covert integrity tests to coaching and faking. *Psychol. Sci.* 7:32–39

Anderson GD, Viswesvaran C. 1998. *An update of the validity of personality scales in personnel selection: a meta-analysis of studies published between 1992–1997.* Presented at Annu. Meet. Soc. Ind. Organ. Psychol., 13th, Dallas

Anderson LE, Stone-Romero EF, Tisak J. 1996. A comparison of bias and mean squared error in parameter estimates of interaction effects: moderated multiple regression versus errors-in-variables regression. *Multivariate Behav. Res.* 31:69–94

Anderson N, Herriot P, eds. 1997. *International Handbook of Selection and Assessment*, Vol. 13. Chichester, UK: Wiley. 652 pp.

Anderson N, Ostroff C. 1997. Selection as socialization. See Anderson & Herriot 1997, pp. 413–40

Arthur W, Bennett W. 1995. The international assignee: the relative importance of factors perceived to contribute to success. *Pers. Psychol.* 48:99–114

Arthur W, Doverspike D, Barrett GV. 1996. Development of a job analysis-based procedure for weighting and combining content-related tests into a single test battery score. *Pers. Psychol.* 49:971–85

Arthur W, Tubre T. 1999. The assessment center construct-related validity paradox: a case of construct misspecification? See Quiñones 1999

Arthur W, Woehr DJ, Maldegen R. 1999. Convergent and discriminant validity of assessment center dimensions: a conceptual and empirical re-examination of the assessment center construct-related validity paradox. *J. Manage.* In press

Aryee S. 1997. Selection and training of expatriate employees. See Anderson & Herriot 1997, pp. 147–60

Ashton MC. 1998. Personality and job performance: the importance of narrow traits. *J. Organ. Behav.* 19:289–303

Austin JT, Klimoski RJ, Hunt ST. 1996. Dilemmatics in public sector assessment: a framework for developing and evaluating selection systems. *Hum. Perform.* 9:177–98

Averill JR. 1997. The emotions: an integrative approach. See Hogan et al 1997, pp. 513–41

Barrett RS, ed. 1996. *Fair Employment Strategies in Human Resource Management.* Westport, CT: Quorum Books. 319 pp.

Barrett RS. 1998. *Challenging the Myths of Fair Employment Practices.* Westport, CT: Quorum Books. 190 pp.

Barrick MR, Mount MK. 1991. The Big Five personality dimensions and job performance: a meta-analysis. *Pers. Psychol.* 44:1–26

Barrick MR, Mount MK. 1996. Effects of impression management and self-deception on the predictive validity of personality constructs. *J. Appl. Psychol.* 81:261–72

Barrick MR, Stewart GL, Neubert MJ, Mount MK. 1998. Relating member ability and personality to work-team processes and team effectiveness. *J. Appl. Psychol.* 83:377–91

Barry B, Stewart GL. 1997. Composition, process, and performance in self-managed groups: the role of personality. *J. Appl. Psychol.* 82:62–78

Bauer TN, Maertz CP Jr, Dolen MR, Campion MA. 1998. Longitudinal assessment of applicant reactions to employment testing and test outcome feedback. *J. Appl. Psychol.* 83:892–903

Bernstein J. 1999. *Computer-based assessment of spoken language.* Presented at Annu. Meet. Soc. Ind. Organ. Psychol., 14th, Atlanta

Bobko P, Roth PL, Potosky D. 1999. Derivation and implications of a meta-analytic matrix incorporating cognitive ability, alternative predictors, and job performance. *Pers. Psychol.* 52:1–31

Bobrow W, Leonards JS. 1997. Development and validation of an assessment center during organizational change. *J. Soc. Behav. Pers.* 12(5):217–36

Borman WC, Motowidlo SJ, eds. 1997. Organizational citizenship behavior and contextual performance. *Hum. Perform.* 10:67–192

Bruyére S. 1999. Disability nondiscrimination in the employment process: the role for psychologists. See Ekstrom & Smith 1999. In press

Burke MJ, Rupinski MT, Dunlap WP, Davison HK. 1996. Do situational variables act as substantive causes of relationships between individual difference variables? Two large-scale tests of "common cause" models. *Pers. Psychol.* 49:573–98

Burnett JR, Fan C, Motowidlo SJ, Degroot T. 1998. Interview notes and validity. *Pers. Psychol.* 51:375–96

Burnett JR, Motowidlo SJ. 1998. Relations between different sources of information in the structured selection interview. *Pers. Psychol.* 51:963–83

Burroughs SM, Bing MN, James LR. 1999. Reconsidering how to measure employee reliability: an empirical comparison and integration of self-report and conditional reasoning methodologies. See Williams & Burroughs 1999

Bushman BJ, Wells GL. 1998. Trait aggressiveness and hockey penalties: predicting hot tempers on the ice. *J. Appl. Psychol.* 83:969–74

Campbell JP. 1996. Group differences and personnel decisions: validity, fairness, and affirmative action. *J. Vocat. Behav.* 49:122–58

Campbell JP. 1999. The definition and measurement of performance in the new age. See Ilgen & Pulakos 1999, pp. 399–429

Campbell JP, Gasser MB, Oswald FL. 1996. The substantive nature of job performance variability. See Murphy 1996, pp. 258–99

Campion MA, Palmer DK, Campion JE. 1997. A review of structure in the selection interview. *Pers. Psychol.* 50:655–702

Carlson KD, Scullen SE, Schmidt FL, Rothstein H, Erwin F. 1999. Generalizable biographical data validity can be achieved without multi-organizational development and keying. *Pers. Psychol.* 52:731–55

Carretta TR, Doub TW. 1998. Group differences in the role of *g* and prior job knowledge in the acquisition of subsequent job knowledge. *Pers. Individ. Differ.* 23:585–93

Carretta TR, Ree MJ. 1996. Factor structure of the Air Force officer qualifying test: analysis and comparison. *Mil. Psychol.* 8:29–42

Carretta TR, Ree MJ. 1997. Negligible sex differences in the relation of cognitive and psychomotor abilities. *Pers. Individ. Differ.* 22:165–72

Carretta TR, Retzlaff PD, Callister JD, King RE. 1998. A comparison of two U.S. Air Force pilot aptitude tests. *Avation, Space, Environ. Med.* 69:931–35

Cascio WF. 1995. Whither industrial and organizational psychology in a changing world of work? *Am. Psychol.* 50:928–39

Chan D. 1997. Racial subgroup differences in predictive validity perceptions on personality and cognitive ability tests. *J. Appl. Psychol.* 82:311–20

Chan D. 1998a. The conceptualization and analysis of change over time: an integrative approach incorporating longitudinal mean and covariance structures analysis (LMACS) and multiple indicator latent growth modeling (MLGM). *Organ. Res. Methods* 1:421–83

Chan D. 1998b. Functional relations among constructs in the same content domain at different levels of analysis: a typology of composition models. *J. Appl. Psychol.* 83:234–46

Chan D, Schmitt N. 1997. Video-based versus paper-and-pencil method of assessment in situational judgment tests: subgroup differences in test performance and face validity perceptions. *J. Appl. Psychol.* 82:143–59

Chan D, Schmitt N, Jennings D, Sheppard L. 1999. Developing measures of basic job-relevant English proficiency for the prediction of job performance and promotability. *J. Bus. Psychol.* In press

Chan D, Schmitt N, Sacco JM, DeShon RP. 1998. Understanding pretest and posttest reactions to cognitive ability and personality tests. *J. Appl. Psychol.* 83:471–85

Cliff N, Caruso JC. 1998. Reliable component analysis through maximizing composite reliability. *Psychol. Methods* 3:291–308

Cohen SG, Bailey DE. 1997. What makes teams work: group effectiveness research from the shop floor to the executive suite. *J. Manage.* 23(3):239–90

Coleman V, Borman W. 1999. Investigating the underlying structure of the citizenship performance domain. *Hum. Resour. Res. Rev.* In press

Colihan J, Burger GK. 1995. Constructing job families: an analysis of quantitative techniques used for grouping jobs. *Pers. Psychol.* 48:563–86

Collins JM, Gleaves DH. 1998. Race, job applicants, and the five-factor model of personality: implications for black psychology, industrial/organizational psychology, and the five-factor theory. *J. Appl. Psychol.* 83:531–44

Collins JM, Schmidt FL, Sanchez-Ku M, Thomas LE, McDaniel M. 1999. Predicting assessment center ratings from cognitive ability and personality. See Quiñones 1999

Conway JM, Jako RA, Goodman DF. 1995. A meta-analysis of interrater and internal consistency reliability of selection interviews. *J. Appl. Psychol.* 80:565–79

Cronshaw SF. 1997. Lo! The stimulus speaks: the insider's view on Whyte and Latham's "The futility of utility analysis." *Pers. Psychol.* 50:611–15

Cudeck R. 1996. Mixed-effects models in the study of individual differences with repeated measures data. *Multivariate Behav. Res.* 31:371–403

Dalessio AT, Crosby MM, McManus MA. 1996. Stability of biodata keys and dimensions across English-speaking countries: a test of the cross-situational hypothesis. *J. Bus. Psychol.* 10:289–96

Deadrick DL, Bennett N, Russell CJ. 1997. Using hierarchical linear modeling to examine dynamic performance criteria over time. *J. Manage.* 23:745–57

Dean MA, Russell CJ, Muchinsky PM. 1999. Life experiences and performance prediction: toward a theory of biodata. In *Research in Personnel and Human Resources Management,* Vol. 17, ed. G Ferris. Greenwich, CT: JAI. In press

DeShon RP, Alexander RA. 1996. Alternative procedures for testing regression slope homogeneity when group error variances are unequal. *Psychol. Methods* 1:261–77

DeShon RP, Ployhart RE, Sacco JM. 1998a. The estimation of reliability in longitudinal models. *Int. J. Behav. Dev.* 22:493–515

DeShon RP, Smith MR, Chan D, Schmitt N. 1998b. Can racial differences in cognitive test performance be reduced by presenting problems in a social context. *J. Appl. Psychol.* 83:438–51

Dipboye R. 1997. Structured selection interviews: Why do they work? Why are they underutilized? See Anderson & Herriot 1997, pp. 455–73

Douglas EF, McDaniel MA, Snell AF. 1996. The validity of non-cognitive measures decays when applicants fake. In *Proc. Acad. Manage.,* ed. JB Keyes, LN Dosier, pp. 127–31. Madison, WI: Omnipress. 594 pp.

Dunnette M. 1976. Aptitudes, abilities, and skills. In *Handbook of Industrial and Organizational Psychology,* ed. M Dunnette, pp. 473–520. Chicago: Rand McNally. 1740 pp.

Dunnette MD. 1997. Emerging trends and vexing issues in industrial and organizational psychology. *Appl. Psychol. Int. Rev.* 47(2):129–53

Dwight SA, Donovan JJ. 1998. *Warning: Proceed with caution when warning applicants not to dissimulate (revised).* Presented at Annu. Conf. Soc. Ind. Organ. Psychol., 13th, Dallas

Ekstrom R, Smith D, eds. 1999. *Assessing Individuals with Disabilities: a Source-book* Washington, DC: Am. Psychol. Assoc. In press

Ellingson JE, Sackett PR, Hough LM. 1999a. Social desirability corrections in personality measurement: issues of applicant comparison and construct validity. *J. Appl. Psychol.* 84:155–66

Ellingson JE, Smith DB, Sackett PR. 1999b. Investigating the influence of social desirability on personality factor structure. *J. Appl. Psychol.* In press

Fox HR. 1999. Task force describes test user qualifications. *Score Newsl.* 21(3):3–4

Frei RL, McDaniel MA. 1998. Validity of customer service measures in personnel selection: a review of criterion and construct evidence. *Hum. Perform.* 11:1–27

Gandy JA, Dye DA, MacLane CN. 1994. See Stokes et al 1994, pp. 275–309

Ghiselli EE. 1966. *The Validity of Occupational Aptitude Tests.* New York: Wiley & Sons. 155 pp.

Gilliland SW, Steiner DD. 1999. Causes and consequences of applicant perceptions of unfairness. In *Justice in the Workplace,* ed. R Cropanzano, Vol. 2 Mahwah, NJ: Lawrence Erlbaum. In press

Goffin RD, Rothstein MG, Johnston NG, 1996. Personality testing and the assessment center: incremental validity for managerial selection. *J. Appl. Psychol.* 81:746–56

Goldstein H, Riley Y, Yusko KP. 1999. Exploration of Black-White subgroup differences on interpersonal constructs. *Subgroup differences in employment testing.* Symp. Annu. Meet. Soc. Ind. Organ. Psychol., 14th, Atlanta

Goldstein HW, Yusko KP, Braverman EP, Smith DB, Chung B. 1998. The role of cognitive ability in the subgroup differences and incremental validity of assessment center exercises. *Pers. Psychol.* 51:357–74

Gottfredson LS. 1986. Occupational Aptitude Patterns map: development and implications for a theory of job aptitude requirements. *J. Vocat. Behav.* 29:254–91

Gottfredson LS. 1997. Why g matters: the complexity of everyday life. *Intelligence* 24:79–132

Gottfredson LS. 1999. Skills gaps, not tests, make racial proportionality impossible. *Psychol. Public Policy Law.* In press

Gough HG. 1968. *The Chapin Social Insight Test Manual.* Palo Alto, CA: Consult. Psychol. Press. 14 pp.

Gough HG. 1994. Theory, development, and interpretation of the CPI Socialization scale. *Psychol. Rep.* 75:651–700 (Suppl.)

Graves LM, Karren RJ. 1996. The employee selection interview: a fresh look at an old problem. *Hum. Res. Manage.* 35:163–80

Guion RM. 1998. *Assessment, Measurement, and Prediction for Pers. Decisions.* Mahwah, NJ: Lawrence Erlbaum Assoc. 690 pp.

Guzzo AR, Salas E, eds. 1995. *Team Effectiveness and Decision Making in Organizations.* San Francisco: Jossey-Bass. 413 pp.

Hakel M, ed. 1998. *Beyond Multiple Choice: Evaluating Alternatives and Traditional Testing for Selection.* Hillsdale, NJ: Erlbaum. 221 pp.

Hambleton RK. 1999. Guidelines for adapting educational and psychological tests. *Bull. Int. Test Commiss.*

Hancock GR. 1997. Correlation/validity coefficients disattenuated for score reliability: a structural equation modeling approach. *Educ. Psychol. Meas.* 57:598–606

Hattrup K, Jackson SE. 1996. Learning about individual differences by taking situations seriously. See Murphy 1996, pp. 507–41

Hattrup K, O'Connell MS, Wingate PH. 1998. Prediction of multidimensional criteria: distinguishing task and contextual performance. *Hum. Perform.* 11:305–19

Hattrup K, Rock J, Scalia C. 1997. The effects of varying conceptualizations of job performance on adverse impact, minority hiring, and predicted performance. *J. Appl. Psychol.* 82:656–64

Hayden vs County of Nassau. No. 98–6113, 1999. WL 373636 (2nd Cir June 9, 1999)

Heilman ME. 1996. Affirmative action's contradictory consequences. *J. Soc. Issues* 52(4): 105–9

Heilman ME, Battle WS, Keller CE, Lee RA. 1998. Type of affirmative action policy: a determinant of reactions to sex-based preferential selection? *J. Appl. Psychol.* 83:190–205

Helms JE. 1992. Why is there no study of cultural equivalence in standardized cognitive ability testing? *Am. Psychol.* 47:1083–101

Herriot P, Anderson N. 1997. Selecting for change: How will personnel and selection psychology survive? See Anderson & Herriot 1997, pp. 1–34

Highberger W. 1996. Current evidentiary issues in employment litigation. *Empl. Relat. Law J.* 22(1):31–56

Hoffman CC, McPhail SM. 1998. Exploring options for supporting test use in situations precluding local validation. *Pers. Psychol.* 51:987–1003

Hoffman CC, Thornton GC III. 1997. Examining selection utility where competing predictors differ in adverse impact. *Pers. Psychol.* 50:455–70

Hofmann DA. 1997. An overview of the logic and rationale of hierarchical linear models. *J. Manage.* 23:723–44

Hofstede G. 1980. *Culture's Consequences: International Differences in Work-Related Values.* Thousand Oaks, CA: Sage

Hogan J, Brinkmeyer K. 1997. Bridging the gap between overt and personality-based integrity tests. *Pers. Psychol.* 50:587–99

Hogan J, Ones DS. 1997. Conscientiousness and integrity at work. See Hogan et al 1997, pp. 513–41

Hogan J, Rybicki SL. 1998. *Performance Improvement Characteristics Job Analysis.* Tulsa, OK: Hogan Assessment Systems

Hogan R. 1968. Develoment of an empathy scale. *J. Consult. Clin. Psychol.* 33:307–16

Hogan R. 1998. Reinventing personality. *J. Soc. Clin. Psychol.* 17:1–10

Hogan R, Johnson J, Briggs S, eds. 1997. *Handbook of Personality Psychology.* San Diego: Academic. 987 pp.

Hornick CW, Fox KA, Axton TR, Wyatt BS. 1999. The relative contribution of conditional reasoning and multiple intelligence measures in predicting firefighter and law enforcement officer job performance. See Williams & Burroughs 1999

Hough LM. 1992. The 'Big Five' personality variables—construct confusion: description versus prediction. *Hum. Perform.* 5(1&2): 139–55

Hough LM. 1997. The millennium for personality psychology: new horizons or good old daze. *Appl. Psychol. Int. Rev.* 47(2):233–61

Hough LM. 1998a. Effects of intentional distortion in personality measurement and evaluation of suggested palliatives. *Hum. Perform.* 11:209–14

Hough LM. 1998b. Personality at work: issues and evidence. See Hakel 1998, pp. 131–59

Hough LM, Ones DS, Viswesvaran C. 1998. Personality correlates of managerial performance constructs. See Page 1998

Hough LM, Paullin C. 1994. Construct-oriented scale construction: the rational approach. See Stokes et al 1994, pp. 109–45

Hough LM, Schneider RJ. 1996. Personality traits, taxonomies, and applications in organizations. See Murphy 1996, pp. 31–88

House RJ, Wright NS, Aditya RN. 1997. Cross-cultural research on organizational leadership: a critical analysis and a proposed theory. In *New Perspectives on International Industrial/Organizational Psychology,* ed. PC Earley, M Erez, pp. 535–625. San Francisco: New Lexington Press. 790 pp.

Howard A, ed. 1995. *The Changing Nature of Work.* San Francisco: Jossey-Bass. 590 pp.

Howard A. 1999. Discussant comments. See Quiñones 1999

Huffcutt AI, Roth PL. 1998. Racial group differences in employment interview evaluations. *J. Appl. Psychol.* 83:179–89

Huffcutt AI, Woehr DJ. 1999. Further analysis of employment interview validity: a quantitative evaluation of interviewer-related structuring methods. *J. Organ. Behav.* 20(4):549–60

Hunter JE. 1997. Needed: a ban on the significance test. *Psychol. Sci.* 8:3–7

Hunter JE, Schmidt FL. 1996. Cumulative research knowledge and social policy formulation: the critical role of meta-analysis. *Psychol. Public Policy Law* 2:324–47

Ilgen DR, Pulakos ED. 1999. *The Changing Nature of Performance: Implications for Staffing, Motivation, and Development.* San Francisco: Jossey-Bass. 452 pp.

James LR. 1998. Measurement of personality via conditional reasoning. *Organ. Res. Methods* 1(2):131–63

James LR. 1999. *Use of a conditional reasoning measure for aggression to predict employee reliability.* Presented at Annu. Meet. Soc. Ind. Organ. Psychol., 14th, Atlanta

James LR, Demaree RG, Mulaik SA, Ladd RT. 1992. Validity generalization in the context of situational models. *J. Appl. Psychol.* 77:3–14

Jeanneret R. 1998. Ethical, legal, and professional issues for individual assessment. In *Individual Psychological Assessment: Predicting Behavior in Organizational Settings,* ed. R Jeanneret, R Silzer, pp. 88–131. San Francisco: Jossey-Bass. 495 pp.

Johnson JW. 1999. A heuristic method for estimating the relative weight of predictor variables in multiple regression. *Multivariate Behav. Res.* In press

Johnson JW, Schneider RJ, Oswald FL, 1997. Toward a taxonomy of managerial performance profiles. *Hum. Perform.* 10:227–50

Joint Committee on Testing Practices. 1999. *Test Taker Rights and Responsibilities: Guidelines and Expectations.* Washington, DC: Am. Psychol. Assoc. In press

Judge TA, Erez A, Bono JE. 1998. The power of being positive: the relation between positive self-concept and job performance. *Hum. Perform.* 11:167–87

Kataoka HC, Latham GP, Whyte G. 1997. The relative resistance of the situational, patterned behavior, and conventional structured interviews to anchoring effects. *Hum. Perform.* 10:47–63

Katigbak MS, Church AT, Akamine TX. 1996. Cross-cultural generalizability of personality dimensions: relating indigenous and imported dimensions in two cultures. *J. Person. Soc. Psychol.* 70:99–114

Kehoe JF, ed. 1999. *Managing Selection Strategies in Changing Organizations.* San Francisco: Jossey-Bass. In press

Kiker S, Motowidlo S. 1999. Main and interaction effects of task and contextual performance on supervisory reward decisions. *J. Appl. Psychol.* 84:602–09

Klimoski R, Zukin LB. 1999. Selection and staffing for team effectiveness. See Sundstrom 1999, pp. 63–91

Kraut AI, Korman AK. 1999a. The "DELTA Forces" causing change in human resource management. See Kraut & Korman 1999b, pp. 3–22

Kraut AI, Korman AK, eds. 1999b. *Evolving Practices in Human Resource Management.* San Francisco: Jossey-Bass. 376 pp.

Kravitz DA, Harrison DA, Turner ME, Levine EL, Chaves W, et al. 1997. *Affirmative Action: a Review of Psychological and Behavioral Research.* Bowling Green, OH: Soc. Ind. Organ. Psychol. 50 pp.

Kuncel NR, Hezlett SA, Ones DS. 1999. Comprehensive meta-analysis of the predictive validity of the graduate record examinations: implications for graduate student selection and performance. *Psychol. Bull.* In press

Latham GP, Whyte G. 1994. The futility of utility analysis. *Pers. Psychol.* 47:31–46

Lefkowitz J, Gebbia MI, Balsam T, Dunn L. 1999. Dimensions of biodata items and their relationships to item validity. *J. Occup. Organ. Psychol.* In press

Legree PJ, Pifer ME, Grafton FC. 1996. Correlations among cognitive abilities are lower for higher ability groups. *Intelligence* 23:45–57

LePine JA, Hollenbeck JR, Ilgen DR, Hedlund J. 1997. Effects of individual differences on the performance of hierarchical decision-making teams: much more than g. *J. Appl. Psychol.* 85:803–11

Levine EL, Spector PE, Menon S, Narayanan L, Cannon-Bowers J. 1996. Validity generalization for cognitive psychomotor, and perceptual tests for craft jobs in the utility industry. *Hum. Perform.* 9:1–22

Li H, Rosenthal R, Rubin DB. 1996. Reliability of measurement in psychology: from Spearman-Brown to maximal reliability. *Psychol. Methods* 1:98–107

Lievens F. 1998. Factors which improve the construct validity of assessment centers: a review. *Int. J. Select. Assess.* 6:141–52

Lowman RL, ed. 1998. *The Ethical Practice of Psychology in Organizations.* Washington, DC: Am. Psychol. Assoc. 299 pp.

Lubinski D. 2000. Scientific and social significance of assessing individual differences: "Sinking shafts at a few critical points." *Annu. Rev. Psychol.* 51:405–44

Lubinski D, Benbow C. 1999. States of excellence: a psychological interpretation of their emergence. *Am. Psychol.* In press

Mael FA. 1998. Privacy and personnel selection: reciprocal rights and responsibilities. *Empl. Responsib. Rights J.* 11:187–214

Mael FA, Connelly M, Morath RA. 1996a. None of your business: parameters of biodata invasiveness. *Pers. Psychol.* 49:613–50

Mael F, Kilcullen R, White L. 1996b. Soldier attributes for peacekeeping and peacemaking. In *Reserve Component Soldiers as Peacekeepers,* ed. R Phelps, B Farr, pp. 29–57. Alexandria, VA: U.S. Army Res. Inst. Behav. Sci. 449 pp.

Matthews G. 1997. The Big Five as a framework for personality assessment. See Anderson & Herriot 1997, pp. 475–92

McCrae RR, Costa PT Jr. 1997. Personality trait structure as a human universal. *Am. Psychol.* 52:509–16

McManus MA, Kelly ML. 1999. Personality measures and biodata: evidence regarding their incremental predictive value in the life insurance industry. *Pers. Psychol.* 52:137–48

Migetz DZ, James LR, Ladd RT. 1999a. *A validation of the conditional reasoning measurement.* Presented at Annu. Meet. Soc. Ind. Organ. Psychol., 14th, Atlanta

Migetz DZ, McIntyre M, James LR. 1999b. Measuring reliability among contingent workers. See Williams & Burroughs 1999

Millsap RE. 1995. Measurement invariance, predictive invariance, and the duality paradox. *Multivariate Behav. Res.* 30:577–605

Millsap RE. 1997. Invariance in measurement and prediction: their relationship in the single-factor case. *Psychol. Methods* 2:248–60

Miner JB, Capps MH. 1996. *How Honesty Testing Works.* Westport, CT: Quorum Books. 192 pp.

Mone MA, Mueller GC, Mauland W. 1996. The perceptions and usage of statistical power in applied psychology and management research. *Pers. Psychol.* 49:103–20

Morgeson FP, Campion MA. 1997. Social and cognitive sources of potential inaccuracy in job analysis. *J. Appl. Psychol.* 82:627–55

Moss FA, Hunt T, Omwake KT, Woodward LG. 1955. *Social Intelligence Test Manual.* Washington, DC: Cent. Psychol. Serv. 4 pp.

Motowidlo SJ, Burnett JR. 1995. Aural and visual sources of validity in structured employment interviews. *Organ. Behav. Hum. Decis. Process.* 61(3):239–49

Mount MK, Barrick MR. 1995. The Big Five personality dimensions: implications for research and practice in human resource management. *Res. Pers. Hum. Resour. Manage.* 13:153–200

Mount MK, Barrick MR, Stewart GL. 1998. Five-factor model of personality and performance in jobs involving interpersonal interactions. *Hunt. Perform.* 11:145–65

Muchinsky PM. 1999. Biodata: a mirror of moxie. See Stennett et al 1999. In press

Mumford MD, Costanza DP, Connelly MS, Johnson JF. 1996. Item generation procedures and background data scales: implications for construct and criterion-related validity. *Pers. Psychol.* 49:361–98

Mumford MD, Stokes GS. 1992. Developmental determinants of individual action: theory and practice in the application of background data measures. In *Handbook of Industrial and Organizational Psychology,* ed. MD Dunnette, LM Hough, 2:61–138. Palo Alto, CA: Consult. Psychol. Press. 957 pp. 2nd ed.

Murphy vs United Parcel Service, Inc. No. 97–1992 (119 S Ct 2133, June 22, 1999)

Murphy KR, ed. 1996. *Individual Differences and Behavior in Organizations.* San Francisco: Jossey-Bass. 606 pp.

Murphy KR. 1997. Meta-analysis and validity generalization. See Anderson & Herriot 1997, pp. 323–42

Murphy KR, Luther N. 1997. Assessing honesty, integrity, and deception. See Anderson & Herriot 1997, pp. 369–88

Murphy KR, Myors B. 1999. Testing the hypothesis that treatments have negligible effects: minimum-effect tests in the general linear model. *J. Appl. Psychol.* 84:234–47

Murphy KR, Shiarella AH. 1997. Implications of the multidimensional nature of job performance for the validity of selection tests: multivariate frameworks for studying test validity. *Pers. Psychol.* 50:823–54

Nelson JB. 1997. The boundaryless organization: implications for job analysis, recruitment, and selection. *Hum. Resour. Plan.* 20(4):39–49

Nyfield G, Baron H. 1999. Cultural context in adapting selection practices across borders. See Kehoe 1999. In press

O'Neil HF Jr, ed. 1997. *Workforce Readiness: Competencies and Assessment.* Mahwah, NJ: Erlbaum. 467 pp.

O'Neil HF Jr, Allred K, Dennis RA. 1997a. Use of computer simulation for assessing the interpersonal skill of negotiation. See O'Neil 1997, pp. 205–28

O'Neil HF Jr, Allred K, Dennis RA. 1997b. Validation of a computer simulation for assessment of interpersonal skills. See O'Neil 1997, pp. 229–54

Ones DS, Hough LM, Viswesvaran C. 1998. Personality correlates of managerial performance constructs. See Page 1998

Ones DS, Viswesvaran C. 1996. *What do pre-employment customer service scales measure? Explorations in construct validity and implications for personnel. selection.* Presented at Annu. Meet. Soc. Ind. Organ. Psychol., 11th, San Diego

Ones DS, Viswesvaran C. 1998a. Gender, age, and race differences on overt integrity tests: results across four large-scale job applicant data sets. *J. Appl. Psychol.* 83:35–42

Ones DS, Viswesvaran C. 1998b. Integrity testing in organizations. In *Dysfunctional Behavior in Organizations:* Vol. 2, *Nonviolent Behaviors in Organizations,* ed. RW Griffin, A O'Leary-Kelly, JM Collins, pp. 243–76. Greenwich, CT: JAI. 318 pp.

Ones DS, Viswesvaran C. 1998c. The effects of social desirability and faking on personality and integrity assessment for personnel selection. *Hum. Perform.* 11:245–69

Ones DS, Viswesvaran C. 1999. Job-specific applicant pools and national norms for personality scales: implications for range restriction corrections in validation research. *J. Appl. Psychol.* In press

Ones DS, Viswesvaran C, Reiss AD. 1996. Role of social desirability in personality testing for personnel selection: the red herring. *J. Appl. Psychol.* 81:660–79

Ones DS, Viswesvaran C, Schmidt FL, Reiss AD. 1994. *The validity of honesty and violence scales of integrity tests in predicting violence at work.* Presented at Annu. Meet. Acad. Manage., Dallas

Ostroff C, Harrison D. 1999. Meta-analysis, level of analysis, and best estimates of population correlations: cautions for interpreting meta-analytic results in organizational behavior. *J. Appl. Psychol.* 84:260–70

Oswald FL, Ferstl KL. 1999. Linking a structure of vocational interests to Gottfredson's (1986) Occupational Aptitude Patterns map. *J. Vocat. Behav.* 54:214–31

Oswald FL, Johnson JW. 1998. On the robustness, bias, and stability of statistics from meta-analysis of correlation coefficients: some initial Monte Carlo findings. *J. Appl. Psychol.* 83:164–78

Oswald FL, Saad SA, Sackett PR. 1999. The homogeneity assumption in differential prediction analysis: Does it really matter? *J. Appl. Psychol.* In press

Page RC, chair. 1998. In *Personality determinants of managerial potential performance, progression and ascendancy.* Symp. Annu. Meet. Soc. Ind. Organ. Psychol., 13th, Dallas

Patton TW, Walton W, James LR. 1999. Measuring personal reliability via conditional reasoning: identifying people who will work reliably. See Williams & Burroughs 1999

Pearlman K. 1997. Twenty-first century measures for twenty-first century work. In *Transitions in Work and Learning: Implications for Assessment,* ed. A Lesgold, MJ Feuer, A Block, pp. 136–79. Washington, DC: Natl. Acad. Press. 283 pp.

Pearlman K, Barney MF. 1999. Selection for a changing workplace. See Kehoe 1999. In press

Peterson NG, Mumford MD, Borman WC, Jeanneret PR, Fleishman EA. 1999. *An Occupational Information System for the 21st Century: the Development of O*NET.* Washington, DC: Am. Psychol. Assoc. 319 pp.

Ployhart RE, Hakel MD. 1998. The substantive nature of performance variability: predicting interindividual differences in intraindividual performance. *Pers. Psychol.* 51:859–901

Ployhart RE, Ryan AM, Bennett M. 1999. Explanations for selection decisions: applicants' reactions to informational and sensitivity features of explanations. *J. Appl. Psychol.* In press

Plutchik R, Conte HR, eds. 1997. *Circumplex Models of Personality and Emotions.* Washington, DC: Am. Psychol. Assoc. 484 pp.

Pulakos ED, Schmitt N. 1996. An evaluation of two strategies for reducing adverse impact and their effects on criterion-related validity. *Hum. Perform.* 9:241–58

Quiñones MA, chair. 1999. *Assessment centers, 21st century: new issues, and new answers to old problems.* Symp. Annu. Meet. Soc. Ind. Organ. Psychol., 14th, Atlanta

Quiñones MA, Ford JK, Teachout MS. 1995. The relationship between work experience and job performance: a conceptual and meta-analytic review. *Pers. Psychol.* 48:887–910

Raju NS, Bilgic R, Edwards JE, Fleer PF. 1997. Methodology review: estimation of population validity and cross-validity, and the use of equal weights in prediction. *Appl. Psychol. Meas.* 21:291–305

Raju NS, Bilgic R, Edwards JE, Fleer PF. 1999. Accuracy of population validity and cross-validity estimation: an empirical comparison of formula-based, traditional empirical, and equal weights procedures. *Appl. Psychol. Meas.* 23:99–115

Raykov T. 1997. Estimation of composite reliability for congeneric measures. *Appl. Psychol. Meas.* 21:173–84

Raymark PH, Schmit MJ, Guion RM. 1997. Identifying potentially useful personality constructs for employee selection. *Pers. Psychol.* 50:723–36

Ree MJ, Carretta TR, Teachout MS. 1995. Role of ability and prior job knowledge in complex training performance. *J. Appl. Psychol.* 80:721–30

Robertson I, Callinan M. 1998. Personality and work behaviour. *Eur. J. Work Organ. Psychol.* 7:321–40

Rosse JG, Stecher MD, Levin RA, Miller JL. 1998. The impact of response distortion on preemployment personality testing and hiring decisions. *J. Appl. Psychol.* 83:634–44

Roth PL, Bobko P. 1997. A research agenda for multi-attribute utility analysis in human resource management. *Hum. Resource Manage. Rev.* 7:341–68

Roth PL, Campion JE, Jones SD. 1996. The impact of four missing data techniques on validity estimates in human resource management. *J. Bus. Psychol.* 11:101–12

Russell CJ. 1999. Toward a model of life experience learning. See Stennett et al. 1999. In press

Russell CJ, Dean MA, Broach D. 1998. *Guidelines for Bootstrapping Validity Coefficients in ATCS Selection Research.* Norman, OK: Univ. Okla. 58 pp.

Russell JA, Carroll JM. 1999. On the bipolarity of positive and negative affect. *Psychol. Bull.* 125:3–30

Ryan AM, Greguras GJ. 1998. Life is not multiple choice: reactions to the alternatives. See Hakel 1998, pp. 183–202

Ryan AM, Ployhart RE, Friedel LA. 1998a. Using personality testing to reduce adverse impact: a cautionary note. *J. Appl. Psychol.* 83:298–307

Ryan AM, Ployhart RE, Greguras GJ, Schmit MJ. 1998b. Test preparation programs in selection contexts: self-selection and program effectiveness. *Pers. Psychol.* 51:599–621

Sackett PR, Ellingson JE. 1997. The effects of forming multi-predictor composites on group differences and adverse impact. *Pers. Psychol.* 50:707–21

Sackett PR, Gruys ML, Ellingson JE. 1998. Ability-personality interactions when predicting job-performance. *J. Appl. Psychol.* 83:545–56

Sackett PR, Roth L. 1996. Multi-stage selection strategies: a Monte Carlo investigation of effects on performance and minority hiring. *Pers. Psychol.* 49:549–72

Sackett PR, Wanek JE. 1996. New developments in the use of measures of honesty, integrity, conscientiousness, dependability, trustworthiness, and reliability for personnel selection. *Pers. Psychol* 49:787–829

Sager CE, Peterson NG, Oppler SH, Rosse RL, Walker CB. 1997. An examination of five indexes of test battery performance: analysis of the ECAT battery. *Mil. Psychol.* 9:97–120

Salgado JF. 1997a. The five factor model of personality and job performance in the European community. *J. Appl. Psychol.* 82:30–43

Salgado JF. 1997b. VALCOR: a program for estimating standard error, confidence intervals, and probability of corrected validity. *Behav. Res. Methods Instrum. Comput.* 29:464–67

Salgado JF. 1998. Big Five personality dimensions and job performance in army and civil occupations: a European perspective. *Hum. Perform.* 11:271–88

Sanchez J, Levine E. 1999. Is job analysis dead, misunderstood, or both? New forms of work analysis and design. See Kraut & Korman 1999b, pp. 43–68

Sanchez J, Prager I, Wilson A, Viswesvaran C. 1998. Understanding within-job title variance in job-analytic ratings. *J. Bus. Psychol.* 12:407–19

Sánchez-Meca J, Marín-Martínez F. 1997. Homogeneity tests in meta-analysis: a Monte Carlo comparison of statistical power and Type I error. *Qual. Quant.* 31:385–99

Sands WA, Waters BK, McBride JR. 1997. *Computerized Adaptive Testing.* Washington, DC: Am. Psychol. Assoc. 292 pp.

Saucier G, Goldberg LR. 1998. What is beyond the Big Five? *J. Pers.* 66:495–524

Schmidt FL, Hunter JE. 1996. Measurement error in psychological research: lessons from 26 research scenarios. *Psychol. Methods* 1:199–223

Schmidt FL, Hunter JE. 1998. The validity and utility of selection methods in personnel psychology: practical and theoretical implications of 85 years of research findings. *Psychol. Bull.* 124:262–74

Schmidt FL, Rader M. 1999. Exploring the boundary conditions for interview validity: meta-analytic validity findings for a new interview type. *Pers. Psychol.* 52:445–64

Schmidt FL, Viswesvaran V, Ones DS. 1997. Validity of integrity tests for predicting drug and alcohol abuse: a meta-analysis. In *Meta-Analysis of Drug Abuse Prevention Programs,* ed. WJ Bukoski, pp. 69–95. Rockville, MD: NIDA National Institute on Drug Abuse Press. 263 pp.

Schmit MJ, Kilm JA, Robie C. 1999. Refining a personality test to be used in selection across several cultures. In *Personality and Performance: Boundary Conditions for Measurement and Structural Models,* chair WC Borman, Symp. Annu. Meet. Soc. Ind. Organ. Psychol., 14th Atlanta

Schmit MJ, Ryan AM. 1997. Applicant withdrawal: the role of test-taking attitudes and racial differences. *Pers. Psychol.* 50:855–76

Schmitt N, Chan D. 1998. *Personnel Selection.* Thousand Oaks, CA: Sage. 378 pp.

Schmitt N, Chan D. 1999. The status of research on applicant reactions to selection tests and its implications for managers. *Int. J. Manage. Rev.* In press

Schmitt N, Jennings D, Toney R. 1999. Can we develop measures of hypothetical constructs? *Hum. Resour. Manage. Rev.* In press

Schmitt N, Nason E, Whitney DJ, Pulakos ED. 1995. The impact of method effects on structural parameters in validation research. *J. Manage.* 21:159–74

Schmitt N, Ployhart RE. 1999. Estimates of cross-validity for stepwise regression and with predictor selection. *J. Appl. Psychol.* 84:50–57

Schmitt N, Pulakos ED. 1998. Biodata and differential prediction: some reservations. See Hakel 1998, pp. 167–82

Schmitt N, Rogers W, Chan D, Sheppard L, Jennings D. 1997. Adverse impact and predictive efficiency of various predictor combinations. *J. Appl. Psychol.* 82:719–30

Schneider RJ, Ackerman PL, Kanfer R. 1996. To "act wisely in human relations": exploring the dimensions of social competence. *Pers. Individ. Differ.* 21:469–81

Schoenfeldt LF. 1999. From dust bowl empiricism to rational constructs in biographical data. *Hum. Resour. Manage. Rev.* In press

Segall DO. 1999. General ability measurement: an application of multidimensional adaptive testing. Presented at Meet. Natl. Council Meas. Educ., Montreal, Canada

Shackleton V, Newell S. 1997. International assessment and selection. See Anderson & Herriot 1997, pp. 81–95

Sharf JC, Jones DP. 1999. Employment risk management See Kehoe 1999. In press

Smith M, DeMatteo JS, Green P, James LR. 1995. *A comparison of new and traditional measures of achievement motivation.* Presented at Annu. Meet. Am. Psychol. Assoc., 103rd, New Orleans

Snell AF, McDaniel MA. 1998. *Faking: getting data to answer the right questions.* Poster presented at Annu. Meet. Soc. Ind. Organ. Psychol., 13th, Dallas

Snell AF, Sydell EJ, Lueke SB. 1999. Towards a theory of applicant faking: integrating studies of deception. *Hum. Resour. Manage. Rev.* In press

Spychalski A, Quiñones M, Gaugler BB, Pohley K. 1997. A survey of assessment center practices in organizations in the United States. *Pers. Psychol.* 50:71–90

Stajkovic AD, Luthans F. 1998. Self-efficacy and work-related performance: a meta-analysis. *Psychol. Bull.* 124:240–61

Stanush P, Arthur W, Doverspike D. 1998. Hispanic and African American reactions to a simulated race-based affirmative action scenario. *Hispanic J. Behav. Sci.* 20(1):3–16

Stennett RB, Parisi AG, Stokes GS, eds. 1999. *A Compendium: Papers Presented at the First Biennial Biodata Conference.* Athens, GA: Univ. Georgia. In press

Stokes GS, Mumford MD, Owens WA, eds. 1994. *Biodata Handbook.* Palo Alto, CA: Consult. Psychol. Press. 650 pp.

Stokes GS, Searcy CA. 1999. Specification of scales in biodata form development: rational vs. empirical and global vs. specific. *Int. J. Select. Assess.* 7:72–85

Stricker LJ, Rock DA. 1998. Assessing leadership potential with a biographical measure of personality traits. *Int. J. Select. Assess.* 6:164–84

Sundstrom E, ed. 1999. *Supporting Work Team Effectiveness.* San Francisco: Jossey-Bass. 388 pp.

Sutton vs United Airlines, Inc. No. 97–1943, 119 S. Ct. 2139, (June 22, 1999)

Task Force on Assessment Center Guidelines. 1989. Guidelines for ethical considerations. *Public Pers. Manage.* 18:457–70

Terpstra DE, Mohamed AA, Kethley B. 1999. An analysis of federal court cases involving nine selection devices. *Int. J. Select. Assess.* 7:26–34

Terris W. 1997. The traditional regression model for measuring test bias is incorrect and biased against minorities. *J. Bus. Psychol.* 12:25–37

Thorsteinson TJ, Ryan AM. 1997. The effect of selection ratio on perceptions of the fairness of a selection test battery. *Int. J. Select. Assess.* 5:159–68

Tippins NT. 1999. The Americans with Disabilities Act and employment testing. See Ekstrom & Smith 1999. In press

Tisak J, Tisak MS. 1996. Longitudinal models of reliability and validity: a latent curve approach. *Appl. Psychol. Meas.* 20(3):275–88

Tokar DM, Fischer AR, Subich LM. 1998. Personality and vocational behavior: a selective review of the literature, 1993–1997. *J. Voc. Behav.* 53:115–53

Truxillo DM, Bauer TN. 1999. Applicant reactions to test score banding in entry-level and promotional contexts. *J. Appl. Psychol.* 84:322–39

U.S. Equal Employment Opportunity Commission. 1999. *Enforcement Guidance: Reasonable Accommodation and Undue Hardship under the Americans with Disabilities Act.* Washington, DC: Equal Empl. Opportun. Comm.

U.S. Equal Employment Opportunity Commission, Civil Service Commission, Department of Labor, and Department of Justice. 1978. Uniform guidelines on employee selection procedures. *Fed. Regist.* 43:38290–315

Van Scotter JR, Motowidlo SJ. 1996. Interpersonal facilitation and job dedication as separate facets of contextual performance. *J. Appl. Psychol.* 81:525–31

Verive JM, McDaniel MA. 1996. Short-term memory tests in personnel selection: low adverse impact and high validity. *Intelligence* 23:15–32

Vinchur AJ, Schippmann JS, Switzer FS, Roth PL. 1998. A meta-analytic review of predictors of job performance for salespeople. *J. Appl. Psychol.* 83:586–97

Viswesvaran C, Ones DS. 1999. Meta-analyses of fakability estimates: implications for personality measurement. *Educ. Psychol. Meas.* 59:197–210

Viswesvaran C, Ones DS, Schmidt FL, 1996. Comparative analysis of the reliability of job performance ratings. *J. Appl. Psychol.* 81:557–74

Wang T. 1998. Weights that maximize reliability under a congeneric model. *Appl. Psychol. Meas.* 22:179–87

West M, Allen N. 1997. Selecting for teamwork. See Anderson & Herriot 1997, pp. 493–506

Whitney DJ, Diaz J, Mineghino ME, Powers K. 1999. Perceptions of overt and personality-based integrity tests. *Int. J. Select. Assess.* 7:35–45

Whitney DJ, Schmitt N. 1997. Relationship between culture and responses to biodata employment items. *J. Appl. Psychol.* 82:113–29

Whyte G, Latham G. 1997. The futility of utility analysis revisited: when even an expert fails. *Pers. Psychol.* 50:601–10

Wiggins JS, Trapnell PD. 1997. Personality structure: the return of the Big Five. See Hogan et al 1997, pp. 737–65

Wilk SL, Sackett PR. 1996. Longitudinal analysis of ability-job complexity fit and job change. *Pers. Psychol.* 49:937–67

Williams LJ, Burroughs SM, chairs. 1999. *New developments using conditional reasoning to measure employee reliability.* Symp. Annu. Meet. Soc. Ind. Organ. Psychol., 14th, Atlanta

Williamson LG, Campion JE, Malos SB, Roehling MV, Campion MA. 1997. Employment interview on trial: linking interview structure with litigation outcomes. *J. Appl. Psychol.* 82:900–12

Woehr DJ, Arthur W Jr. 1999. The assessment center validity paradox: a review of the role of methodological factors. See Quiñones 1999

Wright TA, Cropanzano R. 1998. Emotional exhaustion as a predictor of job performance and voluntary turnover. *J. Appl. Psychol.* 83:486–93

Wright TA, Staw BM. 1999. Affect and favorable work outcomes: two longitudinal tests of the happy-productive worker thesis. *J, Organ. Behav.* 20:1–23

Zickar MJ, Drasgow F. 1996. Detecting faking on a personality instrument using appropriateness measurement. *Appl. Psychol. Meas.* 20:71–87

64

EPISTEMOLOGY AND WORK PSYCHOLOGY

New agendas

Phil Johnson and Catherine Cassell

Source: *Journal of Occupational and Organizational Psychology* 74 (2001): 125–143.

Abstract

The aim of this paper is to examine current epistemological debates within psychology and social science generally, and to explicate their significance for the way in which work psychology research is conducted. It is argued that although there have been a number of recent critiques of the epistemological and methodological base of psychology, the research base of work psychology has come in for little such attention. The result has been a lack of reflexivity on the part of work psychologists. One potential challenge to this *status quo* comes from postmodernism which has had a significant impact on other areas of social science. This paper illustrates some of the key tensions and debates that result from extending these epistemological debates to the realm of work psychology. It is argued that a consideration of epistemology is important for work psychologists; and that different approaches to positivism, such as postmodernism, can provide us with different ways of examining and conducting work psychology research. The importance of epistemological reflexivity is highlighted within the paper: that is the researcher makes explicit, and critically reflects upon, the epistemological assumptions that underlie their own work. Finally, the authors assess the implications of this for work psychology research and practice generally.

These are challenging times for those of us who investigate the world of work where the future is seen to entail a radical break with the past. Not surprisingly, work psychologists have spent considerable time discussing the impact of changing times on work, manifested through new psychological contracts and career structures, more sophisticated methods of selecting, assessing, rewarding and training employees, advancing technologies and post-bureaucratic organizational forms (e.g. Clegg *et al.,* 1997; Rousseau, 1995; Sparrow, 1998). However, despite these recent developments in the concerns of work psychology, there has been little change in the underlying epistemological assumptions that influence how research is construed, undertaken and evaluated within the discipline.

At first sight, compared with recent discussions of 'a new paradigm' in other areas of psychology (e.g. Smith, Harre, & Van Langenhove, 1995), work psychology research still seems entrenched in the positivist paradigm (Symon & Cassell, 1998*a*). However, within other social science disciplines, debates about epistemology and its methodological imperatives have raged for a long time (Woolgar, 1996). There is evidence that these debates have been extended into the realm of psychology. The origins of this reorientation are located in the critique of social psychology that emerged in the 1970s. While Shotter (1975) questioned the epistemological authority underpinning experimental design, others (e.g. Henriquez, Hollway, Urwin, Venn, & Walkerdine, 1984) challenged the whole notion of the role of the 'subject' upon which psychology is based. Indeed, Smith *et al.* suggest that the impact of this disaffection is that psychology has clearly moved away from the 'hegemony of the laboratory experiment in the last twenty years' (1995, p. 2). Despite this ostensible paradigm shift in the work of some psychologists, much of this debate still remains the 'ghost' at work psychology's 'banquet'. As Sparrow (1999) suggests in his editorial reflecting on the future of this journal and the discipline in general:

> Paradigm change is in the air. Many managerial and social science disciplines have put themselves through a period of critical analysis. Strangely the occupational and organizational psychologists seem not to have entered into such an analysis. (p. 261)

The consequent silence is all the more surprising given the impact that alternatives such as postmodernism have had in closely related disciplines, such as organization studies (e.g. Hassard & Parker, 1993), human resource management (e.g. Townley, 1994), corporate strategy (e.g. Knights & Morgan, 1991) and even accountancy (e.g. Miller & O'Leary, 1987). Although some work psychologists have engaged with these debates (e.g. Hollway, 1991), there have been few systematic internal challenges to the positivist *status quo*. Nevertheless, there are external challenges which both researchers and practitioners will eventually have to take some note.

This paper addresses the current epistemological challenges faced by the discipline. Our aim is to examine current epistemological debates within psychology and social science generally, and to explicate their significance for the way in which work psychology research and practice is understood and conducted. We begin with an examination of the implications of the dominance of positivist epistemology for the research base of work psychology. The ways in which positivism is undermined by a highly sceptical form of social constructivism called postmodernism are then considered. Through the use of examples from work psychology we illustrate some of the key tasks, tensions and dilemmas that emerge from these debates. Throughout we show how these debates necessitate the development of a more reflexive work psychology, where the assumptions that underlie an epistemological approach are identified and critiqued. First, we briefly examine why epistemology and reflexivity are such important issues.

Epistemology and reflexivity

Although philosophers have debated epistemological questions since the time of Plato, those debates have too often appeared far removed from the concerns of work psychologists. However, behind this esoteric appearance are issues which, despite often remaining unnoticed, influence the ways in which all work psychologists undertake their research or engage with their clients. This significance is revealed by the Greek etiology of the term epistemology, *episteme,* which means 'knowledge' or 'science'; *logos* which means 'knowledge', 'information', 'theory' or 'account'. In other words, epistemology is the study of the criteria by which we can know what does, and does not, constitute warranted, or scientific, knowledge. As Rorty (1979) has observed epistemology seems to offer a vantage point, one step removed from the actual practice of science itself, which at first sight promises to provide some foundation for scientific knowledge. By seeking to explain ourselves as knowers, by telling us how we ought to arrive at our beliefs, epistemology is pivotal to science since 'proper' scientific theorizing can only occur after the development of epistemological theory. It follows that a key question must be how can we develop epistemological theory—a science of science?

Almost 60 years ago Neurath (1944) pointed to the paradox that epistemology confronts: a fundamental problem of circularity, from which it cannot escape, in that any theory of knowledge (i.e. any epistemology) presupposes knowledge of the conditions in which knowledge takes place. In effect, this prevents any grounding of epistemology in what purports to be scientific knowledge, psychological or otherwise, because one cannot use science in order to ground the legitimacy of science. For Neurath, such circularity means that we cannot dump philosophy by detaching ourselves from our epistemological commitments so as to assess those commitments objectively—indeed we would depend upon them in order to undertake that reflexive task. It follows that there are no secure foundations from which we can begin any consideration of our knowledge of knowledge—rather what we have are competing philosophical assumptions about knowledge that lead us to engage with work psychology in particular ways.

Perhaps the most we can hope for in considering epistemology is to become more consciously reflexive by thinking about our own thinking, by noticing and criticizing our own epistemological pre-understandings and their effects on research, and by exploring possible alternative commitments (Alvesson & Skoldberg, 2000).

Although this new spirit has gained much influence in related areas, the received view of research in work psychology is centred upon positivist epistemological commitments. A silence reigns around such commitments so that they are 'forgotten' and any reflexivity is 'skilfully avoided' (Chia, 1996, pp. 7–8). Presumably, if pressed, this silence would be justified by the claim that such commitments are so innocent and commonsensical they are not worth discussing. But to make unexamined epistemological assumptions and remain unaware of their origins has to be poor practice, particularly when even a cursory examination of the philosophy of science would suggest that not only is epistemological commitment unavoidable in any work psychology, but also that any epistemological commitment is highly contentious.

Positivism: the epistemological orthodoxy of work psychology

The term work psychology is used here because as Arnold, Cooper, and Robertson (1995) suggest it is a simple term that encompasses both the individual and organizational levels of analysis, typically covered by both occupational and organizational psychology approaches. The aim is to be inclusive about the content of work psychology as a discipline, rather than focusing on a specific content area, such as personnel practice. In defining the work psychology domain, a key element to take into account is the role of practice. In differentiating work psychology from other social science disciplines, it is evident that work psychology has an identifiable practitioner community. At both practitioner and researcher levels, an underlying feature of the discipline is a tacit commitment to positivism.

This commitment supports the methodological unity of natural and social science and the presupposition of a theory neutral observational language. This implies that the researcher can be a neutral collector of data who can objectively access the facts of an *a priori* reality. The enduring importance and relevance of such commitments derive from positivism's social origins in the anti-authoritarian cultural changes that occurred in 18th century Western Europe which have been dubbed the Enlightenment (Gray, 1995, pp. 136–137). Drawing upon Descartes, Locke, and Bacon, the Enlightenment philosophers (e.g. David Hume) embraced empiricism and used it to launch attacks upon metaphysical speculation and theocratic revelation. In doing so, empiricism aimed to make all truth-claims objectively assessable. So later, when Comte coined the term positivism (1853), he was expressing the desire to rid science of dogma by the examination of the 'positively given'—that which is directly available to sensory perception. At this stage Comte saw that 'the human mind' rejected all religion and metaphysics as a distraction from sense-data and '... confines itself to the discovery, through reason and observation combined, of the actual laws that govern the succession and similarity of phenomena' (quoted in Andreski, 1974, p. 20).

In this light, the tacit adoption of a theory neutral observational language by work psychologists allows the settling of knowledge claims through appeal to empirical facts and thus protects it from metaphysical dogmatism. Therefore, positivism has clearly been crucial to the development, security and credibility of work psychology as a discipline. But these certain gains have resulted in a series of costs. The over-reliance on positivism has resulted in there being:

> ... virtually no debate about the status of the knowledge which makes up work psychology and this state of affairs is the result of the uncritical identification of work psychology with behavioural science, which in turn identifies with natural science.
>
> (Hollway, 1991, p. 7)

Such lack of epistemological reflexivity has other dangers. As Herriot and Anderson (1997) observe in their discussion of selection and assessment within personnel psychology:

> The maturation of personnel psychology as a scientific discipline, whilst reaping the benefits of increasingly robust and sophisticated empirical research, has led to a predominant cultural code of mass epistemological conformity. No other sub-discipline in the organizational sciences has exhibited such a paucity of theoretical perspectives, such a lack of debate over guiding paradigmatic assumptions and such unquestioned conformity to naive, managerialist positivism. And if the discipline fails to stimulate a diversity of theoretical perspectives and epistemological approaches, then it runs the risk of becoming an overheated engine house of remote, blind empiricism. (p. 13)

Besides the problems created by a lack of epistemological reflexivity (to which we shall return) another significant consequence is the tendency to exclude human subjectivity from the realm of warranted science so as to preserve the unity of the sciences (i.e. *monism*). This occurs through the deployment of a deterministic deductive experimental logic where human behaviour is conceptualized as measurable responses to external stimuli. Stimuli may be either administered by an experimenter or operationalized through the use of metrics such as those, for instance, encoded into questionnaire *pro forma*. Evidence of how the resultant methods underpin much of what we know as work psychology research is presented in content reviews of the key international journals (Schaubroeck & Kuehn, 1992; Symon & Cassell, 1998a). As Anderson (1998) observes, the most prestigious work psychology research, demonstrates little variation from an unreflexive and deterministic positivist norm. Indeed, such homogeneity is all the more surprising when it is evident that positivism has been under attack in both the natural and social sciences, from a variety of perspectives, for most of the 20th century (see Delanty, 1997).

One popular attack, which focuses upon the exclusion of human subjectivity from the domain of legitimate science, has led to the development of a wide range of interpretative approaches for accessing human subjectivity within psychological research. An outcome has been an almost unanimous presentation of a case for the use of qualitative methods (e.g. Gillet, 1995; Henwood & Pidgeon, 1992; Potter & Wetherall, 1987). Usually, this case has been based on highlighting: the appropriateness of such techniques for the areas that psychologists research; the added value that such methods provide; and the creative use of theory that can emerge from using qualitative methods or even the 'qualitative paradigm' (Henwood & Nicolson, 1995). Indeed, the use of qualitative methods is becoming more common within work psychology research (Symon & Cassell, 1998*b*).

Nevertheless, what is also evident is that the epistemological stance underlying the use of so-called qualitative methods rarely entails a significant departure from positivism beyond questioning methodological monism. Instead a neo-positivist stance is often adopted which retains positivism's key epistemic characteristic—the presupposition of a theory neutral observational language. So when researchers use qualitative methods in a neo-positivist framework, they still see themselves as neutrally reporting the *cultural* worlds of their participants and reflexivity is thus avoided. Through the use of qualitative techniques they are merely accessing that cultural world in a different way. This is hardly a radical departure from the positivist norm.

While the retention of positivist epistemology has an important impact on how research is conducted and evaluated, it is also important to realize that it influences the kinds of question we ask in the first place (Hosking, Dachler, & Gergen, 1995). For Dachler (1998) the result is that work psychologists are:

> ... caught in a certain way of thinking about the world—if you wish, caught in a dominant logic—which so far has served us well, but whose central questions seem increasingly problematic in the face of challenges never before encountered. (p. 1)

The point is that if we become more reflexive we will challenge and change those epistemological assumptions and work psychology as a discipline will change. This will create a number of opportunities and choices which will be outlined in more detail later.

The epistemological undermining of positivism

Positivistic epistemological commitments have been undermined in both the natural and social sciences by a disparate group of critics often labelled 'social constructivists' who, just as they are united by their repudiation of a theory neutral observational language, are simultaneously divided over the ontological implications of this epistemological stance, as is explained below.

While Burr (1995) identifies Berger and Luckmann's work (1967) as a pivotal influence upon the social sciences, it would seem that social constructivism has a longer history in the natural sciences. Here social constructivism had already been expressed by Heisenberg's (1958) 'uncertainty principle'—that it is impossible to study something without influencing what is seen. Therefore, what a scientist observes is not independent of the process of observing but is an outcome of the scientists' methodological interaction with, and conceptual constitution of, his/her objects of knowledge.

In a similar manner, Wittgenstein (1958) and Hanson (1958) argued that language did not allow access to reality, instead our renditions of reality are located in language itself rather than anything independent of it. There cannot be any neutral foundation for science located in the passive registration of sensory inputs since the scientist's language-in-use, their theories and hypotheses influence what will be observed *before* any empirical observations are made. This thesis in effect socializes science and was subsequently highly influential upon Kuhn's theory of scientific development (1957; 1962/1970) which used historical examples to demonstrate how, in practice, natural science neither proceeds inductively through verification and proof of theory nor deductively through falsification of theory. Especially during the 1970s and 1980s, social constructivists popularized the view that the positivist ideal of a neutral observer was an impracticable ideal—what counts as warranted knowledge, truth and reason are always conditioned by the sociohistorical context of the scientist. Far from articulating universal scientific truths any scientists' account will be a local social construction created through the operation of: community language games (e.g. Rorty, 1979); paradigms (e.g. Burrell & Morgan, 1979); metaphors (e.g. Ortony, 1979); interests (Habermas, 1972, 1974); traditions (Gadamer, 1975); discourses (Foucault, 1977); inescapable frameworks (Taylor, 1985); or world views (Geertz, 1989) and so on.

It is only with this realization that social construction must embrace *both* the lay and the scholarly domains, that the importance of reflexivity has been extended and brought to the fore in social science (e.g. Beck, 1992; Bourdieu, 1990; Holland, 1999; Steier, 1991). Bordieu (1990) argues that any science is embedded in, and conditioned by, an underlying socially derived collective unconsciousness that forms a subtext of research which conditions any account. Reflexivity entails the work psychologist attempting to think about his/her own thinking by excavating, articulating, evaluating and in some cases transforming the collective unconscious she or he deploys in structuring research activities as well as in apprehending and interpreting what is observed. Here, the implication is that we must hold our own 'research structures and logics as themselves researchable and not immutable, and by examining how we are part of our own data, our research becomes a reciprocal process' (Steier, 1991, p. 7).

However, as Fay (1987) pointed out, because reflexivity insists that researchers must confront and question the taken-for-granted assumptions which give meaning to our lives, then resistance can only be expected. As Habermas (1972, p. 67) forcefully shows, a key source of resistance is the protection afforded by positivist epistemology. The commitment to a theory neutral observational language implies that positivists, due to their methodological training etc., are able to accumulate facts passively from an ontologically prior world—thus rendering their own involvement in the research process, beyond seemingly technical methodological issues, unproblematic.

Besides using different terminologies, where such writers also disagree is regarding the ontological implications of their constructivism—a matter which is illustrated by Kuhn's own earlier equivocation. Kuhn's thesis leads to two very different sets of implications which are both tacitly invoked by his statement that after a change in paradigm 'scientists are responding to a different world' (1962, 1970, p. 135). Although it is evident that he means that any scientific statement is a social construction, are these statements just different versions of an independently existing social/natural reality which we can never fully know because our theories are always underdetermined (i.e. ontological realism), or does it mean that reality is created and determined by the socially constructed theory (i.e. ontological subjectivism)? While some social constructivists seem to inadvertently oscillate between ontological realism and subjectivism (e.g. Morgan, 1986, 1993), a tendency towards a subjectivist stance, usually called postmodernism, has become increasingly influential in the last 10 years or so.

Postmodernism

Despite the attention that the term 'postmodernism' has attracted since the early 1980s, it remains difficult to define as avowed postmodernists themselves reject a single correct position in favour of a multiplicity of perspectives that emphasize indeterminacy. A key theme, however, is the rejection of positivism's 'grand' narrative—that it is possible to develop a rational and generalizable basis to scientific inquiry that 'pictures' and explains the world from an objective standpoint (Berg, 1989; Best & Kellner, 1991; Harvey, 1989; Parker, 1992; Vattimo, 1992).

Through what is called the 'linguistic turn' postmodernists advocate a de-differentiation of relations between subject and object (e.g. Chia, 1995; Jeffcutt, 1994; Kilduff & Mehra, 1997) thereby replacing epistemic privilege, grounded in what Dachler and Hosking (1995) term an 'entitative and egocentric reasoning', with a social constructivist view of science and knowledge. For postmodernists the notion of an external world is precarious since our linguistic representations are seen to *create* what positivists assume *to be* an independent external reality. For Baudrillard (1983) all that we are left with are 'simulacra'—images which refer to nothing but themselves: a 'hyper-reality', divorced from extra-linguistic reference points, in which there is nothing to see save simulations which appear to be real. Reality as an independent referent is destroyed and 'the boundary between hyper-reality and everyday life is erased' (Best & Kellner, 1991, p. 120). Since nothing exists outside discursive texts, it is language which needs to be reflexively illuminated so as to display its constructive processes.

In this vein, Rorty (1979, 1982) argues that whatever counts as truth or reality is a changeable sociolinguistic artefact where justification lies in the consensus arising out of the culturally specific discourses. Different discourses constructed in diverse forms of life are incommensurable. It follows then that there is a need to focus attention upon the arguments that are reasonable and persuasive to members of a particular scientific community. In this project Rorty suggests that philosophy can no longer presume to rise above everyday language games so as to '... underwrite or debunk claims to knowledge made by science' (1979, p. 3). Rather postmodernism must accept diversity and be concerned to gain knowledge of variable and socially contingent understandings so as to '... refine our sensitivity to differences and reinforce our ability to tolerate the incommensurable' (Lyotard, 1984, p. xxv). The toleration of dissensus is vital so as to avoid the hegemony of a particular discourse which serves to silence alternative possible voices and prevent the heteroglossia which would otherwise ensue (Gergen, 1992; Rosenau, 1992).

So for postmodernists whatever work psychology is, it cannot be justified through meta-narratives which commit us to thinking that it entails accurate representations of the external world. For postmodernists multiple truths are always possible—the question then is which truths are being allowed to be voiced, how, why and what are their effects upon people. The postmodernists' mission is to deploy their rhetorical skills so as to: unsettle the language of representation; erode traditions and orthodoxies; carve out the new domains of intelligibility thereby giving voice to 'truths' previously suppressed. Obviously, this has implications for how we understand work psychology as a discourse in its own right and how people who identify themselves as work psychologists may develop alternative understandings of their domains of interest.

If work psychology's current legitimacy is primarily located in its claim to a rational picturing of people in their organizations so as to ensure progress through improved performance and so on, postmodernists erode these apparently self-evident meta-narratives through undertaking several interrelated tasks: to identify the particular ways of seeing and acting that such a discourse takes and excludes; to analyse the social processes that make it possible for such a discourse to be historically constituted; to analyse how it is reconstituted into new discursive formations; and to identify the effects of such a discourse upon people. Below we review how postmodernists deal with these tasks—first through deconstruction, second through genealogy and third by examining truth-effects.

The deconstruction of work psychology

The outcome of the linguistic turn is the notion that since language cannot depict the real it must rhetorically produce what we take to be real. Phenomena such as motivation, stress and personality cannot refer to real objects, but are merely linguistic constructs which work psychologists take to be real. So rather than deploying conceptual resources for analysing aspects of reality, work psychology is seen as a set of discourses which constructs and certifies particular meaningful versions of reality that are taken to be neutral and thereby accorded scientific status. Here, the eight knowledge areas of work psychology recognized by the Division of Occupational Psychology would be presented as discourses which create what is known as legitimate work psychology and serve to regulate the discipline by excluding both the non-qualified from domains of practice and alternative knowledge bases from consideration. Claims to science would be seen as a self-serving rhetoric which bolster claims to the status of a 'profession'. Indeed; from a postmodern stance it is through its discursive activity that work psychology produces the behaviour it seeks to describe (see Turner, 1987) since empirical findings would 'reflect preexisting intellectual categories' (Hassard, 1993, p. 12). For instance, personality tests used in selection and assessment rather than reflecting something which the individual has, would be seen as creating accounts of the personality which enable certain interventions: discourses which may be deconstructed.

Deconstruction is the reflexive dismantling of linguistic constructions so as to reveal their inherent contradictions, assumptions and different layers of meaning—issues which are hidden from the naïve reader and unrecognized by the author. Any body of knowledge, any behaviours or organizational practices can be treated as a text which can be deconstructed. In conducting a deconstructive reading of a text several questions are asked:

> Why are certain authors, topics or schools excluded from the text? Why are certain themes never questioned, whereas other themes are condemned? Why, given a set of premises, are certain conclusions not reached? The aim of such questions is not to point out textual errors but to help the reader understand the extent the text's objectivity and persuasiveness depend upon a series of strategic exclusions.
> (Kilduff, 1993, pp. 15–16)

Hence all texts are understood to contain elements that counter their author's assertions. For instance Kilduff (1993) deconstructs March and Simon's book *Organizations* (1958) to identify its gaps and silences and show how the Tayloristic assumptions it overtly condemns are simultaneously replicated elsewhere in the text in order to produce their narrative. Deconstruction also entails showing how their texts contain taken-for-granted ideas which depend upon the exclusion of something (Cooper, 1989; Linstead, 1993). Often this will involve identifying the assumptions which underpin and thereby produce the 'fixed' truth claim (Gergen, 1992). These assumptions are then disrupted through their denial and the identification of the 'absent' alternatives whose articulation produces an alternative text, or re-reading of reality.

For instance Knights (1992) and Townley (1994), respectively show how strategic and human resource management discourses reflect and reproduce masculine regimes of rationality which exclude and suppress the binary opposite—women as irrational. This issue has not been ignored by work psychologists. Thus, selection tests have been shown to encapsulate values and qualities that are associated with those in powerful positions. In this spirit, Alimo-Metcalf (1994) discusses how the norms operationalized by management selection tests are based on samples of current managers, therefore embedding assumptions surrounding a 'male white' norm beneath an appearance of objectivity thereby disabling any interventions that can be made regarding the development of equal opportunities.

Hence, deconstruction denies that any text can be ever settled or stable: it can always be questioned as layers of meaning are reflexively removed to reveal those meanings which have been suppressed. So in organizational life, meaning is always precarious and local (Linstead & Grafton-Small, 1992) and may be deconstructed even, as Cooper (1990) shows, the notion of organization itself. Simultaneously deconstruction leads to questions about how something becomes seen as factual. Usually, we remain blithely unaware of these sociolinguistic processes and although the ontological result may appear as 'out there' through the action of discourses we are participants in creating what we apprehend. So in Chia's (1995) terms postmodern deconstruction is about remembering these formative processes that attribute a false concreteness to our objects of analysis and which positivists have sublimated or forgotten. The result is a relativistic position for deconstruction does not get the deconstructor closer to a 'fixed' truth. At most it only offers alternative meanings within a text which are themselves then available to further parasitic deconstruction and thereby are not allowed to rest in any finalized truth.

Genealogy of work psychology discourse

As we have shown, deconstruction is concerned with reflexively examining the logics and contradictions embedded in discourses—a process for Linstead (1993) that is consistent with Foucault's genealogical method (1977, 1986). The latter extends reflexivity by revealing how discourses are constructed, highlighting the tacit meta-narratives that underpin them, and opening up the potential for articulating alternative ways of knowing.

In undertaking a genealogy of work psychology the first task is to isolate and describe the discourses of work psychology, their ways of seeing organizations and members, and excavate the systems of rules that enable and limit what is knowable. This analysis disrupts established discourses' claims to report observed reality and to be essential tools for rendering the management of organizational processes more rational by pointing to how those discourses create the objects which they presume to analyse. The next step is to examine the sociohistorical conditions which make it possible for a particular discourse of work psychology to emerge and develop thereby further unsettling its epistemological authority. Hence, genealogy would not be a history of stress or motivation *per se*, rather it would be a history about how such phenomena were discursively produced and became taken for granted.

For example, a number of authors have argued that work psychologists have neglected the area of emotion at work (Briner, 1999; Fineman, 1993). If we examine where psychologists have directed their attentions in this area, generally they have focused on two key concepts: job satisfaction and stress (Cassell, 1999). Taking stress as an example, a key (positivist) assumption is that stress exists 'out there' and constitutes a condition which is independent of our conceptualizations of it. Therefore, it can be objectively measured and its variable impact upon individuals explained in terms of their work contexts (e.g. job characteristics) or personal attributes (e.g. gender). Thus, various occupational groups, such as women managers have been investigated to assess the extent to which they experience more stress than others (Davidson & Cooper, 1992). At the practitioner level a whole number of interventions designed to alleviate stress at work have been developed, leading to the development of what Briner (1997) describes as a stress industry dominated by stressologists. In contrast, a genealogy would construe stress as linguistic: a relational concept (Hosking *et al.*, 1995) that is produced and reproduced by individuals in their discursive interactions and which is specific to a set of sociohistorical conditions.

Genealogy is, however, not just concerned with the emergence of discourses but also how existing discourses are adapted or transformed into new discourses. For instance Barry and Elmes (1997) construe strategic discourses as stories and then use narrative theory to highlight how different rhetorical devices can increase or decrease the appeal of a discourse in the eyes of any audience/readership. In other words, the appropriation of a particular narrative has nothing to do with its truth but is located in audience approval and their identification with the characterizations and plot provided by the story. Hence, the increased interest in the public domain about stress generally would suggest that the public at large find its narrative aesthetically pleasing and hence plausible.

In summary genealogy would focus upon the description of work psychology's discourses/narratives and the analysis of their development and change. In part Hollway (1991) has undertaken these tasks by describing 80 years of work psychology and its relationships to management practice. Some of the key questions posed by such a genealogy are: Who gets to write and read any discourse? Who is marginalized and subjugated by that writing and reading? How is the writing and reading of work psychology's discourses linked to power in organizations? Pivotal to answering these questions is what the postmodernists would call the truth-effects of work psychology.

Discursive truth-effects of work psychology

Any discourse 'produces reality ... domains of objects and rituals of truth' (Foucault, 1977, p. 194) which in effect surpress and even destroy the articulation of alternative possible 'truth-effects'. This stance leads postmodernists to *de-centre the subject*: to reject the individual knower as the autonomous origin of meanings and as the focus of any analysis. Instead, through the language we use and gain in social interaction we obtain and propagate shared discourses. The individual is thereby constituted through exposure to historically and socially contingent discourses: through learning to speak a discourse, the discourse speaks to the individuals by structuring their experiences and definitions of who they are. An example here is the way in which workers are discursively produced through the work psychologists' use of the language of attitudes. The attitudinal labels used in investigations (e.g. job involvement, organizational commitment, and job satisfaction) accord visibility to the worker through forms of categorization, measurement and intervention that inscribe images of what it is to be 'normal'. Power is not possessed by conscious agents, whether they be individuals or collectivities; rather, like knowledge, power is seen to reside in discourses themselves (Foucault, 1980) so that knowledge and power 'inhabit each other' (Cooper, 1989).

A key task has been to apply de-centring to investigate how all forms of work-based identity and subjectivity are discursively constituted and hence vary. For instance, by examining contemporary retailing Du Gay (1996) traces how discourses of organizational change take hold in particular contexts and 'make up' the identities of employees in their everyday working lives. He shows how an all pervasive enterprise-excellence discourse has, through the image of the sovereign consumer, reimagined and blurred the distinction between the identities of consumers and employees. Both are now constituted as autonomous, responsible, calculating individuals seeking to maximize his or her worth through self-regulated acts of choice in a market-based world. For Du Gay a person's sense of identity is negotiated, constituted and confirmed by his or her positioning within relations of power: they become inscribed with the ethos of enterprise in all aspects of their lives, an ethos which encourages them to transform themselves by building 'resources in themselves rather than rely[ing] on others' (Du Gay, 1996, p. 183).

Du Gay's Foucauldian understanding of identity has influenced the recent work of some work psychologists. For instance Dick (2000) suggests that traditional approaches within work psychology have usually attributed women's lack of progression within the UK police force to the nature of the 'canteen culture' and male attitudes to female officers. However, the large amount of research on this issue has failed to address why the nature of policing is discursively constructed in the ways it is and how this clashes with female identities. She outlines how certain discourses gain dominance and are reflected in working practices. Thus, the idea that policing is not compatible with being a mother is an effect of how the police identity is discursively produced as excessively demanding, and the 'good' officer as one who subordinates non-work aspects of life to those demands. In contrast, she observes that the adult female identity continues to be largely constructed through the site of motherhood and while that construction continues to emphasize the importance of 'being there' for the children, the vertical subordination of policewomen will continue.

Another truth-effect arises here. Organizational members may be differentiated according to their participation in a discourse which shapes their subjectivity. For instance, those groups who accept and deploy discourses enjoy an aura of expertise and material privilege within organizational hierarchies while those who are unable to deploy that discourse lose status. Indeed, the deployment of any discourse is seen as empowering those people with the right to speak and analyse while subordinating others who are the object of the knowledge and disciplinary practices produced by the discourse. Such experts, as Hollway (1991) has noted with regard to work psychologists and Townley (1994) with regard to human resource management practitioners, together with the knowledge that they articulate, serve to mask what postmodernists see as the arbitrary nature of their normative judgments which subordinate employees. Thus, not all people are equal within the web of power relations which defines and orchestrates them. Here claims to detached reason and objective analysis merely serve to mask the self-aggrandizement of the 'speaker' who, through the discourse, dominates and oppresses those who are analysed and categorized. The disempowered may collude in the establishment of this power relationship in two ways. First, they accept the authority of discourse speakers to analyse and categorize thereby empowering them. Second, as Du Gay notes (1996), a discourse defines and constrains the subjectivities and identities of the disempowered to the extent that they engage in self-surveillance and correction of their behaviour towards the norms it articulates. Likewise, those with privileged access to the discourse gain a sense of meaning and identity from the practices it sanctions (Knights & Morgan, 1991).

In summary, postmodernists portray human subjectivity deterministically, as an outcome of the exercise of power—'a game in which the rules are never revealed or understood by the players' (Delanty, 1997, p. 106). In this sense postmodernists see power as being everywhere yet nowhere: as a relationship between subjects yet also independent of subjects where 'it is not possible for power to be exercised without knowledge it is impossible for knowledge not engender power' (Foucault, 1980, p. 52). In this manner individuals and collectivities become constructed, classified, known and transformed into self-disciplining subjects through a power that they may exercise but do not possess. However, this does not mean that resistance is always absent. For instance in the case of strategy Knights and Morgan (1991) argue that not everyone has taken up a strategic discourse: some managers reject its rationalism preferring intuition; many employees remain incorrigibly cynical; and there is a time lag between different parts of the world in the uptake of strategy.

To summarize, a work psychology inspired by postmodernism poses a considerable sceptical challenge to the positivist *status quo*. Post-modernism demands that work psychologists be sceptical about: how they engage with the world; the categories they deploy; the assumptions that they impose and the interpretations that they make. By 'not finding answers to problems, but ... [by] ... problematizing answers' (Cooper & Burrell, 1988, p. 107) postmodernism makes people think about their own thinking and question the taken-for-granted. It encourages irony and humility as well as rebellion against the imposition of any totalizing meta-narrative which erases plurality through discursive closure.

Like all epistemological approaches, postmodernism has its own set of problems that have been critiqued extensively in the literature (e.g. Parker, 1992; Thompson, 1993). While postmodernism's reflexive value seems self-evident, caution is required as its reflexivity can be simultaneously and paradoxically problematized through its relativistic tendencies. For some postmodernists truth is relative to one's mode of engagement with the 'world' for which no independently existing evaluative criteria exist. The intellectual mirroring of reality that sustains positivism is thereby replaced by the relativist's intellectual production of reality. If we follow through the implications of this to the extreme, then there is no possibility of adjudicating between different realities because there are no independent criteria upon which to judge. Therefore, it follows that there are no criteria through which we can engage in any form of criticism of the status quo. Criticism becomes either a pointless juxtaposition of incommensurable narratives or the critic's unsustainable assertation of an epistemologically privileged meta-narrative. Any intervention implies the exercise of choice and closure based upon some kind of evaluative criteria—anathema to postmodernists. The practical effect of this is that 'the problems of (fictional) individuals in (mythical) organizations are safely placed behind philosophical double glazing and their cries are treated as interesting examples of discourse' (Parker, 1992, p. 11).

Despite our call for some caution, postmodernism proffers a sustainable alternative to the positivist orthodoxy of work psychology which could give voice to a more reflexive work psychology. Clearly, a number of work psychologists already actively work in this way, though it would seem their approaches are tacit and rarely reported in the esteemed journals of the field even though practitioners, researchers, and the clients/stakeholders on the receiving end, must have much to gain.

Implications

The aim of our analysis has been to examine some current epistemological debates and to focus on the implications of those debates for work psychology research. In doing this we have focused on positivism, neo-positivism, social constructivism and postmodernism. We are not suggesting here that an approach such as postmodernism is either the right or wrong way of conducting research, but rather that work psychologists need to be aware of the current debates and the impact they have on the discipline. In criticizing the overemphasis on positivism within work psychology research we have highlighted the attendant problems of epistemological conformity and lack of reflexivity. In particular we have called for more epistemological reflexivity within work psychology generally. Increasing epistemological reflexivity creates many choices for work psychologists, but with it comes a set of responsibilities. We now turn to the implications of our analysis for future research and practice.

The first key implication is that a decrease in epistemological conformity and increased use of alternative epistemological approaches can provide access to new and interesting types of research questions within work psychology research. If we look at the area of selection as an example, Herriot and Anderson (1997) suggest that there are a whole range of questions about the selection process that are rendered inaccessible by the positivist paradigm. However, some of those questions lay themselves open to investigation from a social constructivist approach for example. A key issue from that perspective would be a focus on the processes of selection, as opposed to the validity of individual methods. Our research questions would be about how different individuals construe, make sense of, and experience the selection process. Rather than seeking to represent those constructions correctly from the perspective of a neutral observer, our emphasis would be on how individuals in their accounts draw on particular discourses to explain or legitimize their experiences of different selection techniques. Additionally, we could focus on the interactive nature of the process of selection and the relationship between the assessor and assessee. For example, a focus could be on how the notion of the 'ideal candidate' is produced and reproduced through the interview process. Other questions that alternative epistemological approaches could also address include impression management within the selection process by recruiters and candidates, and how the psychological contract is formed and developed by both parties through the selection experience (Herriot & Anderson, 1997). Therefore, exploration of different perspectives creates different ways of asking and investigating new work psychology questions.

A second related implication of considering alternatives to positivism is that the work psychology researcher can access a range of different insights into traditional work psychology questions. Symon (2000) demonstrates how alternative approaches to traditional positivism can augment the explanatory power of research in work psychology. She applied rhetorical analysis within a social constructivist framework to a case study of the implementation of a networked personal computer system in a public sector organization. In this study one of the foci was 'resistance' to change. This analysis enabled an illustration of 'how arguments against computerization were embedded in local and more global contexts, how opposition was legitimated and the role the construction of identity plays in this process' (Symon, 2000, p. 10). Therefore within the area of organizational change and development, Symon argues that this form of analysis enables researchers or interventionists to understand how different viewpoints are constructed and maintained, rather than just provide evidence that they exist. This therefore enables them to engage more effectively with a diversity of positions, thereby ultimately providing an in-depth analysis of the change process (Symon, 2000).

At the methodological level, throughout this paper we have argued that work psychology is currently dominated by a particular form of positivist epistemology, which encourages an exclusive focus upon deductive and often quantitative methodologies. However, challenging this orthodoxy could encourage a range of multi-methodological approaches to thrive. If we accept that no methodology can be epistemically superior to any other, that all are partial and fallible modes of engagement which simultaneously socially construct, and consequently, obstruct different renditions of reality, then methodological pluralism can be the norm. For those schooled in the positivist way of conducting research this means that the traditional quantitative notions of reliability and validity may not be appropriate for assessing the integrity of a piece of research. However, other sets of criteria can be applied. For example, with the increased use of qualitative methods in the social sciences generally, a number of authors have derived appropriate criteria for assessing research using those techniques (e.g. Flick, 1998; Guba & Lincoln, 1989). Nevertheless, a key reflexive criterion for all pieces of research is epistemological coherence, that is the extent to which the methods used are fitting, given the underlying epistemological assumptions.

In considering different epistemological approaches, the role of different interests comes to light. For example, postmodernists would be interested to consider how alternative ways of understanding what work psychology is about are created by a range of individuals and groups, including those who traditionally remain silent, such as those on the receiving end of work psychology interventions. Accessing those groups is not a new idea in work psychology research and practice. Indeed, some researchers have made this a deliberate part of their research strategies, particularly in intervention research (e.g. Fryer & Feather, 1994) or new paradigm research (Reason & Rowan, 1981). Reason and Rowan (1981) outline a variety of strategies that can lead to more participative or collaborative research, the collaborators being those traditionally excluded from the research process. In other areas where work psychologists intervene, for example in the design of new technology systems (Clegg *et al.*, 1996), tools have been designed that encourage those traditionally on the receiving end of organizational change programmes to become more actively involved in the planning and change process. In the alternative approaches to positivism we have outlined in this paper, the researched become an active group with an impact on the research process. Therefore, in the same way that epistemological reflexivity calls on the researcher to interrogate their own assumptions and their own impact on the research process, so account needs to be taken of the ways in which the researched actively create their own view of that process.

In conclusion, we have argued that work psychology as a discipline and the work psychology researcher need to be more epistemologically reflexive. We need to be aware of the range of choices that are available to researchers, and to confront and challenge one's own epistemological commitments in the light of possible challenges. Such reflexivity is important for the development of a mature research-based discipline. It emphasizes the need to think through methodological alternatives. The resulting more pluralist work psychology, with the wider set of questions it presents, enables us to cope theoretically and methodologically with the continuously changing subject matter of the discipline. The process of thinking about the assumptions that underlie a piece of research is not about academic navel gazing. Rather, it is about escaping from the ivory tower of epistemic privilege and producing more reflexive research that can address the ongoing challenges in the world of work.

Acknowledgements

The authors would like to thank Rene Bouwen, Paul Sparrow, Gillian Symon and three anonymous referees for their encouragement, helpful comments and critical insights.

References

Alimo-Metcalfe, B. (1994). 'Waiting for fish to grow feet! Removing organizational barriers to women's entry into leadership positions'. In M. Tanton (Ed.), *Women in management: A developing presence* (pp. 27–45). London: Routledge.

Alvesson, M., & Skoldberg, K. (2000). *Reflexive methodology: New vistas for qualitative research.* London: Sage.

Anderson, N. (1998). The practitioner–researcher divide in work and organizational psychology. *The Occupational Psychologist, 34,* 7–16.

Andreski, S. (1974). *The essential Comte* (M. Clark, Trans.). London: Croom Helm.

Arnold, J., Cooper, C. L., & Robertson, I. T. (1995). *Work psychology: Understanding human behaviour in the workplace* (2nd ed.). London: Pitman.

Ayer, A. J. (1971). *Language, truth and logic.* Harmondsworth: Penguin.

Barry, D. (1997). Telling changes: From narrative family therapy to organizational change and development. *Journal of Organizational Change Management, 10*(1), 30–46.

Barry, D., & Elmes, M. (1997). Strategy retold: Toward a narrative view of strategic discourse. *Academy of Management Review, 22(2),* 429–452.

Baudrillard, J. (1983). *Simulation.* New York: Semiotext(e).

Beck, U. (1992). *The risk society: Towards a new modernity.* Cambridge: Polity.

Berg, P. O. (1989). Postmodern management? From facts to fiction in theory and practice. *Scandinavian Journal of Management, 5*(3), 201–217.

Berger, P., & Luckmann, T. (1967). *The social construction of reality.* London: Allen Lane.

Best, S., & Kellner, D. (1991). *Postmodern theory: Critical interrogations.* London: Macmillan.

Bourdieu, P. (1990). *The logic of practice.* Cambridge: Polity.

Briner, R. B. (1997). Feeling and smiling. *The Psychologist, 12*(1), 16–19.

Briner, R. B. (1999). Beyond stress and satisfaction: Alternative approaches to understanding psychological well-being at work. *Proceedings of the British Psychological Society Occupational Psychology Conference,* 95–100.

Burr, V. (1995). *Introduction to social constructionism.* London: Routledge.

Burrell, G., & Morgan, G. (1979). *Sociological paradigms and organizational analysis.* London: Heinemann.

Cassell. C. M. (1999). Exploring feelings in the workplace: Emotion at work. *The Psychologist, 12*(1), 16–19.

Chia, R. (1995). From modern to postmodern organizational analysis. *Organization Studies, 16*(4), 579–604.

Chia, R. (1996). *Organizational analysis as deconstructive practice.* Berlin: De Gruyer.

Clegg, C., Axtell, C., Damodaran, L., Farbey, B., Hull, R., Lloyd-Jones, R., Nicholls, J., Sell, R., & Tomlinson, C. (1997). Information technology: A study of performance and the role of human and organizational factors. IWP memo, Sheffield.

Clegg, C., Coleman, P., Hornby, P., Maclaren, R., Robson, J., Carey, N., & Symon, G. (1996). Tools to incorporate some psychological and organizational issues during the development of computer-based systems. *Ergonomics, 39*(3), 482–511.

Comte, A. (1853). *The positive philosophy of Auguste Comte.* London: Chapman.

Cooper, R. (1989). Modernism postmodernism and organizational analysis 3: The contribution of Jacques Derrida. *Organization Studies, 10*(4), 479–502.

Cooper, R. (1990). Organization/disorganization. In J. Hassard, & D. Pym (Eds.), *The theory and philosophy of organizations: Critical issues and new perspectives* (pp. 167–197). London: Routledge.
Cooper, R., & Burrell, G. (1988). Modernism postmodernism and organizational analysis: An introduction. *Organization Studies, 9*(1), 91–112.
Dachler, H. P. (1998). Relational theorizing, power and the 'ecology' of W/O psychology. Presidential address to the 24th International Congress of Applied Psychology, San Francisco, 9–14 August.
Dachler, H. P., & Hosking, D. M. (1995). The primacy of relations in socially constructing organizations. In D. M. Hosking, H. P. Dachler, & K.J. Gergen (Eds.), *Management and organization: Reasonable alternatives to individualism* (pp. 1–28). Aldershot: Avebury Press.
Davidson, M. J., & Cooper, C. L. (1992). *Shattering the glass ceiling: The woman manager.* London: Paul Chapman.
Delantey, G. (1997). *Social science: Beyond constructivism and realism.* Buckingham: Open University Press.
Dick, P. (2000). *The social construction of policing: Gender, discourse and identity.* Unpublished Phd thesis, University of Sheffield.
Du Gay, P. (1996). *Consumption and identity at work.* London: Sage.
Fay, B. (1987). *Critical social science.* Cambridge: Polity.
Fineman, S. (1993). *Emotion at work.* London: Sage.
Flick, U. (1998). *An introduction to qualitative research.* London: Sage.
Foucault, M. (1977). *Discipline and punish: The birth of the prison.* Harmondsworth: Penguin.
Foucault, M. (1980). *Power/Knowledge.* Brighton: Harvester.
Foucault, M. (1986). *History of sexuality.* Harmondsworth: Penguin.
Fryer, D., & Feather, N. T. (1994). Intervention techniques. In C. M. Cassell, & G. Symon (Eds.), *Qualitative methods in organizational research: A practical guide* (pp. 230–246). London: Sage.
Gadamer, G. (1975). *Truth and method.* London: Sheed and Ward.
Geertz, C. (1989). Anti Anti-Relativism. In M. Krausz (Ed.), *Relativism: Interpretation and confrontation* (pp. 51–72). Notre Dame: Notre Dame University Press.
Gergen, K. (1992). Organization theory in the postmodern era. In M. Reed, & M. Hughes (Eds.), *Rethinking organization* (pp. 207–226). London: Sage.
Gillet, G. (1995). The philosophical foundations of qualitative psychology. *The Psychologist, 8*(3), 111–114.
Gray, J. (1995). *Isaiah Berlin.* London: Harper Collins.
Guba, E., & Lincoln, Y. (1989). *Fourth generation evaluation.* Newbury Park, CA: Sage.
Habermas, J. (1972). *Knowledge and human interest.* London: Heinemann.
Habermas, J. (1974). *Theory and practice.* London: Heinemann.
Hammersley, M. (1992). *What is wrong with ethnography?* London: Routledge.
Hanson, N. R. (1958). *Patterns of discovery.* Cambridge: Cambridge University Press.
Harvey, D. (1989). *The condition of postmodernity: An enquiry into the origin of social change.* Oxford: Blackwell.
Hassard, J. (1993). Postmodernism and organizational analysis. In J. Hassard, & J. Parker (Eds.), *Postmodernism and organizations* (pp. 1–23). London: Sage.
Hassard, J., & Parker, M. (Eds.) (1993). *Postmodernism and organizations.* London: Sage.

Heisenberg, W. (1958). *Physics and philosophy.* New York: Harper Brothers.
Henriquez, J., Hollway, W., Urwin, C., Venn, C., & Walkerdine, V. (1984). *Changing the subject: Psychology, social relations and subjectivity.* London: Methuen.
Henwood, K. L., & Nicholson, P. (1995). Qualitative research. *The Psychologist, 8*(3), 109–110.
Henwood, K. L., & Pidgeon, N. F. (1992). Qualitative research and psychological theorizing. *British Journal of Psychology, 83,* 83–111.
Herriott, P., & Anderson, N. (1997). *International handbook of selection and assessment.* Chichester: John Wiley.
Holland, R. (1999). Reflexivity. *Human Relations, 52,* 463–83.
Hollway, W. (1991). *Work psychology and organizational behaviour: Managing the individual at work.* London: Sage.
Hosking, D. M., Dachler, H. P., & Gergen, K. J. (1995). *Management and organization: Relational alternatives to individualism.* Aldershot: Avebury Press.
Jeffcutt, P. (1994). The interpretation of organization: A contemporary analysis and critique. *Journal of Management Studies, 31,* 225–250.
Jewell, L. N., & Siegall, M. (1990). *Contemporary industrial/organizational psychology* (2nd ed.). St Paul: West Publishing Company.
Kilduff, M. (1993). Deconstructing organizations. *Academy of Management Review, 18*(1), 13–31.
Kilduff, M., & Mehra, A. (1997). Postmodernism and organizational research. *Academy of Management Review, 22*(2), 453–481.
Knights, D. (1992). Changing spaces: The disruptive impact of a new epistemological location for the study of management. *Academy of Management Review, 17*(3), 514–535.
Knights, D., & Morgan, G. (1991). Strategic discourse and subjectivity. *Organization Studies, 12*(2), 251–274.
Kuhn, T. (1957). *The Copernican revolution.* Cambridge, MA: Harvard University Press.
Kuhn, T. (1962/1970). *The structure of scientific revolutions* (2nd ed.). Chicago, IL: Chicago University Press.
Linsted, S. (1993). Deconstruction in the study of organizations. In J. Hassard, & M. Parker (Eds.), *Postmodernism and organizations* (pp. 49–70). London: Sage.
Linstead, S., & Grafton-Small, R. (1992). On reading organization culture. *Organization Studies, 13*(3), 331–355.
Lyotard, J-F. (1984). *The postmodern condition: A report on knowledge.* Manchester: Manchester University Press.
March, J. G., & Simon, H. A. (1958). *Organizations.* New York: Wiley.
Milter, P., & O'Leary, T. (1987). Accounting and the construction of the governable person. *Accounting, Organizations and Society, 12*(3), 235–261.
Morgan, G. (1986). *Images of organization.* London: Sage.
Morgan, G. (1993). *Imaginization.* London: Sage.
Neurath, O. (1944). *Foundations of the social sciences.* Chicago, IL: University of Chicago Press.
Ortony, A. (Ed.) (1979). *Metaphor and thought.* Cambridge: Cambridge University Press.
Parker, M. (1992). Post-modern organizations or postmodern organization theory. *Organization Studies, 13,* 1–17.
Parker, M. (1993). Life after Jean-Francois. In J. Hassard, & M. Parker (Eds.), *Postmodernism and organizations* (pp. 204–212). London: Sage.

Potter, J., & Wetherall, M. (1987). *Discourse and social psychology.* London: Sage.
Reason, P., & Rowan, J. (1981). *Human inquiry: A sourcebook of new paradigm research.* Chichester: Wiley.
Rorty, R. (1979). *Philosophy and the mirror of nature.* Princeton, NJ: Princeton University Press.
Rorty, R. (1982). *Consequences of pragmatism (Essays 1972–80).* Minneapolis, MN: University of Minnesota Press.
Rosenau, P. M. (1992). *Post-modernism and the social sciences: Insights, inroads and intrusions.* Princeton, NJ: Princeton University Press.
Rousseau, D. M. (1995). *Psychological contracts in organizations.* London: Sage.
Schaubroeck, J., & Kuehn, K. (1992). Research design in industrial and organizational psychology. In C. L. Cooper, & I. T. Robertson (Eds.), *International review of industrial and organizational psychology* (Vol. 7, pp. 99–121). Chichester: Wiley.
Shotter, J. (1975). *Images of man in psychological research.* London: Methuen.
Smith, J. A., Harre, R., & Van Langenhove, L. (1995). *Rethinking methods in psychology.* London: Sage.
Sparrow, P. R. (1998). New organizational forms, processes, jobs and psychological contracts: Resolving the issues. In P. Sparrow, & M. Marchington (Eds.), *HRM: The new agenda* (pp. 117–141). London: Pitman.
Sparrow, P. R. (1999). Editorial. *Journal of Occupational and Organizational Psychology,* 72(3), 261–264.
Steier, F. (1991). *Research and reflexivity.* London: Sage.
Symon, G. (2000). Everyday rhetoric: argument and persuasion in everyday life. *European Journal of Work and Organizational Psychology, 9,* 477–488.
Symon, G., & Cassell, C. M. (1998a). *Qualitative methods in work psychology.* Paper presented to the 24th International Congress of Applied Psychology, San Francisco, 9–14 August.
Symon, G., & Cassell, C. M. (1998b). *Qualitative methods and analysis in organizational research.* London: Sage.
Taylor, C. (1985). *Philosophy and the human sciences: Philosophical Papers 2.* Cambridge: Cambridge University Press.
Thompson, P. (1993). Postmodernism: Fatal distraction. In J. Hassard, & M. Parker (Eds.), *Postmodernism and organizations* (pp. 183–203). London: Sage.
Townley, B. (1994). *Reframing human resource management: Power, ethics and the subject at work.* London: Sage.
Turner, B. S. (1987). *Medical power and social knowledge.* London: Sage.
Vattimo, G. (1992). *The transparent society.* Cambridge: Polity.
Wittgenstein, L. (1958). *Philosophical investigations.* Oxford: Blackwell.
Woolgar, S. (1996). Psychology, qualitative methods and the ideas of science. In J. T. E. Richardson (Ed.), *Handbook of qualitative research methods for psychology and the social sciences* (pp. 11–24). Leicester: BPS.

65

THE PRACTITIONER–RESEARCHER DIVIDE IN INDUSTRIAL, WORK AND ORGANIZATIONAL (IWO) PSYCHOLOGY

Where are we now, and where do we go from here?

Neil Anderson, Peter Herriot and Gerard P. Hodgkinson*

Source: *Journal of Occupational and Organizational Psychology* 74 (2001): 391–411.

Abstract

There is current concern that the researcher, or academic, and the practitioner wings of our discipline are moving further apart. This divergence is likely to result in irrelevant theory and in untheorized and invalid practice. Such outcomes will damage our reputation and ultimately result in our fragmentation. We present a simple 2 × 2 model along the dimensions of relevance and rigour, with the four cells occupied by Popularist, Pragmatic, Pedantic, and Puerile Science, respectively. We argue that there has been a drift away from Pragmatic Science, high in both relevance and rigour, towards Pedantic and Popularist Science, and through them to Puerile Science. We support this argument by longitudinal analyses of the authorship of academic journal articles and then explain this drift in terms of our stakeholders. Powerful academics are the most immediate stakeholders for researchers, and they exercise their power in such a way as to increase the drift towards Pedantic Science. Organizational clients are the most powerful stakeholders for practitioners, and in their effort to address their urgent issues, they push practitioners towards Popularist Science. In the light of this analysis, we argue that we need to engage in political activity in order to reduce or redirect the influence of the key stakeholders. This can be done either directly, through our relationship with them, or indirectly, through others who influence them. Only by political action can the centrifugal forces away from Pragmatic Science be countered and a centripetal direction be established. Finally, we explore the implications of our analysis for the future development of members of our own profession.

Industrial and organizational psychology's major challenge for the future is to convince both our academic and non-academic patrons to develop a more complex and multifaceted definition of what constitutes our own performance effectiveness . . . then, our impact on both the science and practice of industrial and organizational psychology will be far more profound and will no longer be so dependent upon simply counting publications or on promoting faddish techniques that have often been prematurely foisted upon organizational systems.

(Dunnette, 1990, p. 21)

Following almost 100 years of research and several decades of flourishing practice in the field of Industrial, Work and Organizational (IWO) psychology, growing concerns are being expressed across a number of European countries (e.g. Britain, Germany, The Netherlands) and in the United States that there is an increasing divide between researchers/academics and practitioners opening up within our discipline (e.g. Anderson, 1998a; Dunnette, 1990; Hodgkinson & Herriot, in press; Rice, 1997; Sackett, 1994; Weinreich, Barandon, Franko, Lubahn, & Nutzhorn, 1997). In this, the Centenrary Special Issue of the *Journal of Occupational and Organizational Psychology* (JOOP), it is timely to take stock of the current state of relations between the scientific and practitioner wings of our discipline, particularly in view of the concentration of all other papers in the present issue upon key knowledge and practice areas in IWO psychology. One of the defining characteristics of IWO psychology, from its inception, has been the high level of synergy between research and practice (Anderson, Ones, Sinangil, & Viswesvaran, 2001; Cooper & Locke, 2000; Shimmin & Wallis, 1994; Viteles, 1959). As demonstrated by the other articles in this Special Issue of JOOP, throughout much of its history, robust research has informed best professional practice, whilst simultaneously, informed practice in the field has stimulated new directions for research and theorizing in IWO psychology. However, we believe that researchers and practitioners are currently moving further apart. In this article, we seek to establish that this is the case, to explore why it is happening, and to propose an approach to address the issue, based upon this analysis.

Rigorous research and relevant practice

Practitioners and researchers have often held stereotypical views of each other, with practitioners viewing researchers as interested only in methodological rigour whilst failing to concern themselves with anything in the real world, and researchers damning practitioners for embracing the latest fads, regardless of theory or evidence. These stereotypes have received academic support in analyses of the nature of the production of knowledge. Such analyses have led scholars to propose a set of binary dimensions along which disciplines differ. For example, Becher (1989) suggests that there are four such dimensions:

(i) hard vs. soft, defined in terms of the degree to which a single agreed paradigm exists;
(ii) pure vs. applied, or the degree of concern for application to practical problems;
(iii) convergent vs. divergent, or the degree to which common assumptions and values are shared; and
(iv) urban vs. rural, or the degree to which the discipline addresses relatively few, well-defined research problems.

Whilst the first-mentioned pole of each of these continua is more characteristic of the physical sciences, some applied social scientists have also aspired to move towards them. Pfeffer (1993), for example, argues that only when the supporting science is 'secure' (i.e. towards the first-mentioned poles) can professional practice become effective. Clearly, this analysis of the creation of knowledge takes a traditional view of the relationship between sound, generalizable, fundamental science and its transitory, specific application. It is an account that many on the academic side of our discipline have embraced, asserting that research in the sub-discipline of applied psychology is followed by its dissemination, which in turn results, in time, in the application of its findings in the real world.

In reaction, some theorists of science have proposed two contrasting modes of research (Gibbons *et al.*, 1994; Tranfield & Starkey, 1998). The first, 'scientific inquiry' or 'Mode 1', follows the above physical-sciences model, whereby theoretical models are tested against empirical data, each successive study adding to previous findings. This corresponds to Kuhn's (1970) model of normal science. The second mode is termed 'problem solution' or 'Mode 2', and adopts a more action-centred approach. Mode 2 research constitutes a more socially distributed form of knowledge production in which knowledge is generated in the context of application by multi-stakeholder teams, drawn from a range backgrounds that transcend the boundaries of traditional disciplines, and results in immediate or short time to market dissemination/exploitation. The origin of the problem to be addressed is likely to be found in working life and experience rather than in the extant scientific literature, and the process of knowledge creation involves continuous feedback between eclectic theory and the outcomes of various interventions. Problem solution is arrived at directly rather than subsequently inferred, but is not necessarily transferable to other situations.

These two modes of knowledge production are often put forward as alternative accounts of the knowledge creation process, and proposals for science policy are based upon the assumptions of one or the other model.

Rigorous practice and relevant research

It is against this backdrop that we propose a simple 2 × 2 working model (see Fig. 1). This model does not require us to choose between practical relevance and methodological rigour. On the contrary, we argue that both requirements are of crucial importance to our discipline, but that they are not always both met.

Where practical relevance is high but methodological rigour low, *Popularist Science* is generated (Quadrant 1). Studies falling within this category address a theme widely recognized as relevant, but fail to do so with sufficient rigour to permit any reliance upon their findings. In the USA, research of this sort has been termed 'junk science', and has been viewed as inadmissible evidence in a court of law. It is typically executed where fast-emerging business trends or management initiatives have spawned ill-conceived or ill-conducted studies, rushed to publication in order to provide a degree of legitimacy and marketing support. Another characteristic of popularist studies is that fields in which they proliferate fail to apply appropriate peer review and refereeing procedures prior to publication, resulting in a notable absence of quality control over reports of studies available in the public domain. Several examples of Popularist Science afflict IWO psychology currently, including popularist books on emotional intelligence, unvalidated claims in respect of team-building and OD interventions, and self-produced 'validation' studies by less reputable test publishers that have been dashed into press to support recently published psychometric tests. Popularist Science, of course, can be dangerous if practice is founded upon such badly conceived, unvalidated, or plain incorrect research, since ineffectual or even harmful practical methods may result (Lévy-Leboyer, 1988). Moreover, such work illustrates only too clearly the importance of the anonymous review procedures applied by all of the reputable

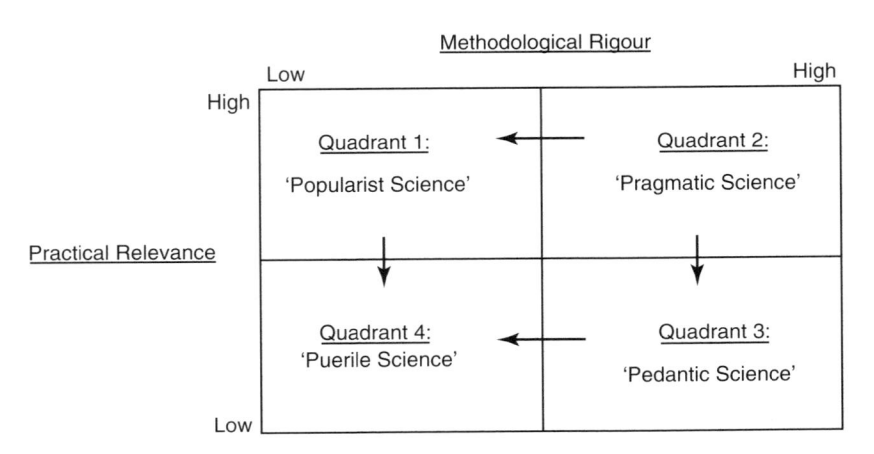

Figure 1 Fourfold typology of research in industrial, work and organizational psychology (arrows indicate current environmental pressures toward different quadrants acting upon researchers and practitioners).

journals in IWO psychology to the robustness of the research base which underpins our discipline.

Quadrant 2, where both practical relevance and methodological rigour are high, we term *Pragmatic Science*. Such work simultaneously addresses questions of applied psychological relevance and does so in a methodologically robust manner (Hackman, 1985). Clearly, we believe that this particular form of research is the form that should dominate our discipline, and many excellent examples are described in the rest of this issue of the journal. It is difficult to overstate the importance of basing our practical interventions in IWO psychology upon a strong foundation of Pragmatic Science, and any balanced review of the current state of our discipline would need to acknowledge that examples of this happening litter our history and indeed present-day practice. For instance, the area of selection and assessment can be cited as one of the most flourishing sub-areas within IWO psychology, which, for many years, has benefited from a symbiotic relationship between good science and good practice (Salgado, Viswesvaran, & Ones, 2001). The use of assessment centres, tests of cognitive ability and personality, structured interviewing techniques, and biodata forms are all examples of this symbiotic relationship between robust research and practice in selection, and it is important that any critical self-reflection over the state of health of our discipline acknowledges these undoubted strengths built up over the years by researchers and practitioners being sympathetic to the views and objectives of one another, both groups being mindful of the superordinate goals of the longer term development of the profession internationally. Nevertheless, we would not wish to be accused as a profession or as professionals of becoming complacent; hence, we feel that the time has now come to engage in a process of constructive self-appraisal.

Where methodological rigour is high but practical relevance is low (Quadrant 3), *Pedantic Science* is generated. We employ this term in respect of studies that are fastidious in their design and analytical sophistication yet fail to address an issue of current organizational or psychological relevance. Such research usually derives its questions from theory or from existing published studies, the sole criterion of its worth being the evaluation of a small minority of other researchers who specialize in a narrow field of inquiry. Again considering the area of selection and assessment as an exemplar, Herriot and Anderson (1997) have criticized utility theory studies on precisely these grounds. Utility theory, in its original conceptualization, was intended as a comparatively simple, rational, cost–benefit-driven method to persuade organizations to use more reliable and predictively valid techniques of employee selection, the formulaic calculations of utility value being only a part of this process. Regrettably, the field has witnessed an ever-increasing preoccupation by some researchers active in this area over the minutiae of formulaic expressions and the calculation of job performance standard deviation estimates, with successive papers becoming ever more myopic and technical in nature. This reductionistic, pedantic orientation was only thrown into some turmoil by more recent studies casting doubt upon the basic effectiveness of utility theory as a means for persuading selection practitioners to adopt different methods. Indeed, it can be argued that the march of technically pedantic scientific papers was abruptly curtailed by these recent studies, which returned to the crucial question of the practical relevance of utility theory—a rare example perhaps of robust Pragmatic Science halting the drift towards Pedantic Science. (See Herriot & Anderson (1997) and Hodgkinson, Herriot & Anderson (2001) for an extended debate of this example, and Hodgkinson & Herriot (in press) for a similar discussion in relation to the criterion problem in personnel selection research.)

Finally, in Quadrant 4, what we term *Puerile Science* can emerge. Here, misguided authors have pursued issues of unacceptably low practical relevance, and have done so using research designs and methods lacking in rigour. Such research incurs huge opportunity costs, ruins the reputation of IWO psychology, and will have damaging effects if actions are taken as a result. Finding clear examples of Puerile Science in the field of IWO psychology to denigrate at this point is, thankfully, quite problematic. However, many journal editors and reviewers will have had the unfortunate experience, as we ourselves have experienced, of receiving papers addressing irrelevant problems through studies or experiments that lack even the basic foundations of scientific robustness. Most are summarily rejected for publication by all of the reputable journals, but we should be conscious of the fact that there are plenty of outlets for such studies and that Puerile Science does exist in our field; the question is how to minimize its existence and its impact upon organizational practices. Unfortunately, it also has to be acknowledged that Puerile Science can gain exposure through professional and other media and influence indirectly the organizational *Zeitgeist*.

Defining practical relevance and methodological rigour

Our four-quadrant model identifies practical relevance and methodological rigour as the two key dimensions underpinning the entire research endeavour of IWO psychology. More problematic, however, is to define precisely what is meant by each of these terms.

Even if we accept as a given that our ultimate goal, as a knowledge-based profession, is the enhancement of employee well-being and organizational effectiveness, it has to be recognized that these are socially constructed phenomena, with fundamentally different meanings across differing stakeholder groups. Consequently, the question of relevance is multifaceted. We need to consider the question of relevance in relation to several other questions, not least relevance for whom, for what ultimate purposes, and to what ends? What constitutes 'practically relevant research', therefore, is the subject of a series of ongoing negotiations between the various stakeholding parties concerned and will vary at any given point in time, depending upon which particular stakeholders are involved in the research process. For this reason, it is difficult to offer a categorical definition of 'relevance'. Nevertheless, as we shall seek to demonstrate shortly, the range of stakeholders directly and indirectly involved in the research process has widened considerably over recent years. Clearly, therefore, any research in our field that fails to consider this broader, evolving context is likely to meet a similar fate to that of personnel selection, as discussed above.

The question of 'methodological rigour' is fraught with similar difficulty. Standards of evidence vary according to the ontological assumptions and epistemological orientations underpinning particular schools of thought. In keeping with our earlier discussion of Mode 1 and Mode 2 approaches to knowledge production, historically, many researchers in IWO psychology have tended to follow the lead of their counterparts in the other areas of psychology in defining methodological rigour. In turn, researchers in these other areas have tended to follow the physical sciences, attempting to establish general laws and cause–effect relations, mostly, although by no means exclusively, through the adoption of laboratory experimental research methods, which permit the control and manipulation of variables in isolation from their context.

As noted by Hodgkinson and Herriot (in press), many of the most pressing problems confronting contemporary organizations do not necessarily lend themselves to the wholesale adoption of this conventional, Mode 1 approach, and there is a need to broaden our search for, and acceptance of, methodological alternatives that meet the twin imperatives of rigour and relevance. One such alternative, identified by Hodgkinson and Herriot, is 'scholarly consulting' (Argyris, 1999), major elements of which have been termed action research. This approach entails the development of propositions that are both valid and actionable; they are both generalizable *and* applicable to the specific case. Such propositions are generated in the context of solving particular organizational problems. However, the fact that alternative outcomes to those intended in the implementation of the propositions are both possible and tested for means that falsification, the bedrock of scientific method (Popper, 1962), is central to this whole approach. Hence, scholarly consulting and closely related approaches, such as action research, fall within our definition of pragmatic science and illustrate the fact that pragmatic science is much broader than the overly narrow conceptions of science characteristic of the natural science model of knowledge production that has historically underpinned the development of so much of the work in our field.

The drift from pragmatic science

We contend that there are current trends away from the conduct of Pragmatic Science, and towards the other three approaches outlined in Fig. 1. These movements are represented by means of the various arrow-headed pathways in this figure. First, we seek to establish the existence of these trends.

One form of evidence relates to the degree of involvement of practitioners in the publication process. Although it is only one indicator of a general structural problem, the decline of such involvement is an important concern (Dunnette, 1990). When we consider three refereed journals, the *Journal of Occupational and Organizational Psychology*, the *Journal of Applied Psychology* (JAP), and *Personnel Psychology* (PP), a clear trend emerges over five decades (see Table 1, which

Table 1 Changing practitioner involvement in scientific journal publishing

	Journal of Applied Psychology/ Personnel Psychology		Occupational Psychology/ Journal of Occupational Psychology		Journal of Applied Psychology	Personnel Psychology	Journal of Occupational and Organizational Psychology
	1949–1964[a]	1967–1982[b]	1949–1964[c]	1967–1982[c]	1990–2000[d]	1990–2000[e]	1990–2000[f]
All authors academics	63%	77%	78%	81%	96%	92%	89%
All authors practitioners	31%	15%	17%	13%	1%	3%	3%
Mix of academics and practitioners	5%	8%	5%	6%	3%	5%	8%

[a,b] Figures from Sackett et al. (1986) reproduced in Dunnette (1990).
[c] Journal of Occupational and Organizational Psychology was formerly titled Occupational Psychology until 1973, then Journal of Occupational Psychology until 1991.
[d] Figures cover February 1990 [75, (1)] to October 2000 [85, (5)] and include JAP research reports.
[e] Figures cover Spring 1990 [43, (1)] to Autumn 2000 [53, (3)] and include scientist–practitioner forum papers.
[f] Figures cover March 1990 [63, (1)] to September 2000 [73, (3)] and include JOOP Short Research Notes introduced in 1996.

is developed from Sackett, Callahan, DeMeuse, Ford, & Kozlowski, 1986, cited in Dunnette, 1990). First, there has been a sizeable increase in the proportion of papers where all authors are academics, especially in JAP and PP.

Second, there has been an equally strong decline in papers where all authors are practitioners, to the point of virtual extinction. Collaborative papers between academics and practitioners have remained at a low, but relatively constant, level.

When we consider the origins of those questions that published research addresses, we find a similar picture. The vast majority of studies follow on from other published studies, with relatively few aimed at testing theory, and even fewer at addressing a relevant problem issue (Anderson, 1998b; Sackett & Larson, 1990). Sackett and Larson (1990) carried out a careful content analysis of all papers published in JAP, PP, and *Organizational Behavior and Human Decision Processes* (OBHDP) over three years—1977, 1982, and 1987. The 577 published papers were coded on a number of dimensions, including the origin of the research question, under three sources: (i) questions derived from theory; (ii) questions derived from real-world problems; and (iii) questions derived from existing studies, so-called 'coupling' research or 'replication–extension' studies (Anderson, 1998a). Their findings are somewhat unsettling: 13% of studies were theory-driven, and a paltry 3% addressed real-world problems, whereas an overwhelming 84% were replication–extension studies. Of course, the original studies on a given topic may have been relevant to real-world issues, but later additions often engage in ever more methodologically refined and analytically sophisticated research, which soon loses any relevance for practitioners. The continued proliferation of studies investigating outmoded research questions and refinements of measurement procedures in relation to peripheral methodological concerns exemplifies this trend (cf. Herriot, 1993; Herriot & Anderson, 1997; Hodgkinson & Herriot, in press), as does the withdrawal of researchers from field studies back into laboratory experiments and the excessive use of student participants in such laboratory manipulations. Clearly, such trends are indicative of a general drift away from Pragmatic Science towards Pedantic Science.

The move from Pragmatic to Popularist Science is also clear, though harder to evidence unambiguously. Urgent needs have been expressed, for example, to evaluate Human Resource Management processes in terms of their organizational impact (Huselid, 1995; Schuler, 1998). Clearly, the perception by HR professionals of the need to evaluate is very welcome, given the sequence of unevaluated management fads practised in organizations over the last two decades. However, such is the pressure for rapid results that the establishment of causality by means of longitudinal research designs has been the exception rather than the rule. Journal editors have been forced to make explicit policy statements pointing to the undesirability of relying upon cross-sectional designs (Sparrow, 1999; Zjilstra, 2000).

More generally, there is considerable pressure to engage in research that draws upon concepts or methods that constitute currently fashionable solutions to issues. These often have little theoretical underpinning, and hence it is very difficult to establish any degree of construct validity. Arguably, much of the recent research in the areas of emotional intelligence and managerial competencies exemplifies this trend.

Finally, the trend towards Puerile Science may be construed as the further decay of Pedantic and Popularist Science, respectively. Pedantic Science rapidly becomes Puerile when academics engage in self-indulgent mental jousting over questions of dubious epistemological or pragmatic value, even over the longer term. The increase in the number of journals published by and for specific partisan groups of academics points to a growth in Puerile Science. Popularist Science, however, deteriorates into Puerility when the choice of topic is not based upon what practitioners feel to be important, but is rather aimed at achieving media attention. True popularization, that is, the clear communication of Pragmatic Science to a wide audience, is one thing; its perverted version, the attempt to provide a story that will heighten one's media profile, is quite another.

There are other indications that the trends away from Pragmatic Science are gathering pace. One such indication is the formation in several countries of professional groups that claim to represent only the interests of practitioners, asserting that the interests of academic members predominate, to their own disadvantage (St Ather, 1999). Another, is the growth of special interest groups of practitioners, exchanging specific, local information and methods without reference to broader areas of practice or to sources of validation.

As depicted in Fig. 2, we can envisage these trends continuing in the centrifugal directions outlined above, unless we act now to reverse them. Left unchecked, the results will be catastrophic for our discipline. Within this doomsday scenario (McIntyre, 1990), we may expect to see Pedantic and Popularist Science, often descending into Puerility, pursued by academic and practitioner groups, respectively. Links between the two groups will be largely severed, with

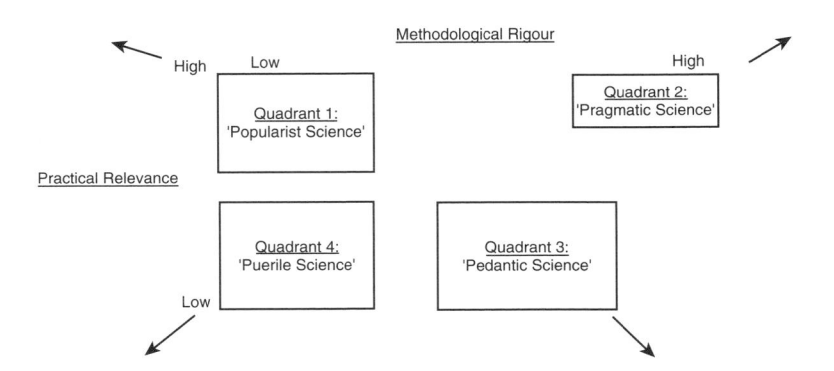

Figure 2 Scenario 1: Increasing fragmentation (arrows indicate centrifugal forces/environmental pressures toward fragmentation with each quadrant becoming increasingly isolated; quadrants are shown approximately to scale to represent the volume of research in each quadrant).

untheorized practice and irrelevant replication–extension studies as the unavoidable consequences. When not engaged in producing Pedantic and Popularist Science, the two groups will spend what remains of their time and energy fighting internal and/or external battles (based largely upon mutually reinforced stereotypical views of one another) in a quest for supremacy. Practitioner groups will subdivide into sects, each enjoying the luxury of believing fervently in specific methods, which, in the absence of sound research, cannot be evaluated. Academics, however, will engage in increasingly internecine theoretical disputes, unencumbered by any imperative to relate to the real world of work. Pockets of Pragmatic Science will survive only in a few applied academic departments and in those large consultancies that base their services upon sound research and evaluation. In sum, left unchecked, the growing divide between academic and practitioner groups will result in the wholesale fragmentation of our field, a wide range of highly disparate subgroups emerging on both sides of the divide.

Stakeholder claims

So how might the centrifugal forces depicted in Fig. 2 be replaced by the centripetal ones shown in Fig. 3? We contend that unless we recognize the existence of the various stakeholders in our professional environment, and understand the ways in which they are exercising their power, we will not address the real issues that face us.

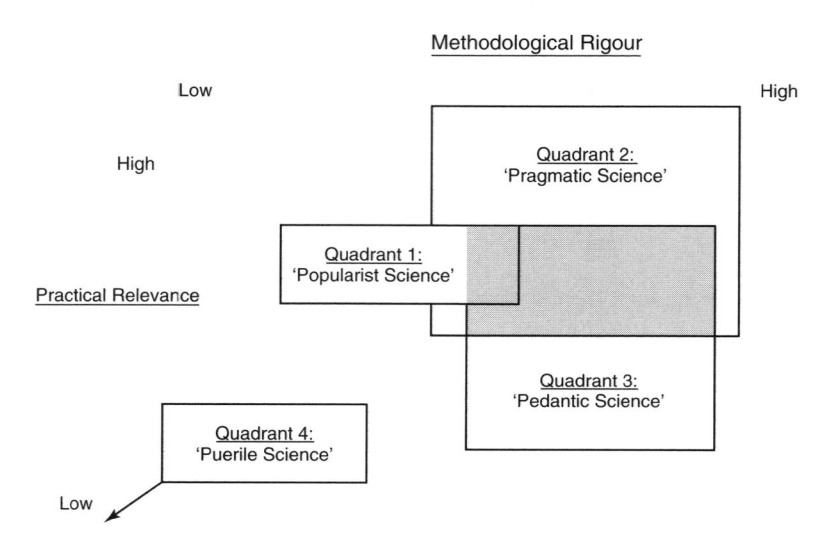

Figure 3 Scenario 2: Synergistic science and practice (arrows indicate mechanisms and opportunities for constructive exchanges between research and practice in both directions; quadrants are drawn approximately to scale with overlaps illustrated by shaded areas again drawn approximately to scale).

Many of the remedial recommendations that have been made so far address the symptoms rather than the causes. For example, Hyatt *et al.* (1997) invite academics and practitioners to communicate more using information technology, to exchange speakers, to exchange sabbaticals, to both be involved in graduate training, to provide graduate projects inside organizations, and to form collaborative research groups. Whilst all of these initiatives are worthy they will not have the desired effect unless political issues of stakeholder power are addressed.

First, we need to define what we mean by stakeholders. Stakeholders are 'any group or individual who can affect or is affected by the achievement of objectives' (Freeman, 1984, p. 24). In this case, we are referring to the objectives of an institution, i.e. the profession of IWO psychology. Stakeholders, in other words, are those who have an interest in our activities and their outcomes. Note that there is no normative element in this definition; stakeholders are not defined as those with a *legitimate* interest in our activities. The implication is clear: if we are to pay attention to our environment in order to discover how we might survive in it, we have to review it as it is, and as it is becoming, not as we would like it to be. Hence, arguments about academic independence are important in their own right, but not of great relevance at this juncture. Indeed, we would argue that as an *applied* discipline, those who do the applying and those in receipt of the application *are* legitimate stakeholders.

When we examine those stakeholders who both have an interest in our objectives and who also exercise considerable power in their efforts to maintain those interests, an overarching generalization is immediately apparent: different key stakeholder groups, in varying ways, have exerted pressures upon academics and practitioners (see Fig. 4). In the case of academics, a nexus of government, universities, and the academic discipline community exercise power, represented by powerful academic decision-makers. In the case of practitioners, the client is undisputed king (although, of course, there is often some ambiguity as to who is or are

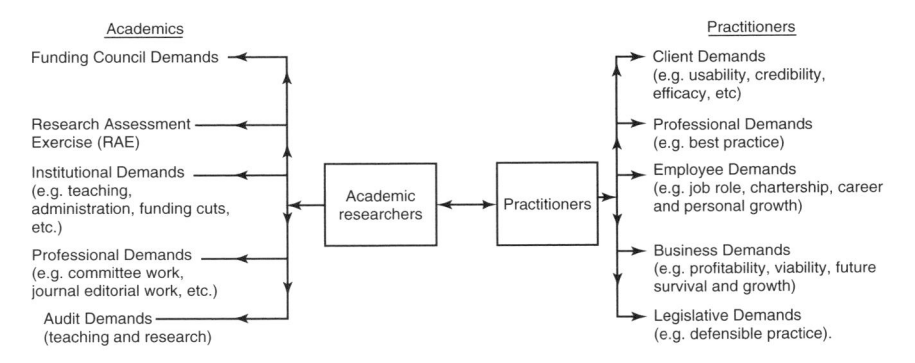

Figure 4 Stakeholder pressures on practitioners and academics in IWO psychology.

the clients). If the perceived interests of these two sets of stakeholders are different, then the strong resource power that they each wield will pull in different directions. The results, we suggest, are the centrifugal forces depicted in Fig. 2.

Stakeholders in research

First, we examine the stakeholder influences upon academics. Governments are under increasing pressure to ensure that taxpayers are receiving value for their money. Hence, a major increase in the auditing of public services has recently occurred, including that of universities (where these are funded partly by the state).

Aware of the value placed upon academic independence and integrity, governments have tended to allocate most auditing functions, except the financial functions, to other academics. Thus, for example, in the UK, powerful academics review the research performance of other departments in their subject discipline (e.g. psychology). Traditional academic criteria, especially publications in the most reputable refereed journals, are used in the evaluation, as a result of which, research ratings are awarded and resources allocated, with more going to those rated more highly.

This process handicaps IWO psychology in the following ways. First, it normally takes longer to do real-world research than laboratory studies, since access has to be negotiated and participation is normally very low on employers' and employees' lists of priorities. Second, the most reputable journals are considered to be American, and these journals set stringently high standards for methodological rigour and expect research to be designed in particular ways, which few research groups outside the USA are accustomed to. Given that the career progression of academics is also dependent upon the extent and 'quality' of their publications list, the pull towards Pedantic Science becomes overwhelming. Moreover, departments of psychology have often decreased the numbers of IWO psychologists in favour of cognitive neuroscientists and experimental cognitive psychologists, who can produce more research that is published in journals with higher citation impact factors. The higher impact factors enjoyed by these journals, of course, are determined, to a certain extent, by the fact that there are more active researchers in these subfields. A key consequence of this dysfunctional resource allocation process has been the growth of mass teaching in IWO psychology, since it is the area most in demand by students, yet understaffed in many research-led psychology departments. As a result, hard-pressed academics are being forced to retreat into more Pedantic and less Pragmatic research. The situation is little better in many business schools. Again, demand for IWO psychology teaching often outstrips supply, with a consequent negative impact on research performance. In this environment, however, academics are increasingly faced with additional pressures: to pursue consultancy opportunities, both as a means of generating additional sources of income for their paymasters, and in order to add to their credibility as executive educators.

Whilst the picture in Europe resembles to a degree that of the UK, the USA, easily the largest and most influential producer of research in IWO psychology, is somewhat different. There, the power exercised by academics over the production of knowledge is even greater. The resources for research are generously bestowed by a wide variety of governmental and voluntary agencies, but the advisory function for their allocation and monitoring is, to a considerable extent, in the hands of a relatively small number of elite academics.

Stakeholders in practice

Whilst their primary stakeholders pull academics towards Pedantic Science, practitioners' stakeholders exercise their considerable reward power towards Popularist Science. The primary stakeholders of practitioners are their clients, an ever greater proportion of whom are private sector organizations as the privatization of previously public sector services proceeds apace. Every management text (e.g. Hamel & Prahalad, 1994) recounts the litany of changes in the business environment that profoundly affect organizations and the people who work within them. Globalization, competition, deregulation and technological change combine to make organizational survival ever more dependent upon the skills and motivation of employees (Cascio, 1995; Cooper & Jackson, 1997; Herriot & Anderson, 1997; Hodgkinson & Herriot, in press). How to engage employees in an employment relationship that enhances their contribution and the organization's performance has become one of the most urgent problems facing clients (Herriot, 2001). In response, organizations have lavished resources on those who lay claim to be able to help them with these pressing problems, to the extent that consultancy is one of the fastest growing and most profitable sectors in business.

A host of suppliers has developed to compete for this rich market. Areas of professional practice, which historically have been considered the territory of IWO psychologists, have been annexed by others. Assessment services, for example, previously the jewel in the crown of IWO psychologists, are offered by Human Resource consultants, recruitment agencies, outplacement agencies, IT consultants, and accountancy firms, among others. Other Human Resource interventions, such as organizational change management and employee development, are offered in a bewildering variety of forms by a host of different suppliers (Cascio, 1995).

Given this degree of competition in the provision of services, clients are able to demand that their criteria be met stringently by suppliers. Amongst the foremost of these criteria are speed of response, solutions tailored to their own issues, the thorough implementation of these solutions, and cost-competitive service. These criteria often militate against Pragmatic Science. The requirement for speed often precludes the gathering of the evidence over time that methodological rigour requires. The expectation for tailored solutions implies that well-established and valid instruments and procedures may have to be adapted in unvalidated ways, or that new solutions will have to be designed without the faintest hope of prior validation. The emphasis on implementation highlights processual skills, such as political influencing and project management, rather than analysis, design, and evaluation, the strengths of Pragmatic Science. Finally, when cost is of prime concern, it will always be cheaper (though not necessarily more effective) to engage in Popularist, rather than Pragmatic Science.

Self-harm by stakeholders

We have argued that it is primarily the resource power of the two key sets of stakeholders (Pfeffer, 1981) that is pulling the two wings of our discipline in different directions away from Pragmatic Science. Does this spell the death knell of our profession? We argue that it does not, for the following fundamental reason: both sets of stakeholders are currently exercising their power in ways that are detrimental to their own longer term interests. Instead of causing the drift to Pedantic or Popularist Science, as they are at present, they both need to support Pragmatic Science if they are to realize their ultimate, longer term interests. Only when they both do so will the centrifugal process be replaced by a centripetal process.

First, we argue that stakeholders are damaging their long-term interests by the ways in which they exercise their resource power at present. Powerful academics in the applied social sciences are currently the main arbiters of what research is valued, published, and funded. At present, they use their resource power to enable them and their colleagues to continue engaging in activities that they enjoy and at which they excel. This they achieve through their role as gatekeepers of what gets published, who gets appointed to academic positions, which areas of work get funded, and who receives academic awards. This is yet another case of professionals regulating themselves and acting as though they were the only stakeholders in their own activities.

However, there is increasing evidence that more distal stakeholders, such as governments, are becoming less inclined to entrust the policy, management, and evaluation of research to academics alone. For instance, the UK Government has recently become far more directive in its stance towards social science research. It has directed its funding towards specific, nationally relevant issues, such as innovation, for example. Moreover, it has rewarded collaboration between academics and external organizations, and has included representatives of such organizations in its regulating committees.

These political developments place a check upon the descent into Pedantic Science, and applied social science academics who continue to engage in research that is perceived as irrelevant are unlikely to receive Government funding. Governments as stakeholders in research are impelled by a greater expectation from their citizens of accountability in the expenditure of their taxes. They are also sometimes driven by a belief that social science should be able to help to devise solutions to the immense political, social, and economic problems that they face.

Similarly, organizational stakeholders may not be serving their own best interests in the ways in which they influence practitioners through their resource power. Their use of the criteria of speed, cost, and ease of implementation in local settings in their selection of practitioner suppliers may be inimical to their interests over the longer term.

Specifically, the following areas are likely to suffer:

- the clear analysis of what the real problems are, on the basis of reliable, current evidence;
- the search through the records of previous attempts to understand and address these issues;
- the choice or development of interventions that are validly based on theory and research;
- the monitoring and evaluation of the processes and outcomes of interventions in terms of their total systemic effects;
- the incorporation of the theory and practice of the interventions into the capability set of the organization.

All of these key success factors of organizational interventions are apt to suffer, and so as a consequence are their outcomes. The drift towards Popularist Science, therefore, is not helpful.

Finally, there is the sensitive issue of scientists and researchers in IWO psychology themselves damaging the health of our discipline by engaging in excessively self-interested agendas, to the harm of the wider profession. Any widening of the divide between academics and researchers we would argue is going to be necessarily detrimental in the longer term to both groups; yet the stakeholder pressures identified earlier in this article may already be irreversibly forcing apart practitioners and researchers. One reason for this is the qualitatively different sets of objectives held by each group—researchers striving for generalizable cause–effect relations, often using longitudinal designs, practitioners needing immediately applicable techniques and methods, which have 'faith validity' for clients in the short term. The stakeholder pressures towards these different objectives have become more intensified over recent years, making it almost impossible to cope with the model of being a scientist-practitioner, able to contribute to both 'sides' of the discipline (Anderson, 1998a). Early career specialization, either as a researcher or as a practitioner, has become the accepted norm in IWO psychology. Indeed, this occurs for most immediately upon completion of their Masters degree, whereupon the decision is taken over whether to continue studying to complete a Ph.D. or to gain practical experience as a junior consultant or as an in-house IWO psychologist. We seriously doubt whether such early specialization is healthy for the development of a profession that has exalted the model of the scientist-practitioner as one that should be striven for by younger recruits entering our field, hoping to make a career in it.

The management of stakeholder relationships

If the drift towards Pedantic and Popularist Science is a consequence of the influence of key stakeholder groups with resource power, then it follows that it can only be reversed if that power is reduced or redirected. Our discipline can pursue these political objectives directly or indirectly (Wood, 1994).

Directly, we can attempt to influence the key stakeholders themselves. Thus, for example, we might point out to organizational stakeholders the costs of Popularist Science and the benefits of Pragmatic Science. This rational persuasion, together with other sorts of influencing activities, may well result in a redirection of their resources towards suppliers who use or practice Pragmatic Science. In another form of political influence, we could seek to replace Pedantic academics in funding bodies, or on editorial boards of journals, or as heads of department, by Pragmatic academics. The direct management of each stakeholder relationship is an important activity worth pursuing.

However, the sources of power and its exercise are complex and inter-related. Stakeholders are frequently involved in power relationships with each other. It is very possible that more distal stakeholders have a very strong influence over more proximal stakeholders. Moreover, there may be organizations or institutions that are not stakeholders at all themselves, but which exercise considerable influence over those who are.

We have already cited an example of the first of these two cases. The Government is a more distal stakeholder in academic research than are powerful academics, yet Government already exercises considerable influence over them as a consequence of its resource and its legitimate power. It can bypass them by appointing more amenable academics to its funding and policy committees, for example; and it can reduce their power by refusing to fund Pedantic Science. Hence, influencing such distal stakeholders may be more profitable than targeting the more proximal stakeholders. Pragmatic Scientists will be influencing Government by indicating that they are capable of helping Government address relevant issues, but only if they are permitted to practice sound science.

Additionally, our influence attempts can be directed through third parties, who have little apparent stakeholder status, but nevertheless can have a powerful influence on the key stakeholders themselves. For example, trade unions and professional associations can affect organizations profoundly, as can pressure groups and shareholders. The media notoriously influence Government and organizations, both directly and indirectly.

In sum, the only way in which to reverse the current trend away from Pragmatic Science is to engage in political activity. Unfortunately, political activity, defined as furthering our interests and our values as a united discipline, has not hitherto been considered the most important of activities for IWO psychologists. On the contrary, such activity has historically been criticized, on the grounds that it is likely to compromise our independence and integrity. The precise opposite is true. The more actual and potential stakeholders with whom we engage, the more likely are our activities to exemplify and promote our values. For example, if trade unions, Government, and private-sector companies all have a stakeholder input, then we are less likely to engage in work that benefits one group at the expense of another.

Summary and implications

Recently, a number of commentators (Gibbons *et al.*, 1994; Tranfield & Starkey, 1998) have identified two contrasting forms of knowledge production within the natural/physical and social sciences alike. Mode 1, characterized as the 'scientific inquiry' approach, comes closest to the way in which knowledge has traditionally been developed and applied within the field of IWO psychology, corresponding to the Kuhnian model of normal science. Concerns that IWO psychology may be perpetuating an excessively normal science in the face of fundamentally changing environmental circumstances have been voiced by the present authors elsewhere (Anderson, 1998b; Herriot & Anderson, 1997; Hodgkinson & Herriot, in press). According to Gibbons and his colleagues, in recent years and across a wide variety of fields, the Mode 1 approach to knowledge production has increasingly been giving way to a second approach, characterized as 'problem solution' or 'Mode 2' research. The latter approach constitutes a more socially distributed form of knowledge production in which knowledge is generated in the context of application by multi-stakeholder teams, drawn from a range of backgrounds that transcend the boundaries of traditional disciplines, and results in immediate or short time to market dissemination/exploitation.

In this article, we have presented evidence that suggests that there is a divide opening up between the researcher/academic and practitioner wings of our profession. Left unchecked, the trends that we have identified in our analysis of the ways in which knowledge is produced and consumed within the field of IWO psychology can only lead, over the longer term, to our ultimate demise. On the basis of the evidence that we have presented, it is tempting to conclude that the wholesale adoption of Mode 2 methods and tactics is the one best way forward for the long-term health of our field as a whole. Since real-world problems seldom come discipline-shaped, it makes sense to involve a wider range of stakeholders, from a variety of backgrounds, in the research process. Moreover, the adoption of a problem-led approach might well resolve some of the growing tensions we have identified between the various disparate subgroups within our profession. However, we contend that a closer examination of the underlying issues we have identified reveals that such a simplistic prescription is clearly unwarranted.

Undoubtedly, a greater involvement of a wider range of stakeholders in all aspects of the research process, from the initial stages of problem definition to final dissemination, is not only desirable, but also essential at this juncture. Historically, as our analysis has shown, the fact that we have not involved a sufficiently wide range of stakeholders in our scientific endeavours has been very much to our own detriment. Many of the complexities and uncertainties facing modern organizations are simply too great for IWO psychologists alone to provide all the answers. In a number of key areas, both as researchers *and* as practitioners, we do not even fully appreciate what are the most appropriate questions that need to be addressed, let alone what form the answers might take. Such are the complexities involved, that the same is true of managers and other key stakeholders. Nevertheless, by involving these wider stakeholders in the research process, from the outset, we maximize the likelihood that, in future, we will pursue research that addresses problems of pressing concern to those who ultimately fund our scientific endeavours, through taxation and other mechanisms.

However, it does not follow from this analysis that the wholesale abandonment of Mode 1 in favour of a Mode 2 approach to the production of knowledge is either necessary or desirable. As Huff (2000) has observed, there are considerable benefits to be gained from seeking to combine the virtues of both approaches, while minimizing the associated weaknesses of each, a strategy that she has aptly termed Mode 1.5. This approach shares several features in common with what we have presently characterized as 'Pragmatic Science'. Crucially:

> Mode 1.5 should accommodate fault finders as well as facilitators. Critical observations ... have a particularly important role to play ... However, the critic's role cannot be undertaken credibly without familiarity with Mode 2 practices. Critics who adopt a Mode 1.5 position add an important element of diversity.
>
> (Huff, 2000, p. 292)

Our analysis also has considerable implications for the ways in which we train and develop researchers and practitioners in the field of IWO psychology over the longer term. Not least among these is the need to ensure that both groups possess the requisite socio-political skills to develop the new negotiated order that we undoubtedly require as a professional body of scientist-practitioners. Unfortunately, the development of finely honed, highly practical, processual skills has not, hitherto, featured highly in the curricula of our specialist Masters and Doctoral degree programmes. Historically, we have tended to regard the development of a critical awareness of the limitations of the extant knowledge base in the main substantive topic areas of our field (purely at a conceptual level), together with a thorough grounding in research design and statistical analysis, as the vital pre-requisites for pursuing a successful career either as a researcher and/or as a practitioner. Whilst such content-based skills are undoubtedly essential, it is equally clear that the development of key social and political skills (especially negotiation, leadership and influencing skills) is also required, if we are to remain viable as a profession over the longer term. However, given the increasing numbers of students being accepted onto Masters programmes, to meet targets imposed by universities seeking to maximize fee income, it is difficult to see how the teaching of these much needed processual skills might be accommodated.

As noted by Hodgkinson and Herriot (in press), the widespread development of process know-how (and the accompanying social and political skills necessary to put this knowledge to good use), throughout the academic and practitioner communities alike, is one key to ensuring that our scientific endeavours remain centred on issues that matter. Moreover, if we are to survive the rigours of competition and, thus, remain intact as a knowledge-based profession in these turbulent times, it is vital that such skills are deployed with immediate effect by our leading academics and practitioners. Only then can we hope to heal the researcher–practitioner divide that has become apparent over recent years.

Conclusion

We began this article with a quote from Marvin Dunnette, one of the founding fathers of modern IWO psychology, in which he challenges us to re-appraise the criteria against which we ourselves and others measure our own success (Dunnette, 1990). In the 11 years that have elapsed since Dunnette and Hough published their four-volume *Handbook of I/O Psychology* (1990–1994), his words have become even more poignant—academics are being evaluated on the quantity (and quality) of their publications, and consultancies are becoming ever more pressured to achieve financial targets set by non-psychologist owners and/or shareholders. Have we as a profession, therefore, failed spectacularly in the challenge that Dunnette laid down for us with such foresight little over a decade ago? Undoubtedly, the increasing separation of the practitioner and academic wings of our discipline has not been a positive development, and the likelihood is that the underlying stakeholder pressures toward potential fragmentation will not subside without our fighting them in mutually constructive and effective ways. The consequence of our historical unwillingness as a professional institution to engage politically is that we are unused to exercising what power and influence we have. We are not always aware of the nature and extent of the power that we possess, we are not in the habit of exercising it, and institutionally (though perhaps not individually), we have failed to build up an extensive network of allies. Yet, we have the resources to do so, and we have already developed some islands of excellence. Failure to attend to the centrifugal forces discussed in this article will surely hamper the development and societal impact of IWO psychology well into the future. What remains for the coming decades into the 21st century, therefore, is for IWO psychologists to exercise their political will and skill in such a way as to ensure that Pragmatic Science dominates our field, to the benefit of individuals, teams, and organizations alike, in this period of major organizational and social change.

Note

* The authorship of this article is strictly alphabetical, reflecting the fact that this work is the product of a joint and equal contribution on the part of all three authors.

References

Anderson, N. (1998a). The practitioner–researcher divide in work and organizational psychology. *The Occupational Psychologist, No. 34,* 7–16.

Anderson, N. (1998b). The people make the paradigm. *Journal of Organizational Behavior, 19,* 323–328.

Anderson, N., Ones, D. S., Sinangil, H. K., & Viswesvaran, C. (Eds.) (2001). *Handbook of industrial, work, and organizational psychology* (Vols I and II). London: Sage.

Argyris, C. (1999). *On organizational learning* (2nd ed.). Oxford: Blackwell.

Becher, A. (1989). *Academic tribes and territories: Intellectual enquiry and the cultures of discipline.* Milton Keynes, UK: Open University Press.

Cascio, W. F. (1995). Whither industrial and organizational psychology in a changing world of work? *American Psychologist, 50, (11),* 928–939.

Cooper, C. L., & Jackson, S. E. (1997). Introduction. In C. L. Cooper & S. E. Jackson (Eds.), *Creating tomorrow's organizations: A handbook for future research in organizational behavior.* Chichester, UK: Wiley.

Cooper, C. L., & Locke, E. A. (Eds.) (2000). *Industrial and organizational psychology: Linking theory with practice.* Oxford: Blackwell.

Dunnette, M. D. (1990). Blending the science and practice of industrial and organizational psychology: Where are we and where are we going? In M. D. Dunnette & L. M. Hough (Eds.), *Handbook of industrial and organizational psychology* (2nd ed., Vol. 1). Palo Alto, CA: Consulting Psychologists Press.

Freeman, R. E. (1984). *Strategic management: A stakeholder approach.* New York: Harper Collins.

Gibbons, M., Limoges, C., Nowotny, H., Schwartzman, S., Scott, P., & Trow, M. (1994). *The new production of knowledge: The dynamics of science and research in contemporary societies.* London: Sage.

Hackman, J. R. (1985). Doing research that makes a difference. In E. E. Lawler III, A. M. Mohrman Jr., S. A. Mohrman, G. E. Ledford Jr., & T. G. Cummings (Eds.), *Doing research that is useful for theory and practice.* San Francisco, CA: Jossey-Bass.

Hamel, G., & Prahalad, C. K. (1994). *Competing for the future.* Boston, MA: Harvard Business School Press.

Herriot, P. (1993). A paradigm bursting at the seams. *Journal of Organizational Behavior, 14,* 371–375.

Herriot, P. (2001). *The employment relationship: A psychological perspective.* London: Routledge.

Herriot, P., & Anderson, N. (1997). Selecting for change: How will personnel and selection psychology survive? In N, Anderson & P. Herriot (Eds.), *International handbook of selection and assessment.* Chichester, UK: Wiley.

Hodgkinson, G. P., & Herriot, P. (in press). The role of psychologists in enhancing organizational effectiveness. In I. Robertson, M. Callinan, & D. Bartram (Eds.), *Organizational effectiveness: The role of psychology.* Chichester, UK: Wiley.

Hodgkinson, G. P., Herriot, P. & Andesson, N. (2001). Re-aligning stakeholders in management research: Lessons from industrial, work and organizational psychology. *British Journal of Management, 12,* special issue, S41–S48.

Huff, A. S. (2000). Changes in organizational knowledge production. *Academy of Management Review, 25,* 288–293.

Huselid, M. A. (1995). The impact of Human Resource Management practices on turnover, productivity, and corporate financial performance. *Academy of Management Journal, 38,* 635–672.

Hyatt, D., Cropanzano, R., Finfer, L. A., Levy, P., Ruddy, T. M., Vandaveer, V., & Walker, S. (1997). Bridging the gap between academics and practice: Suggestions from the field. *The Industrial–Organizational Psychologist, 35, (1),* 29–32.

Kuhn, T. S. (1970). *The structure of scientific revolutions* (2nd ed.). Chicago, IL: University of Chicago Press.

Lévy-Leboyer, C. (1988). Success and failure in applying psychology. *American Psychologist, 43,* 779–785.

McIntyre, R. M. (1990). Our science-practice: The ghost of industrial–organizational psychology yet to come. In K. R. Murphy & E. E. Saal (Eds.), *Psychology in organizations: Integrating science and practice.* Hillsdale, NJ: Erlbaum.

Pfeffer, J. (1981). *Power in organizations.* Marshfield, MA: Pitman.

Pfeffer, J. (1993). Barriers to the advance of organizational science: Paradigm development as a dependent variable. *Academy of Management Review, 18,* 599–620.

Popper, K. (1962). *Conjectures and refutations.* London: Routledge and Kegan Paul.

Rice, E. E. (1997). Scenarios: The scientist–practitioner split and the future of psychology. *American Psychologist, 52, (11),* 1173–1181.

Sackett, P. R. (1994). *The content and process of the research enterprise within industrial and organizational psychology.* Presidential address to the Society for Industrial and Organizational Psychology conference, Nashville TN, April 1994.

Sackett, P. R., Callahan, C., DeMeuse, K., Ford, J. K., & Kozlowski, S. (1986). Changes over time in research involvement by academic and nonacademic psychologists. *The Industrial–Organizational Psychologist, 24, (1),* 40–43.

Sackett, P. R., & Larson, J. R. (1990). Research strategies and tactics in industrial and organizational psychology. In M. D. Dunnette & L. M. Hough (Eds.), *Handbook of industrial and organizational psychology* (2nd ed., Vol. 1). Palo Alto, CA: Consulting Psychologists Press.

Salgado, J., Viswesvaran, C., & Ones, D. (2001). Predictors used for personnel selection: An overview of constructs, methods and techniques. In N. Anderson, D. S. Ones, H. K. Sinangil, & C. Viswesvaran (Eds.), *Handbook of industrial, work, and organizational psychology* (Vols I and II). London: Sage.

Schuler, R. S. (1998). Human resource management. In M. Poole & M. Warner (Eds.), *The handbook of human resource management.* London: International Thomson Business Press.

Shimmin, S., & Wallis, D. (1994). *Fifty years of occupational psychology in Britain.* Leicester, UK: British Psychological Society.

Sparrow, P. (1999). Editorial. *Journal of Occupational and Organizational Psychology, 72,* 261–264.

St Ather, T. (1999). Where do we go from here ... again? *The Occupational Psychologist, No. 38,* 59–61.

Tranfield, D., & Starkey, K. (1998). The nature, social organization, and promotion of management research: Towards policy. *British Journal of Management, 9,* 341–353.

Viteles, M. S. (1959). Fundamentalism in industrial psychology. *Occupational Psychology, 33,* 1–13.

Weinreich, U., Barandon, R., Franko, Z., Lubahn, G., & Nutzhorn, H. (1997). Are occupational psychologists missing the boat to Europe? *EAWOP Newsletter, 7, (4),* 5–6.

Wood, D. J. (1994) *Business and society* (2nd ed.). New York: Harper Collins.

Zjilstra, F. (2000). Editorial. *European Journal of Work and Organizational Psychology, 9, (3),* 305–306.

66

ANY NEARER A "BETTER" APPROACH?

A critical view

Karen Legge

Source: D. Holman, T.D. Wall, C.W. Clegg, P. Sparrow and A. Howard (eds), *The New Workplace: A Guide to the Human Impact of Modern Working Practices*, Chichester: John Wiley, 2005, pp. 393–412.

The brief I was given for writing this chapter suggested that I "summarise and evaluate the previous chapters ... in particular, to critically assess the evidence for the effectiveness of new working practices, discuss the extent to which they have had a positive or negative effect on the experience of work, and propose ways in which the gaps in our practice and theory may be overcome".

In responding to this brief, I intend to focus on four issues. The first issue is to consider what really is new about the organisational and work designs discussed in these chapters. Is twenty-first century teamworking much different from the semi-autonomous work groups of the 1970s or call centre work different from any 1950s factory organised on Tayloristic lines? Have issues about new technologies and work design advanced much beyond the early work of the socio-technical systems theorists of the 1950s and 1960s (Rice, 1958; Trist & Bamford, 1951; Trist *et al.*, 1963) or even the work of the 1980s and 1990s (Clark *et al.*, 1988; Clark, 1995)? Second, what evidence do we really have of employees' experience of work? As has been discussed elsewhere (Mabey *et al.*, 1997), even when we purport to talk of employees' "experience", too much of our "evidence" relies at best on employees responding to highly structured questionnaires or on managers speaking on their behalf. In any case, in the globalised world to which Sparrow (Chapter 19) refers, with the extended supply chains that Kerrin & Icasati-Johanson (Chapter 5) discuss, who are the employees that we are (or should be) referring to? Surely not just those handily placed for Western researchers to access with questionnaires based on ethnocentric, Western theories of organisational psychology? Third, there is the related issue of the inadequacies of positivistic methodologies (even in their own terms) to deliver meaningful findings about the relationships between working practices and various outcome measures, notably organisational performance. Fourth, when considering gaps between theory and practice, we perhaps need to query whether some of these reflect psychology's neglect of political dimensions to behaviour at work, including the "political" behaviours of academics themselves.

In the light of the above agenda, I should declare an interest. Unlike most of the other contributors to this volume, my background is not in organisational psychology but in radical organisational theory, oscillating between sympathies for postmodernist and critical realist approaches to organisational analysis. Hence, although I will attempt to assess this work in its own terms, as a devil's advocate, I will also critique it from an agnostic—or should I say excommunicated—position.

Plus ça change, plus c'est la même chose?

Reading the chapters in this collection, at first sight, is like returning to debates and issues of the 1970s and 1980s. Old familiar friends raise their heads, such as those of organisational choice/technological determinism (e.g. Cooney & Sohal, Chapter 3, in relation to TQM; Holman, Chapter 7, in relation to call centres), job characteristics [e.g. discussions of autonomy, job enrichment, job enlargement and empowerment feature in Chapter 15, by Batt & Doellgast, on service sector work, Lamond and colleagues (Chapter 11) on teleworking and Benson & Lawler (Chapter 9) on employee involvement], work systems design [e.g. Cordery (Chapter 6) on team working, Unsworth & Parker (Chapter 10) on promoting a proactive and innovative workforce] and socio-technical systems analysis [e.g. Mumford & Axtell (Chapter 17) on tools and methods to support the design and implementation of new work systems]. As would be expected from organisational psychologists, concepts such as motivation, job satisfaction and stress feature heavily as dependent variables. All this is very familiar ground.

However, as Sparrow (Chapter 19) is at pains to point out, whether we use such buzz words as "disorganised capitalism", "globalisation" or "unprecedented economic transition", there is an academic discourse of "hypercompetition" which is translated into management-speak as the "search for competitive advantage". Either way, to quote Sparrow, it refers to the *response expected to these changes* and puts a different slant on *some* of the job and work system design changes that we have seen at the end of the twentieth and beginning of the twenty-first century [of course, as Grey & Mitev (1995) have suggested in relation to the "revolution" of business process re-engineering, by its advocacy and implementation of competitive techniques it *constitutes* the competition, which is then the problem that the organisation must address].

The new slant on task and work systems design, as compared to the 1970s is the backgrounding of quality of working life (QWL) issues and the foregrounding of organisational performance. In the tight Western labour markets of the 1970s, before south-east Asian competition in manufactured consumer goods began to bite in western Europe and the USA, before the ascendancy of the new right liberal economics and the demise of corporatism and Keynsianism in the Anglo-Saxon world, job and work system design "experiments", such as the famous experiments by Volvo at Kalmar and Uddevalla, were chiefly aimed at securing worker retention (and hopefully, motivation and commitment) through attention to QWL issues. Although improved performance was central to the agenda, it was conceptualised as improved *worker* performance (invariably in manufacturing industry) through enhanced motivation, resultant on job designs that adhered to the tenets of the job characteristics model, embedded in work system designs that embraced the socio-technical systems principle of joint optimisation. Although the action researchers involved in such experiments did not fall into the managerial fantasy of reverse causality, that "the happy worker is the productive worker", there was often an explicit commitment to the idea that work should be designed in such a way that workers could fulfil at least some higher-order needs and gain intrinsic satisfactions that would enhance their experience of work.

Contrast that position with work system designs and research conducted in the 1990s, generally featuring initiatives in business process engineering, JIT and TQM. Business process engineering, in theory at least, rests on the logic of cutting out anything within the organisation or along its supply chain (people, structures, technologies, materials) that does not add value. As such, it is a key ingredient of lean manufacturing. "Lean manufacturing", as Delbridge (Chapter 2) makes only too clear, is based, via JIT and its symbiotic relationship with TQM and continuous improvement (*kaizen*), on the removal of organisational slack (defined as "waste" or anything that does not add value), both within and between members of the supply chain. Removal of waste is aimed first and foremost at reducing costs and so improving productivity, while the "bottom line" may be yet further enhanced by greater responsiveness to the customer in terms of speed of delivery, price and quality competitiveness. The object of such designs (and recognised as such by employees) (Bacon & Blyton, 2000; Collinson *et al.*, 1998) is preeminently to improve the financial performance of the organisation or, to put it in late-1990s managerial-speak, to "increase shareholder value". Certainly there is a recognition (at least in theory and among academics) that "lean" organisations, being extremely fragile systems, need to secure a workforce that is both flexible and reliable and that this is likely to have implications for skill enhancement and the generation of employee commitment. There is recognition that this points logically to some form of "high-commitment" (in the USA, significantly termed "high-performance" HRM (Becker & Gerhart, 1996; Becker & Huselid, 1998; Delery & Doty, 1996; Huselid, 1995), which may address many of the concerns of the QWL protagonists. However, this is seen very much as a corollary of a work system design aimed at efficiency, rather than being the object of the design. Whereas the designs of the 1970s were intended to enhance worker motivation and performance and so *indirectly* organisational performance, some of the designs of the 1990s and 2000s, notably those involving BPR and "lean" manufacturing, are intended *directly* to improve financial returns, with a "high-commitment" HRM strategy being regarded by way of an ongoing servicing and insurance policy, rather as an end in itself and, as such, as a potential cost just as much as a benefit.

Of course, this is not the whole story. It could be argued that initiatives involving the adoption of "high-commitment" HRM policies, no less than the QWL experiments of the 1970s, rest on the assumption that such policies will generate highly skilled, flexible and motivated employees who will be highly productive, enabling enhanced organisational performance. But a key issue here is whether one adopts a universalistic or a contingency approach to task and work system design. Although the sociotechnical systems approach of the 1970s was contingent in the sense that organisational choices about design should match the exigencies of the context in order to achieve joint (social and technical) optimisation—the "composite shortwall" design in the British coal-mining industry being a classic example (Trist *et al.*, 1963)—it was universalistic in its concern for QWL issues and in its belief that these were best served by designing jobs high in the requisite task attributes of autonomy, variety, skill, feedback and task identity (Hackman & Oldham, 1976).

Similarly, today, there are universalistic and contingency approaches in relation to the choice of HRM policies, including task and work system design, skill levels sought, training and reward system policy. The universalistic approach maintains that there is an identifiable "bundle" of best ("high-commitment"/"high-performance") HR policies and practices that have universal, additive, positive effects on organisational performance, irrespective of external circumstances or business strategy (e.g. Guest, 1987; Huselid, 1995; MacDuffie, 1995; Pfeffer, 1994; Walton, 1985). This is consistent with institutional theory about organisational isomorphism—that organisations survive because they identify and implement the "best" policies and practices and that, as a result, successful organisations get to look more and more like each other (DiMaggio & Powell, 1983).

In contrast, the contingency approach argues that, to achieve high organisational performance, HRM policies and practices must be congruent with other organisational characteristics, such as culture, and be in alignment with the firm's business strategy (e.g. Arthur, 1994; Purcell, 1999). The contingency approach, in contrast to the universalistic, would also argue that "high-commitment" HRM practices, while appropriate to high-skill, high-value-added activities, are inappropriate to low-skill, mass production or service activities, if the objective is to maximise profitability. The contingent assumption seems to be that designs based on the control of the workforce suit mass production or service activities, while the generation of commitment is necessary where high-value-added activities are involved. This position is consistent with resource-based theories that argue that sustained competitive advantage rests not on imitating "best" practice, but on developing unique and non-imitable competences (Barney, 1991).

A third approach to task and work system design is a muddling-through, seat-of-the-pants pragmatism guided by a concern for short-term cost-effectiveness. This lacks the coherence of either a commitment to "best" practice or to consistent strategic alignment.

Where the "one best way" philosophy of "high-commitment"/"high-performance" HRM is adopted, there is much overlap with the designs proposed by the socio-technical systems, QWL movement of the 1970s, *except* that belief in

QWL values appears purely instrumental, not as an end in itself. This is consistent with the prevailing liberal economics of the late twentieth and early twenty-first century, just as adherence to QWL values for their own sake was consistent with the corporatism of the post-war decades, pre-1980s. Rather than having any position on QWL issues, a contingency approach to task and work system design, however, where strategic integration or alignment is a priority, would suggest that Tayloristic designs in some circumstances might be deemed more appropriate than those based on the investment in training, multiskilling and empowerment strategies of "high commitment" HRM. This is indeed what we find in the studies cited in many of the chapters. There is evidence of organisations taking both the "high" and the "low" road, to use Bacon and Blyton's (2000) terminology. Let us consider team working and "lean manufacturing" by way of example.

"High" road team working, as typified by Bacon & Blyton's research in the UK steel industry, is characterised by task variety (maintenance tasks integrated into production tasks, frequent job rotation, flexible job descriptions, no job classification system), identification with team tasks (skilled maintenance workers integrated into the team), expertise in teams (integration of craft expertise in teams), stability and belief in teams (workers in teams have similar skills), participative management (delayered management, teams responsible for some production targets and some measure of financial performance, team leaders selected with team input) and common rewards (few pay bands and few grades within the teams). This is very much the sort of team working discussed in Cordery's chapter and reported in the US steel industry (Ichniowski *et al.*, 1997). In contrast, "low" road team working is typified by Bacon & Blyton (2000, p. 1429) as involving a "low-skill-low-wage strategy". A key difference seems to lie in management's rationale for introducing team working. Although, irrespective of the type of team work, an economic rationale was perceived by their respondents as predominating, in the case of "high" road team working, social and cultural objectives, such as improving job satisfaction and increasing worker commitment and motivation, were scored more highly than where "low" road team working prevailed. Clearly, the latter is a far cry from the team working Cordery appears to have in mind when he speaks of the employee benefits it may afford of increased scope to satisfy higher-order needs and to obtain important intrinsic rewards through work, such as task variety and autonomy, increased social interaction, etc. Perhaps more recognition of, and research into, situations where "low" road team working is the norm might be appropriate, at least in the UK, given the finding from the Workplace Employee Relations Survey (WERS), that, of the 65% of workplaces reporting team working, only 5% had teams with features of autonomous team working (Cully *et al.*, 1999).

A similar story seems to emerge with respect to "lean" manufacturing. Delbridge's analysis finds evidence of a lean manufacturing that, at least in many employees' experience, falls well short of the ideal type marriage of the "hardware" of TQM, JIT and associated "Japanese" production processes with the "software" of "high-commitment" HRM (Rees *et al.*, 1996) to provide a "tripod of success" (Wickens, 1987), where employees work "smarter not harder". Delbridge points to the down-side of "lean" manufacturing as involving labour intensification, low trust–high surveillance control, "peer controls turning poisonous" and high stress levels—a state of affairs which elsewhere has been termed the "tripod of subjugation": management-by-stress, management-through-blame and management-through-compliance (Garrahan & Stewart, 1992). This is not surprising, at least in relation to UK research evidence. For it is highly debatable to what extent the "Japanese" model of "lean" manufacturing can be applied to UK manufacturing, let alone to services.

Indeed, based on an analysis of the largest 200 British-owned firms (size measured by capitalisation), Ackroyd & Proctor (1998) suggest that a different form of lean organisation exists in the bulk of British manufacturing industry. They emphasise that the typical British manufacturing firm has grown through merger and acquisition, comprising a large number of decentralised production facilities producing a wide range of "cash cow" goods for retail in mature markets. These are firms that favour a tight control of financial performance from the centre, with a good deal of operational freedom allowed to plant management and which are characterised by the shortism of much of British industry (Storey & Sisson, 1993). In terms of production systems and working practices, there is little evidence here of high levels of investment in advanced technology or of multi-skilling or of "high-commitment" HRM practices. Rather, they argue, the characteristics of the typical British manufacturing firm are as follows:

- Production is organised as cellular manufacture as it facilitates the calculation of marginal costs and the identification of unprofitable activities, while limiting the need for employees to develop a broad spectrum of skills.
- Advanced manufacturing technology is little used, except as additions to existing configurations of equipment.
- Labour flexibility is achieved by teams of semi-skilled workers performing a range of specific tasks and given some on-the-job training.
- Employees do not enjoy privileged status or high employment security, but compete with sub-contracted labour and alternative suppliers.
- Production operations are considered as dispensable, separate segments, about which calculations of cost are regularly made.
- Management takes the form of intensified indirect control, based on the allocation of costs.
- The high-surveillance management regimes associated with "Japanese" lean manufacturing are not typical of British manufacturing, as they exaggerate the quality of information typically available and the willingness and ability of managers to appraise such information, even if available, given the much reduced ranks of middle management and supervision.

This model of lean organisation lacks the coherency and logic of the "ideal-type" "Japanese" model. Indeed, it smacks of a policy of "asset management" rather than "value-added", to use Capelli & McKersie's (1987) well-known distinction. Even where working practices are used that are associated with Japanese-style lean manufacturing, such as team working, the motivation for their introduction may be pragmatic rather than due to any concern for strategic and operational integration. This form of leanness, motivated exclusively by financial concerns, is often accused of "cutting muscle" rather than fat, of giving rise to the stressed-out anorexic organisation. In the context of this argument, it is not surprising that Cordery's chapter on team-working finds studies where it is associated with lay-offs, decreases in average real wages for core staff, with the employment of fewer managers and fewer temporary or contract staff. Cordery also finds considerable variability in the findings regarding the consequences for productivity, work attitudes and employee behaviour (Goodman *et al.*, 1988; Guzzo & Dickson, 1996; Hackman, 1990; Osterman, 2000).

One noticeable difference between job and work systems design research in the 1970s and 2000 reflects the changing structure of Western economies. In the 1970s research was focused largely on manufacturing industry and, in so far as the service sector got a look-in, the focus was on task design for office workers and computer operators (e.g. Mumford, 1972). A major concern in the late 1990s and 2000s is the "office factories" of call centres (Batt, 1999, 2000; Deery *et al.*, 2002; Frenkel *et al.*, 1999; Hutchinson *et al.*, 2000; Knights & McCabe, 1998; Taylor & Bain, 1999) and those retail services where the worker has direct contact with the customer and is involved in "emotional labour" (retail stores, fast food outlets, hotels, airlines, health care) (Hochschild, 1983). Another issue is the changing patterns of work that arise from new information and communication technologies—not just the call centres, whose very existence relies on computer and telephone-based technologies—but teleworking (see Lamond *et al.*, Chapter 11) and E-business (see Clegg *et al.*, Chapter 13) (I will consider E-business in a later section of this chapter).

Holman (Chapter 7) on call centres echoes some of the themes already discussed with reference to teamworking and lean manufacturing. In call centres, similarly, there seems to be the choice between a Tayloristic, mass service model of task design (the "low" road), aimed at cost minimisation and a high commitment, customer service-orientated model, aimed at customer satisfaction (the "high" road). The "low" road is characterised by task fragmentation, little variety or task interdependence, low autonomy (rigid adherence to set scripts) and potentially punitive performance monitoring (listening in to calls for disciplinary purposes). In contrast, the "high" road, aiming to provide a customised service, is characterised by more variety involving the use of extensive product or service knowledge, more autonomy (unscripted calls apart from the opening and closing formulae) and higher degrees of task interdependence, as staff often need to draw on others' knowledge and performance monitoring that is less intense and focused on support and development rather than sanctions. Not surprisingly, the "low" road, in particular, is often associated with stress, exacerbated by the strains of surface acting associated with emotional labour.

Furthermore, the pragmatism inherent in the UK version of lean manufacturing (Ackroyd & Proctor, 1998) also seems evident in design choices in call centres. As Holman points out, there are many anomalies in the data, in that some mass service call centres adopt some high-commitment work practices (Batt, 2000) and some high-commitment service call centres adopt some mass service work practices (Kinnie *et al.*, 2000). He argues that this implies that true alignment, consistent with contingency theory, may not be possible. For example, if local labour markets are very competitive, it may not be possible to use low pay and Tayloristic work practices, which exacerbate recruitment and turnover problems, even if the logic of a mass low cost service calls for this strategy. Pragmatic choices may emerge as managers juggle the contradictions of a call centre environment—between service quality and quantity; ensuring employee empathy with the customer and instrumentality; providing a customised service and having standardised procedures; balancing employee control and commitment.

Lamond and colleagues (Chapter 11) on teleworking again introduce the "high" road/"low" road distinction. Where teleworking involves knowledge intensive professional work and is seen as part of the creation of an "organic informated organisation" (Travic, 1998) designed to transcend, in a globalised economy, traditional time/space constraints, the outcomes may be high employee autonomy and flexible task completion combined with high intra-organisational contact and little of the reported experience of social isolation that may afflict home-based teleworkers. In contrast, where teleworking involves low knowledge intensity and is introduced to achieve cost reductions through downsizing, delayering and shedding accommodation costs, then, as the authors suggest, "notions of 're-engineering' may be code for cost-cutting, and teleworking introduced with stringent electronic controls and greater use of contingent workers".

In their broader discussion of the service sector, Batt & Doellgast (Chapter 15) interestingly, find evidence that could be interpreted as supportive of both contingency and universalistic approaches. On the one hand, similarly to Holman, they found that intensified price competition in the industries studied (airlines, financial services, telecommunications and hotels) led firms to focus more on cost reduction than on quality-enhancing strategies. Where the latter are adopted, they are typically reserved, as contingency theory would lead us to expect, for business or high-value-added customers. On the other hand, Batt & Doellgast found that investments in IT, when coupled with complementary high-commitment HR practices, are consistently associated with higher productivity, product and service innovations, customization and order-processing efficiencies. Also, fairly consistent evidence was found that collaborative forms of work "are associated with better performance in front-line service work".

The experience of work

I deliberately ended the preceding paragraph with a quotation that talks of *associations*. Most of the studies reviewed in these chapters are survey-based empirical research that seeks statistical associations between responses representing independent and dependent variables. The ontology is realist (measurable variables) and the epistemology is positivistic, one "which seek(s) to explain and predict what happens in the social world by searching for regularities, and causal relationships between its constituent elements" (Burrell & Morgan, 1979, p. 5). The majority of the authors in this book represent people's experience of work in these terms, e.g. "team processes such as sharing, norms, task orientation and participation significantly affect innovation levels" (Unsworth & Parker, Chapter 10); "the technological methods that allow managers to monitor the actions of teleworkers as closely as they could monitor on-site workers have been associated with low employee morale" (Lamond *et al.*, Chapter 11); "trust in buyer–seller interaction influences satisfaction with profit, sales outcomes and performance. In contrast, a lack of trust has been associated with partnering failure" (Kerrin & Icasati-Johanson, Chapter 5).

While fully accepting the importance of strong positivistic designs, such as experimental and *strong* quasi-experimental designs (such as the interrupted time series with comparison series design) in establishing the internal validity of causal attributions, and while recognising the problems of external validity associated with qualitative case-study designs, I query whether positivistic designs give us much insight into the *experience* of work (see Legge, 1984, for an extended critique of the use of positivistic designs in evaluation research). In the case of weak correlational designs, I wonder if they give us much insight into anything.

In my view, the review of positivistic studies with which the chapters are largely concerned gives rise to two problems. First, in relation to causal attributions, with respect, some of the chapters contain statements that are at best unsurprising, not to say trite, even tautological, e.g. "Too many extroverts or neurotics in a team will diminish effectiveness" (Cordery); "Proactivity determinants tend to be those that promote action, such as need for achievement, self-esteem, extraversion and conscientiousness" (Unsworth & Parker); "The provision of such training is, however, contingent, with low-skill redesigns entailing minimal training while high-skill designs require significantly more" (Cooney & Sohal); "Hill has suggested that a trust based approach to inter-organisational relationships, reduces motivation to behave opportunistically ... because 'behavioural repertoires are biased towards cooperation rather than opportunism" (Kerrin & Icasati-Johanson). Exceptionally, this can result in chapters arguing what may seem self-evident. For example, the message of Kerrin & Icasati-Johanson's chapter seems to be largely that trust and perspective taking (the affective response of empathy) is important in developing successful supply-chain partnering. This level of generality can exist because contextual variation is not adequately explored.

Second, many of the chapters refer to mixed or contradictory findings about outcomes (but cf. Clegg *et al.*, (Chapter 13 on e-business) who report consistent findings!). For example, Batt & Doellgast find evidence that the effectiveness of high-commitment practices on a quality or up-market service strategy is "inconclusive", that several organisational studies of TQM have shown "mixed results", as have studies on the effects of supervisory support. Holman finds that studies aimed to discover whether call centre work is more stressful than comparable forms of work "show no clear pattern of findings", while there are many "anomalies" in findings on the degree of strategic alignment of "bundles" of HR practices with customer segment. Cordery finds very mixed evidence of the benefits of teams to organisations and their employees. The fact that findings may be mixed or contradictory is hardly surprising, as the independent variables may be differently specified (e.g. "high" road vs. "low" road team working) and intervening variables, such as contextual factors, may differ. Indeed, Batt & Doellgast repeatedly call for research designs that are more contextually sensitive, while Clegg et al., in relation to e-business, argue for detailed case studies of companies and supply chains that are introducing relatively advanced forms of e-business and for the importance of contextual issues. A better understanding of the context to which findings refer can help explain contradictory results.

However, most importantly, an understanding of context is essential in understanding people's experience of work. "Experience of work" is not just about measurable attitudinal and behavioural responses to task and work systems design interventions, but about people's *situated* sense-making through processes of human action and interaction (Weick, 1995). Even if one rejects a fully social constructionist position, where the reality of the work context "is created afresh in each encounter of everyday life as individuals impose themselves (by language, labels, actions and routines) on their world to establish a realm of meaningful definition" (Morgan & Smircich, 1980), it must be recognised that people's experience is grounded in daily interactions that are located in specific times and spaces and which generate meaning. Most of the research studies reviewed in these chapters, given their epistemological stance, cannot access experience in these terms and hence their discussion is inevitably partial.

For example, there is no way that Cordery's discussion of positivistic studies of team working can access the subtle shades of meaning yielded by rich ethnographic data such as that of McCabe's case study of the "bewitched, bothered and bewildered" employees of an automobile company (McCabe, 2000; Knights & McCabe, 2000). Drawing on formal and informal interview data, McCabe identifies three types of employees and their experience of team working. First (by far the minority of those interviewed), there are those who seem to have been "bewitched" by the discourse of team working and who, in a wholehearted manner, have internalised its norms and values. Second, there are those who are "bothered" by team working in the sense that they are disturbed by what they perceive to be its incessant intrusion into their lives. They are concerned that some of their colleagues seem to be enthralled by the team discourse and alarmed at what they see as psychological warfare waged by management through an ideology of team working. Third, there are employees who are "bewildered" by team working, less because of its ideological overtones than because of its attack on established ways of doing things and the working practices and trade demarcations that reflect and reinforce their own sense of identity. The bewildered are ambivalent or confused because, while approving of the quality standards promoted by team working, they feel no necessity to change their practices to achieve them. Rather, such changes threaten their pride (and hence their identity) in having always worked to high standards. Knight & McCabe's (2000, p. 1489) comment on the identification of these three categories should act as a warning to those who think that the experience of work can be captured by the instruments of survey-based positivistic studies:

> These ideal types are used as a heuristic device and we recognize that there are dangers of forcing complex human experiences into simplistic constructions. Moreover, we also acknowledge that the employees we identify as bewitched or bothered may respond differently under different circumstances or at different times. Indeed, employees may disagree with our "labels" and their position in relation to them and, as such, it is important to see this typology as fluid and dynamic.

One further point. In talking of employees' experience of work, the implicit assumption in all the chapters is that we are referring to the experience of workers in the Western developed World. This seems an odd omission in the context of Sparrow's comments (Chapter 19) about globalisation and the boundaryless company, and given the recognition of the importance of supply-chain partnerships (Kerrin & Icasati-Johanson, Chapter 5). Nevertheless, this probably reflects how little research on developing countries is published in UK- and USA-refereed organisational psychology and management journals. I will return to this point in my conclusions.

Assessing the outcomes of new working practices and "high-commitment"/"high-performance" HRM

I mentioned earlier the importance of strong positivistic designs in establishing the internal validity of causal attributions. In theory, then, they should come into their own in demonstrating the effects of new working practices and associated HRM interventions. However, Wright & Gardner's excellent chapter (Chapter 16) on the theoretical and empirical challenges in studying the HR practice–firm performance relationship casts doubts on the methodological adequacies of much of the positivistic research conducted in this area and its ability to provide cumulative knowledge. In this section I will consider their arguments, along with the doubts I have already expressed elsewhere (Legge, 2001a).

First there is the problem that there is no agreed conceptualisation of HRM ("strategic", "descriptive" or "prescriptive" approach?), little consensus about what precise practices should be included in the operationalization of "high-commitment"/"high-performance" HRM and, even where there is some agreement on the inclusion of a particular "high-commitment/performance" working practice, none on its specification and measurement. There is concern, too, about the validity and reliability of measures of HR practices (see Legge, 2001a, pp. 23–26).

Second, there are problems in conceptualising and measuring performance. In the US studies, the measures of performance are invariably those relating to financial performance and productivity, rather than to employee outcomes (Rogers & Wright, 1998) (cf. Guest, 1999; Cully *et al.*, 1999, who *do* look at UK employee reactions to HRM initiatives). The US studies seem misguided, as all the theoretical rationales of how HRM affects performance rest on the assumption that it occurs *through* these employee outcomes. Apart from this very limited and questionable conceptualisation of organisational performance and, with the exception of Guest (1997, p. 267), no recognition that the financial and productivity measures are but social constructions, there are problems with measurement. As Wright & Gardner point out, with the notable exception of Huselid's (1995) study, there is a tendency not to assess multiple performance measures in any single study. As a result, researchers are unable to examine the interrelationships among outcomes, although Huselid's study suggests that these may be significant (at least some of the effect of HR practices on firm performance was mediated by the reduction in employee turnover).

Third, these problems pale into insignificance when compared to those associated with examining the *relationship* between HRM and performance, however conceptualised. Leaving aside the lack of agreement on the conceptualisation of the relationship between HRM and performance ("universalistic"? "contingency"?— or even "configurational"?) (Delery & Doty, 1996), Wright & Gardner raise serious methodological problems in establishing valid findings.

First, there is the practical issue of trade-offs in selecting an appropriate level of analysis in testing HRM–performance relationships. Plant-level studies have three strengths: the risk of variance in HR practices is minimised; the respondent(s) is likely to have first-hand knowledge of HR practices—both espoused and in-use—increasing the validity of the responses; and there is the potential of providing the most proximal measures of performance. The drawback is that research at this level may not allow assessing the "fit" between HR practices and business strategy and there are perennial issues about generalisability. Organisational or business level studies are optimal for assessing relationships between HR practices and business strategy, but given that businesses often have multiple locations, categories of employees and jobs, precise assessments of HR practices become problematic, especially when—as is often the case—the research design relies on just one senior management respondent. The bulk of research linking HR practices and performance has been conducted at corporate level, given the reliance on financial measures of performance, as it is at this level that much of the publicly available financial data exists. However, this exacerbates problems associated with the validity of single-respondent assessments, given the complexity of assessing HR practices over a range of businesses, the problem that there may be variance between the business strategies across businesses within some corporations (hence, identifying *a* business strategy is likely to be problematic) and, because these studies cross industries, the difficulty in partialling out all of the industry effects.

Not only are there methodological issues here, but what is worrying theoretically is that, if the majority of the research studies remains located at the corporate level, given the US obsession with measures of financial performance, this is not conducive to assessing the enacted aspects of employee behaviour that constitute the intervening variable in explaining the relationship between HR practices, operating and financial performance. It is difficult to see how such studies can *test* causal relationships, as opposed to making theory-derived inferences about the correlations they find.

This brings us to the issue of establishing causality, where Wright and Gardner's critique is trenchant. First, with some exceptions, the majority of the US studies are cross-sectional rather than longitudinal and, hence, while causality may be *inferred* from correlation, technically, it is not tested. This gives rise to three possibilities. A causal relationship may exist in the direction inferred, i.e. HRM policies and practices may give rise to positive outcomes, although as Purcell (1999, p. 30) has pointed out, this may be no more than a temporary "Hawthorne" effect [of course, it is possible, with the same direction of causality, that HRM, particularly "hard" HRM, may give rise to negative outcomes or, as Guest & Hoque (1994) report, positive outcomes on organisational performance measures but negative outcomes on HR–employee outcomes]. Or, reverse causality may exist (a possibility also recognised by Batt & Doellgast in this book). In other words, as a firm becomes more profitable or its share price rises, it may invest in "high-commitment/performance" HRM practices, such as expenditure on training or profit sharing. As Wright & Gardner point out, this may be due to a belief that such practices will further increase performance, or that they will reduce the risk of performance declines, or from a belief in the justice and efficacy of wealth distribution. However, it is the profits that generate HR practices, rather than vice versa.

A further possibility that they identify is that the observed relationship between HR practices and performance may not stem from any true relationship (i.e. "true" from a positivistic perspective), but from implicit theories of organisational survey respondents. In other words, if a respondent has little detailed knowledge of HR practices in his/her firm (highly likely if the firm is large, diverse and multi-sited), but knows the firm is performing well in terms of productivity and profitability, he/she may infer that "high-performance" HR practices *must* exist, given this level of performance, based on the implicit theory that such practices are related to high performance (Gardner *et al.*, 1999).

Finally, Wright & Gardner raise the issue of how little has been done to unlock the "black box" of the processes that link HRM (however conceptualised) with performance (however conceptualised). But unless this is done, e.g. by developing models that include theory-derived, key intervening variables, it is not possible to rule out unequivocally alternative causal models that explain empirical associations between HR practices and organisational outcomes.

The question then becomes how many and what intervening variables should there be in the "black box" (employee behaviour/skills? strategy implementation? operating performance?) and how should these variables be specified? For example, "operating performance" might be defined and measured in terms of customer satisfaction, customer retention, sales revenues, quality defects, scrap, down-time, productivity, labour costs. Then there is the issue of distinguishing between espoused and actual HR practices and employee skills and behaviours. And, as Wright & Gardner point out, the greater the number of intervening variables identified and the greater the level of specificity, the greater the multiplicative effect in determining the processes of a model, as the model building requires the specification of the relationships between each of the specifications of the major intervening variables.

If this complexity is problematic when a universalistic approach to HR practices/performance relationships is adopted, it becomes additionally so when a contingency or a configurational approach is preferred. With contingency models of HRM–performance relationships, there are issues of causal ambiguity and path-dependent contingencies that add up to idiosyncratic choices (Boxall, 1992; Collis & Montgomery, 1995; Purcell, 1999). Causal ambiguity refers to the numerous and subtle interconnections between contingent factors that make each organisation's experience, in a sense, unique. Path dependency recognises the emergent nature of strategy and the dependence of policy choices on the organisation's history and culture. Put the two together and the resultant idiosyncratic contingency suggests that each organisation has to make choices of HR policy and practice based on its judgement, not only of appropriateness to business and operational strategies but of what "suits" the history and culture of the organisation, what "feels" right (Purcell, 1999, p. 35). Such potential complexity sits uneasily with the large-scale surveys and quantitative approaches of positivistic research designs.

I have focused here on Wright & Gardner's critique of theoretical and methodological problems in researching HRM outcomes, but much of the critique could also be applied to studies about the effects of task and work system design. Certainly this must be considered in the light of the contradictory and inconsistent findings I mentioned earlier. Can the inconsistencies be explained by different contextual factors or are they methodological artefacts? Or is it a question of not "either/or", but "and/both"?

The (absent) political dimension

In reading the chapters which, fundamentally, are about resource allocation and change, I was struck by a curious absence of reference to a political dimension. For example, the concept of "empowerment" is generally treated as non-problematic, although clearly it means different things to managers and mainstream organisational psychology researchers than it does to critical organisation theorists

(Hardy & Leiba-O'Sullivan, 1998). In Pritchard & Payne's otherwise excellent discussion (Chapter 12) of the relationship between performance management practices and their variant of an expectancy theory of motivation, there is no questioning of the implicit managerial agenda which they appear wholeheartedly to embrace, nor a recognition of what is marginalised by a focus on "motivation". That is, to look for "performance" improvements (as defined by managerial interests) in terms of an *individual* level concept, "motivation", deflects attention from the *societal* and *organisational structures* of inequality, which not only allow the powerful (including academics from leading US business schools) to set the agenda, but to place responsibility for "poor" performance on the individual rather than on the economic and social system. Scarbrough (Chapter 8) provides a very interesting discussion of cognitive vs. community perspectives on knowledge management, of codification vs. personalization knowledge management strategies and of the constraints on the use of IT for knowledge management. Here, issues of power and politics are clearly apparent (e.g. in the tensions between knowledge sharing and career paths in bureaucratic, hierarchical structures; in general issues of the ownership and control of knowledge), but they are not highlighted. Sonnentag's chapter (Chapter 18) on designing evaluation studies contains one reference to a potentially political issue in evaluation research ("there might be some reluctance in initiating an evaluation project at all ... stakeholders within an organisation might be afraid of the evaluation outcomes or anticipate negative specific results"), but otherwise treats it as a purely technical, rationalistic exercise. Indeed, the chapter treats evaluation research as something that may present technical problems, but is otherwise unproblematic.

I would take a very different view, but admittedly from a different epistemological and from a political standpoint. Almost 20 years ago, I too was asking questions about the evaluation of organisational change (Legge, 1984). As a result of my researches, I came to very different conclusions from Sonnentag about the role of positivistic evaluation designs.

Briefly, in the 1980s, several prominent evaluation researchers (such as Patton, Guba and Lincoln) were openly sceptical about positivistic methods as a result of their tendency to produce "weak" or uninterpretable findings about change outcomes. In part the problem appeared to have resulted from difficulties in maintaining internal validity and the conflicting requirements of internal and external validity in organisation settings. Some disbelievers were more a product of the paradigm warfare that was prevalent in the 1980s and early 1990s, when debates raged about paradigm incommensurability and the need for minority, non-positivistic voices to form breakaway movements, such as the Standing Conference of Organisational Symbolism or European Group of Organization Studies to protect their epistemological positions (and careers) from US-led, functionalist imperialism (see Pfeffer, 1993, 1995; van Maanen, 1995a,b). How then do you account for the continued prevalence of positivistic designs? The imperialism of entrenched, traditionalist academic interests on both sides of the Atlantic—and the publishing policies of top US journals—might be one explanation. Another is this.

The exact data that positivistic designs in theory should yield are only required if rationality is at a premium. But, in practice, the more important the decision, the more likely are political rather than rational considerations to prevail (Buchanan & Badham, 2000). The more trivial the decision, the less likely is the decision maker to bother with exact information, irrespective of how rationally he/she is able to make the decision. In which case, it could be argued that positivistic designs also prosper through acting as a rhetoric for an evaluation ritual, whereby the lack of formal rationality of actual decision making and the accountability and responsibility demanded of the idealised decision maker are reconciled.

Furthermore, as Hollway (1991, p. 187) reminds us more generally about the discourses of organisational psychology, they are "conditioned by the history of the management of regulation at work ... (and) through power relations and language, produce subjectivity" (read identity, "experience of work"). Writing from a Foucauldian perspective, Hollway makes the valuable point, missing from the chapters in this book, that:

> The individual at work whom work psychology is so intent on discovering (feeling that it is getting nearer to an efficacious truth as discovery succeeds discovery) is the individual that work psychology is involved, with others, in producing: the trainable hands; the fatiguable body; the individual abilities, skills and aptitudes; the sentiment; the interpersonal skills; the leadership qualities; the motivation; the boredom and satisfaction; the irrational opposition to management. The individual is all over the place, the product of diverse problems in practice not of theory, nor even of scientific experiment. *The changes in the individual over time reflect the shifting problems of regulation* (my own italics).

What we are witnessing in the mantras of "team working", "flexibility", "employee involvement", "empowerment", "lean" organisation, "business process re-engineering", "high-commitment/performance" HRM is the production of new boundaries in the frontiers of control, where commitment and control strategies are not juxtaposed (either/or), but exist side by side (both/and), if differentially applied to differently constituted groups ("core"/"periphery"; "knowledge" workers/"McDonaldized" workers). The regulation of work in a globalised economy constitutes a discourse about the "bottom line" (worker as value-adding commodity), not about QWL (worker as human being). As Hollway (1991, pp. 187–188) puts it:

> The power of work psychology is that it can reflect back the preoccupations of employers and managers in systematic, formal, apparently scientific discourses which are tied to developments in the practice of workplace regulation ... They are always based on that same problematic: enhancing workplace regulation; and by reflecting back this problematic

as scientific, work psychology increases the legitimacy of management practices and their justification in the workplace.

Back to the future?

I will now return to the brief I began with and attempt to assess the effectiveness of new working practices, their positive/negative effects on the experience of work and to suggest ways in which the gaps in our theory and practice might be overcome.

It was often observed in the 1980s and 1990s that technical changes, such as new IT systems and CIM, took longer to disperse and to work effectively than early protagonists imagined (e.g. McLoughlin & Clark, 1988). Indeed, in spite of the prevalence of PCs in offices of the developed world, the paperless office (indeed, teleworking) is still the experience of a minority. Scarbrough's chapter on knowledge management similarly concludes that "the available evidence tends to suggest that KM's influence on management thinking has been somewhat greater than its impact on organisational practices". Further, Clegg and his colleagues, with reference to E-business, found that the majority of companies in the UK are in the "early stages" of adoption (mainly using E-mail and on-line marketing facilities) and that the impacts, not surprisingly, have been "low key". Although team working has been widely adopted in the UK, the evidence suggests that only a very small minority of initiatives involve teams with features of autonomous group working (Ackroyd & Proctor, 1998; Cully *et al.*, 1999). Again, business process re-engineering was widely adopted in the UK and USA in the 1990s, but there is little evidence that it delivers the results it promises (Grint, 1994: Grint & Willcocks, 1995; Kinnie *et al.*, 1996; Mumford & Hendricks, 1996; Oram & Wellins, 1995; Willmott, 1994). The initiatives that are essentially about cost cutting and control (reorganising work in the context of delayering and downsizing) may deliver in the short run, but we have to question the long-term consequences in terms of potential loss of organisational memory and learning (Sparrow, 1998), work intensification, low morale, "survivor syndrome" and so on (see, Legge, 2000, for a summary of research on these issues).

An important question about effectiveness is "effectiveness for whom and on the basis of what criteria?" There is evidence, referenced throughout the chapters, that initiatives in the context of "high-commitment/performance" HRM are correlated with productivity and good financial performance, but we cannot be sure of the direction of causality. Where employees have been questioned they seem to like "high-commitment" HRM, where it has been introduced (Guest, 1999), but the evidence cited in the chapters would suggest that the "low" road (or "hard" HRM) is more prevalent. Nevertheless, it would be unwise to assume that workers' experience of "low" road practices is necessarily and uniformly negative. Much will depend on their social construction of their working experience, in the light of their expectations and situated experiences of work in general. It is popularly claimed that the neo-liberal policies of the 1980s in the UK did much to realign workers' expectations about job security and work rates. As Ron Todd (Secretary General of the TGWU at that time) is famously reported to have said in the mid-1980s, "We have 3 million unemployed and 23 million scared to death".

However, questionnaire-based research findings are often difficult to interpret. For example, the Collinson et al. (1998) study of TQM initiatives found that, generally speaking, it had failed to improve trust between management and workers. Nevertheless, they found that most of their respondents enjoyed working as hard as they did; that the organisations where the workers were most likely to say that they were working harder and more subject to managerial monitoring were also those where trust in management and the acceptance of quality programmes were highest; and that workers subject to output targets and most aware of the monitoring of their work were clearly the most, not the least, likely to be favourable to quality initiatives and to express trust in management. How do we interpret this finding? Collinson et al. (1998) conclude that employees had pragmatic expectations of TQM; that while they did not necessarily seek empowerment and retained a sense of distance from management, nevertheless they welcomed the principles of quality management and involvement in problem solving, even though this involvement was limited to immediate work tasks. Rather than being characterised in terms of "work intensification", the authors suggest that the idea of the "disciplined worker" might more appropriately describe their situation and reactions. This is a classic pluralist interpretation. However, a commentator of a unitarist persuasion might find evidence here that the more trusting workers are of management, the more positive they are about management's initiatives, do not see legitimate control systems as oppressive (cf. Delbridge's findings, this volume; Garrahan & Stewart, 1992) and are happy to give of their best (work harder). A critical theorist would be more likely to interpret the data in terms of co-optation strategies producing "docile bodies" (Foucault, 1977).

A major omission in this collection, in spite of Sparrow's chapter on the future of work and Kerrin & Icasati-Johanson's on supply chains, is a recognition of the impact of globalisation and the boundaryless organisation on *how we might approach the subject of the experience of work*. Space constraints prevent a full discussion of this issue (but see Legge, 2001b), but two points may be highlighted. First, the chapters here pay no attention to the nature of work and the experience of work among people in developing countries, to whom we increasingly sub-contract commodity production (and some knowledge work, as in the case of software programmers in India) *as a direct result of many of the initiatives discussed here*. Perhaps the Western ethnocentricism of many of the concepts and theories discussed in these chapters preclude such a consideration, although a good place to start might be in exploring the use of social and human capital theory (referred to specifically by Sparrow & Doellgast as promising avenues of research) in relation to developing countries. After all, as Handy (1979, p. 24) once remarked, whereas in the West (at that time) we tend to think of labour as a scarce resource and capital as a plentiful one, in developing countries the reverse is the case.

Secondly, in spite of reference to TQM and JIT, where the producer is conceptualised as a customer, and in spite of an interesting chapter on performance in services, there is very little attempt to consider how our experience as workers, in Western developed economies, is intimately related to the identities we seek and our expectations as customers. Our expectations about fashion, brands, quality, cost and the nature of leisure products and services are the drivers behind the design of flexible working and flexible, "hollowed-out" organisations, that, in Sennett's (1998) terms, result in "illegible" jobs, ambiguous career structures, low trust and a "corrosion of character", as employees can no longer develop a long-term, coherent narrative of their working lives.

The problem is that if we seek to achieve the meaningful identity denied to many of us at work, through the consumption of, literally, *meaningful* brands (Klein, 2000), we collude with the large, often global, corporations that have been instrumental in creating the conditions that "corrode character" in the first place. There are many ironies in this process. When we speak of shopping as "retail therapy", the implication is that it unwinds the stresses induced by the flexibalisation deemed necessary to produce the products and services we now seek to consume at a price we are prepared to pay. As producers, we may be stressed by the work intensification inherent in functional flexibility and the "contingent worker" status afforded us by numerical flexibility; as shoppers, we welcome low prices and extended opening hours. In purchasing brands we may feel we acquire a distinctive image, yet in following "fashion" we lose uniqueness. We may deplore the instabilities in our working life, yet embrace it in some of our consumption as we seek to identify and follow the latest trends. We may find no meaning in poorly paid, casualised "McJobs", but as consumers, whether of hamburgers, financial services or supermarkets, we collude with our conversion into unpaid, part-time workers, clearing tables, pushing trolleys and performing the role of bank clerks and sales assistants as we engage with call centres and cash machines. In so far as we retreat into "retail therapy" to establish identities threatened by demeaning work experiences, we perpetuate a vicious circle. And the irony is that those most in need of alternative experiences, to compensate for a "McJob" working life, are least able to afford them. What has organisational psychology to say about the producer–consumer relationship?

Finally, how may the gaps between our theory and practice be addressed? It is conventional to call for better research and certainly all the chapters have ideas here. For example, Wright and Gardner's ideas on methodological improvements in researching the HRM–performance relationship are to be welcomed. There seems to be a wide measure of agreement about the need to open up the "black box" of the processes that link HRM with organisational performance/outcomes. Guest's (1997) ideas about using expectancy theory and the psychological contract (cf. Pritchard & Payne, this volume) to explore HRM-performance linkages are promising. Purcell's (1999) approach of using in-depth case studies to explore how organisations develop successful transition management, build unique sets of competencies and distinctive organisational routines and, in situations of leanness, with greater dependency on all core workers, develop inclusiveness and trust, is yielding interesting results (Hutchinson et al., 2000).

However, in addressing the gap between theory and practice, I would urge organisational psychologists to reflect on the role of power in working lives: first, as it influences their own commitment to mainstream positivism and, second, in its role in constituting their discipline, their subjects and the world their subjects inhabit.

References

Ackroyd, S. & Proctor, S. (1998). British manufacturing organization and workplace relations: some attributes of the new flexible firm. *British Journal of Industrial Relations*, **36**(2), 163–183.

Arthur, J. B. (1994). Effects of human resource systems on manufacturing performance and turnover. *Academy of Management Journal*, **37**, 670–87.

Bacon, N. & Blyton, P. (2000). High road and low road teamworking: perceptions of management rationales and organizational and human resource outcomes. *Human Relations*, **53**(11), 1425–1458.

Barney, J. (1991). Firm resources and sustained competitive advantage. *Journal of Management*, **17**, 99–120.

Batt, R. (1999). Work organization, technology and performance in customer service and sales. *Industrial and Labor Relations Review*, **52**, 539–564.

Batt, R. (2000). Strategic segmentation in front line services: matching customers, employees and human resource systems. *International Journal of Human Resource Management*, **11**, 540–561.

Becker, B. & Gerhart, B. (1996). The impact of human resource management on organizational performance, progress and prospects. *Academy of Management Journal*, **39**(4), 779–801.

Becker, B. & Huselid, M. (1998). High performance work systems and firm performance: a synthesis of research and managerial implications. In G. R. Ferris (Ed.), *Research in Personnel and Human Resource Management*, Vol. 16, (pp. 53–101). Greenwich, CT: JAI Press.

Boxall, P. (1992). Strategic human resource management: beginnings of a new theoretical sophistication? *Human Resource Management Journal*, **2**(3), 60–78.

Buchanan, D. & Badham, R. (2000). *The Politics of Organizational Change*. London: Sage.

Burrell, G. & Morgan, G. (1979). *Sociological Paradigms and Organisational Analysis*. London: Heinemann.

Capelli, P. & McKersie, R. B. (1987). Management strategy and the redesign of work rules. *Journal of Management Studies*, **24**(5), 441–462.

Clark, J. (1995). *Managing Innovation and Change*. London: Sage.

Clark, J. et al. (1988). *The Process of Technological Change*. Cambridge: Cambridge University Press.

Collinson, M., Rees, C. & Edwards, P. K. (with Inness, L.) (1998). *Involving Employees in Total Quality Management: Employee Attitudes and Organizational Context in Unionized Environments*. London: DTI.

Collis, D. J. & Montgomery, C. A. (1995). Competing on resources: strategy for the 1990s. *Harvard Business Review*, **73**(4), 118–128.

Cully, M., Woodland, S., O'Reilly, A. & Dix, G. (1999). *Britain at Work*. London: Routledge.
Deery, S. J., Iverson, R. D. & Walsh, J. T. (2002). Work relationships in telephone call centres: understanding emotional exhaustion and employee withdrawal. *Journal of Management Studies*, **39**(4), 471–496.
Delery, J. & Doty, H. (1996). Models of theorizing in strategic human resource management: tests of universalistic, contingency and configurational performance predictions. *Academy of Management Journal*, **39**(4), 802–835.
DiMaggio, P. J. & Powell, W. W. (1983). The iron cage revisited: institutional isomorphism and collective rationality in organizational fields. *American Sociological Review*, **48**, 147–160.
Foucault, M. (1977). *Discipline and Punish*. Harmondsworth: Penguin.
Frenkel, S., Korczyniski, M. & Shire, K. (1999). *On the Front-Line: Organization of Work in the Information Economy*. Ithaca, NY: Cornell University Press.
Gardner, T. M., Wright, P. M. & Gerhart, B. (1999). The HR-performance relationship: can it be in the mind of the beholder? Working Paper, Center for Advanced Human Resources Studies, Cornell University, Ithaca, NY.
Garrahan, P. & Stewart, P. (1992). *The Nissan Enigma*. London: Mansell.
Goodman, P. S., Devadas, R. & Griffiths-Hughson, T. L. (1988). Groups and productivity: analyzing the effectiveness of self-managed teams. In J. P. Cambell & R. J. C. & Associates (Eds), *Productivity in Organizations* (pp. 295–327). San Francisco, CA: Jossey-Bass.
Grey. C. & Mitev, N. (1995). Re-engineering organizations: a critical appraisal. *Personnel Review*, **24**(1), 6–18.
Grint, K. (1994). Re-engineering history: social resonances and business process re-engineering. *Organization*, **1**(1), 179–201.
Grint, K. & Willcocks, L. (1995). Business process re-engineering in theory and practice: business paradise regained?' *New Technology, Work and Employment*, **19**(2), 99–109.
Guest, D. E. (1987). Human resource management and industrial relations. *Journal of Management Studies*, **24**(5), 503–521.
Guest, D. E. (1997). Human resource management and performance: a review and research agenda. *International Journal of Human Resource Management*, **8**(3), 263–90.
Guest, D. E. (1999). Human resource management—the workers' verdict. *Human Resource Management Journal*, **9**(3), 263–290.
Guest, D. E. & Hoque, K. (1994). The good, the bad and the ugly: human resource management in new non-union establishments. *Human Resource Management Journal*, **5**(1), 1–14.
Guzzo, R. A. & Dickson, M. W. (1996). Teams in organizations: recent research on performance and effectiveness. *Annual Review of Psychology*, **47**, 307–338.
Hackman, J. R. (1990). *Groups that Work (and Those that Don't)*. San Francisco, CA: Jossey-Bass.
Hackman, J. R. & Oldham, G. R. (1976). Motivation through the design of work: test of a theory. *Organizational Behavior and Human Performance*, **15**, 250–279.
Handy, C. (1979). The shape of organisations to come. *Personnel Management*, **June**, 24–26.
Hardy, C. & Leiba-O'Sullivan, S. (1998). The power behind empowerment: implications for research and practice. *Human Relations*, **51**(4), 451–483.

Hochschild, A. (1983). *The Managed Heart.* Berkeley, CA: University of California Press.
Hollway, W. (1991). *Work Psychology and Organizational Behaviour.* London: Sage.
Huselid, M. (1995). The impact of human resource management practices on turnover, productivity, and corporate financial performance. *Academy of Management Journal,* **38**(1), 635–672.
Hutchinson, S., Purcell, J. & Kinnie, N. (2000). Evolving high commitment management and the experience of the RAC call centre. *Human Resource Management Journal,* **10,** 63–78.
Ichniowski, C., Shaw, K. & Prennushi, G. (1997). The effects of human resource management practices on productivity; a study of steel finishing lines. *American Economic Review,* **87**(3), 291–313.
Kinnie, N., Hutchinson, S. & Purcell, J. (1996). The people management implications of leaner ways of working. Report of the University of Bath. *Issues in People Management,* No. 15 (pp. 6–63). London: Institute of Personnel and Development.
Kinnie, N., Purcell, J. & Hutchinson, S. (2000). Managing the employment relationship in call centres. In Purcell, K. (Ed.), *Changing Boundaries in Employment* (pp. 163–194). Bristol: Bristol Academic Press.
Klein, N. (2000). *No Logo.* London: Flamingo.
Knights, D. & McCabe, D. (1998). 'What happens when the phones go wild?' Staff, stress and spaces for escape in a BPR telephone banking call regime. *Journal of Management Studies,* **35,** 163–194.
Knights, D. & McCabe, D. (2000). Bewitched, bothered and bewildered: the meaning and experience of teamworking for employees in an automobile company. *Human Relations,* **53**(11), 1481–1517.
Legge, K. (1984). *The Evaluation of Planned Organizational Change.* London: Academic Press.
Legge, K. (2000). Personnel management in the lean organisation. In S. Bach & K. Sisson (Eds), *Personnel Management,* 3rd Edn (pp. 41–69). Oxford: Blackwell.
Legge, K. (2001a). Silver bullet or spent round? Assessing the meaning of the "high commitment management"/performance relationship. In J. Storey (Ed.), *Human Resource Management, A Critical Text,* 2nd Edn (pp. 21–36). London: Thomson Learning.
Legge, K. (2001b), 'Why kid ourselves? Is social justice possible in global markets?' Keynote address presented at the AIRAANZ Conference, Wollongong, Australia, February.
Mabey, C., Clark, T. & Skinner, D. (Eds) (1997). *Experiencing Human Resource Management.* London: Sage.
MacDuffie, J. P. (1995). Human resource bundles and manufacturing performance: organizational logic and flexible production systems in the world auto industry. *Industrial and Labor Relations Review,* **48,** 197–221.
McCabe, D. (2000). The team dream: the meaning and experience of teamworking for employees in an automobile manufacturing company. In S. Proctor & F. Mueller (Eds), *Teamworking* (pp. 203–221). Basingstoke: Macmillan.
McLoughlin, I. & Clark, J. (1988). *Technological Change at Work.* Milton Keynes: Open University.
Morgan, G. & Smircich, L. (1980). The case for qualitative research. *Academy of Management Review,* **5**(4), 491–500.
Mumford, E. (1972). *Job Satisfaction.* London: Longman.

Mumford, E. & Hendricks, R. (1996). 'Business process re-engineering RIP'. *People Management*, **3**(9), 22–29.

Oram, M. & Wellins, R. (1995). *Re-engineering's Missing Ingredient: the Human Factor*. London: Institute of Personnel and Development.

Osterman, P. (2000). Work reorganization in an era of restructuring: trends in diffusion and effects on employee welfare. *Industrial and Labor Relations Review*, **53**, 179–196.

Pfeffer, J. (1993). Barriers to the advance of organizational science: paradigm development as a dependent variable. *Academy of Management Review*, **18**(4), 599–620.

Pfeffer, J. (1994). *Competitive Advantage through People*. Boston, MA: Harvard Business School Press.

Pfeffer, J. (1995). 'Mortality, reproducibility, and persistence of styles of theory'. *Organization Science*, **6**(6), 681–686.

Purcell, J. (1999). Best practice and best fit: chimera or cul-de-sac? *Human Resource Management Journal*, **9**(3), 26–41.

Rees, C., Scarbrough, H. & Terry, M. (1996). *The People Management Implications of Leaner Ways of Working*. Report by IRRU, Warwick Business School, University of Warwick; Issues in People Management, No. 15 (pp. 64–115). London: Institute of Personnel and Development.

Rice, A. K. (1958). *Productivity and Social Organisation*. London: Tavistock.

Rogers, E. W. & Wright, P. M. (1998). Measuring organizational performance in strategic human resource management: problems, prospects, and performance information markets. *Human Resource Management Review*, **8**, 311–331.

Sennett, R. (1998). *The Corrosion of Character*. New York: Norton.

Sparrow, P. (1998). New organizational forms, processes, jobs and psychological contracts: resolving the HRM issues. In P. Sparrow & M. Marchington (Eds), *Human Resource Management: The New Agenda* (pp. 117–141). London: Financial Times/Pitman.

Storey, J. & Sisson, K. (1993). *Managing Human Resources and Industrial Relations*. Milton Keynes: Open University Press.

Taylor, P. & Bain, P. (1999). An assembly line in the head: the call centre labour process. *Industrial Relations Journal*, **30**, 101–117.

Travic, B. (1998). Information aspects of new organizational designs: exploring the non-traditional organization. *Journal of the American Society for Information Science*, **49**, 1224–144.

Trist, E. & Bamford, K. (1951). Some social and psychological consequences of the longwall method of coal-getting. *Human Relations*, **4**(1), 3–38.

Trist, E., Higgen, G., Murray, H. & Pollock, A. (1963). *Organisational Choice*, London: Tavistock.

van Maanen, J. (1995a). Style as theory. *Organization Science*, **6**(1), 133–143.

van Maanen, J. (1995b). Fear and loathing in organization studies. *Organization Science*, **6**(6), 687–692.

Walton, R. (1985). From control to commitment in the workplace. *Harvard Business Review*, **63**(2), 77–85.

Weick, K. E. (1995). *Sensemaking in Organizations*. Thousand Oaks, CA: Sage.

Wickens, P. (1987). *The Road to Nissan*. London: Macmillan.

Willmott, H. (1994). Business process re-engineering and human resource management. *Personnel Review*, **23**(3), 34–46.

67

WHITHER INDUSTRIAL AND ORGANIZATIONAL PSYCHOLOGY IN A CHANGING WORLD OF WORK?

Wayne F. Cascio

Source: *American Psychologist* 50(11) (1995): 928–939.

Abstract

Dramatic changes are affecting the world of work. Examples include increased global competition, the impact of information technology, the re-engineering of business processes, smaller companies that employ fewer people, the shift from making a product to providing a service, and the growing disappearance of "the job" as a fixed bundle of tasks. These trends are producing a redefinition of work itself. They provide great opportunities for industrial and organizational psychologists to contribute to the betterment of human welfare. This article identifies 6 key areas in which to start: job analysis, employee selection, training and development, performance appraisal, compensation (including incentives), and organizational development. Relevant research in these areas can provide substantial payoffs for individuals, organizations, and society as psychology moves into the 21st century.

As citizens of the 20th century, we have witnessed more change in our daily existence and in our environment than anyone else who ever walked the planet. But if you think the pace of change was fast in this century, expect it to accelerate in the next one. The 21st century will be even more complex, fast paced, and turbulent. It will also be very different. Industrial and organizational psychology potentially has much to contribute to this new world of work. It has the potential to lead change rather than to simply react to it, but to do so it must seize opportunities to provide research-based answers to pressing organizational problems. This article is organized into two parts. The first part describes some of the dramatic changes that are affecting the world of work; the second proposes a research agenda in six key areas in which applied psychologists often practice. I begin by considering the changing nature of economic competition.

Changing nature of economic competition

Just as wars—two World Wars, the Korean conflict, Vietnam, and Desert Storm—dominated the geopolitical map of the 20th century, economics will rule over the 21st. The competition that is normal and inevitable among nations increasingly will be played out, not in aggression or war but in the economic sphere. The weapons used will be those of commerce: growth rates, investments, trade blocs, and imports and exports (Nelan, 1992).

These changes reflect the impact of globalized product and service markets, coupled with increased domestic competition (largely fueled by deregulation in telecommunications, airlines, and banking) and new business start-ups. By a wide margin, however, global competition is the single most powerful economic fact of life in the 1990s. In the relatively sheltered era of the 1960s, only 7% of the U.S. economy was exposed to international competition. In the 1980s, that number zoomed past 70%, and it will keep climbing (Gwynne, 1992). Today, one in five American jobs is tied directly or indirectly to international trade. Merchandise exports are up more than 40% since 1986, and every $1 billion in U.S. merchandise exports generates approximately 20,000 new jobs. For the most part these are good jobs that pay about 22% more than average ("Investing in people," 1994).

The results of accelerated global competition have been almost beyond comprehension—free political debate throughout the former Soviet empire, democratic reforms in Central and South America, the integration of the European community, the North American Free Trade Agreement, and an explosion of free market entrepreneurship in Southern China. In short, the free markets and free labor markets that we in the United States have enjoyed throughout our national history have now become a global passion (Doyle, 1992).

There is no going back. Today, firms and workers in America must compete for business with firms and workers in the same industries in England, France, and Germany; in Poland, Hungary, and the former Russian republics; in Mexico, Brazil, Argentina, and Chile; and in Japan, Korea, Malaysia, Taiwan, Singapore, Hong Kong, and China, just to name a few of our competitors. However, it takes more than trade agreements, technology, capital investment, and infrastructure to deliver world-class products and services. It also takes the skills, ingenuity, and creativity of a competent, well-trained workforce. Our competitors know this, and they are spending unstintingly to create one.

The *World Competitiveness Report* (1994) provides a ranking of countries that combines the quality of public education, levels of secondary schooling and on-the-job training, computer literacy, and worker motivation. The United States ranks sixth, behind (in descending order) Singapore, Denmark, Germany, Japan, and

Norway. Although none of the higher-ranking countries is as heterogeneous as the United States, the lesson for decision makers is clear: The race to create a broad, technically literate labor pool has no finish line!

Impact on jobs in the United States

As nations around the world move from wartime to peacetime economies, from industrial societies to information societies, we are witnessing wrenching structural changes in our economy. These changes have impacted most profoundly in terms of jobs (Cascio, 1993). In the United States, more than 7 million permanent layoffs have been announced since 1987. That number includes 6 million between 1987 and 1992 (Baumohl, 1993), 615,000 is 1993 (Byrne, 1994), and 516,000 in 1994 (Murray, 1995).

Companies are not downsizing because they are losing money. Fully 81% of companies that downsize in a given year were profitable in that year. Major reasons, according to the American Management Association's 1994 survey on downsizing, were strategic or structural in nature: to improve productivity, transfers of location, new technological processes, mergers and acquisitions, or plant obsolescence ("1994 AMA").

Laid-off workers who must return to the job market often must take huge pay cuts. Downward mobility is the rate rather than the exception ("Downside," 1994). Of roughly 2,000 workers let go by RJR Nabisco, for example, 72% found jobs subsequently but at wages that averaged only 47% of their previous pay ("Jobs," 1993).

Surprisingly, older, higher-paid workers may fare better. A recent study of 311 workers (285 men and 26 women) whose average age and salary were 57 and $75,000, respectively, took an average of 5.6 months to land jobs that paid an average of $61,500 (Drake, Beam, Morin, Inc., 1994). Whether young or old, however, the bottom line for most reemployed workers is that both their spending power and their standards of living have dropped.

What's happening here? In a nutshell, as an executive in the pharmaceutical industry noted, we're moving from an economy where there are a lot of hard-working people to one where there are fewer, smarter-working people (Pilon, 1993). Jobs aren't being lost temporarily because of a recession; rather, they are being wiped out permanently as a result of new technology, improved machinery, and new ways of organizing work. In the following sections, I briefly examine the impact of these changes and then discuss how organizations are responding, particularly to the changes affecting managers and workers.

Effects of technology on organizations and people

Fifty million workers use computers every day along with other products of the digital age—faxes, modems, cellular phones, and E-mail. This is breaking down departmental barriers, enhancing the sharing of vast amounts of information, creating "virtual offices" for workers on the go, collapsing product development cycles, and changing the ways that organizations service customers and relate to their suppliers and to their employees. To succeed and prosper in the changing world of work, companies need motivated, technically literate workers.

A caveat is in order here, however. It relates to the common assumption that because production processes have become more sophisticated, high technology can substitute for skill in managing a workforce. Beware of such a "logic trap." On the contrary, high technology actually makes the workforce even more important for success, as Pfeffer (1994) has noted,

> This is because more skill may be necessary to operate the more sophisticated and advanced equipment, and with a higher level of investment per employee, interruptions in the process are increasingly expensive. This means that the ability to effectively operate, maintain, and repair equipment—tasks all done by first-line employees—become even more critical. (p. 8)

Ideally, therefore, technology will help workers make decisions in organizations that encourage them to do so ("Workplace of the Future," 1993). However, organizations of the future will look very different from organizations of the past, as the next section illustrates.

Changes in the structure and design of organizations

In today's world of fast-moving global markets and fierce competition, the windows of opportunity are often frustratingly brief (Byrne, 1993).The features that dominated industrial society's approach to designing organizations throughout the 19th and 20th centuries—mass production and large organizations—are disappearing. Trends such as the following are accelerating the shift toward new forms of organization for the 21st century (Kiechel, 1993): (a) smaller companies that employ fewer people; (b) the shift from vertically integrated hierarchies to networks of specialists; (c) technicians, ranging from computer repair persons to radiation therapists, replacing manufacturing operatives as the worker elite (see Barley, 1991); (d) pay tied less to a person's position or tenure in an organization and more to the market value of his or her skills; (e) the change in the paradigm of doing business from making a product to providing a service; and (f) the redefinition of work itself—growing disappearance of "the job" as a fixed bundle of tasks (see Bridges, 1994) and increased emphasis on constantly changing work required to fulfill the ever-increasing demands of customers. This will require constant learning, more higher order thinking, and the availability to work outside the standard hours of 9 a.m. to 5 p.m.

In this emerging world of work, more and more organizations will focus carefully on their core competencies and outsource everything else. They will be characterized by terms such as *virtual*, *boundary-less*, and *flexible*, with no guarantees to workers or managers. Hundreds of big companies have outsourced noncore operations: Continental Bank Corporation has contracted its legal, audit, cafeteria, and mailroom operations to outside companies. American Airlines is doing the same with customer service jobs at 30 airports.

This approach to organizing is no short-term fad. The fact is, organizations are becoming leaner and leaner, with better and better trained "multispecialists"— those who have in-depth knowledge about a number of different aspects of the business. Eschewing narrow specialists or broad generalists, organizations of the future will come to rely on cross-trained multispecialists to get things done. One such group whose roles are changing dramatically is that of managers.

The changing role of the manager

In the traditional hierarchy that used to comprise most bureaucratic organizations, rules were simple. Managers ruled by command from the top (essentially one-way communication), used rigid controls to ensure that fragmented tasks (grouped into clearly defined jobs) could be coordinated effectively, and partitioned information into neat compartments—departments, units, and functions. Information was (and is) power, and, at least in some cases, managers clung to power by hoarding information. This approach to organizing, that is, 3-C (command, control, and compartmentalization) logic, was geared to achieve three objectives: stability, predictability, and efficiency.

In today's reengineered, hypercompetitive work environments, the autocratic, top-down command-and-control approach is out of step with the competitive realities that many organizations face. To survive, organizations have to be able to respond quickly to shifting market conditions. In this kind of an environment, a key job for all managers, especially top managers, is to articulate a vision of what the organization stands for and what it is trying to accomplish. The next step is to translate that vision into everything that is done and to use the vision as a benchmark to assess progress over time.

A large and growing number of organizations now recognize that they need to emphasize workplace democracy to achieve the vision. This involves breaking down barriers, sharing information, using a collaborative approach to problem solving, and an orientation toward continuous learning and improvement. For many managers, these kinds of skills simply weren't needed in organizations designed and structured under 3-C logic.

Does this imply that we are moving toward a universal model of organizational and leadership effectiveness? Hardly. Contingency theories of leadership such as path-goal theory (House, 1971), normative decision theory (Vroom & Yetton, 1973), or least-preferred coworker (LPC) contingency theory (Fiedler, 1967) suggest that an autocratic style is appropriate in some situations. In recent years many organizations (e.g., Eaton Corporation and Levi Strauss & Co.) have instituted formal information-sharing and workplace education programs that reduce or eliminate a key condition that makes autocratic leadership appropriate—workers who lack the information or knowledge needed to make meaningful suggestions or decisions. More often, today's networked, interdependent, culturally diverse organizations require transformational leadership (Bass, 1985). The ability of leaders to transform followers to bring out their creativity, imagination, and best efforts requires well-developed interpersonal skills, founded on an understanding of human behavior in organizations. Industrial and organizational psychologists are well-positioned to help managers develop these kinds of skills.

In addition, although by no means universal, much of the work that results in a product, service, or decision is now done in teams—intact, identifiable social systems (even if small or temporary) whose members have the authority to manage their own task and interpersonal processes as they carry out their work. Such teams go by a variety of names—autonomous work groups, process teams, and self-managing work teams. All of this implies a radical reorientation from the traditional view of a manager's work.

In this kind of an environment, workers are acting more like managers, and managers more like workers. The managerial roles of controllers, planners, and inspectors are being replaced by coaches, facilitators, and mentors (Wellins, Byham, & Wilson, 1991). This doesn't just happen—it requires good interpersonal skills, continuous learning, and an organizational culture that supports and encourages both.

Flattened hierarchies also mean that there are fewer managers in the first place. The empowered worker will be a defining feature of such organizations.

The empowered worker—no passing fad

It should be clear by now that we are in the midst of a revolution—a revolution at work. Change isn't coming only from large, high-profile companies doing high-technology work. It has also permeated unglamorous, low-tech work. As an example, consider Toronto-based Cadet Uniform Services, which outfits the employees of some of North America's leading corporations (Henkoff, 1994).

Cadet doesn't just hire people to drive trucks, deliver clean uniforms, and pick up dirty ones. Rather, its concept of customer service representatives (CSRs) extends much further. They are mini-entrepreneurs who design their own routes, manage their own accounts, and, to a large extent, determine the size of their paychecks.

Cadet ties compensation almost entirely to measures of customer satisfaction. Lose a customer on your watch and your salary sinks. CSR pay is about $40,000 a year, nearly twice the industry average. In practice, Cadet rarely loses a customer; its annual defection rate is less than 1%. Employees don't leave either; turnover is a low 7%. To a large extent this is because Cadet spends considerable time and effort on selecting employees—who take pride in their work, are exceedingly neat, and are outgoing. In all, 46 ethnic groups are represented at Cadet.

How has the company done? Its annual growth has averaged 22% for the past 20 years, and it boasts double-digit profit margins that exceed the industry norm. Says Quentin Wahl, chief executive officer, "The jobs we do aren't so special—the pay is good, but it's not great. The main thing we have to sell to employees is the culture of the organization" (Henkoff, 1994, p. 122).

Organizations of the 1990s, both large and small, differ dramatically in structure, design, and demographics from those of even a decade ago. Demographically, they are far more diverse. They comprise more women at all levels, more multiethnic, multicultural workers, more older workers, workers with disabilities, robots, and contingent workers. Paternalism is out; self-reliance is in. There's constant pressure to do more with less and steady emphasis on empowerment, cross-training, personal flexibility, self-managed work teams, and continuous learning. Workers today have to be able to adapt to changing circumstances and be prepared for multiple careers. Industrial and organizational psychologists are helping to educate prospective, current, and former workers to these new realities. In the future, they will be expected to do much more, as I describe later, but first I consider some organizational responses to these new realities.

Implications for organizations and their people

What do these trends imply for the ways that organizations will compete for business? In a world where virtually every factor that affects the production of goods or the delivery of services—capital, equipment, technology, and information—is available to every player in the global economy, the one factor that doesn't routinely move across national borders is a nation's workforce. In the years to come, the quality of the American workforce will be a crucial determinant of America's ability to compete and win in world markets.

Human resources can be sources of sustained competitive advantage as long as they meet three basic requirements: (a) They add positive economic benefits to the process of producing goods or delivering services; (b) the skills of the workforce are distinguishable from those of competitors (e.g., through education and workplace learning); and (c) such skills are not easily duplicated (Barney, 1991). Human resource systems (the set of interrelated processes designed to attract, develop, and maintain human resources) can either enhance or destroy this potential competitive advantage (Lado & Wilson, 1994).

Perhaps a quote attributed to Albert Einstein, the famous physicist, best captures the position of this article. After the first atomic reaction in 1942, Einstein remarked, "Everything has changed, except our way of thinking" ("Workplace of the Future," 1993, p. 2). As psychology in general, and industrial and organizational psychology in particular, stands poised on the brink of the 21st century, I believe that our greatest challenge will be to change the way we as a field think about organizations and their people. The first part of this article addressed some key changes in the world of work; the remainder identifies some pressing research questions that must be addressed if our science is to remain relevant to 21st-century organizations.

A research agenda for industrial and organizational psychologists

Each of the following sections identifies traditional practices, new developments, and research questions that require attention if the field is to lead organizational change rather than react to it. These sections are job analysis, employee selection, training and development, performance appraisal, compensation (including incentives), and organization development. Admittedly, these areas represent only some of the broad range of activities that psychologists are engaged in and that relate to the management of people in work settings. In total, however, they comprise much of the work in this area.

Job analysis: identifying the work to be done and the personal characteristics necessary to do the work

Traditional task-based "jobs" were once packaged into clusters of similar tasks and assigned to specialist workers. Today, many firms have no reason to package work that way. Instead, they are unbundling tasks into broader chunks of work that change over time. Such shifting clusters of tasks make it difficult to define a job, at least in the traditional sense. Practices such as flex time, job sharing, and telecommuting, not to mention temporary workers, part-timers, and consultants, have compounded the definitional problem.

Job analysis is a common activity of industrial and organizational psychologists, and there exists a well-defined technology for doing such analysis (Gael, 1988; Harvey, 1991; Ilgen & Hollenbeck, 1991; McCormick, 1979). Terms such as *job element*, *task*, *duty*, *position*, *job*, *job description*, and *job family* are well-understood parts of the lexicon of industrial and organizational psychologists everywhere.

Today, however, there is a detectable shift away from a task-based toward a process-based organization of work. A *process* is a collection of activities (such as procurement, order fulfillment, product development, or credit issuance) that takes one or more kinds of input and creates an output that is of value to a customer (M. Hammer & Champy, 1993). Customers may be internal or external. Individual tasks are important parts of the process, but the process itself cuts across organizational boundaries and traditional functions, such as engineering, production, marketing, and finance.

Consider credit issuance as an example. Instead of the separate jobs of credit checker and pricer, the two may be combined into one "deal structurer." Such integrated processes cut response time and increase efficiency and productivity. Bell Atlantic created a "case team"—a group of people who have among them all of the skills necessary to handle an installation order. Members of the team—who previously were located in different departments and in different geographical areas—were brought together into a single unit and given total responsibility for installing the equipment. Such a process operates, on average, ten times faster than the assembly line version it replaces. Bell Atlantic, for example, reduced the time it takes to install a high-speed digital service link from 30 days to 3 (M. Hammer & Champy, 1993).

Employees involved in the process are responsible for ensuring that customers' requirements are met on time and with no defects, and they are empowered to experiment in ways that will cut cycle time and reduce costs. Result: Less supervision is needed, while workers take on broader responsibilities and a wider purview of activities. Moreover, the kinds of activities that each worker does are likely to shift over time.

In terms of traditional job analysis, this leaves many unanswered questions and a number of challenges. Some of these questions follow.

What will be the future of traditional task-based descriptions of jobs and job activities? Should other types of descriptors replace task statements that describe what a worker does, to what or whom, why, and how? Will "task cluster" statements or "subprocess" statements become the basic building blocks for describing work? What does a job description look like in a process-based organization of work? Will job specifications (which identify the personal characteristics—knowledge, skills, abilities, and other characteristics—necessary to do the work) supersede job descriptions? Does identification of the environmental, contextual, and social dimensions of work become more important in a process-based structure? Will emphasis shift from describing jobs to describing roles?

Managers often look to industrial and organizational psychologists to help them analyze jobs and describe work processes as a foundation for other human resource management activities, such as employee selection, training, compensation, work and organization design, and performance appraisal. In the next section, I discuss the implications of the new organization of work for employee selection.

Selecting employees

In the traditional paradigm, so-called "one-shot" selection–placement programs worked as follows: analyze the job, identify relevant job performance criteria, identify job-related predictors of performance, validate predictors, and then select candidates who score highest on the set of validated predictors. As with job analysis, the technology for working within this paradigm is also well developed (see, e.g., Cascio, 1991; Guion, 1991; Schmitt & Borman, 1993).

I just described the problems associated with analyzing jobs under a process-based organization of work. To compound those problems, consider that relatively few jobs in today's economy are performed independently of others and that most are interdependent or coordinate in nature—that is, they are a function of group efforts, not just the sum of individual talents. For example, both Xerox Corporation and General Electric (GE) now develop new products through multidisciplinary teams that work in a single process, instead of vertical functions or departments. At GE a senior team of 9–12 people oversees nearly 100 processes or programs worldwide, from new product design to improvement of the yield on production machinery. The senior team—consisting of managers with multiple competencies rather than narrow specialists—exists to allocate resources and ensure coordination of the processes and programs. "They stay away from the day-to-day activities, which are managed by the teams themselves," explains Harold Giles, manager of human resources in GE's lighting business ("The Horizontal Corporation," 1993, p. 79). That's quite a change from the traditional role of a supervisor.

Let us add just one more complicating factor to this mix: In some cases workers will join intact work teams that stay together to perform different kinds of work, such as assembly of different models of an automobile, or different products entirely, as under a flexible manufacturing system. In project-based work, such as research and development, consulting, legal defense, or movie production, "virtual" teams consisting of multidisciplinary players are created to work on a project and then are disbanded when the project is finished. In these cases, the nature of the work changes, as does the composition of the teams that do the work.

From the point of view of industrial and organizational psychology, the challenge is to move beyond valid, job-based predictors because the work to be done changes constantly. This raises a number of research issues relevant to the selection of employees (including managers): How does the selection process influence team effectiveness? As Klimoski and Jones (1995) noted, selecting the right mix of individuals to comprise a team implies attention to worker requirements on at least three dimensions: ability, values and personality, and politics (a team member's future role in making things happen once a decision is reached).

Will the role of tests of cognitive abilities focus on identifying candidates with general (as opposed to specific) abilities, such as basic verbal and numeracy skills, the ability to think critically, to reason logically, and to draw conclusions from a body of facts? If so, this would comport with recent findings that general cognitive ability is an efficient predictor in terms of job performance (Ree & Earles, 1992; Ree, Earles, & Teachout, 1994) and training performance (Ree & Earles, 1991).

How can psychology contribute to the optimal use of people with lower levels of cognitive abilities? Because not all jobs require high levels of cognitive ability (e.g., many types of service jobs), what other types of predictors of work performance will validly forecast success in such jobs? Services, which now account for 74% of the gross domestic product, and 79% of all employment in the United States, are expected to account for all of the net growth in jobs in the next decade. Will measures of personality characteristics—for example, adaptability, empathy, and ability to work under stress—receive relatively more attention man cognitive ability tests in jobs whose primary objective is customer service? To be sure, the ability to select, train, and retain front-line, customer-contact workers will be a top priority for many organizations. Companies such as Marriott and Disney now require the same skills of workers that they once demanded of managers—" people who are resilient and resourceful, empathetic and enterprising, competent and creative" (Henkoff, 1994, p. 110).

There is no question that well-developed measures of personality characteristics can account for additional variance in the prediction of behavior on the job (Hogan, 1991; Ones, Mount, Barrick, & Hunter, 1994; Tett, Jackson, Rothstein, & Reddon, 1994). Although a wide variety of such measures exists, they have not been used routinely to select employees. However, given the emphasis on effective interpersonal interaction in the new forms of work organization, more and more managers insist that such characteristics be taken into account. This poses another question of interest to industrial and organizational psychologists, namely the following:

Do alternative modes of pre-hire personality assessment—paper-and-pencil measures, interactive video, computer-based, structured individual or group interviews, or situational tests, for example—provide equivalent psychometric properties? Do they measure the same constructs? As Campbell and Fiske (1959) noted, any test or other measurement procedure is really a trait–method unit—that is, a test measures a given trait by a single method. Hence if one wants to know the relative contribution of trait and method variance to test scores, one must study more than one trait (e.g., dominance and affiliation) and use more than one method (e.g., paper and pencil and interactive video). Second-order confirmatory factor analysis (Marsh & Hocevar, 1988) may be especially helpful in this context.

To probe personality characteristics, pre-hire assessment procedures, especially those used by large organizations, often include patterned behavior description interviews, in which candidates are asked to provide detailed accounts of actual situations (Alderman, 1995). For example, instead of asking, "How would you reprimand an employee?" now it's "Give me a specific example of a time you had to reprimand an employee. What action did you take, and what was the result?" Answers tend to be remarkably consistent with actual (i.e., subsequent) job behavior (Dipboye & Gaugler, 1993; Weekley & Gier, 1987).

Alternatively, interviewers may pose "What would you do if ...?" questions. Such questions compose the situational interview, which is based on the assumption that a person's expressed behavioral intentions are related to subsequent behavior. In the situational interview, candidates are asked to describe how they think they would respond in certain job-related situations. Validities for both types of interviews vary from about 0.22 to 0.28 (Motowidlo et al., 1992). This brings up the following questions. (a) Does it matter whether patterned behavior description interview questions or situational interview questions are administered face-to-face or by computer? (b) Do they (interview questions) measure the same constructs and yield equivalent validities? (c) Will work samples or situational tests be used more frequently to assess the compatibility of potential team members, especially members of self-managed work teams? Such procedures measure the ability to do, not just the ability to know. Group-based situational tests (e.g., the leaderless group discussion) have long been used in management selection (e.g., Bass, 1954).

How should they be designed to fit the context of a self-managed team—whether intact or virtual?

"Why is it that I always get a whole person when what I really want is a pair of hands?" Henry Ford lamented (Labich, 1994, p. 64). In today's (and tomorrow's) world of work, characteristics of the whole person—cognitive as well as personality—are required to improve continuously the business processes that satisfy the needs of internal and external customers. Managers know this, and increasingly they are turning to industrial and organizational psychologists for answers.

Training and development

The old Chinese proverb, "Give a man a fish and you feed him for a day; teach a man to fish and you feed him for life," fits neatly into today's emphasis on self-reliance and career resiliency. Career-resilient workers are dedicated to continuous learning. They stand ready to reinvent themselves to keep pace with change, they take responsibility for their own career management, and they are committed to their company's success (Waterman, Waterman, & Collard, 1994). This implies two things: (a) Companies must make it easy for employees to learn and to become flexible, and (b) workers should have the right to obtain ongoing training.

For example, at Sun Microsystems, a core value is "We acknowledge the essential link between company growth and the development of individuals" ("Career," 1994). To make this link a reality, Sun supports training and development activities in three areas: (a) assessment of interests, values, and temperament (to help employees understand who they are and where they are going); (b) assessment and development of technical and functional work skills (to help employees benchmark and improve their work performance); and (c) assessment and development of work strategies (to help employees understand and improve their performance in areas such as problem-solving and conflict resolution).

Compelling as the idea of training may seem, there are strong disincentives for implementing it. To illustrate, consider just three macrolevel structural issues in the design and delivery of training (Cascio, 1994b):

1   Corporate commitment is lacking and uneven. Most companies spend nothing at all on training. Those that do spend tend to concentrate on managers, technicians, and professionals, not rank-and-file workers. Fully 89% of American workers never receive any formal training from their employers ("Labor Letter," 1991).
2   Poaching trained workers is a major problem for U.S. businesses and provides a strong disincentive for training. Unlike in Germany, where local business groups pressure companies not to steal one another's employees, there is no such system in the United States (Salwen, 1993). This has profound consequences for "selling" senior managers on the value of training in the United States.

3 Despite the rhetoric about training being viewed as an investment, current accounting rules require that it be treated as an expense. Business might spend more on training if accounting rules were revised. Unlike investments in plant and equipment, which show up on the books as an asset, training expenditures are seen merely as expenses to be deducted in the year they are incurred ("Labor Letter," 1991).

Industrial and organizational psychologists have little control over these macrolevel problems. However, there is much that they can contribute. For example, with respect to the poaching problem, it is important to point out the "training paradox," as described by Robert Waterman (Filipczak, 1995). The paradox runs both ways. That is, if employees take charge of their own employability by keeping their skills updated and varied so they can work for anyone, de facto they build more job security with their current employer—assuming the employer values highly skilled, motivated employees. Similarly, the company that provides lots of training and learning opportunities is more likely to retain workers because it creates an interesting and challenging environment. In theory, therefore, increasing an individual's employability outside a company simultaneously increases his or her job security and desire to stay with the current employer.

A related area in which psychologists can contribute on the basis of strong inferences from data is that of training evaluation. The literature on training evaluation shows that whereas the potential returns from well-conducted training programs can be substantial, there is often considerable variability in the effectiveness with which any given training method or content area is implemented (Cascio, 1994a). Considerable planning (through needs analysis) and follow-up program evaluation efforts are necessary to realize these returns. Both needs analysis and program evaluation are well-developed areas in industrial and organizational psychology (Goldstein, 1989, 1994; Kraiger, Ford, & Salas, 1993).

For example, one issue that often vexes employers is whether to spend money on reskilling programs for older workers with shorter payback periods. Another is whether to invest in training for the hard-core unemployed or for workers who lack basic literacy skills. In both cases, business sees lower payback probabilities. Utility analyses can play an important role in dispelling myths about the costs of training relative to its benefits. The technology is available now to do such analyses (Cascio, 1989), and a number of them already have been reported in the personnel psychology literature (Cascio, 1994a). However, what generally has not been reported, and that will be essential in the future, is objective evidence of the extent to which the financial returns forecasted by utility analyses actually do materialize.

One area in which objective evidence does indicate positive payoffs for individual and organizational performance is that of high-performance work practices (HPWPs), of which training is an integral component. Such practices provide workers with the information, skills, incentives, and responsibility to make decisions essential for innovation, quality improvement, and rapid response to change

(U.S. Department of Labor, 1993). A recent study based on a national sample of nearly 1,000 publicly-traded firms found that HPWPs have an economically and statistically significant impact both on employee turnover and productivity on short-term and long-term measures of corporate financial performance (Huselid, 1995).

Earlier I showed how the roles of workers and managers are changing dramatically, from controlled to empowered, from boss to mentor. Both groups will require extensive training and support to change entrenched attitudes and beliefs to function effectively in the new world of work. For example, empowered employees need to develop the kind of understanding of business and financial issues that no one but an owner or an executive used to be concerned with (Bridges, 1994). Moreover, several studies have supported the novel proposition that the "skills gap" is really about attitudes (Cappelli, 1992). Thus a 1989 employer survey by Towers Perrin found that the most common reasons for firing new employees were absenteeism and failure to adapt to the work environment; only 9% of the workers were dismissed because of difficulties in learning how to perform their jobs. A 1990 survey by the National Association of Manufacturers found that the belief that applicants would not have the work attitudes and behaviors needed to adapt to the work environment was almost twice as common a reason for rejecting applicants as the next most important factor. This raises several intriguing research questions:

If attitudes play such an important role in work performance, then constructs such as adaptability, consistency, and prosocial behavior become particularly important components of workplace learning programs. To what extent can such characteristics be taught? How should they be taught? To what extent can research findings in applied social psychology, cognitive psychology, and instructional technology inform training practice in these areas?

In designing training systems to promote team development and workplace learning, what are the most effective methods for developing skill, knowledge, and attitudinal competencies (Cannon-Bowers, Tannenbaum, Salas, & Volpe, 1995)? Do results hold up when teams must operate in stable as opposed to rapidly changing environments?

Senior managers are looking for evidence of the extent to which workers and managers can change their attitudes and behavior to fit new organizational designs. Research is needed to identify methods and activities that will facilitate and maintain such change. The relapse prevention model, a cognitive–behavioral model of self-control strategies designed to reduce the likelihood of relapse, is a good place to start (Marx, 1982).

Performance appraisal

Performance appraisal refers to the systematic description of the job-relevant strengths and weaknesses of an individual or group. In recent years, one issue that has generated considerable debate is the relevance and appropriateness of performance appraisal in work contexts that emphasize total quality management (TQM).

TQM emphasizes the continuous improvement of products and processes to ensure long-term customer satisfaction. Its group problem-solving focus encourages employee empowerment by using the job-related expertise and ingenuity of the workforce. Cross-functional teams develop solutions to complex problems, often shortening the time taken to design, develop, or produce products and services. Because a team may not include a representative of management, the dividing line between labor and management often becomes blurred in practice, as workers themselves begin to solve organizational problems. Thus adoption of TQM generally requires cultural change within the organization as management reexamines its past methods and practices in light of the demands of the new philosophy (Wiedman, 1993).

If the "father of TQM," W. Edwards Deming, had his way, appraisal systems that tie individual performance to salary adjustments would be eliminated. In his view, such systems hinder teamwork, create fear and mistrust, and discourage risk-taking behavior, thereby stifling innovation. Worse yet, Deming believes, most appraisal systems are based on the faulty assumption that individuals have significant control over their own performance—that is, that most individuals can improve if they choose to do so by putting forth the necessary effort (Deming, 1986).

Most industrial and organizational psychologists would agree that as a basis for implementing a "pay-for-performance" philosophy, performance appraisal is a meaningful tool only if workers have significant control over the variables that impact their individual performance. If not, then it is true, as Deming (1986) believes, that appraisals only measure random statistical variation within a particular system. Here are three suggestions for harmonizing these two processes (Wiedman, 1993): Let customer expectations (a) generate individual or team performance expectations, (b) include results expectations that identify actions to meet or exceed those expectations, and (c) include behavioral skills that make the real difference in achieving quality performance and total customer satisfaction.

Here are several other pressing research issues in appraisal:

1   Traditionally, the immediate supervisor is responsible for rating subordinates (Bernardin & Beatty, 1984; Murphy & Cleveland, 1991). New organizational designs that incorporate self-managed work teams or manufacturing "cells" (small teams of workers) may not have an immediate supervisor. Research is needed to provide answers to questions such as Who should rate performance under these circumstances and on what criteria? What should be the relative role (if any) of customers or suppliers? McIntyre and Salas (1995) have identified a number of behavioral indicators of team performance, and their work can help guide future research in this area.
2   To create greater allegiance to a process, rather than to a boss, GE has begun to put in place so-called "360-degree appraisals" in which peers and others above and below the employee evaluate the performance of an individual

in a process ("The Horizontal Corporation," 1993; see also Tornow, 1993). Research is needed to identify the relative weights of the various raters as well as optimal means for combining information. Moreover, given that multiple perspectives are represented (e.g., peers, subordinates, and supervisors), and that each is best able to rate different aspects of performance (Borman, 1974; Mabe & West, 1982), what should each rater rate?

3   In work that is highly coordinate in nature (e.g., grant proposal writing and process reengineering), it is simply not possible to disaggregate individual from team performance. Although individual behaviors can be rated (e.g., initiative, flexibility, and effort), individual outcomes cannot. As McIntyre and Salas (1995) pointed out, teamwork and task work are distinct. Research is needed to identify the components and mechanics of team-based performance appraisal.

4   What is the most appropriate format and method for communicating performance feedback when multiple perspectives are represented? Should a single individual serve as the conduit for such feedback? Who is responsible for following up to ensure that goals are set and progress is monitored? What is the long-term impact of such feedback on behavior and work outcomes (Smither et al. 1995)?

Answers to these kinds of questions are particularly relevant to the changing world of work. Industrial and organizational psychologists have the tools and know-how to advance cumulative knowledge in this area while making genuine contributions to better management of human resources.

Compensation and incentives

Traditionally, pay systems were job-based. That is, each job had an intrinsic worth (identified through the process of job evaluation) so that, in theory at least, pay stayed relatively constant regardless of who performed the job. Individual contributions were rewarded, as was position in the hierarchy and tenure on the job. Base salaries tended to increase year after year, as percentage increases yielded larger and larger amounts of money added to the base.

In today's flatter, less hierarchical organizations, the old assumptions about pay systems are being questioned. Some organizations are rewarding employees not just for individual performance but also for the development of their skills and for team or organizational performance (Ost, 1995). Others are asking employees to put more of their pay at risk. Consider each of these trends.

In a skill- or knowledge-based pay system, workers are not paid on the basis of the job they currently are doing but rather on the basis of the number of jobs they are capable of doing, or on their depth of knowledge. In such a "learning environment," the more workers learn, the more they earn. Workers at American Steel & Wire can boost their annual salaries by up to $12,480 by acquiring as many as 10 skills. Is there any impact on productivity or morale? A recent survey of 27 companies with such programs revealed that 70% to 88% reported higher job satisfaction, product quality, or productivity. Some 70% to 75% reported lower operating costs or reduced turnover ("Skill-Based Pay," 1992).

Such systems cannot work in all situations. They seem to work best when the following conditions exist (Gomez-Mejia & Balkin, 1992): (a) A supportive human resource management (HRM) philosophy underpins all employment activities (such a philosophy is characterized by mutual trust and the conviction that employees have the ability and motivation to perform well); (b) HRM programs such as profit sharing, participative management, empowerment, and job enrichment complement the skill- or knowledge-based pay system; (c) technology and organization structure change frequently; (d) employee exchanges (i.e., assignment and rotation) are common; (e) there are opportunities to learn new skills; (f) employee turnover is relatively high; and (g) workers value teamwork and the opportunity to participate.

A second trend among many firms is to increase the proportion of pay that is at risk or variable, thereby reducing fixed costs. A third trend is to use team or organization-wide incentives, such as profit sharing or productivity gain sharing, to provide broader motivation than is furnished by incentive plans geared to individual employees. Their aim is twofold: to increase productivity and to improve morale by giving employees a feeling of participation in and identification with the company (Florkowski, 1987).

It is important to distinguish *gain sharing* from *profit sharing*. The two approaches differ in three important ways (T. H. Hammer, 1988): (a) Gain sharing is based on a measure of productivity. Profit sharing is based on a global profitability measure. (b) Gain sharing, productivity measurement, and bonus payments are frequent events, distributed monthly or quarterly, whereas the measures and rewards of profit-sharing plans are annual. (c) Gain-sharing plans are current distribution plans, in contrast to most profit-sharing plans, which have deferred payments. Hence gain-sharing plans are true incentive plans rather than employee benefits. As such, they are more directly related to individual behavior and therefore can motivate worker productivity.

Does profit sharing improve productivity? One review of 27 econometric studies found that profit sharing was positively related to productivity in better than 9 of every 10 instances. Productivity was generally 3% to 5% higher in firms with profit-sharing plans than in those without plans (U.S. Department of Labor, 1993).

Does gain sharing improve productivity? Of 72 companies using Improshare (Fein, 1982)—production standards based on time-and-motion studies, plus a sharing of productivity gains 50–50 between employees and the company—38 companies were nonunion and 34 were represented by 18 international unions. The average gain in productivity over all companies using the plan after one year was 22.4%. Productivity gains tended to be larger if workers were provided with training and information; gains tended to be smaller, none, or negative (i.e., productivity deteriorated) if workers perceived that there was "nothing in it" for them.

Such changes in compensation and incentive systems raise several important research questions:

1. American culture emphasizes "rugged individualism" rather than a group orientation. What specific contextual issues are relevant when team or organization-wide incentives are applied in such a culture?
2. Empowerment emphasizes an active role for employees in determining outcomes. Yet employees sometimes feel powerless to influence profits, as under a profit-sharing program. How can firms deal with this inconsistency?
3. Logically, team-based performance appraisals should form the basis for team-based incentives. However, there is almost no extant research on team-based appraisals (an exception is Norman & Zawacki, 1991), with respect either to process or to format.
4. Although firms such as General Foods, General Motors, Procter and Gamble, and Anheuser-Busch have been experimenting with skill- or knowledge-based pay (Tosi & Tosi, 1987), job evaluation methods remain more popular. Why? What employee or work-related factors might enhance the applicability of such systems in a changing world of work?

Organizational development

Organizational development (OD) can be described broadly as the use of planned, behavioral science-based interventions in work settings for the purpose of improving organizational functioning and individual development (Porras & Robertson, 1992). At its core, OD is about change, and in the future world of work, "the core competitive advantage for companies will be their capacity for mastering revolutionary change at all levels of the organization" (Tichy, 1994).

For many organizations, this will require a metamorphosis into a "learning organization." Yet as compelling a notion as that is, in-depth interviews with 350 executives in 14 industries found that in attempting to implement change, from work redesign to organization culture, many firms had not learned from their past mistakes, or else somehow felt doomed to repeat them (Arthur D. Little, Inc., 1994). As many as 70%–80% of change initiatives had failed; 40% of the executives surveyed were very unhappy, finding change too slow or patchy; there were no significant benefits from the change initiatives; and 80% of the companies expected to be going through other major changes within a few years.

These results are not encouraging, but they certainly increase opportunities and raise some important research issues for industrial and organizational psychologists. These issues span two broad areas: planning for change (based on theory) and implementing change (based on practice). With respect to planning, the most pressing need is to develop a well-specified theory about the process of organizational change. Indeed, a comprehensive review of literature in the field of OD concluded, "It is a major weakness of the field that, as a group, the theories supposed to define the dynamics of the planned change process are so vague" (Porras & Robertson, 1992, p. 760). Specifically, two types of research are needed:

1. Identification and specification of alternative models of organizations on which to base change process theories. As has been shown, both the structure and variety of organizational forms are changing dramatically as organizations strive to meet the ever-changing demands of the marketplace. Change process theory is not keeping pace.
2. More comprehensive frameworks, categorization schemes, or models that will allow industrial and organizational psychologists to make sense of the theory and knowledge that already exists (Woodman, 1989).

In the Arthur D. Little (1994) survey, those who were successful in implementing change were able to help managers and employees fundamentally change the way they think about and approach change. This can be done in a number of ways. From the perspective of implementing change, a variety of OD intervention techniques exists, from simple to complex, from short-term to long-term, from affecting one individual to affecting an entire organization, and from affecting only one organizational variable (e.g., social factors) to affecting several (e.g., organizing arrangements, technology, and physical setting; Porras & Robertson, 1992).

If OD interventions are to be maximally effective, however, practitioners must identify the best change technique or combination of techniques to apply to a given situation, while at the same time addressing fundamental characteristics such as underlying assumptions, beliefs, and attitudes. Unfortunately, present OD theory does not provide sufficient guidance for determining the best techniques to use in particular situations. As a result, practice is leading theory, instead of the other way around (Mirvis, 1988).

What can be done?

Perhaps the greatest need in this area today, as in the past, is for methodologically sound evaluations of the relative impact of alternative OD interventions. Problems such as the unit of analysis and random assignment of individuals to groups make classic experimental designs difficult to implement in field settings. This should not be cause for abandonment of efforts to evaluate the relative impact of alternative interventions. Application of quasi-experimental designs, qualitative research methods (Van Maanen, 1979), and assessment of the agreement of laboratory and field results (Gersick, 1989) all can contribute to the advancement of knowledge and practice.

Thousands of change efforts are initiated every year. If the field is to maintain a scientific basis for its continued existence, then it is essential to evaluate change efforts to determine which interventions have the greatest impact on which organizational variables. The ultimate objective is to develop cumulative knowledge that can be translated into a science-based practice of OD that is directly useful to organizations. Such knowledge will be critical to mastering change at all levels and ensuring a sustained competitive advantage for organizations that rely on behavioral science-based change interventions to do so.

Summary and conclusions

Dramatic changes are affecting the world of work. Some of these include increased global competition, the impact of information technology, the reengineering of business processes, the shift from vertically integrated hierarchies to networks of specialists, smaller companies that employ fewer people, and the change in the paradigm of doing business from making a product to providing a service. Beyond those, there is an emerging redefinition of work itself: growing disappearance of the job as a fixed bundle of tasks, along with an emphasis on constantly changing work required to fulfill the ever-increasing demands of customers.

There are great opportunities for industrial and organizational psychologists to contribute to the betterment of human welfare in the context of these changes. To lead change rather than to follow it, however, will require a break with traditional practices and a focus on rigorous research that addresses emerging trends. This article identified six key areas in which to start: job analysis, employee selection, training and development, performance appraisal, compensation (including incentives), and organizational development. These challenges provide an exciting agenda with large potential payoffs for individuals, organizations, and society as psychology moves into the 21st century.

Author's note

Portions of this article were presented as part of a presidential address to the Society for Industrial and Organizational Psychology at its Eighth Annual Convention, San Francisco, May 1993.

References

Alderman, L. (1995, April). What you need to ace today's rough-and-tough job interviews. *Money*, pp. 35, 36, 38.

Arthur D. Little, Inc. (1994, September). *Managing organizational change: How leading organizations are meeting the challenge.* Cambridge, MA: Author.

Barley, S. (1991). *The new crafts: The rise of the technical labor force and its implications for the organization of work.* Philadelphia: National Center on the Educational Quality of the Workforce, University of Pennsylvania.

Barney, J. (1991). Firm resources and sustained competitive advantage. *Journal of Management, 17*, 99–120.

Bass, B. M. (1954). The leaderless group discussion. *Psychological Bulletin, 51*, 465–492.

Bass, B. M. (1985). *Leadership and performance beyond expectations.* New York: Free Press.

Baumohl, B. (1993, March 15). When downsizing becomes "dumbsizing." *Time*, p. 55.
Bernardin, H. J., &. Beatty, R. W. (1984). *Performance appraisal: Assessing human behavior at work*. Boston: Kent.
Borman, W. C. (1974). The rating of individuals in organizations: An alternative approach. *Organizational Behavior and Human Performance, 12*, 105–124.
Bridges, W. (1994, September 19). The end of the job. *Fortune*, pp. 62–64, 68, 72, 74.
Byrne, J. A. (1993, February 8). The virtual corporation. *Business Week*, pp. 98–103.
Byrne, J. A. (1994, May 9). The pain of downsizing *Business Week*, pp. 60–69.
Campbell, D. T., & Fiske, D. W. (1959). Convergent and discriminant validation by the multitrait–multimethod matrix. *Psychological Bulletin, 56*, 81–105.
Cannon-Bowers, J. A., Tannenbaum, S. I., Salas, E., & Volpe, C. E. (1995). Defining competencies and establishing team training requirements. In R. A. Guzzo & E. Salas (Eds.), *Team effectiveness and decision making in organizations* (pp. 333–380). San Francisco: Jossey-Bass.
Cappelli, P. (1992). *Is the "skills gap" really about attitudes?* Philadelphia: National Center on the Educational Quality of the Workforce. (Educational Quality of the Workforce Catalog No. WP01).
Career management services @ Sun. (1994). Milpitas, CA: Author.
Cascio, W. F. (1989). Using utility analysis to assess training outcomes. In I. Goldstein (Ed.), *Training and development in organizations* (pp. 63–88). San Francisco: Jossey-Bass.
Cascio, W. F. (1991). *Applied psychology in personnel management* (4th ed.). Englewood Cliffs, NJ: Prentice Hall.
Cascio, W. F. (1993, February). Downsizing: What do we know? What have we learned? *Academy of Management Executive, 7(1)*, 95–104.
Cascio, W. F. (1994a). *Documenting training effectiveness in terms of worker performance and adaptability* (Educational Quality of the Workforce Catalog No. WP23). Philadelphia: University of Pennsylvania, National Center for the Educational Quality of the Workforce.
Cascio, W. F. (1994b). *Public investments in training: Perspectives on macro-level structural issues and micro-level delivery systems* (Educational Quality of the Workforce Catalog No. WP24). Philadelphia: University of Pennsylvania, National Center for the Educational Quality of the Workforce.
Deming, W. E. (1986). *Out of the crisis*. Cambridge, MA: MIT Center for Advanced Engineering Study.
Dipboye, R. L., & Gaugler, B. B. (1993). Cognitive and behavioral processes in the selection interview. In N. Schmitt & W. C. Borman (Eds.), *Personnel selection in organizations* (pp. 135–170). San Francisco: Jossey-Bass.
Downside to the jobs upturn. (1994, November 14). *Business Week*, p. 26.
Doyle, F. P. (1992, June). Unpublished keynote address, National Academy of Human Resources, Santa Fe, NM.
Drake, Beam, Morin, Inc. (1994). *Career transition study, November 1993 to August 1994*. Washington, DC: Author.
Fein, M. (1982, August). *Improved productivity through worker involvement*. Paper presented at the annual meeting of the Academy of Management, New York.
Fiedler, F. E. (1967). *A theory of leadership effectiveness*. New York: McGraw-Hill.
Filipczak, B. (1995, January). You're on your own: Training, employability, and the new employment contract *Training*, pp. 29–36.

Florkowski, G. W. (1987). The organizational impact of profit sharing. *Academy of Management Review, 12,* 622–636.

Gael, S. (Ed.). (1988). *The job analysis handbook for business, industry, and government.* New York: Wiley.

Gersick, C. J. G. (1989). Marking time: Predictable transitions in task groups. *Academy of Management Journal, 32,* 274–309.

Goldstein, I. L. (Ed.). (1989). *Training and development in work organizations.* San Francisco: Jossey-Bass.

Goldstein, I. L. (1994). *Training in organizations: Needs assessment, development, and evaluation* (4th ed.). Monterey, CA: Brooks/Cole.

Gomez-Mejia, L. R., & Balkin, D. B. (1992). *Compensation, organizational strategy, and firm performance.* Cincinnati, OH: Southwestern.

Guion, R. M. (1991). Personnel assessment, selection, and placement. In M. D. Dunnette & L. M. Hough (Eds.), *Handbook of industrial and organizational psychology* (2nd ed., Vol. 2, pp. 327–397). Palo Alto, CA: Consulting Psychologists Press.

Gwynne, S. C. (1992, September 28). The long haul. *Time,* pp. 34–38.

Hammer, M., & Champy, J. (1993). Reengineering the corporation. New York: *Harper Business,* p. 90.

Hammer, T. H. (1988). New developments in profit sharing, gainsharing, and employee ownership. In J. P. Campbell & R. J. Campbell (Eds.), *Productivity in organizations* (pp. 328–366). San Francisco: Jossey-Bass.

Harvey, R. J. (1991). Job analysis. In M. D. Dunnette & L. M. Hough (Eds.), *Handbook of industrial and organizational psychology* (2nd ed., Vol. 2, pp. 71–163). Palo Alto, CA: Consulting Psychologists Press.

Henkoff, R. (1994, October 3). Finding, training, and keeping the best service workers. *Fortune,* pp. 110–122.

Hogan, R. T. (1991). Personality and personality measurement. In M. D. Dunnette & L. M. Hough (Eds.), *Handbook of industrial and organizational psychology* (2nd ed., Vol. 2, pp. 873–919). Palo Alto, CA: Consulting Psychologists Press.

House, R. J. (1971). A path-goal theory of leader effectiveness. *Administrative Science Quarterly, 16,* 321–339.

Huselid, M. A. (1995). The impact of human resource management practices on turnover, productivity, and corporate financial performance. *Academy of Management Journal, 38,* 635–672.

Ilgen, D. R., & Hollenbeck, J. R. (1991). The structure of work: Job design and roles. In M. D. Dunnette & L. M. Hough (Eds.), *Handbook of industrial and organizational psychology* (2nd ed., Vol. 2, pp. 165–207). Palo Alto, CA: Consulting Psychologists Press.

Investing in people and prosperity. (1994, May). U.S. Department of Labor, Washington, DC, p. 7.

Jobs in an age of insecurity. (1993, November 22). *Time,* p. 35.

Kiechel, W., III. (1993, May 17). How we will work in the year 2000. *Fortune,* pp. 38–52.

Klimoski, R., & Jones, R. G. (1995). Staffing for effective group decision making: Key issues in matching people and teams. In R. A. Guzzo & E. Salas (Eds.), *Team effectiveness and decision making in organizations* (pp. 291–332). San Francisco: Jossey-Bass.

Kraiger, K., Ford, J. K., & Salas, E. (1993). Application of cognitive, skill-based, and affective theories of learning outcomes to new methods of training evaluation. *Journal of Applied Psychology, 78,* 311–328.

Labich, K. (1994, November 14). Why companies fail. *Fortune*, pp. 52–54, 58, 60, 64, 68.
Labor letter. (1991, October 22). *The Wall Street Journal*, p. A1.
Lado, A. A., & Wilson, M. C. (1994). Human resource systems and sustained competitive advantage: A competency-based perspective. *Academy of Management Review, 19*, 699–727.
Mabe, P. A., & West, S. G. (1982). Validity of self-evaluation of ability: A review and meta-analysis. *Journal of Applied Psychology, 67*, 280–296.
Marsh, H. W., & Hocevar, D. (1988). A new, more powerful approach to multitrait–multimethod analyses: Application of second-order confirmatory factor analysis. *Journal of Applied Psychology, 73*, 107–117.
Marx, R. D. (1982). Relapse prevention for managerial training: A model for maintenance of behavior change. *Academy of Management Review, 7*, 435–441.
McCormick, E. J. (1979). *Job analysis: Methods and applications.* New York: AMACOM.
McIntyre, R. M., & Salas, E. (1995). Measuring and managing for team performance: Emerging principles from complex environments. In R. A. Guzzo & E. Salas (Eds.), *Team effectiveness and decision making in organizations* (pp. 9–45). San Francisco: Jossey-Bass.
Mirvis, P. H. (1988). Organization development: Part 1: An evolutionary perspective. In W. A. Passmore & R. W. Woodman (Eds.), *Research in organizational change and development* (Vol. 2). Greenwich, CT: JAI Press.
Motowidlo, S. J., Carter, G. W., Dunnette, M. D., Tippins, N., Werner, S., Burnett, J. R., & Vaughan, M. J. (1992). Studies of the structured behavioral interview. *Journal of Applied Psychology, 77*, 571–587.
Murphy, K. R., & Cleveland, J. N. (1991). *Performance appraisal: An organizational perspective.* Boston: Allyn & Bacon.
Murray, M. (1995, May 4). Thanks, goodbye: Amid record profits, companies continue to lay off employees. *The Wall Street Journal*, pp. A1, A5.
Nelan, B. W. (1992, Fall). How the world will look in 50 years (Special issue: Beyond the Year 2000), *Time*, pp. 36–38.
1994 AMA survey on downsizing and assistance to displaced workers. New York: American Management Association.
Norman, C. A., & Zawacki, R. A. (1991, September). Team appraisals—team approach. *Personnel Journal*, pp. 101–104.
Ones, D. S., Mount, M. K., Barrick, M. R., & Hunter, J. E. (1994). Personality and job performance: A critique of the Tett, Jackson, and Rothstein (1991) meta-analysis. *Personnel Psychology, 47*, 147–156.
Ost, E. J. (1995). Team-based pay: New wave strategic initiatives. In J. B. Miner & D. P. Crane (Eds.), *Advances in the practice, theory, and research of strategic human resource management* (pp. 353–366). New York: Harper Collins.
Pffefer, J. (1994). *Competitive advantage through people.* Boston: Harvard Business School Press, p. 8.
Pilon, L. J. (1993, February 22). Quoted in "Jobs, Jobs." *Business Week*, p. 74.
Porras, J. I., & Robertson, P. J. (1992). Organizational development: Theory, practice, and research. In M. D. Dunnette & L. M. Hough (Eds.), *Handbook of industrial and organizational psychology* (2nd ed., Vol. 3, pp. 719–822). Palo Alto, CA: Consulting Psychologists Press.
Ree, M. J., & Earles, J. A. (1991). Predicting training success: Not much more than g. *Personnel Psychology, 44*, 321–332.

Ree, M. J., & Earles, J. A. (1992). Intelligence is the best predictor of job performance. *Current Directions in Psychological Science, 1*, 86–89.

Ree, M. J., Earles, J. A., & Teachout, M. S. (1994). Predicting job performance: Not much more than g. *Journal of Applied Psychology, 79*, 518–524.

Salwen, K. G. (1993, April 19). The cutting edge: German-owned maker of power tools finds job training pays off. *The Wall Street Journal*, pp. A1, A7.

Schmitt, N., & Borman, W. C. (Eds.). (1993). *Personnel selection in organizations.* San Francisco: Jossey-Bass.

Skill-based pay boosts worker productivity and morale. (1992, April 18). *The Wall Street Journal*, p. A1.

Smither, J. W., London, M., Vasilopoulos, N. L., Reilly, R. R., Millsap, R. E., & Salvemini, N. (1995). An examination of the effects of an upward feedback program over time. *Personnel Psychology, 48*, 1–34.

Tett, R. P., Jackson, D. N., Rothstein, M., & Reddon, J. R. (1994). Meta-analysis of personality–job performance relations: A reply to Ones, Mount, Barrick, & Hunter (1994). *Personnel Psychology, 47*, 157–172.

The horizontal corporation. (1993, December 20). *Business Week*, pp. 77–81.

Tichy, N. (1994, May). The future of workplace learning and performance. *Training and Development*, p. S46.

Tornow, W. W. (1993). Perceptions or reality: Is multi-perspective measurement a means or an end? *Human Resource Management, 32*, 221–230.

Tosi, H., & Tosi, L. (1987). What managers need to know about knowledge-based pay. In D. A. Balkin & L. R. Gomez-Mejia (Eds.), *New perspectives on compensation* (pp. 43–48). Englewood Cliffs, NJ: Prentice Hall.

U.S. Department of Labor. (1993, August). *High performance work practices and firm performance.* Washington, DC: U.S. Government Printing Office.

Van Maanen, J. (Ed.). (1979). Qualitative methodology [Special issue]. *Administrative Science Quarterly,* 24(4).

Vroom, V. H., & Yetton, P. W. (1973). *Leadership and decision making.* Pittsburgh, PA: University of Pittsburgh Press.

Waterman, R. H., Jr., Waterman, J. A., & Collard, B. A. (1994, July–August). Toward a career-resilient workforce. *Harvard Business Review*, pp. 87–95.

Weekley, J. A., & Gier, J. A. (1987). Reliability and validity of the situational interview for a sales position. *Journal of Applied Psychology, 72*, 484–487.

Wellins, R. S., Byham, W. C., & Wilson, J. M. (1991). *Empowered teams: Creating self-directed work groups that improve quality, productivity, and participation.* San Francisco: Jossey-Bass.

Wiedman, T. G. (1993, October). Performance appraisal in a total quality management environment. *The Industrial–Organizational Psychologist, 31(2),* pp. 64–66.

Woodman, R. W. (1989). Organizational change and development New arenas for inquiry and action. *Journal of Management, 15*, 205–228.

Workplace of the future: A Report of the Conference on the Future of the American Workplace. (1993). New York: U.S. Departments of Commerce and Labor.

World Competitiveness Report. (1994). Lausanne, Switzerland: World Economic Forum and Institute for Management Development.

INDEX

(Tables and Figures in Italics)

adjustment **I** 22; to full-time work **I** 19; to new job **I** 20; to relocation **I** 18–19
age: and careers **I** 33–5; employee **I** 14; and job-related well-being **I** 395, 418; and motivational traits **II** *110*, 112–14, *113*
agreeableness **II** 39–40, *45*, 45, *46*, 48, *49, 50*, 55, 62–3, 132
anxiety, and job well-being (*see* well-being, job related)
applicant(s): assessment centers **I** 27, **II** 22–3, 143, **IV** 340–1; assessment methods **IV** 339–40 (*See also* personnel selection methods); biodata **I** 52–3, **II** *12, 15*, 22, **IV** 341; preferences **IV** 156–60, 317–18; reactions to technology **IV** 156–63, 165; research on **IV** 164–6, 172; undergraduates as **IV** 165–6. *See also* employee(s)
appraisal theory **II** 83–4
Army General Classification Test (GCT) **II** 119, *120–1*
ASA framework. *See* attraction-selection-attrition (ASA) framework
aspiration **I** 388–9. *See also* well-being, job-related
assessment centers **I** 27, **II** 22–3, 143; explanations for predictive validity of **II** 144–51; future research on **II** 153–4; managerial use of **II** 152–3; validity of **II** *12*, 23, 142–3
AT&T **II** 81, 152, 455, 458
attitude **I** 341; -behavior relationship **I** 240–1. *See also* job attitudes; job performance; work experience: attitudes and
attitudinal commitment: affective attachment component of **I** 286–8; obligation (normative) component of **I** 287–9, 300; perceived costs (continuance) component of **I** 287–9; research on antecedents of components of **I** 293–301, *296–7*, 302–3; research on measuring components of **I** 289–93, *291–2*, 299–301
attraction-selection-attrition (ASA) framework **I** 51–6, *56*, 95; implications of **I** 56–60. *See also* person-organization (P-O) fit
attribution: processes, cultural differences in **IV** 16–17; theory **II** 231–2
attrition **I** 53

Beck Depression Inventory (BDI) **I** 398
behavioral competency **II** 296–8, 300, 304; validity issues **II** 300–2
behavioral-modeling training **II** 336, *370*, 382, 386–7
behavior constraints: external-distal **IV** 12–13; internal-proximal **IV** 11–12; taxonomy **IV** 12
behaviorism **II** 68
behavior theory **I** 49–51
beliefs: internal-proximal constraints and **IV** 11–12; locus-of-control **IV** 12
benchmarking **II** 454–5
benefits. *See* job benefits
Big Five model of personality factors: cultural differences in **IV** 17; development of **II** 36–7; interpretations

INDEX

of **II** 37–8, 130–1; and job performance (*see* personality traits and job performance: meta-analysis of validity studies of Big Five); vs. motivational traits **II** 105; traits included in (*see* agreeableness; conscientiousness; emotional stability; extraversion; openness to experience)
biodata predictions **I** 52–3, **II** *12, 15*, 22, **IV** 341

call centers: customer-employee interaction in **IV** *181*, 181–2; definition **IV** 179; employee reactions to **IV** 178–9; history **IV** 178; human resource management in **IV** 185, 187–9; job design in **IV** 184–5; models **IV** *186*; performance **IV** 193–4; performance monitoring in **IV** 182; stress in **IV** 189–92, 195–6; technology in **IV** 178–80
career(s): boundaryless **I** 14, 145, 148; changes **I** 15; concepts of **I** 12–13, 23; counseling **I** 28–9; decision processes and **I** 30–1; development **I** 27–8, 32–3, 164–5; employment (*see* long-term employment); interventions **I** 23–9; management **I** 23–4, 27–8; personality and **I** 29–30; Protean **I** 14; -related literature reviews **I** 11; study of **I** 13
Career Commitment Measure (CCM) **I** 23
Career Transitions Inventory **I** 17
cashier(s): control strategies used by **I** 323–7, *324*; -co-worker relationship **I** *314*, 315; customer view of service from **I** 320–2; -customer relationship **I** 308–12, *314*, 315–20, 327; -management relationship **I** *314*, 314–15; view of customer encounters **I** 322–3
change, resistance to: group standards and **III** 356; theories of **III** 342–7; transfer learning curve and **III** 340, *341*, 342
China: career management in **IV** 80–1; compensation strategies in **IV** 80; competency components in **IV** 85; E-commerce in **IV** 75 (*See also* E-commerce); economic reform in **IV** 74–6, 80, 87; human resource competency in **IV** 80–3; leadership competency in **IV** 75–9; motivational strategies in **IV** 80, *81*; organizational commitment in **IV** 80; organizational competency in **IV** 83–4, 86; organizational psychology in **IV** 74, 87; risk perception in **IV** 76; technological innovation in **IV** 75; workplace assessment in **IV** 76–8; work teams in **IV** 75, 83
Chinese Personality Assessment Inventory 79
cognitive ability. *See* general mental ability
cognitive consistency theories **II** 234
commensurate measurement **I** 98–9
commitment: career **I** 23; organizational (*see* organizational commitment)
communication: changes in **IV** 262; I/O psychologists and **IV** 271–2
company(ies): boards (*see* corporate board(s)); characteristics **IV** *62*, 168, 435–6; compensation strategies in **IV** 80; competitiveness of **IV** 267–8; cross-organizational studies in **IV** 42–3; demographics **IV** 66; development (*see* organizational development); ethics in **IV** 84; founder's values and **IV** 66; information processing in **IV** 231–2; innovation in **IV** 153, 168 (*see also* technology); inventory shrinkage **III**, 368, *368–9*; job boards **IV** 120; leadership competencies in **IV** 75–9; learning (see organizational learning); management **IV** *62*, 63–4, 436 (*See also* management); mergers and acquisition **III** 205–6; motivational strategies in **IV** 80, *81*; multinational **IV** 42; organization **IV** 51, *56, 62*; orientation **IV** *56*; practices by **IV** 59–60, *67*; web sites **IV** 119–20, 124, 157; within-firm memory **IV** 233–4. *See also* organizational culture
competency **I** 388, **II** 295–6; approach, future research **II** 307; behavioral **II** 296–8, 300–2, 304; core **II** 296, 302–4; HRM and **II** *299*, 303–7; management **II** 296–7. *See also* job performance; personnel assessment; well-being, job-related
complementary fit **I** 93, *94*, 95, 99
concreteness **IV** 125
Confucian work dynamism **IV** 25, 42
congruence: goal **I** 95, 104, 113–15, 122; value **I** 95, 99, 104, 106, 109–11, 113–15
conscientiousness: future research on **II** 53; as job performance predictor **II**

458

39–40, *45*, 45, *47*, 48, *49, 51*, 52–3, 55–6, 59, 61–3, 131–2, 289; tests **II** *12, 15*, 17–18, 27–8
consensus estimates **I** 102
consistency estimates **I** 102
constraints on behavior: external-distal **IV** 12–13; internal-proximal **IV** 11–12; taxonomy **IV** 12
contextual performance **II** 254–6, **IV** 320
contractual employment. *See* employment, nonstandard
control, perceived **I** 413; in workplace **I** 414–16
corporate culture. *See* organizational culture
corporate board(s): characteristics **III** 165–6; cohesiveness **III** 172–3, *177*; conflict **III** 168–9, *177*; demography **III** 174–7; dynamics **III** 177–80; effectiveness **III** 166–7, *174*; effort norms in **III** 167–8, *177*; knowledge and skill level **III** 170–2, *177*; models **III** 164–7, 180; processes **III** 167–74, *174, 177*; size **III** 176–7; tenure **III** 177; variation by corporation type **III** 178–80
corporations. *See* company(ies)
counterproductive behaviors (CWBs): causes **III** 364; classification **III** 360–3, 391; deceit **III** 384–6, *386*; espionage **III** 386–9, *390*, 390–1; fraud **III** 377–8, *379*, 380–2, *383*; individual difference factors in **III** 366–7; inventory shrinkage and **III** 368, *368, 369*; models **III** *364–5*; resignations **III** 406–7; sabotage **III** 399–406; theft **III** 366–72, *372*, 372–7; typology **III** *363*; whistle-blowing and **III** 375, 391–5, *395–6*, 396–9
crew resource management (CRM) training **II** 336–7
cross cultural psychology: approaches to **IV** 8–9; Asian cultures and **IV** 9; attribution processes and **IV** 16–17; competency models **IV** 84–6; coping behavior and **IV** 78–9; decision-making and **IV** 22; equivalence of measurement in **IV** 10; emotion and **IV** 15–16; ethnic identity and **IV** 14–15; group processes and **IV** 19–23; history **IV** 9; internal-proximal constraints in **IV** 11–12; interpersonal attraction and **IV** 18; justice and **IV** 18–19; leadership and **IV** 20–1; meta-analysis and **IV** 321–2; methodology **IV** 26–7; negotiation **IV** 22–3; organizational behavior and **IV** 23–6, *82*; self-esteem and **IV** 15; work motivation and **IV** 23–4; work patterns and **IV** 78–9
cultural competence **IV** 85
cultural constructs, measurements of **IV** 12
culture: collectivism and **IV** 13, 19; definition, **IV** 10–11; individualistic **IV** 18; interpersonal attraction and **IV** 18; language in **IV** 17–18; leadership differences and **III** 11; models of, **IV** 13, 17; national **IV** 41–2, *67*; occupation and **IV** *67*; organizational (*see* organizational culture)
customer: -employee interactions **I** 308–12, *314*, 315–20, 327, **IV** *181*, 181–2, 190–1; service **I** 320–2, **IV** 162, 178, 180, 184, 191–2, 196, 201–2, 238, 336, 415, 436–7

Deci effect **II** 78–9
demands-control model: components **III** 262; conjunctive moderator effects and **III** 283–93; cross-sectional research and **III** 265–6; history **III** 263–5; longitudinal research and **III** 266–7; methods in **III** 273–7; tests of **III** 269–72, 278, 283, 298;
demands-decision latitude model **III** 278
depression, and job well-being (*see* well-being, job-related)
development: center **I** 27; on-the-job **I** 27–8
Development Challenge Profile **I** 28
difference scores **I** 104–6
distance learning systems **II** 334–5, 341
distributive justice **I** 431–7, 441–3, 446, 449, 451, **II** 86, 161–3, *165*, 165; combining procedural and **II** 163–4, 185–6; future research issues **II** 192–3; rules and fairness perceptions **II** *165*, 179–85, 187–90
dominant paradigm: bimodal prediction **IV** 315–6; cultural assumptions of **IV** 303–5; framework for **IV** 311–3; maladaptations **IV** 309; validation cycles in **IV** 316–7. *See also* personnel and selection psychology
downsizing **I** 16, 91, 121, 137–8, 140, 144–5, 148, 150, 405–6, 408–9, **IV** 259–60, 299–300

459

INDEX

E-commerce **IV** 75, 88, 97
economy, competition in **IV** 433–4
education: as hiring predictor **II** *12*, 23; and job-related learning **II** *15*, 23
elaboration likelihood model **IV** 126–43
emotional contagion **I** 372–3
emotional stability **II** 39–40, *45*, 45, *46, 49–50*, 55, 62, 131
emotions: cultural differences in **IV** 15–16; and group dynamics **I** 371–4; and motivation **I** 369–70; normalizing **I** 367–8; and organizations **I** 359, 361–4, *363*, 367–8 (*See also* emotions: regulation of workplace); perspectives on **I** 360–1; and rationality **I** 359, 361–5, *363*, 368; regulation of workplace **I** 364–8, 377; research on workplace **I** 359, 365, 375–7; symbolic management and **I** 370–1; and transformational leadership **I** 374–5. *See also* emotional stability
employee(s): age of **I** 14, **II** 263; absenteeism **III** 3, 73–4, 76, 98, 144, 234, 241, *242, 250*, 251, 268, 277, 299, 338, 343, 360, *365*, **IV** 61, *62*, 65, 76, 83, 220, 445; academic achievement and **IV** 333; alternative work environments and **IV** 209–14, 265; assessment (*see* personnel assessment); attitudes towards older workers **IV** 257; attraction **IV** 93; career management **IV** 302–3; compensation and incentives **IV** 74, 80, 222, 224–5, 230–1, 421, 439–40, 447–9, 451; conscientiousness **IV** 335; counterproductive behaviors (*see* counterproductive behaviors); -customer interactions **I** 308–12, *314*, 315–323, 327, **IV** *181*, 181–2, 190–1; empowerment of **IV** 437–8; gender of **I** 14; growth need strength and **III** 234, *235*, 238–9, 247, 249, *250*, 253–5; group standards and **III** 356–8; hiring selection (*see* personnel assessment); internet based information use by **IV** 126–7; interrelationships **IV** 226–8; job knowledge (*see* job knowledge); job performance (*see* job performance); language proficiency **IV** 333; and management (*see* management); motivation (*see* motivation); non-work support for **IV** 237–8; products and services **IV** 265; recruitment (*see* recruitment); resignation **III** 406–7; retirement **I** 20, **IV** 258; rewards **III** 226, 339, **IV** 222–6; self-evaluation **II** 260–1, *358*, 415–16, **IV** 336–7; selection (*see* personnel selection); service (*see* service employees); stress **IV** 189–92, 195–6; technology and **IV** 434–5 (*See also* technology); training (*see* training); transition **III** 227, **IV** 236; turnover **III** 60–1, 73–4, 98, 167, 338, 358, 343–4, *344*, 345, 351, 358–9, 368, 398, 407–8, **IV** 76, 124, 127–9, 188, 194, 220, 227, 229, 233–4, 416, 420, 437, 445, 448 (*see also* organizational commitment); utility assessment of **II** 265–8; well-being (*see* well-being, job-related); whistle-blowing **III** 375, 391–5, *395–6*, 396–9; work roles and **IV** 297–9. *See also* work force
Employee Reliability **II** 56
employment interviews **II** *12, 15*, 18, 29
employment, nonstandard **I** 138–9; rates **I** 143–4
epistemology **IV** 365–72, 379–80
equity **II** 180–2, 193; theory **I** 189, **II** 86, 160–1. *See also* distributive justice
ethnic identity **IV** 14–15
expectancy **II** 72, 390–1
expectations, met **I** 20–1
experience curves **II** 458
extraversion **II** 39–40, *45*, 45, *46, 49–50*, 53–6, 59, 61–2, 132

fairness heuristic theory **I** 442–5
fairness perceptions: distributive justice and (*see* distributive justice: rules and fairness perceptions); outcomes of **II** 186–92, 231; of personnel selection methods **II** 164–6, *165, 167*; procedural justice and (*see* procedural justice: rules and fairness perceptions)
fairness theory **I** 443–5, 455–6
Fifth Discipline, The (Senge) **II** 444–5
Five-Factor Model (FFM) of personality. *See* Big Five model of personality factors
frame of reference (FOR) training **II** 264–5

GATB. *See* General Aptitude Test Battery
GCT. *See* Army General Classification Test

gender: and job performance **II** 263, 311–13; self-concept **IV** 14; stereotypes and management, research on **II** 313–19, *315, 316, 317*
General Aptitude Test Battery (GATB) **II** 119, 123, 125, **IV** 322
General Health Questionnaire **I** 397
general mental ability (GMA) **II** 118; as hiring selector **II** 8, *12–13*, 14, 16–18, 27–9, **IV** 332; Internet and **IV** 158, 162, 166; and job performance **II** 122–4, *124, 125, 128*, 128–9, 131–5, *134*, 289, **IV** 332; and job-related learning **II** 14, *15*, 16, 27, *124*–5, 125–7, *127*, 289, 328–9, **IV** 332; and occupational level **II** 119, *120–1*, 121–2
globalism **IV** *296*, 296–7
GMA. *See* general mental ability
goal(s): ability and **II** 80; and affect **II** 84–6, *85*; commitment and **II** 77–9; congruence **I** 95, 104, 113–15, 122; feedback and **II** 76, 82; and motivation **II** 70–6, *71, 72*; orientation **II** 330; rewards and **II** 77–9, *78*, 82; self-efficacy and (*see* self-efficacy); setting **II** 73–4, 79–81, 426–8, *430*; task complexity and **II** 80–1; task strategies and **II** 75–6
graphology **II** 24–5
group(s): demographic composition of **I** 97; dynamics (*see* group dynamics/processes); mergers and acquisitions **III** 205; subgroup structure **III** 202–3; sociodemographic **III** 203–5
group dynamics/processes **IV** 19–23; ability in **III** 144–7; aggressiveness **III** 134–7, *135, 137–8*; change and **III** 128–9, 142–3, *143–4*, 144, 149–58; conduct and **III** 151–2; in corporate boards **III** 177–80; decision-making **III** 153–4, *154–5*, 155, **IV** 22, 82; force-fields in **III** 149, *152*, 164; leadership and **IV** 20–1; negotiation **IV** 22–3; objectivity in **III** 148; phase spaces and **III** 129; scapegoating **III** 138–40; social fields and **III** 128; standards and **III** 150–1; subjectivity in **III** 148
GTE **II** 459

half-life curve **II** *459*, 459–61
happy/productive worker **I** 201–3, *202*

hierarchical storage **II** 411
human resource management: call centers and **IV** 185, 187–9; high-commitment/high-performance **IV** 419–22, 425; influence **IV** 307–8; policies **IV** 412–3; requirements **IV** 438
human rights: individual views on **IV** 19; resource allocation and **IV** 19

industrial/organizational (I/O) psychologists: decision-making by **IV** 287; diversity **IV** 272; internet skills of **IV** 285; training **IV** 270–3
industrial/organizational (I/O) psychology: associations in **IV** 417; conflicts within **IV** 400–1; fragmentation **IV** *395*, 403, 427; interactions among **IV** *396*, 396–7, *397*, 402–3; journals **IV** 392, *393*; political dimensions in **IV** 422–5; positivism **IV** 368–70; postmodernism **IV** 372–3; practitioners **IV** 387–90, *393*, 399–400; relevance in **IV** 391–2; researchers **IV** 387–90, 398–9; situationist perspective **I** 51
industrial, work and organizational psychology. *See* industrial/organizational (I/O) psychology
information technology: as change agent **IV** 296–7. *See also* Internet; technology
innovation, definition of **IV** 153. *See also* technology
instrumental model of justice judgement process **I** 440–1
integrity tests **II** *12, 15*, 17, 29, 132–3
intelligence tests **II** 150–1
interactional justice **I** 431–7, 446–8, **II** 162
interactional psychology **I** 49–50
Internet: acceptance **IV** 286–7; access **IV** 107–9, *109–10*, 111, 162; assessment **IV** 104, 105–12; computer-based assessment and **IV** 94–5; employee recruitment by **IV** 93, 98–103; employee selection **IV** 103–5; growth **IV** 95, *96*, 97–8; inequality of access to **IV** 97–8; I/O psychology and **IV** 283; job advertisement **IV** 100, *101*; job interview **IV** 103–4, 159–60; job simulations **IV** 159; objective testing **IV** 105; privacy concerns and **IV** 285–6; recruitment **IV** 118–29, 161, 287–9; references check **IV** 104; relationship

INDEX

recruiting **IV** 121; second generation users **IV** 111; security **IV** 106–7; testing (*see* Internet-based testing); training (*see* distance learning systems); use **IV** 282–4

Internet-based testing: advantages **IV** 129; applicant perceptions of **IV** 135–6, 158–9; approaches to **IV** 130–3; equivalence in **IV** 160; measurement equivalence and **IV** 133–5, 137; psychological theories and **IV** 139–42

interpersonal behavior **IV** 17–18

item response theory **IV** 10, 93, 130, 332

job analysis **IV** 439–40

job attitudes: changing **I** 203–4; consistency of **I** 204–6; dispositional sources of **I** 205–6, 225, 346; -job performance relationship future research **I** 243–9, *245*; -job performance relationship meta-analyses **I** 227–43, *235, 236, 238, 251–62*; -job performance relationship models **I** 217–27, *218*, 230, 240–1, 243–4, *243, 245*; organizational change and **I** 208–13; past research on job performance and **I** 216–17. *See also* job performance; work attitudes; work experience: attitudes and

job benefits **I** 146, 149, 151, **IV** 230, 421, 448–9. *See also* employee(s): compensation and incentives

job changes **I** 15–18, 150; and learning **I** 21–2. *See also* job loss; job rotation

job characteristics theory **II** 86

job experience: and job performance **II** *12, 15*, 21, 23, 27–8; predictive validity of **II** *128*, 129–30, *130*

job demands-job control model **I** 414–15

job insecurity, perceived: and job well-being **I** 406–8; reasons for **I** 405–6. *See* also job security

job knowledge **II** *134*, 134–5; ability and **IV** 332–3; tests **II** *12*, 18–19. *See also* job-related learning

job loss **I** 148, 186; age related **I** 141, 151; and earnings loss **I** 145, 151, 153; rates **I** 138, 141–2, 148–9

job performance: age and **II** 263; change **III** *146*, **IV** 331–2; compensation and **IV** 447–9; consistency of **I** 206–7; definition of **II** 252–5, 280, **IV** 330–1 (*See also* job performance: models of); demographics and **III** 163; dimensions, antecedents of **II** 287–8; encouragement **IV** 213; evaluation **II** 9, 255–65, 278–9, 289–90; evaluation training **II** 264–5; facilitation **IV** 212–3; gender and **II** 263, 311–13; GMA and **II** 122–4, *124, 125, 128*, 128–9, 131–5, *134*; goals and (*see* goal(s)); GPA and **IV** 333; -job attitudes relationship future research **I** 243–9, *245*; -job attitudes relationship meta-analyses **I** 227–43, *235, 236, 238, 251–62*; -job attitudes relationship models **I** 217–27, *218*, 230, 240–1, 243–4, *243, 245*; job difficulty and **III** 354; measurement of **II** 9, 255–65, 278–9, 287–8; models of **II** *279*, 279–87; organizational change and **I** 208–13; past research on job satisfaction and **I** 216–17; personality and (*see* personality traits and job performance); predictors, validity of **II** 11, *12–13*, 14, 16–25, 36, 39–45, *45, 46–7*, 48, *49–51*, 52–6, 60–6, 123–6, *124, 125, 128*, 128–9; race and **II** 261–3, **IV** 333–4; and specific aptitudes **II** 126; strain avoidance and **III** 354–5; and VAM model **I** 351–2. *See also* job attitudes; job-related learning

job quality: and low-wage workers **I** 153; measures of **I** 143–4

job-related learning: GMA and (*see* general mental ability: and job-related learning); predictors, validity of **II** 14, *15*, 16–18, 21–5, *124, 125*, 125–6, 132; specific aptitudes and **II** 126–7, *127*. *See also* job performance

job rotation **I** 27–8

job satisfaction/dissatisfaction: factors influencing **I** 113, 349, 446, 448, **II** 84–9, *85* (*See also* person-organization (P-O) fit); mood and **I** 349; responses to **II** 90–1; value congruence and **I** 113. *See also* job attitudes; organizational commitment

job security **I** 137–8, 141–3, 149, 187, 406. *See also* job insecurity, perceived; job loss

job tryout **II** *12*, 19–20

justice: cultural differences and **IV** 18–19; distributive (*see* distributive justice); interactional **I** 431–7, 446–8, **II** 162;

judgement process **I** *440*, 440–5; judgement process effects **I** 445–52; organizational (*see* organizational justice); procedural (*see* procedural justice); types of, distinctions between **I** 431–7, *438–9*

Kalecki effect **I** 145
Kirkpatrick's model of training evaluation **II** 338, 352–3, 406; relationships between levels in **II** 353–60, *355, 357, 358, 359*
knowledge: declarative **II** 409–11, *430*; organization **II** *430*; procedural **II** 409, 411; production/operating stages of **II** *453*; strategic **II** 409; tacit **II** 409; verbal **II** 409–10, *430*

labor market, factors affecting **I** 144–6
layoff. *See* job loss
leader–follower relations **III** 9–10, 31, 44
leadership: achievement competence and **IV** 85; characteristics **III**, 8, **IV** 78–9; charismatic **III** 29; competence **IV** 75–9; cultural competence and **IV** 85; cultural differences in **III**, 11, 19, **IV** 20–1; decision competence and **IV** 85; development **IV** 84–6, 268–9; effectiveness **III** 29–30; emergence **III** 30; group level processes in **III** 34–7, *37*; groupthink and **III** 200; managerial skills and **IV** 78; minority **III**, 200; models **III** 11–12, 15–16, 31–2, *32*, 34, 38, 197–8, **IV** 78–9; power in **III** 200–2; predisposition for **IV** 78; professional knowledge and **IV** 79; prototypical **III**, 200; psychological traits and **IV** 78; reinforcement by **III** 12; risk perception by **IV** 76; "romance of" (*see* romance of leadership); situational adaptability by **IV** 76; as social construction **III** 28; team competence and **IV** 85; top management teams (TMT) and **III** 163–5, 171; transactional (*see* transactional leadership); transformational (*see* transformational leadership)
learning curves **II** 458
learning organizations **II** 444–5, 461–2; definition of **II** 445–7, *446*; experimentation and **II** 448, *449*, 450–2; measuring learning and **II** 458–60

(*See also* learning outcomes); outside perspective and **II** 454–5; past experience and **II** 452–4; and stages of knowledge **II** *453*; systematic problem solving and **II** 447–8; transfer of knowledge and **II** 456–8
learning outcomes **II** 407–8, *408*; affective **II** *408*, 421–8, *430*; classification for training evaluation **II** 429, *430–1*, 432–5; cognitive **II** *408*, 408–16, *430*; skill-based **II** *408*, 416–21, *430–1*. *See also* training effectiveness models; training evaluation; training transfer
lifespan development **I** 32–5
locus of control **I** 456, *458*, 459, **II** 72, 88, 368, *374, 377*, 389, 390, **IV** 12
long-term employment **I** 140–3
low-wage workers, problems faced by **I** 153
loyalty, employee. *See* organizational commitment

management: career **IV** 302–3; of change **IV** 261–2, 235–236; communication and **IV** 262; control practices **IV** 192; gender **II** 311–13, 318–19; performance **IV** 211; pressure **III** 355–6; project **IV** 210, 400; resistance to **IV** 192–3, *193*; self- **IV** 229–31; training **IV** 206–9
manager(s): changing role of **IV** 436–7; competency **IV** 86–8; cross cultural training **IV** 84–5; motivation of **IV** 80. *See also* management
managerialism **III** 412, 427, 430–32
manufacturing: characteristics **IV** 414–5; lean **IV** 413–4
Maslow's need hierarchy theory **II** 82–3
mastery orientation **II** 424–5, *431*
mathematical economics **III** 158
mental health, job-related (*see* well-being, job-related)
mental model **II** 411–13, *430*
mentoring **I** 25–6
metacognition **II** 413–15, *430*
MMPI **II** 56, **IV** 322
motivation: behaviorist approach to **II** 68–9, *431*; conscious approach to **II** 69; and emotions **I** 369–70; and goals **II** 70–3, *71–2*, 74–6, 79–80; self-efficacy and (*see* self-efficacy); rewards and **IV** 222–5; subconscious approach to **II** 69;

work (*see* work motivation). *See also* motivational traits; personality
motivational traits: and age **II** *110*, 112–14, *113*; vs. approach/avoidance motivational orientations **II** 105–6 (*See also* Motivational Traits Questionnaire); vs. Five-Factor Model of personality **II** 105; and gender **II** *110*, 112–14, *113*; and intelligence **II** 111–14; and personality traits **II** *110*, 111, 113–14; and training **II** 368–9, 424–8, *431*. *See also* motivation
Motivational Traits Questionnaire (MTQ) **II** 107–14, *113*
Multidimensional Personality Questionnaire (MPQ) **II** 109–11
multidimensional scaling (MDS) **IV** 241, *242–3*
multifactor leadership questionnaire (MLQ) **III** 8–9, 13, 15–19
multivariate analysis **IV** 52

National Longitudinal Survey **I** 205
need-press theory **I** 95
need(s): distributive justice and **II** 183–4; theories **II** 82–3, 161
negotiation: intracultural **IV** 23; intercultural **IV** 23

openness to experience: future research on **II** 54–5; as job performance predictor **II** 39–40, *45, 47*, 48, *49, 51*, 54, 56, 59, 61, 63, 131
organization(s): changing structure of **IV** 263–4; definition **III** 188; responsibility of **III** 228; transition in **III** 227
organizational behavior **I** 60–1; attraction-selection-attrition (ASA) framework for **I** 51–6, *56*; employee interrelationships and **IV** 226–8; goal setting and **IV** 229–31; learning and **IV** 232; network formation **IV** 234–5; organizational change and **IV** 219–20; research in **IV** 220, *240*. *See also* organizational culture
organizational change: combined system of **I** 212–13; continuous **III** *315*, 323–30; episodic **III** *315*, 316–23; forms of **III** 311; group-oriented system of **I** 209–10; individually-oriented system of **I** 208–9; internationalization and **IV** 260–1;

intervention theory in **III** 328; organizationally-oriented system of **I** 210–11; organizational structure and **IV** 263–4; personal restructuring and **IV** 319–20; reasons for **III IV** 259–61, 312; resistance to (*see* change, resistance to); sociotechnical design and **III** 227; theories of **III** 314; work teams and 74–8
organizational citizenship behavior (OCB) **II** 191, 281
organizational climate: comparative research in **III** 429–10; comparison with organizational culture **III** *419*, 421–22, 432–8; literature **III** 413–16, *417*; methodology and epistemology in **III** 422, *423*, 424–6; social construction and **III** *427*, 427–8, **IV** 221, 371–2, 425; theories of **III** 418–21, 426–7. *See also* organizational culture
organizational commitment **I** 22–3, 150–1, **II** 89: attitudinal (*see* attitudinal commitment); consequences of **I** 301–2; and VAM model **I** 352–3. *See also* long-term employment
Organizational Commitment Questionaire (OCQ) **I** 287, 290, *292*, 292–3, 301, 303
organizational culture **IV** 25–6: authority and **IV** *55;*changes in (*See also* organizational change); comparison with organizational culture **III** *419*, 421–2, 432–8; company characteristics and **IV** 56; comparative research in **III** 429–30; corporate competency and **IV** 83–6; definition **IV** 39–40; determinants **IV** 60–5; diversity and **IV** 272; ecological analyses of **IV** 51–3; employee security **IV** 55; heroes **IV** 44, *45*; history of study of **III** 411–13; innovation and **IV** 152; interdisciplinarity and **IV** 272–3; literature **III** 413–6, *417* **IV** 40; methodology and epistemology in **III** 422, *423*, 424–6, **IV** 43–4, 51–2; models for **IV** 67–8; rituals **IV** 44, *45*; social construction and **III** *425*, 425–6, **IV** 221, 371–2, 425; symbols **IV** 44, *45*; theories of **III** 418–21, 426–7; values **IV** 44, *45*, 49, 59–60, 65–6, *67*, 83–4; virtual workplaces and **IV** 203–4; within-firm memory and **IV** 233–4; work centrality in **IV** 55. *See also*

464

organizational behavior; organizational climate
organizational development (OD) **III**, 312, 318, 323, **IV** 86, 220, 235, 261, 267, 443–5, 449–50
organizational goals **I** 54–5
organizational justice: effects, boundary conditions of **I** 452–60, *458*; judgement process (*see* organizational justice judgement process); and leadership **I** 460–1; and motivation **I** 463–4; and organizational climate **I** 461–2; theory **II** *167*; types of **I** 431–7, *438–9*
organizational justice judgement process: effects **I** 445–52; models/theory **I** *440*, 440–5, **II** 160–1. *See also* distributive justice; interactional justice; personnel assessment; procedural justice
organizational learning **II** 445, *446*, **IV** 234–5. *See also* learning organizations
organizational psychology **I** 2–4; in China **IV** 74, 87; history of **IV** 1, 74; internet use and **IV** 2; research in **IV** 220–2. *See also* industrial/organizational (I/O) psychology; organizational behavior; organizational climate; organizational culture
organizational socialization **I** 21, 85–6: of police **I** 73–85
organizational spontaneity **II** 281

particularism **IV** 125
part-time employment. *See* employment, nonstandard
peer ratings **II** *12, 15*, 19, 20, 256, 260–1
P-E fit. *See* person-group (P-G) fit; person-job (P-J) fit; person-organization (P-O) fit; person-vocation (P-V) fit
performance: group **III** 61, 140, *141–2*, 142; management **IV** 211, 228–9, 289–90, 445–7; monitoring **IV** 183–4, 190; motivation and group **III** 62; organizational **IV** 228–9; organizational change and **IV** 262–5; orientation **II** 424–5, *431*; team **IV** 212
personality: assessment **IV** 318; Big Five factors of (*see* Big Five model of personality factors); and careers **I** 29–30; 5-factor model of (*see* Big Five model of personality factors); and job performance (*see* personality traits and job performance); and motivational

traits **II** *110*, 111, 113–14; and personnel selection **IV** 334–8; vocational **I** 29, 52–3. *See also* personality traits
Personality and Assessment (Mischel) **I** 49–50
personality traits: Big Five (*see* Big Five model of personality factors); and intelligence **II** 108–9, *110*; and job performance (*see* personality traits and job performance); and motivational traits **II** *110*, 111, 113–14. *See also* personality
personality traits and job performance: mediators of **II** 82, *83*; meta-analysis of validity studies of Big Five **II** 39–45, *45–7*, 48, *49–51*, 52–6, 60–6. *See also* motivational traits
person-culture fit. *See* person-organization (P-O) fit
person-environment (P-E) fit. *See* person-group (P-G) fit; person-job (P-J) fit; person-organization (P-O) fit; person-vocation (P-V) fit
person-group (P-G) fit **I** 96, **IV** 319–20; and person-organization fit **I** 119. *See also* person-job (P-J) fit; person-organization (P-O) fit; person-vocation (P-V) fit
person-job (P-J) fit **I** 97–8, 125, **IV** 75, 302, 315, 319–20. *See also* person-group (P-G) fit; person-organization (P-O) fit; person-vocation (P-V) fit
personnel and selection psychology: changing nature of **IV** *296*; cognitive abilities **IV** 332; cross-cultural perspectives **IV** *312*; national cultures and **IV** 313–14. *See also* personnel selection
personnel assessment **II** 159–60, 249; computer-based **IV** 93–5; globalization and **IV** 111–12; Internet and **IV** 94–5, 104–6; methods, validity of **II** 11, *12–13*, 14, 16–25; performance predictors **II** 8, 39–45, *45, 46–7*, 48, *49–51*, 52–6, 60–6; research on **II** 250–69; selection methods (*see* personnel selection; personnel selection methods); virtual reality technology (VRT) in **IV** 159–60. *See also* assessment centers; training evaluation
personnel selection: cognitive ability and **IV** 332; cross cultural issues in **IV** 347; ethical standards for **IV** 349–50; I/O

465

psychology and **IV** 440–3; job knowledge and **IV** 332; language proficiency and **IV** 333; legal standards for **IV** 348–9; measurement issues in **IV** 342; methods (*see* personnel selection methods); personality and **IV** 334–8; professional standards for **IV** 348; race and ethnicity and **IV** 338; systems for **IV** 343–6; of team members **IV** 346–7; validity generalization and **IV** 343. *See also* personnel and selection psychology

personnel selection methods **IV** 93, 103–5, 155–6; applicants' perceptions of, determinants of **II** *204–18*, 221–7; applicants' perceptions of, future research on **II** 232–4, *235*, 236–7; applicants' perceptions of, outcomes of **II** *204–18*, 227–32, 237–8; applicants' perceptions of, research on **II** 201–3, *204–18*, 219–21, 231–2, **IV** 161 (*See also* fairness perceptions); applicants' reactions to **II** 164–6, *165, 167*, 200–1, 231, **IV** 158 (*See also* distributive justice: rules and fairness perceptions; procedural justice: rules and fairness perceptions); fairness of **II** 164; utility of **II** 8–11

person-organization (P-O) fit **I** 91–2; applications of **I** 119–20, 123–7, **IV** 319–20; actual **I** 100, 103, 120–2; complementary **I** 93, *94*, 95, 99, 117–18, 125, 128; consequences of **I** 126–7; definition of **I** 93–4, *94*, 117–19; future research **I** 118, 121–4; measuring **I** 98–106, 120–1; operationalizations of **I** 94–5; organizational entry and **I** 108–11, 121; perceived **I** 99–100, 118–19, 120–2; and person-group fit **I** 119; and person-vocation fit **I** 119–20; socialization and **I** 111–12, 122, 125–6; studies of **I** 106, *107*, 108–117, 122; supplementary **I** 93–4, *94*, 95, 99, 109, 117–18, 125, 128. *See also* person-group (P-G) fit; person-job (P-J) fit

person-vocation (P-V) fit **I** 96; and person-organization fit **I** 119–20

P-O fit. *See* person-organization (P-O) fit

police recruit socialization **I** 73–85

positivism **IV** 368–72, 380

power: coercive **III** 46–7; expert **III** 51–2; interactions between forms of **III** 53;

legitimate **III** 47–50; referent **III** 50–1; social (*see* social power); tests **II** 410, *430*

procedural justice **I** 431–7, 441–3, 446–9, 451–3, 456, **II** 86, *87*, 161–2, *165*; combining distributive and **II** 163–4, 185–6; future research issues **II** 192–3; rules and fairness perceptions **II** *165*, 166–79, *167*, 187–90

PROFILOR® **II** 283

profit sharing **IV** 230, 421, 448–9. *See also* employee(s): compensation and incentives; job benefits

prosocial organizational behavior (POB) **II** 281

psychological contracts: concept criticisms **I** 180–3, 185, 188–91; concept utility **I** 191–2; definition of **I** 161–2, 181–3, 188, **IV** 224; equity theory and **I** 189; expectations vs. **I** 161–3, 174–5, 181, 188; formation of **IV** 104, 224, *296*, 306, 323, 380 ; future research **I** 176, 188–9; research studies on **I** 162, 165–75, 183–6; social exchange theory and **I** 190; theory advancement of **I** 192–6; violations effects **I** 162–5, 174, **IV** 225, 299–300; violations types **I** *173*

psychology: American dominance in **IV** 9; cross cultural (*see* cross cultural psychology); developmental **IV** 13; ethnocentrism **IV** 9; generalization in **IV** 8; goals **IV** 8; industrial/organizational (*see* industrial/organizational (I/O) psychology)

quasi-stationary equilibrium **III** 43, 120, 127, 129–35, 138, 140, 150, 157, 321, 351–2, *352–3*, 353, 357

race: and cognitive ability tests **IV** 333–4; ethnicity and personnel selection **IV** 338; ethnicity and work force **IV** 256, 333; and job performance **II** 261–3, **IV** 333–4; and vocational behavior **I** 33

rationality: and emotions **I** 359, 361–5, *363*; and organizations **I** 359, 361–4, *363*

recruiters: new technology and **IV** 156–71; personal characteristics **IV** 158; research on **IV** 166–7

recruitment: costs **IV** 128–9; internet **IV** 93, 98–103, 118–29, 287–8; models **IV** *169*, 170; moderator variables in **IV** 171; new technology in **IV** 152–5, 160, 168–75
reference checks **II** *12, 15*, 20–1, **IV** 104
referent cognitions theory (RCT) **I** 441–2, 443
reflexivity **IV** 367
regulation: economic **I** 152–3; social **I** 152
relational model of justice judgement process **I** 440–1, 451
relocation **I** 17–18; international **I** 18–19
requisite task attributes (RTA) index **III** 234
resource exchange theory **IV** 125, 143
retirement **I** 20, **IV** 258
Revised Causal Dimension Scale **IV** 16
romance of leadership: definition **III** 28; models **III** 31–2, *32*; perspective on leadership **III** 28–9

self-categorization: depersonalization in **III** 190; prototype groups in **III** 191, 194; theory **III** 190, 192
self-concept: clarity (SCC) **IV** 13; gender and **IV** 13
self-efficacy **II** 72; increasing **II** 79, 425–6; and learning **II** 329, 425–8, *431*; and performance **II** *72*, 74–5, 76, 77, 81, 147–8, 329, 425; and task interest **II** 78
self-esteem, cultural differences in **IV** 15
self-rating **II** 260–1, *358*, 415–16, **IV** 336–7
service employees **I** 306–7, 327: cashier (*see* cashier(s)); research and management of **I** 327–30 (*See also* cashier(s)); workplace emotions and **I** 365, 366–7
side-bet theory **I** 287–9, 301, 303
simulation/simulators and training **II** 335–6
situational specificity, theory of **II** 123
social cognition: definition **III** 189; self-concept and **IV** 13
social construction **III** *427*, 427–8, **IV** 221, 371–2, 425
social exchange theory and psychological contracts **I** 190
social identity: cohesion in **III**, 194–5; leadership and, 197–202; mergers and acquisition and **III** 205–6; rational demography in **III** 195–7; self-categorization theory and **III** 190, 193–4, 198; self-esteem hypothesis and **III** 192; social attraction hypothesis **III** 194–6; social contexts and **III** 193; theory **III** 189–90, 192, 194, 197, 205; uncertainty reduction hypothesis **III** 192
socialization **I** 22; of cashiers **I** 312–13, *313*; of newcomers **I** 20, 85–6, 111–12 (*See also* organizational socialization: of police); and person-organization fit **I** 111–12, 122, 125–6; organizational (*see* organizational socialization)
social power: definition **III** 42–3; objective elements in **III** 125–7; psychological change and **III** 41; social influence on **III** 41; subjective elements in **III** 125–7. *See also* power
social relationships: domains of **IV** 13; emotion and **IV** 16
social sciences: developmental stages of **III** 120; existence and **III** 120–1, 123–5; legitimacy of **III** 121–2; methodology **III** 123–4
sociotechnical design: boundary location **III** 224; compatibility and **III** 222–3, 228; information flow **III** 225; minimal critical specification **III** 223–4; multifunction principle **III** 226; power and authority **III** 225; support congruence and **III** 226; theory **III** 233; transitional organization in **III** 227; variance control **III** 224–5
specific aptitude theory **II** 126
speed tests **II** 410, *430*
stress. *See* employee(s): stress
stress-based models: and international relocation **I** 18–19; and work-role transitions **I** 17
stress-exposure training (SET) **II** 334
Strong-Campbell Interest Inventory **I** 52
subconscious motivation **II** 69
succession, executive **I** 26
supervisor(s): and performance rating **II** 19–20, 53, 129, *134*, 135, 255–6, 258, 260–3, 266, 268–9; and racial bias **II** 262; subordinates, performance ratings and **II** 185, 258, 261
supplementary fit **I** 93–5, *94*, 99

team(s): composition **I** 97; training **II** 336–7; work (*see* work team(s))

technology: organizational change and **IV** 264, 415, 425, 434–5; in recruitment **IV** 152–6, 172–3; uptake **IV** 155
teleworking **IV** 208–10, 416. *See also* virtual workplace
temporary employment. *See* employment, nonstandard
testing: computerized **IV** 129, 131, 136–7, 142, 157, 160; ethical standards for **IV** 349–50; Internet-based (*see* Internet-based testing); legal standards for **IV** 348–9; professional standards for **IV** 348. *See also* personnel assessment
Theory of Work Adjustment **I** 17, 20, 95
360-degree performance measures **II** 261, **IV** 446–7
training: antecedent conditions and **II** 328; benefits, optimizing **II** 331–2 (*See also* training transfer); costs **II** 323, 363; evaluation of **II** 338–9, 341–2, 352–60; Internet **IV** 290–1; of I/O psychologists **IV** 270–3; I/O psychologists' role in **IV** 443–5; methods **II** 332–7; motivation **II** 330, 424, 427–8; needs analysis **II** 325–8, 331; and organizational change **IV** 262; technology and **II** 334–5, 341; for telework **IV** 209–10; theories **II** 324–5; transfer of (*see* training transfer) **II** 339–40. *See also* job-related learning
training & experience (T & E): behavioral consistency **II** *12*, 19–20; points **II** *12*, 23
training effectiveness models **II** 406–7. *See also* learning outcomes; training evaluation; training transfer
training evaluation **II** 338–9, 341–2, 352–60, 405–7, 426. *See also* learning outcomes; training effectiveness models; training transfer
training transfer **II** 339–40, 363–4; environmental characteristics and, future research on **II** 391–3, 396–7; environmental characteristics and, research on **II** 369, *380–1*, 384–5; generalization aspect **II** 393–4; maintenance aspect **II** 394–6, *395*; process **II** 364–5, *365*; research on **II** 365–9, *370–81*; supervisory support and **II** 391–2; trainee characteristics and, future research on **II** 389–91, 397;

trainee characteristics and, research on **II** 368–70, *374–9*, 382–4; training design and, future research on **II** 385–9, 397; training design and, research on **II** 366–9, *370–3*, 382. *See also* learning outcomes; training effectiveness models; training transfer
transactional leadership: active management by exception in **III** 14–15; contingent reward and **III** 10, 14–20; laissez-faire leadership and **III** 14–15; passive management by exception and **III** 14–15; one-way augmentation effect and **III** 17; organizational characteristics and **III** 20
transactional-transformational leadership paradigm: applicability **III** 9; definition **III** 7
transformational leadership: characteristics **III** 20; contextual cues and **III** 33; cultural considerations in **III** 19–21; idealized influence (charisma) and **III** 13, 15; individualized consideration **III** 14–15; inspirational motivation and **III** 14–15; intellectual stimulation and **III** 14–15; international aspects of **III** 18; military **III** 17; one-way augmentation effect and **III** 17; organizational characteristics and **III** 20
total quality management (TQM) **IV** 410–11, 413, 417, 426–7, 446

universalism **IV** 10

valence-instrumentality-expectancy (VIE) theory **II** 70–1, 79, 85, 87
value(s): congruence **I** 95, 99, 104, 106, 109–11, 113–15; internal-proximal constraints and **IV** 11–12; instrumental **I** 339; terminal **I** 339; work **I** *338*, 338–40
VAM model: components of **I** 344–9; and extra-role behavior **I** 350–1; and future research **I** 353; and job performance **I** 351–2; and social loafing **I** 352; and turnover/absenteeism **I** 352–3
virtual reality technology (VRT) **IV** 159–60
virtual workplace: business justification for **IV** 202–3; communication in **IV** 211; culture **IV** 203–4; economics **IV**

203–4; disadvantages **IV** 203–4; managerial challenges in **IV** 201–2, 210–14; suitability **IV** 204–5; teams in **IV** 205–6; training in **IV** 206–10

wages **I** 147
Web-based training (*see* distance learning systems)
welfare capitalism **I** 137–9, 150–2
well-being, affective **I** 385–8, *386*. *See also* well-being, job-related
well-being, job-related: health and **I** 418–20, **IV** 190; managers and **I** 416–18; organizations and negative **I** 406–8, 413; perceived control and **I** 415–16; research on mental health and **I** 389–400, *392–4, 396–8*; workforce diversity and **I** 419–20. *See also* workplace: wellness
Wonderlic Personnel Test **II** 123, **IV** 322
work analysis **IV** 330–1
work attitudes: and P-O fit **I** 113–14; and work experience (*see* work experience: attitudes and). *See also* job attitudes
work behavior, cross cultural aspects of **IV** 23–4
work characteristics **III** 267–9
work control: curvilinear effects of **III** 296; demands-control model and **III** 261–3; forms **III** 281–2; indirect effects of **III** 295; main effects of **III** 293–5; personal control and **III** 260–1, 278–9, 286–90; relationship to work stress **III** 270
work design: activation theory in **III** 232–3; growth need strength and **III** 234, *235,* 238–9, 247, 249, *250,* 253–5; job characteristics and **III** 234, *235,* 236–9, *242, 245,* 255–6; motivation in **III** 231 (*See also* motivation); psychological states in **III** 230, 235–6, 239–40, *241, 243,* 243–5, *246,* 247–52, *250,* 255; redesign and **III** 230–1; theory **III** 231–5
Work Orientation Scale **II** 56
worker, happy/productive **I** 201–3, *202*
work experience **I** 337; attitudes and **I** *338,* 340–2, 345, 347–9 (*See also* job attitudes); dimensions of **I** *344,* 344–8; emotions and (*see* emotions; work experience moods and); models of (*see* VAM model); moods and **I** 342–3, 345, 347–9; values and **I** 113, *338,* 338–40, 345–9

work force: academic **IV** 308–9; aging **IV** 256–7; changes in **IV** 254–9, 434; gender **IV** 255–6; diversity in **III** 79; familiarity in **III** 79; job attitudes in **IV** 258–9; job creation **IV** 301; numbers **IV** 254; race/ethnicity and **IV** 256, 333; segmentation **IV** 302; skills **IV** 254–5; teamworking in **IV** 301, 413–4. *See also* employee(s); person-job (P-J) fit; person-organization (P-O) fit
work motivation: cross cultural aspects of **IV** 25–6; goals and **II** 70–3, *71, 72,* 74–6; individualist cultures and **IV** 24; model of **II** 92, *93,* 94–5
workplace: change in **IV** 265–6; globalization **IV** 426; products and services **IV** 265; virtual (*see* virtual workplace); wellness **IV** 269–70 (*See also* well-being, job-related)
work psychology: deconstruction **IV** 373–5; genealogy **IV** 375–6; postmodernism and **IV** 372–9
work roles: emergence **IV** 299–300; flexibility in **IV** 300–1
work-role transitions **I** 16–20: executive succession **I** 26; retirement **I** 20, **IV** 258; school to employment **I** 19
work sample tests **II** *12,* 17
work schedules/hours, alternative **I** 408–9, 427, 429; and employee well-being **I** 408–12, 428–30
work team(s): in China **IV** 75; cohesiveness **III**, 58–9, **IV** 83; comparison between countries **IV** 22; competency **IV** 82–3, 85; composition **III** 59–60; computer-assisted **III** 68–71, 80–1; conflict in 103–5; context **III** 81; creativity in **III** 91–2; decision making in **III** 102–3, **IV** 82–3; for defined problems **III** 71–4; definition of **III** 57–8; diversity in **III** 95–8; external forces and **III** 98–101; flight crews as **III** 64–8; goals of **III** 62–3, 102; heterogeneity of **III** 60; innovation **III** 91–3, *92, 101,* 105, 110; integration skills **III** 108–9; motivation **III** 62; multicultural **IV** 78; organizational change and **III** 74–8; performance **III**

469

58, 60–1, 81; processes **III** *101*, 101–5; psychological safety in 106–7; reflexivity in **III**, 108; task characteristics and **III** 93–5; team boundaries in **III** 79–80; types of **III** 64–7; virtual **IV** 205–6

World Trade Organization (WTO): China and **IV** 74–5; human resource requirements for **IV** 74–5
World Wide Web (*see* Internet)

XEROX **II** 448, *449*, 455, 457